MEDIA/IMPACT

AN INTRODUCTION TO MASS MEDIA

ELEVENTH EDITION

MEDIA/IMPACT

AN INTRODUCTION TO MASS MEDIA

ELEVENTH EDITION

SHIRLEY BIAGI
CALIFORNIA STATE UNIVERSITY, SACRAMENTO

CENGAGE
Learning·

Australia • Brazil • Mexico • Singapore • United Kingdom • United States

Media/Impact: An Introduction to Mass Media, Eleventh Edition
Shirley Biagi

Product Director: Monica Eckman

Product Manager: Kelli Strieby

Content Developer: Laurie Dobson

Associate Content Developer: Erin Bosco

Product Assistant: Rachel Schowalter

Media Developer: Jessica Badiner

Marketing Manager: Jillian Borden

Senior Content Project Manager: Michael Lepera

Senior Art Director: Marissa Falco

Manufacturing Planner: Doug Bertke

Senior Rights Acquisition Specialist: Jennifer Meyer Dare

Production Service/Compositor: Lachina Publishing Services

Text Designer: Ke Design

Cover Designer: Wing Ngan

Cover Image: FRONT COVER: Man in yellow surfing web in Nairobi: Tony Karumba/AFP/Getty Images; Muslim girl in purple with cell phone: Rouf Bhat/AFP/Getty Images; Baltimore Orioles at NY: Lloyd Fox/Baltimore Sun/MCT via Getty Images; Jennifer Lawrence at marquee: Rebecca Sapp/WireImage/Getty Images; Man holding Kindle: Will Ireland/Future Publishing/Getty Images; Gov. Deval Patrick in Watertown, MA: Essdras M Suarez/The Boston Globe via Getty Images; BACK COVER: Stevie Wonder: Jamie McCarthy/Wire Image/Getty Images; Chicago Bulls mascot: Jonathan Daniel/Getty Images; RCA radio ad: LCDM Universal History Archive/Getty Images

Library of Congress Control Number: 2013946058

ISBN-13: 978-1-133-31138-6

ISBN-10: 1-133-31138-5

Cengage Learning
200 First Stamford Place, 4th Floor
Stamford, CT 06902
USA

Cengage Learning is a leading provider of customized learning solutions with office locations around the globe, including Singapore, the United Kingdom, Australia, Mexico, Brazil and Japan. Locate your local office at **international.cengage.com/region**.

Cengage Learning products are represented in Canada by Nelson Education, Ltd.

For your course and learning solutions, visit **www.cengage.com**.

Purchase any of our products at your local college store or at our preferred online store **www.cengagebrain.com**.

Instructors: Please visit **login.cengage.com** and log in to access instructor-specific resources.

Printed in China
2 3 4 5 6 7 17 16 15 14

BRIEF CONTENTS

CONTENTS

PART ONE
THE MASS MEDIA INDUSTRIES

AFP/Getty Images

1 MASS MEDIA AND EVERYDAY LIFE

2 BOOKS: REARRANGING THE PAGE

3 NEWSPAPERS: EXPANDING DELIVERY

Mario Tama/Getty Images

4 MAGAZINES: TARGETING THE AUDIENCE

Chris McKay/Getty Images

5 RECORDINGS: DEMANDING CHOICES

Cindy Ord/Getty Images

6 RADIO: RIDING THE WAVE

Rebecca Sapp/WireImage/Getty Images

7 MOVIES: PICTURING THE FUTURE

Robyn Beck/AFP/Getty Images

8 TELEVISION: CHANGING CHANNELS

Gareth Cattermole/Getty Images
Entertainment/Getty Images

9 DIGITAL MEDIA: WIDENING THE WEB

PART TWO
SELLING THE MESSAGE

Fotosearch/Getty Images

10 ADVERTISING: CATCHING CONSUMERS

Luis Sinco/Los Angeles Times

11 PUBLIC RELATIONS: PROMOTING IDEAS

PART THREE
CHANGING MESSAGES

Stuart C. Wilson/Getty Images

12 NEWS AND INFORMATION: CHOOSING SOURCES

Jewel Samad/AFP/Getty Images

13 SOCIETY AND POLITICAL ISSUES: SHAPING THE ARGUMENTS

Saul Loeb/AFP/Getty Images

14 LAW AND REGULATION: REWRITING THE RULES

Suzanne Kreiter/The Boston Globe via
Getty Images

15 ETHICS: PLACING RESPONSIBILITY

16 GLOBAL MEDIA: DISCOVERING NEW MARKETS

Welcome to the world of *Media/Impact*.

Media/Impact's energetic new design—inside and out—reflects the excitement and intensity that is inherent in the study of mass media today. Dozens of new charts, illustrations and photographs in this 11th edition enhance the totally revised and updated text, making *Media/Impact*, 11th edition, the most current, accessible, challenging way for students to study the central role that America's mass media play in the global media marketplace.

Accompanying this new edition are many new digital tools offered by Cengage Learning, including MindTap, to organize and enhance student thinking. The result for students and teachers is *Media/Impact*'s best edition ever.

NEW FEATURES IN THE ELEVENTH EDITION

- More than 50 new Impact Boxes—The Impact Boxes feature current articles and information on the latest topics and trends from the best sources covering the media business, such as *The New York Times*, *The Washington Post*, CNET, *Advertising Age*, the *International Herald Tribune*, *Los Angeles Times*, the Pew Center for People & the Press and *The Guardian*.

- Five Impact Box Subject Areas—Impact Boxes are now divided into five essential subject areas: Convergence, Money, Audience, Profile and Global. For example:

    ▶ **Impact/Convergence**. "Broadcasters Worry About 'Zero TV' Homes Migrating to the Internet."

    ▶ **Impact/Money**. "How Much Do Businesses Spend Annually to Advertise on the Internet?"

    ▶ **Impact/Audience**. "What the Explosion in Mobile Audiences Means for News."

    ▶ **Impact/Profile**. "'You've Got to Find What You Love,' Steve Jobs Says."

    ▶ **Impact/Global**. "What Are the World's Largest Markets for Advertising?"

- Expanded Examination of Convergence—The addition of a new Impact/Convergence Box emphasizes the increasing integration of the mass media industries, which has turned mobile phones and tablets into the fastest-growing media marketplaces.

- Current Statistics on the Mass Media Industries—Statistical information is beautifully displayed in 34 new illustrations to reflect current research on key issues such as: Internet Ad Spending, Sales of Digital Content, Top 10 Internet News Sites, Top 10 Social Media Sites, and Top 10 International Cities with Public Wireless Hot Spots.

- Timely Cartoons, Photographs and Illustrations to Capture Students' Attention—More than 250 carefully selected new photos, cartoons and illustrations throughout the book emphasize timely trends and important topics in today's media business.

- Impact/Action Videos—Four new Impact/Action videos bring contemporary issues in mass communication to life, with content customized to expand on the text. Specialized narration accompanies images and videos to tell the story of how mass communication is changing and transforming the world. These four Impact/Action videos, matched to chapters throughout the book, expand student understanding of how mass communication affects today's world:

    ▶ Learn how international political movements use social networking in *Impact/Action: Communicating Change*.

    ▶ Discover the importance of—and dangers facing—journalists around the world in *Impact/Action: Reporters at Risk*.

    ▶ Watch the evolution and application of 3D movie and TV technology in *Impact/Action: Living in 3D*.

    ▶ Explore the transition of words from print to digital in *Impact/Action: Moving Pages*.

CONTINUING FEATURES IN THE ELEVENTH EDITION

- **Comprehensive Coverage of the Latest Trends in Digital Media.** *Media/Impact* details the latest innovations and controversies surrounding the Internet, mobile media, 3-D, video games, intellectual property rights, government regulation and social media.

- **Analysis of Changing Delivery Systems for News and Information.** Chapter 12 chronicles the declining audience for broadcast news as consumers personalize their information and use the Internet to stay current, as well as social media's transformative role in gathering and sharing information. First introduced in the sixth edition, when few people understood how consumers' changing news habits would affect news delivery, Digital Media, Chapter 9, also has proven extremely popular with faculty and students.

- **Discussion of Current Media Issues.** Beginning with the first graphic illustration in Chapter 1, "Average Time People Spend Using Mass Media Each Day," *Media/Impact* offers students a realistic picture of the central role mass media play in their lives.

- **Margin Definitions.** Designed to help students build a media vocabulary while they read, key terms and definitions are highlighted separately at the bottom of the page, giving students concise definitions incorporated into the text.

- **Comprehensive End-of-Chapter Review.** Each chapter's concluding materials include these essential resources:

  ▶ **Chapter Summaries.** Organized by headings that correspond to the chapter's major topics, the section **Review, Analyze, Investigate** uses bullet points to summarize major concepts.

  ▶ **Key Terms.** A list of important terms with corresponding page numbers appears at the end of each chapter and in the comprehensive **Glossary** at the end of the book.

  ▶ **Critical Questions.** Following the key terms, five questions focus students' analysis of each chapter to help deepen their understanding and engage their critical thinking skills.

  ▶ **Working the Web.** Finishing each chapter, a list of 10 Web sites specific to the chapter includes a brief annotation to describe each site and encourage mass media students to pursue further research.

- **Media Information Resource Guide.** This invaluable student reference on page 379 provides hundreds more resources to help students explore media topics and assist them with media research, including an alphabetical listing of more than 200 Web site references from the text.

FORMAL REVIEWERS KEEP MEDIA/IMPACT'S FOCUS ON STUDENTS

A special thank you to the many professors who contributed valuable ideas in their formal reviews of *Media/Impact*. I especially appreciate the extra time and dedicated effort the video reviewers gave, which greatly helped shape the new concept of Impact/Action Videos as an integral part of *Media/Impact* for students. The eleventh edition's reviewers are:

Ron Allman, Indiana University Southeast
Megan Burnett, Alice Lloyd College
Dan Close, Wichita State University
Adrienne Hacker Daniels, Illinois College
Allen Levy, Chapman University
John Marlow, Hawaii Community College
Judith Menezes, College of the Sequoias
James Mueller, University of North Texas

CENGAGE TEACHING AND LEARNING TOOLS FOR TEACHERS AND STUDENTS

Resources for Students

MindTap from Cengage Learning represents a new approach to a highly personalized, online learning platform. A fully online learning solution, MindTap combines all of a student's learning tools—readings, multimedia (including Impact/Action videos), activities, and assessments—into a singular Learning Path that guides the student through the curriculum. Educators personalize the experience by customizing the presentation of these learning tools to their students, even seamlessly introducing their own content into the Learning Path via "apps" that integrate into the MindTap platform. MindTap can also be integrated into an institution's Learning Management System (LMS) through a service called MindLinks.

CourseMate from Cengage Learning brings course concepts to life with interactive learning, study, and exam preparation tools that support the printed textbook. MindTap™ Reader is included. Watch student comprehension soar as your class works with the printed textbook and the textbook-specific website. Communication CourseMate goes beyond the book to deliver what you need.

Resources for Instructors

Instructor's Edition (IE): Examination and desk copies of the Instructor's Edition of *Media/Impact*, Eleventh Edition, are available upon request.

Instructor's Web site: This dedicated online resource for instructors provides access to the Instructor's Manual and Test Bank, Microsoft® PowerPoint® lecture slides covering key concepts from the text, and book-specific JoinIn™ content for response systems that allows you to transform your classroom and assess your students' progress with instant in-class quizzes and polls. There's also a Test Bank powered by **Cognero®**, a flexible, online system that allows you to author, edit, and manage test bank content from multiple Cengage Learning solutions; create multiple test versions in an instant; and deliver tests from your Learning Management System, your classroom, or wherever you want.

Instructor's Manual: *Media/Impact*'s Instructor's Manual provides a comprehensive teaching guide featuring the following tools for each chapter: chapter goals and an outline; suggestions for integrating print supplements and online resources; suggested discussion questions and activities and a comprehensive Test Bank with an answer key that includes multiple choice, true/false, short answer, essay, and fill-in-the-blank test questions. The Manual also includes discussion questions for each of the Impact/Action Videos. This Manual is available on the password-protected instructor's Web site.

Thank you for your continuing support for *Media/Impact*. Comments? Questions? Suggestions? Please contact your local Cengage sales representative or our Cengage Learning Academic Resource Center at 1-800-423-0563.

BECKY HAYDEN is the reason *Media/Impact* is now being published in its eleventh edition. Becky was Mass Communications Editor in 1987 at Wadsworth Publishing when Wadsworth released the first edition of *Media/Impact*. She was already a legendary figure in book publishing because she had sponsored so many excellent texts in mass communications and journalism. Her support and enthusiasm for *Media/Impact* carried me through two years of writing and researching the first edition. Every edition since the first carries her indelible imprint. I feel privileged to be a part of Becky Hayden's publishing legacy.

Wadsworth is now part of Cengage Learning, and *Media/Impact* has evolved from a print-only U.S. product to a multimedia learning experience also produced as an e-book and published in Korean, Spanish, Greek, Chinese and Canadian editions. To be successful, this evolution demands committed leadership. For the eleventh edition I was very lucky to have the dedicated energy of Monica Eckman, who, along with Kelli Strieby, joined the project after it was underway. Laurie Dobson, who has shepherded several editions of *Media/Impact*, continued her superb, patient and persistent project stewardship. Marissa Falco oversaw the splendid new design, and Matt Orgovan of Lachina contributed his careful eye for detail, detail, detail. And Tom Biondi contributed important Web site research.

Special thanks also to Michael Lepera, Cengage Senior Content Project Manager, for overseeing the eleventh edition; Jillian Borden, Cengage Marketing Manager; Erin Bosco, Associate Content Developer; Jessica Badiner, Media Developer; Rachel Schowalter, Product Assistant; Jennifer Meyer Dare, Senior Rights Acquisition Specialist; Meg Shanahan, Permissions Project Manager, PreMediaGlobal; and Punitha Rajamohan, Associate Project Manager Text Permissions, PreMediaGlobal.

Most important with his help and support for this edition is my favorite photo editor and video producer, Vic Biondi. He believes, as I do, that the visuals in *Media/Impact* are as important as the text, and his imprint and contributions are on every page.

And, to all the students and teachers who continue to value *Media/Impact* as a way to explore the exciting field of mass media, thank you for your enduring support.

Shirley Biagi

Christopher Briscoe

SHIRLEY BIAGI is a professor in the Department of Communication Studies at California State University, Sacramento. Her bestselling text, *Media/Impact*, is also published in Canadian, Greek, Spanish, Chinese and Korean editions. Biagi has authored several other Wadsworth/Cengage Learning communications texts, including *Media/Reader: Perspectives on Mass Media Industries, Effects and Issues* and *Interviews That Work: A Practical Guide for Journalists*. She is co-author, with Marilyn Kern-Foxworth, of *Facing Difference: Race, Gender and Mass Media*.

From 1998 to 2000, she was editor of *American Journalism*, the national media history quarterly published by the American Journalism Historians Association.

She has served as guest faculty for the University of Hawaii, the Center for Digital Government, the Poynter Institute, the American Press Institute, the National Writers Workshop and the Hearst Fellowship Program at the *Houston Chronicle*. She has also been an Internet and publications consultant to the California State Chamber of Commerce.

She also was one of eight project interviewers for the award-winning Washington (D.C.) Press Club Foundation's Women in Journalism Oral History Project, sponsored by the National Press Club. Interviewers completed 57 oral histories of female pioneers in journalism, available free on the Press Club's Web site at http://www.wpcf.org.

In 2007, Biagi was nominated and served as a delegate to the Oxford Round Table's conference on Ethical Sentiments in Government at Pembroke College in Oxford, England. Biagi's other international experience includes guest lectureships at Al Ahram Press Institute in Cairo, Egypt, and at Queensland University in Brisbane, Australia.

MASS MEDIA
AND EVERYDAY LIFE

Today mass media is an essential
element of everyday life. On January 21, 2013,
members of the crowd at President Barack Obama's
Inaugural Ball use their mobile phones to capture and
share the event.

"Consumers need to have an internal compass where they're able to balance the capabilities that technology offers them for work, for search, with the qualities of the lives they live offline."

—RICHARD HERNANDEZ, EXECUTIVE COACH, GOOGLE

You are connected.

In today's world mass media are waiting to bombard you every waking hour. When was the last time you spent 24 hours without the media? From the moment you wake up until the time you go to sleep, mass media are available to help you share information, keep you updated and entertained and—most importantly—sell you products.

MASS MEDIA ARE EVERYWHERE YOU ARE

Online news offers national and local news with constant updates and alerts for breaking stories. Radio news gives you traffic reports on the freeway. Magazines describe new video games, show you the latest fashion trends and help plan your next camping trip.

Should you do your homework now or power up your Kindle to read the latest romance novel or stream a video on your iPad from Netflix? Maybe you should grab your iPhone to check Facebook or schedule DirecTV to record the latest episode of your favorite sitcom tonight. Perhaps you should answer e-mail or text your friends to ask what they're doing, while downloading some new songs through iTunes. All those media choices certainly are more compelling than your homework.

According to industry estimates, adults spend an average of 11 hours of each day using mass media—more than half their waking hours. (See **Illustration 1.1**, p. 4.) Some form of mass media touches you every day—

economically, socially and culturally. Mass media can affect the way you vote and the way you spend your money. Sometimes mass media influence the way you eat, talk, work, study and relax. This is the impact of mass media on you individually and, collectively, on American society.

The media's wide-ranging global presence means today's mass media capture more time and attention than ever. The media affect almost all aspects of the way people live, and the media earn unprecedented amounts of money for delivering information and entertainment. (See **Illustration 1.2**, p. 5.)

Today's American society has inherited the wisdom, mistakes, creativity and vision of the people who work in the mass media industries and the society that regulates and consumes what the mass media produce. Consider these situations:

- You are shopping online at Amazon.com, trying to decide between James Patterson's latest e-book and a travel guide to Brazil. What are the economic consequences of your book-buying decision for the book publishing industry? (See **Chapter 2**.)

- You are an entrepreneur with a lot of ideas but very little money. You decide to start an online cooking magazine. What are the chances your new magazine will succeed? (See **Chapter 4**.)

- On the Internet, a friend shares a new song from your favorite recording artist, which you download and publish on your personal Web site. You get the

TIMEFRAME

3500 B.C.–TODAY

DEA/De Agostini/Getty Images

Three Information Communications Revolutions Form the Basis for Today's Digital Media

3500 B.C. The first known pictographs are carved in stone.

2500 B.C. The Egyptians invent papyrus.

1000 B.C. The First Information Communications Revolution: Phonetic Writing

200 B.C. The Greeks perfect parchment.

A.D. 100 The Chinese invent paper.

1300 Europeans start to use paper.

1445 The Chinese invent the copper press.

1455 The Second Information Communications Revolution: Movable Type

1640 The first American book is published.

1690 The first American newspaper is published.

1741 The first American magazine is published.

1877 Thomas Edison first demonstrates the phonograph.

1899 Guglielmo Marconi first uses his wireless radio.

Hulton Archive/Stringer/Getty Images

1927 *The Jazz Singer*, the first feature-length motion picture with sound, premieres in New York City.

1939 NBC debuts TV at the New York World's Fair. On display are 5-inch and 9-inch television sets priced from $199.50 to $600.

1951 The Third Information Communications Revolution: Digital Computers That Can Process, Store and Retrieve Information

1980 The Federal Communications Commission begins to deregulate the broadcast media.

1989 Tim Berners-Lee develops the first Internet Web browser.

2007 Amazon introduces the Kindle e-reader. Apple introduces the iPhone.

2008 Internet advertising income reaches $23 billion annually, more than twice what it was in the year 2000.

2010 Apple introduces the iPad tablet.

2011 Apple introduces iCloud.

2013 Pebble introduces the Smart Watch.

TODAY Wireless digital technology is the standard for all mass media. Mass media is personalized and mobile.

Rouf Bhat/AFP/Getty Images

IMPACT/Audience

Illustration 1.1

Average Time Americans Spend Using Mass Media Each Day

On average, Americans spend more waking time each day with the mass media than without them.

Source: emarketer.com/ Article/Trends-Consumers- Time-Spent-with- Media/1008138

Total minutes in a day = 1,440

46%
Using media
660 minutes

33%
Sleeping
480 minutes

21%
Not using media
300 minutes

---

music you want, but the artist's licensing company sues you because you haven't paid for the song. Will you be prosecuted? (See **Chapter 5**.)

- You are a reporter for a major news organization. To try to scoop the competition, you hack into a celebrity's cell phone. How does your company respond when it learns what you've done? (See **Chapter 15**.)

People who work in the media industries, people who own media businesses, people who consume media and people who regulate what the media offer face decisions like these every day. The choices they make continue to shape the future of the American mass media.

Wi-Fi An abbreviation for *Wireless Fidelity*. The new mass media are as convenient as your cell phone, complete with graphics and sound, offering massive choices of information, entertainment and services whenever and wherever you want them.

MASS COMMUNICATION BECOMES WIRELESS

In the 1930s, to listen to the radio, your house needed electricity. You plugged your radio into an electrical outlet, with the furniture positioned near the radio so the family could listen to the programs. In the 1950s, you had to add an antenna to your roof so you could watch your new TV set, which was connected at the wall to an electrical outlet and the antenna. To be wired was to be connected. In the 1990s, you still needed an electrical outlet at home and at work to be connected to your computer, and the furniture in your family room still was arranged to accommodate the cable, satellite and/or telephone connection for your television set.

Today's technology makes mass media wireless (*Wi-Fi*, an abbreviation for *Wireless Fidelity*). New technologies give you access to any mass media in almost any location without wires. You can sit on your front porch and watch movies on your laptop, listen to radio by satellite and

IMPACT/Money

Illustration 1.2

U.S. Media Industries Annual Income 1987–Today

This historical graphic shows how the distribution of media industry income has shifted since 1987.

Sources: *U.S. Industrial Outlook 1987, McCann-Erickson Insider's Report 1987, The Veronis, Suhler & Associates Communications Industry Forecast, 1997–2001,* publishers .org, hoovers.com, naa.org, adage.com, forrester.com, emarketer.com, riaa.org.

1987

The consumer Internet industry does not exist and print media industry revenue (newspapers, magazines and books combined) is 55% of all media industry income.

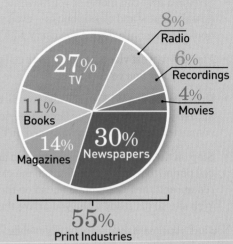

1999

The Internet first emerges as a viable media industry. Income for newspapers and magazines begins to drop dramatically, although book industry income increases. Overall, print media industry income drops to 49% of the total.

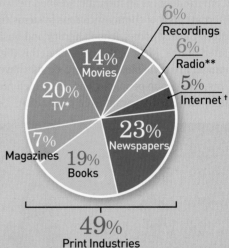

Today

Internet advertising income totals 10% of all media industry income. Movie income is up. TV and radio revenue have stabilized. Recording industry income is half what it was in 1999, and print media collect only 31% of total media industry revenue, about half of what it was in 1987.

* Broadcast, cable & satellite
** Includes Internet downloads
*** Includes Internet editions

† Internet advertising revenue
†† Includes e-book sales

download music, books, newspapers and video games to the cell phone you carry in your pocket. You also can:

- Check Twitter to see what your friends are saying.

- Stream a first-run movie or your favorite TV sitcom or download new and classic books—even your textbook—to a mobile device you carry with you.

- Play the newest video game on your cell phone with three people you've never met.

- Drink coffee in a Wi-Fi café while you check your family ancestry to create an online family tree, leading you to connect with overseas relatives you didn't know existed.

- Stop on the street corner in a new town and use your cell phone to retrieve directions to the closest Italian restaurant; then order pizza ahead on the restaurant's Web site so it's ready when you arrive there.

You and your mass media are totally mobile. Today's digital environment is an intricate, webbed network of many different types of communications systems that connects virtually every home, school, library and business in the United States. Most of the systems in this digital environment are invisible. Electronic signals have replaced wires, freeing up people to stay connected no matter where or when they want to communicate.

Gus Stewart/Redferns/Getty Images

Nanna Bryndis Hilmarsdottir and Ragnar Thohallsson from the band Of Monsters and Men perform in London, England, on March 5, 2013. If a friend e-mails you a copy of the group's latest song, and you use it on your Web site without permission, can you be prosecuted for violating their music copyright?

Mass Communication   Communication from one person or group of persons through a transmitting device (a medium) to large audiences or markets.

This global communications system uses broadcast, telephone, satellite, cable and computer technologies to connect everyone in the world to a variety of services. Eventually, this communications system will be accessible and affordable everywhere in the world. As futurist George Gilder phrased it: "Who will ride the next avalanche of bits on the information superhighway—and who will be buried under it?"

HOW THE COMMUNICATION PROCESS WORKS

To understand mass media in the digital age, first it is important to understand the process of communication. Communication is the act of sending messages, ideas and opinions from one person to another. Writing and talking to each other are only two ways human beings communicate. We also communicate when we gesture, move our bodies or roll our eyes.

Three ways to describe how people communicate are

- *Intrapersonal communication*

- *Interpersonal communication*

- *Mass communication*

Each form of communication involves different numbers of people in specific ways. If you are in a grocery store and you silently debate with yourself whether to buy an apple or a package of double-chunk chocolate chip cookies, you are using what scholars call *intra*personal communication—communication within one person. To communicate with each other, people rely on their five senses—sight, hearing, touch, smell and taste. This direct sharing of experience between two people is called *inter*personal communication. **Mass communication** is communication from one person or group of persons through a transmitting device (a medium) to large audiences or markets.

In *Media/Impact* you will study *mass communication*. To describe the process of mass communication, scholars use a communications model. This includes six key terms: *sender, message, receiver, channel, feedback* and *noise*. (See **Illustration 1.3**, p. 7.)

Pretend you're standing directly in front of someone and say, "I like your Detroit Tigers hat." In this simple communication, you are the sender, the message is "I like your Detroit Tigers hat," and the person in front of you is the receiver (or audience). This example of interpersonal communication involves the sender, the message and the receiver.

In mass communication, the *sender* (or *source*) puts the *message* on what is called a *channel*. The sender (source) could be a local business, for example. The

IMPACT/Audience

Illustration 1.3

Elements of Mass Communication

The process of mass communication works like this: A *sender* (source) puts a message on a *channel* (medium) that delivers the message to the *receiver*. *Feedback* occurs when the receiver responds, and that response changes subsequent messages from the source. *Noise* (such as static or a dropped connection) can interrupt or change the message during transmission.

Noise

Channel (medium)

Message

Noise

Channel (medium)

Sender (source)

Company

Receiver (consumer)

Feedback

Survey

☒ yes

☐ no

© Cengage Learning

channel (or **medium**) delivers the message (electronic signal). The channel could be the cable, satellite or internet provider. A medium is the means by which a message reaches an audience. (The plural of the word *medium* is *media*; the term **media** refers to more than one medium.) Your television set or mobile device is the medium that delivers the message simultaneously to you and many other people.

The *receiver* is the place where the message arrives, such as you, the consumer. **Noise** is any distortion (such as static or a briefly interrupted signal) that interferes with clear communication. **Feedback** occurs when the receiver processes the message and sends a response (such as a survey) back to the sender (source).

As a very simple example, say your satellite company (sender/source) sends an advertisement for a movie-on-demand (the message) through the signal (channel) into your TV set (medium). If you (the receiver) use the controls on your TV remote to stream the movie, the order you place (feedback) ultimately will bring you a movie to watch. This entire loop between sender and receiver, and

Nicolas Asfouri/AFP/Getty Images

Wireless technology means you can carry your media with you and send and receive messages anytime. In Queenstown, Singapore, people use their cell phones to try to get a picture of Britain's Prince William and his wife Catherine, the Duchess of Cambridge, during their visit to the country on September 12, 2012.

Medium   The means by which a message reaches the audience. Also, the singular form of the word *media*.

Media   Plural of the word *medium*.

Noise   Distortion (such as static) that interferes with clear communication.

Feedback   A response sent back to the sender from the person who receives the communication.

the resulting response (feedback) of the receiver to the sender, describes the process of mass communication.

Using a general definition, mass communication today shares three characteristics:

1. A message is sent out on some form of mass communication system (such as the Internet, print or broadcast).

2. The message is delivered rapidly.

3. The message reaches large groups of different kinds of people simultaneously or within a short period of time.

Thus, a telephone conversation between two people does *not* qualify as mass communication, but a message from the president of the United States, broadcast simultaneously by all of the television networks and carried via the Internet, would qualify because mass media deliver messages to large numbers of people at once.

WHAT ARE THE MASS MEDIA INDUSTRIES?

The term *mass media industries* describes eight types of mass media businesses. The word *industries*, when used to describe the media business, emphasizes the primary goal of mass media in America—to generate money. The eight media industries are

- Books
- Newspapers
- Magazines
- Recordings
- Radio
- Movies
- Television
- The Internet

Books, newspapers and magazines were America's only mass media for 250 years after the first American book was published in 1640. The first half of the 20th century brought four new types of media—recordings, radio, movies and TV—in fewer than 50 years. The late-20th-century addition to the media mix, of course, is the Internet. To understand where each medium fits in

Mass Media Industries   Eight types of media businesses: books, newspapers, magazines, recordings, radio, movies, television and the Internet.

Movies such as *Iron Man 3*, which are available to large groups of different types of people simultaneously, represent one form of mass communication.

the mass media industries today, you can start by examining the individual characteristics of each media business.

Books

Publishers issue about 150,000 titles a year in the United States, although many of these are reprints and new editions of old titles. Retail bookstores in the United States account for one-third of all money earned from book sales. The rest of book publishing income comes from books that are sold online, in college stores, through book clubs, to libraries and to school districts for use in elementary and high schools. Book publishing, the oldest media industry, is a static industry. Publishers see expanded revenue potential in the sale of e-books (downloaded copies of books), but the transition from print-only sales to print-and-digital sales is expensive.

Newspapers

Newspapers today are struggling to make a profit. Advertising revenues in the last five years have plummeted, partly because of difficult economic conditions in the United States but also because newspaper readers have migrated to other sources for their news. Between 2008 and 2010, eight major newspaper chains declared bankruptcy, and many laid off reporters and cut salaries.

Advertising makes up more than two-thirds of the printed space in daily newspapers. Most newspapers have launched Internet editions to try to expand their reach, and some newspapers have converted to online-only publication, but increased Internet ad revenue has not compensated for advertising declines in the printed product.

Magazines

According to the Association of Magazine Media, about 25,000 magazines are published in the United States. To maintain and increase profits, magazines are raising their subscription and single-copy prices and fighting to sustain their advertising income. Many magazines have launched Internet editions, and a few magazines (such as *Slate*) are published exclusively online. Magazine subscriptions and newsstand sales are down. Magazine income is expected to decline over the next decade, primarily because advertising revenue is down substantially.

Recordings

People older than age 25 are the most common buyers of recordings today because people younger than 25 download or stream music from the Internet, both legally and illegally, and buy very few CDs. CDs and Internet downloads account for almost all recording industry income, with a small amount of money coming from music videos. Industry income has been declining sharply because new technologies allow consumers to share music over the Internet rather than pay for their music. The only growing revenue source for the recording companies among people younger than 25 is individual music downloads, sold through Internet sites such as iTunes. In 2010, Apple announced that iTunes had sold its 10 billionth download, becoming the nation's largest music retailer.

Radio

About 14,000 radio stations broadcast programming in the United States, evenly divided between AM and FM stations. About 2,900 radio stations are public stations, most of them FM. Satellite radio, such as Sirius XM, generates revenue through subscriptions, offering an almost unlimited variety of music and program choices without commercials. As a result, over-the-air broadcast radio revenue from commercials is declining because the price of a commercial is based on the size of the audience, which is getting smaller. To expand their audience, more than 6,000 traditional radio stations also distribute their programs online. Pandora, Rhapsody and Spotify are radio services, available only on the Internet. In 2013, Apple announced plans to launch its own radio service, iRadio.

Mick Stevens/www.cartoonbank.com

"It was much nicer before people started storing all their personal information in the cloud."

Movies

About 40,000 theater screens exist in the United States. The major and independent studios combined make about 600 pictures a year. The industry is collecting more money because of higher ticket prices, but more people watch movies at home and online than in theaters, so the number of movie theaters is declining. Fewer people are buying DVDs and instead are getting movies through Redbox and streaming through Netflix. The increases in income to the U.S. movie industry have been from overseas movie sales, movie downloads and the introduction of 3-D movies. Overall movie industry income began declining in 2005, and that trend continued until 2012, when industry income stabilized.

Television

About 1,700 television stations operate in the United States. One out of four stations is a public station. Many stations are affiliated with a major network—NBC, CBS, ABC or Fox—although a few stations, called *independents*, are not affiliated with any network. More than 90 percent of the homes in the United States are wired for cable or satellite delivery. To differentiate cable and satellite TV from over-the-air television, cable and satellite television services are now lumped together in one category, called ***subscription television***.

TV network income is declining while income to cable operators and satellite companies for subscription

Subscription Television A new term used to describe consumer services delivered by cable and satellite program delivery.

Eamonn McCormack/WireImage/Getty Images

They are affected in turn by changes in our beliefs, tastes, interests and behavior. Three important concepts can help to organize your thinking about mass media and their impact on American society:

1. The mass media are profit-centered businesses.

2. Technological developments change the way mass media are delivered and consumed.

3. Mass media both reflect and affect politics, society and culture.

American mass media are very popular overseas, representing substantial income potential for U.S. media companies. Hugh Jackman attends the British premiere of *The Wolverine* **in London, England, on July 16, 2013.**

services is increasing, so all the television networks have invested heavily in subscription TV programming. The nation's largest cable operator, Comcast Corp., also owns the E! Entertainment cable network. In 2008, AT&T began offering subscription television services using fiber cable through its U-verse system. Total television industry revenue—including cable, satellite and fiber delivery—is expected to grow steadily in the next decade.

The Internet

The newest media industry also is growing the fastest. About 80 percent of all U.S. adults have Internet access, and the amount of money businesses spent for Internet advertising increased from $8 billion in the year 2000 to $37 billion in 2012. Internet media have become a new mass medium as well as an integrated delivery system for traditional print, audio, video and interactive services (such as video games). The Internet also offers access to many other consumer services, such as shopping and social networking, and a place for businesses to sell their products using advertising and product promotion.

THREE KEY CONCEPTS TO REMEMBER

The mass media are key institutions in our society. They affect our culture, our buying habits and our politics.

MASS MEDIA ARE PROFIT-CENTERED BUSINESSES

What you see, read and hear in the mass media may tease, entertain, inform, persuade, provoke and even perplex you. But to understand the American mass media, the first concept to grasp is that the central force driving the media business in America is the desire to make money. American media are businesses, vast businesses.

The products of these businesses are information and entertainment that depend on attracting an audience of media consumers to generate income. Of course, other motives shape the media in America: the desire to fulfill the public's need for information, to influence the country's governance, to disseminate the country's culture, to offer entertainment and to provide an outlet for artistic expression. But American media are, above all, profit-centered.

To understand the mass media industries, it is essential to understand who owns these important channels of communication. In the United States, all media are privately owned except the Public Broadcasting Service (PBS) and National Public Radio (NPR), which survive on government support, private donations and minimal corporate sponsorship. The annual budget for all of public broadcasting (PBS and NPR combined) is less than 2 percent of the amount advertisers pay every year to support America's commercial media.

In some media industries, the same number of companies control ownership today as in the 1950s. There are five major movie studios today, for example, compared to the same number of major studios in the 1940s. The number of broadcast stations and the number of magazines has increased since the 1940s, but the number of newspapers and recording companies has declined.

Overall, however, American media ownership has been contracting rather than expanding. This is because large companies are buying small companies. The trend is for media companies to cluster together into big groups, which means that a small number of companies now control many aspects of the media business. This trend, called *concentration of ownership*, takes four different forms: chains, broadcast networks, conglomerates and vertical integration.

CHAINS. Benjamin Franklin established America's first newspaper chain in the 1700s, when he was publishing his own newspaper, the *Pennsylvania Gazette*, as well as sponsoring one-third of the cost of publishing the *South Carolina Gazette*. (He also collected one-third of the *South Carolina Gazette*'s profits.) William Randolph Hearst expanded this tradition in the 1930s. At its peak, the Hearst newspaper chain accounted for nearly 14 percent of total national daily newspaper sales and 25 percent of Sunday sales. Today's U.S. newspaper chain giant is Gannett Co., with 82 daily newspapers, including *USA Today*. The word *chain* is used to describe a company that owns several newspapers.

BROADCAST NETWORKS. A broadcast network is a collection of radio or television stations that offers programs during designated program times. Unlike newspaper ownership (which is not regulated by the government), the Federal Communications Commission (*FCC*) regulates broadcast station ownership and operations. The FCC is a government regulatory body whose members are appointed by the president.

The four major TV networks are ABC (American Broadcasting Co.), NBC (National Broadcasting Co.), CBS (originally the Columbia Broadcasting System) and Fox. NBC, the oldest network, was founded in the 1920s. NBC and the two other original networks (CBS and ABC) first were established to deliver radio programming across the country and continued the network concept when television was invented. Fox is the youngest major network, founded in 1986, and originally was created to deliver only television programming.

Broadcast networks can have as many *affiliates* as they want. Affiliates are stations that use network programming but are owned by companies other than the networks. No network, however, can have two affiliates in the same geographic broadcast area, due to government regulation of network affiliation.

In 2006, the TV networks announced they would offer shows on demand for downloading. Apple and

CBS is one of the original U.S. broadcast networks and earned an early reputation as the nation's best TV news operation, beginning in the 1960s. On October 21, 1968, CBS news anchor Walter Cronkite explained America's *Apollo 7* mission from North American Rockwell Space Center in Houston, Texas.

Disney agreed to make series programming available through video downloads. One month later, CBS and NBC announced they planned to offer series programs on demand for 99 cents an episode through Comcast and DirecTV. Today broadcast network programming is available by streaming on all mobile media, such as cell phones and iPads. To generate revenue, the broadcast networks today take the programming to their viewers instead of waiting for viewers to come to them.

Concentration of Ownership   The current trend of large companies buying smaller companies so that fewer companies own more types of media businesses.

FCC   Federal Communications Commission.

Affiliates   Stations that use network programming but are owned by companies other than the networks.

CONGLOMERATES. When you watch a Sony Pictures Entertainment film or listen to Sony music, you might not realize that Sony also owns Micronics, a medical diagnostics company. Sony is a *conglomerate*—a company that owns media companies (Sony Pictures Entertainment, Sony Music Entertainment, and Sony Electronics) as well as other businesses that are unrelated to the media business.

VERTICAL INTEGRATION. The most widespread trend among today's media companies is *vertical integration*—where one company controls several related aspects of the media business at once, with each part of the company helping the others. Many media companies own more than one type of media property: newspapers, magazines, radio and TV stations, for example.

Gannett, which owns the nation's largest chain of newspapers, also owns television and radio stations, so Gannett is a newspaper chain that is also a vertically integrated company.

The media company Viacom owns MTV, Comedy Central, Nickelodeon and Black Entertainment Television (BET). The Walt Disney Co. owns Disneyland amusement parks, Walt Disney Motion Pictures Group, the ABC TV network, the ESPN cable network and *ESPN: The Magazine*. Time Warner owns Warner Bros. Pictures, HBO, Turner Broadcasting, CNN, TNT, TBS, *Sports Illustrated*, SI.com and the Cartoon Network.

CONVERGENCE DOMINATES THE MEDIA BUSINESS

To describe the financial status of today's media industries is to talk about intense competition. Media companies are buying and selling each other in unprecedented numbers and forming media groups to position themselves in the marketplace to maintain and increase their income. Since 1986, all three original TV networks (NBC, CBS and ABC) have been sold to new owners—sometimes more than once—making each of the three original networks smaller parts of giant publicly owned

Conglomerates   Companies that own media companies as well as businesses that are unrelated to the media business.

Vertical Integration   An attempt by one company to simultaneously control several related aspects of the media business.

Convergence   The melding of the communications, computer and electronics industries. Also used to describe the economic alignment of the various media companies with each other to take advantage of technological advancements.

Thomas Samson/AFP/Getty Images

The Walt Disney Company is a vertically integrated media corporation—a company that owns several different types of media businesses, with each part of the company contributing to the others. Mickey and Minnie pose at the 20th anniversary party for Paris Disneyland.

media companies. Fox Broadcasting Co. is a part of the larger international media company, Rupert Murdoch's News Corp., which also owns *The Wall Street Journal*, TV stations, magazines and Twentieth Century Fox Film Corp. In 2013, the leading cable operator Comcast acquired full ownership of NBC Universal, with its cable channels, theme parks and the NBC broadcast network. Since shares in most of today's media companies are publicly traded, they face heavy pressure to deliver hefty profits to their shareholders.

Media companies today also are driven by media *convergence*. The word *convergence* describes two developments taking place simultaneously. First, it means the melding of the communications, computer and electronics industries because of advances in digital technology. Second, *convergence* also means the economic alignment of different types of media companies with each other so they can offer the variety of services that technical advancements demand.

The people who manage U.S. media companies today want to make money. As in all industries, there are people who want to make money quickly and people who take the long-term view about profits, but certainly none of them wants to lose money. One way to expand a company to take advantage of technological and economic convergence is to acquire an already established business that's successful. Such media acquisitions have skyrocketed for two reasons—public ownership and deregulation.

PUBLIC OWNERSHIP. Most media companies today are publicly traded, which means their stock is sold on one of the nation's stock exchanges. This makes acquisitions relatively easy. A media company that wants to buy another publicly owned company can buy that company's stock when the stock becomes available.

The open availability of stock in these public companies means any company or individual with enough money can invest in the American media industries, which is exactly how the Australian Rupert Murdoch, owner of Fox Broadcasting, joined the U.S. media business and was able to accumulate so many media companies in such a short time.

DEREGULATION. Beginning in 1980, the Federal Communications Commission gradually deregulated the broadcast media. *Deregulation* means the FCC withdrew many regulatory restrictions on broadcast media ownership. Before 1980, for example, the FCC allowed a broadcast company to own only five TV stations, five AM radio stations and five FM radio stations. Companies also were required to hold onto a station for three years before the owners could sell it.

The post-1980 FCC eliminated the three-year rule and raised the number of broadcast holdings allowed for one owner. Today, there are very few FCC restrictions on broadcast media ownership.

Why Media Properties Converge

Ownership turnover is highest in the newspaper and broadcast industries. Six factors have affected the economic alignment of these properties:

1. Media properties can be attractive investments. Many broadcast companies have historically earned profits of 10 percent or more a year, for example, which is about double the average amount that a U.S. manufacturing company earns.

2. Newspapers and broadcast stations are scarce commodities. Because the number of newspapers has been declining and the government regulates the number of broadcast stations that are allowed to operate, a limited number of established media outlets are available. As with all limited commodities, this makes them attractive investments.

3. Newspapers and broadcast stations have moved past their early cycle of family ownership. If the heirs to the founders of a family business are not interested in running the company, the only way for them to collect their inheritance is to sell the business, and the only companies with enough money to buy individual media businesses are large corporations and investment companies.

4. Newspapers and broadcast stations are easier businesses to buy than to create. Because these businesses require huge investments in equipment and people, they are expensive to start up. In broadcasting, the major factor that encouraged ownership changes, beginning in the 1980s, was deregulation. This allowed investors who had never been in the broadcast business before to enter the industry, using bank loans to pay for most of their investment. Some new owners of broadcast media companies see these companies the way they would look at any business— hoping to invest the minimum amount necessary. They hold onto the property until the market is favorable, planning to sell at a huge profit.

5. In the 1990s, the introduction of new technologies, especially the Internet, changed the economics of all the media industries. Each industry had to adapt to the Internet quickly, and the fastest way to gain Internet expertise was to buy a company or to invest in a company that already had created an Internet presence or a successful Internet product.

6. The economic downturn that began in 2007 hit the newspaper business especially hard. Heavily dependent on real estate advertising and classifieds and challenged by the dynamics of the Internet, many publicly owned newspaper companies began losing money at an unprecedented rate. This fall in profits drove down their stock prices to new lows, which made them vulnerable to takeovers and buyouts as the companies struggled to survive. Several newspaper companies, such as the Tribune Company (which publishes the *Chicago Tribune* and the *Los Angeles Times*), filed for bankruptcy protection, and in 2013 the investors who own the Tribune Company put it up for sale.

Deregulation   Government action that reduces government restrictions on the business operations of an industry.

Supporters of concentrated ownership and convergence say a large company can offer advantages that a small company could never afford—training for the employees, higher wages and better working conditions.

The major arguments against the concentration and convergence of group ownership are that concentration of so much power limits the diversity of opinion and the quality of ideas available to the public and reduces what scholars call *message pluralism*. More than 30 years ago, Ben H. Bagdikian, dean emeritus, Graduate School of Journalism at the University of California, Berkeley, described how the loss of message pluralism can affect every aspect of communication:

> It has always been assumed that a newspaper article might be expanded to a magazine article which could become the basis for a hardcover book, which, in turn, could be a paperback, and then, perhaps a TV series and finally, a movie. At each step of change an author and other enterprises could compete for entry into the array of channels for reaching the public mind and pocketbook. But today several media giants own these arrays, not only closing off entry points for competition in different media, but influencing the choice of entry at the start.

Today, ownership concentration is an ongoing trend in the media business.

Advertisers and Consumers Pay the Bills

Most of the income the American mass media industries collect comes from advertising. Advertising directly supports newspapers, radio and television. Subscribers actually pay only a small part of the cost of producing a newspaper. Advertisers pay the biggest portion. Magazines receive more than half their income from advertising and the other portion from subscriptions. Income for movies, recordings and books, of course, comes primarily from direct purchases and ticket sales.

This means that companies that want to sell you products pay for most of the information and entertainment you receive from the Internet, TV, radio, newspapers and magazines. You support the media industries *indirectly* by

---

Message Pluralism   The availability to an audience of a variety of information and entertainment sources.

Pictograph   A symbol of an object that is used to convey an idea.

---

buying the products that advertisers sell. General Motors Corp. spends $3 billion a year on advertising. Verizon Communications Inc. spends $200 million a year just on print advertising. Multiply the spending for all this advertising for all media, and you can understand how easily American media industries accumulate billions in annual profits.

You also pay for the media *directly* when you buy a book or a video game or go to a movie. This money buys equipment, underwrites company research and expansion, and pays stock dividends. Advertisers and consumers are the financial foundation for American media industries because different audiences provide a variety of markets for consumer products.

Technology Changes Mass Media Delivery and Consumption

The channels of communication have changed dramatically over the centuries, but the idea that a society will pay to stay informed and entertained is not new. In Imperial Rome, people who wanted to find out what was going on paid professional speakers a coin (a *gazet*) for the privilege of listening to the speaker announce the day's events. Many early newspapers were called *gazettes* to reflect this heritage.

The history of mass communication technology involves three information communications revolutions: phonetic writing, printing and computer technology. (See TimeFrame, p. 3.)

Phonetic Writing: The First Information Communications Revolution

Early attempts at written communication began modestly with *pictographs*. A pictograph is a symbol of an object that is used to convey an idea. If you have ever drawn a heart with an arrow through it, you understand what a pictograph is. The Sumerians of Mesopotamia carved the first known pictographs in stone in about 3500 B.C.

The stone in which these early pictographic messages were carved served as a medium—a device to transmit messages. Eventually, people imprinted messages in clay, and then they stored these clay tablets in a primitive version of today's library. These messages weren't very portable, however. Heavy clay tablets don't slip easily into someone's pocket.

In about 2500 B.C., the Egyptians invented papyrus, a type of paper made from a grasslike plant called sedge, which was easier to write on, but people still communicated using pictographs.

Pictographs as a method of communication developed into *phonetic writing* in about 1000 B.C. when people began to use symbols to represent sounds. Instead of drawing a picture of a dog to convey the idea of a dog, scholars represented the sounds d-o-g with phonetic writing. The invention of phonetic writing has been called *the first information communications revolution.* "After being stored in written form, *information could now reach a new kind of audience, remote from the source and uncontrolled by it,*" writes media scholar Anthony Smith. "Writing transformed knowledge into information."

About 500 years later, the Greek philosopher Socrates anticipated the changes that widespread literacy would bring. He argued that knowledge should remain among the privileged classes. Writing threatened the exclusive use of information, he said. "Once a thing is put in writing, the composition, whatever it may be, drifts all over the place, getting into the hands not only of those who understand it, but equally of those who have no business with it."

In about 200 B.C., the Greeks perfected parchment, made from goat and sheepskins. Parchment was an even better medium on which to write. By about A.D. 100, before the use of parchment spread throughout Europe, the Chinese had invented paper, which was much cheaper to produce than parchment. Europeans didn't start to use paper until more than a thousand years later, in about A.D. 1300. The discovery of parchment and then paper meant that storing information became cheaper and easier.

As Socrates predicted, when more people learned to write, wider communication became possible because people in many different societies could share information among themselves and with people in other parts of the world. But scholars still had to painstakingly copy the information they wanted to keep or pay a scribe to copy for them. In the 14th century, for example, the library of the Italian poet Petrarch contained more than 100 manuscripts that he himself had copied individually.

In Petrarch's day, literate people were either monks or members of the privileged classes. Wealthy people could afford tutoring, and they also could afford to buy the handwritten manuscripts copied by the monks. Knowledge—and the power it brings—belonged to an elite group of people.

Printing: The Second Information Communications Revolution

As societies grew more literate, the demand for manuscripts flourished, but a scribe could produce only one copy at a time. What has been called *the second information communications revolution* began in Germany in 1455, when Johannes Gutenberg printed a Bible on a press that used movable type.

More than 200 years before Gutenberg, the Chinese had invented a printing press that used wood type, and the Chinese also are credited with perfecting a copper press in 1445. But Gutenberg's innovation was to line up individual metal letters that he could ink and then press onto paper to produce copies. Unlike the wood or copper presses, the metal letters could be reused to produce new pages of text, which made the process much cheaper.

The Gutenberg Bible, a duplicate of the Latin original, is considered the first book printed by movable type (47 copies still survive today, 559 years later). As other countries adopted Gutenberg's press, the price for Bibles plummeted. In 1470, the cost of a French, mechanically printed Bible was one-fifth the cost of a hand-printed Bible.

The second information communications revolution—printing—meant that *knowledge, which had belonged to the privileged few, would one day be available to everyone.* The key development of printing was one of the essential conditions for the rise of modern governments, as well as an important element of scientific and technological progress.

From the Gutenberg Bible, printed in the workshop of Johannes Gutenberg, 1455 (parchment), German School, (15th century)/Universitatsbibliothek, Gottingen, Germany/ Bildarchiv Steffens/The Bridgeman Art Library

The Gutenberg Bible, published by Johannes Gutenberg in Germany in 1455, was the first book printed using movable type. Although the printing was done mechanically, hand-colored decorative drawings (called *illuminations*) often were added to artistically enhance the text.

Phonetic Writing The use of symbols to represent sounds.

Illuminations Hand-colored decorative drawings used to enhance printed text.

Before the Gutenberg press, a scholar who wanted specialized information had to travel to the place where it was kept. But once information could be duplicated easily, it could travel to people beyond the society that created it. The use of paper instead of the scribes' bulky parchment also meant that books could be stacked end to end. *For the first time, knowledge was portable and storable.*

Libraries now could store vast amounts of information in a small space. And because people could easily carry these smaller, lighter books, all different kinds of people in many different cities could read classical works simultaneously. Another benefit of the development of printing was that societies could more easily keep information to share with future generations. *Knowledge now was accessible to many; knowledge no longer belonged to just the chosen few.*

This effort to communicate—first through spoken messages, then through pictographs, then through the written word and finally through printed words—demonstrates people's innate desire to share information with one another. *Storability, portability and accessibility* of information are essential to today's concept of mass communication. By definition, *mass communication is information that is available to a large audience quickly.*

Computer Technology: The Third Information Communications Revolution

Today's age of communication has been called the *third information communications revolution* because computers have become the electronic storehouses and

The introduction of digital delivery represents the third information communications revolution and affects all aspects of politics, society and culture. In Barcelona, Spain, on February 25, 2013, a visitor takes his picture on the first day of the Mobile World Congress, where major communications companies unveil their latest products.

transmitters of vast amounts of information that previously relied on the written word.

Electronic technology, which processes and transmits information much more efficiently than mechanical devices, is driving the majority of changes affecting today's media. This has become possible with the development of digital computers, beginning around 1950. Digital delivery means that changes in today's media industries happen much faster than in the past. Satellite broadcasts, digital recordings and the international computer network called the Internet are just three examples of the third information communications revolution.

Although each medium has its own history and economic structure, today all of the media industries compete for consumers' attention. Digital technology is transforming the media business more than we can foresee—enabling faster transmission of more information to more people than ever before.

Media Take Advantage of Digital Delivery

The economics of the communications industries makes digital delivery very important. All the industries involved in building and maintaining this interconnected network—broadcast, cable, telephone, computer, software, satellite and the consumer electronics industries—want a piece of the estimated $1 trillion in global revenue that digital delivery represents.

Leaders of the media industries in the United States are among the central driving forces in this network because many of the companies that are developing digital products—such as Apple, Microsoft and Intel—are based in the United States.

Because the United States already contributes so many of the digital environment's necessary elements, it has become logical—and very profitable—for the media industries in this country to drive converging technologies that package and deliver information worldwide.

One-Way Versus Two-Way Communication

The classic model of mass communication (see **Illustration 1.3** on page 7) describes a process that begins with a *sender* (or source), who puts a *message* on a *channel* (a medium). The channel then delivers the message to the *receiver*. This is the equivalent of a one-way road—sender to receiver.

Digital delivery begins in the same way. The *channel* carries information and entertainment (*messages*) from many different sources (*senders*) to many different people (*receivers*). The messages that return from the receiver to the sender are called *feedback*. In the digital

David Ramos/Getty Images

environment, messages and feedback can occur almost instantly because the sender and the receiver can communicate with each other simultaneously. This makes digital systems *interactive*.

To take advantage of this interactivity, today's delivery system has evolved from a communications system that works like an ordinary television (sending messages and programming one way from the sender to the receiver) into a two-way, interactive system that can send and receive messages simultaneously and that works more like a combination television, telephone and computer.

Dumb Versus *Smart* Communication

A standard television set is a "dumb" appliance; it can only deliver programming. You can change the channel to receive different programs, but you can't talk back to the people who send the programming to your television set to tell them when you'd like to see a particular program. You can record something to watch later or pick a specific program to watch. But you can't rearrange a television network schedule to show all your programs exactly when you want to see them. You also can't add anything to the programs on your TV, such as your personal commentary about a football game or a bad movie. This type of mass communication—in which the programs are sent to you on an established schedule with you as a passive receiver (a couch potato) for the program—is *one-way*.

As communications devices, however, telephones are smarter. When you talk on the telephone, the person on the other end of the conversation can listen to you and talk back right away (and, in the case of a teleconference, this can involve several people at the same time). This makes telephone communication interactive, giving you the ability to talk back—to receive as well as to transmit messages. Telephone communications are *two-way*.

To communicate rapidly, telephone communication uses a system of digitized information. When you talk, the telephone system uses electronic signals to transform your voice into a series of digits—ones and zeroes—and then reassembles these digits into an exact reproduction of your voice on the other end of the line. This method of storing and transmitting data is called *digital communication*.

Like telephone communications, computers also operate using digitized information and are interactive. Written words, audio and video are translated and stored as *bits*. These bits can easily be transmitted, using two-way

communication. This is the reason that someone can, for instance, connect to the Internet on a computer and receive and send information. To communicate via the Internet, a computer uses a *modem* to connect to a telephone line or a cellular signal, making two-way communication possible.

And, unlike television and telephones, computers can store digital information for future use. This ability to store information makes the computer different from broadcast, cable, telephone and satellite communications.

HOW TODAY'S COMMUNICATIONS NETWORK OPERATES

Today's communications network combines many different elements from existing media industries. The broadcast industry produces content and delivers one-way communication by antenna and satellite; the cable industry delivers one-way communication and two-way communication by underground (or overhead) cable; the telephone companies deliver digital two-way communication using fiber, satellite and cellular technology; and the computer industry offers digital storage capability.

A digital communications network combines all these elements: content, two-way digital communication and digital storage. **Illustration 1.4** on page 18 shows how this communications network operates.

Interactive   A message system that allows senders and receivers to communicate simultaneously.

Digital Communication   Data in a form that can be transmitted and received electronically.

IMPACT/Convergence

Illustration 1.4

How the Communications Network Works

Today's communications network combines different elements of broadcast, cable, telephone, satellite, cellular and computer technology to create a global digital communications service.

National-International Network

Telephone company

Satellite company

Cable company

Video phone services　Video game services　Interactive services
Audio and video program services　Television-on-demand services

Computer

Mobile media device

Television

© Cengage Learning

The Receiver (You, the Subscriber)

A digital network begins with you, the receiver/subscriber. For example, you go online to check your *e-mail* and then look around to decide which other services you want, such as

- First-run movies, TV episodes and music streaming
- Worldwide video news feeds, including access to overseas news channels in a variety of languages

- Newspaper and video services, offering real-time access to today's stories from news outlets around the globe on topics you've preselected
- Internet video games and gambling sites
- Twitter feeds, social networks, blogs and video indexed by subject

As you glance through the offerings of each service and make your choices, the screen shows several windows simultaneously so you can use various services at the same time, each on a different screen. For example, you check your bank balance while you play poker online and check your text messages while you watch overseas news headlines.

All these services, which you take for granted today, weren't available ten years ago. The Internet's digital communications network is what makes all this possible.

E-mail　Mail that is delivered electronically over the Internet.

The Channel (Cable, Telephone, Satellite and Cellular Companies)

Cable, telephone, satellite and cellular companies provide Internet communications delivery, acting as a conduit—gathering all the services from national and international networks. Some companies offer only specific services, or they package services together (local, national and international news services, for example), or they offer an unlimited menu of all the available services and let you choose what you want. Cable, telephone, satellite and cellular companies are competing today for consumers' Internet business.

You can choose the type of service you want based on each company's offerings and pricing. Some services are billed as pay-per-use (a $6 charge to view a first-run movie, for example) or per retrieved item (to use a newspaper's archive for research, for example).

This international communications network and the satellite system to support it already are in place—long-distance carrier networks run by a communications company such as AT&T or a satellite service such as DirecTV or Dish Network. The *Internet*, as an international web of computer networks, forms the backbone of this communications network, which is available to any consumer who has a screen and a cable, satellite, cellular or telephone connection to the system.

The Sender (Internet Service Providers)

Internet service providers (*ISPs*), such as MSN, provide a way of organizing the information to help you find what you want. Today's broadcast networks, as well as cable and satellite channels, essentially are video program services, offering a group of programs for a specific subscription fee. Telephone companies are also beginning to compete to deliver programs directly to consumers.

Program services are moving toward a different model, however, which eventually will make it possible for you to choose programs from NBC and ABC and not CBS, for example, or pick 10 channels from a list of available channels, rather than having to accept a large number of channels—many that you don't necessarily want to watch—packaged together as they are now. When the complete communications network is in place, the ISP will offer customized *bundles*, and you will be able to select the specific bundle you want.

The Message (Content)

All text, audio and video that are digitized into bits are potential content for a digitized communications system. In a world of networked, rapid, digitized communications, *any* digitized textbook, novel, movie, magazine article, recording, video segment or news story, for example, qualifies as content.

Information and entertainment that already have been produced, stored and digitized form the basic content for this communications network. Companies that hold the copyrights for information and entertainment can quickly and easily market the content they already own as products, along with the ongoing information-entertainment they are producing, because they own the rights to their content and don't have to buy the rights from someone else.

Today, media companies that traditionally have produced content, such as newspaper publishers, book publishers, TV program producers and movie producers, are busy creating and buying more "inventory" for the online world. "Movie companies have been increasing production," says *The Wall Street Journal*, "because there is a general feeling that as 'content providers' they will be big winners."

Once information and entertainment products are digitized, they are available in many different formats. This is the reason a music video of Disney songs is available online as soon as—even before—Disney releases a new movie; a profile of a well-known musician, complete with video, can be made available on the musician's Internet site during the musician's worldwide concert tour; and a publisher can assemble excerpts and photos from a new book, along with a video interview with the author, and make them available on the Internet to promote the book before it hits the bookstores. With convergence, the availability of digital content means all the mass media industries have become technologically interdependent and interconnected.

MASS MEDIA BOTH REFLECT AND AFFECT POLITICS, SOCIETY AND CULTURE

The media industries provide information and entertainment, but mass media also can affect political, social and cultural institutions. Although the media actively influence society, they also mirror it, and scholars constantly strive to delineate the differences.

Internet   An international web of computer networks.

ISP   Internet service provider.

Bundle   The combination of telecommunications services that the media industries can offer consumers.

Current news events often focus attention on the role of mass media in society. For example, when a gunman killed 20 children and 6 adults in Newtown, Connecticut, on December 14, 2012, the public conversation about the relationship between violence in society and mass media portrayals of violence in movies and video games exploded. Does violence portrayed in the mass media directly cause violent copycat crimes? Does the mass media set the national agenda on issues like gun violence, or does the mass media simply reflect current issues on the public's mind? Did media attention to the event inflame the dialogue? What role did the mass media play in setting the political agenda and the call for stricter national gun control legislation? If you were a scholar studying the mass media, how would you view these developments?

This example shows the difficulty scholars face when analyzing mass media's political, social and cultural effects. Early media studies analyzed each message in the belief that once a message was sent, everyone would receive and react to the message in the same way. Then studies proved that different people process messages differently—a phenomenon described as *selective perception*. This occurs because everyone brings many variables—family background, interests and education, for example—to each message.

Complicating the study of mass media's political, social and cultural effects is the recent proliferation of media outlets. The multiplying sources for information and entertainment today mean that very few people share identical mass media environments. This makes it much more difficult for scholars to analyze the specific or cumulative effects of mass media on the general population.

Still, scholars' attempts to describe mass media's political, social and cultural roles in society are important because, once identified, the effects can be observed. The questions should be asked so we do not become complacent about mass media in our lives, so we do not grow immune to the possibility that our society may be cumulatively affected by mass media in ways we cannot yet accurately quantify. (See **Impact/Audience**, "Silicon Valley Says Step Away from the Device," p. 21.)

Advertising also is often the focus of media analysis—does advertising cause you to buy products you don't

Connecticut State Police Lieutenant Paul Vance addresses a press conference after 20 children and 6 adults were killed at Sandy Hook Elementary School in Newtown, Connecticut, on December 14, 2012. The event revived questions about the role that portrayals of violence in the mass media play in provoking violence in society.

need? Is there a one-to-one relationship between how much money a company devotes to advertising a product and the success of that product? And, if so, how does an advertiser reach a specific customer for a product when mass media delivery today is so diffused? "Marketers used to try their hardest to reach people at home, when they were watching TV or reading newspapers or magazines. But consumers' viewing and reading habits are so scattershot now that many advertisers say the best way to reach time-pressed consumers is to try to catch their eye at literally every turn," reports *The New York Times*.

The market research firm Yankelovich reports that a person living in a city 30 years ago saw up to 2,000 ad messages a day, compared with up to 5,000 today. According to *The New York Times*, about half the people surveyed by Yankelovich said they thought marketing and advertising today was "out of control."

WHY YOU SHOULD UNDERSTAND MASS MEDIA AND EVERYDAY LIFE

In the United States, Europe and Asian countries that have encouraged technological advancements,

---

Selective Perception   The concept that each person processes messages differently.

IMPACT/Audience

Silicon Valley Says Step Away from the Device

By Matt Richtel

Stuart Crabb, a director in the executive offices of Facebook, naturally likes to extol the extraordinary benefits of computers and smartphones. But like a growing number of technology leaders, he offers a warning: log off once in a while, and put them down.

In a place where technology is seen as an all-powerful answer, it is increasingly being seen as too powerful, even addictive.

The concern is that the lure of constant stimulation—the pervasive demand of pings, rings and updates—is creating a profound physical craving that can hurt productivity and personal interactions.

"If you put a frog in cold water and slowly turn up the heat, it'll boil to death—it's a nice analogy," said Mr. Crabb, who oversees learning and development at Facebook. People "need to notice the effect that time online has on your performance and relationships."

Google has started a "mindfulness" movement at the company to teach employees self-awareness and to improve their ability to focus. Richard Fernandez, an executive coach at Google and one of the leaders of the mindfulness movement, said the risks of being overly engaged with devices were immense.

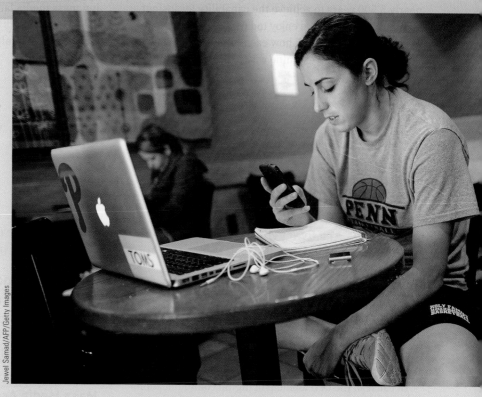

Jewel Samad/AFP/Getty Images

While today's mobile media devices offer many advantages, experts caution that the lure of constant communication can become addictive. A woman at a Starbucks in Silver Spring, Maryland, simultaneously uses her smartphone, laptop and iPod.

"Consumers need to have an internal compass where they're able to balance the capabilities that technology offers them for work, for search, with the qualities of the lives they live offline," he said. "It's about creating space, because otherwise we can be swept away by our technologies."

Excerpted from Matt Richtel, "Silicon Valley Says Step Away from the Device," nytimes.com, July 23, 2012.

communications changes are moving faster than ever before. For the media industries, this means increasing costs to replace old equipment and expand to meet demand. For consumers, this means a confusing array of products that need to be replaced soon after they buy them—video streaming replacing Blu-ray disc players, which replaced DVD players, which replaced VCRs;

HDTV replacing conventional TVs and iPods replacing CD players, for example.

The development of communications technology directly affects the speed with which a society and culture evolve. A town with only one telephone or one radio may be impossible for people in the United States to imagine, but there still are many countries in which ten families share a single telephone, and people consider a television set to be a luxury.

By today's standards, the earliest communications obstacles seem unbelievably simple: how to transmit a single message to several people at the same time and how to share information inexpensively. Yet it has taken nearly 5,500 years to achieve the capability for instant communication that we enjoy today.

After you understand how each type of media business works, you can examine why people who work in the media make the business decisions they do and the effects these decisions have on the United States and the global economy. Once you have traced the history of mass media development, you can consider their present-day effects on you and on society as a whole.

With a better grasp of technology's role in the evolving mass media landscape, you can see how technological change affects the media business. Only then can you truly begin to analyze the *impact* of mass media on your everyday life.

Review, Analyze, Investigate

Reviewing Chapter 1

Mass Media Are Everywhere You Are

- Adults spend more than half of their waking lives with the media.
- Some form of media touches your life every day— economically, socially and culturally.

Mass Communication Becomes Wireless

- Historically, to be connected to media meant that you had to be near an electrical outlet.
- Because of the development of digital communication, most of today's mass media is wireless.
- Electronic signals have replaced wires, freeing people up to stay connected no matter where or when they want to communicate.

How the Communication Process Works

- Communication is the act of sending messages, ideas and opinions from one person to another.
- *Intra*personal communication means communication within one person.
- *Inter*personal communication means communication between two people.
- Mass communication is communication from one person or group of persons through a transmitting device (a medium) to large audiences or markets.
- By definition, mass communication is information that is made available to a large audience quickly.

What Are the Mass Media Industries?

- There are eight mass media businesses: books, newspapers, magazines, recordings, radio, movies, television and the Internet.

- Books were the first mass medium.
- The Internet is the newest mass medium.

Three Key Concepts to Remember

- Mass media are profit-centered businesses.
- Technological developments change the way mass media are delivered and consumed.
- Mass media both reflect and affect politics, society and culture.

Mass Media Are Profit-Centered Businesses

- All U.S. media are privately owned except the Public Broadcasting Service and National Public Radio, which survive on government support and private donations.
- Overall, American mass media ownership has been contracting rather than expanding, with fewer companies owning more aspects of the media business. This trend is called *concentration of ownership*.
- Concentration of ownership takes four forms: chains, broadcast networks, conglomerates and vertical integration.
- The mass media industries—books, newspapers, magazines, recordings, radio, movies, television and the Internet—earn billions in revenue annually.
- Above all, the major goal of the American mass media is to make money. Except for National Public Radio and the Public Broadcasting Service, all U.S. media operate primarily as profit-centered businesses.

Convergence Dominates the Media Business

- Media acquisitions in the United States have skyrocketed because most conglomerates today are publicly traded companies and because, beginning in 1980, the federal government deregulated the broadcast industry.

- The economic downturn that began in 2007 made publicly owned newspapers especially vulnerable to takeovers and acquisitions.

- The trend of mergers and acquisitions is expected to continue as changing technology expands the global market for media products.

Why Media Properties Converge

- U.S. media industries continue to prosper, but the share of profits is shifting among the different types of media industries.

- Supporters of concentrated ownership and convergence say a large company offers advantages that a small company can never afford; critics say concentrated ownership and convergence interfere with message pluralism.

Advertisers and Consumers Pay the Bills

- Most of the income the mass media industries collect comes from advertising.

- People who want to sell you products pay for most of the information and entertainment you receive through the American mass media.

- Consumers support the media indirectly by buying the products that advertisers sell.

Technology Changes Mass Media Delivery and Consumption

- The invention of phonetic writing in 1000 B.C. was considered the *first information communications revolution*.

- The invention of movable type in 1455 marked the *second information communications revolution*.

- The invention of digital computers in 1951 ushered in the *third information communications revolution*.

- The new world of mass media uses wireless communications technology, an intricate webbed network of many different types of communications systems.

- The development of communications technology directly affects the speed with which a society evolves.

- Storability, portability and accessibility of information are essential to today's concept of mass communication.

Media Take Advantage of Digital Delivery

- Today's information network uses broadcast, telephone, cable, satellite and computer technology.

- The traditional delivery system for information and entertainment is primarily a one-way system.

- The ability to talk back—to receive as well as transmit messages—makes the telephone interactive.

- Today's communications network is a two-way, interactive system.

How Today's Communications Network Operates

- The communications network needs content, two-way digital communication and digital storage.

- Cable companies, satellite services, telephone and cellular companies deliver services on the new communications network.

- Many Americans already have all the tools that a digital communications system needs—television, telephone, cellular, cable and satellite services and computers.

- Information and entertainment that already have been produced, stored and digitized provided the first content for the communications network.

- Many motives shape the American mass media, including the desire to fulfill the public's need for information, to influence the country's governance, to disseminate the country's culture, to offer entertainment and to provide an outlet for creative expression.

- Media industries expand and contract in the marketplace to respond to the audience.

Mass Media Both Reflect and Affect Politics, Society and Culture

- The media are political, social and cultural institutions that both reflect and affect the society in which they operate.

- Multiplying sources of information and entertainment mean that, today, very few people share identical mass media environments.

Why You Should Understand Mass Media and Everyday Life

- In the United States, Europe and Asian countries that have encouraged technological advancements, communication changes are moving faster than ever before.

- For the media industries, this means increasing costs to replace old equipment. For consumers, this means a confusing array of products that need to be replaced soon after you buy them.

- The development of communications technology directly affects the speed with which a society and culture evolve.

- It has taken nearly 5,500 years to achieve the capability for instant communication that we enjoy today.

Key Terms

These terms are defined in the margins throughout this chapter and appear in alphabetical order with definitions in the Glossary, which begins on page 373.

Critical Questions

1. Discuss the differences between one-way and two-way communication, and explain why two-way communication is important for the new communications network.

2. Give three examples of how consumers pay both directly and indirectly for mass media in America.

3. Identify the three communications revolutions and discuss how each one drastically changed the world's mass media.

4. Summarize the advantages and disadvantages of the concentration of ownership in today's mass media business.

5. In traditional media, advertising aimed at consumers pays for delivery of entertainment and information. How has digital delivery changed the way people pay for mass media?

Working the Web

This list includes both sites mentioned in the chapter and others to give you greater insight into mass media and everyday life.

CBS Corporation
cbscorporation.com

CBS Corp. has operations in every field of media and entertainment. The company consists of mass media brands, including CBS Radio, Showtime, Simon & Schuster Publishers, The CW (a joint venture with Warner Bros. Entertainment), CBS Sports Network, Smithsonian Network, CBS Television Studios, CBS Outdoor, CBS Global Distribution Group, CBS Interactive, CBS Consumer Products, CBS Home Entertainment, CBS Films and CBS EcoMedia.

Comcast Corporation (owner of NBC Universal)
comcast.com

Comcast Corp. is a global media and technology company with two primary businesses, Comcast Cable and NBC Universal. It provides video, high-speed Internet and phone service to individuals and businesses throughout the United States under the Xfinity brand. NBC Universal operates 30 news and entertainment cable networks, including the NBC and Telemundo broadcast networks, television production networks, television production operations, television station groups, Universal Pictures and Universal Parks and Resorts.

Gannett Company (owner of *USA Today*)
gannett.com

The United States' largest newspaper chain, Gannett publishes 82 daily newspapers, including *USA Today*. The Web site usatoday.com is one of the most popular news sites on the Web. The company operates 23 television stations, Gannett Digital (CareerBuilder.com and 100 online mobile properties) and Newsquest (one of the U.K.'s leading regional community news providers). Gannett's broadcasting group also delivers news and advertising to specific audiences through video screens in office building elevators and select hotels in North America.

News Corporation
newscorp.com

News Corp. is Rupert Murdoch's diversified media empire and home of the various Fox media. Its operations include filmed entertainment, television cable digital (Hulu.com—a joint venture with NBC Universal and Disney that is the leading online video site, helping people find and enjoy the world's premium video content), satellite, and books. The company began in Australia and has many media outlets there and in Europe and Asia as well as in the United States. In 2007 News Corp. bought *The Wall Street Journal*.

Sony Corporation of America

sony.com

This U.S. subsidiary of Sony Corp. is based in New York City. Its parent company, based in Tokyo, Japan, is a leading manufacturer of audio, video, communications and information technology. Sony's principal media businesses include Sony Electronics, Sony Pictures and Sony Music Entertainment.

Time Warner Inc.

timewarner.com

A leading media and entertainment company, Time Warner Inc.'s businesses include cable and broadcast television, interactive services, filmed entertainment and publishing. In addition to entertainment companies (HBO, CNN and Warner Bros.), Time Warner also owns AOL and investment and global media groups.

Tribune Company

tribune.com

Tribune Co. operates businesses in publishing, interactive and broadcast media. The company's leading daily newspapers include the *Los Angeles Times*, the *Chicago Tribune* and *The Baltimore Sun*. In 2009, the Tribune Company filed for bankruptcy protection.

Twitter

twitter.com

Twitter describes itself as "a real-time information network powered by people all around the world that lets you share and discover what's happening now. Twitter asks 'what's happening' and makes the answer spread across the globe to millions, immediately." Users can follow personal or celebrity blogs and breaking news, find out more about a local traffic jam and sales at their favorite stores plus receive and send messages to friends.

U.S. Census Bureau Statistical Abstract: Information and Communications

census.gov/compendia/statab/cats/information_communications.html

This source presents statistics on the various information and communications media: publishing, motion pictures, recordings, broadcasting, telecommunications and information services such as libraries. Internet-use statistics also are included.

Viacom Inc. (owner of Nickelodeon, Comedy Central and Nick at Nite)

viacom.com

This publicly traded company was formerly known as the Viacom Corporation before it split from CBS in 2005. Its well-known cable networks and entertainment brands include Nickelodeon, Nick at Nite, Comedy Central and CMT: Country Music Television. Viacom Inc. also owns Rhapsody, a membership-based music service, and Shockwave, a library of Web-based and mobile games.

Walt Disney Company (owner of ABC)

disney.com

This vertically integrated entertainment pioneer began as an animated cartoon studio in 1923. Today, Disney is divided into five major business segments: Studio Entertainment (Walt Disney Pictures and Touchstone Pictures), Parks and Resorts, Consumer Products, Disney Interactive Media Group and Media Networks (which includes the Disney-ABC Television Group, ESPN and The Walt Disney Internet Group). Disney's latest acquisitions are Pixar and Marvel Comics.

YouTube

youtube.com

Founded in 2005 and acquired by Google Inc. just a year later, YouTube is the leader in online video. Users can watch anything from current events to quirky and unusual content and can browse categories such as comedy, news and politics, pets and animals and sports.

Impact/Action Videos are concise news features on various topics created exclusively for *Media/Impact*. Go online to access MindTap at cengagebrain.com. MindTap for Media/Impact sequences all of your learning tools—Chapter Readings with highlighting and note taking, Impact/Action Videos, activities and assessments—into chapter driven learning units that guide you through the curriculum.

BOOKS:
REARRANGING THE PAGE

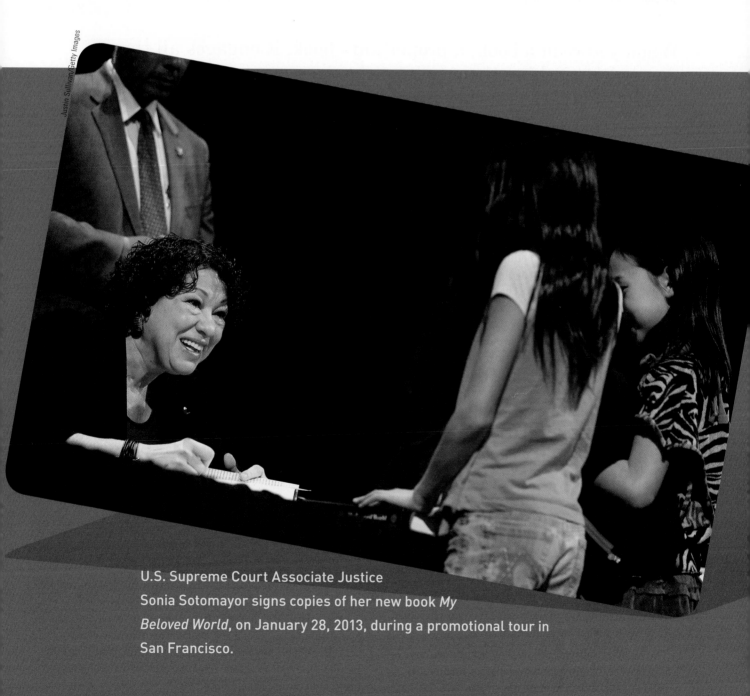

Justin Sullivan/Getty Images

U.S. Supreme Court Associate Justice Sonia Sotomayor signs copies of her new book *My Beloved World*, on January 28, 2013, during a promotional tour in San Francisco.

"When you read a book, a proper kid's book, it engages all the senses. It's teaching them to turn the page properly. You get the smell of paper, the touch."

—ALEXANDRA TYLER, KINDLE USER AND MOTHER OF A 7-YEAR-OLD, TALKING ABOUT WHY SHE PREFERS PRINTED BOOKS FOR HER YOUNG SON.

"I'm not sure I can

explain how to write a book," said essayist and author E. B. White, who wrote 19 books, including *Charlotte's Web.* "First you have to want to write one very much. Then, you have to know of something that you want to write about. Then, you have to begin. And, once you have started, you have to keep going. That's really all I know about how to write a book." The process of writing a book today is much more complex than White suggests, and every year in the United States publishers produce about 150,000 book titles. This number includes revised editions of previously published books, but most of the books are new.

Publishers Nurture Ideas and Try to Make a Profit

The publishing industry always has been tugged by what publishing scholars Lewis A. Coser, Charles Kadushin and Walter W. Powell call "the culture and commerce of publishing"—the desire to preserve the country's intellectual ideas versus the desire to make money. But a publisher who doesn't make a profit cannot continue to publish books.

Coser and his colleagues describe the four characteristics of book publishing in America:

1. The industry sells its products—like any commodity— in a market that, in contrast to that for many other products, is fickle and often uncertain.

2. The industry is decentralized among a number of sectors whose operations bear little resemblance to each other.

3. A mixture of modern mass media production methods and craftlike procedures characterizes these operations.

4. The industry remains perilously poised between the requirements and restraints of commerce and the responsibilities and obligations that it must bear as a prime guardian of the symbolic culture of the nation.

Many new owners of publishing houses try to bring some predictability to the market. Says Coser, "Publishers attempt to reduce . . . uncertainty . . . through concentrating on 'sure-fire' blockbusters, through large-scale promotion campaigns or through control over distribution, as in the marketing of paperbacks. In the end, however, publishers rely on sales estimates that may be as unreliable as weather forecasts in Maine."

How American Book Publishing Grew

Today, the book publishing industry divides responsibilities among many people. But when Americans first started publishing books, one person often did all the work.

Aboard the *Mayflower* in 1620, there were two dogs and 70 adults and only a few books. The pilgrims were very practical. They brought a map of Virginia and John Smith's *Description of New England,* but the main books they carried were their Bibles.

TimeFrame

1620–TODAY

Book Publishing Becomes Big Business

Stock Montage/Archive Photos/Getty Images

1620 Imported books arrive in the colonies on the *Mayflower*.

1640 America's first book, *The Bay Psalm Book*, is printed at Cambridge, Mass.

1731 Benjamin Franklin creates the first lending library.

1776 Thomas Paine publishes the revolutionary pamphlet *Common Sense*.

1891 Congress passes the International Copyright Law of 1891, which requires publishing houses to pay royalties to all authors.

1900 Elementary education becomes compulsory, which means increased literacy and more demand for textbooks.

1926 Book-of-the-Month Club is founded, increasing the audience for books.

1939 Robert de Graff introduces Pocket Books, America's first series of paperback books.

Buyenlarge/Archive Photos/Getty Images

1948 New American Library begins publishing serious fiction by and about African Americans.

1960 Publishing houses begin to consolidate, concentrating power in a few large corporations.

1970S Book marketing changes significantly with the growth of retail bookstore chains.

1980S Publishers begin producing audiobooks of popular titles.

1990S Amazon.com begins doing business as an Internet retailer for books.

2000 Publishers launch e-books, electronic versions of paper books.

2004 Google announces the Google Book Project to scan the books of major research libraries and make their contents searchable.

2007 Amazon introduces the Kindle e-reader tablet.

2009 U.S. Department of Justice opposes a settlement by the Google Book Project with authors, putting the project's future in doubt.

Noah Berger/Bloomberg/Getty Images

2010 Apple introduces the iPad, making books available as instant downloads.

2011 Chain book retailer Borders files for bankruptcy and eventually shuts down.

2012 Apple introduces the iPad mini, a smaller, less expensive version of the iPad.

TODAY Most books are sold through Internet retailers and chain bookstores, and independent booksellers are struggling. Publishers are promoting e-books, including e-textbooks, as a cheaper, convenient alternative to traditional printed books.

The first books in the United States were imports, brought by the new settlers or ordered from England after the settlers arrived. In 1638, the colonists set up a press at Cambridge, Mass., and in 1640 they printed America's first book: *The Bay Psalm Book*. As the only book, it became an instant best-seller. There were only about 3,500 families in the colonies at the time, and the book's first printing of 1,750 sold out.

By 1680, Boston had 17 booksellers, but most of the books still came from England. Between 1682 and 1685, Boston's leading bookseller, John Usher, bought 3,421 books to sell. Among the books he ordered were 162 romance novels.

In 1731, Benjamin Franklin decided that Philadelphia needed a library. So he asked 50 subscribers to pay 40 shillings each to a library company. The company imported 84 books, which circulated among the subscribers. This circulating library was America's first.

The year after he established the circulating library, Franklin published *Poor Richard's Almanack*. Unlike most printers, who waited for someone to come to them with a manuscript, Franklin wrote his own books. The typical author sought a patron to pay for the book's printing and then sold the book at the print shop where it was published.

To expand readership, early publishers sold political pamphlets, novels, poetry and humor. In addition, three events of the 19th century ensured that the book publishing industry would prosper in the 20th century: the International Copyright Law, the creation of publishing houses and the establishment of compulsory education.

Political Pamphlets

The big seller of the 1700s was Thomas Paine's revolutionary pamphlet *Common Sense*, which argued for the colonies' independence from Great Britain. From January to March 1776, colonial presses published 100,000 copies of Paine's persuasive political argument—one copy for every 25 people in the colonies—a true best-seller. Throughout the Revolutionary War, Paine was America's best-read author.

Novels and Poetry

Political pamphlets became much less important once the new nation was established, and printers turned their attention to other popular reading, especially fiction. Historians credit Benjamin Franklin with selling *Pamela* by Samuel Richardson in 1744, the first novel published in the United States, although it was a British import that first had appeared in England in 1740.

Because there was no international copyright law, colonial printers freely reprinted British novels like *Pamela* and sold them. It was cheaper than publishing

William Haefeli/The New Yorker Collection/Cartoonbank.com

"Actually, I'm sitting here reading a book—just to see if I can still do it."

American authors, who could demand royalties. (See "International Copyright Law of 1891," p. 31.)

Like other media industries, book publishing always has faced moral criticism. Novels, for example, didn't start out with a good reputation. One critic said the novel "pollutes the imaginations." Women wrote one-third of all the early American novels, and women also bought most of them.

Especially popular after the Civil War and before the turn of the century were dime novels, America's earliest paperbacks. Dime novels often featured serial characters, like many of today's mystery novels. The stories and characters continued from one novel to the next. Most of them cost only a nickel, but some early paperbacks were as expensive as 25 cents.

Poetry generally has been difficult to sell, and it is correspondingly difficult for poets to get published. Literary scholar James D. Hart says that although poetry was never as popular as prose, the mid-1800s was "the great era of poetry. . . . It was more widely read in those years than it has been since."

Humor

Humor has been a durable category in book publishing since the days of humorist Mark Twain. Made famous by his short story "The Celebrated Jumping Frog of Calaveras County," Twain became a one-man publishing enterprise. One reason his books sold well was that he was the first American author to recognize the importance of advance publicity. Like most books, Twain's novels were sold door to door. Sales agents took advance orders before the books were published so the publisher could estimate how many to print. Before 1900, more than three-fourths of the popular books people bought were sold door to door.

International Copyright Law of 1891

Before 1891, publishers were legally required to pay royalties to American authors but not to foreign authors. This hurt American authors because books by American authors cost more to publish.

After the International Copyright Law of 1891, all authors—foreign and American—had to give permission for their works to be published. For the first time, American authors cost publishing houses the same amount as foreign authors. This motivated publishers to look for more American writers. In fact, after 1894, American writers published more novels in the United States than foreign writers did.

Publishing Houses

Many publishing houses that began in the late 18th century or during the 19th century continued into the 20th century. Nineteenth-century book publishing houses were just that—book publishing houses. They were nothing like today's multimedia corporations.

These pioneering companies housed all aspects of publishing under one roof: They sought out authors, reviewed and edited copy, printed and then sold the books.

Compulsory Education

By 1900, 31 states had passed compulsory education laws. This was important to book publishing because schools buy textbooks, and education creates more children who can read. Widespread public education meant that schools bought more books, and textbook and children's publishing flourished. Expanded public support for education also meant more money for libraries—more good news for the publishing industry. (See **Impact/Audience**, "For Their Children, Many E-Book Fans Insist on Paper," p. 32.)

CHEAPER BOOKS CREATE A MASS MARKET

The first quarter of the 20th century enabled still more publishing houses, such as Simon & Schuster and McGraw-Hill, to meet the public's needs. Publishers that specialized in paperbacks started in the 1930s and 1940s: Pocket Books (1939), Bantam Books (1946) and New American Library (1948). If you drop a product's price drastically, sales can explode. That's exactly what happened to book publishing with the introduction of book clubs and paperbacks, beginning in the 1920s.

Book Clubs

Book clubs replaced door-to-door sales agents as a way to reach people who otherwise wouldn't buy books.

Book-of-the-Month Club was founded in 1926, and Literary Guild in 1927. By 1946, there were 50 book clubs in America, and the Book-of-the-Month Club was selling nearly 12 million copies a year.

Paperbacks

In 1939, Robert de Graff introduced America's first series of paperback best-sellers, called Pocket Books, which issued titles that had already succeeded as hardbound books. They were inexpensive (25 cents), and they fit in a pocket or a purse. Suddenly, a book could reach millions of people who had never owned a book before. Paperbacks democratized reading in America.

The books were so small, however, that people at first thought paperback books were shortened versions of the original. So publishers printed messages to readers on the cover to assure them that the paperbacks were the "complete novel, as originally published" or "complete and unabridged."

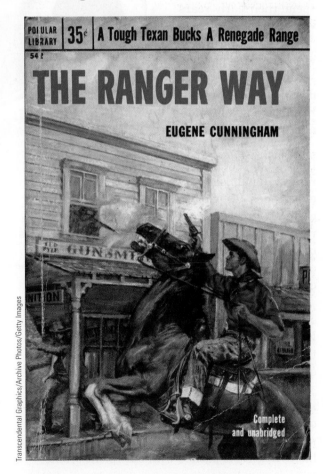

When publishers first issued paperbacks in 1939, consumers thought the smaller books were abridged versions of the originals. So publishers printed messages on the covers of paperbacks like *The Ranger Way* to assure readers that the books were "Complete and unabridged."

IMPACT/Audience

For Their Children, Many E-Book Fans Insist on Paper

By Matt Richtel and Julie Bosman

Print books may be under siege from the rise of e-books, but they have a tenacious hold on a particular group: children and toddlers. Their parents are insisting this next generation of readers spend their early years with old-fashioned books.

This is the case even with parents who themselves are die-hard downloaders of books onto Kindles, iPads, laptops and phones.

As the adult book world turns digital at a faster rate than publishers expected, sales of e-books for titles aimed at children under 8 have barely budged. They represent less than 5 percent of total annual sales of children's books, several publishers estimated, compared with more than 25 percent in some categories of adult books.

"There's definitely a predisposition to print," said Jon Yaged, president and publisher of Macmillan Children's Publishing Group. "And the parents are the same folks who will have no qualms about buying an e-book for themselves."

That is the case in the home of Ari Wallach, a tech-obsessed New York entrepreneur who helps companies update their technology. He himself reads on Kindle, iPad and iPhone, but the room of his twin girls is packed with only print books.

Suzanne DeChillo/The New York Times/Redux Pictures

Ari Wallach (left), a technology entrepreneur, reads books on a Kindle, an iPad and an iPhone but only buys print books for his children. Ari and Sharon Wallach say they want to teach their children to appreciate the value of the printed page.

"I know I'm a Luddite on this, but there's something very personal about a book and not one of one thousand files on an iPad, something that's connected and emotional, something I grew up with and that I want them to grow up with," he said.

Excerpted from Matt Richtel and Julie Bosman, "For Their Children, Many E-Book Fans Insist on Paper," nytimes.com, November 20, 2011.

More publishers joined Pocket Books to produce paperbacks: New American Library (NAL), Avon, Popular Library, Signet and Dell. NAL distinguished itself by being the first mass-market publisher willing to issue serious books by and about African Americans—Richard Wright's *Native Son*, Lillian Smith's *Strange Fruit* and Ralph Ellison's *Invisible Man*. Signet's unexpected hit in the 1950s was J. D. Salinger's novel *Catcher in the Rye*, still popular today.

Grove Press Tests Censorship

Book publishers always have resisted any attempts by the government to limit freedom of expression. One of the first publishers to test those limits was Grove Press. In 1959, Grove published the sexually explicit *Lady Chatterley's Lover* by D. H. Lawrence (originally published in Italy in 1928); in 1961, the company published *Tropic of Cancer* by Henry Miller (originally published in Paris in 1934). Both books had been banned from the United States as obscene. The legal fees to defend Miller's book against charges of pornography cost Grove more than $250,000, but eventually the U.S. Supreme Court cleared the book in 1964.

The publisher again challenged conventional publishing in 1965, when it issued in hardback the controversial *The Autobiography of Malcolm X*, the story of the leader of the African American nationalist movement, by Alex Haley, as told by Malcolm X. The book became a best-seller.

INVESTORS BUY UP PUBLISHING COMPANIES

Forecasts for growing profits in book publishing in the 1960s made the industry attractive to corporations looking for new places to invest. Before the 1960s, the book publishing industry was composed mainly of independent companies whose only business was books. Then, rising school and college attendance from the post-World War II baby boom made some areas of publishing, especially textbooks, lucrative investments for media companies that had not published books before.

Beginning in the 1960s, publishing companies began to consolidate. Publishing expert John P. Dessauer says, "Publishing stocks, particularly those of educational companies, became glamour holdings. And conglomerates began to woo every independent publisher whose future promised to throw off even a modest share of the forecast earnings." Dessauer acknowledges that the new owners often brought a businesslike approach to an industry that was known for its lack of attention to making a profit.

But, according to Dessauer, another consequence of these large-scale acquisitions was that "in many cases

they also placed the power of ultimate decision and policymaking in the hands of people unfamiliar with books, their peculiarities and the markets." The same pace of acquisitions continued through the end of the 20th century, and today large media corporations own most of the major book publishing companies. (See **Illustration 2.1**, p. 34.)

In 2012, publishing companies Random House and Penguin announced they would merge into a new company called Penguin Random House, which creates the largest consumer book publisher in the world. With the merger, Penguin Random House gained a 25 percent share of the global market for consumer books.

"Publishers are increasingly worried about the leverage wielded by Internet giants like Google, Apple and, especially, Amazon," reports *The New York Times*. "These companies have vast resources to invest in new technology, like digital sales platforms, and the size to let them negotiate better terms on prices."

BOOK PUBLISHING AT WORK

When authors get together, often they tell stories about mistakes publishers have made—manuscripts that 20 or 30 publishers turned down but some bright-eyed editor eventually discovered and published. The books, of course, then become best-sellers. Some of the stories are true. But the best publishing decisions are made deliberately, to deliver an awaited book to an eager market. Successful publishing companies must consistently anticipate both their competitors and consumers.

Not only must books be written, but they also must be printed, they must be promoted and they must be distributed in print and electronic formats. This whole process usually takes at least 18 months from the time a project is signed by an editor until the book is published, so publishers are always working ahead. The classic publisher's question is, "Will someone pay $25 (or whatever the projected price of the book is) for this book 18 months after I sign the author?"

BOOKS BEGIN WITH AUTHORS AND AGENTS

Publishers acquire books in many ways. Some authors submit manuscripts "over the transom," which means they send an unsolicited manuscript to a publishing house, hoping the publisher will be interested. However, many of the nation's larger publishers refuse to read unsolicited manuscripts and accept only books that agents submit.

IMPACT/Money

Illustration 2.1

**Consumer Book Publishing's
Five Global Giants**

Book publishing is an international business. With the merger of Random House and Penguin in 2012, the global consumer book publishing business consolidated into five companies owned by large corporations located in the United States and Europe.

Source: Eric Pfanner and Amy Chozick, "Random House and Penguin Merger Creates Global Giant," nytimes.com, October 29, 2012.

Publishers pay authors a *royalty* for their work. A royalty amount is based on an established percentage of the book's price and may run anywhere from 6 to 15 percent of the cover price of the book. Some authors receive an *advance*, which is an amount the publisher pays the author before the book is published. Royalties the book earns once it is in print are charged against the advance payment, so the book first must sell enough copies to pay off the advance before the author gets additional money.

Agents who represent authors collect fees from the authors they represent. Typically, an agent's fee is 10 to 15 percent of the author's royalty. If a publisher prices a book at $20, for example, the author receives from $2 to $3 per book, depending on the author's agreement with the publisher; the agent then receives 20 cents to 45 cents of the author's $2 to $3, depending on the agent's agreement with the author.

Royalty   An amount the publisher pays an author, based on an established percentage of the book's price; royalties run anywhere from 6 to 15 percent.

Advance   An amount the publisher pays the author before the book is published.

HOW DO BOOKS GET PUBLISHED?

In most cases, books start with the *author*, who proposes a book to an acquisitions editor, usually with an outline and some sample chapters. Often an agent negotiates the contract for the book, but some authors negotiate their own contracts. Today the author is only one part of publishing a book. Departments at the publishing house called *acquisitions, media, design, production, manufacturing, marketing* and *fulfillment* all participate in the process. At a small publishing house, these jobs are divided among editors who are responsible for all the steps.

The *acquisitions editor* looks for potential authors and projects and works out an agreement with the author. The acquisitions editor's most important role is to be a liaison among the author, the publishing company and the book's audience. Acquisitions editors also may represent the company at book auctions and negotiate sales of **subsidiary rights**, which are the rights to market a book for other uses—to make a movie, for example, or to use the image of a character in the book on T-shirts.

The *media editor* works with the author to create electronic materials to enhance the book. This could be simply an e-book version of the printed book or any other type of multimedia (such as archival photographs, slide shows or video). For textbooks, this might mean a Web site where students can take sample tests and download chapter outlines.

The *designer* decides what a book will look like, inside and out. The designer chooses the typefaces for the book and determines how the pictures, boxes, heads and subheads will look and where to use color. The designer also creates a concept—sometimes more than one—for the book's cover. Designers also must help with the format for the e-book version of a text, which is different from the printed version.

The *production editor* manages all the steps that turn a double-spaced typewritten manuscript into a book. After the manuscript comes in, the production editor sets up a schedule and makes sure that all the production work gets done on time.

The *manufacturing supervisor* buys the typesetting, paper and printing for the book. The book usually is sent outside the publishing company to be manufactured.

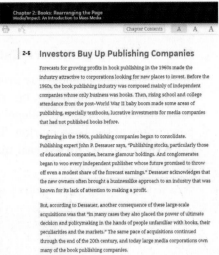

Book designers use digital technology to help them create the way a book looks inside and out. The cover is a vital part of the book's design. Publishers also adapt the book's printed format to be used as an e-book. A page from *Media/Impact* formatted as an e-book is shown on the right.

Marketing, often the most expensive part of creating a book, is handled by several departments. *Advertising* designs ads for the book. *Promotion* sends the book to reviewers. Sales representatives visit bookstores and college campuses to tell book buyers and, in the case of textbooks, potential adopters about the book.

Fulfillment makes sure that the books get to the bookstores on time. This department watches inventory so that if the publisher's stock gets low, more books can be printed.

BOOK INDUSTRY HAS THREE MAJOR MARKETS

Today, adult and juvenile trade books account for almost half of the books people buy, and textbooks make up more than a third of all books sold. The number of new books and new editions has stabilized, but publishers are charging more for each book. Today, paperbacks and hardbacks cost nearly three times what they cost 30 years ago, while e-books typically cost less than hardback editions of new books but more than paperback editions.

Books fall into three major categories: adult and juvenile trade books; textbooks; and professional and scholarly books. Originally, many publishing houses

Subsidiary Rights The rights to market a book for other uses—to make a movie or to print a character from the book on T-shirts, for example.

IMPACT/Money

Illustration 2.2

How Do Book Publishers Make Their Money?

Most of the books people buy are adult and juvenile fiction and nonfiction trade books, but textbooks (kindergarten through 12th grade and college) account for a substantial percentage of the book market. **Today e-books account for 8 percent of the overall market, and e-book sales are growing rapidly.**

Source: Jim Milliot, "Tracking the Transition: Bookstats," August 12, 2011, publishersweekly.com.

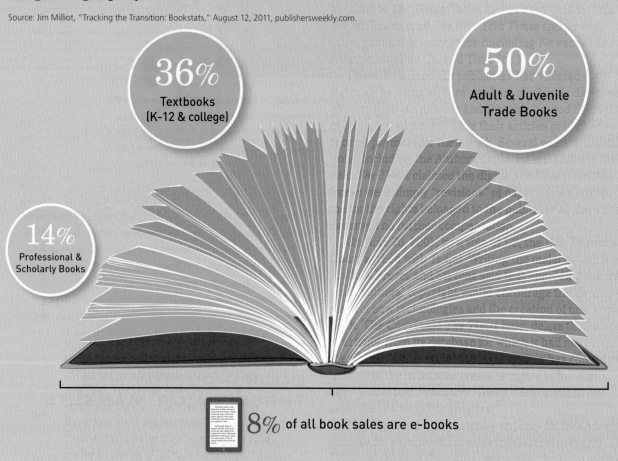

36%
Textbooks
(K-12 & college)

50%
Adult & Juvenile
Trade Books

14%
Professional &
Scholarly Books

8% of all book sales are e-books

were classified based on the type of publisher that produced the books. A company that was called a textbook publisher produced only textbooks, for example. Today, one publishing house often publishes several kinds of books—trade books and textbooks, for example—although it may be organized as separate divisions of the same company. (See **Illustration 2.2**.)

Adult and Juvenile Trade Books

Usually sold through bookstores and to libraries, trade books are designed for the general public. These books include hardbound books and trade (or "quality")

paperbound books for adults and children. Typical trade books include hardcover fiction, current nonfiction, biography, literary classics, cookbooks, travel books, art books and books on sports, music, poetry and drama. Many college classes use trade books as well as textbooks. Juvenile trade books can be anything from picture books for children who can't read yet to novels for young adults. Included under trade books are mass-market paperbacks, such as detective series or romance novels. Many are reprints of hardcover trade books; others are only published as mass-market paperbacks. Generally, they're made from cheaper paper and cost less than trade paperbacks.

Textbooks

Textbooks are published for elementary and secondary school students (called the "el-hi" market) as well as for college students. Most college texts are paid for by the students but are chosen by their professors.

Very little difference exists between some college texts and some trade books. Often the only real difference is that textbooks include what publishers call *apparatus*—for example, test questions and chapter summaries with extra assignments. The difference in content may be difficult to discern, so the Association of American Publishers classifies these two types of books (that is, trade books and textbooks) according to where they are sold the most. A book that is used mainly in grammar school, high school or college classrooms, for example, is called a textbook.

Professional and Scholarly Books

University presses publish a small number of scholarly books every year and are defined solely by who publishes them: A university press book is one that a university publishes. Most university presses are nonprofit and are connected to a university, museum or research institution. These presses produce mainly scholarly materials in hardcover and softcover. Most scholarly books are sold through direct mail and in college bookstores.

Professional books are designed for a specific profession. Often these are reference books, such as an auto-repair manual or an encyclopedia of veterinary terms.

AUDIOBOOKS AND E-BOOKS MULTIPLY THE AUDIENCE

Audiobooks

Since they were first introduced in the 1980s, *audiobooks* have been a small sales category for book publishers, aimed at people who would rather listen to a book than read it. Audiobooks can be abridged or complete versions of the originals.

Initially, book publishers produced classics and popular audiobooks on CDs, but now most audiobooks are sold as Internet downloads. Digital formats such as MP3 mean that, for a fee, consumers can download audiobooks from the Internet to be played on any device designed to play downloaded files. The availability of audiobooks on mobile devices has revived interest in audiobooks because they are available so easily.

Electronic Books

Always looking for more income from the content they own, book publishers today are producing some books only as electronic books (*e-books*) as well as e-book versions of printed books. E-books can be downloaded and then read on an electronic tablet or even a mobile phone.

The introduction of e-books is a promising way for publishers to expand the market for their products. With the introduction of e-readers such as the Amazon Kindle and Apple's iPad, e-books have become a very popular and portable way to read a book. In 2010, Google launched Google eBooks, which makes e-books available on smartphones and computers as well as electronic tablets. E-books now account for 8 percent of all book sales.

"As with digital music, multiple books—say, Shakespeare's collected works—can be stored on a memory card the size of a stick of gum, making them popular with travelers, students and professionals," says Reuters columnist Franklin Paul. According to software developer Adobe's Russell Brady, "Two audiences that will benefit best are young people who loathe the idea of a library . . . and aging people who want the convenience of large type on demand, or freedom from lugging heavy hardcover tomes.

"We think that in the long term, e-book technology has a great future. Market acceptance has not taken off quite as quickly as was predicted, but we are certainly continuing to invest in this area." Many publishers now believe that e-books are the only way that the book publishing business can expand. Publishers must absorb the huge costs of electronic delivery and settle new copyright issues about who owns an e-book once it's downloaded. (See **Impact/Convergence**, "E-Book Restrictions Leave 'Buyers' with Few Rights," p. 38.)

CORPORATIONS DEMAND HIGHER PROFITS

Consolidation in the book business means the giants in today's publishing industry are demanding increasingly higher profits. The companies look for extra income in three ways: subsidiary and international rights, blockbuster books and chain and Internet marketing.

Subsidiary and International Rights

Trade and mass-market publishers are especially interested in, and will pay more for, books with the potential for subsidiary- and international-rights sales. The rights to make a video game version of a book, for example, are subsidiary rights.

Audiobooks Abridged or complete versions of classic books and popular new titles available on CDs and as Internet downloads.

E-books Electronic books.

IMPACT/Convergence

E-Book Restrictions Leave "Buyers" with Few Rights

By Michael Hiltzik

There's a crass old joke about how you can never buy beer, just rent it. Who would think that the same joke applies to book buying in the digital age?

But that's the case. Many people who'll be unwrapping iPads, Amazon Kindles or Barnes & Noble Nooks on [Christmas] morning and loading them with bestsellers or classics won't have any idea how limited their rights are as their books' "owners."

In fact, they won't be owners at all. They'll be licensees. Unlike the owners of a physical tome, they won't have the unlimited right to lend an e-book, give it away, resell it or leave it to their heirs. If it's bought for their iPad, they won't be able to read it on their Kindle. And if Amazon or the other sellers don't like what they've done with it, they can take it back, without warning.

All these restrictions "raise obvious questions about what 'ownership' is," observes Dan Gillmor, an expert on digital media at Arizona State University. "The companies that license stuff digitally have made it clear that you own nothing."

Typically, e-book buyers have no idea about these complexities. How could they? The rules and limitations are embodied in "terms of service" documents that Amazon, Apple, B&N and other sellers shroud in legalese and bury deep in their Web sites. That tells you how little they want you to know.

The rules are based, in turn, on the 1998 Digital Millennium Copyright Act, with which Congress hoped to balance the rights of copyright holders and content users.

Both camps have important rights to protect. Let's start with copyright owners.

In the non-digital world, copyright ends with the first sale of each copyrighted object. Under the "first sale" doctrine, once you buy a book, that physical book is yours to lend, give away, or resell.

Will Ireland/Future Publishing/Getty Images

E-books are a growing market for publishers, making books electronically available on mobile devices such as the new Kindle Paperwhite, introduced in 2013 and about the same size as a traditional book. But consumers don't own an e-book; they are licensed users, and the publisher retains the rights to the book.

In digital-dom, however, technology allows infinite copies to be made, with no loss of quality. Absent the usual restrictions, one could give away an e-book and still have it to read. Unrestricted transferability becomes a genuine threat to the livelihood of authors, artists, filmmakers, musicians.

So some limitation is sensible. The question is whether the balance has tipped too far in favor of the booksellers, at the consumers' expense. The answer is yes.

It should be a top priority for Congress to clear out the murk. The guiding principle must be that an e-book owner's rights and responsibilities parallel those of a book owner, and the same must go for authors, publishers and booksellers. Clarify these rules of e-book commerce, and the book market will reap the benefit. The power of electronic booksellers over publishers might be reduced, and consumers would know what they were buying—and would own what they bought. Leave the rules as vague as they are, and the victims will be authors, consumers and publishers.

Michael Hiltzik, "E-Book Restrictions Leave 'Buyers' with Few Rights," latimes.com, December 22, 2012.

In the 19th century, the number of copies of books that individual readers bought determined a book's profit. Today, profits also come from the sale of subsidiary rights to movie companies, book clubs, foreign publishers, paperback reprint houses and e-book publishers. The same rights govern whether a character in a book becomes a star on the front of a T-shirt or a video game or an e-book. For some publishing houses, subsidiary- and international-rights sales make the difference between making a profit and going out of business.

Blockbusters

Selling a lot of copies of one book is easier and cheaper than selling a few copies of many books. This is the concept behind publishers' eager search for *blockbuster* books. Publishers are attracted to best-selling authors because usually they are easy to market. Brand loyalty draws loyal readers to buy every book by a favorite author, so publishers often try to capitalize on an author's media visibility, which can help sell their books.

Following are some amounts that publishers recently paid for potential blockbusters:

- In 2012, the 26-year-old writer and star of the HBO series *Girls*, Lena Dunham, received an advance of more than $3.5 million for an essay collection called *Not That Kind of Girl: A Young Woman Tells You What She's Learned*.

- In December 2010, WikiLeaks founder Julian Assange received a $1.3 million advance for American and British rights to write his memoirs.

- Little, Brown & Company reportedly signed a $5 million deal with TV comedian Tina Fey in late 2008 for a book called *Bossypants*, which was published in 2013 as a printed book and a Kindle e-book.

Only the big publishing houses can afford such a bidding game. Some publishers have even developed computer models to suggest how high to bid for a book and still make a profit, but these high-priced properties are a very small part of book publishing, perhaps 1 percent. The majority of editors and writers rarely get involved in an argument over seven-figure advances. Most authors would be pleased to see five-figure advances in a contract.

Many critics believe that what has been called a *blockbuster complex* among publishing houses hurts authors who aren't included in the bidding. One Harper & Row editor told *The Wall Street Journal* that seven-figure advances "divert money away from authors who really need it and center attention on commercial books instead of less commercial books that may nonetheless be better. God help poetry or criticism."

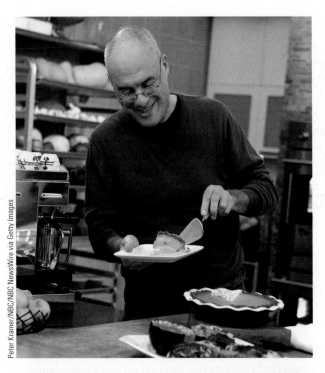

Publishers try to capitalize on an author's media visibility, which can help sell their books. Popular *New York Times* food columnist and cookbook author Mark Bittman appears on NBC's *TODAY* show on October 24, 2012, to promote his new cookbook.

Chain Bookstores and Internet Retailers Compete

The most significant change in book marketing in the past 40 years has been the growth of bookstore chains and Internet retailers. Until 2010, the big chains, such as Borders and Barnes & Noble, accounted for more than half the bookstore sales of trade books. They brought mass-marketing techniques to the book industry, offering book buyers an environment that was less like the traditional cozy atmosphere of an independent bookstore and more like a department store.

"Blockbusters are going to be published anyway, but with a marginal book, like a volume of poetry, a chain's decision about whether to order it can sometimes determine whether the book is published," says Joan M. Ripley, a former president of the American Booksellers Association. But in 2010, Barnes & Noble reported declining sales at its retail outlets, and in 2011 Borders bookstore filed for bankruptcy protection and eventually all the Borders bookstores closed. The reason? Internet

Blockbuster A book that achieves enormous financial success.

booksellers are rapidly stealing business from chains and independent booksellers.

Online booksellers, such as Amazon, have become a major factor in book marketing. Internet retailers can buy in huge volume, and they buy books only from publishers that give them big discounts, so they're able to sell most books cheaper and carry a bigger inventory than retail booksellers. Even books that are published by smaller publishing houses can today easily reach online buyers through Amazon. For blockbusters and specialty books alike, the Internet retailer is a very important outlet.

Amazon also has been buying up smaller publishing companies to add titles to its Kindle book collection. In June 2012, Amazon bought Avalon Books, which publishes romances and mysteries. Books that are issued in a series and often read quickly—such as romances and mysteries—have been among the most popular titles on Kindle readers.

Like the resistance to book clubs when they first were introduced, the skepticism among book publishers about chain bookstores, Internet retailers and e-books has changed into an understanding that they can expand the market to people who didn't buy many books before.

Internet book retailers like Amazon, which offer lower prices and a larger inventory, threaten independent booksellers like Mari's Books in the coastal town of Yachats, Oregon. Mari's has survived by offering personal service and catering to customers' local interests.

But the competitive pricing and the power over content that Internet retailers bring emphasizes what can happen when a few companies control the distribution of an industry's products, as they do in book publishing.

Small Presses Seek Specialized Audiences

The nation's large publishing houses (those with 100 or more employees) publish 80 percent of the books sold each year, but some of the nation's publishers are small operations with fewer than 10 employees. These publishers are called *small presses*, and they counterbalance the corporate world of large advances and multimedia subsidiary rights.

Small presses do not have the budgets of the large houses, but their size means they can specialize in specific topics, such as the environment or bicycling, or in specific types of writing that are unattractive to large publishers, such as poetry.

Small presses are, by definition, alternative. Many of them are clustered together in locations outside of the New York City orbit, such as Santa Fe, N.M., and Berkeley, Calif. Specialization and targeted marketing are the most important elements of small press success. However, because they have limited distribution capabilities, and because they don't have the money to invest heavily in e-book production, most small presses today struggle to survive.

New Technologies Affect Production and Consumption

Technology is a major factor in all aspects of book publishing. Because books cost so much to publish, advances in technology can lower the cost of producing printed books, which benefits the industry. But the investment required to publish e-books has crowded out many smaller publishers who can't afford the new technology.

Changes in Production

Technological advances in the last 30 years have led to seven important changes in the way books are produced, distributed and promoted:

1. Because computers monitor inventories more closely, publishers can easily order new printings of books that are selling quickly so booksellers can keep the books in stock.

2. Book publishing is an on-screen industry. Publishers now receive most manuscripts from authors electronically via the Internet. Editors process the

manuscripts on computers and then send the books into production online. This means books can be printed anywhere, often overseas.

3. Electronic graphics make books more interesting, and many book publishers are using online content to produce expanded versions of traditional books and to add materials that enhance a book's marketability.

4. Publishers are using Web sites to promote their books and to advertise blockbusters.

5. Large publishers are continuing to consolidate, and the number of small publishers is decreasing.

6. Many aspects of the publishing process, such as copy-editing, photo research and design, are contracted to freelancers who work outside the publishing house. Because publishing can be done online, book projects can be managed from any location. This means that publishers have fewer in-house employees today and much of the work is contracted and sent overseas.

7. To try to maintain and expand the market for books, publishers are exploring all aspects of digital delivery for e-books so that books can be made available on all mobile devices as well as in printed form.

Changes in Consumption

Imagine a world in which every book ever written is available to search online. This is the vision of the Google Book Project, which began contracting in 2004 with several of the nation's libraries to scan the contents of the books the libraries hold so that eventually the books' contents could be available through Google online. You could enter the word "romance," for instance, and call up a list of all the books in which the word had appeared. Or you could call up a famous phrase and trace its origin to the author who first used it. Google Inc. began to digitize millions of books to make them searchable. This concept introduced a huge shift in the way books could be consumed in the future.

This project was as controversial as it was ambitious. Authors and publishers had legal questions about copyright and royalties; booksellers wondered whether anyone would buy books if they're all available online; scholars wondered what would happen to the value of knowledge and information once it was searchable on such a wide scale. Still, Google Inc. said the company was committed to the project.

In 2008, Google paid $125 million to settle two copyright lawsuits brought by publishers and authors over the company's right to digitize books for online use. However, the settlement still "left unresolved the question of whether Google's unauthorized scanning of copyrighted

Mick Stevens/Cartoonbank.com

"Let's say you want to write an award-winning short story—you just push this key, here . . . "

books was permissible under copyright laws," according to *The New York Times*.

In September 2009, the U.S. Department of Justice asked that the settlement be delayed indefinitely, citing antitrust problems. The U.S. District Court with jurisdiction over the agreement agreed. This leaves unresolved the fate of Google's ambitious project and Google has stopped scanning books.

BOOK PUBLISHING TODAY IS A COMPETITIVE, COMPLEX BUSINESS

Because book publishing has been part of America's culture for so long, the contrast between its simple beginnings and its complicated future is especially startling. On August 2, 2010, book retailer Amazon.com announced that, for the previous three months, the company had sold more e-books than hardcover printed books—143 Kindle books for every 100 hardcover books.

By the end of 2010, 100 million e-books had been sold, according to Forrester Research. Books are getting smaller and more portable—small enough for more than 100 electronic books to fit on an iPad or a Kindle in a space 9 inches square and 1 inch deep—the same size as a single copy of one hardback book.

"The real competition [at Amazon.com] is not . . . between the hardcover book and the e-book," Amazon executive Russ Grandinetti told *The New Yorker* magazine. "TV, movies, Web browsing, video games are all competing for people's valuable time. And if the book doesn't compete we think that over time the industry will suffer."

Book publishing, which had simple beginnings in America that still evoke romantic ideas about the way books were individually produced and sold, today has become a highly competitive corporate media industry.

Review, Analyze, Investigate

Reviewing Chapter 2

Publishers Nurture Ideas and Try to Make a Profit

- U.S. book publishers produce about 150,000 book titles every year.

- Publishers have always been torn between the goal of preserving the country's intellectual ideas and the need to make money.

- Many new owners of publishing houses are trying to limit uncertainty by publishing blockbusters and by spending money on promotional campaigns.

How American Book Publishing Grew

- Early publishers widened their audience by publishing political pamphlets, novels, poetry and humor.

- The International Copyright Law of 1891 expanded royalty protection to foreign writers, which also benefited American authors.

- The creation of publishing houses in the 19th and early 20th centuries centralized the process of producing books.

- The adoption of compulsory education throughout the United States was important for book publishing because schools buy textbooks, and education creates more people who can read.

Cheaper Books Create a Mass Market

- Beginning in the 1920s, publishers dropped prices and introduced book clubs and paperbacks.

- Early book clubs, such as Book-of-the-Month, expanded the market for books and widened the audience.

- The introduction of paperbacks that sold for as little as 25 cents meant the books could reach people who had never owned a book before.

Grove Press Tests Censorship

- Grove Press challenged book censorship by publishing *Lady Chatterley's Lover* in 1959 and *Tropic of Cancer* in 1961. Both books had been banned in the United States as obscene.

- The publication by Grove Press of *The Autobiography of Malcolm X* in 1965 was another challenge to censorship. The book became a best-seller.

Investors Buy Up Publishing Companies

- Before the 1960s, the book publishing industry was composed mainly of independent companies whose only business was books.

- Publishing company consolidation began in the 1960s, and this pattern of consolidation continues today.

- In 2012, Random House and Penguin merged into a new company called Penguin Random House, which created the largest consumer book publisher in the world.

Book Publishing at Work

- Successful publishers consistently anticipate both their competitors and the market.

- The process of publishing a book usually takes at least 18 months from the time an author is signed until the book is published.

Books Begin with Authors and Agents

- Publishers acquire books in many ways. Some authors submit unsolicited manuscripts, hoping the publisher will be interested. However, many publishers refuse to read unsolicited manuscripts and accept only books that agents submit.

- Publishers pay authors a royalty for their work.

- Agents who represent authors collect fees from the authors they represent.

How Do Books Get Published?

- Book publishing requires an author, an acquisitions editor, a media editor, a designer, a production editor, a manufacturing supervisor, a marketing department and a fulfillment department.

- Most publishing houses are small, with fewer than 20 employees.

- Textbooks account for about one-third of book publishing income.

Book Industry Has Three Major Markets

- Books fall into three major categories: adult and juvenile trade books; textbooks; and professional and scholarly books.

Audiobooks and E-Books Multiply the Audience

- Audiobooks allow consumers to download and purchase book files on the Internet and listen to books on their computers or a mobile phone or iPod.

- Electronic books (e-books) offer digital copies of thousands of titles instantly on an electronic tablet or even on a mobile phone.

Corporations Demand Higher Profits

- Publishers are especially interested in books with subsidiary- and international-rights potential.

- To reduce their risks, many publishers look for blockbuster books (and best-selling authors) that they can sell through large-scale promotion campaigns.

- Chain bookstores and Internet retailers, such as Amazon, are big factors in book marketing.

- Chain bookstores and Internet retailers can buy in huge volume, and often they buy books only from publishers that give them big discounts.

- Internet retailing has expanded the book market and has introduced competitive pricing.

- In 2011 Borders bookstore filed for bankruptcy protection and eventually all the Borders bookstores closed.

- In June 2012, Amazon bought Avalon Books, which publishes romances and mysteries. Books that are issued in a series and often read quickly—such as romances and mysteries—have been among the most popular titles on Amazon's Kindle readers.

Small Presses Seek Specialized Audiences

- Small presses are, by definition, alternative.

- Many small presses exist outside the New York City orbit.

- Specialization and targeted marketing are important elements of small press success.

New Technologies Affect Production and Consumption

- Computers monitor inventories more closely.

- Publishers now receive and process manuscripts electronically via the Internet. Many aspects of the publishing process, such as copyediting and photo research, are contracted to freelancers who work outside the publishing house, including overseas.

- Electronic graphics make books more interesting to look at, and many book publishers use Web sites to promote books and enhance the content.

- Large publishers are continuing to consolidate, and the number of small publishers is decreasing.

- To try to maintain and expand the market for books, publishers are exploring all aspects of electronic delivery for e-books so that books can be made available on all mobile devices as well as in printed form.

- Beginning in 2004, the Google Book Project contracted with several of the nation's libraries to scan the contents of books the libraries hold. Google Inc. planned to make the books' contents available online.

- In 2008, Google Inc. paid $125 million to settle copyright infringement claims.

- In 2009, the U.S. Justice Department and the U.S. District Court with jurisdiction over the case delayed the settlement indefinitely, citing antitrust objections, so the copyright issues inherent in the project remain unresolved and Google Inc. has stopped scanning books.

Book Publishing Today Is a Competitive, Complex Business

- On August 2, 2010, book retailer Amazon.com announced that, for the previous three months, the company had sold more e-books than hardcover printed books—143 Kindle books for every 100 hardcover books.

- By the end of 2010, book buyers had purchased an estimated 100 million e-books.

- Book publishing, which had simple beginnings in America that still evoke romantic ideas about the way books were produced and sold, today has become a highly competitive corporate media industry.

Key Terms

These terms are defined in the margins throughout this chapter and appear in alphabetical order with definitions in the Glossary, which begins on page 373.

Critical Questions

1. Why was passage of the International Copyright Law of 1891 so important to American authors?

2. List five ways the economics of book publishing changed from Benjamin Franklin's day to today.

3. Will e-books totally replace print books? Why or why not?

4. Why are textbooks so important to the publishing industry?

5. What is the biggest challenge facing the book publishing industry today?

Working the Web

This list includes both sites mentioned in the chapter and others to give you greater insight into book publishing.

Amazon

amazon.com

Since this pioneer Internet bookseller started in 1995, Amazon has expanded its e-commerce offerings to include a wide variety of products in multiple categories including Movies, Music & Games, Digital Downloads and even Grocery. In 2007, Amazon released Kindle, a wireless, portable reading device with instant access to books at more than 50 percent savings from the print price, as well as blogs, newspapers and magazines. Amazon.com operates sites internationally, including the United Kingdom, France, Japan, China, Canada and Germany.

American Booksellers Association (ABA)

bookweb.org

This national not-for-profit trade association for independent booksellers exists to protect and promote the interests of its members: independently owned bookstores, large and small, with storefront locations in towns and cities nationwide. The ABA provides "advocacy, education, opportunities for peer interaction, support services and new business models." Its IndieBound program (evolved from Book Sense, indiebound .org) is a national marketing program to raise consumer awareness of the value of independent bookstores.

American Booksellers Foundation for Free Expression (ABFFE)

abffe.org

Founded by the American Booksellers Association in 1990, ABFFE is "The bookseller's voice in the fight against censorship." The Foundation opposes book banning and other restrictions on free speech, participates in legal cases about First Amendment rights and provides education on the importance of free expression to many entities including the public, the press and politicians.

Association of American Publishers

publishers.org

This organization deals with broad issues concerning publishers, as well as specific concerns in particular industry segments. Committees attend to such issues as intellectual property; new technology; First Amendment rights, censorship and libel; funding for education and libraries; postal rates and regulations; and international copyright enforcement.

Barnes & Noble

barnesandnoble.com

Barnes & Noble.com uses mass-marketing techniques to sell books, DVDs, music and other merchandise. BN.com maintains that it has one million titles available for immediate delivery as well as used and out-of-print-titles. The Web site features include online Book Clubs, B&N Review and B&N Studio, a video library with hundreds of webcasts where viewers can learn more about authors, musical artists and fellow book lovers.

Biblio

biblio.com

Based in Asheville, N.C., Biblio is an online marketplace for used, rare and out-of-print books and textbooks. The booksellers are located around the world, and the list of links to specialists is very long (use the Bookstores tab and go to the "Find specialist" link). Users can search 50 million used and rare books, browse by subject or author, or browse collectible and rare books by featured category.

BookFinder

bookfinder.com

BookFinder.com is an e-commerce search engine for new, used, rare and out-of-print books and textbooks. It searches all the major online catalogs (such as Amazon.com and Barnes & Noble) and independent sources. Searches can be conducted in English, French, Dutch, Spanish, German and Italian. BookFinder's global network of book search engines includes JustBooks.de, JustBooks.co.uk and JustBooks.fr.

Google Book Search

books.google.com

This controversial project between Google and several libraries (including the University of Michigan, Harvard University, Stanford University, New York Public Library and Oxford University) has expanded to include partnerships with book publishers and authors. Google's plan "to digitize the world's books in order to make them easier for people to find and buy" has encountered legal obstacles and its future is in doubt.

IndieBound

indiebound.org

Evolved from the ABA's Book Sense program, IndieBound "rallies passionate readers around a celebration of independent stores and independent thinking." Independently owned ABA member bookstores are automatically part of the program and are encouraged to use the logos, spirit lines, posters, buttons, T-shirts and more provided by the ABA.

Scholastic Corporation

scholastic.com

The world's largest publisher of children's books, Scholastic creates a variety of educational and entertainment materials and products for home and school use and distributes them through various channels including school-based book clubs and book fairs, retail stores, television networks and Scholastic.com.

 Impact/Action Videos are concise news features on various topics created exclusively for *Media/Impact*. Go online to access MindTap at cengagebrain.com. MindTap for Media/Impact sequences all of your learning tools—Chapter Readings with highlighting and note taking, **Impact/Action Videos**, activities and assessments—into chapter driven learning units that guide you through the curriculum.

NEWSPAPERS: EXPANDING DELIVERY 3

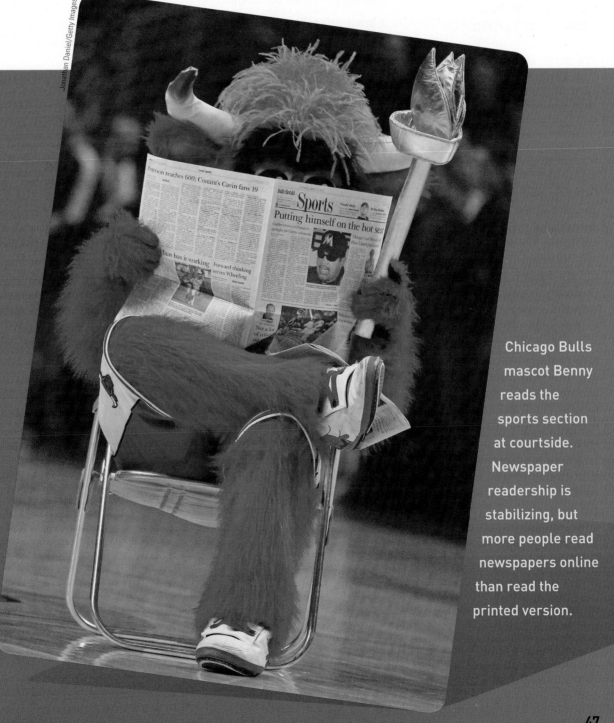

Jonathan Daniel/Getty Images

Chicago Bulls mascot Benny reads the sports section at courtside. Newspaper readership is stabilizing, but more people read newspapers online than read the printed version.

What's Ahead?

- First Mass Medium to Deliver News
- Publishers Fight for an Independent Press
- Technology Helps Newspapers Reach New Audiences
- Newspapers Seek Mass Audiences and Big Profits
- Newspapers Dominate the Early 20th Century
- Unionization Encourages Professionalism
- Television Brings New Competition
- Alternative Press Revives Voices of Protest
- Newspapers Expand and Contract
- Newspapers at Work
- Newspapers Struggle to Retain Readers
- Technology Transforms Production
- Consolidation Increases Chain Ownership
- Today's Newspaper Audience Is a Moving Target

"If the newspaper industry had theme music in 2013, it might use 'Been down so long it looks like up to me.'"

—PEW RESEARCH CENTER'S PROJECT FOR EXCELLENCE IN JOURNALISM

In 1882, Harrison

Gray Otis bought a 25 percent share of the *Los Angeles Times* for $6,000. In 2000, the Chandler family (Otis' descendants) sold Times Mirror Co., which included the *Los Angeles Times, Newsday, The Baltimore Sun* newspapers, the *Hartford Courant* and other media properties to Chicago-based Tribune Co. for $8.3 billion. Then in 2007, Chicago real estate tycoon Sam Zell paid $8.2 billion for Tribune Co. (including *Times Mirror*), less than Tribune Co. had paid for *Times Mirror* alone seven years earlier.

One year later, in December 2008, the Tribune Company filed for bankruptcy protection, citing the rapid decline in newspaper revenue. In 2013, the company announced that it was putting its newspaper group up for sale. The Tribune Company's uncertain future is an example of the precarious economics of the newspaper business today.

American newspapers began in colonial America more than three centuries ago as one-page sheets that consisted primarily of announcements of ship arrivals and departures and old news from Europe. Today's large urban newspapers such as the *Los Angeles Times* sometimes run 300 pages on Sunday. (*The New York Times* holds the record for the largest single-day's newspaper. On November 13, 1987, *The Times* published a 1,612-page edition that weighed 12 pounds.) Most newspapers today are just one part of large media companies rather than family-run operations.

FIRST MASS MEDIUM TO DELIVER NEWS

Technological developments in the 21st century have changed the role of newspapers and the way news is delivered. From 1690 until the introduction of radio in 1920, newspapers were the only mass news medium available, attempting to deliver news and information as soon as it happened. Until 1920, newspapers were the only way for large numbers of people to get the same news simultaneously. There was no competition.

The invention of broadcasting in the early 20th century changed newspapers' exclusive access to news because broadcasting offered quicker access to information. In the late 20th century, the expansion of the Internet challenged newspapers' delivery system, and advertisers fled printed newspapers for an online audience. Yet, despite increasing competition for its audience, newspapers continue to be a significant source of information and news.

The newspaper industry also historically has played an important role in defining the cultural concept of an independent press, based on the belief that the press must remain independent from government control to fulfill its responsibility to keep the public informed. Concepts about what the public should know, when they should know it and who should decide what the public needs to know developed in America during a time when newspapers were the primary news outlet.

TIMEFRAME

1690–TODAY

Newspapers Adapt to Try to Maintain Their Audience Share

1690 *Publick Occurrences*, America's first newspaper, is published.

1721 James Franklin publishes *The New England Courant*, the first newspaper to appear without the Crown's "Published by Authority" sanction.

1734 John Peter Zenger is charged with sedition. While he is in jail, his wife, Anna Zenger, continues to publish *The New York Weekly Journal*, making her America's first woman publisher.

1808 *El Misisipi*, America's first Spanish-language newspaper, begins publication in Georgia.

1827 John B. Russwurm and the Reverend Samuel Cornish launch *Freedom's Journal*, the nation's first newspaper directed specifically at an African American audience.

1828 Elias Boudinot (Galagina Oowati) launches the *Cherokee Phoenix*.

1831 In Boston, William Lloyd Garrison launches the abolitionist newspaper *The Liberator*.

1847 Frederick Douglass introduces the weekly *North Star*, considered America's most important African American pre-Civil War newspaper.

1848 Jane Grey Swisshelm publishes the first issue of the abolitionist newspaper the *Pittsburgh Saturday Visiter*, which also promotes women's rights.

1889 Ida B. Wells becomes part owner of the *Memphis Free Speech and Headlight* and begins her anti-lynching campaign.

1900 One-third of the nation's newspapers follow the popular trend toward yellow journalism.

1950 Newspaper readership begins to decline following the introduction of television.

1982 Gannett Co. creates *USA Today*, using a splashy format and color throughout the paper.

1990s Newspapers launch special sections to appeal to declining audiences—teens and women. Some newspapers launch Spanish-language editions.

2009 Tribune Co. files for bankruptcy protection. Denver's *Rocky Mountain News* and the *Seattle Post-Intelligencer* close down.

2011 *The New York Times* begins charging for online content.

2013 Amazon founder Jeff Bezos buys *The Washington Post*.

TODAY The newspaper business is consolidating. To attract younger readers, newspapers have expanded their Internet editions and news-on-demand features. Declining ad revenue has forced many newspapers to close.

Hulton Archive/Stringer/Getty Images

Hulton Archive/Archive Photos/Getty Images

Tim Boyle/Bloomberg/Getty Images

PUBLISHERS FIGHT FOR AN INDEPENDENT PRESS

The issue of government control of newspapers surfaced early in the history of the colonies. At first, newspapers were the mouthpieces of the British government, and news was subject to British approval. The British government subsidized many colonial newspapers, and publishers actually printed "Published by Authority" on the first page of the paper to demonstrate government approval.

The first colonial newspaper angered the local authorities so much that the newspaper issued only one edition. This newspaper, *Publick Occurrences*, which was published in Boston on September 25, 1690, often is identified as America's first newspaper.

The first and only edition of *Publick Occurrences* was just two pages, each page the size of a sheet of today's binder paper (then called a half-sheet), and was printed on three sides. Publisher Benjamin Harris left the fourth side blank so people could jot down the latest news before they gave the paper to friends. Harris made the mistake of reporting in his first issue that the French king was "in much trouble" for sleeping with his son's wife. Harris' journalism was too candid for the governor and council of the Massachusetts Bay Colony, who stopped the publication four days after the newspaper appeared.

Seditious Language   Language that authorities believe could incite rebellion against the government.

The nation's first consecutively issued (published more than once) newspaper was *The Boston News-Letter*, which appeared in 1704. It was one half-sheet printed on two sides. In the first issue, editor John Campbell reprinted the queen's latest speech, some maritime news and one advertisement telling people how to put an ad in his paper. Like many subsequent colonial publishers, Campbell reprinted several items from the London papers.

James Franklin's *New England Courant* Establishes an Independent Press Tradition

The next challenge to British control came when James Franklin started his own newspaper in Boston in 1721. His *New England Courant* was the first American newspaper to appear without the crown's "Published by Authority" sanction. *Thus, James Franklin began the tradition of an independent press in this country.*

Benjamin Franklin Introduces Competition

In 1729, Benjamin Franklin, James' younger brother, moved to Philadelphia and bought the *Pennsylvania Gazette* to compete with the only other newspaper in town, the *American Weekly Mercury* published by Andrew Bradford. The *Pennsylvania Gazette* became the most influential and most financially successful of all the colonial newspapers. In the same print shop that printed the *Gazette*, Franklin published *Poor Richard's Almanack* in 1732, an annual book that sold about 10,000 copies a year for the next 25 years. *Benjamin Franklin proved that a printer could make money without government sanctions or support.*

Truth Versus Libel: The Zenger Trial

In New York, John Peter Zenger started the *New York Weekly Journal* in 1733. The *Journal* continually attacked Governor William Cosby for incompetence, and on November 17, 1734, Zenger was arrested and jailed, charged with printing false and seditious writing. (*Seditious language* is language that authorities believe could incite rebellion against the government.) While Zenger was in jail, his wife Anna continued to print the paper, making her America's first woman publisher.

Numb. L.

THE
New - York Weekly JOURNAL.

Containing the freſheſt Advices, Foreign, and Domeſtick.

MUNDAY October 14*th*, 1734.

Mr. *Zenger* ;

I Have been Reading, the arguments of Mr. *Smith*, and *Murray*, with Regard to the Courts, and there is one Thing, I can't comprehend, *viz.* If it is the ſame Court, I take it, that all the Writs ought to be taken out in *England*, and teſted by the Judges there ; if they are taken out here, the ſame Judges ought to teſt them here. If it is a like Court, it is not the ſame ; and if not the ſame, it is not that fundamental Court which is e-ſtabliſhed by immemorial Cuſtom. I would be glad ſome of your Correſ-pondents would clear up this Point ; becauſe in my poor Oppinion, if the Exchequer Court here is not the ſame identical Court as the Exchequer Court in *England*, it is without Law-ful Authority.

FOREIGN AFFAIRS.

Dantzick, Auguſt 4.

Yeſterday the Biſhop of Cracow, in the King's Name, received Homage of this City, and the Ceremony was very magnificent. His Majeſty, be-fore his Departure, iſſued the Univer-ſalia for holding of the Petty-Dyets in the Provinces. Thoſe in Poliſh Pruſ-ſia, will be held in 15 Days. The Ruſſian and Saxon Troops will march ſuddenly to the Places where the Pro-vincial Aſſemblies are to be opened ; and the reſt are to go and poſt them-

ſelves in Great Poland. M. Rewuſki, the Crown Carver, is declared Regi-mentary, and is to command a Body of Troops, conſiſting of 2000 Ruſſian Dragoons, 11000 Coſſacks, and the Regiment Guards formerly in the Ser-vice of King Staniſlaus.

Bruſſels, Auguſt 6.

Letters from Rome of the 17*th* paſt adviſe. That they had Advice there that the Siege of Gaeta was not yet formed, altho' the Spaniards had there 70 Cannon, and Mortars, and were working on Batteries, but that all they raiſed in the Night was beat down next Morning by the Cannon of the Palace ; and that the Heats be-ing already Exceſſive, the Spaniards were in Fear of looſing a vaſt Num-ber of Men in the Reduction of that Fortreſs.

Hamburg, Auguſt 10.

According to Letters from the Camp before Dantzick, the Veſſels there were taken up by Order of the Gene-rals in Chief, to ſerve for carrying the heavy Artillery and Baggage by Water to Thorn and Warſaw. We have certain Advice, that King, Staniſlaus was departed from Branden-burg Pruſſia, and arrived ſafe in the Crown Army, under the Command of M. Kiowſki, near Peterkow the 24*th* paſt, and immediately afterwards held a Council of War, wherein it was reſolved to draw all the diſperſed Troops into a Body, and march di-rectly to Volhinia in Podolia.

Amſt.

On November 17, 1734, John Peter Zenger, publisher of the *New York Weekly Journal*, **was arrested and jailed, charged with printing false and seditious writing. While Zenger was in jail, his wife Anna continued to publish the paper.**

Zenger's trial began on August 4, 1735, nine months after his arrest. His defense attorney argued that *truth was a defense against libel*, and that if Zenger's words were true, they could not be libelous. (A *libelous* statement is a false statement that damages a person by questioning that person's character or reputation.)

The trial established a *landmark precedent for freedom of the press in America—the concept that truth is the best defense for libel*. If what someone publishes is true, the information cannot be considered libelous. (The issue of libel is explained in **Chapter 14**.)

Women's Early Role as Publishers

Colonial women were not encouraged to work outside the home at all. Therefore, women who published newspapers

during the colonial period are especially notable because so few women managed businesses early in the nation's history. Early colonial women printers, such as Anna Zenger, usually belonged to printing families that trained wives and daughters to work in the print shops. By the time the American Revolution began, at least 14 women had worked as printers in the colonies. One of these family-trained printers was Elizabeth Timothy.

Timothy became editor of the weekly *South Carolina Gazette* in Charleston when her husband, Lewis, died unexpectedly and their son, Peter, was only 13. Elizabeth Timothy published her first edition on January 4, 1737, under her son's name. Her first editorial appealed to the community to continue to support the "poor afflicted widow and six small children." Mother and son ran the paper together until 1746, when Peter formally took over the business.

Birth of the Partisan Press

As dissatisfaction with British rule grew in the colonies, newspapers became political tools that fostered the debate that eventually led to the colonies' independence. By 1750, 14 weekly newspapers were being published in the colonies.

The Stamp Act

Opposition to the British Stamp Act in 1765 signaled the beginning of the revolutionary period. The Stamp Act taxed publishers a halfpenny for each issue that was a half-sheet or smaller and one penny for a full sheet. Each advertisement was taxed two shillings. All the colonial newspapers, even those loyal to the crown, fought the act.

Many newspapers threatened to stop publication, but only a few of them did. Most editors published newspapers that mocked the tax. William Bradford III issued the famous tombstone edition of the *Pennsylvania Journal* on October 31, 1765. The front page, bordered in black, showed a skull and crossbones where the official stamp should have been.

The Stamp Act Congress met in New York in October 1765 and adopted the now-familiar slogan "No taxation without representation." Parliament, facing united opposition from all the colonial publishers, repealed the Stamp Act on March 18, 1766.

Libelous A statement is libelous if it damages a person's character or reputation by exposing that person to public ridicule or contempt.

MPI/Archive Photos/Getty Images

Furious colonists reacted to the Stamp Act in 1765 by throwing stamped documents onto a bonfire in Boston. Newspaper publishers threatened to stop publication but instead printed editions that mocked the tax. The Stamp Act was repealed a year later.

The Alien and Sedition Laws

During the early part of the country's history, journalists often used newspapers as a way to oppose the new government. The Alien and Sedition Laws, passed by Congress in 1798, were the federal government's first attempt to control its critics. Congress said that anyone who "shall write, print, or publish . . . false, scandalous and malicious writing or writings against the government of the United States, or either house of the Congress of the United States, or the President of the United States" could be fined up to $2,000 and jailed for two years.

Several journalists went to jail. A Boston publisher was jailed for libeling the Massachusetts legislature. A New York editor was fined $100 and jailed for four months. By 1800, the angry rhetoric had dissipated. The Alien and Sedition Laws expired after two years and were not renewed. However, *throughout American press history, the tradition of an independent press, established by* *James Franklin in 1721, continued to confront the government's desire to restrain criticism.*

Technology Helps Newspapers Reach New Audiences

Technological advances of the 19th century—such as cheaper newsprint, mechanized printing and the telegraph—meant newspapers could reach a wider audience faster than before. Confined to eastern cities and highly educated urban audiences during the 1700s, newspaper publishers in the 1800s sought new readers—from the frontier, from among the nation's growing number of immigrants and from within the shrinking Native American population. This expansion resulted in three new developments for American newspapers: frontier journalism, ethnic and cultural newspapers and the alternative press.

Frontier Journalism

Gold, silver and adventure lured people to the West, and when the people arrived, they needed newspapers. The *Indiana Gazette*, the *Texas Gazette*, the *Oregon Spectator*, the *Weekly Arizonian* and Colorado's *Rocky Mountain News* met that need, aided by the telegraph, which moved news easily from coast to coast.

The wide-open land beckoned many journalists. The most celebrated journalist to chronicle the frontier was Samuel Clemens, who traveled to Nevada in 1861, prospecting for silver. Clemens didn't find any silver, but a year later Virginia City's *Territorial Enterprise*—the area's largest paper—hired him for $25 a week. Clemens first signed his name as Mark Twain on a humorous travel letter written for the *Enterprise*.

On the frontier, journalists learned to improvise. This press operation, assembled to publish the *New York Herald*, was set up in a field under a tree.

Ethnic and Native American Newspapers

English-language newspapers did not satisfy everyone's needs. In the first half of the 19th century, many newspapers sought to succeed by catering to ethnic and cultural interests. In the early 1800s, Spanish-speaking people in Georgia could read *El Misisipi*. Herman Ridder's German newspaper, *New Yorker Staats-Zeitung*, founded in 1845, was the most successful foreign-language newspaper in the United States. It formed the financial basis for today's Knight Ridder chain, which was bought by McClatchy Co. in 2006.

People outside the mainstream of society, such as Spanish and German immigrants, used newspapers to create a sense of community and ethnic identity. In the 1800s, Native Americans who had been displaced by the settlers also felt a need to express their culture through a newspaper. As a non-mainstream group, they especially wanted to voice their complaints.

On February 21, 1828, the nation's first Native American newspaper appeared. Elias Boudinot, a Native American who had been educated at a Connecticut seminary, launched the *Cherokee Phoenix*, a weekly newspaper. Boudinot's native name was Galagina (The Buck) Oowati. (He took the name Elias Boudinot as a tribute to one of his early mentors.)

The Cherokee nation held exclusive control over the four-page paper, which was printed half in English and half in an 86-character alphabet that represented the Cherokee language. Boudinot resigned because of editorial differences with some of his partners in August 1832, and the *Phoenix* published its last issue on May 31, 1834.

Dissident Voices Create the Early Alternative Press

Two strong social movements—emancipation and women's suffrage—brought new voices to the American press. This *alternative press* movement signaled the beginning of a significant American journalistic tradition. Newspapers became an outlet for the voices of social protest, a tradition that continues today. (The alternative press also is called the *dissident press*.)

Six early advocates for domestic change who used the press to advance their causes—the abolition of slavery and suffrage for women—were John B. Russwurm, the Reverend Samuel Cornish, Frederick Douglass, William Lloyd Garrison, Jane Grey Swisshelm and Ida B. Wells.

Library of Congress

The Granger Collection, NYC

Elias Boudinot [Cherokee name: Galagina (The Buck) Oowati] published the first Native American newspaper (right), the *Cherokee Phoenix*, from 1828 to 1832. The newspaper used the Cherokee language.

Stock Montage/Archive Photos/Getty Images

Stock Montage/Archive Photos/Getty Images

Frederick Douglass (left) established the weekly newspaper *North Star*, often called the most important African American pre–Civil War newspaper. William Lloyd Garrison (right), a Boston abolitionist, founded the New England Anti-Slavery Society and published *The Liberator*, another important abolitionist newspaper.

Alternative (Dissident) Press   Media that present alternative viewpoints that challenge the mainstream press.

Ida B. Wells Uses Her Pen to Fight 19th-Century Racism

By Shirley Biagi

Ida B. Wells didn't start out to be a journalist, but the cause of emancipation drew her to the profession. Wells, who eventually became co-owner of the *Free Speech and Headlight* in Memphis, Tennessee, documented racism wherever she found it. She is known for her pioneering stand against the unjustified lynching of African Americans in the 1890s.

In 1878, both of Wells' parents and her infant sister died in a yellow fever epidemic, so 16-year-old Wells took responsibility for her six brothers and sisters, attended Rush College, and then moved the family to Memphis, where she became a teacher.

A Baptist minister who was editor of the Negro Press Association hired Wells to write for his paper. She wrote under the pseudonym Iola.

In 1892, Wells wrote a story about three African American men who had been kidnapped from a Memphis jail and killed. "The city of Memphis has demonstrated that neither character nor standing avails the Negro, if he dares to protect himself against the white man or become his rival," she wrote. "We are outnumbered and without arms." While in New York, she read in the local paper that a mob had sacked the *Free Speech* office.

Ida B. Wells, part owner of the *Memphis Free Speech and Headlight*, wrote under the pseudonym Iola. Wells' struggle for social justice represents an early example of the role of the dissident press in American history.

Wells decided not to return to Memphis. She worked in New York and lectured in Europe and then settled in Chicago, where she married a lawyer, Ferdinand Lee Barnett. Ida Wells-Barnett and her husband actively campaigned for African American rights in Chicago, and she continued to write until she died at age 69 in 1931.

In 1827, Russwurm and Cornish, who were African American, started *Freedom's Journal* in New York City with very little money. They launched their newspaper to respond to racist attacks in several local newspapers. *Freedom's Journal* lasted for two years and reached only a few readers, but it was the beginning of an African American press tradition that eventually created more than 2,700 newspapers, magazines and quarterly journals.

What often has been called the most important African American pre-Civil War newspaper was Frederick Douglass' weekly *North Star*. "Right is of no Sex—Truth is of no Color—God is the Father of us all, and we are all Brethren" read the masthead. Beginning in 1847, Douglass struggled to support the *North Star* by giving lectures. The newspaper eventually reached 3,000

subscribers in the United States and abroad with its emancipation message.

In 1831, William Lloyd Garrison began publishing *The Liberator*, a weekly abolitionist paper in Boston. As a white man fighting slavery and advocating women's rights, Garrison was attacked by a mob in 1835 but survived when the Boston mayor jailed him for his own protection. Garrison continued to publish *The Liberator* for 30 years.

Like Douglass and Garrison, Ida B. Wells and Jane Grey Swisshelm campaigned for civil rights. Swisshelm's first byline appeared in 1844 in the *Spirit of Liberty*, published in Pittsburgh. Four years later, she began her own abolitionist publication, the *Pittsburgh Saturday Visiter*, which also promoted women's rights. (See **Impact/Profile**, "Ida B. Wells Uses Her Pen to Fight 19th- Century Racism.")

As a correspondent for Horace Greeley's *New York Tribune* in Washington, D.C., Swisshelm convinced Vice President Millard Fillmore to let her report from the Senate press gallery. The gallery had been open to male journalists for 55 years, and on May 21, 1850, Swisshelm became the first female journalist to sit in the gallery.

These pioneers—Russwurm, Cornish, Douglass, Garrison, Wells and Swisshelm—used newspapers to lobby for social change. Dissident newspapers offered a forum for protest and reform, which is an important cultural role for an independent press.

Bettmann/CORBIS Bettmann/CORBIS

The battle for New York readers between Joseph Pulitzer (left) and William Randolph Hearst (right) provoked the Spanish-American War and popularized the term *yellow journalism.*

NEWSPAPERS SEEK MASS AUDIENCES AND BIG PROFITS

The voices of social protest reached a limited, committed audience, but most people could not afford to subscribe to a daily newspaper. Newspapers were sold by advance yearly subscription for $6 to $10 at a time when most skilled workers earned less than $750 a year. Then, in 1833, Benjamin Day demonstrated that he could profitably appeal to a mass audience by dropping the price of a newspaper to a penny and selling the paper on the street every day.

Benjamin Day's *New York Sun* published sensational news and feature stories for the working class. He was able to lower the price to a penny by filling the paper with advertising and by hiring newsboys to sell the paper on street corners. In its four pages, this first successful penny paper reported local gossip and sensationalized police news and carried a page and a half of advertising.

Newsboys (and some newsgirls) bought 100 papers for 67 cents and tried to sell them all each day to make a profit. Even *The New York Times,* founded by Henry J. Raymond in 1851, was a *penny paper* when it began. The legacy of these early penny papers continues in today's gossip columns and crime reporting.

NEWSPAPERS DOMINATE THE EARLY 20TH CENTURY

For the first 30 years of the 20th century—before radio and television—newspapers dominated the country. Newspapers were the nation's single source of daily dialogue about political, cultural and social issues. This also was the era of the greatest newspaper competition for readers.

Competition Breeds Sensationalism

In large cities such as New York, as many as ten newspapers competed for readers at once, so the publishers looked for new ways to expand their audience. Two New York publishers—Joseph Pulitzer and William Randolph Hearst—revived and refined the *penny press* sensationalism that had begun in 1833 with Benjamin Day's *New York Sun.* Like Benjamin Day, Pulitzer and Hearst proved that newspapers could reap enormous fortunes for their owners. They also demonstrated that credible, serious reporting is not all that people want in a newspaper. Pulitzer and Hearst promoted giveaways, included gossip and fabricated stories.

An ambitious man who knew how to grab his readers' interest, Joseph Pulitzer published the first newspaper comics and sponsored journalist Nellie Bly on an around-the-world steamship and railroad trip to try to beat the fictional record in the popular book *Around the World in 80 Days.* Bly finished the trip in 72 days, 6 hours and 11 minutes, and the stunt brought Pulitzer the circulation he craved. In San Francisco, young William Randolph Hearst, the new editor of the *San Francisco Examiner,* sent a reporter to cover Bly's arrival.

In 1887, William Randolph Hearst convinced his father, who owned the *San Francisco Examiner,* to let him run the paper. Hearst tagged the *Examiner* "The Monarch

Penny Press or Penny Paper   A newspaper produced by dropping the price of each copy to a penny and supporting the production cost through advertising.

of the Dailies," added a lovelorn column and attacked several of his father's influential friends in the newspaper. He spent money wildly, buying talent from competing papers and staging showy promotional events.

Yellow Journalism Is Born: Hearst's Role in the Spanish-American War

In New York, Hearst bought the *New York Journal*, hired Pulitzer's entire Sunday staff and cut the *Journal*'s price to a penny, so Pulitzer dropped his price to match it. Hearst bought a color press and printed color comics. Then he stole Pulitzer's popular comic "Hogan's Alley," which included a character named the Yellow Kid.

Hearst relished the battle, as the *Journal* screamed attention-grabbing crime headlines, such as "Thigh of the Body Found," and the paper offered $1,000 for information that would convict the murderer. Critics named this sensationalism *yellow journalism* after the Yellow Kid, a term that is still used to describe highly emotional, exaggerated or inaccurate reporting that emphasizes crime, sex and violence. By 1900, about one-third of the metropolitan dailies were following the trend toward yellow journalism.

Beginning in 1898, the Spanish-American War provided the battlefield for Pulitzer and Hearst to act out their newspaper war. For three years, the two newspapers unrelentingly overplayed events in the Cuban struggle for independence from Spain, each trying to beat the other with irresponsible, exaggerated stories, many of them invented.

The overplayed events that resulted from the sensational competition between Pulitzer and Hearst showed that newspapers could have a significant effect on political attitudes. The Spanish-American War began a few months after the sinking of the U.S. battleship *Maine* in Havana harbor, which killed 266 crew members. The cause of the explosion that sank the ship was never determined, but Pulitzer's and Hearst's newspapers blamed the Spanish.

Hearst dubbed the event "the *Journal*'s War," but in fact Hearst and Pulitzer shared responsibility because both men had inflamed the public unnecessarily about events in Cuba. *The serious consequences that resulted from their yellow journalism demonstrate the importance of press responsibility.*

Tabloid Journalism: Selling Sex and Violence

The journalistic legacy of Day, Pulitzer and Hearst surfaced again in the tabloid journalism of the 1920s, also called jazz journalism. In 1919, the publishers of the *New York Daily News* sponsored a beauty contest to inaugurate the nation's first tabloid. A *tabloid* is a small-format newspaper, usually 11 inches by 14 inches, featuring illustrations and sensational stories.

The *Daily News* merged pictures and screaming headlines with reports about crime, sex and violence to exceed anything that had appeared before. It ran

New York Daily News/Getty Images

NY Daily News/Getty Images

Yellow Journalism News that emphasizes crime, sex and violence; also called jazz journalism and tabloid journalism.

Tabloid A small-format newspaper that features large photographs and illustrations along with sensational stories.

This 1928 photo of Ruth Snyder's execution (left) in the *New York Daily News* exemplifies the screaming headlines and large photographs of early tabloids that still populate today's *Daily News* (right). At the Snyder execution, a reporter from the *Daily News* strapped a small hidden camera to his leg and secretly snapped a picture of Snyder as she was executed. During a sensational trial, fueled by tabloid headlines, an all-male jury convicted Snyder of helping her boyfriend kill her husband. Snyder and her boyfriend were executed on the same day.

full-page pictures with short, punchy text. Love affairs soon became big news and so did murders. In the ultimate example of tabloid journalism, a *Daily News* reporter strapped a camera to his ankle in 1928 and took a picture of Ruth Snyder, who had conspired to kill her husband, as she was electrocuted at Sing Sing prison.

Snyder's picture covered the front page, and the caption stated, "This is perhaps the most remarkable exclusive picture in the history of criminology." Photojournalism had taken a sensational turn. Today, yellow journalism's successors are the supermarket tabloids, such as the *National Enquirer*, which feature large photographs and stories about sex, violence and celebrities.

Transcendental Graphics/Archive Photos/Getty Images

In the 1950s, newspaper readership declined as TV became America's primary source for news and entertainment. The *Howdy Doody Show* celebrates its tenth anniversary in 1957.

UNIONIZATION ENCOURAGES PROFESSIONALISM

The first half of the 20th century brought the widespread unionization of newspaper employees, which standardized wages at many of the nation's largest newspapers. Labor unions were first established at newspapers in 1800, and the International Typographical Union went national in the mid-1850s.

Other unions formed to represent production workers at newspapers, but reporters didn't have a union until 1934, when *New York World-Telegram* reporter Heywood Broun called on his colleagues to organize. Broun became The Newspaper Guild's first president. Today, the Guild continues to cover employees at many of America's urban newspapers.

With the rise of unions, employee contracts, which once had been negotiated in private, became public agreements. In general, salaries for reporters at union newspapers rose, and this eventually led to a sense of professionalism, including codes of ethics for journalists.

TELEVISION BRINGS NEW COMPETITION

The invention of television dramatically affected the newspaper industry. Newspaper publishers had learned

how to live with only one other 20th-century news industry—radio. In the 1920s, when radio first became popular, newspapers refused to carry advertising or time logs for the programs, but eventually newspapers conceded the space to radio.

In the 1950s, however, television posed a larger threat: TV offered moving images of the news, along with entertainment programs. The spread of television demonstrated how interrelated the media were. The newspaper industry gave up its position as the number one news medium and was forced to share the news audience with broadcasting. Eventually, television's influence changed both the look and the content of many newspapers.

ALTERNATIVE PRESS REVIVES VOICES OF PROTEST

The social movements of the 1960s briefly revived one portion of the early newspaper industry—the alternative press. Like their 1800s predecessors in the abolitionist and emancipation movements, people who supported the revival of the alternative press in the 1960s believed the mainstream press was avoiding important issues, such as the anti-Vietnam War movement, the civil rights movement and the gay rights movement.

In 1964, as a way to pass along news about the antiwar movement, the *Los Angeles Free Press* became the first underground paper to publish regularly. The *Barb* in Berkeley, Calif., *Kaleidoscope* in Chicago and *Quicksilver Times* in Washington, D.C., soon followed. In 1965, Jim Michaels launched the nation's first gay newspaper, the Los Angeles *Advocate*. What the 1960s underground press proved already had been proven in the 19th century: In America, causes need a voice, and if those voices are not represented in the mainstream press, publications emerge to support alternative views.

Newspapers Expand and Contract

Since the 1970s, the overall number of newspapers has declined. Many afternoon papers died when TV took over the evening news. Other afternoon papers changed to morning papers. Then, newspaper publishers realized television could provide the news headlines, but newspapers could offer the background that television news could not.

Newspaper publishers also began to exploit the popularity of television personalities and expanded their entertainment, business and sports news. Eventually, advertisers realized that newspapers gave people the broader news that TV couldn't deliver. Also, viewers couldn't clip coupons out of their television sets or retrieve copies of yesterday's TV ads, so advertisers began to use newspapers to complement television advertising campaigns. To try to match television's visual appeal, newspapers introduced advanced graphics and vivid color.

Today newspapers are facing declining readership, especially among young readers, and many major newspapers have announced staff cuts in an attempt to stay as profitable as they have been in the past. (See **Illustration 3.1**, "Percentage of Adults Who Say They Use Newspapers as Their Main News Source," p. 59.)

Syndicates News agencies that sell articles for publication to a number of newspapers simultaneously.

To survive, most of today's dailies have become part of a chain; most cities have only one newspaper.

Newspapers at Work

Many colonial publishers handled all the tasks of putting out a newspaper single-handedly, but today's typical newspaper operation is organized into two separate departments: the editorial side and the business side. The *editorial side* handles everything that you read in the paper—the news and feature stories, editorials, cartoons, photographs and online editions. The *business side* handles everything else—production, advertising, distribution and administration.

On the editorial side at a medium-size daily newspaper, different *editors*—a news editor, a sports editor, a features editor and a business editor, for example—handle different parts of the paper. The managing editor oversees these news departments. A copyeditor checks the reporters' stories before they are set in type, and a layout editor positions the stories. Editorial writers and cartoonists usually work for an editorial page editor. The editorial department usually also manages all aspects of the newspaper's Internet editions. Editorial employees report to the *editor-in-chief* or the *publisher* or both.

A *business manager* and his or her staff run the business side of the paper: getting the paper out to subscribers, selling advertising and making sure the paper gets printed every day. These people also ultimately report to the editor-in-chief or the publisher. Sometimes the publisher also owns the paper. If a corporation owns the paper, the publisher reports to its board of directors.

Almost all newspapers today run Web sites, and many newspapers have created New Media departments to introduce strong graphic and video elements to their Internet editions.

Syndicates

Newspapers also can add to their content without having to send their own reporters to stories by using *syndicates*, which are news agencies that sell articles for publication to a number of newspapers simultaneously. The first syndicated column was a fashion letter distributed in 1857.

Today, many newspapers syndicate their columns and features to try to add income. Syndicates mainly provide columnists such as Dear Abby as well as comics and editorial cartoons. The price of the syndicated copy for each newspaper is based on the newspaper's circulation.

IMPACT/Audience

Illustration 3.1

Percentage of Adults Who Say They Use Newspapers as Their Main News Source (includes Internet and mobile phone readers)

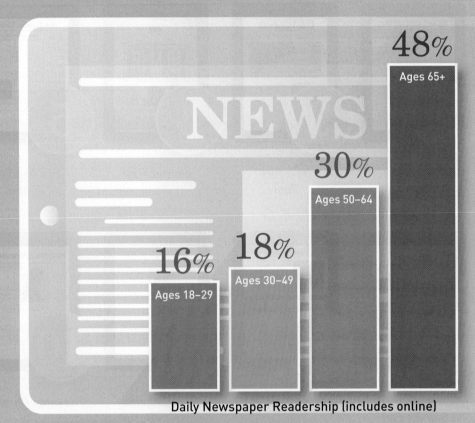

48%
Ages 65+

30%
Ages 50–64

18%
Ages 30–49

16%
Ages 18–29

Daily Newspaper Readership (includes online)

Adults between 18 and 35 today are much less likely to read a daily newspaper—even online—than mature adults (age 45 and older).

Source: "In Changing News Landscape, Even Television is Vulnerable," Pew Research Center for the People & the Press, September 27, 2012. Retrieved from people-press.org.

A large newspaper pays more for syndicated copy than a small newspaper, but revenue from syndication is limited.

NEWSPAPERS STRUGGLE TO RETAIN READERS

In the 1980s, newspaper companies looking for new ways to make money rediscovered and expanded on some old ideas. Gannett Co. introduced a new national newspaper, *USA Today*, in the 1980s with bold graphics and shorter stories, and more newspaper organizations joined the syndication business. Many newspapers introduced Internet editions in the 1990s, and today digital publishing is an essential element of any newspaper business. (See **Illustration 3.2**, "Top 10 U.S. Newspapers with Daily Digital Editions," p. 60.)

IMPACT/Convergence

Illustration 3.2

Top 10 U.S. Newspapers with Daily Digital Editions

1 *The New York Times*

2 *The Wall Street Journal*

3 *New York Post*

4 *Denver Post*

5 *Los Angeles Times*

6 *New York Daily News*

7 *Newark Star-Ledger*

8 *Newsday (N.Y.)*

9 *Los Angeles Investors Business Daily*

10 *Houston Chronicle*

About one-third of the nation's daily newspapers charge for their digital editions. This list shows U.S. newspapers with the largest number of digital readers. Some of the top-ranked digital newspapers are available only by paid subscription; others are free to online readers.

Source: Rick Edmonds, Emily Guskin, Amy Mitchell and Mark Jurkowitz, *The State of the News Media 2013*, An Annual Report on American Journalism, The Pew Research Center's Project for Excellence in Journalism. Retrieved from stateofthemedia.org/2013/network-news-a-year-of-change-and -challenge-at-nbc/

Newspapers depend primarily on advertising for support. Subscriptions and newsstand sales account for only a small percentage of newspaper income.

During the 20th century, big-city newspapers lost readers as people moved to the suburbs, and suburban newspapers grew, as did suburban editions of big-city papers.

Today's newspapers are maintaining most of their audience but only because they've added Internet editions.

As people stopped reading the printed newspaper and migrated to the Internet in the 21st century, and as younger readers abandoned newspapers altogether (even online), newspaper revenues declined very

quickly. Hundreds of newspapers have been shut down. More than 100 newspapers closed in the United States in the first six months of 2009. Seattle lost Washington state's oldest newspaper, the *Seattle Post-Intelligencer*, and Denver lost the *Rocky Mountain News*. "In 2009 and 2010, all the two-newspaper markets will become one-newspaper markets," said Mike Simonton of Fitch Ratings, a company that analyzes the newspaper industry, "and you will start to see one-newspaper markets become no-newspaper markets." By 2011, Simonton's prediction had come true, as the number of newspapers continued to drop.

National Newspapers

In 1982, the Gannett newspaper chain (which owns more newspapers than any other chain) created *USA Today*, which it calls "The Nation's Newspaper." Gannett designed *USA Today* to compete with the country's two other major national newspapers, *The Wall Street Journal* and *The New York Times*. Dubbing it "McPaper" with only "McNuggets" of news, critics called *USA Today* the fast-food approach to news. It features expensive color graphics, a detailed national weather report, comprehensive sports coverage and news stories that rarely run longer than 600 words.

USA Today went after a different audience—people who don't want to spend a lot of time reading but who want to know the headlines. Someone in an airport or someone who likes something to read on a coffee break, Gannett argued, may not need a paper the size of *The Wall Street Journal* or a large metropolitan daily. *USA Today* succeeded, and Gannett's innovations also have influenced many other newspapers, which added graphics and color and shortened the average length of stories.

Today, *The Journal*, *USA Today* and *The Times* publish regional editions by satellite so that a local bank, for example, can place an ad in a regional edition of a national newspaper. Each area's regional edition is distributed in a defined geographic area, so a local advertiser (such as the bank) pays a lower price than someone who advertises nationwide.

USA Today (owned by Gannett), *The Journal* (owned by Rupert Murdoch's News Corp.) and *The Times* (owned by The New York Times Co.) are in constant competition to become the nation's number one newspaper. Each paper has more than a million daily readers for its print edition, with an expanded audience online. Still, even the expanded online audience is not enough to consistently maintain profits, so they are always trying to find new readers or grab them from their competitors.

In 2010, *The Wall Street Journal* announced that it would add a local news section to its New York edition, in direct competition with *The New York Times*. The same year, Gannett launched HighSchoolSports.net, to offer comprehensive local high school sports coverage throughout the country. For newspapers, high school sports have been a mainstay of local news coverage. Many weekly newspapers focus on high school sports reporting, targeted at a younger audience and their parents to help maintain readership.

Internet Editions

Newspaper publishing companies first launched Internet editions in the late 1990s to try to capture new audiences for the information they gather. Today, newspapers

©Glenn and Gary McCoy/Distributed by Universal Uclick via CartoonStock.com

McCoy, Glenn and Gary/CartoonStock

arriving on-screen are an essential part of newspapers' reader-friendly strategy, but Internet editions generate a lot less revenue than print editions because a print edition can carry much more advertising than an online version. Print editions also generate revenue from newsstand sales and subscriptions but, of course, many Internet editions are available free.

In 2010, the results of a Pew Research Center survey showed that for the first time, more people (34 percent) went online for news than got their news from a newspaper (31 percent). Internet editions publish shorter highlights of the day's news, as well as special features that don't appear in the daily newspaper. Chat rooms offer subscribers the chance to discuss the news, for example, and other interactive features offer Internet links to more information, lists of archived stories on related topics and updated photos and audio and video clips from breaking news events.

Many newspapers are beginning to establish a fee structure for access (called a *paywall*). Newspapers may offer a sampling of the current week's news free online, for example, but charge a fee to retrieve the full

Paywall A fee-for-access system set up by a newspaper to charge readers for Internet content.

Large-city daily newspapers, such as *The Miami Herald* (left), and small-town weeklies, such as *The Garden Island* (right), published on the Hawaiian island of Kauai, offer Internet editions to boost their audience and attract advertising revenue.

text of longer stories and for access to their archives. Some newspapers offer free Internet access only to people who also subscribe to their daily print edition. *The Wall Street Journal* charges a subscription fee for access to its complete online edition, and in 2010 *The New York Times* began charging frequent users for content.

Technology Transforms Production

Since their colonial beginnings, newspapers have shown their ability to appeal to changing audiences, adapt to growing competition and continue to attract advertisers. The Newspaper Association of America and other newspaper analysts describe these recent advances:

- Reporters and photographers in the field send their stories from laptop computers using wireless technology. Photographers use video and digital cameras, transmitting their pictures to the newsroom electronically. News photography systems can reproduce still pictures for newspapers from video images and digital cameras.

- Newspapers use the Internet to sell more of the information they gather. Once a story is in a digital format, the information and photographs can easily be sold to people who want that information, such as lawyers and researchers.

- Satellite publishing brings customized national newspapers to readers in regional editions so advertisers can choose their audiences more selectively.

Today's technology also means that machines are doing work formerly done by people. For newspaper unions, this shift to technology has meant a consistent effort among newspaper owners to challenge union representation.

Before 1970, newspapers needed typographers to handset metal type, and labor unions represented most of these typographers. With the introduction of photocomposition, newspaper management slowly moved to eliminate the typographers' jobs. The unions fought the transition, and many newspaper workers went on strike—notably at the *New York Daily News* in 1990, at the *San Francisco Chronicle* and *San Francisco Examiner* in 1994 and at the *Detroit News* in 1996.

With the threat of new technologies eliminating even more jobs, newspaper unions are understandably worried. And as the number of newspapers declines, membership in The Newspaper Guild (which covers reporters) and other newspaper unions has dropped. Union influence at most big-city newspapers continues, but employees at most smaller newspapers are not unionized.

Consolidation Increases Chain Ownership

Because newspaper circulation is declining, large corporations have bought up many newspapers that once were family-owned. Instead of editors competing locally within a community, like Hearst battling Pulitzer, national chains now compete with one another.

Chain ownership doesn't necessarily mean that every newspaper in a chain speaks with the voice of the chain owner. Chains can supply money to improve a newspaper's printing plant and to add more reporters. But critics say the tendency to form chains consolidates and limits the traditional sources of information for readers. (See **Chapter 1** for more discussion of media consolidation.)

TODAY'S NEWSPAPER AUDIENCE IS A MOVING TARGET

Although newspapers still hold power for advertisers, recent studies reveal that younger readers are deserting the medium. According to Grant Podelco, arts editor of the Syracuse (New York) *Herald-Journal*, "It dawned on us that if we don't start luring teenagers into the paper and start them reading us now, they may not subscribe in the future."

To stop the slide among young readers, many newspapers have added inserts directed to, and sometimes written by, teenagers. *The Wall Street Journal* introduced a high school classroom edition. At the *Chicago Tribune*, five teenage film reviewers appear in the newspaper every Friday with their choices, and a "Preps Plus" section covers high school sports. *The Dallas Morning News* runs a half-sheet called "The Mini Page," subtitled "Especially for Kids and Their Families," which carries puzzles, explanatory stories about current issues and a teacher's guide.

Female readers also are abandoning newspapers in unprecedented numbers. Karen Jurgensen, editorial page editor of *USA Today*, says that readership surveys show women today are less likely to read a daily newspaper than men. "Women across the board are more likely than men to feel that the paper doesn't speak to them," she says. To attract more female readers, *The Charlotte Observer* created a daycare beat, and some newspapers are attempting to devote more space to women's sports. Newspapers also are experimenting with a section targeted specifically for women.

In some cities with large Latino populations, English-language newspapers are expanding the market by publishing Spanish-language editions, and existing Spanish-language newspapers are finding a wider audience. In areas like Dallas-Fort Worth, for example, where about a fifth of the population is Latino, newspaper companies see an ever-increasing audience with a desire for information in Spanish.

Newspapers are competing to maintain their audience because audiences attract advertisers—and profits. People who don't read a printed copy of a newspaper may still want to read the news online. Some large newspapers have even introduced free newspapers, hoping the advertising revenue will support the free editions. (See **Impact/Money**, "Newspapers: Stabilizing, but Still Threatened," p. 64.)

The challenge facing newspaper owners today is how to make money with something people can get free— either a free printed newspaper or a newspaper online.

Matthew Staver/Bloomberg/Getty Images

Unionization of newspaper employees began in the 1800s when printing was entirely mechanical. Today's new technologies have reduced the number of people required to produce a newspaper, but unions are still an important factor at urban newspapers. In this photo, an employee at the Denver Newspaper Agency checks a newspaper at the press where the *Denver Post, USA Today* and *The Wall Street Journal* are printed.

The average daily printed newspaper is about two-thirds advertising, and in some printed newspapers advertising runs as high as 80 percent. National advertisers (such as Procter & Gamble) buy much more television time than printed newspaper space, but small community businesses still need local newspapers to advertise their products and services.

Newspapers are racing to figure out how to make a profit by bringing the news to an audience that is distracted by other free media and by the personal demands of their own lives. Newspapers also traditionally have brought the public information about controversies and conflicts that people sometimes would rather ignore. "It's not always our job to give readers what they want," says Dean Baquet, former editor of the *Los Angeles Times*, now at *The New York Times*. "The job of newspapers is to help readers understand the world," he told *The New Yorker*. "If we don't do that, who will?"

As the country's first mass medium for news, today's newspaper companies are no longer necessarily the first place people go for information. Today's newspapers are trying to rediscover how they can continue to fulfill their responsibility to keep the public informed and still stay profitable.

IMPACT/Money

Newspapers: Stabilizing, but Still Threatened

By Rick Edmonds of the Poynter Institute and Emily Guskin, Amy Mitchell and Mark Jurkowitz of the Pew Research Center

I f the newspaper industry had theme music in 2013, it might use "Been down so long it looks like up to me," the much-recycled line from a 1920s blues song.

For the first time since the deep recession that began in 2007, newspaper organizations have grounds for a modicum of optimism:

- Companies have started to experiment in a big way with a variety of new revenue streams and major organizational changes. They show signs of stabilizing revenue.
- Digital pay plans are being adopted at 450 of the country's 1,380 dailies and appear to be working not just at *The New York Times* but also at small and mid-sized papers.
- Publicly traded newspaper companies saw their share prices rise in 2012, with several up 30 percent or more.
- Although the sale prices are low, newspapers coming onto the market are finding buyers.
- Even halting improvement in the general economy helps the industry. . . . Auto advertising has come back, and some markets, like Miami, are beginning to see recovery in real estate and employment ads as well.

All those positives, however, are for the time being mostly promise rather than performance. The most basic indicators have not turned around. The industry is little more than half the size it once was. Considerable dangers persist:

- Print advertising fell for a sixth consecutive year in 2012, and not by just a little—it dropped about $1.5 billion, or 7.3 percent, in a slowly improving economy. National advertising is a particular weakness, suggesting that corporations are shifting their advertising dollars to other platforms.
- Digital advertising, now up to 15 percent of total newspaper ad revenue, has grown anemically the past two years and does not come close to covering print ad losses.

(Marvin Joseph / The Washington Post)

Post to be sold to Amazon's Jeff Bezos

The Washington Post, www.washingtonpost.com

On August 6, 2013, The Washington Post Company announced on its mobile site that the paper had been sold to Amazon founder Jeff Bezos. The paper cited declining ad revenue as the main reason for the sale.

- While newspaper organizations have been successful at attracting readers who read news on mobile devices, particularly smartphones, advertising has not yet materialized.
- Though the great majority of newspaper organizations are profitable on an operating basis, many companies continue to struggle with debt and pension obligations assumed in better times.
- Papers continue to reduce traditional newsroom staff with smaller expansion on the digital side. A few have also cut print frequency to three times a week.
- Newspapers are abandoning the grand head-quarters buildings that used to help anchor downtowns in favor of smaller, less expensive offices.

So the industry entered 2013 with some positive signs but still dealing with difficult economic realities.

Excerpted from Rick Edmonds , Emily Guskin, Amy Mitchell and Mark Jurkowitz. "Newspapers: Stabilizing, but Still Threatened," *The State of the News Media 2013*, An Annual Report on American Journalism, The Pew Research Center's Project for Excellence in Journalism, stateofthemedia.org

Review, Analyze, Investigate

Reviewing Chapter 3

First Mass Medium to Deliver News

- Between 1690 and 1920, newspapers were the only mass news medium.
- Newspapers are historically important in defining the cultural concept of an independent press.

Publishers Fight for an Independent Press

- The issue of government control of newspapers surfaced early in colonial America, when the authorities stopped *Publick Occurrences* in 1690 after a single issue because the paper angered local officials.
- The tradition of an independent press in this country began when James Franklin published the first newspaper without the heading "Published by Authority."
- The John Peter Zenger case established an important legal precedent: If what a newspaper reports is true, the paper cannot successfully be sued for libel.
- By the time the American Revolution began, at least 14 women had worked as printers in the colonies.
- As dissatisfaction grew over British rule, newspapers became essential political tools in the effort to spread revolutionary ideas, including opposition to the British Stamp Act and the Alien and Sedition Laws.

Technology Helps Newspapers Reach New Audiences

- The technological advances of the 19th century, such as cheaper newsprint, mechanized printing and the telegraph, meant that newspapers could reach a wider audience faster than ever before.
- In the 1800s, newspapers sought new readers—Native Americans, immigrants and those on the nation's frontiers.
- Elias Boudinot [Galagina (The Buck) Oowati] published the first issue of the nation's first Native American newspaper, the *Cherokee Phoenix*, on February 21, 1828.
- The abolitionist and women's suffrage campaigns fostered the first alternative press movements.
- Six early advocates for domestic change were John B. Russwurm, the Reverend Samuel Cornish, Frederick Douglass, William Lloyd Garrison, Jane Grey Swisshelm and Ida B. Wells.

Newspapers Seek Mass Audiences and Big Profits

- Penny papers made newspapers affordable for virtually every American.
- The penny press made newspapers available to the masses.
- The legacy of the penny press continues today in gossip columns and crime reporting.

Newspapers Dominate the Early 20th Century

- Newspapers were the nation's single source of daily dialogue about politics, culture and social issues.
- Intense competition bred yellow journalism.

Unionization Encourages Professionalism

- Unions standardized wages at many of the nation's largest newspapers.
- Unions raised wages and created a sense of professionalism.

Television Brings New Competition

- The introduction of television contributed to a decline in newspaper readership that began in the 1950s.
- Newspapers were forced to share their audience with broadcasting.

Alternative Press Revives Voices of Protest

- The social causes of the 1960s briefly revived the alternative press.
- People who supported the alternative press believed the mainstream press was avoiding important issues such as the anti-Vietnam War movement, the civil rights movement and the gay rights movement.

Newspapers Expand and Contract

- Since the 1970s, the overall number of newspapers has declined.
- To try to match TV's visual appeal, newspapers introduced advanced graphics and vivid color in the 1990s.
- Today newspaper audiences are still declining, especially among young readers.

Newspapers at Work

- Newspaper operations are divided into two areas: business and editorial.
- The editorial department usually also manages all aspects of the newspaper's Internet editions.
- Editorial employees report to the editor-in-chief or the publisher or both.
- Almost all newspapers today produce Internet editions to capture new audiences.

Newspapers Struggle to Retain Readers

- Big-city newspapers are losing readers.
- Newspapers depend primarily on advertising for support.
- Hundreds of newspapers have been shut down in the last ten years.
- More than 100 newspapers closed in the United States in the first six months of 2009.
- According to the Pew Research Center for the People and the Press, in 2010 more people got their news online than read a printed newspaper.
- The nation's three national newspapers are *USA Today*, *The New York Times* and *The Wall Street Journal*.
- In 2010, *The Wall Street Journal* announced that it would add a local news section to its New York edition, in direct competition with *The New York Times*.
- In 2010, Gannett launched a national local high school sports site, HighSchoolSports.net, to try to attract younger readers.
- Many larger newspapers like *The Wall Street Journal* and *The New York Times* have added paywalls, which require subscribers to pay for access to the Internet editions.

Technology Transforms Production

- Wireless technology has simplified field reporting.
- Newspapers are using the Internet to sell more of the information they gather.
- Satellite publishing means national newspapers can publish regional editions.

Consolidation Increases Chain Ownership

- Large corporations have bought up newspapers that once were family-owned.
- Instead of competing locally, national chains now compete with one another.

Today's Newspaper Audience Is a Moving Target

- The future financial success of newspapers depends on their ability to appeal to a shifting audience and meet growing competition.
- Newspapers still hold power for advertisers, but recent studies reveal that younger readers are deserting the medium faster than any other group. Readership among women also has declined. To stop this slide in readership, many newspapers have introduced features and special sections targeted toward teenagers and women.
- In cities with large Latino populations, newspapers have introduced Spanish-language editions, and existing Spanish-language newspapers have expanded.
- Some large newspapers are distributing free editions in order to attract advertisers. The average daily newspaper is about two-thirds advertising.
- To survive economically, many newspapers have started charging for online content.
- Newspapers must continue to fulfill their responsibility to keep the public informed yet still stay profitable.

Key Terms

These terms are defined in the margins throughout this chapter and appear in alphabetical order with definitions in the Glossary, which begins on page 373.

Alternative (Dissident) Press **53**

Libelous **51**

Paywall **61**

Penny Press or Penny Paper **55**

Seditious Language **50**

Syndicates **58**

Tabloid **56**

Yellow Journalism **56**

Critical Questions

1. Describe the circumstances surrounding the John Peter Zenger decision. Which important precedent did the case set for the American mass media? Why is this precedent so important?

2. Describe the contributions of two early colonial American women publishers.

3. Describe the impact on American society of the competition that developed between the Hearst and Pulitzer newspaper empires. Describe the style of news coverage that characterized that competition. Give an example of sensationalized reporting from your experience.

4. Discuss the growing importance of newspapers published in Spanish and other languages and of newspapers published in digital editions. Consider both the informational and the economic impacts of these changing audiences on local communities and the nation.

5. Describe some of the Internet services newspapers offer and discuss how they make newspapers more accessible to readers. Do you read a newspaper online? How often? Under which circumstances, if any, would you be willing to pay for online news content?

Working the Web

This list includes sites mentioned in the chapter and others to give you greater insight into newspaper publishing.

American Society of News Editors (ASNE)
asne.org

This professional organization for daily newspaper editors has committees and annual conventions that address such issues as ethics, diversity and the Freedom of Information Act. ASNE also is concerned about improving journalism training and education. It was known as the American Society of Newspaper Editors until 2009.

The Dallas Morning News
dallasnews.com

One of the major daily newspapers in Texas, *The Dallas Morning News* was a pioneer in creating an online version, DallasNews.com. The paper was the first major news organization to run an exclusive online story of convicted Oklahoma City bomber Timothy McVeigh before the printed version was distributed.

Honolulu Star-Advertiser
staradvertiser.com

In June 2010, the longstanding competition between Honolulu's two major newspapers—the 128-year-old *Honolulu Star-Bulletin* and the 154-year-old *Honolulu Advertiser*—ended when the two newspapers merged to become the *Honolulu Star-Advertiser*.

Los Angeles Times
latimes.com

As one of California's major urban newspapers, the *Los Angeles Times* is known for the quality of its reporting and its coverage of entertainment-industry news. Since 1942, it has won 35 Pulitzer Prizes. On the Web site, viewers can personalize their news pages around the content that interests them.

The Miami Herald
miamiherald.com

South Florida's daily newspaper, owned by McClatchy Co., has developed a reputation for its coverage of Caribbean and Latin American news due to Miami's large Latino population. The paper has published an international edition for readers in the Caribbean and Latin America since 1946 and in Mexico since 2002. When McClatchy Co. bought Knight Ridder in 2006, *The Herald* was the largest paper acquired in the purchase.

The New York Times
nytimes.com

Long regarded as the nation's most credible and complete newspaper, *The Times* has won over 100 Pulitzer Prizes, more than any other news organization. The New York Times Co. also owns the *International Herald Tribune* and *The Boston Globe*.

Newspaper Association of America (NAA)
naa.org

As the lobbying organization of the newspaper industry, NAA's goals are to improve newspapers' market shares, advocate their interests to the government, encourage a diverse workforce and provide business and technological guidance.

Topix
topix.net

A customizable news site founded in 2002 by developers of the Open Directory Project, Topix LLC is a privately held company with investment from Gannett Co., McClatchy Co. and Tribune Co. The Web site links news from 50,000 sources to 360,000 user-generated forums. In 2007, Topix opened its Web site to give all users the power to discuss, edit and share the news important to them.

The Washington Post
washingtonpost.com

The Post is the major daily newspaper of Washington, D.C., and the preeminent newspaper for national political news. The Washington Post Co. also owns other media, including Cable One, six television stations and Kaplan Inc., a global provider of educational services, serving over one million students annually operating in more than 30 countries.

Impact/Action Videos are concise news features on various topics created exclusively for *Media/Impact*. Go online to access MindTap at cengagebrain.com. MindTap for Media/Impact sequences all of your learning tools—Chapter Readings with highlighting and note taking, Impact/Action Videos, activities and assessments—into chapter driven learning units that guide you through the curriculum.

MAGAZINES:
TARGETING THE AUDIENCE

4

Mario Tama/Getty Images

Newsstand and subscription sales still account for most of magazine industry revenue, but the future of magazines depends on their ability to expand readership to a digital audience.

> "We spent a lot of time debating whether we were the best magazine with a Web site or the best Web site with a magazine. And at the end of the day, I don't think we care."
>
> —HOWARD MITTMANN, VP-PUBLISHER *WIRED* MAGAZINE

By the early 1950s,

magazine mogul Henry Luce's *Time* and *Fortune* were well established. He often traveled with his wife, Ambassador Clare Boothe Luce, and many of the people Henry Luce met overseas wanted to talk with him about sports instead of international politics.

"Luce knew nothing about sports," says *Los Angeles Times* sports columnist Jim Murray, who in the early 1950s was writing about sports for *Time* magazine. "But every place he'd go, all over the world, the conversation would veer to the World Cup or the British Open or whatever. He got fascinated and irritated, I guess, and finally said, 'Why this all consuming interest in games?' We said, 'Well, that's the way the world is, Henry.' He said, 'Well, maybe we ought to start a sports magazine.'" The result was *Sports Illustrated*, which today is ranked among the nation's most profitable magazine brands and is published by the media giant Time Warner Inc.

Sports Illustrated was one of the earliest magazines to anticipate today's trend in magazines targeted to a specific audience. Today, successful magazines cater to their audiences with articles and advertising that reflect what each audience wants. What advertisers like most about magazines is that their readers are usually good targets for the products they see advertised around the articles.

You probably have seen a copy of *Sports Illustrated* recently, or perhaps you read *Glamour* or *Parenting*. These publications, ranked among the country's top magazines, give their readers information they can't find anywhere else, and their vast readership might surprise you.

MAGAZINES REFLECT TRENDS AND CULTURE

Glamour, published by Condé Nast, reaches more than 2 million readers every month and is ranked among the nation's top ten women's magazines, and women have always been magazines' best audience. *Parenting*, the nation's most successful family magazine, caters primarily to new parents and parents with small children, and the magazine's readership is very attractive to advertisers, who pay $200,000 a page to reach its readers.

Glamour and *Parenting* demonstrate a significant fact about the history of the magazine industry: *Magazines reflect the surrounding culture and the characteristics of the society.* As readers' needs and lifestyles change, so do magazines. The current trend toward specialty and Internet magazines, in response to the shrinking number of print magazine readers, is the latest development in this evolution.

COLONIAL MAGAZINES COMPETE WITH NEWSPAPERS

In 1741, more than 50 years after the birth of the colonies' first newspaper, magazines entered the American media marketplace. Newspapers covered daily crises for local readers, but magazines could reach beyond the parochial concerns of small communities to carry their cultural, political and social ideas to help foster a national identity.

TimeFrame

1741–TODAY

Magazines Grow as a Specialized Medium That Targets Readers

1741 Benjamin Franklin and Andrew Bradford publish America's first magazines, *General Magazine* (Franklin) and *American Magazine* (Bradford).

1821 *The Saturday Evening Post* becomes the first magazine to reach a wide public audience.

1830 Louis A. Godey hires Sarah Josepha Hale as the first woman editor of a general circulation women's magazine, *Godey's Lady's Book*.

1865 *The Nation*, featuring political commentary, appears in Boston.

1887 Cyrus Curtis begins publishing *The Ladies' Home Journal*.

1893 Samuel A. McClure founds *McClure's Magazine*, featuring muckrakers Ida Tarbell and Lincoln Steffens.

1910 W. E. B. Du Bois and the National Association for the Advancement of Colored People (NAACP) start *The Crisis*.

1923 Henry Luce creates *Time*, the nation's first newsmagazine, and then *Fortune* and *Life*, and eventually *Sports Illustrated*.

1925 Harold Ross introduces *The New Yorker*.

1945 John Johnson launches *Ebony* and then *Jet*.

1985 Advance Publications buys *The New Yorker* for more than $185 million, beginning the era of magazine industry consolidation.

1993 *Newsweek* launches an Internet edition.

1997 Dennis Publishing, which owns *Rolling Stone* magazine, launches *Maxim*, the most successful magazine launch in the last decade.

2000 Oprah Winfrey launches the lifestyle magazine *O, The Oprah Magazine*.

2005 *Slate* magazine grows popular as an Internet magazine, one of the first magazine-type publications to be issued exclusively online.

2009 Magazine publisher Condé Nast shuts down several formerly successful magazines, such as *Gourmet* and *Modern Bride*.

2010 Condé Nast launches mobile and tablet editions of its most popular printed magazines.

2012 *Newsweek* magazine stops publishing a printed version.

2013 *Wired* magazine becomes the nation's most successful combined print and digital magazine, with 50 percent of its ad revenue derived online.

TODAY Large media companies publish most magazines, and some magazines are published only on the Internet. Magazine income is stabilizing, after suffering a large drop in overall advertising revenue since 2008. Magazines are expanding their readership through digital editions.

From the beginning, women have been magazines' best audience, and *Seventeen* magazine continues today to attract a loyal female following.

The U.S. magazine industry began in 1741, in Philadelphia, when Benjamin Franklin and Andrew Bradford raced each other to become America's first magazine publisher. Franklin originated the idea of starting the first American magazine, but Bradford issued his *American Magazine* first, on February 13, 1741. Franklin's first issue of *General Magazine* came out three days later. Neither magazine lasted very long. Bradford published three issues, and Franklin published six, but their efforts initiated a rich tradition.

Because they didn't carry advertising, early magazines were expensive, and their circulations remained very small, limited to people who could afford them. Like colonial newspapers, early magazines primarily provided a means for political expression.

Magazines Travel Beyond Local Boundaries

Newspapers flooded the larger cities by the early 1800s, but they circulated only within each city's boundaries, so national news spread slowly. Colleges were limited to the wealthy because they cost too much to attend, and books were expensive. Magazines became America's only national medium to travel beyond local boundaries, and subscribers depended on them for news, culture and entertainment.

The magazine that first reached a large public was *The Saturday Evening Post*, started in 1821. The early *Post*s cost a nickel each and were only four pages, with no illustrations. One-fourth of the magazine was advertising, and it was affordable.

Publishers Locate New Readers

Magazines like *The Saturday Evening Post* reached a wide readership with their general interest content, but many other audiences were available to 19th-century publishers, and they spent the century locating their readership. Four enduring topics that expanded the magazine audience in the 1800s were women's issues, social crusades, literature and the arts, and politics.

Women's Issues

Because women were a sizable potential audience, magazines were more open to female contributors than newspapers. A central figure in the history of women's magazines in America was Sarah Josepha Hale. In 1830, Louis A. Godey was the first publisher to capitalize on a female audience. Women, most of whom had not attended school, sought out *Godey's Lady's Book* and its gifted editor, Sarah Josepha Hale, for advice on morals, manners, literature, fashion, diet and taste.

When her husband died in 1822, Hale sought work to support herself and her five children. As the editor of *Godey's* for 40 years beginning in 1837, she actively supported higher education and property rights for women. By 1860, *Godey's* had 150,000 subscribers. Hale retired from the magazine when she was 89, a year before she died.

Social Crusades

Magazines also became important instruments for social change. *The Ladies' Home Journal* is credited with leading a crusade against dangerous medicines. Many of the ads in women's magazines in the 1800s were for patent medicines like Faber's Golden Female Pills ("successfully used by prominent ladies for female irregularities") and Ben-Yan, which promised to cure "all nervous debilities."

The Ladies' Home Journal was the first magazine to refuse patent medicine ads. Founded in 1887 by Cyrus Curtis, the *Journal* launched several crusades. It offered columns about women's issues, published popular fiction and even printed sheet music.

Sarah Josepha Hale was the nation's first female editor of a major magazine. Beginning in 1837, she served as editor of *Godey's Lady's Book* for 40 years. She fervently supported access to higher education and property rights for women.

Editor Edward Bok began his crusade against patent medicines in 1892, after he learned that many of them contained more than 40 percent alcohol. Next, Bok revealed that a medicine sold to soothe noisy babies contained morphine. Other magazines joined the fight against dangerous ads, and partly because of Bok's crusading investigations, Congress passed the Pure Food and Drug Act of 1906.

Fostering the Arts

In the mid-1800s, American magazines began to seek a literary audience by promoting the nation's writers. Two of today's most important literary magazines—*Harper's* and *The Atlantic*—began more than a century ago. *Harper's New Monthly Magazine*, known today as *Harper's*, first appeared in 1850.

The American literary showcase grew when *The Atlantic Monthly* appeared in 1857 in Boston. The magazine's purpose was "to inoculate the few who influence the many." That formula continues today, with *The Atlantic* and *Harper's* still publishing literary criticism and promoting political debate in print and digital editions.

Political Commentary

With more time (usually a month between issues) and space than newspapers had to reflect on the country's problems, political magazines provided a forum for public arguments by scholars and critical observers. Three of the nation's progressive political magazines that began in the 19th and early 20th centuries have endured: *The Nation*, *The New Republic* and *The Crisis*.

The Nation, founded in 1865, is the oldest continuously published opinion journal in the United States, offering critical literary essays and arguments for progressive change. This weekly magazine has survived a succession of owners and financial hardship. It is published by a foundation, supported by benefactors and subscribers.

Another outspoken publication, which began challenging the establishment in the early 1900s, is *The New Republic*, founded in 1914. The weekly's circulation has rarely reached 60,000, but its readers enjoy the role it plays in regularly criticizing political leaders.

An important organization that needed a voice at the beginning of the century was the National Association for the Advancement of Colored People (NAACP). For 24 years, beginning in 1910, that voice was W. E. B. Du Bois, who founded and edited the organization's monthly magazine, *The Crisis*. Du Bois began *The Crisis* as the official monthly magazine of the NAACP. In

***The Crisis*, founded by W. E. B. Du Bois in 1910 as the monthly magazine of the NAACP, continues to publish today as a quarterly. This photo, taken around 1910, shows workers in the magazine's offices. W. E. B. Du Bois is the man standing on the far right near the door.**

The Crisis, he attacked discrimination against African American soldiers during World War I, exposed Ku Klux Klan activities and argued for African American voting and housing rights. By 1919, circulation was more than 100,000. Today, *The Crisis* continues to publish quarterly.

Postal Act Helps Magazines Grow

The Postal Act of 1879 encouraged the growth of magazines. Before the Act passed, newspapers traveled through the mail free while magazine publishers had to pay postage. With the Postal Act of 1879, Congress gave magazines second-class mailing privileges and a cheap mailing rate. This meant quick, reasonably priced distribution for magazines, and today magazines still travel on a preferential postage rate.

Aided by lower mailing costs, the number of monthly magazines grew from 180 in 1860 to more than 1,800 by 1900. However, because magazines travel through the mail, they are vulnerable to censorship. (See **Chapter 14**.)

McCLURE'S LAUNCHES INVESTIGATIVE JOURNALISM

Colorful, campaigning journalists began investigating big business just before the turn of the 20th century. They became known as ***muckrakers***. The strongest editor in the first ten years of the 20th century was legendary magazine publisher Samuel S. McClure, who founded *McClure's Magazine* in 1893.

McClure and his magazine were very important to the Progressive era in American politics, which called for an end to the close relationship between government and big business. To reach a large readership, McClure priced his new monthly magazine at 15 cents an issue, while most other magazines sold for 25 or 35 cents. He hired writers such as Lincoln Steffens and Ida Tarbell to investigate wrongdoing. Ida Tarbell joined *McClure's* in 1894 as associate editor. Her series about President Lincoln boosted the magazine's circulation. Subsequently, Tarbell tackled a series about Standard Oil Co. (See **Impact/Profile**, "Muckraker Ida Tarbell Exposes Standard Oil's John D. Rockefeller," page 75.)

Tarbell peeled away the veneer of the country's biggest oil trust. Her 19-part series began running

in *McClure's* in 1904. Eventually the series became a two-volume book, *History of the Standard Oil Company*, which established Tarbell's reputation as a muckraker. The muckrakers' targets were big business and corrupt government. President Theodore Roosevelt coined the term *muckraker* in 1906 when he compared reformers like Tarbell and Steffens to the "Man with the Muckrake" who busily dredged up the dirt in John Bunyan's book *Pilgrim's Progress*.

By 1910, many reforms sought by the muckrakers had been adopted, and this particular type of magazine journalism declined. The muckrakers often are cited as America's original investigative journalists.

Published since 1925, *The New Yorker* is one of the nation's most successful magazines and continues today to be the primary showcase for American writers and artists. The magazine is available in print and digital editions.

THE NEW YORKER AND TIME SUCCEED DIFFERENTLY

Magazines in the first half of the 20th century matured and adapted to absorb the invention of radio and then television. As with magazines today, magazine publishers had two basic choices:

Muckrakers Investigative magazine journalists who targeted abuses by government and big business.

IMPACT/Profile

Muckraker Ida Tarbell Exposes Standard Oil's John D. Rockefeller

By Shirley Biagi

When John D. Rockefeller refused to talk with her, Ida Tarbell sat at the back of the room and watched him deliver a Sunday-school sermon. In her autobiography, *All in the Day's Work*, written when she was 80, Tarbell described some of her experiences as she investigated Standard Oil:

The impression of power deepened when Mr. Rockefeller took off his coat and hat, put on a skullcap and took a seat commanding the entire room, his back to the wall. It was the head which riveted attention. It was big, great breadth from back to front, high broad forehead, big bumps behind the ears, not a shiny head but with a wet look. The skin was as fresh as that of any healthy man about us. The thin sharp nose was like a thorn. There were no lips; the mouth looked as if the teeth were all shut hard. Deep furrows ran down each side of the mouth from the nose. There were puffs under the little colorless eyes with creases running from them.

Wonder over the head was almost at once diverted to wonder over the man's uneasiness. His eyes were never quiet

J.E. Purdy/Historical/Corbis

In 1904 as a reporter for *McClure's* magazine, muckraker Ida Tarbell targeted oil magnate John D. Rockefeller, who called her "that misguided woman."

but darted from face to face, even peering around the jog at the audience close to the wall. . . .

My two hours' study of Mr. Rockefeller aroused a feeling I had not expected, which time has intensified. I was sorry for him. I know no companion so terrible as fear. Mr. Rockefeller, for all the conscious power written in face and voice and figure, was afraid, I told myself, afraid of his own kind.

1. Publishers could seek a *definable, targeted loyal audience*, or

2. Publishers could seek a *broad, general readership*.

Harold Ross, founding editor of *The New Yorker*, and Henry Luce, who started Time Inc., best exemplify these two types of American publishers in the first half of the 20th century.

Harold Ross and *The New Yorker*

Harold Ross' *The New Yorker* magazine launched the wittiest group of writers that ever gathered around a table at New York's Algonquin Hotel. The "witcrackers," who met there regularly for lunch throughout the 1920s,

included Heywood Broun, Robert Benchley, Dorothy Parker, Alexander Woollcott, James Thurber and Harpo Marx. Because they sat at a large round table in the dining room, the group came to be known as the Algonquin Round Table.

Harold Ross persuaded Raoul Fleischmann, whose family money came from the yeast company of the same name, to invest half a million dollars in *The New Yorker* before the magazine began making money in 1928, three years after its launch. Ross published some of the country's great commentary, fiction and humor, sprinkled with cartoons that gave *The New Yorker* its charm. Ross edited the magazine until he died in 1951, and William Shawn succeeded him.

After one owner—the Fleischmann family—and only two editors in 60 years, *The New Yorker* was sold in 1985 to Advance Publications, the parent company of one of the nation's largest magazine groups, Condé Nast. *The New Yorker* continues today to be the primary showcase for contemporary American writers and artists.

Henry Luce's Empire: *Time*

Henry Luce is the singular giant of 20th-century magazine publishing. Unlike Harold Ross, who sought a sophisticated, wealthy audience, Luce wanted to reach the largest possible readership. Luce's first creation was *Time* magazine, which he founded in 1923 with his Yale classmate Briton Hadden. Luce and Hadden paid themselves $30 a week and recruited their friends to write for the magazine.

The first issue of *Time* covered the week's events in 28 pages, minus 6 pages of advertising—half an hour's reading. "It was of course not for people who really wanted to be informed," wrote Luce's biographer W. A. Swanberg. "It was for people willing to spend a half-hour to avoid being entirely uninformed." The brash news magazine became the foundation of Luce's media empire, which eventually also launched *Fortune, Life, Sports Illustrated, Money* and *People Weekly*. Today, *Time* is only a small part of the giant company Time Warner Inc., which includes television stations, movie studios, book publishing companies, Home Box Office, CNN and America Online.

Luce's magazine fostered a *Life* magazine look-alike called *Ebony*, an African American magazine introduced in the 1940s by John H. Johnson. The Johnson chain also launched *Jet* magazine. At the beginning of the 21st century, *Ebony* and *Jet* had a combined readership of 3 million people. Johnson groomed his daughter, Linda Johnson Rice, to manage the company, a job Rice assumed in 2005 when her father died.

SPECIALIZED MAGAZINES TAKE OVER

In the 1950s, television began to offer Americans some of the same type of general interest features that magazines provided. General interest magazines collapsed. Readers wanted specialized information they could not get from other sources. These new targeted magazines segmented the market, which meant each magazine attracted fewer readers.

Very few general interest magazines survive today. The trend, since television expanded the media marketplace, is for magazines to find a specific audience interested in the information that magazines can deliver. This is called *targeting an audience*, which today magazines can do more effectively than any other medium.

COMPANIES CONSOLIDATE OWNERSHIP AND DEFINE READERSHIP

In 1984, for the first time, the price paid for individual magazine companies and groups of magazines bought and sold in one year reached $1 billion. *U.S. News & World Report* sold for $100 million. *Billboard* sold for $40 million. Like other media industries, magazines are being gathered together under large umbrella organizations, and this trend continues today. A single magazine publishing company, such as Condé Nast, may publish 200 or more different magazines each month.

These companies tend to seek more refined audience targeting. As the audience becomes more segmented, magazine publishers envision a time when they will deliver to each reader exactly what he or she wants to read. This means an infinitely defined readership, so advertisers will be able to reach only the people they want.

MAGAZINES DIVIDE INTO THREE TYPES

Today's magazines can be categorized into three types:

1. Consumer magazines

2. Trade, technical and professional magazines

3. Company magazines

You probably are most familiar with **consumer magazines**, which are popularly marketed: *Time, Glamour, Parenting* and *Sports Illustrated* are examples. In the magazine business, consumer magazines are not just those that give buying advice. This term refers to all magazines sold by subscription or at newsstands, supermarkets and bookstores. As a group, consumer magazines make the most money because they have the most readers and carry the most advertising. (See **Illustration 4.1**, p. 77.)

People in a particular industry read **trade, technical and professional magazines** to learn more about their business. *Veterinary Practice Management*, for example, is a trade magazine, published as "a

---

Consumer Magazines All magazines sold by subscription or at newsstands, supermarkets and bookstores.

Trade, Technical and Professional Magazines Magazines dedicated to a particular business or profession.

IMPACT/Audience

Illustration 4.1

Top 10 U.S. Consumer Magazines

Magazines that target a female audience have always been the most successful type of magazine. Half the nation's top ten magazines are considered women's magazines (*Better Homes and Gardens, Good Housekeeping, Woman's Day, Family Circle* and *Taste of Home*). In 2010, *Game Informer Magazine* joined the top-ten list for the first time. By 2012, it was the number one consumer magazine—reflecting the growing interest in video games.

Source: Alliance for Audited Media (formerly the Audit Bureau of Circulation) figures for 6-month period ending June 30, 2012. Retrieved from Adage.com/datacenter.

| 1 Game Informer Magazine | 2 Better Homes and Gardens | 3 Reader's Digest | 4 Good Housekeeping | 5 National Geographic |
| 6 Family Circle | 7 People | 8 Woman's Day | 9 Time | 10 Taste of Home |

business guide for small animal practitioners." Other examples of trade magazines are the *Columbia Journalism Review* (published by Columbia University) and *American Medical News* (published by the American Medical Association).

Media companies issue these magazines for their specific subscribers (*Veterinary Practice Management*, for example); universities or university-connected organizations, for their subscribers (*Columbia Journalism Review*, for example); or professional associations, for their members (*American Medical News*, for example). Most trade, technical and professional magazines carry advertising directed at the professions they serve.

Company magazines are produced by businesses for their employees, customers and stockholders. These magazines usually don't carry advertising. Their main purpose is to promote the company. Chevron Corp., for instance, publishes a company magazine called *Chevron USA Odyssey*.

Company Magazines   Magazines produced by businesses for their employees, customers and stockholders.

Magazines at Work

Magazine employees work in one of five divisions:

1. Editorial
2. Circulation sales
3. Advertising sales
4. Manufacturing and distribution
5. Administration

The *editorial* department handles everything regarding the content of the magazine, except the advertisements. Magazine editors work in this department, and they decide the subjects for each magazine issue, oversee the people who write the articles and schedule the articles for the printed and online magazine. Designers who determine the "look" of the magazine and the magazine's Web site also are considered part of the editorial department, as well as the artists and photographers who provide illustrations and photographs.

Guy and Rodd/CartoonStock

© Guy & Rodd/Distributed by Universal Uclick via CartoonStock.com

AAM   Alliance for Audited Media (formerly Audit Bureau of Circulations). An independent agency of media market research that verifies and publishes circulation figures for member magazines.

The *circulation* department manages the subscription information. Workers in this department enter new subscriptions and handle address changes and cancellations, for example. The *advertising* department is responsible for finding companies that would like to advertise in the magazine. Advertising employees often help the companies design their ads to be consistent with the magazine format.

Manufacturing and *distribution* departments manage the production of the magazine and get it to readers. This often includes contracting with an outside company to print the magazine and to publish the magazine on the Internet. Many magazine companies also contract with an outside distribution company rather than deliver the printed magazines themselves.

Administration, as in any media company, takes care of the organizational details—the paperwork of hiring, paying bills and managing the office, for example.

Because advertisers provide nearly half a magazine's income, tension often develops between a magazine's advertising staff and its editorial staff. The advertising staff may lobby the editor for favorable stories about potential advertisers, but the editor is responsible to the audience of the magazine. The advertising department might argue with the editor, for example, that a local restaurant will not want to advertise in a magazine that publishes an unfavorable review of the restaurant. If the restaurant is a big advertiser, the editor must decide how best to maintain the magazine's integrity.

The Alliance for Audited Media (*AAM*), an independent agency of print media market research, verifies and publishes circulation figures for member magazines. Advertisers use AAM figures to help them decide which magazines will reach their audience. Circulation figures (how many readers each magazine has) determine how much each magazine can charge for ads in the magazine.

Putting the magazine together and selling it (circulation, advertising, administration, manufacturing and distribution) cost more than organizing the articles and photographs that appear in the magazine (editorial). Often a managing editor coordinates all five departments.

The magazine editor's job is to keep the content interesting so people will continue to read the magazine. Good magazine editors can create a distinctive, useful product by carefully choosing the best articles for the magazine's audience and ensuring the articles are well written.

Full-time magazine staffers write many of the articles, such as a food editor who creates recipes or a columnist who writes commentary. Some magazines use articles by *freelancers*. Freelancers do not receive a salary from the magazine; instead, they are paid for each article published in the magazine. Many freelancers write for several magazines simultaneously. Some freelancers specialize—just writing travel articles, for example. Other freelancers work just as the tradition of their name implies: They have a pen for hire, and they can write about any subject a magazine editor wants.

Magazines Compete for Readers in Crowded Markets

Today, trends in magazine publishing continue to reflect social and demographic changes, but magazines no longer play the cutting-edge social, political and cultural role they played in the past. Instead, most magazines are seeking a specific audience, and many more magazines are competing for the same readers.

Time and *The Week* compete in the newsweekly category to serve the reader who wants a weekly news roundup. Joining *Fortune* in the category of business magazines are *Bloomberg Businessweek* and *Nation's Business*, among others. Younger readers are less likely to read magazines than their parents. In 1990, for the first time, the number of magazines published in the United States stopped growing, and today the number is declining.

Still, women continue to be the single most lucrative audience for magazines. *Family Circle* and *Woman's Day* are called ***point-of-purchase magazines*** because they are sold mainly at the checkout stands in supermarkets and are one part of the women's market. *Vogue, Glamour* and *Cosmopolitan* cater to the fashion-conscious, and women's magazines have matured to include the working women's audience with *Savvy, Self* and *Working Woman*, for example. The market is divided still further by magazines like *Essence*, aimed at professional African American women, and the specifically targeted *Today's Chicago Woman* for female executives who live in Chicago.

The need for magazines to specialize based on current cultural trends and interests is reflected in the very different audience targets for two of today's fastest growing magazines, *Off-Road Adventures* and *Women's Health*.

Magazine publishers are seeking readers with a targeted interest and then selling those readers to the advertisers who want to reach that specific audience—skiers, condominium owners, motorcyclists and toy collectors. Besides targeting a special audience, such as gourmet cooks or computer hackers, magazines also can divide their audience further with regional and

Brian Bedder/Getty Images

Photographers are considered part of a magazine's editorial staff. Actress Jaime King poses for an *InStyle* magazine photo session on November 12, 2012.

special editions that offer articles for specific geographic areas along with regional advertising, or they can use *webzines* (also called *zines*), which are digital magazines available on the Internet. National magazines, such as *Time*, can insert advertising for a local bank or a local TV station next to national ads. This gives the local advertiser the prestige of a national magazine at a lower cost than a national ad.

Readers Represent a Valuable Audience for Advertisers

The average magazine reader is a high school graduate, is married, owns a home and works full-time. This is a very attractive audience for advertisers. Advertisers also like magazines because people often refer to an ad weeks after they first see it. Many readers say they read a magazine

Freelancers   Writers who are not on the staff of a magazine but who are paid for each individual article published.

Point-of-Purchase Magazines   Magazines that consumers buy directly, not by subscription. They are sold mainly at checkout stands in supermarkets.

Webzines   (also called **zines**) Online magazines available only on the Internet.

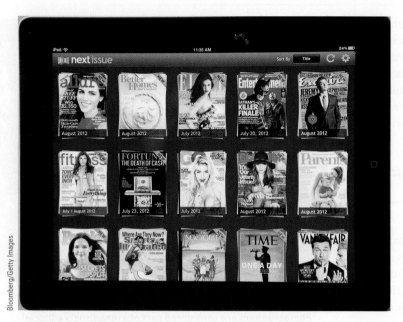

Magazines are expanding their readership by offering digital editions of the printed magazine. In July 2012, Next Issue Media offered a new iPad application that offers unlimited access to a group of popular digital magazines for one monthly fee.

as much for the ads as they do for the articles. This, of course, is also very appealing to advertisers. ***MPA***—The Association of Magazine Media—estimates that people keep a magazine issue an average of 17 weeks and that each issue has at least four adult readers on average. This magazine sharing is called ***pass-along readership***.

Advertisers can target their audiences better in magazines than in most other media because magazines can divide their audiences for advertisers by geography, income, interests and even zip code. This means that advertisers can promote special offers in separate portions of the country or market expensive products in regional issues of the magazine that go to wealthy zip codes.

Most new magazines are small-scale efforts produced on the Internet and financed by loyal relatives or friends. Sex is a favorite category for new magazines, followed by lifestyle, sports, media personalities and home improvement. In 2000, television personality Oprah Winfrey

MPA The Association of Magazine Media, originally the Magazine Publisher's Association.

Pass-Along Readership People who share a magazine with the original recipient.

launched a lifestyle magazine called *O, The Oprah Magazine*, and it was very successful. She sold the magazine to the Hearst Corporation in 2012.

But only a few new magazines succeed. Today, only one in three new magazines will survive more than five years. The reason most magazines fail is that many new companies do not have the money to keep publishing long enough to be able to refine their editorial content, sell advertisers on the idea and gather subscribers—in other words, until the magazine can make a profit. Today, many well-established magazines are struggling to survive. In 2009, Condé Nast Publications (which publishes *Vogue, Vanity Fair* and *The New Yorker*) announced that it was shutting down *Gourmet* and *Modern Bride*, which had been publishing for more than half a century.

All magazines are vulnerable to changing economic and even technology trends. In 2005, *TV Guide* announced that it was discontinuing the magazine's role as a publisher of local TV schedules and, instead, relaunching the magazine in a new format exclusively devoted to celebrity news. Changing technology, and the expansion of TV channels, made it too hard for the magazine to keep up with TV programming, so the magazine chose to focus on the most popular part of the magazine—celebrity features.

Today's consumers are buying fewer print magazines, and advertising revenues are declining. Although magazines once were very inexpensive and advertising paid for most of the cost of production, publishers gradually have been charging more, even charging for digital content, to see if subscribers will be willing to pay for specific content they want. For example, some magazines like *The Economist* recently announced plans to charge for digital content separately, so a print subscriber who wants to read the digital magazine will have to pay extra for a digital subscription. (See **Impact/Money**, "Digital Cracks 50 Percent of Ad Revenue at *Wired* Magazine," p. 81.)

Even though the audiences are smaller, magazines have increased the price they charge advertisers because magazine readers are a very good consumer audience. They're more likely to be interested in the specific products advertised in a magazine that's devoted to a subject that interests them.

However, today's changing economic outlook means that people are less willing to buy magazines when they believe they can find most of the information they want for free on the Internet. In 2009, when he announced that Condé Nast Publications was shutting down several

IMPACT/Money

Digital Cracks 50 Percent of Ad Revenue at *Wired* Magazine

First for the Title Is an Encouraging Sign for the Industry

By Nat Ives

Digital contributed half of all ad revenue at *Wired* magazine in the final three months of 2012, a first for the title and an encouraging sign for an industry where most big brands still rely overwhelmingly on the difficult business of print. Across the year as a whole, digital ads comprised 45 percent of total ad sales at *Wired*, according to the magazine.

The Atlantic has ratcheted digital ad revenue to an even higher share of the total, saying today that digital delivered 59 percent of its ad revenue in 2012. But *Wired* has a larger print business, guaranteeing advertisers a paid and verified circulation of 800,000 last year and running 885 ad pages, according to the *Media Industry Newsletter*, compared with *The Atlantic*'s rate base of 450,000 and 463 ad pages.

Digital revenue for most magazines still runs at a significantly lower level.

Digital advertising contributed to about 10 percent of *Wired* ad revenue in 2006, when parent company Condé Nast bought Wired.com and reunited it with the magazine, according to Howard Mittman, VP-publisher at *Wired*.

"We spent a lot of time debating whether we were the best magazine with a Web site or the best Web site with a magazine," Mr. Mittman said. "And at the end of the day, I don't think we care. Hitting 50 percent is proof that there is a successful template inside of this industry that can be followed by others and that having a magazine doesn't necessarily need to be an analog anchor around your technological neck."

Wired ad pages declined 5.7 percent in 2012, according to the *Media Industry Newsletter*,

but Mr. Mittman said digital's rise did not depend on a drop in print. "Real-world print dollars were flat year over year," he said.

Roughly 90 percent of *Wired*'s digital ad revenue is coming from the traditional Web, he added. "The tablet is becoming a significant contributor to all this but, candidly, the bulk of this is coming from the Web site," Mr. Mittman said.

Source: "Digital Cracks 50 Percent of Ad Revenue at Wired Magazine," January 3, 2013. Retrieved from adage.com.

popular magazines, including *Gourmet* and *Modern Bride*, CEO Chuck Townsend said, "In this economic climate it is important to narrow our focus to titles with the greatest prospects for long-term growth." Townsend's comment described the challenge facing the magazine industry as a whole—how to maintain the audience that advertisers want.

Yet even though *Gourmet* shut down, the same year the cable channel Food Network launched *Food Network Magazine*. One year later the magazine had 1.25 million readers.

DIGITAL EDITIONS OFFER NEW PUBLISHING OUTLETS

The way magazines do business in the future will be affected by technology as well as by the shifting economics of the industry. The latest innovation in magazine publishing is digital editions as a way to expand readership and give advertisers access to an online audience.

As early as 1994, *Business Week* began offering its magazine online, including a feature that gives readers access to Internet conferences with editors and newsmakers and forums where readers can post messages related to topics covered in each issue of the magazine. Many major consumer magazines today publish Internet editions. (See **Illustration 4.2**, "What's Your Magazine's Digital IQ?," p. 83.)

The economics of Internet publishing also make it possible for someone using a personal computer, a scanner, a digital camera and desktop publishing software to publish a magazine just online, dedicated to a fairly small audience, with none of the expense of mail distribution. Some large magazine publishing companies also have launched literary-political online magazines, such as *Salon.com* and *Slate*, which have attracted a very loyal Internet readership.

In 2005, *Slate* editor Michael Kinsley launched online **podcasts**, available by subscription on *Slate*'s Web site. Kinsley said *Slate* would offer "weekday podcasts of one or more of our articles read aloud (mostly by me, *Slate*'s resident radio guy). Think of this as books on tape—only

King, Jerry/CartoonStock

"Our last cell phone call, and instead of getting us help, you renew your subscription to some car magazine?"

without the books and without the tape." With podcasts, Kinsley said, readers would be able to "listen to some of your favorite *Slate* features while you're commuting or working out or sitting in a tedious meeting (make sure the boss can't see your earbuds)." Podcasts are one way the Internet has helped magazines expand their audiences beyond the printed page.

MAGAZINES' FUTURE IS DIGITAL

Magazines complement other media yet have their own special benefits. Magazines' survival has always depended on their ability to adapt to new trends. To maintain and expand their audience and revenue, the magazine industry must maintain their print audience and seek new readers online. "There is clear demand for good content on mobile devices as evidenced by the amazing growth of e-books and the terrific response to the magazine apps launched on the iPad," according to Mark Edmiston, CEO for digital travel publications. "We believe that there is even greater potential for content designed from the ground up for mobile rather than taking an existing format and converting it to mobile."

Podcast An audio or video file made available on the Internet for anyone to download, often available by subscription.

IMPACT/Convergence

Illustration 4.2

What's Your Magazine's Digital IQ?

In a study conducted by the digital research group L2, these magazines ranked highest in Digital IQ, which means that the magazines' digital content:

1. Is distinctive.

2. Is available on all digital platforms (tablets, mobile phones, iTunes, computers).

3. Expands advertising opportunities.

4. Includes social platforms.

Source: "L2 Digital IQ Index: Magazines," July 24, 2012. Retrieved from L2ThinkTank.com.

① Wired[1]	② The New Yorker[1]	③ Entertainment Weekly[2]	④ Glamour[1]
⑤ Better Homes & Gardens[4]	⑥ Time[2]	⑦ Elle[3]	⑧ Seventeen[3]

Tied

⑨ Sports Illustrated[2]

⑩ Cosmopolitan[3] — Forbes[5]

People[2] — The Economist[6]

[1] Condé Nast   [2] Time Inc.   [3] Hearst
[4] Meredith   [5] Forbes   [6] The Economist Group

In 2010, magazine giant Condé Nast announced plans to create tablet versions of some of its top magazines, such as *GQ, Vanity Fair* and *Wired*. "We feel confident enough that consumers will want our content in this new format that we are committing the resources necessary to be there," says Charles H. Townsend, President and Chief Executive of Condé Nast. "How large a revenue stream digitized content represents is an answer we hope to learn through this process." By 2013, *Wired* was the number one digital magazine in America.

Review, Analyze, Investigate

Reviewing Chapter 4

Magazines Reflect Trends and Culture

- Magazines mirror the society.
- Today, magazines target specific audiences.
- Internet editions expand magazines' traditional reach.

Colonial Magazines Compete with Newspapers

- American magazines began in 1741 when Andrew Bradford published *American Magazine* and Benjamin Franklin published *General Magazine*.
- Like colonial newspapers, early magazines provided a means for political expression.
- *The Saturday Evening Post*, first published in 1821, was the nation's first general interest magazine.
- Early magazines were expensive and had small circulations.

Magazines Travel Beyond Local Boundaries

- The Postal Act of 1879 encouraged the growth of magazines because it ensured quick, reasonably priced distribution for magazines. Today's magazines still travel on a preferential postal rate.
- *The Saturday Evening Post* was the first national magazine with a large circulation.

Publishers Locate New Readers

- Magazines widened their audience in the 1800s by catering to women, tackling social crusades, becoming a literary showcase for American writers and encouraging political debate.
- Sarah Josepha Hale and Edward Bok were central figures in the development of early magazines in the United States.
- In 1910, W. E. B. Du Bois launched *The Crisis*, published for an African American audience.

McClure's Launches Investigative Journalism

- *McClure's Magazine* pioneered investigative reporting in the United States early in the 20th century. *McClure's* published the articles of Ida Tarbell, who was critical of American industrialists.
- Early investigative magazine reporters were called muckrakers.

The New Yorker and *Time* Succeed Differently

- Magazines in the first half of the 20th century adapted to absorb the invention of radio and television. To adapt, some publishers sought a defined, targeted audience; others tried to attract the widest audience possible. *The New Yorker* and *Time* magazines are media empires that began during the early 20th century.

Specialized Magazines Take Over

- Magazines in the second half of the 20th century survived by targeting readers' special interests.
- Specialization segments an audience for advertisers, making magazines the most specific buy an advertiser can make.
- Publishers can target their magazines by geography, income and interest group, as well as by zip code.

Companies Consolidate Ownership and Define Readership

- Magazines are consolidating into large groups just like other media.
- Magazine publishers envision a time when their readership will be even more specialized than today.

Magazines Divide into Three Types

- There are three types of magazines: consumer magazines; trade, technical and professional magazines; and company magazines.
- Consumer magazines make the most money because they have the most readers and carry the most advertising.

Magazines at Work

- Magazine employees work in one of five areas: editorial, circulation sales, advertising sales, manufacturing and distribution, and administration.
- Alliance for Audited Media (formerly the Audit Bureau of Circulations) monitors and verifies readership.
- Advertisers provide nearly half a magazine's income.

Magazines Compete for Readers in Crowded Markets

- The audience for magazines is growing older, and young readers are less likely to read magazines.
- The number of magazines being published in the United States has been declining since 1990.
- Women continue to be the single most lucrative audience for magazines.

Readers Represent a Valuable Audience for Advertisers

- Each issue of a magazine, according to the Magazine Publishers Association, has at least four adult readers on average, and people keep an issue an average of 17 weeks.
- Magazines can target readers better than other media because they can divide their readers by geography, income and interests.

Digital Editions Offer New Publishing Outlets
- Many magazines have launched Internet sites to expand their readership.
- Today's digital technology means people can start an online magazine without the production and mailing expense of a printed publication.
- Some magazines, such as *Salon.com* and *Slate*, are published only on the Internet.

Magazines' Future Is Digital
- Magazines complement other media.
- Magazines are a very personal product.
- To maintain their audience and revenue, the magazine industry today is expanding its presence on the Internet.

Key Terms

These terms are defined in the margins throughout this chapter and appear in alphabetical order with definitions in the Glossary, which begins on page 373.

AAM *78*

Company Magazines *77*

Consumer Magazines *76*

Freelancers *79*

MPA *80*

Muckrakers *74*

Pass-Along Readership *80*

Podcast *82*

Point-of-Purchase Magazines *79*

Trade, Technical and Professional Magazines *76*

Webzines (zines) *79*

Critical Questions

1. What important tradition in magazine journalism did Ida Tarbell and other muckrakers establish? Describe how Tarbell reported on Standard Oil Co. Why is her reporting significant?

2. Why do today's magazines target specialized audiences for readership? Give at least three specific examples of this phenomenon and the reasons for each.

3. Discuss the role that magazines like *Ebony* and *Jet*, targeted to a specific audience, play in the development of American society.

4. If you started a magazine, what kind would you launch? How would you fund it? Who would read and advertise in it? Would you print it or put it just on the Internet or publish both printed and Internet editions? Using lessons from this chapter, how would you ensure its success?

5. What impact are digital technologies having on magazines' future direction? Consider the audience for magazines, the way in which magazines are delivered to their readers and the impact on advertisers and advertising.

Working the Web

This list includes both sites mentioned in the chapter and others to give you greater insight into the magazine industry.

AllYouCanRead.com
allyoucanread.com

The largest database of magazines and newspapers on the Internet, AllYouCanRead.com lists more than 22,000 media sources from all over the world. Listings are organized by topic and country of origin, and they can also be searched by name or keyword. Registered users can personalize their news collections, and visitors can read their favorite sources online. Subscriptions to printed materials are also available.

American Society of Journalists and Authors (ASJA)
asja.org

The ASJA is a national organization for freelance writers where members can share information about writing rates, publishing contracts, editors and agents. It also provides a referral service where editors and others can search the membership list to hire experienced authors and journalists, as well as health insurance plans for members and a writers' emergency fund.

Condé Net—Web Site for Condé Nast Publications

condenast.com

An Internet unit of Condé Nast publications, condenast.com is the leading creator and developer of upscale lifestyle brands online. It serves as a portal for prestigious online publications in fashion, men's lifestyle, food, travel and more. Users can link to style.com (the online home of *Vogue*), gq.com (*Details* and *GQ*) and epicurious.com ("for people who love to eat").

Folio: The Magazine for Magazine Management

foliomag.com

This online magazine for managers in all sectors of the magazine publishing industry reports industry trends and news. Information topics range from Audience Development to Sales and Marketing. The site also includes a Careers section, Industry Events and Webinars, and its own professional and social network, Folio: MediaPro.

Hearst Corporation

hearst.com

Starting with the publication of the *San Francisco Examiner* in 1887, The Hearst Corporation has grown to now include 200 businesses in more than 150 countries. The company owns media properties including newspapers (*San Francisco Chronicle* and *Houston Chronicle*), magazines (*Esquire; Car and Driver; O, The Magazine*), broadcast stations (WCVB-TV, Boston; KCRA-TV, Sacramento; WBAL Radio, Baltimore), and entertainment and syndication (A&E Networks, King Features Syndicate) as well as business media (B2B Information Services) and real estate.

MPA—The Association of Magazine Media and the American Society of Magazine Editors (ASME)

magazine.org

As the "Definitive Resource for the Magazine Industry," MPA (formerly Magazine Publishers of America) represents more than 300 domestic and international publishing companies from AARP to Time Warner. Departments include Government and International Affairs, Consumer Marketing, and Professional Development. ASME supports the editorial division of the site and serves its members through awards, internship programs, forums and career development workshops.

Newsweek

thedailybeast.com/newsweek.html

First published in 1933, *Newsweek* is only available today as an electronic publication and no longer offers a print edition. *Newsweek* holds more National Magazine Awards than any other newsweekly. *Newsweek.com* offers columns from the magazine's top writers, as well as podcasts, mobile content and archives.

Salon

salon.com

This pioneer online magazine, headquartered in San Francisco with offices in New York City and Washington, D.C., was founded in 1995. Because of the quality of its content, it has won many online journalism awards (such as the Webby).

Slate

slate.com

This online magazine of The Washington Post Co. includes links to news stories in current issues of *The Washington Post* and *Newsweek*. Selected *Slate* stories can be heard on National Public Radio on "Day to Day." SlateV.com is an extensive webcast library of entertaining editorials from various interviewers as well as advice from "Dear Prudence." Users can also customize their news through "build your own Slate."

Sports Illustrated

sportsillustrated.cnn.com

Known for its use of color photos shot from dramatic perspectives and its talented sportswriters, *Sports Illustrated* is the preeminent weekly sports magazine owned by Time Warner. Its online counterpart, SI.com, offers scores, news, schedules, stats and more, all organized by sport. Users can personalize their views by favorite professional or college teams.

Impact/Action Videos are concise news features on various topics created exclusively for *Media/Impact*. Go online to access MindTap at cengagebrain.com. MindTap for Media/Impact sequences all of your learning tools—Chapter Readings with highlighting and note taking, Impact/Action Videos, activities and assessments—into chapter driven learning units that guide you through the curriculum.

RECORDINGS:
DEMANDING CHOICES

Chris McKay/Getty Images

Artist income from music sales is declining, which makes live concerts a crucial source of revenue. In Atlanta on September 21, 2012, a crowd arrives at the Music Midtown Festival.

What's Ahead?

▸ Edison Introduces His Amazing Talking Machine

▸ Peter Goldmark Perfects Long-Playing Records

▸ William S. Paley Battles David Sarnoff for Record Format

▸ Hi-Fi and Stereo Rock In

▸ Recording Industry at Work

▸ Concerts Bring In Important Revenue

▸ Three Major Companies Dominate

▸ Music Sales and Licensing Drive Industry Income

▸ Industry Struggles to Protect Content Labeling

▸ Recording Industry Association Sues Downloaders

▸ U.S. Supreme Court Rules Against Illegal File Sharing

▸ Music Industry Wins Legal Action Against Downloader

▸ Digital Technology Transforms Delivery

▸ Internet Brings New Obstacles and New Opportunities

"Right now, all the conversations we have are about how do we accelerate this business."

—JEFF LEVICK, CHIEF MARKETING OFFICER, SPOTIFY MUSIC SERVICE

For the first time in more

than ten years, the music industry announced in 2013 that global sales had increased, instead of declined. "For years, the music industry's decline looked terminal, with record companies seemingly unable to come up with digital business models that could compete with the lure of online piracy," reported *The New York Times*. In 2012, however, "digital sales and other new sources of revenue grew significantly enough to offset the continuing decline in CD sales."

The sudden decline in music sales that began in 1999, primarily because of illegal downloading, meant that musicians could no longer rely on music sales to support their music. Concert performances that can draw a huge audience became a necessity, as the recording business struggled to find a financial model to sustain the industry. Ironically, the very technology that led to the music industry's decline may now be its savior. "At the beginning of the digital revolution it was common to say that digital was killing music," Sony Music executive Edgar Berger told *The Times*. Now, he said, "digital is saving music."

Most of the music people listen to each year is categorized as popular music—rock, rap/hip-hop, urban, country and pop—according to the Recording Industry Association of America (RIAA). Other types of music—religious, classical, big band, jazz and children's recordings—make up the rest, but most of the profits and losses in the recording business result from the mercurial fury of popular songs.

Of all the media industries, the recording industry is the most vulnerable to piracy and suffered the biggest

losses as a result of digital technology. Like the radio and television industries, the recording industry is challenged by Internet access to music. The recording industry also is at the center of recent debates over the protection of artistic copyright. In 2003, RIAA sued 261 people for downloading music from the Internet, saying CD shipments dropped 15 percent from the year before.

Carlos Alvarez/Redferns/Getty Images

More than half the music people buy each year, and a majority of recording industry profits, comes from sales of popular artists such as Patrick Carney (left) and Dan Auerbach of The Black Keys, performing in Madrid, Spain, on November 28, 2012.

TIMEFRAME

1877–TODAY

The Recording Industry Caters to a Young Audience

RB/Redferns/Getty Images

NICHOLAS KAMM/AFP/Getty Images

RIAA Keep your Hands Off My iPod

Justin Sullivan/Getty Images

Virgin

1877 Thomas Edison first demonstrates the phonograph.

1943 Ampex develops tape recorders, and Minnesota Mining and Manufacturing perfects plastic recording tape. Singer Bing Crosby was one of the first recording artists to use tape.

1947 Peter Goldmark develops the long-playing record.

1956 Stereophonic sound arrives.

1958 Motown, promoted as "Hitsville USA," introduces the Detroit Sound of African American artists, including The Supremes, popularizing rock 'n' roll.

1979 Sony introduces the Walkman as a personal stereo.

1985 The recording industry begins to consolidate into six major international corporations. Only one of these companies is based in the United States.

1999 MP3 technology, developed by Michael Robertson, makes it easy for consumers to download music files from the Internet.

2001 Napster, which used file-sharing software designed to download music on the Internet, shuts down after the Recording Industry Association of America (RIAA) sues for copyright infringement.

Apple introduces the iPod portable music player.

2003 Apple opens the online music store iTunes, offering music downloads for 99 cents per song.

2005 The U.S. Supreme Court says that the makers of file-sharing software can be sued for helping people violate recording industry copyright protections.

2007 RIAA sues online music consumer Jammie Thomas for copyright infringement and a jury fines her $222,000 for sharing 24 songs.

2009 Virgin Music closes all of its U.S. Megastores, marking the end of large-store music retailing.

2013 The U.S. Supreme Court refuses to hear Jammie Thomas' file-sharing case, exhausting her appeals, which means she must pay the $222,000 fine.

TODAY Three major companies dominate the recording industry. The industry earns most of its revenue from popular music. The industry is fighting copyright infringement and illegal Internet file sharing, and industry income is stabilizing. The iTunes online music store is the nation's dominant music retailer.

In 2009, a jury found one of the plaintiffs in the downloading case guilty of copyright infringement, and the case reached the U.S. Supreme Court in 2013.

But in 1877, when Thomas Edison first demonstrated his phonograph, who could foresee that the music business would become so complicated?

EDISON INTRODUCES HIS AMAZING TALKING MACHINE

Today's recording industry would not exist without Thomas Edison's invention, more than a century ago, of what he called a phonograph (which means "sound writer"). In 1877, *Scientific American* reported Edison's first demonstration of his phonograph. Edison's chief mechanic had constructed the machine from an Edison sketch that came with a note reading, "Build this."

In 1887, Emile Berliner developed the gramophone, which replaced Edison's cylinder with flat discs. Berliner and Eldridge Johnson formed the Victor Talking Machine Company (later to become RCA Victor) and

Today's recording industry would not exist without Thomas Edison's invention of the phonograph in 1877. Edison is shown in 1901 in his laboratory in West Orange, N.J.

Hulton Archives/Getty Images

RPM Revolutions per minute.

LP Long-playing record.

sold recordings of opera star Enrico Caruso. Edison and Victor proposed competing technologies as the standard for the industry, and eventually the Victor disc won. Early players required large horns to amplify the sound. Later the horn was housed in a cabinet below the actual player, which made the machine a large piece of furniture.

In 1925, Joseph Maxfield perfected the equipment to eliminate the tinny sound of early recordings. The first jukeboxes were manufactured in 1927 and brought music into restaurants and nightclubs.

By the end of World War II, 78 *rpm* (*r*evolutions *p*er *m*inute) records were standard. Each song was on a separate recording, and "albums" in today's sense did not exist. An album in the 1940s consisted of a bound set of ten envelopes about the size of a photo album. Each record, with one song recorded on each side, fit in one envelope. (This is how today's collected recordings got the title "album," even though they no longer are assembled in this cumbersome way.) Each shellac hard disc recording ran three minutes.

Peter Goldmark, working for Columbia Records (owned by CBS), changed that.

PETER GOLDMARK PERFECTS LONG-PLAYING RECORDS

In 1947, engineer Peter Goldmark was listening with friends to Brahms' Second Piano Concerto played by pianist Vladimir Horowitz and led by the world-famous conductor Arturo Toscanini. The lengthy concerto had been recorded on 6 records, 12 sides.

Goldmark hated the interruptions in the concerto every time a record had to be turned over. He also winced at the eight sound defects he detected. After several refinements, Peter Goldmark created the long-playing (*LP*) record, which could play for 23 minutes, but LPs were larger than 78 rpm records.

WILLIAM S. PALEY BATTLES DAVID SARNOFF FOR RECORD FORMAT

William Paley, who owned CBS radio and also CBS records, realized he was taking a big risk by introducing LP records when most people didn't own a record player that could play the bigger 33 1/3 rpm discs. While the LP record was being developed, Paley decided to contact RCA executive David Sarnoff, since RCA made record players, to convince Sarnoff to form a partnership with CBS to manufacture LPs. Sarnoff refused.

classical music conductor Arturo Toscanini convinced Sarnoff to manufacture LPs and to include the 33 1/3 speed on RCA record players to accommodate classical-length recordings.

CBS, in turn, agreed to use 45s for its popular songs. Later, players were developed that could play all three speeds (33 1/3, 45 and 78 rpm). A limited number of jazz artists were recorded, but most of the available recorded music was big band music from artists like Tommy Dorsey, Broadway show tunes and songs by popular singers like Frank Sinatra.

Hi-Fi and Stereo Rock In

In the 1950s, the introduction of rock 'n' roll redefined the concept of popular music. Contributing to the success of popular entertainers like Elvis Presley were the improvements in recorded sound quality that originated with the recording industry. First came *high fidelity*, developed by London Records, a subsidiary of Decca. Tape recorders grew out of German experiments with recorders during World War II.

Ampex Corp. built a high-quality tape recorder, and Minnesota Mining and Manufacturing (3M) perfected the plastic tape. The use of tape meant that recordings could be edited and refined, something that couldn't be done on discs.

Stereo arrived in 1956, and soon afterward came groups like The Supremes with the Motown sound, which featured the music of African American blues and rock 'n' roll artists. With an $800 loan from his family, songwriter Berry Gordy, 29, founded Motown studios in 1958 in a small two-story house in Detroit. He named the label after Detroit's nickname Mo(tor)town and called the building "Hitsville USA."

"Everything was makeshift," he told *Fortune* in 1999. "We used the bathroom as an echo chamber." In July 1988, Gordy sold Motown Records for $61 million. The Detroit house where Motown began is now a historical museum, and Motown Records is part of Universal Music Group.

During the same time that Berry Gordy was creating Motown, the Federal Communications Commission (FCC) approved "multiplex" radio broadcasts so that monaural (one source of sound) and stereo (two sound sources) could be heard on the same stations. The development of condenser microphones also helped bring truer sound.

In the 1960s, miniaturization resulted from the transistor. Portable transistor radios that could be carried around meant that people could listen to radio wherever they wanted—on the beach, at the park, even in the shower. Eventually the market was overwhelmed with tape players smaller than a deck of playing cards. Quadraphonic

Eric Schaal/ *Time Magazine*/Time & Life Pictures/Getty Images

Engineer Peter Goldmark invented the long-playing record format. LPs could play for 23 minutes and offered better sound quality than 78 rpm records. Goldmark stands next to a tall storage tower holding hundreds of 78 rpm records, which equals the amount of music recorded on the smaller stack of long-playing records he holds in his hands.

Stubbornly, Sarnoff introduced his own 7-inch, 45 rpm records in 1948. The 45s had a quarter-size hole in the middle, played one song on a side and required a different record player, which RCA started to manufacture. The 45s were a perfect size for jukeboxes, but record sales slowed as the public tried to figure out what was happening. Eventually Peter Goldmark and

Gilles Petard/Redferns/Getty Images

Berry Gordy founded Motown Records in 1958 and popularized the Detroit sound of singers like The Supremes. In January 1965, Gordy joined The Supremes (left to right) Mary Wilson, Florence Ballard and Diana Ross in Motown's recording studio.

(four-track) and eight-track tapes seemed ready to become the standard in the 1970s, but cassette tapes proved more adaptable and less expensive.

In 1979, Sony introduced the Walkman as a personal stereo. (The company is Japanese, but the name Sony comes from the Latin *sonus* for "sound" and *sunny* for "optimism.") Walkmans were an ironic throwback to the early radio crystal sets, which also required earphones.

Today's compact discs (CDs) deliver crystal-clear sound, transforming music into digital code on a 4.7-inch plastic and aluminum disc read by lasers. Discs last longer than records and cassettes ever did, making CDs a much more adaptable format.

Launched in the year 2000, CD players that included a *CD recorder* (also known as a CD writer or CD burner) and computers with *CD-RW (Re-Writable) drives* meant consumers could burn data to a blank CD, allowing them to copy music, play it and then re-record on the same disc. Recordable discs gained widespread

CD-RW (Re-Writable) Drives Computer drives that are used to read data and music encoded in digital form and can be used to record more than once.

acceptance quickly after they were introduced, and these players and computer drives made it even harder for the recording industry to police unauthorized use of copyrighted material.

Music videos, the music channels MTV and VH1 and the availability of iPod music downloads also have expanded the audience and potential income for music artists. The Apple iPod portable music player, first introduced in 2001, allows users to store and play music downloads. Apple launched iTunes, its online music store, in 2003, charging 99 cents per song.

The Apple iPhone, launched in 2007, combined mobile phone technology with the capabilities of the iPod, expanding Apple's dominance in music retailing. Today, the iTunes online music store has become the dominant consumer source for contemporary music. In February 2010, the iTunes store recorded its 10 billionth download, the song "Guess Things Happen That Way" by Johnny Cash. (See **Impact/Convergence**, "*Rolling Stone* Lands on iPad with iTunes Integration in Tow," p. 95.)

RECORDING INDUSTRY AT WORK

Recordings, like books, are supported primarily by direct purchases. But a recording company involves five separate levels of responsibility before the public hears a sound:

1. Artists and repertoire

2. Operations

3. Marketing and promotion

4. Distribution

5. Administration

Artists and repertoire (or A&R) functions like an editorial department in book publishing; it develops and coordinates talent. Employees of this division are the true talent scouts. They try to find new artists and also constantly search for new songs to record.

Operations manages the technical aspects of the recording, overseeing the sound technicians, musicians, even the people who copy the discs. This work centers on creating the master recording, from which all other recordings are made. Before stereophonic recording was developed in 1956, a recording session meant gathering all the musicians in one room, setting up a group of microphones and recording a song in one take. If the first take didn't work, the artists all had to stay together to do another, and then another.

It was common in the 1950s for a recording group to go through 50 takes before getting the right one. Today, artists on the same song—vocals, drums, bass, horns and guitars—can be recorded individually, and then the separate performances are mixed for the best sound. They don't have to be in the same room or even in the same country because the sound can be mixed after each of the artists has recorded his or her portion.

The producer, who works within the operations group, can be on the staff of a recording company or a free-lancer. Producers coordinate the artist with the music, the arrangement and the engineer.

Marketing and promotion decides the best way to sell the recording. These employees oversee the cover design and the copy on the cover (jacket or sleeve). They also organize giveaways to retailers and to reviewers to find an audience for their product. Marketing and promotion might decide that the artist should tour or that the group should produce and distribute a music video on Facebook to succeed. Recording companies also often use promoters to help guarantee radio play for their artists. This has led to abuses such as payola (see **Chapter 6**).

Distribution gets the recording into the stores. There are two kinds of distributors: independents and branches. Independents contract separately with different companies to deliver their recordings. But independents, usually responsible for discovering music that is outside of the mainstream, are disappearing as the big studios handle distribution through their own companies, called branches. Because branches are connected with the major companies, they typically can offer the music retailer better discounts.

Administration, as in all industries, handles the bills. *Accounting* tracks sales and royalties. *Legal departments* handle wrangles over contracts.

All these steps are important in the creation of a recording, but if no one hears the music, no one will buy it. This makes *marketing* and *promotion* particularly important. Live concerts have become the best way for artists to promote their music. Many recording artists say that music sales alone don't make them any money and that the only way to make a living is to perform before a live audience.

CONCERTS BRING IN IMPORTANT REVENUE

Concerts have become high-profile showcases for technological innovation and provide an essential source of revenue for today's big bands. For example, the group Coldplay performed in 2008 at the three-day Pemberton Music Festival in Pemberton, British Columbia, along with Jay-Z, Tom Petty and the Heartbreakers and 40 other music acts. A three-day pass for the festival cost $239.50.

"While the recording industry frets about the financial impact of music trading over the Internet, innovative bands . . . are embracing the latest technologies to create spectacular live concerts and phantasmagoric festival experiences that are more like computer-controlled theme parks than like the rock festivals of yesteryear," reports *The New York Times*.

Richard Goodstone, a partner at Superfly Productions, told *The New York Times*, "The real difference between your normal rock festival like Lollapalooza and Ozzfest is that there's a lot of music, but now we're trying to make it a complete experience in terms of the activities that really interact with the patrons out there, so it's not just a one-element kind of event." Digital technology has become an important element of selling a band to its fans, as well as selling the band's music. (See **Illustration 5.1**, "What Types of Music Do People Buy?," p. 94.)

Jamie McCarthy/WireImage/Getty Images

Live concerts demand expensive digital engineering, using new technologies to create a memorable audience experience. On October 24, 2012, Stevie Wonder and Janelle Monae perform at the United Nations Day Concert in New York City.

IMPACT/Audience

Illustration 5.1

What Types of Music Do People Buy?

The recording industry's success rests on trends in popular music. For more than 50 years, rock music has maintained its lead as the most popular type of music.

Source: Recording Industry Association of America, Consumer Profile, riaa.com.

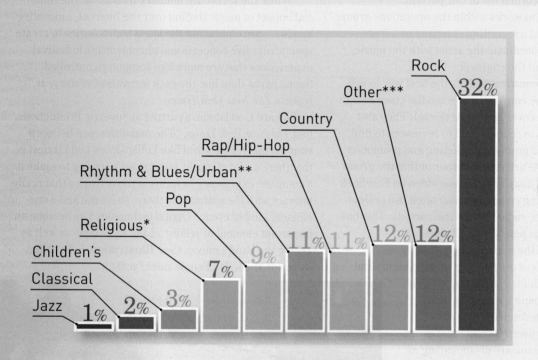

* Includes Christian, Gospel, Inspirational, Religious, Spiritual.
** Includes R&B, Blues, Dance, Disco, Funk, Fusion, Motown, Reggae, Soul.
*** Includes Soundtracks, Oldies, New Age, Big Band, Broadway Shows, Comedy, Ethnic, Folk, Holiday Music.

THREE MAJOR COMPANIES DOMINATE

Three companies dominate the global music business: Sony/BMG, Universal and Warner. In 2011, for the first time, half the music consumers bought was digital. The main recording centers in the United States are Los Angeles, New York and Nashville, and many large cities have at least one recording studio to handle local productions.

The recording industry, primarily concentrated in large corporations, generally chooses to produce what has succeeded before. "Increasingly, the big record companies are concentrating their resources behind fewer acts," reports *The Wall Street Journal*, "believing that it is easier to succeed with a handful of blockbuster hits than with a slew of moderate sellers. One result is that fewer records are produced."

Most radio formats today depend on popular music, and these recordings depend on radio to succeed. The main

IMPACT/Convergence

Rolling Stone Lands on iPad with iTunes Integration in Tow

Newsstand holdout *Rolling Stone* magazine is now on the App Store, with some iTunes music integration to let people buy tracks.

By Josh Lowensohn

Longtime Apple Newsstand holdout *Rolling Stone* magazine has caved, and is now available on Apple's subscription service.

Rolling Stone's new app works like any other publication in Newsstand, with a way to buy a single issue or subscribe using an iTunes account. *Rolling Stone* is pricing issues at $4.99 apiece, and there are two subscription options: one month for $1.99 (Rolling Stone comes out twice a month), or one year for $19.99—both with the first month for free.

The addition is noteworthy given comments made by publisher Jann Wenner of Wenner Media, who in 2011 said he was "not in any rush to break what I consider fundamental principles of what the magazine industry is" in order to make a deal with Apple that "will mortgage me into the future on the basis of getting 2,000 copies sold a month."

Nonetheless, a few months after that interview, Wenner's position appeared to have softened.

Given the music-oriented focus of the magazine, what's worth noting is that the app ties into Apple's iTunes store. Reviews of entire albums or mentions of particular songs get linked so you can stream, and potentially buy, without switching devices.

The app was made with Adobe's Digital Publishing Suite, the nearly 2-year-old software Adobe sells to companies that want to make interactive publications on tablets.

The Washington Post, www.washingtonpost.com

In an example of converging technologies, in 2013 *Rolling Stone* magazine created a mobile application that allows subscribers who read the magazine on a mobile device to buy music featured in the magazine on iTunes.

The *Rolling Stone* app is already drawing some ire from early users, who are complaining that they don't get access to a free copy of the digital version with their existing print subscription. That practice has been popularized by others, including publisher Condé Nast.

Source: Josh Lowensohn, "*Rolling Stone* Lands on iPad with iTunes Integration in Tow," January 17, 2013, cnet.com.

measurement of what is popular comes from *Billboard*, the music industry's leading trade magazine. *Billboard* began printing a list of the most popular vaudeville songs and the best-selling sheet music in 1913. In 1940, the magazine began publishing a list of the country's top-selling records.

Today, *Billboard* offers more than two dozen charts that measure, for example, airplay and album sales for popular artists such as Janelle Monae and The Black Keys. Radio, governed by ratings and what the public demands, tends to play proven artists, so new artists are likely to get more radio attention if their recordings make one of the *Billboard* lists. This radio play, in turn, increases the artists' popularity and promotes their music.

MUSIC SALES AND LICENSING DRIVE INDUSTRY INCOME

The industry also collects income from direct sales and from music licensing for radio, television and movies.

Direct Sales

The promotional tour once was the only way a company sold recordings. But in the 1980s, music videos became a very visible form of promotion for an artist. This shift changed the industry's economics. Jennifer Lopez, for example, is attractive to music companies because she is a recording artist who can perform well in videos and also makes movies.

Music Licensing: ASCAP Versus BMI

For the first 30 years of commercial radio, one of the reasons broadcasters used live entertainment was to avoid paying royalties to the recording companies. Today, two licensing agencies handle the rights to play music for broadcast: the American Society of Composers, Authors and Publishers (ASCAP) and Broadcast Music, Inc. (BMI).

ASCAP, founded in 1914, was the first licensing organization. As noted in **Chapter 6**, ASCAP sued radio stations in the 1920s that were playing recorded music. Eventually some radio stations agreed to pay ASCAP royalties through a licensing agreement, which meant that each station that paid ASCAP's fee could play any music that ASCAP licensed.

New recording artists like Alabama Shakes strive to make it to the top of the *Billboard* magazine popular music charts so they will be included in radio station playlists. Radio stations license the music they play from either ASCAP or BMI.

Throughout the 1930s, many stations refused to pay ASCAP because they didn't have enough money. These stations agreed to explore the idea of forming a separate organization so they could license the music themselves.

In 1939, broadcasters came together to establish a fund to build their own music collection through *BMI*. ASCAP and BMI became competitors—ASCAP as a privately owned organization and BMI as an industry-approved cooperative. BMI used the same blanket licensing agreement, collecting payments from broadcasters and dividing royalties among its artists. ASCAP licensed the majority of older hits, but rhythm and blues and rock 'n' roll gravitated toward BMI.

Today, most broadcasters subscribe to both BMI and ASCAP. They also agree to play only licensed artists, which makes getting on the air more difficult for new talent. BMI and ASCAP, in turn, pay the authors, recording artists, producers and sometimes even the recording companies—whoever owns the rights to use the music.

Recording industry income originally received a boost from the widespread pricing increases for music CDs. However, Internet piracy and file sharing on the Internet are the main reasons recording income declined.

ASCAP   American Society of Composers, Authors and Publishers.

BMI   Broadcast Music, Inc.

Industry Struggles to Protect Content Labeling

Three issues face today's recording industry: content labeling, overseas piracy and artists' copyright protection from file sharing on the Internet.

In 1985, the Parents Music Resource Center (PMRC) called for recording companies to label their recordings for explicit content. The new group was made up primarily of the wives of several national political leaders, notably Susan Baker, wife of then-Treasury Secretary James A. Baker III, and Tipper Gore, wife of then-Senator Al Gore.

Saying that recordings come under the umbrella of consumer protection, the PMRC approached the National Association of Broadcasters and the Federal Communications Commission with their complaints. "After equating rock music with the evils of 'broken homes' and 'abusive parents,' and labeling it a 'contributing factor' in teen pregnancy and suicide, they single[d] out Madonna, Michael Jackson, Mötley Crüe, Prince, Sheena Easton, Twisted Sister and Cyndi Lauper for their 'destructive influence' on children," reported journalism law professor Louis P. Sheinfeld.

The result was that, beginning in January 1986, the *Recording Industry Association of America* (RIAA), whose member companies account for 95 percent of U.S. recording sales, officially urged its members either to provide a warning label or to print lyrics on albums with potentially offensive content. Like the movie industry when it adopted its own ratings system (see **Chapter 7**), the recording industry favored self-regulation rather than government intervention.

In 1990, the nation's two largest record retailers ordered all their outlets to stop stocking and selling sexually explicit recordings by the controversial rap group 2 Live Crew. A Florida judge ruled that the group's album *As Nasty As They Wanna Be* was obscene, even though it carried a warning about explicit lyrics. The Luke Skywalker record label, which produced the album, said the controversy increased sales, but the ban meant that more than 1,000 stores nationwide refused to sell the music. Eventually, the decision was overturned, but sales of the album already had plummeted.

Overseas Piracy

Overseas pirates who copy prerecorded music that is then sold in the United States cost the recording industry a lot of money. RIAA says pirates control 18 percent of album sales, and this represents $1 billion a year in lost income.

Besides the lost revenue, counterfeit copies can easily fool consumers and usually are inferior quality, which doesn't truly represent the artist's music. This is a continuing battle for the music industry because many of the countries responsible for the counterfeit copying do not have agreements with the United States to force them to honor U.S. copyrights and prosecute the pirates.

File Sharing on the Internet

Portable MP3 players—electronic devices that allow users to download music to a computer chip-based player—were introduced in 1999. In 1999, a software-sharing program available at a Web site called Napster.com skyrocketed into popularity. With the program, computer users could download music over the Internet for free, called *file sharing*. Then, using MP3 technology (which provides high-quality sound and requires very little computer storage space), users could keep and use the music. RIAA immediately sued Napster, claiming violation of copyright.

In April 2000, the heavy-metal rock group Metallica sued Napster for copyright infringement. Rapper Dr. Dre filed suit two weeks later. In July 2000, an appeals court ordered Napster to shut down the site, but Napster delayed. Napster finally shut down in 2001.

Jack Ziegler/The New Yorker Collection/Cartoonbank

"Wow, thanks. I'm a big fan. I've downloaded all your stuff."

Recording Industry Association of America (RIAA) Industry association that lobbies for the interests of the nation's major recording companies. Member companies account for 95 percent of all U.S. recording company sales.

File Sharing The peer-to-peer distribution of copyrighted material on the Internet without the copyright owner's permission.

Recording Industry Association Sues Downloaders

In 2003, Apple opened its online iTunes Music Store, offering a place where consumers could download music legally for 99 cents per song. Still, people continued to download free music, aided by new free online music services such as Kazaa and Grokster. So in 2003, RIAA sued 261 individual music downloaders across the United States, intensifying its efforts to stop music piracy. On average, each defendant had shared 1,000 songs each.

"A lot of people think they can get away with what they are doing because peer-to-peer file sharing allows them to hide behind made-up screen names," the president of RIAA told *The New York Times*. "They are not anonymous. The law is very clear. What they are doing is stealing." Copyright laws allowed the industry to seek $750 to $150,000 for each violation.

The lawsuits included copies of screen shots of many users' entire online music-sharing accounts, showing the names of each song and how many times the user downloaded music. RIAA offered not to pursue the individual lawsuits for people who were willing to sign a notarized statement saying they would stop sharing music files and delete files they now had. A subsequent court ruling stopped the prosecution of people who downloaded free music, but the case headed to the U.S. Supreme Court.

U.S. Supreme Court Rules Against Illegal File Sharing

In June 2005, the U.S. Supreme Court announced a decision that eventually shut down many free music software providers. In *MGM Studios v. Grokster*, the Court said the makers of Grokster, which allowed Internet users to browse freely and copy songs from each other, could be sued for their role in helping people violate recording industry copyright protections.

This Supreme Court decision gave the recording companies the legal ammunition they needed to shut down file-sharing services, and the services quickly closed.

Music Industry Wins Legal Action Against Downloader

In 2007, a federal jury ruled that a Minnesota woman, Jammie Thomas, was liable for copyright infringement because she had shared music online. The jury imposed a penalty against Thomas of $222,000—calculated at

$9,250 in damages for each of the 24 songs involved in the trial. In September 2008, the judge set aside the original verdict and ordered a retrial.

The verdict represented the first time a federal jury had imposed a legal fine on someone for music piracy. Earlier in the summer, however, a judge dismissed record labels' claims that an Oklahoma woman had used an Internet address to share music.

AP Photo/Julia Cheng, File

In 2007, a federal jury ruled that Jammie Thomas was liable for copyright infringement because she shared music online, and the jury imposed a penalty of $222,000 ($9,250 in damages for each of the 24 songs involved). In 2013, the U.S. Supreme Court let the verdict stand.

According to evidence presented at the Thomas trial, the music downloads were linked to a Kazaa account user name that belonged to Thomas. Thomas denied she had a Kazaa account. Bringing the charges against Thomas were Capitol Records, the Universal Music Group, Sony BMG Entertainment and the Warner Music Group.

In late 2008, however, RIAA announced that it was dropping the legal actions it had initiated against about 35,000 other people for music downloading. Instead, the association said it planned primarily to pursue agreements with Internet service providers where RIAA would notify the provider when RIAA learned that the provider's customers were making music available online to share with others. The provider would then, after notification, cancel the customers' account.

The decision to drop the suits originally was viewed as an admission by RIAA that their initial legal strategy had failed to stop online file sharing. However, RIAA continued to pursue the Thomas case. The case eventually reached

Pat Byrnes/The New Yorker Collection/CartoonBank

"Come on, we're all going to sit around the campfire and play our iPods."

the U.S. Supreme Court, and on March 18, 2013, the Court let the original $222,000 judgment against Thomas stand.

Digital Technology Transforms Delivery

From the beginning, profits in the recording industry have been tied to technology. Ever since William S. Paley and David Sarnoff decided to produce LPs and 45s, the consumer has followed equipment manufacturers, looking for better, more convenient sound. The recent expansion of MP3 digital technology signaled a new era for music lovers, making quality music available on the Internet. (See **Illustration 5.2**, "How Does the Recording Industry Make Money?," p. 100.)

But recording companies claim that people's ability to download and copy digitized music on the Internet is financially ruining the industry. Once digitized, the music is available to anyone and can be sent through the Internet around the world.

Music company executives originally thought that the way to protect their music was to develop new technology that would make free downloads impossible. Yet despite aggressive attempts by RIAA to stop music file sharing, it is still a widespread practice with vast copyright and income implications for recording artists and music companies.

Aware of the potential damage to recording company income, RIAA joined an international crackdown on overseas companies that sell pirated music and people who download copyrighted music on the Internet. But policing the international community for music piracy

and monitoring the Internet for illegal music sharing is difficult and expensive.

One solution to combat illegal downloading emerged with the introduction of subscription music services, such as Rhapsody, Spotify, Rdio and Deezer. Some services are free (supported by advertising), and some charge a monthly fee for access to an almost unlimited selection of music. Others offer the option of free or subscription music.

In 2011, RIAA reported that revenue from subscription music services grew to a new high of $241 million, with 1.8 million users. (See **Impact/Global**, "Worldwide Music Service Spotify: Growing Like Mad, Yet So Far to Go," p. 101.)

Internet Brings New Obstacles and New Opportunities

Because of the Internet, music can be shared globally in an instant, which is a huge benefit for artists and consumers. Yet the Internet also makes music piracy so easy that many people consider it a harmless act, and the economic implications for recording artists are substantial. In 2007, RIAA estimated the industry had lost nearly $1 billion in revenue just from illegal music downloads. In 2009, RIAA announced that music sales in 2008 were down 18 percent worldwide from 2007—the lowest level ever.

In 2010, RIAA estimated that "globally only one of 20 downloads is authorized, and online piracy rates in many markets is in the vicinity of 99 percent." In 1999, recording company income was $38 billion; in 2011, it was less than half that—$16.5 billion.

No industry can survive for long on such a rapid loss of income. So the recording companies have no choice but to pursue copyright infringement wherever they find it. Licensed music is governed by national and international copyright law, and the recording industry continues to aggressively pursue all the legal remedies available to curtail illegal music downloads in the United States and reduce piracy, especially overseas. The industry, of course, also encourages all legal music download services, such as iTunes, and subscription sites such as Spotify and Rhapsody.

By April 2008, the iTunes store had become the largest music retailer in the United States. By 2010, according to Apple, customers had downloaded 10 billion songs. And Spotify has 6 million users. Because of the Internet, music artists today can find a bigger audience than Thomas Edison ever could have imagined—through music downloads and subscription services. However, the music business cannot escape the challenges of the Internet. Recording

IMPACT/Money

Illustration 5.2

How Does the Recording Industry Make Money?

In 2011, for the first time, recording industry income from digital music sales equaled income from what the industry calls "physical" units, such as CDs. However, physical CDs still account for substantial revenue. Here is the sales breakdown.

Source: Recording Industry Association of America, "2011 Year-End Shipment Statistics," riaa.org.

Digital Sales (50%)

Music Videos 1%
Subscription 3%
Mobile* 4%
Other** 5%
Download Albums 16%
Download Singles 21%

Physical Sales (50%)

CD Singles 1%
Vinyl Singles 1%
DVD Videos 2%
Music Videos 2%
CD 44%

Total Income = $7 Billion

* Includes ringtones, full-length downloads, and kiosks.
** Performance royalties

IMPACT/Global

Worldwide Music Service Spotify: Growing Like Mad, Yet So Far to Go

By Paul Sloan

AUSTIN, Texas—It's not a bluegrass jam on the legendary Austin City Limits stage, but for Spotify CEO Daniel Ek, it nonetheless will be a heady moment.

When Ek sits for a fireside chat at the South By Southwest (SXSW) Interactive Festival here, the Swedish-born, aspiring music industry mogul will be able to share some fresh bragging rights: Spotify has signed another one million subscribers since December (2012), bringing the total to 6 million and cementing its position as the fastest-growing digital music company ever—second in reach only to Internet radio company Pandora.

It's no small accomplishment. Music-streaming startups have come and gone like one-hit wonders in recent years. And yet, through a mixture of hype, a quality product, great timing, and shrewd execs and backers, Spotify has risen to prominence even as deep-pocketed behemoths like Google and Apple appear ready to jump into the music streaming business.

"Right now," said Spotify Chief Marketing Officer Jeff Levick, "all the conversations we have are about how do we accelerate this business."

That growth comes as Spotify expands its global footprint. Over the past year, it has doubled to 20 the number of countries in which it's available. In February (2013), it added Italy, Poland, and Portugal. In the coming months, launches are planned across South America and Southeast Asia.

Spotify also has cut deals with automakers Ford and Volvo, ensuring the music-streaming service is available with some new vehicles. The company also is seeking partnerships with Internet providers and wireless companies to find ways to bundle its service, which has played a key role in some of its success in European markets.

Since it burst on the scene in the U.S. 17 months ago, Spotify has caught flak from artists bitter about the paltry payouts they get when their music is streamed on Spotify. Where artists

James Martin/CNET

In less than two years since its launch in 2011, international music streaming company Spotify, based in Sweden, signed up 6 million subscribers. As of March 2013, the service was available in 20 countries.

might earn 7 to 10 cents from a 99-cent song purchased from iTunes, they'll usually make a fraction of a penny when that same song is streamed on Spotify.

One way that problem can go away is through sheer size. Those penny payouts grow to dollars the more people listen. The bigger Spotify gets, the better off things become for the artists and labels.

As it stands, Spotify is on track to bring in more than $684 million this year (2013) from subscribers alone, because roughly 90 percent of those 6 million people pay $10 a month—or the local currency equivalent. The rest pay the $5-a-month version for desktop access.

Still, it will be a challenge for Spotify to become more than a single-digit-margin business, assuming it can turn a profit. Its aim is to get big fast and bring in so much money for the labels that they'll be willing to offer more favorable terms. The clock is ticking, but Ek and company are getting used to defying the odds.

Source: Paul Sloan, "Spotify: Growing Like Mad, Yet So Far to Go," March 12, 2013, cnet.com.

companies must learn how to produce music consumers want to buy, delivered in a format and/or through a service that can sustain the industry financially.

When Edison demonstrated his phonograph for the editors of *Scientific American* in 1877, the magazine reported that "Mr. Thomas Edison recently came into this office, placed a little machine on our desk, turned a crank, and the machine inquired as to our health, asked how we liked the phonograph, informed us that it was very well, and bid us a cordial good night. These remarks were not only perfectly audible to ourselves, but to a dozen or more persons gathered around."

None of the discoveries by Edison's successors has been a new invention, only refinements. Berliner flattened the cylinder; Goldmark and Sarnoff slowed down the speed; hi-fi, stereo and quadraphonic sound increased the fidelity; cassettes, compact discs, digital recorders

and MP3 players refined the sound further; and file-sharing software allowed people to share copyrighted music. While advances in technology have dramatically improved the quality of recordings, they have also made free copying possible, robbing the recording companies of their profitability.

Still, the basic foundation of the recording industry today is the same as it was for Thomas Edison in 1877. Reflecting on the movie version of Edison's life, Robert Metz describes the development of the phonograph: An Edison employee was tinkering with "a makeshift device consisting of a rotating piece of metal with a pointed piece of metal scratching its surface. The device was full of sound and fury—and signified a great deal. . . . And thus, supposedly through idle play, came the first permanent 'record' of ephemeral sound. By any measure, it was an invention of genius."

Review, Analyze, Investigate

Reviewing Chapter 5

Edison Introduces His Amazing Talking Machine

- Thomas Edison first demonstrated his phonograph in 1877.
- Emile Berliner developed the gramophone in 1887.
- Berliner and Eldridge Johnson formed the Victor Talking Machine Company (later RCA Victor) to sell recordings.
- Joseph Maxfield perfected recording equipment to eliminate the tinny sound.
- The first standard records were 78 rpm.

Peter Goldmark Perfects Long-Playing Records

- Peter Goldmark, working for CBS' William S. Paley, developed the long-playing (LP) record (33 1/3 rpm).
- The first long-playing records played for 23 minutes and were larger than 78s.

William S. Paley Battles David Sarnoff for Record Format

- David Sarnoff's staff at RCA developed the 45 rpm record.
- Eventually record players that could play all the different speeds—33 1/3 rpm, 45 rpm and 78 rpm—were sold.

Hi-Fi and Stereo Rock In

- Rock 'n' roll redefined the concept of popular music.
- Recording industry efforts to improve recorded sound quality contributed to the success of rock 'n' roll entertainers like The Supremes.
- The introduction of transistor radios in the '60s and the Walkman in the late '70s made music personal and portable.
- CD-RWs, compact discs that could record as well as play, meant consumers could create their own CDs.
- The Apple iPod music player, first introduced in 2001, allowed users to store and play music downloads.
- Apple launched iTunes, its online music store, in 2003, charging 99 cents per song and allowing legal music downloads.
- The Apple iPhone, introduced in 2007, combined mobile phone technology with the capabilities of the iPod, expanding Apple's dominance in music retailing.
- Today, Apple's iTunes store has become the primary consumer source for contemporary music.

Recording Industry at Work

- A recording company is divided into artists and repertoire, operations, marketing and promotion, distribution and administration.
- CD sales alone don't generate enough revenue to support most music groups.

Concerts Bring In Important Revenue

- Concerts require high-tech innovation.
- Concert ticket sales are an essential source of revenue for large bands.

Three Major Companies Dominate

- Three large corporations dominate the recording industry.
- Recording companies sell more than 2 billion recordings a year.
- Radio depends on popular music to succeed.

Music Sales and Licensing Drive Industry Income

- The recording industry collects income from direct sales, music licensing, music videos and music downloads, but recording income today is declining.
- Today two licensing agencies—ASCAP and BMI—handle the rights to play music for broadcast.

Industry Struggles to Protect Content Labeling

- Three issues facing today's recording industry are attempts to control music content through labeling, overseas piracy and copyright protection for music file sharing.
- The recording industry responded to threats of government regulation of music lyrics by adopting its own standards for music labeling.
- MP3 digital technology, perfected in 1999, allowed consumers to download and store good-quality music directly from the Internet.
- Music-sharing company Napster was sued in 1999 for copyright infringement by the Recording Industry Association of America and shut down in 2001.
- Consumers continued to use music-sharing sites such as Kazaa and Grokster, even though the downloaded songs were covered by copyright.

Recording Industry Association Sues Downloaders

- In 2003, the Recording Industry Association of America sued 261 individual music downloaders, hoping to stop the flow of free music on the Internet, but people still continue to download.
- The lawsuits included specific names of people who had downloaded music.

U.S. Supreme Court Rules Against Illegal File Sharing

- In June 2005, the U.S. Supreme Court in *MGM Studios v. Grokster* ruled that the makers of Grokster, which allowed Internet users to browse freely and copy songs from each other, could be sued for helping people violate recording industry copyright protections.
- *MGM Studios v. Grokster* gave the recording industry the legal standing it needed to try to stop illegal file sharing.

Music Industry Wins Legal Action Against Downloader

- In 2007, a federal jury imposed a penalty for file sharing of $222,000 against a woman named Jammie Thomas— calculated at $9,250 in damages for each of the 24 songs involved in the trial, the first time a federal jury had imposed a legal fine on someone for music piracy.
- In late 2008, RIAA dropped suits against 35,000 downloaders and said it primarily would pursue downloaders through their Internet service providers.
- The Thomas case eventually reached the U.S. Supreme Court, and on March 18, 2013, the Court let the original $222,000 judgment against Thomas stand.

Digital Technology Transforms Delivery

- Apple introduced the iPod portable music player in 2001.
- Apple's iTunes music store, launched in 2003, provides a legal way for people to download music.
- Subscription services, such as Rhapsody and Spotify, are growing in popularity as a legal source of digital music.

Internet Brings New Obstacles and New Opportunities

- The Apple iPhone, introduced in 2007, combines the functions of the Apple iPod and a mobile phone, making Apple the dominant music retailer.
- In 2007, RIAA estimated the industry had lost nearly $1 billion in revenue just from illegal music downloads.
- By April 2008, the iTunes store had become the largest music retailer in the United States.
- In 2010, RIAA estimated that "globally only one of 20 downloads is authorized, and online piracy rates in many markets is in the vicinity of 99 percent."
- The recording companies have no choice but to pursue copyright infringement wherever they find it.
- Licensed music is governed by national and international copyright law, so the recording industry aggressively pursues all the legal remedies available to curtail illegal music downloads in the United States and reduce piracy, especially overseas.
- The industry also encourages all legal music download services, such as iTunes, and subscription sites, such as Spotify.

Key Terms

These terms are defined in the margins throughout this chapter and appear in alphabetical order with definitions in the Glossary, which begins on page 373.

ASCAP *96*	File Sharing *97*	Recording Industry Association of America (RIAA) *97*
BMI *96*	LP *90*	
CD-RW (Re-Writable) Drives *92*	RPM *90*	

Critical Questions

1. Describe the competition between William Paley's 33 1/3 records and David Sarnoff's 45s. How was that battle resolved? What does that battle tell you about the role that technology plays in the media industries?

2. Why are the recording industry and the radio industry so interdependent?

3. Give a brief history of Motown. Why was the company so important in the history of the music industry?

4. Discuss the response of the music recording industry to file sharing, and evaluate the extent to which it has been successful in protecting recording artists and recording companies. Do you believe the 2013 U.S. Supreme Court decision against Jammie Thomas will stop illegal file sharing? Explain.

5. How have recent technologies, such as the iPod and the iPhone, affected the music recording and performance industries in ways other than file sharing? Discuss.

Working the Web

This list includes both sites mentioned in the chapter and others to give you greater insight into the recording industry.

American Top 40 with Ryan Seacrest

at40.com

Along with America's longest-running popular music weekend countdown, AT40 offers music news, artist pictures and podcasts, and user contests and blogs.

AOL Music

music.aol.com

The music division of America Online, AOL Music, offers streaming radio, music downloads from a variety of genres and entertainment news and live performances on Sessions.

Apple.com/iTunes

apple.com/itunes

iTunes provides "music jukebox" software used to store music on a computer or a hand-held digital player such as an iPod. Apple's online music service opened in 2003, and its popularity has proven the feasibility of online music sales. In addition to music, the iTunes Store features audio books, TV shows, movies, iPod games and cell phone ringtones. The iPod is currently rivaled by Apple's own iPhone, which has all the iPod's

capabilities plus Internet access, GPS mapping, cell phone service and more.

Billboard

billboard.biz and *billboard.com*

Billboard.biz is the official business Web site of *Billboard* magazine, the music industry's bible. It includes breaking news about the music business, top-selling charts in all music categories and even a job bulletin board to lead readers to jobs in the music industry. The companion Web site, Billboard.com, offers samples from best-selling music albums and singles; news articles on artists, products and awards; interactive blogs, games and contests; and even a Billboard fashion store. Billboard.com is also available in Spanish at billboardenespanol.com.

Insound

insound.com

Developed in 1999 by "a bunch of indie rock kids" determined to improve the music mail-order business, Insound presents a wide variety of independent music. The Web site offers CDs, music downloads and vinyl records as well as T-shirts, posters and other merchandise. Favorite music lists created by staff, bands and guests are also available.

Pandora: Radio from the Music Genome Project

pandora.com

With the belief that each listener has an individual relationship with music, Pandora provides a customizable online listening experience. Users enter a favorite artist or song and Pandora's software analyzes melody, harmony, rhythm and more to identify and recommend similar music.

Recording Industry Association of America (RIAA)

riaa.com

As the trade group representing U.S. music companies, RIAA protects intellectual property rights and First Amendment rights globally, conducts consumer and technical research and monitors governmental regulations and policies. It also issues the awards for Gold and Platinum best-selling recordings.

Rhapsody, Inc.

rhapsody.com

Rhapsody's Web site says, "Going on ten years strong, Rhapsody continues to outpace the competition with great social features, millions of songs, and an easy-to-use interface." Users can stream and download music from customized playlists.

Universal Music Group (UMG)

universalmusic.com

Owned by Vivendi, Universal Music Group has worldwide operations that cover recorded music and music publishing. UMG offers the world's largest digital music catalog and holds recording labels including EMI, Interscope Geffen A & M, Universal Motown and Nashville groups, and Universal Music Latino. Its Web site hosts videos in all music genres.

Impact/Action Videos are concise news features on various topics created exclusively for *Media/Impact*. Go online to access MindTap at cengagebrain.com. MindTap for Media/Impact sequences all of your learning tools—Chapter Readings with highlighting and note taking, Impact/Action Videos, activities and assessments—into chapter driven learning units that guide you through the curriculum.

RADIO:
RIDING THE WAVE

Cindy Ord/Getty Images

Radio sports is one of the most popular programming formats. In New Orleans on February 1, 2013, radio hosts (left to right) Rich Davis, Steve Covino and actor Tracy Morgan attend Sirius XM's live broadcast from Super Bowl XLVII.

What's Ahead?

"We call ourselves a radio station, but we're really a multimedia content provider."

—JOHN O. PLATT, COMMUNICATIONS DIRECTOR OF WFUV, FORDHAM UNIVERSITY'S COLLEGE RADIO STATION

Today, the nation's

collective memory and impressions about events that happened in the first half of the 20th century are directly tied to radio. Newspapers offered next-day reports and occasional extras, and magazines offered long-term analysis. But radio gave its listeners an immediate news record at a time when world events demanded attention. Radio also gave people entertainment: sports, big bands, Jack Benny, George Burns and Gracie Allen, Abbott and Costello, Bob Hope, and the original radio character, the Shadow (the Shadow's famous lines were: "The weed of crime bears bitter fruit. Crime does not pay! The Shadow knows!").

Radio transformed national politics by transmitting the sounds of public debate, as well as the words, to the audience. Radio also expanded Americans' access to popular as well as classical culture. Opera played on the same dial as slapstick comedy; drama and music shared the airwaves with sports—all supported by advertising.

RADIO SOUNDS ARE EVERYWHERE

The legacy of news and music remains on radio today, but the medium that once was the center of attention in everyone's front room has moved into the bedroom, the office, the car and the shower. Radio wakes you up and puts you to sleep. Radio goes with you when you run on the trail or sit on the beach. Internet radio even follows

you to your desk at work. Consider these industry statistics about radio today:

- 99 percent of America's homes have radios.

- 95 percent of America's cars have radios, and radio reaches three out of five adults in their cars at least once each week.

- 40 percent of Americans listen to the radio sometime between 6 a.m. and midnight.

- Weekly online radio listening is at an all-time high, nearly 30 percent of the U.S. population.

Although radio is more accessible today, what you hear is not the same as what your great-grandparents heard. Advertisers, who once sought radio as the only broadcast access to an audience, have many more places to put their ads. For audiences, radio has become an everyday accessory rather than a necessity. No one had envisioned radio's place in today's media mix when radio's pioneers began tinkering just before the turn of the 20th century. All these pioneers wanted to do was figure out a way to send sounds along a wire.

RADIO TAKES A TECHNOLOGICAL LEAP

Today we are so accustomed to sending and receiving messages instantaneously that it is hard to imagine a time when information took more than a week to travel

TIMEFRAME

1899–TODAY

Digital Technology and Format Programming Chase the Audience

1899 Guglielmo Marconi introduces his wireless radio to the United States with a report of the America's Cup race.

1906–1907 Reginald Aubrey Fessenden transmits the first voice and music broadcast. Lee de Forest introduces the Audion tube.

1920 Station KDKA in Pittsburgh goes on the air, the nation's first commercial radio station.

1934 Congress establishes the Federal Communications Commission to regulate broadcasting.

1936 Edwin H. Armstrong licenses frequency modulation (FM).

1938 *Mercury Theater on the Air* broadcasts *War of the Worlds*, demonstrating how quickly broadcast misinformation can cause a public panic.

1948 The first transistor radios are sold, making radio portable and expanding radio's reach to audiences outside of the home and the car.

1959 Gordon McLendon introduces format radio at KABL in San Francisco.

1960 The Manhattan grand jury indicts disc jockey Alan Freed for payola.

1970 National Public Radio (NPR) goes on the air. By design, public radio was created as an alternative to commercial radio.

1996 Congress passes the Telecommunications Act of 1996, which encourages unprecedented consolidation in the radio industry.

2001 Sirius Satellite Radio and XM Radio begin offering digital satellite radio service.

2005 New York Attorney General Eliot Spitzer charges that payola still is pervasive in the radio industry.

Radio broadcasters form the HD Digital Radio Alliance to promote HD radio.

Internet radio pioneer Tim Westergren launches Internet radio service Pandora to offer free and subscription music online.

2008 Satellite radio companies XM and Sirius merge to become Sirius XM.

The Nielsen Company, which provides ratings for television, launches a radio ratings service, ending Arbitron's monopoly on radio ratings.

2009 Pandora Internet radio reaches a royalty-fee agreement with a group representing artists and record labels, which frees Pandora to legally expand its Internet radio services.

2012 Nielsen buys Arbitron, consolidating radio ratings into one company.

TODAY The radio industry is concentrated primarily into large groups of stations that use standardized formats, but satellite and Internet radio are splitting the audience into smaller digital pieces.

Lawrence Manning/Corbis

Slaven Vlasic/Getty Images

Bloomberg/Getty Images

from place to place. In the early 1800s, the pony express took ten and a half days to go from St. Joseph, Mo., to San Francisco. Stagecoaches had to travel 44 hours to bring news from New York City to Washington, D.C.

Technological advances brought rapid changes in how quickly information could move throughout the country. First came the invention of the telegraph and the telephone, which depended on electrical lines to deliver their messages, and then wireless telegraphy, which delivers radio signals through the air.

In 1835, *Samuel F. B. Morse* first demonstrated his electromagnetic telegraph system in America. In 1843, Congress gave him $30,000 to string four telegraph lines along the Baltimore & Ohio Railroad right of way from Baltimore to Washington, D.C. Morse sent the first official message—"What hath God wrought?"—from Baltimore to Washington, D.C., on May 24, 1844.

Telegraph lines followed the railroads, and for more than 30 years Americans depended on Morse's coded messages printed on tape, sent from one railroad station to another. On March 10, 1876, *Alexander Graham Bell* sent a message by his new invention, the telephone, to his associate Thomas A. Watson in an adjoining room of their Boston laboratory: "Mr. Watson, come here. I want you." Both Morse's telegraph and Bell's telephone used wires to carry messages.

Then in Germany in 1887, the physicist *Heinrich Hertz* began experimenting with radio waves, which became known as Hertzian waves—the first discovery in a series of refinements that led eventually to the development of radio broadcasting.

BROADCASTING IS BORN

Broadcasting was truly a revolutionary media development. Imagine a society in which the only way you can hear music or enjoy a comedy is at a live performance or by listening to tinny noises on a record machine. The only way you can hear a speech is to be in the audience. Movies show action but no sound.

Without the inventions of broadcasting's early pioneers such as Heinrich Hertz, you could still be living without the sounds of media that you have come to take for granted. Four pioneers besides Hertz are credited with advancing early radio broadcasting in America: Guglielmo Marconi, Reginald Aubrey Fessenden, Lee de Forest and David Sarnoff.

Wireless Breakthrough: Guglielmo Marconi

Twenty-year-old Guglielmo Marconi, the son of wealthy Italian parents, used the results of three discoveries by Morse, Bell and Hertz to expand his idea that messages should be able to travel across space without a wire. Marconi became obsessed, refusing food and working at home in his locked upstairs room, trying to make his invention work. Soon Marconi could ring a bell across the room or downstairs without using a wire. Eventually Marconi was able to broadcast over a distance of 9 miles. "The calm of my life ended then," Marconi said later.

The *New York Herald* invited Marconi to the United States to report the America's Cup race in October 1899. Marconi reported "by wireless!" American business people, intrigued by the military potential of Marconi's invention, invested $10 million to form American Marconi.

To experiment with the new discovery, amateur radio operators created radio clubs. Two experimenters, Reginald Aubrey Fessenden and Lee de Forest, advanced the Marconi discovery to create today's radio.

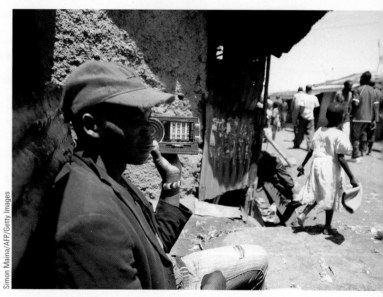

In many parts of the world today, radio is a necessity. In March 2013, a Kenyan man listens to results of his country's just-concluded elections.

Experimental Broadcasts: Reginald Aubrey Fessenden

Reginald Aubrey Fessenden, a Canadian, began wireless experiments in the United States in 1900 when he set up his National Electric Signaling Company to attempt to send voices by radio waves. On Christmas Eve 1906, "ship wireless operators over a wide area of the Atlantic . . . were startled to hear a woman singing, then a violin playing, then a man reading passages from Luke. It was considered uncanny; wireless rooms were soon crowded with the curious," wrote broadcast historian Erik Barnouw.

The noises were coming from Fessenden's experimental station at Brant Rock, Mass. Fessenden's 1906 experiment is considered the world's first voice and music broadcast.

Detecting Radio Waves: Lee de Forest

Lee de Forest called himself the father of radio because in 1907 he perfected a glass bulb called the Audion that could detect radio waves. "Unwittingly then," wrote de Forest, "had I discovered an invisible Empire of the Air." Besides being an inventor, de Forest was a good publicist. He began what he called "broadcasts" from New York and then from the Eiffel Tower.

In 1910, de Forest broadcast Enrico Caruso singing at the Metropolitan Opera House. Later his mother broadcast an appeal to give women the vote. Gradually, the Audion became the technical foundation of modern broadcasting.

A Household Utility: David Sarnoff

In 1912, 21-year-old wireless operator David Sarnoff relayed news from Nantucket Island, in Massachusetts, that he had received a distress call from the *Titanic* on his Marconi wireless. Four years later, when Sarnoff was working for the Marconi Company in New York, he wrote a visionary memo that predicted radio's future, although in 1916 his ideas were widely ignored.

"I have in mind a plan of development which would make radio a household utility. The idea is to bring music into the home by wireless," Sarnoff wrote. Eventually, as commercial manager and then president of RCA, Sarnoff watched his early vision for radio come true, and RCA became the nation's primary radio distributor.

FEDERAL GOVERNMENT REGULATES THE AIRWAVES

The federal government decided to regulate broadcasting almost as soon as it was invented. This decision to regulate broadcasting separated the broadcast media, which are regulated by the federal government, from the print media, which are not regulated directly by any federal government agency.

As amateurs competed with the military for the airwaves, Congress passed the Radio Act of 1912 to license people who wanted to broadcast or receive messages. The federal government decided to license people to transmit signals because there only were a certain number of frequencies available to carry broadcast signals. Many amateurs, trying to send signals on the same frequency, were knocking each other off the air. The government intervened to try to keep the operators out of each other's way.

Then, during World War I, the federal government ordered all amateurs off the air and took control of all privately owned stations, and the military took over radio broadcasting. After the war, the federal government lifted the freeze, and the Navy argued that the military should maintain the monopoly over the airwaves that it had enjoyed during the war.

Government Approves Commercial Broadcasting

Faced with strong arguments by the amateurs that they should be able to return to the airwaves, Congress decided against a Navy monopoly. Instead, the government sanctioned a private monopoly formed by General Electric, Westinghouse, AT&T, Western Electric Company and United Fruit Company. General Electric (GE) bought out American Marconi and its patents, and in 1919, these five sympathetic interests pooled the patents they controlled to form Radio Corporation of America (RCA).

David Sarnoff became RCA's general manager in 1921. Because of this early monopoly, RCA dominated radio development for many years, but eventually smaller operations formed all over the country as radio fever spread from coast to coast.

Experimental Stations Multiply

A plaque placed on a building in San Jose, Calif., in 1959 celebrates the 1909 founding of the experimental station FN: "On this site in 1909, Charles D. Herrold founded a voice radio station which opened the door to electronic mass communication. He conceived the idea of 'broadcasting' to the public, and his station, the world's first, has now served Northern California for half a century." Today, KCBS is based in San Francisco.

Various other stations claim they were among the earliest radio pioneers. Station 9XM broadcast music and weather reports from Madison, Wis.; 6ADZ broadcast concerts from Hollywood, Calif.; 4XD sent phonograph music from a chicken coop in Charlotte, N.C.; and 8MK in Detroit, operated by *Detroit News* publisher William E. Scripps, transmitted election returns.

These stations were run by amateur radio operators who broadcast messages to each other and their friends but not to the general public; nevertheless, they are early examples of broadcast entrepreneurs. They were tinkerers, fascinated with an invention that could carry sounds through the air. One of these tinkerers, Frank Conrad, is credited with creating the beginnings of the nation's first *commercial* radio station.

KDKA Launches Commercial Broadcasting

An ad in the September 29, 1920, *Pittsburgh Sun* changed broadcasting from an exclusive hobby to an easy-to-use

Underwood & Underwood/CORBIS

The nation's first commercial radio station, KDKA in Pittsburgh, went on the air in 1920. KDKA announcer Louis Kaufman stands with members of the Pittsburgh Pirates baseball team in 1925, the year the Pirates won the World Series.

medium available to everyone. The ad described a 20-minute evening concert broadcast from the home of Frank Conrad, a "wireless enthusiast" who worked for Westinghouse.

Conrad often broadcast concerts from his garage on his station, 8XK, but his boss at Westinghouse, Harry P. Davis, had an idea: Why not improve the broadcasts so more people would want to buy radios? Davis talked Conrad into setting up a more powerful transmitter at the Westinghouse plant by November 2, 1920, so Conrad could broadcast election returns.

On October 27, 1920, using the powers of the 1912 Radio Act, the U.S. Department of Commerce licensed station KDKA as the nation's first *commercial* radio station. The broadcast began at 8 p.m. on November 2, 1920,

ASCAP American Society of Composers, Authors and Publishers.

Blanket Licensing Agreement An arrangement whereby radio stations become authorized to use recorded music for broadcast by paying a fee.

BMI Broadcast Music, Inc., a cooperative music licensing organization.

and continued past midnight, reporting that Warren G. Harding was the nation's next president. KDKA immediately began a daily one-hour evening schedule, broadcasting from 8:30 to 9:30 p.m.

RADIO AUDIENCE EXPANDS QUICKLY

The crude KDKA broadcasts proved that regular programming could attract a loyal audience. KDKA was just the beginning of what eventually became radio networks. The radio craze led almost immediately to a period of rapid expansion as entrepreneurs and advertisers began to grasp the potential of the new medium. Almost as quickly, government was compelled to step in to expand its regulation of radio broadcasting.

Radio's potential as a moneymaker for its owners fueled competition for the airwaves. Three important developments for radio's future were the

1. Blanket licensing agreement
2. Decision that radio would accept commercial sponsors
3. Radio Act of 1927.

Blanket Licensing

At first, stations played phonograph records; then they invited artists to perform live in their studios. Some of the nation's best talent sought the publicity that radio could give them, but eventually the performers asked to be paid.

In 1923, the American Society of Composers, Authors and Publishers (***ASCAP***) sued several stations for payment. ASCAP claimed that if radio aired ASCAP-licensed music, people would buy less sheet music, so ASCAP members would be cheated out of royalties. Station owners argued that playing the songs on their stations would publicize the sheet music, which would mean ASCAP members would make more money.

Eventually the stations agreed to pay royalties to ASCAP through a ***blanket licensing agreement***, which meant the stations paid ASCAP a fee ($250 a year at first). In exchange, the stations could use all ASCAP-licensed music on the air. (ASCAP licenses its music to stations the same way today.) Eventually another licensing organization, Broadcast Music, Inc., or ***BMI***, also would collect broadcast royalties.

Commercial Sponsorship

Once station owners agreed to pay for their programs, they had to figure out where they would get the money. AT&T had the answer with an idea pioneered at its station WEAF in New York. WEAF started selling advertising time to sponsors. Its first sponsored program cost the advertiser $100 to sponsor a 10-minute program.

The success of commercial sponsorship as a way to support radio settled the issue of who would pay the cost of airing the programs. Advertisers paid for programs through their advertising; the American public paid for the programs indirectly by supporting the advertisers who supported radio.

Federal Radio Commission

As more stations began to crowd the air, their signals interfered with one another. With only so many good radio frequencies available, the provisions of the Radio Act of 1912 began to seem inadequate. Congress passed the Radio Act of 1927, which formed the Federal Radio Commission under the jurisdiction of the Department of Commerce. The president appointed the commission's five members, with the Senate's approval.

The shortage of air space required that broadcasting in the United States operate under a type of government regulation unknown to newspaper and magazine publishers. The federal government licensed the stations for three years, and the commission mandated that the stations operate "*as a public convenience, interest or necessity requires.*"

The commission, created to protect the stations by allocating frequencies, also became the license holder. The stations could operate only with the government's approval, and the stations needed commission approval to be sold or transferred. The Radio Act of 1927, including the concept that broadcasters must operate in the "*public convenience, interest or necessity,*" became the foundation for all broadcast regulation in the United States.

In 1934, Congress established the Federal Communications Commission (*FCC*) to regulate the expanding wireless medium, making the FCC a separate agency of government and no longer a part of the Department of Commerce. It is important to remember that the commission's original purpose was to allocate the broadcast spectrum so station broadcast signals would not interfere with one another. The FCC was not originally envisioned to oversee broadcast content.

The FCC began work on July 11, 1934, with seven commissioners appointed by the president, with Senate approval. This same basic structure and purpose govern the commission's actions today, but now there are

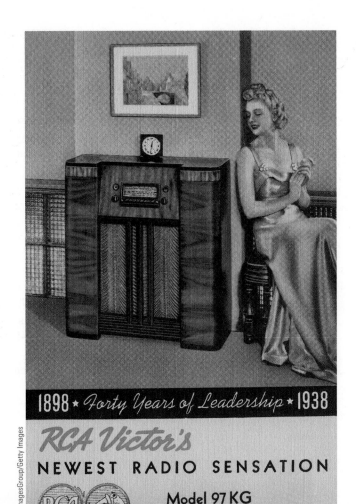

Radio in the 1930s and 1940s became a powerful cultural and political force, offering people an inexpensive source of information and entertainment, and the radio receiver became an essential piece of furniture in many homes. In 1938, RCA Victor offered its newest model for the living room.

only five commissioners. The establishment of the FCC in 1934 also set the precedent for the later regulation of television.

RADIO GROWS INTO A POWERFUL FORCE

Most radio stations mixed entertainment, culture and public service. Radio created a new kind of collective

FCC Federal Communications Commission.

national experience. Radio in the 1930s and 1940s became a powerful cultural and political force and gave millions of people a new, inexpensive source of information and entertainment (see **Illustration 6.1**, "Where Do People Listen to the Radio?," p. 115).

The commercialization of American broadcasting also gave advertisers access to this audience at home. Radio's massive group of listeners sat enraptured with sponsored programming of many types: comedy, music, serials, sports, drama and news. Eventually, all these types of programming migrated to television.

WAR OF THE WORLDS CHALLENGES RADIO'S CREDIBILITY

On Halloween Eve, October 30, 1938, the *Mercury Theater on the Air* broadcast a play based on the H. G. Wells novel *War of the Worlds*. The live 8 p.m. broadcast played opposite the very popular Edgar Bergen program on NBC, and the *Mercury Theater* broadcast rarely had even 4 percent of the audience. Very few people heard the announcement at the beginning of the program that the *Mercury Theater* was performing a version of the Wells story.

The program began with the announcer introducing some band music. A second voice then said, "Ladies and gentlemen, we interrupt our program of dance music to bring you a special bulletin. At 20 minutes before 8 o'clock Central Time, Professor Farrell of Mount Jennings Observatory, Chicago, reports observing several explosions of incandescent gas occurring at regular intervals on the planet Mars."

More dance music followed and then more bulletins about a meteor, with the startling news that 1,500 people near Princeton, N.J., had died when the meteor hit the town. Then the announcer said it was not a meteor but a spaceship carrying Martians armed with death rays.

Two professors from the Princeton geology department actually set out to locate the "meteors." In Newark, N.J., more than 20 families rushed out of their homes, covering their faces with wet handkerchiefs to protect them from the "gas." After a burst of horrified calls, CBS began repeating the announcement that the program was just a play, but the damage had been done.

The episode demonstrated how easily alarming information could be innocently misinterpreted, especially because the listeners had no other source than radio to check the reliability of what they were hearing. Radio listeners truly were a captive audience.

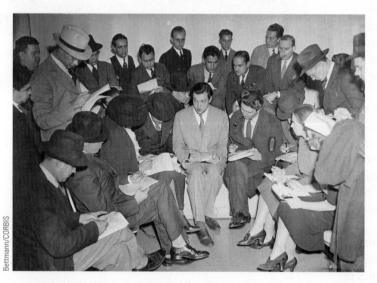

The fear created by Orson Welles' *War of the Worlds* broadcast in 1938 demonstrated how easily unsubstantiated information could be misinterpreted on the radio. Orson Welles (center, in the light-colored suit) met with reporters on October 31, 1938, to answer questions about the broadcast.

Network   A collection of radio or TV stations that offers programs, usually simultaneously, throughout the country during designated program times.

RADIO NETWORKS EXPAND

The formation of radio networks as a source of programming and revenue is a crucial development in the history of American radio. A *network* is a collection of stations (radio or television) that offers programs, usually simultaneously, throughout the country, during designated times.

As the radio networks stretched across the country, they provided a dependable source of programming. Most stations found it easier to affiliate with a network and receive and distribute network programming than to develop local programs.

David Sarnoff Launches NBC

NBC grew out of the government's original agreement with RCA. RCA, GE and Westinghouse formed the National Broadcasting Company in 1926. By January 1927, NBC, headed by David Sarnoff, had formed two networks: the Red network (fed from WEAF in New York) and the Blue network (originating from station WJZ in Newark). Station engineers drew the planned hookups of the two networks with red and blue colored pencils, which is how the networks got their names. RCA faced criticism

Bettmann/CORBIS

IMPACT/Audience

Illustration 6.1

Where Do People Listen to the Radio?

Adults tune into the radio more at work and in the car than they do at home. Advertisers, such as car dealers, use this demographic information to help target radio audiences with their messages.

Source: Radio Advertising Bureau, 2013.

60%
In the Car

30%
At Home

10%
At Work and Other Places

Hulton Archive/Getty Images

Bettmann/CORBIS

David Sarnoff (left), who began his broadcast career as a wireless operator, eventually became president of RCA. William S. Paley (right), who launched CBS radio, often battled with Sarnoff. The continuing competition between Sarnoff and Paley shaped the early development of American radio and TV broadcasting.

about its broad control over the airwaves because it continued to be the world's largest distributor of radios, which were made by Westinghouse and General Electric.

William S. Paley Starts CBS

Twenty-six-year-old William S. Paley, heir to a tobacco fortune, bought the financially struggling Columbia Phonograph Company in 1929. He changed the name to Columbia Broadcasting System, and put his CBS network on the air with 25 stations. Programming originated from WABC in New York. Paley became the nemesis of NBC, then controlled by David Sarnoff, and this early competition between Sarnoff and Paley shaped the development of American broadcasting.

Edward Noble Buys ABC

In 1941, the FCC ordered RCA to divest itself of one of its networks. In 1943, RCA sold NBC-Blue to Edward J. Noble (who had made his fortune as head of the company that produced LifeSavers candy). Noble paid $8 million for the network that became the American Broadcasting Company (ABC), giving the country a three-network radio system.

Radio Adapts to Television

Radio networks prospered from the 1940s to the 1980s, when NBC sold its radio network, and CBS and ABC devoted more attention to their television holdings. When television initially was launched in the 1940s, it seemed it would cause the death of radio. As soon as television proved itself, advertisers abandoned radio, said comedian Fred Allen, "like the bones at a barbecue."

The entertainers fled to television, too—original radio talents such as Bob Hope, Milton Berle and Jackie Gleason soon dropped their radio programs and devoted themselves to TV. Public affairs programs like *Meet the Press* made the move from radio to TV, as did Edward R. Murrow's radio news program, *Hear It Now*, which on television became *See It Now*.

Five developments in the 1940s, 1950s and 1960s transformed the medium of radio as well as guaranteed radio's survival alongside television:

1. FM radio frequency was accepted by the public.

2. Disc jockeys hosted music shows.

3. Radio formats streamlined broadcasts.

4. People started buying clock and car radios.

5. The payola scandals focused on broadcast ethics.

Inventor Edwin H. Armstrong Pioneers FM

After working for more than a decade to eliminate static from radio broadcasts, engineer Edwin H. Armstrong applied to the FCC in 1936 to broadcast using his new technique, frequency modulation (FM). Because of the way FM signals travel through the air, FM offered truer transmission than AM (amplitude modulation) with much less static. Armstrong faced difficult opposition from David Sarnoff at RCA, who had been an early Armstrong sponsor.

The FCC received 150 applications for FM licenses in 1939 but then froze licensing during World War II. After the war, Armstrong again faced Sarnoff, but this time Armstrong lost. RCA was using Armstrong's frequency modulation in its TV and FM sets but refused to pay Armstrong royalties, so Armstrong sued RCA.

RCA fought Armstrong for 20 years, saying that RCA had been among the early developers of FM and citing

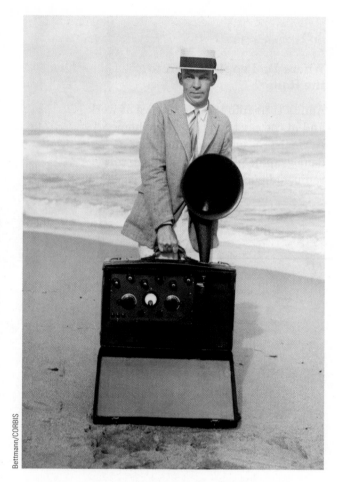

Edwin H. Armstrong's invention of FM made radio signals clearer. For nearly 20 years, Armstrong battled RCA's David Sarnoff for royalties. Disheartened by the legal battle, Armstrong committed suicide, but his widow eventually won the royalty payments. In 1923, Armstrong shows off one of his inventions—radio in a suitcase—on the beach.

RCA's sponsorship of Armstrong's beginning experiments. In 1953, Armstrong became ill and suffered a stroke; then he committed suicide. RCA quickly settled the suit with Armstrong's widow for $1 million. Eventually FM became the spectrum of choice for music lovers, far surpassing the broadcast quality of AM.

Licensed Recordings Launch Disc Jockeys

Early radio station owners avoided playing records because they would have had to pay ASCAP royalties. The FCC also required stations that played records to remind their audiences every half-hour that the audience was listening to recorded music, not a live orchestra. This discouraged record spinning.

In 1935, newscaster Martin Block at New York's independent station WNEW began playing records in between his newscasts, and then he started a program called *Make Believe Ballroom*. He is generally considered America's first disc jockey. In 1940, the FCC ruled that once stations bought a record, they could play it on the air whenever they liked, without the announcements every half hour.

To counteract ASCAP's insistence on royalties, broadcasters formed a cooperative music-licensing organization called Broadcast Music, Inc. Most rhythm and blues, country and rock 'n' roll artists eventually signed with BMI, which charged stations less for recording artists than ASCAP did. This inexpensive source of music also created a new type of media personality—the disc jockey.

Clock, Car and Transistor Radios Make Radio a Necessary Accessory

Clock and car radios helped ensure radio's survival by making it an everyday accessory. Transistor radios, first sold in 1948 for $40, were more reliable and cheaper than tube radios. Clock radios, introduced in the 1950s, woke people up and caused them to rely on radio for the first news of the day.

William Lear, who also designed the Lear jet, invented the car radio in 1928. Early car radios were enormous, with spotty reception, but the technology that was developed during World War II helped refine them.

In 1946, 9 million cars had car radios. By 1963, the number was 50 million. A radio station owner coined the term *drive-time audiences* to describe people who listened in their cars on the way to work from 6 to 9 a.m. and on the way home from 4 to 7 p.m.

Gordon McLendon Introduces Format Radio

How would the stations know which mix of records to use and who would play them? The answer came from Gordon McLendon, the father of format radio. At KLIF in Dallas, McLendon combined music and news in a predictable rotation of 20-minute segments, and eventually KLIF grew very popular. Next he refined the music by creating the Top-40 format.

Top 40 played the top-selling hits continually, interrupted only by a disc jockey or a newscast. By 1959, McLendon launched the beautiful-music format at KABL in San Francisco. In 1964, he created a 24-hour news format for Chicago's WNUS, using three news vans with "telesigns" that showed news on the roofs in lights as the vans drove around town.

Formats meant stations could share standardized programs instead of producing programs individually.

Car Culture/Getty Images

Christian Science Monitor/Getty Images

Drivers have always been an important radio audience. William Lear invented the first car radio in 1928. By 1945, 9 million cars in the United States had radios. Shown here are (top) a 1941 Cadillac dashboard with a luxury push-button radio and (bottom) a 2013 Lexus 450H dashboard, which connects with smartphones and tablets from a hand-operated control stick on the console.

Eventually, formatted programming spread, which made network programming and the networks themselves less important to individual stations.

Drive-Time Audiences People who listen to the radio in their cars during 6 to 9 a.m. and 4 to 7 p.m.

Payola Scandals Highlight Broadcast Ethics

The rise of rock 'n' roll coincided with the development of transistor and portable radios, which meant radio played a central role in the rock revolution. "Rock and radio were made for each other. The relationship between record companies and radio stations became mutually beneficial. By providing the latest hits, record companies kept stations' operating costs low. The stations, in turn, provided the record companies with the equivalent of free advertising," wrote radio historian David MacFarland.

Eventually this relationship would prove too close. On February 8, 1960, Congress began hearings into charges that disc jockeys and program directors had accepted cash to play specific recordings on the air. To describe this practice, the term *payola* was coined from the combination of *pay* and *Victrola* (the name of a popular record player).

In May 1960, the Manhattan grand jury charged eight men with commercial bribery for accepting more than $100,000 in payoffs for playing records. The most prominent among them was Alan Freed, who had worked in Cleveland (where he was credited with coining the term *rock 'n' roll*) and at New York's WABC.

In February 1962, Freed pleaded guilty to two counts of accepting payoffs, paid a $300 fine and received six

months probation. Then he was found guilty of income tax evasion. He died in 1965 while awaiting trial, at age 43. In September 1960, Congress amended the Federal Communications Act to prohibit the payment of cash or gifts in exchange for airplay; nevertheless, the issue of payola surfaced again in 2005 and resulted in stiff fines in 2007.

RADIO AT WORK

A Columbia University report, commissioned by NBC in 1954, defined radio's role after television. "Radio was the one medium that could accompany almost every type of activity. . . . Where radio once had been a leisure-time 'reward' after a day's work, television was now occupying that role. Radio had come to be viewed less as a treat than as a kind of 'companion' to some other activity." Like magazines, radio survived in part because the medium adapted to fill a different need for its audience.

Today, about 10,800 broadcast radio stations are on the air in the United States. They are about evenly divided between FM and AM. Network programming plays a much smaller role than when radio began because most stations play just music and don't need network programming to survive. National Public Radio is the only major public network. Many commercial stations today use *program services*, which provide satellite as well as formatted programming.

Most stations are part of a *group*, which means that a company owns more than one station in more than one broadcast market. Some stations are part of a combination AM/FM (*a combo*), which means that a company owns both AM and FM stations in the same market. A few stations remain family-owned, single operations that run just like any other small business.

The management structure at a radio station usually includes a general manager, a program manager, account executives, the traffic department, production department, engineering department and administration.

The *general manager* runs the radio station. The *program manager* oversees what goes on the air, including the news programs, the station's format and any on-air people. Salespeople, who are called *account executives*, sell the advertising for programs.

The *traffic department* schedules the commercials, makes sure they run correctly and bills the clients. The *production department* helps with local programming, if there is any, and produces local commercials for the station. *Engineering* keeps the station on the air. *Administration* pays the bills, answers the phones and orders the paper clips. A small station requires five employees, or fewer, to handle all these jobs.

Pat Byrnes/The New Yorker Collection/Cartoonbank

P. BYRNES.

"Great! O.K., this time I want you to sound taller, and let me hear a little more hair."

Payola   The practice of accepting payment to play specific recordings on the air.

IMPACT/Convergence

College Radio Heads: Off the Dial

By Kyle Spencer

Inside a broadcast booth, at the radio station of the State University of New York Fredonia, Jud Heussler was presiding over his hourlong comedy show "The Morning Inferno."

"Call, text, Facebook, whatever you want," Mr. Heussler shouted to his listeners as he logged onto Facebook to check out who was posting on the show's wall.

If none of this sounds like classic college radio, it's not. Fredonia has two stations. And WDVL, the more popular, is so far removed from traditional radio it can't even be found on the FM dial. Instead, that station streams on the Internet, constantly encouraging listeners to check out a rolling supply of podcasts, YouTube clips, photos and campus news on the station's Web site.

Most of the Intercollegiate Broadcasting System's 700 college members now stream on the Internet along with, or instead of, their broadcasting efforts.

Three years ago, Fordham started up the *Alternate Side* as an edgier, visually stimulating option to its FM-based station, WFUV. The *Alternate Side* streams 24/7 on the Internet, a few hours a day on the FM dial, and on HD Radio. Student technicians videotape and edit

Michael Appleton for The New York Times

New York's Fordham college radio station WFUV streams its program, *Alternate Side*, 24/7 on the Internet and a few hours on FM and HD Radio. Students like Erica Talbott videotape and edit live jam sessions that are posted on the station's Web site.

live jam sessions that are e-mailed to listeners in a weekly newsletter and posted on the station's page. "We call ourselves a radio station," says John O. Platt, WFUV's communications director. "But we're really a multimedia content provider."

Source: Excerpted from Kyle Spencer, "College Radio Heads: Off the Dial," November 4, 2011, nytimes.com.

CONGRESS CREATES NATIONAL PUBLIC RADIO

The Public Broadcasting Act of 1967 created the Corporation for Public Broadcasting and included funding for public radio and TV stations. National Public Radio launched a national program on FM in 1970, but many radios still didn't have an FM dial. Most public stations—owned by colleges and universities and staffed by volunteers—were staffed irregularly (See **Impact/Convergence**, "College Radio Heads: Off the Dial.")

NPR launched *Morning Edition* in 1979. Still among the most popular news shows on the air, *Morning Edition* offers long interviews on topical issues and international reports. Renee Montagne is one of the *Morning Edition* hosts.

Live sports and sports talk remain popular radio formats. Vic Lombardi, right, and Gary Miller host their morning show on CBS4 in Denver, Colorado.

Then NPR started the program *All Things Considered* for the evening drive-time and in 1979 launched *Morning Edition*. Today, *Morning Edition* and *All Things Considered* have a very loyal audience for their long interviews on topical issues and international reports. By design, public radio is an alternative to commercial radio. Today, NPR still receives some public funding, but it depends primarily on private donations to survive.

PORTABILITY AND IMMEDIACY HELP RADIO SURVIVE

Instead of dying after the spread of television, radio managed to thrive by adapting to an audience that sought the portability and immediacy that radio offers. Nothing can beat radio for quick news bulletins or the latest hits. Radio also delivers a targeted audience much better than television, because the radio station you prefer defines you to an advertiser much better than the television station you watch.

In the 1990s, the advertising potential for an intimate medium like radio attracted entrepreneurs who had never owned a station and group owners who wanted to expand their holdings. When you listen to the radio in your car or through earphones while you jog, for instance, radio is not competing with any other medium for your attention. Advertisers like this exclusive access to an audience. Three important issues for people in broadcast radio today are:

1. Deregulation
2. Ratings
3. Formats.

TELECOMMUNICATIONS ACT OF 1996 OVERHAULS RADIO

The Telecommunications Act of 1996 was the first major overhaul of broadcast regulation since the Federal Communications Commission was established in 1934. Today the legacy of the act is that commercial radio is regulated much less than it was in the 1970s. This is called a policy of *deregulation*.

Before the 1996 act passed, the FCC limited the number of radio stations that one company could own nationwide. The Telecommunications Act removed the limit on the number of radio stations a company can own, and in each local market the number of stations that one owner can hold depends on the size of the market. (For a complete discussion of the Telecommunications Act, see **Chapter 14.**)

Deregulation Government action that reduces government restrictions on the business operations of an industry.

Cross-Ownership The practice of one company owning radio and TV stations in the same broadcast market.

The Telecommunications Act also allows *cross-ownership*, which means that companies can own radio and TV stations in the same market and broadcast and cable outlets in the same market. As soon as the act passed in February 1996, radio station sales began to soar.

Today several radio corporations each own hundreds of broadcast stations. Supporters of the changes say this makes broadcast radio more competitive because these larger companies can give the stations better financial support than small, single owners. Opponents point out that consolidation in the radio industry leads to less program variety for consumers and too much power for companies that own large numbers of radio stations nationwide.

ARE RADIO RATINGS ACCURATE?

Radio station owners depend on ratings to set advertising rates, and the stations with the most listeners command the highest ad rates. Originally, a company called Arbitron gathered ratings for the radio business. To find out what radio stations people were listening to, Arbitron requested that selected listeners complete and return diaries the company sent them.

Arbitron often was criticized because minorities, non-English-speaking listeners and people ages 18 to 24 didn't return the diaries in the same proportion as other people that Arbitron surveyed. The critics contended that Arbitron's ratings hurt rock and urban formats, such as rap/hip-hop and Spanish-language programming, while aiding the contemporary and news/talk/information formats, whose audiences are older and more responsive to the diaries. Arbitron acknowledged the problems and tried filling out diaries for people over the phone and adding bilingual interviewers.

Still, questions persisted. In November 2008, the Nielsen Company, which provides ratings for TV, launched a radio ratings service, in direct competition with Arbitron. Then in 2012, Nielsen bought Arbitron, eliminating their competitor. This makes Nielsen the only company in the United States that provides ratings information for radio.

RADIO DEPENDS ON READY-MADE FORMATS

Today's broadcast radio station owners, looking for an audience, can use one of several ready-made formats. By adjusting their formats, radio managers can test the markets until they find a formula that works to deliver their

John Parra/Getty Images

Popular singers like Loalwa Braz (left) and Don Omar make Spanish-language programming a very popular radio format. Critics say that radio ratings do not accurately reflect the large number of non-English-speaking listeners.

target audience to advertisers. (See **Illustration 6.2**, "Which Radio Formats Are Most Popular?," p. 122.)

If you were a radio station manager today, and you wanted to program your station, you could choose from several popular formats.

COUNTRY. The Grand Ole Opry first broadcast country music on WSM in Nashville in 1925. This radio format is aimed at 25- to 45-year-olds in urban as well as rural areas.

NEWS/TALK/INFORMATION/SPORTS. A station with this format devotes most of its airtime to different types of talk shows, which can include call-in features, where listeners question on-the-air guests. Its typical audience is 35 and older. It is difficult for a small radio station to survive on news alone, so most of these stations are in big cities because of the continuing source of news stories. The immediacy of the live news/talk format also can create problems for broadcasters because talk show hosts sometimes push the limits of commentary with outrageous, potentially libelous statements.

The news/talk category also includes live sports broadcasts, which are very popular because radio is a convenient way to follow live sports in the car and at work.

SPANISH. Spanish stations are the fastest-growing radio format, as radio owners target the nation's expanding Latino population. Spanish-language radio usually

IMPACT/Money

Illustration 6.2

Which Radio Formats Are Most Popular?

The most popular radio formats are country music, news/talk, Spanish, sports, oldies and classic hits. Radio station owners use prepackaged formats to draw the audience they want to deliver to advertisers.

Source: Radio Advertising Bureau Format Analysis, radioadvertisinghome.com, 2013.

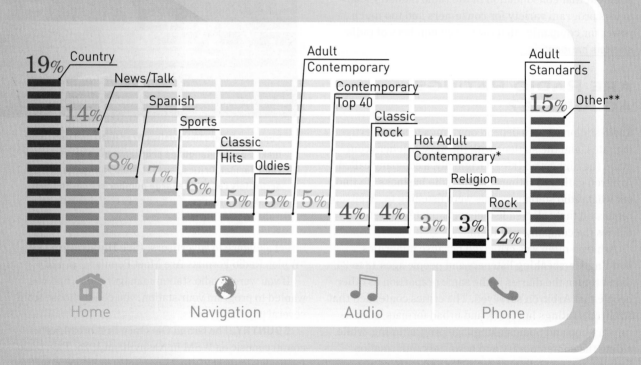

* Formerly known as Adult Hit Radio, tends to play harder rock music than Adult Contemporary, aimed at a younger audience.

** Includes Black Gospel, Southern Gospel, Contemporary Christian, Urban Adult Contemporary, Jazz and Classical.

features news, music and talk. Many Spanish-language stations are AM stations that recently have been converted from less-profitable formats.

ADULT CONTEMPORARY. This program format includes adult rock and light rock music from the 1970s to today and aims to reach 25- to 40-year-olds in all types of markets.

CONTEMPORARY HIT/TOP 40. Playing songs on *Billboard*'s current hits list, a Top 40 station closely follows trends among listeners, especially teenagers.

The most popular radio formats are country music, news/talk, sports and Spanish programming. Although

news/talk radio is very popular in Los Angeles, the most-listened-to radio station in the Los Angeles area is a Spanish-language station. Its popularity in an area with an expanding Spanish-language population shows how cultural changes in urban areas can affect the economics of local radio. Stations can also divide traditional formats into subcategories: Adult Contemporary is splitting into modern rock and oldies; some Spanish-language stations play only love songs.

The use of prepackaged program formats means that a station can specialize its programming simply by what it chooses to play. Most stations operate without any disc jockeys or limit personality programming to morning and evening drive-time. At these stations, engineers and announcers carry the programming. Today, radio networks, which once dominated radio programming, mainly exist to provide national news to their affiliates.

Station managers can program their own stations, mixing local news, music and announcements. Stations also can get programming from syndicated and satellite program services. Syndicates provide prepackaged program formats. Satellites make program distribution easier; satellite networks, such as Satellite Music Network, promise the broadcaster original, up-to-date programming without a large local staff.

Audience Divides into Smaller Segments

The most significant trend in radio is the move toward more segmentation of the audience, similar to the division of audiences in the magazine industry. Identifying a specific audience segment and programming for it is called *narrowcasting*.

"With narrowcasting, advertising efficiency goes way up as overall costs go down.... We are approaching the unstated goal of all radio programmers: to create a station aimed so perfectly that the listener will no longer have to wait, ever, for the song that he wants to hear," says radio historian Eric Zorn.

Competition Revives Payola

As radio technology grows more complex and companies test new formats and different program delivery systems, the competition for your ear expands the choices that advertisers can make to reach you. However, as the competition among stations intensifies, some stations look for profits from a familiar but unethical source.

In 2005, New York Attorney General Eliot Spitzer announced he was investigating the four major music companies to examine their practice of paying independent promoters to influence which songs the stations played on the air. The practice often was criticized as a way for stations to get around laws prohibiting payola that date from the 1960s. Some record labels paid individual stations as much as $100,000 to help promote their songs, Spitzer said. Other companies gave the stations luxury travel for station employees or gifts to use in station giveaways.

"To disguise a payoff to a radio programmer at KHTS in San Diego, Epic Records called a flat-screen television a 'contest giveaway,'" reported *The New York Times*. "Epic ... used the same gambit in delivering a laptop computer

to the program director of WRHT in Greenville, N.C.— who also received PlayStation 2 games and an out-of-town trip with his girlfriend."

After more payoffs like these were uncovered, Sony agreed to a $10 million settlement and fired the top promotion executive at its Epic label. Radio executives at some of the other corporations said they already had stopped paying independent promoters, but Spitzer said, "This is not a pretty picture; what we see is that payola is pervasive." In 2007, the stations agreed to pay an additional $12.5 million to the Federal Communications Commission to settle the complaints.

Digital Audio Delivers Internet and Satellite Radio

A recent technology known as *digital audio broadcast* (DAB) eliminates all the static and hiss of current broadcast signals and means infinite program choices for consumers as all digital radio signals share the same delivery system. Today digital stations can send their digital signals over the Internet as well as over the air.

SATELLITE RADIO. A recent technology in the radio business is *satellite radio*. Launched in 2001, satellite radio offers 140 channels of varied music and

Jack Ziegler/The New Yorker Collection/Cartoonbank

"You've been listening to the mellow sound of Station EZZZ."

Narrowcasting Segmenting the radio audience.

Digital Audio Broadcast A new form of audio transmission that eliminates all static and makes more program choices possible.

Satellite Radio Radio transmission by satellite, with limited or no advertising, available by subscription.

talk, with limited advertising on some stations and no advertising on others. For a subscription fee, two companies—Sirius Satellite Radio (based in New York) and XM (based in Washington)—began offering the service. The companies charged $9.95 to $12.95 a month to hear uninterrupted programming, without commercial announcements.

Satellite radio service requires special radios containing a miniature satellite radio receiver. In 2002, General Motors began offering satellite radios as a factory-installed option on some models. Ford and Daimler-Chrysler began offering the feature in 2003. New car buyers bundled the subscription fee with their automobile financing.

By 2005, XM boasted 4 million subscribers, and the company said it planned to have 10 million subscribers by 2010. In 2008, the Justice Department approved the merger of XM and Sirius, to become Sirius XM. Today, the two program services combined have about 23 million subscribers.

INTERNET RADIO. More than 7,000 stations now send their programming over the Internet. The Internet offers unlimited possibilities for radio to be distributed free beyond the bounds of a local radio audience, and people in the United States can easily hear overseas stations, such as the ***BBC*** (British Broadcasting Corporation),

as well as stations based in the United States but outside their local area.

The streaming Internet radio service Pandora, launched in 2005, allows users to select the programs and music they want to hear, free and by subscription. Other streaming services, such as Rhapsody and Spotify, have followed, and in 2013 Apple launched iTunes Radio. Each streaming service has a different revenue model. Some are available free and supported by advertising; others require subscriptions.

DIGITAL DELIVERY SPLITS RADIO INDUSTRY INCOME

The more stations and digital radio services (such as satellite digital radio and Internet radio) that are available for customers, the harder every station and delivery service must compete for advertising. This means less revenue for each station because each station's potential audience becomes smaller.

Satellite and Internet radio delivery systems change the entire revenue equation for the radio industry. Consumers pay subscription fees to hear radio on satellite without commercials and go to the Internet for access to new channels they couldn't hear before, offering listener-specific programming that isn't available on commercial radio in the United States.

Meanwhile, commercial radio is trying to stay afloat using the same commercial model that has served the industry for more than 90 years. In 2005, commercial radio introduced the concept of ***HD radio***, hybrid digital technology that improves sound quality and also makes it possible for radio stations to transmit real-time text-based information services along with their programming. HD radio can display song titles and artists' names, weather, news and traffic alerts as a digital readout accompanying the audio programming.

HD radio is easier to engineer for FM stations than for AM stations, so more FM than AM stations have HD. "Only a core number of mostly big-wattage, large-market stations are broadcasting in AM digital," says the industry publication *Radio World*. The conversion to HD is more expensive and complicated for AM stations, and many station owners aren't willing to spend the money without a guaranteed return. To receive HD audio and text, consumers must have an HD-enabled radio, so car manufacturers will have to be willing to install HD radios to receive the signal; so far there has been very little consumer demand, so the conversion to HD has been slow.

In the 1930s, radio learned how to compete with newspapers. In the 1950s, radio learned how to compete with television. Today the radio industry must learn how to compete with itself.

iTunes Radio

Hear where your music takes you.

Coming soon

In 2013, Apple launched iTunes Radio, a music service available on the Internet.

Apple, Inc., www.apple.com/itunes

BBC British Broadcasting Corporation.

HD Radio Hybrid digital technology that improves sound quality and makes it possible for radio stations to transmit real-time text messaging along with their programming.

Review, Analyze, Investigate

Reviewing Chapter 6

Radio Sounds Are Everywhere

- Radio transformed national politics and also expanded Americans' access to popular, as well as classical, culture.
- Radio is a commercial medium, supported almost entirely by advertising.

Radio Takes a Technological Leap

- Radio history began with Samuel F. B. Morse's invention of the telegraph, first demonstrated in 1835.
- Alexander Graham Bell invented the telephone, demonstrated in 1876, and Heinrich Hertz first described radio waves in 1887.

Broadcasting Is Born

- Guglielmo Marconi's promotion of wireless radio wave transmission began in 1899 with the America's Cup race.
- Reginald Fessenden advanced wireless technology, but Lee de Forest called himself the father of radio because he invented the Audion tube to detect radio waves.
- David Sarnoff and William S. Paley made radio broadcasting a viable business in the United States.

Federal Government Regulates the Airwaves

- The federal government intervened to regulate broadcasting almost as soon as it was invented.
- Early regulation separated the broadcast media from the print media, which are not regulated directly by the federal government.

Radio Audience Expands Quickly

- Three important developments for commercial radio were blanket licensing, commercial sponsorship and the Radio Act of 1927.
- Blanket licensing meant that radio owners could use recorded music inexpensively.
- Commercial sponsorship established the practice of advertisers underwriting the cost of American broadcasting.
- The Radio Act of 1927 established the concept that the government would regulate broadcasting "as a public convenience, interest or necessity requires."
- The Radio Act of 1927 is the foundation for all broadcast regulation in the United States, including the establishment of the Federal Communications Commission (FCC) in 1934.

Radio Grows into a Powerful Force

- In the 1930s, radio programming expanded to include comedy, music, serials, drama and news.
- Radio also indirectly created a collective national experience that had not existed before.
- Commercials gave advertisers access to an audience at home.

War of the Worlds Challenges Radio's Credibility

- On Halloween Eve, October 30, 1938, *Mercury Theater on the Air* broadcast *War of the Worlds*, a fictional radio drama that sounded to some listeners like a legitimate newscast and featured Martians landing in New Jersey.
- The *War of the Worlds* broadcast demonstrated the vulnerability of a captive broadcast audience.

Radio Networks Expand

- Originally, the three radio networks (NBC, CBS and ABC) provided most radio programming. Today, most stations use a variety of sources to program themselves.
- David Sarnoff launched NBC radio in 1927, William S. Paley started CBS radio in 1929 and Edward Noble bought NBC-Blue, which became ABC, in 1941.

Radio Adapts to Television

- Edwin H. Armstrong is responsible for the invention of FM radio. Today, FM stations are three times as popular as AM stations.
- Clock, car and transistor radios expanded radio's audience, but the role of radio changed with the advent of TV, which meant radio had to compete with visual entertainment and TV news.
- Gordon McLendon launched format radio in 1959.
- In the 1960s, Congress uncovered the unethical practice of payola in the radio industry. Recording companies were paying station disc jockeys to play their songs on the air. These complaints resurfaced in 2005 when the New York attorney general filed payola charges against the four major music companies.

Radio at Work

- Radio is a portable medium that can accompany almost every activity.
- Today the 10,800 broadcast radio stations in the United States are about evenly divided between AM and FM.
- There is one major public network. Many commercial stations are part of a group or a combo and use program services instead of doing original programming.

- The management structure at a radio station includes a general manager; a program manager; account executives; the traffic, production, and engineering departments; and administration.

Congress Creates National Public Radio

- The federal government began funding National Public Radio in 1967, and NPR began broadcasting national programming in 1970.
- Today, NPR programs such as *Morning Edition* and *All Things Considered* still attract a very loyal audience, and public radio depends on private donations to survive.

Portability and Immediacy Help Radio Survive

- Radio is the best medium for quick news bulletins and the latest hits.
- Because it is an intimate medium, radio delivers a targeted audience to advertisers much better than TV.
- Radio is also portable—you can listen to it in your car or take it with you anywhere.

Telecommunications Act of 1996 Overhauls Radio

- The Telecommunications Act of 1996 was the first major overhaul of broadcast regulation since the FCC was established in 1934.
- The act removed the limit on the number of stations one company can own, and in each local market the number of stations one owner can hold depends on the size of the market.

Are Radio Ratings Accurate?

- Arbitron historically has been the primary ratings service for radio.
- Stations use ratings to set their rates for advertising.
- In November 2008, the Nielsen Company launched a radio ratings service, in direct competition with Arbitron.
- In 2012, Nielsen bought Arbitron, leaving the broadcast industry with a single ratings service for radio and TV.

Radio Depends on Ready-Made Formats

- Formats systematize radio broadcasts.

- Stations use formats to target a specific type of radio listener and define the audience for advertisers.
- The most popular radio formats are country music and news/talk.

Audience Divides into Smaller Segments

- The most significant trend in radio today is the move toward more segmentation of the audience, similar to the division of audiences in the magazine industry.
- Identifying a specific audience segment and programming for it is called *narrowcasting*.

Competition Revives Payola

- Payola resurfaced in 2005 when New York's attorney general charged that the four major recording companies paid private promoters to get their songs on the air.
- Sony paid $10 million to settle the charges against it, and in 2007 the radio stations paid the FCC an additional $12.5 million.

Digital Audio Delivers Internet and Satellite Radio

- Digital audio broadcast, Internet radio and satellite radio mean more program choices for listeners.
- Today more than 7,000 radio stations deliver programming over the Internet.
- Streaming Internet radio services like Pandora, launched in 2005, are the latest development in radio delivery systems.
- Recently, Internet services like Spotify and Rhapsody have entered the market to compete with Pandora, offering subscription and free services.

Digital Delivery Splits Radio Industry Income

- The addition of new sources for radio programming, such as satellite and Internet radio, are changing the economics of radio today.
- In 2005, commercial radio introduced the concept of HD radio, digital technology that improves sound quality and also makes it possible for radio stations to transmit real-time text-based information services along with their programming, but only a few stations have been willing to pay for the expensive technology.

Key Terms

These terms are defined in the margins throughout this chapter and appear in alphabetical order with definitions in the Glossary, which begins on page 373.

Critical Questions

1. How did the Radio Act of 1912 set a precedent for American broadcasting?

2. How did the following developments in radio affect the industry? Why is each of them so important?

   a. Blanket licensing
   b. Commercial sponsorship
   c. Establishment of networks

3. Discuss the *War of the Worlds* broadcast and its effects upon its audience. How did it change people's perceptions of radio?

4. Discuss the ethics issues involved in the payola scandals.

5. Briefly discuss the present-day state of radio program delivery, including satellite programming and Internet radio.

Working the Web

This list includes both sites mentioned in the chapter and others to give you greater insight into the radio industry.

The Broadcast Archive

oldradio.com

This is a site for radio historians, with an emphasis on radio technology. The site includes an archive of manuals and schematics, as well as historical narratives and biographies of people who worked in early broadcasting.

Canadian Broadcasting Corporation (CBC) Radio-Canada

cbc.ca/radio

The radio division of Canada's national public broadcasting system, the CBC was created in 1936 in response to concern about the growing U.S. influence in radio. Now encompassing television and new media services, the CBC has a mandate to provide a wide range of programming that is predominantly and distinctively Canadian. The Web site provides live radio streams from CBC Radio One (news and talk) and Radio 2 (jazz, blues and classical music), as well as program schedules, podcasts and forums. It also has links to CBC Radio 3 (rock, pop, hip-hop, electronica and alt-country music) and Sirius XM.

CBS Radio

cbsradio.com

As one of the largest U.S. major-market radio operators, CBS provides broadcast, digital and on-demand radio. In addition to operating 130 radio stations, it is home to more than two dozen professional sports franchises.

Friday Morning Quarterback (FMQB)

fmqb.com

Recently celebrating 40 years of serving the music and radio industries with high-quality content, insightful articles and news, FMQB is the self-proclaimed "premier destination for music and radio industry professionals." The production division is renowned for its one-hour National Radio Series that feature major artists premiering new music. Web site features include breaking radio industry and music news, a voice talent vault, music available for airplay, ratings and job information, and industry links.

Inside Radio

insideradio.com

This radio industry publication features industry news, ratings and classifieds. Inside Radio also publishes *Who Owns What* (a weekly update on station ownership), *Radio Journal* (featuring FCC updates and technical news) and *The Radio Book* (a directory of radio stations in the United States and Canada).

National Public Radio

npr.org

NPR distributes and produces noncommercial news, talk and entertainment programs. Its more than 860 independently operated local stations mix national and local programming to fit the needs of their communities. Audio archives are available for a growing number of nationally produced shows.

Radio Advertising Bureau (RAB)

rab.com

The goal of the RAB, the promotional arm of the commercial radio industry, is to increase the use of radio advertising and develop the skills of radio marketing representatives.

Radio Lovers

radiolovers.com

Radiolovers.com offers hundreds of vintage radio shows online for free. Its goal is to bring the world of Old Time

Radio to a new generation of listeners. Users can browse by show genre or search by title. The site includes a disclaimer stating that the creators believe all show copyrights have expired or never existed and that they will remove any recording that is shown to violate a copyright.

Sirius XM

siriusxm.com

Sirius XM offers 140 channels of satellite radio, including commercial-free music as well as sports, news and talk shows. Radios must be Sirius XM-ready to receive the SiriusXM signal, but Sirius also offers programming to mobile devices such as cell phones and computers over the Internet.

TuneIn

tunein.com

TuneIn allows someone to listen to music, sports and news on over 70,000 radio stations around the world via its Web site. Listeners can access more than 2 million programs such as podcasts, concerts and interviews.

Impact/Action Videos are concise news features on various topics created exclusively for *Media/Impact*. Go online to access MindTap at cengagebrain.com. MindTap for Media/Impact sequences all of your learning tools—Chapter Readings with highlighting and note taking, Impact/Action Videos, activities and assessments—into chapter driven learning units that guide you through the curriculum.

MOVIES:
PICTURING THE FUTURE

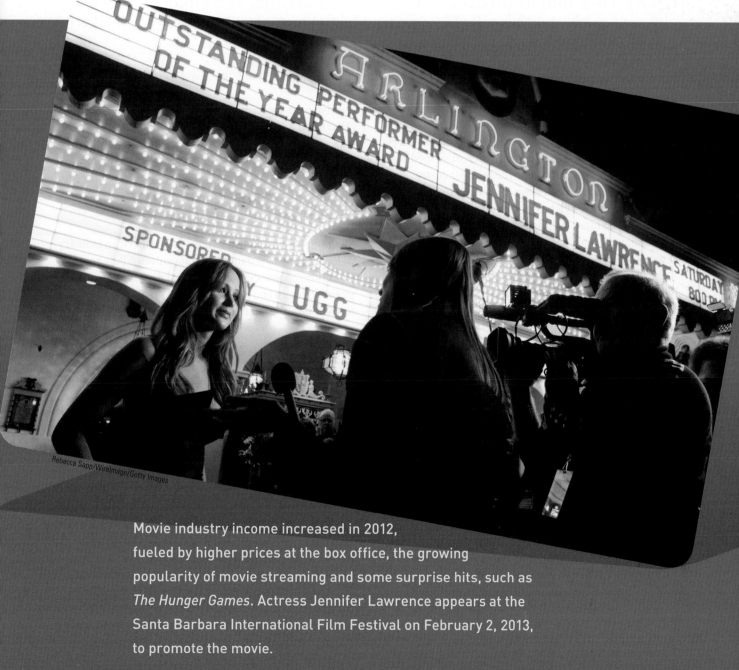

Rebecca Sapp/WireImage/Getty Images

Movie industry income increased in 2012,
fueled by higher prices at the box office, the growing
popularity of movie streaming and some surprise hits, such as
The Hunger Games. Actress Jennifer Lawrence appears at the
Santa Barbara International Film Festival on February 2, 2013,
to promote the movie.

"I love this movie theater. We love our patrons. It's such a positive experience going on, and we're just a little sad this conversion is hitting us. How do we survive?"

—THOM REEVES, OWNER OF THE ISIS THEATER IN CRETE, NEB., COMMENTING ON THE COST OF CONVERTING TO DIGITAL TECHNOLOGY

The movie industry has

been called "an industry based on dreams" because it is a business founded on an imaginative, creative medium. It also would be easy to assume the movie industry is one of the biggest media businesses because the publicity surrounding movie celebrities captures a great deal of attention. So it often surprises people to learn that the movie industry makes less money each year than the newspaper, television or book businesses.

Movies and movie stars thrive on public attention because the size of the audience has a direct effect on whether movies succeed. Movies are expensive to make, and most movies lose money. Investors, therefore, often favor "bankable" talent that brings fans to a movie, rather than new, untested talent. But even movies featuring established talent can fail; no one in the movie industry can accurately predict which movies will be hits.

MOVIES MIRROR THE CULTURE

Perhaps more than any other medium, movies mirror the society that creates them. Some movies offer an underlying political message. Other movies reflect changing social values. Still other movies are just good entertainment. And all movies need an audience to succeed.

Like other media industries, the movie business has had to adapt to changing technology. Before the invention of television, movies were the nation's primary form of visual entertainment. The current use of special effects and 3-D—something you seldom get from television—is one way the movie industry competes with

television for your attention and dollars. But special effects and 3-D don't fit every movie, and they are very expensive. Today, as always, the business of moviemaking is just as important as the movies themselves.

INVENTORS CAPTURE MOTION ON FILM

Movies were invented at a time when American industry welcomed any new gadget, and inventors wildly sought patents on appliances and electrical devices. The motion picture camera and projector were two of the Industrial Revolution's new gadgets.

Early Inventors Nurture the Movie Industry

Movies were not the invention of one person. First, a device to photograph moving objects had to be invented, followed by a device to project those pictures. This process involved six people: Étienne-Jules Marey, Eadweard Muybridge, Thomas Edison, William K. L. Dickson and Auguste and Louis Lumière.

Marey and Muybridge

Étienne-Jules Marey, a scientist working in Paris, sought to record an animal's movement by individual actions—one at a time—to compare one animal to another. He charted a horse's movements on graphs and published the information in a book, *Animal Mechanism*.

Unknown to Marey, photographer Eadweard Muybridge was hired by railroad millionaire and horse

TIMEFRAME

1877–TODAY

Movies Mature as a Popular Medium

Eadweard Muybridge/CORBIS

Bloomberg/Getty Images

Matt Cardy/Getty Images

1877 Eadweard Muybridge catches motion on film when he uses 12 cameras to photograph a horse's movements for Leland Stanford in Palo Alto, Calif.

1915 Director D. W. Griffith introduces the concept of the movie spectacular with *The Birth of a Nation*.

1916 Brothers Noble and George Johnson launch Lincoln Films, the first company to produce movies called "race films," serious narrative movies for African American audiences.

1919 Oscar Micheaux releases *Within Our Gates*, a response to D. W. Griffith's controversial, anti-black epic *The Birth of a Nation*.

1927 *The Jazz Singer*, the first feature-length motion picture with sound, opens in New York City.

1930 The Motion Picture Producers and Distributors Association adopts a production code to control movie content.

1947 The House Un-American Activities Committee calls The Hollywood Ten to testify.

1948 The U.S. Supreme Court breaks up the large studios' control of Hollywood by deciding in the case of *United States v. Paramount Pictures, Inc., et al.* that the studios are a monopoly.

1966 The Motion Picture Association of America introduces a voluntary content-ratings system for the movies.

1994 Steven Spielberg, Jeffrey Katzenberg and David Geffen launch DreamWorks SKG, the first independent movie studio created in the United States since United Artists.

2001 To attempt to stop movie piracy, the Motion Picture Association of America challenges the availability of recordable DVD technology, but eventually DVD-Rs reach the marketplace.

2006 DreamWorks is sold to Viacom Inc., leaving the United States without a major independent movie studio.

2011 3-D movies begin to generate higher revenue for the industry.

2013 Disney buys Lucasfilm, including all rights to the *Star Wars* series, for $40.5 billion.

TODAY Movie theaters collect about 1 billion tickets a year, but more people see movies on video than in theaters. The market for American movies continues to grow overseas. Video streaming is an expanding source of revenue.

breeder Leland Stanford to settle a $25,000 bet. Stanford had bet that during a trot, all four of a horse's feet simultaneously leave the ground. In 1877, Muybridge and Stanford built a special track in Palo Alto, Calif., with 12 cameras precisely placed to take pictures of a horse as it moved around the track. The horse tripped a series of equidistant wires as it ran, which in turn tripped the cameras' shutters. Stanford won his $25,000—one photograph showed that all four of the horse's feet did leave the ground—and the photographic series provided an excellent study of motion.

Muybridge expanded to 24 cameras, photographed other animals and then took pictures of people moving. He traveled throughout Europe showing his photographs. Eventually, Muybridge and Marey met. In 1882, Marey perfected a photographic gun camera that could take 12 photographs on one plate—the first motion picture camera.

Corbis

This rotary disc, demonstrating the movement of a horse's feet, was shown on a machine called a Zoopraxiscope. This series of images photographed by Eadweard Muybridge eventually led to the development of the first motion picture camera.

Thomas Edison

Thomas Edison bought some of Muybridge's pictures in 1888 and showed them to his assistant, William K. L. Dickson. Edison then met with Marey in Europe, where Marey had invented a projector that showed pictures on a continuous strip of film, but the filmstrip moved unevenly across the projector lens, so the pictures jumped.

William K. L. Dickson

Back in America, Dickson perforated the edges of the film so that, as the film moved through the camera, sprockets inside the camera grabbed the perforations and locked the film in place, minimizing the jumps.

Dickson looped the strip over a lamp and a magnifying lens in a box 2 feet wide and 4 feet tall. The box stood on the floor with a peephole in the top so people could look inside. Edison named this device the kinetoscope. On April 11, 1894, America's first kinetoscope parlor opened in New York City. For 25 cents, people could see ten different 90-second black-and-white films, including *Trapeze, Horse Shoeing, Wrestlers* and *Roosters*.

Auguste and Louis Lumière

In France, the Lumière brothers, Auguste and Louis, developed an improved camera and a projector that could show film on a large screen. The first public Lumière showing was on December 28, 1895: ten short subjects with such riveting titles as *Lunch Hour at the Lumière Factory*, which showed workers leaving the building, and *Arrival of a Train at a Station*. Admission was 1 franc and the Lumières collected 35 francs.

Edison Launches American Movies

Four months after the Lumière premiere in France, Edison organized the first American motion picture premiere with an improved camera developed by independent inventor Thomas Armat. Edison dubbed the new machine the Vitascope, and America's first public showing of the motion picture was on April 23, 1896, at Koster and Bial's theater in New York. Edison sat in a box seat, and Armat ran the projector from the balcony.

At first, movies were a sideshow. Penny-arcade owners showed movies behind a black screen at the rear of the arcade for an extra nickel. But soon the movies were more popular than the rest of the attractions, and the arcades were renamed *nickel*odeons. In 1900, there were more than 600 nickelodeons in New York City, with more than 300,000 daily admissions. Each show lasted about 20 minutes. The programs ran from noon until late evening, and many theaters blared music outside to bring in business.

By 1907, Edison had contracted with most of the nation's movie producers, as well as the Lumière brothers and the innovative French producer Georges Méliès, to provide movies for the theaters. Licensed Edison theaters used licensed Edison projectors and rented Edison's licensed movies, many of which Edison produced at his own studio. The important exception to Edison's licensing plan was his rival, the American Mutoscope and Biograph Company, commonly called Biograph.

Biograph manufactured a better motion picture camera than Edison's, and Edison was losing business. In 1908, Biograph signed an agreement with Edison, forming the Motion Picture Patents Company (MPPC).

FILMMAKERS TURN NOVELTY INTO ART

All the early films were black-and-white silent movies. Sound was not introduced to the movies until the 1920s, and color experiments did not begin until the 1930s. Two innovative filmmakers are credited with turning the novelty of movies into art: Georges Méliès and Edwin S. Porter.

Georges Méliès

French filmmaker Georges Méliès added fantasy to the movies. Before Méliès, moviemakers photographed theatrical scenes or events from everyday life. But Méliès, who had been a magician and a caricaturist before he became a filmmaker, used camera tricks to make people disappear and reappear and to make characters grow and then shrink.

His 1902 film, *A Trip to the Moon*, was the first outerspace movie adventure, complete with fantasy creatures. When his films, which became known as *trick films*, were shown in the United States, American moviemakers stole his ideas.

Edwin S. Porter

Edison hired projectionist/electrician Edwin S. Porter in 1899, and in the next decade Porter became America's most important filmmaker. Until Porter, most American films were trick films or short documentary-style movies that showed newsworthy events (although some filmmakers used titillating subjects in movies such as *Pajama Girl* and *Corset Girl* to cater to men, who were the movies' biggest customers). In 1903, Porter produced *The Great Train Robbery*, an action movie with bandits attacking a speeding train.

Instead of using a single location like most other moviemakers, Porter shot 12 different scenes. He also introduced the use of dissolves between shots, instead

Georges Méliès created fanciful creatures for his 1902 film, *A Trip to the Moon*, introducing fantasy to motion pictures. In a scene from the movie, an explorer searches the moon landscape from the top of his shell rocket capsule.

of abrupt splices. Porter's film techniques—action and changing locations—foreshadowed the classic storytelling tradition of American movies.

STUDIO SYSTEM AND INDEPENDENT MOVIEMAKERS FLOURISH

None of the actors in the early movies received screen credit, but then fans began to write letters addressed to "The Biograph Girl," who was Biograph star Florence Lawrence. In 1909, Carl Laemmle formed an independent production company, stole Lawrence from Biograph and gave her screen credit. She became America's first movie star.

Biograph was the first company to make movies using the studio system. The *studio system* meant that a studio hired a stable of stars and production people who were paid a regular salary. These people signed

Studio System   An early method of hiring a stable of salaried stars and production people under exclusive contracts to a specific studio.

contracts with that studio and could not work for any other studio without their employer's permission.

In 1910, Laemmle lured Mary Pickford away from Biograph by doubling her salary. He discovered, says film scholar Robert Sklar, "that stars sold pictures as nothing else could. As long as theaters changed their programs daily—and the practice persisted in neighborhood theaters and small towns until the early 1920s—building up audience recognition of star names was almost the only effective form of audience publicity." (Mary Pickford became one of the most influential women in early Hollywood and helped finance the independent studio United Artists. See page 136.)

The *star system*, which promoted popular movie personalities to lure audiences, was nurtured by the independents. This helped broaden the movies' appeal beyond their original working-class audience. Movie houses began to open in the suburbs. From 1908 to 1914, movie attendance doubled.

In 1915, the first real titan of the silent movies, director D. W. Griffith, introduced the concept of spectacular entertainment. Most early movies were two reels long, 25 minutes. Griffith expanded his movies to four reels and longer, pioneering the feature-length film. In his best-known epic, *The Birth of a Nation* (1915), the Southern-born Griffith presented a dramatic view of the Civil War and Reconstruction, portraying racial stereotypes and touching on the subject of sexual intermingling of the races. The movie's cost—about $110,000—was five times more than any American film before that time.

In 1916, brothers Noble and George Johnson launched Lincoln Motion Picture Company, the first company to produce serious narrative movies for African American audiences, called "race films," paving the way for African American film stars Paul Robeson and Josephine Baker.

Moviemakers like the Johnson brothers and Oscar Micheaux proved that movies produced for specialized audiences could succeed. From 1910 to 1950, filmmakers produced more than 500 movies directed at African American audiences. (See **Impact/Audience**, "Lighting Up a Black Screen: Early 'Race Films' Pioneered the Art of Breaking Stereotypes," p. 135.)

With *The Birth of a Nation* and his subsequent epics, Griffith showed the potential that movies had as a mass medium for gathering large audiences. He also proved

Star System Promoting popular movie personalities to lure audiences.

Block Booking The practice of requiring theaters to take a package of movies instead of showing the movies individually.

that people would pay more than a nickel or a dime to see a motion picture. The Johnson brothers and Oscar Micheaux demonstrated that films also could succeed with specialized audiences. Movies clearly had arrived as a popular, viable mass medium, moving from the crowded nickelodeon to respectability.

MOVIES BECOME BIG BUSINESS

The movie business was changing quickly. Five important events in the 1920s transformed the movie industry:

1. The move to California
2. The adoption of block booking
3. The formation of United Artists
4. The industry's efforts at self-regulation
5. The introduction of sound.

Studios Move to Hollywood

During the first decade of the 20th century, the major movie companies were based in New York, the theater capital. Film companies sometimes traveled to Florida or Cuba to chase the sunshine because it was easier to build sets outdoors to take advantage of the light, but soon they found a new home in California.

In 1903, Harry Chandler, who owned the *Los Angeles Times*, also owned a lot of Los Angeles real estate. He and his friends courted the movie business, offering cheap land, moderate weather and inexpensive labor. Soon the moviemakers moved to Hollywood.

Distributors Insist on Block Booking

People who owned theater chains then decided to make movies, and moviemakers discovered they could make more money if they owned theaters, so production companies built theaters to show their own pictures. The connection between production, distribution and exhibition grew, led by Paramount's Adolph Zukor, who devised a system called *block booking*.

Block booking meant a company, such as Paramount, would sign up one of its licensed theaters for as many as 104 pictures at a time. The movie package contained a few "name" pictures with stars, but the majority of the movies in the block were lightweight features with no stars. Because movie bills changed twice a week, the exhibitors were desperate for something to put on the screen. Often, without knowing which movies they were getting in the block, exhibitors accepted the package and paid the distributor's price.

IMPACT/Audience

Lighting Up a Black Screen: Early "Race Films" Pioneered the Art of Breaking Stereotypes

By Teresa Moore

The halcyon age for African Americans on the big screen was the period between 1910 and 1950 when blacks—and some whites—produced more than 500 "race movies," showcasing all-black casts in a variety of genres, including Westerns, mysteries, romances and melodramas.

In the naturally sepia-toned world of race movies, African Americans could—and did—do just about anything.

Lena Horne shone as the *Bronze Venus*. Crooner Herb Jeffries was the *Bronze Buckaroo*. There were black millionaires and black detectives, black sweethearts and socialites. Black heroines who swooned—tender, wilting ladies who never swept a broom or donned a do-rag. Black heroes who could be gentle and genteel, tough and smart. Black villains of both genders, out to separate black damsels and grandees from their virtue or fortune.

Race movies were so called because they were made for black Southern audiences barred from white-owned theaters. The films were shown either in the black-owned movie palaces of the urban North and Midwest or in "midnight rambles"—special midnight-to-2 a.m. screenings in rented halls or segregated theaters of the South.

Under segregation, the moviemakers created an onscreen world that not only reflected the accomplishments of the rising black middle class but also transformed reality into a realm where race was no impediment to love, power or success . . . .

The leading directors and producers—Oscar Micheaux and the brother team of Noble and George Johnson—wanted to uplift African Americans. Besides presenting black images more appealing to black audiences, they also offered black perspectives on racial injustice.

The New York Public Library/Art Resource, NY

Oscar Micheaux (center) was a pioneering African American filmmaker who produced "race movies," showing all-African American casts in a variety of roles. Micheaux's *Within Our Gates* was designed to counter the racism in D. W. Griffith's epic *The Birth of a Nation*.

"In some ways these filmmakers were more free because they were making the movies for themselves," said Michael Thompson, a professor of African American history at Stanford. In *Within Our Gates*, Micheaux's filmic response to D. W. Griffith's controversial, anti-black epic *The Birth of a Nation*, a white man tries to rape a young black woman—stopping only when he recognizes her as his illegitimate daughter.

According to *Midnight Ramble*, Bestor Cram and Pearl Bowser's 1994 documentary on the black film industry, that industry developed alongside—and initially in reaction against—the white film industry. Virtually shut out of Hollywood, where a handful of black actors were usually cast as Indians and in various "ethnic" or "exotic" roles while whites in blackface cavorted onscreen, African Americans formed their own production companies, making hundreds of features and shorts.

Source: Excerpted from Teresa Moore, "Lighting Up a Black Screen: Early 'Race Films' Pioneered the Art of Breaking Stereotypes," sfgate.com, February 25, 1997. Copyright 1997 by *San Francisco Chronicle*.

United Artists Champions the Independents

In 1919, the nation's five biggest movie names—cowboy star William S. Hart, Mary Pickford, Charlie Chaplin, Douglas Fairbanks and D. W. Griffith—rebelled against the strict studio system of distribution and formed their own studio. Eventually Hart withdrew from the agreement, but the remaining partners formed a company called United Artists (UA). They eliminated block booking and became a distributor for independently produced pictures, including their own.

In its first six years, UA delivered many movies that today still are considered classics, including *The Mark of Zorro, The Three Musketeers, Robin Hood* and *The Gold Rush*. These movies succeeded even though UA worked outside the traditional studio system, proving that it was possible to distribute films to audiences without using a major studio.

(Left) Mary Pickford, D. W. Griffith, Charlie Chaplin and Douglas Fairbanks founded United Artists in 1919. (Right) In 1994, David Geffen, Jeffrey Katzenberg and Steven Spielberg launched DreamWorks SKG, the first major independent movie studio created in the United States since United Artists. In 2006, the media conglomerate Viacom bought DreamWorks Animation, leaving the United States without a major independent studio (although Spielberg retained a partnership in the live-film division called DreamWorks SKG).

Moviemakers Use Self-Regulation to Respond to Scandals

In the 1920s, the movie industry faced two new crises: scandals involving movie stars and criticism that movie content was growing too provocative. As a result, the moviemakers decided to regulate themselves.

The star scandals began when comedian Roscoe "Fatty" Arbuckle hosted a marathon party in San Francisco over Labor Day weekend in 1921. As the party was ending, model Virginia Rappe was rushed to the hospital with stomach pains. She died at the hospital, and Arbuckle was charged with murder. Eventually the cause of death was listed as peritonitis from a ruptured bladder, and the murder charge was reduced to manslaughter. After three trials, two of which resulted in hung juries, Arbuckle was acquitted.

Then director William Desmond Taylor was found murdered in his home. Mabel Normand, a friend of Arbuckle's, was identified as the last person to see Taylor alive. Eventually Norman was cleared, but then it was revealed that "Taylor" was not the director's real name, and there were suggestions he was involved in the drug business. Hollywood's moguls and businesspeople were shocked. The Catholic Legion of Decency announced a movie boycott. Quick to protect themselves, Los Angeles business leaders met and decided that Hollywood should police itself.

Los Angeles Times owner Harry Chandler worked with movie leaders to bring in Will Hays, a former postmaster general and Republican Party chairman, to respond to these and other scandals in the movie business. Hays' job was to lead a moral refurbishing of the industry. In March 1922, Hays became the first president of the Motion Picture Producers and Distributors Association (MPPDA), at a salary of $100,000 a year. A month later, even though Arbuckle had been acquitted, Hays suspended all of Fatty Arbuckle's films, ruining Arbuckle's career.

Besides overseeing the stars' personal behavior, Hays decided that his office also should oversee movie content. The MPPDA, referred to as the Hays Office, wrote a code of conduct to govern the industry. In 1930, the MPPDA adopted a production code, which began with three general principles:

1. No picture shall be produced which will lower the moral standards of those who see it. Hence the sympathy of the audience shall never be thrown to the side of crime, wrongdoing, evil or sin.

2. Correct standards of life, subject only to the requirements of drama and entertainment, shall be presented.

3. Law, natural or human, shall not be ridiculed, nor shall sympathy be created for its violation.

The code then divided its rules into 12 categories of wrongdoing, including

- Murder: "The technique of murder must be presented in a way that will not inspire imitation."

- Sex: "Excessive and lustful kissing, lustful embraces, suggestive postures and gestures are not to be shown."

- Obscenity: "Obscenity in word, gesture, reference, song, joke, or by suggestion (even when likely to be understood only by part of the audience) is forbidden."

- Costumes: "Dancing costumes intended to permit undue exposure or indecent movements in the dance are forbidden."

An acceptable movie displayed a seal of approval in the titles at the beginning of the picture. Producers balked at the interference, but most of them, afraid of censorship from outside the industry, complied with the monitoring.

Although standards have relaxed, the practice of self-regulation of content still operates in the motion picture industry today in the form of the movies ratings system.

New Technology Brings the Talkies

By the mid-1920s, silent movies were an established part of American entertainment, but technology soon pushed the industry into an even more vibrant era—the era of the talkies. MPPDA President Will Hays was the first person to appear on screen in the public premiere of talking pictures on August 6, 1926, in New York City. Warner Bros. and Western Electric had developed the movie sound experiment, which consisted of seven short subjects, called *The Vitaphone Preludes*.

The Warner brothers—Sam, Harry, Jack and Albert— were ambitious, upstart businessmen who beat their competitors to sound movies. On October 6, 1927, *The Jazz Singer*, starring Al Jolson, opened at the Warners' Theater in New York and was the first feature-length motion picture with sound. The movie was not an all-talkie but instead contained two sections with synchronized sound.

Ham Khan/CartoonStock

The success of *The Jazz Singer* convinced Warners' competitors not to wait any longer to adopt sound. By July 1, 1930, 22 percent of theaters still showed silent films. By 1933, less than 1 percent of the movies shown in theaters were silents.

BIG FIVE STUDIOS DOMINATE

In the 1930s, the Big Five—Warner Bros., Metro-Goldwyn-Mayer, Paramount, RKO and Twentieth Century Fox—dominated the movie business. They collected more than two-thirds of the nation's box office receipts. United Artists remained solely a distribution company for independent producers.

The Big Five all were vertically integrated: They produced movies, distributed them worldwide and owned theater chains, which guaranteed their pictures a showing. The studios maintained stables of stars, directors, producers, writers and technical staff. Film scholar Tino Balio calls the studios at this point in their history a "mature oligopoly"—a group of companies with so much control over an industry that any change in one of the companies directly affected the future of the industry.

In the 1930s, Walt Disney was the only major successful Hollywood newcomer. He had released *Steamboat Willie* as "the first animated sound cartoon" in 1928. Disney was 26 years old, and he had sold his car to finance the cartoon's soundtrack. After some more short-animated-feature successes, Disney announced in 1934 that his studio would produce its first feature-length animated film, *Snow White and the Seven Dwarfs*. The film eventually cost Disney $2.25 million, more than MGM usually spent on a good musical. *Snow White* premiered December 21, 1937, at the Cathay Circle Theater in Hollywood and became an instant hit and the foundation for the Disney movie empire.

Box office receipts sagged in the 1930s as the Depression settled into every aspect of America's economy. Facing bankruptcy, several theaters tried to buoy their profits by adding bingo games and cut-rate admissions. The one innovation that survived the 1930s was the double feature: two movies for the price of one.

Labor Unions Organize Movie Workers

The Depression introduced another factor into motion picture budgets: labor unions. Before the 1930s, most aspects of the movie business were not governed by union agreements. But in 1937, the National Labor Relations Board held an election that designated the Screen Actors Guild to bargain for wages, working conditions and overtime.

The Screen Writers Guild was certified in 1938 and the Screen Directors Guild soon afterward. Unionization limited the studios' power over the people who worked for them, and by the late 1930s all the major studios had signed union agreements. Union agreements also introduced professionalism into the movie business. Then the Depression ended, and the studios once again prospered.

Movies Glitter During the Golden Age

With glamorous stars and exciting screenplays, supported by an eager pool of gifted directors, producers and technical talent, plus an insatiable audience, the movie industry reached its apex in the late 1930s and early 1940s. The most successful studio in Hollywood was MGM, which attracted the best writers, directors and actors. MGM capitalized on its star lineup with movies such as *The Great Ziegfeld*, *The Wizard of Oz* and *Gone with the Wind*.

Not only did *Gone with the Wind*'s phenomenal success demonstrate the epic character that movies could provide, but the movie also was a technological breakthrough, with its magnificent use of color. The movie business was so profitable that even MGM's dominance didn't scare away the competition. Many other studios, such as RKO, created enduring stars, such as Fred Astaire and Ginger Rogers, in films with light plots but stunning production numbers.

Silver Screen Collection/Moviepix/Getty Images

The late 1930s and early 1940s have been called the Golden Age of Movies. Although *The Wizard of Oz* was not an instant hit when it was released in 1939, the movie eventually became a blockbuster for MGM studios.

CONGRESS AND THE COURTS CHANGE HOLLYWOOD

Before television arrived throughout the country in 1948, two other events of the late 1940s helped reverse the prosperous movie bonanza that began in mid-1930:

1. The hearings of the House Un-American Activities Committee (HUAC)

2. The 1948 antitrust decision of the U.S. Supreme Court in *United States v. Paramount Pictures, Inc., et al.*

The House Un-American Activities Committee

In October 1947, America was entering the Cold War. This was an era in which many public officials, government employees and private citizens seemed preoccupied with the threat of Communism and people identified as "subversives." The House of Representatives Committee on Un-American Activities, chaired by J. Parnell Thomas, summoned ten "unfriendly" witnesses from Hollywood to testify about their Communist connections. (Unfriendly witnesses were people whom the committee classified as having participated at some time in the past in "un-American activities." This usually meant that the witness had been a member of a left-wing organization in the decade before World War II.) These eight screenwriters and two directors came to be known as the Hollywood Ten.

The Ten's strategy was to appear before the committee as a group and to avoid answering the direct question "Are you now or have you ever been a member of the Communist Party?" Instead, the Ten tried to make statements that questioned the committee's authority to challenge their political beliefs. In a rancorous series of hearings, the committee rejected the Ten's testimony; the witnesses found themselves facing trial for contempt. All of them were sentenced to jail and some were fined. By the end of November 1947, all the Hollywood Ten had lost their jobs. Many more movie people would follow.

In an article for the *Hollywood Review*, Hollywood Ten member Adrian Scott reported that 214 movie employees eventually were ***blacklisted***, which means that many studio owners refused to hire people who were suspected of taking part in subversive activities. The movie people who were not hired because of their political beliefs included 106 writers, 36 actors and 11 directors. This effectively gutted Hollywood of some of its best talent.

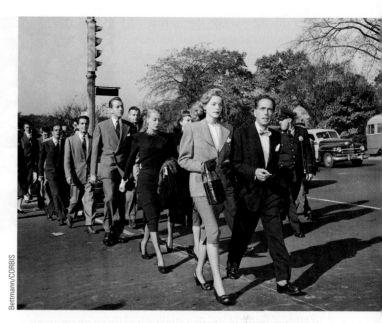

Bettmann/CORBIS

The Hollywood Ten, targeted in 1947 by the House Un-American Activities Committee, eventually went to jail for refusing to answer questions before the committee about their political beliefs. In October 1947, a group of Hollywood stars, led by Humphrey Bogart and Lauren Bacall, represented 500 of their colleagues in Washington, D.C., protesting the way the Hollywood Ten investigation was being conducted.

United States v. Paramount Pictures, Inc., et al.

The U.S. Justice Department began an antitrust suit against the studios in 1938. In 1940, the studios came to an agreement with the government, while admitting no guilt. They agreed to

1. Limit block booking to five films.

2. Stop ***blind booking*** (the practice of renting films to exhibitors without letting them see the films first).

3. Stop requiring theaters to rent short films as a condition of acquiring features.

4. Stop buying theaters.

Blacklisting   Studio owners' refusal to hire someone who was suspected of taking part in subversive activities.

Blind Booking   The practice of renting films to exhibitors without letting them see the films first.

After this agreement, the Justice Department dropped its suit with the stipulation that the department could reinstitute the suit again at any time.

By 1944, the government still was unhappy with studio control over the theaters, so it reactivated the suit. In 1948, *United States v. Paramount Pictures, Inc., et al.* reached the Supreme Court. Associate Justice William O. Douglas argued that although the five major studios—Paramount, Warner Bros., MGM-Loew's, RKO and Twentieth Century Fox—owned only 17 percent of all theaters in the United States, these studios held a *monopoly* over first-run exhibition in the large cities. As a result of the Supreme Court decision, by 1954 the five studios had given up ownership or control of all their theaters. Production and exhibition were now split; vertical integration was crumbling.

When the movie companies abandoned the exhibition business, banks grew reluctant to finance film projects because the companies could not guarantee an audience—on paper. Soon the studios decided to leave the production business to the independents and became primarily distributors of other peoples' pictures. The result was the end of the studio system.

MOVIES LOSE THEIR AUDIENCE TO TELEVISION

In the 1950 Paramount movie *Sunset Boulevard*, aging silent screen star Norma Desmond (played by Gloria Swanson) romances an ambitious young screenwriter (played by William Holden) by promising him Hollywood connections.

> "You're Norma Desmond. You used to be in silent pictures. You used to be big," says the screenwriter.
> "I am big," says Desmond. "It's the pictures that got small."

Desmond could have been talking about the movie business itself, which got much smaller after 1948, when television began to offer home-delivered entertainment across the nation. The House hearings and the consent decrees in the *Paramount* case telegraphed change in the movie business, but television truly transformed Hollywood forever. In the 1950s, the number of television sets people owned grew by 400 percent, while the number of people who went to the movies fell by 45 percent.

Theaters tried to make up for the loss by raising their admission prices, but more than 4,000 theaters closed

In the 1950s, the movie business used technological gimmicks, such as very primitive 3-D, to try to compete with television. In 2011, the movie studios, faced with declining audiences because of the Internet, launched an updated version of 3-D.

between 1946 and 1956. Attendance has leveled off or risen briefly a few times since the 1950s, but the trend of declining movie attendance continues today. The movie industry has tried several methods to counteract this downward trend.

Wide-Screen and 3-D Movies

Stunned by television's popularity, the movie business tried technological gimmicks in the 1950s to lure its audience back. First came 3-D movies, using special effects to create the illusion of three-dimensional action. Rocks, for example, seemed to fly off the screen and into the audience. To see the 3-D movies, people wore special plastic glasses. The novelty was fun, but the 3-D movie plots were weak, and most people didn't come back to see a second 3-D movie.

Next came Cinerama, CinemaScope, VistaVision and Panavision—wide-screen color movies with stereophonic sound. All these techniques tried to give the audience a "you are there" feeling—something they couldn't get from television.

Changes in Censorship

On May 26, 1952, the Supreme Court announced in *Burstyn v. Wilson* that motion pictures were "a significant medium for the communication of ideas," designed "to entertain as well as to inform." The effect of this decision was to protect movies under the First Amendment, which meant fewer legal restrictions on what a movie could show.

In 1953, Otto Preminger challenged the movies' self-regulating agency, the Production Code Administration (PCA). United Artists agreed to release Preminger's movie *The Moon Is Blue*, even though the PCA denied the movie a certificate of approval because it contained such risqué words as *virgin* and *mistress*. Then, in 1956, United Artists released Preminger's *Man with the Golden Arm*, a film about drug addiction, and the PCA restrictions were forever broken.

Buoyed by the *Burstyn* decision and the United Artists test, moviemakers tried sex and violence to lure audiences away from television. In the 1950s, Marilyn Monroe and Jayne Mansfield offered generously proportioned examples of the new trend. Foreign films also became popular because some of them offered explicit dialogue and love scenes.

Spectaculars

One by one, the studio moguls retired, and they were replaced by a new generation of moviemakers. This second generation "inherited a situation where fewer and fewer pictures were being made, and fewer still made money," says film historian Robert Sklar, "but those that captured the box office earned enormous sums. It was as if the rules of baseball had been changed so that the only hit that mattered was a home run."

Spectaculars like *The Sound of Music* (1965) and *The Godfather* (1971) and its sequels rewarded the rush for big money. But then a few majestic flops taught the studios that nothing demolishes a studio's profits like one big movie bomb.

Movie Ratings

In 1966, Jack Valenti, former adviser to President Lyndon Johnson, became president of the Motion Picture Producers Association (MPPA) and renamed it the Motion Picture Association of America (MPAA). The MPAA protects the business interests of movie companies by lobbying Congress about issues that are important to the movie business, such as freedom from government censorship. One of Valenti's first acts was to respond to continuing public criticism about shocking movie content. (Valenti ran the MPAA until his retirement in 2004.)

The MPAA began a rating system modeled on Great Britain's: G for general audiences, M (later changed to PG) for mature audiences, R for restricted (people under 17 admitted only with an adult), and X for no one under 18 admitted. The PG-13 rating—special parental guidance advised for children younger than 13—was added, and the X rating was changed to NC-17. Standards for the R rating have eased since the ratings system began, further blurring the effectiveness of the ratings system for the public.

MOVIES AND MONEY TODAY

In today's system of moviemaking, each of the major studios (such as Disney, Viacom/Paramount and Sony Pictures Entertainment) usually makes fewer than 20 movies a year. The rest come from independent producers, with production, investment, distribution and exhibition each handled by different companies. Most of these independently produced movies are distributed by one of the large studios.

In an attempt to counteract the strong influence of the traditional movie studios, Steven Spielberg, Jeffrey Katzenberg and David Geffen launched a company called DreamWorks SKG in 1994. DreamWorks was the first major independent movie studio created in the United States since United Artists was formed in 1919. The company survived as an independent studio for 11 years, but in 2006 DreamWorks was sold to Viacom, leaving the United States without a major independent movie studio.

In 2004, the animation division, DreamWorks Animation, was spun off as a publicly traded company, with Katzenberg as CEO, and Viacom/Paramount kept the live-action portion of the studio. Geffen left the live-action studio in 2008, and in 2009, Spielberg, with two partners, bought back the live-action part of the original studio from Paramount. So today there is DreamWorks Animation, a publicly traded company that produces only animated features, and Spielberg and his partners own DreamWorks Studios to produce live-action movies, such as *War Horse* (2011) and *Lincoln* (2012).

Today's movies are created by one group (the writers and producers), funded by another group (the investors), sold by a third group (the distributors) and shown by a fourth group (the exhibitors). No other mass media industry is so fragmented.

The dream merchants aim at a mature audience. Movies are targeted at people of all ages, but especially children and people older than 30. Today's moviemakers try to appeal to an audience older than 30 and to children (who typically bring their parents with them to the show), with films such as *Monster University* and *Despicable Me 2*.

Losing Money: Ticket Sales Drop

In 1946, the movies' best year, American theaters collected more than 4 billion tickets. Today, as more people watch more movies on video and DVD, the number of theater admissions has dropped to about 1.3 billion. Exhibitors believe that if they raise their admission prices, they'll lose more patrons. This is why exhibitors charge so much for refreshments, which account for 10 to 20 percent of their income.

IMPACT/Money

Illustration 7.1

How Much Does It Cost to Make a Movie? The 10 Most Expensive Movies Ever Made

The average cost to make a movie today is more than $100 million, but an average is just that—many movies cost less, and a few movies cost a lot more. Even if a movie is a big box-office success, a movie is a financial success only when it brings in more money than it costs to make. This list shows the most expensive movies ever made, along with how much each movie cost to make and how much global revenue the movie collected, adjusted for inflation. (Note that *Waterworld* cost more to make than it earned.)

Source: "The 25 Most Expensive Movies Ever Made," December 4, 2012, businessinsider.com.

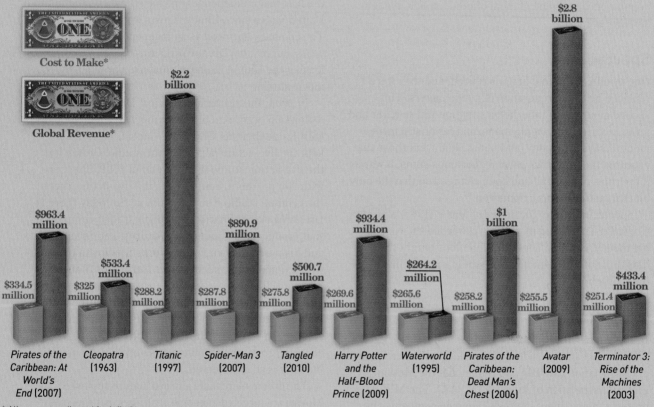

Cost to Make*

Global Revenue*

* All amounts adjusted for inflation.

The movie studios claim they lose money on *most* of the pictures they underwrite. Producers claim that, by hiding behind complicated financing schemes, the studios are able to keep exorbitant profits on the movies they distribute, which raises the cost of making movies for producers.

Movie finance is an important part of the movie business today because movies, like other media industries, are part of publicly owned corporations where loyalty to stockholders comes first. Studios tend to choose safer

projects and seek proven audience-pleasing ideas rather than take risks (see **Illustration 7.1**, "How Much Does It Cost to Make a Movie? The 10 Most Expensive Movies Ever Made").

One way the movie industry collects predictable income is to make movies for television. Half the movies produced every year are made for television and underwritten by the TV networks. Video sales also bring reliable revenues. Another important factor in movie funding is the sale of ancillary rights.

Ancillary Rights Fund Projects

In 1950, a ticket to a movie cost about 50 cents. Today you can still see a movie for 50 cents if you stream a movie for $2.99 and invite five friends to join you at home to watch it, and it is even cheaper if you get a Red Box movie for $1.

The explosion of video rentals and sales since the VCR was first marketed in 1976 had a powerful effect on how the movie business operates today. The sale of movies on video and movie streaming are part of the ***ancillary rights*** market, which means marketing opportunities that are related to a movie (such as video games), in addition to direct income from theater ticket sales for the movie itself.

Today, the studios claim that only two out of ten theatrical movies make money. "Some pictures make a lot of money," says movie analyst David V. Picker, "and a lot of pictures make no money." But the fact is that the large studios usually make a respectable return on investment each year. In 2012, the U.S. movie industry reported record income ticket sales.

Before a theatrical movie starts shooting, the investors want some assurances that they'll make their money back. Moviemakers use the sale of ancillary rights to add to investors' return on their investment. Ancillary rights include the following:

- Subscription television rights
- Network television rights
- Syndication rights (sales to independent TV stations)
- Airline rights for in-flight movies
- Military rights (to show films on military bases)
- College rights (to show films on college campuses)
- Song rights for soundtrack albums
- Book publishing rights (for original screenplays that can be rewritten and sold as books)
- DVD reproduction rights
- Product placement
- Video game rights
- Internet downloads and streaming.

Movies are commercialized in the sense that they are tied to products, which are another way of advertising a movie. A movie that can be exploited as a package of ancillary rights, with commercial appeal, is much more attractive to investors than a movie with limited potential.

Often the only choice for a filmmaker who wants to make a film that doesn't have substantial ancillary-rights

Ruaridh Stewart/ZUMA Press/Corbis

Because of its broad international appeal, *Star Wars* is the most enduring and successful movie project ever produced, with sequels and ancillary rights generating unprecedented income for the movies' creator, George Lucas. In 2012, George Lucas sold Disney all rights to the *Star Wars* series for $40.5 billion.

potential is to settle for a low budget. Once the film is made, the independent filmmaker must then find a way to distribute the movie. This severely limits the number of independent films that make it to the box office.

MOVIES AT WORK

Today the center of the movie industry is movie production. Independent companies produce most of the movies that are distributed by the major studios and exhibited at your local theater under agreements with individual studios. Although these production companies work independently, and each company is organized differently, jobs in movie production fall mainly into the following categories:

1. Screenwriters
2. Producers
3. Directors
4. Actors

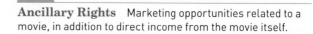

Ancillary Rights Marketing opportunities related to a movie, in addition to direct income from the movie itself.

5. Technical production

6. Marketing and administration

Every movie begins with a story idea, and these ideas come from *screenwriters*. Screenwriters work independently, marketing their story ideas through agents, who promote their clients' scripts to the studios and to independent producers.

Typically, *producers* are the people who help gather the funding to create a movie project. Financing can come from banks or from investors who want to back a specific movie. Sometimes producers or actors help finance the movies they make in exchange for a percentage of the profits.

Once the funding for the story is in place, a *director* organizes all the tasks necessary to turn the script into a movie. The director works with the producer to manage the movie's budget.

Obviously, *actors* are important to any movie project. Sometimes the producer and director approach particular stars for a project even before they seek funding, to attract interest from the investors and also to help assure the investors that the movie will have some box office appeal.

Technical production includes all the people who actually create the movie—camera operators, set designers, film editors, script supervisors and costumers, for example. Once the movie is finished, the *marketing* people seek publicity for the project. They also design a plan to advertise and promote the movie to the public.

As in any media industry, people who work in *administration* help keep all the records necessary to pay salaries

Cable, Carole/CartoonStock

and track the employees' expenses, as well as keep track of the paperwork involved in organizing any business.

DIGITAL TECHNOLOGY DRIVES THE BUSINESS

New digital technologies affect three aspects of today's movie business:

1. Production

2. Distribution

3. Exhibition.

Production

Smaller, portable cameras mean a camera operator can move more easily through a crowd. New types of video mean that filmmakers can shoot more scenes at night and in dark places with less artificial lighting. Directors digitally record scenes as they shoot them and immediately play back the scene to be sure they have the shot they want. Technology also offers exciting special effects possibilities.

The ability to digitize color also means the images in movies can be intensified, adjusted and totally transformed after the movie is shot, in a way that was impossible even 15 years ago.

Distribution

Reproducing copies of films to send to theaters and guaranteeing their arrival is one of the costliest aspects of moviemaking. Some distribution companies already send their movies by satellite-to-satellite dishes on top of each theater and directly to consumers' homes. Live performances, such as a music concert or a major sports event, already are available by satellite at many local theaters, and eventually first-run movies will be sent directly to your home the same day they're released in the theater.

The theater industry is poised to replace the traditional film projector, invented more than 100 years ago, with digital projectors, which can show movies that are sent by satellite or recorded on optical discs. As of 2012, 60 percent of the nation's theaters had converted to digital projection, but the price of the conversion can be prohibitive for small independent film houses (see **Impact/Convergence**, "Small Theaters Struggle as Hollywood Goes Digital," p. 145). Digitized movies are cheaper to distribute and can be shown on more screens or removed quickly from distribution, depending on audience demand.

IMPACT/Convergence

Small Theaters Struggle as Hollywood Goes Digital

By Associated Press

AP Photo/Nati Harnik

Small theaters throughout the country are struggling to convert to digital, which can cost as much as $85,000. Thom Reeves, owner of The Isis Theater in Crete, Neb., ran a fundraising drive to pay for the conversion.

CRETE, Neb.—The Isis Theatre hasn't changed much since it opened 86 years ago, a stone's throw from the grain elevator and railroad tracks that cut through town. But in the past few years, the movie industry has changed dramatically, and unless the Isis' owner comes up with $85,000 to pay for new digital equipment, residents of Crete may have to drive to Lincoln for a night at the movies.

It's a prospect that owner Thom Reeves doesn't want to ponder, but like thousands of small-theater operators across the country, he hasn't found a way out.

"This is my passion, to give back to the community," Reeves said. "I love this movie theater. I love what it does for the students I have employed there. We love our patrons. It's such a positive experience going on, and we're just a little sad this conversion is hitting us. How do we survive?"

For small-theater owners, the problem is the sudden switch from 35 mm film, an industry standard since about 1910, to digital—a format that's cheaper for both studios and distributors, and doesn't scratch as traditional film will. The switch means theater owners must buy new projection equipment, computers and a sound system.

Film studio 20th Century Fox has said it will phase out 35 mm film altogether by the end of 2013, and other production companies are expected to follow suit. Traditional film is expected to vanish during the next few years.

Big chains can afford the digital transition, which can be cheaper when buying in bulk for multi-screen theaters. But those who own smaller theaters with one or two screens typically must take out a bank loan to pay for the equipment.

A film industry program can refund up to 80 percent of the cost to theater owners, but the payments are made gradually through fees based on the number of movies shown. To qualify for the help, theaters must have certain profit levels and show a minimum number of films, leaving many small operators without help.

Some small, independent theaters created a cooperative, the Cinema Buying Group, to pool their resources and participate in the industry program, but the cooperative also required a review of each theater's financial strength and other factors. Many of the smallest theaters didn't qualify or were hesitant to join.

Patrick Corcoran, a spokesman for the National Association of Theatre Owners, said costs of converting to digital average about $70,000 per screen. About 60 percent of the nation's 5,750 theaters have switched to all-digital equipment, he said.

The switch to digital began with the 1999 release of *Star Wars Episode I: The Phantom Menace*, and accelerated with such computer-animated films as Disney's *Chicken Little* and the 2009 Hollywood blockbuster, *Avatar*, Corcoran said. "In some markets, it's going to be a tough climb," he said. "But if you want to be in business as a first-run movie theater, you have to go digital."

NOTE: The Isis fundraising drive was successful and the theater's digital conversion is underway.

Source: Excerpted from Associated Press, "Small Theaters Struggle as Hollywood Goes Digital," September 6, 2012, sfgate.com.

As video technology grew faster and more accessible, established movie studios and independent moviemakers devised a whole new distribution system, based on digital movie downloads delivered directly to consumers. The Internet allows independent and established moviemakers to distribute movies inexpensively by transferring them to the Internet for streaming. In 2008, Apple iTunes launched online movie rentals, which allows customers to download first-run movies to their Macs, PCs, iPods and iPhones for $2.99 each—designed to increase movie revenue by creating another distribution network.

In 2010, Netflix announced agreements with Paramount, Lionsgate and MGM for its "watch instantly" streaming service for new feature films. Subscription TV services, such as DirecTV and cable companies, stockpiled movies as part of a system of video-on-demand, available at home by subscription or pay-per-view.

The global market for American movies accounts for one-third of the movie industry's profits. The movie *42*, a very American story about Jackie Robinson (played by Chadwick Boseman, left) and Branch Rickey (played by Harrison Ford) premiered in Toronto, Canada on April 2, 2013, one week before its premiere in the U.S.

Movie streaming on mobile devices is transforming movie distribution. In November 2012, a child watches the 82-year-old Disney movie *Steamboat Willie* on her iPad.

Exhibition

Theaters are turning to the picture-palace environment that enchanted moviegoers in the 1930s. "The movie theater will have to become an arena; a palace to experience the full grandeur and potential of the theatrical motion picture," says futurist and electronic technology consultant Martin Polon.

"We're looking to marry the movie going experience to different kinds of technological experiences, thereby enhancing the attractiveness of the whole complex," said United Artists chairman Stewart Blair.

To draw people back into theaters, New Line Cinema and DreamWorks began developing a new digital version of 3-D technology similar to what theaters tried in the 1950s. The process, called RealD, uses a single projector to merge two images—one for each eye—to give the movie its realistic effect. To exhibit 3-D movies, theaters must buy new digital projection systems, which cost $75,000 per screen, but they can charge more for a RealD ticket, sometimes twice as much as a regular admission.

By 2009, RealD was available in selected theaters. *Avatar*, released late in 2009, was the first big 3-D hit. Disney released 3-D versions of *Toy Story 3* and *Alice in Wonderland* in 2010, and DreamWorks Studios released *How to Train Your Dragon*. The new technology added more than $1 billion to 2010 industry income, and higher ticket prices for 3-D features help maintain profitability.

INTERNATIONAL MARKETS BRING CONCENTRATED POWER

Today's movie industry is undergoing two major changes. One recent trend in the movie business is global ownership and global marketing. The second trend is the merging of the movie industry with the television industry.

Global Influence

Overseas companies own two of the major studios (Sony owns Sony Pictures Entertainment and Rupert

Murdoch's News Corporation owns Twentieth Century Fox). Foreign ownership gives these companies easier access to overseas markets.

American motion pictures are one of America's strongest exports, and income from foreign sales accounts for more than one-third of the movie industry's profits. "If Hollywood has learned anything the past few years," says *Business Week*, "it's that the whole world is hungry for the latest it has to offer." International ticket sales reached $24 billion in 2011, primarily driven by growth in Russia, Brazil and China.

Concentrating Media Power

In 1993, the Federal Communications Commission voted to allow the TV networks to produce and syndicate their own programs. This opened the door for TV networks to enter the movie business. Today, people in the television business are buying pieces of the movie business, and people in the movie business want to align themselves with television companies.

The result today is consolidated companies that finance movies, make movies and show those movies on their own television stations, on video and on the Internet. By controlling all aspects of the business, a company can have a better chance to collect a profit on the movies it makes.

Sound familiar? The studios held this type of controlling interest in their movies before the courts dismantled the studio system with the 1948 consent decrees (see "*United States v. Paramount Pictures, Inc., et al.,*" p. 139). Today's major studios are trying to become again what they once were: a mature oligopoly in the business of dreams.

Review, Analyze, Investigate

Reviewing Chapter 7

Movies Mirror the Culture

- Before the invention of TV, movies were the nation's primary form of entertainment.
- Like other industries, the movie business has had to adapt to changing technology.

Inventors Capture Motion on Film

- Eadweard Muybridge and Thomas Edison contributed the most to the creation of movies in America. Muybridge demonstrated how to photograph motion, and an Edison employee, William K. L. Dickson, developed a projector, the kinetoscope.
- Auguste and Louis Lumière developed an improved camera and a projector to show film on a large screen.
- Edison also organized the Motion Picture Patents Company to control movie distribution.

Filmmakers Turn Novelty into Art

- French filmmaker Georges Méliès envisioned movies as a medium of fantasy.
- Edwin S. Porter assembled scenes to tell a story.

Studio System and Independent Moviemakers Flourish

- Biograph became the first studio to make movies using what was called the studio system.
- The studio system put the studio's stars under exclusive contract, and the contract could not be broken without an employer's permission.

- The star system promoted popular movie personalities to lure audiences.
- D. W. Griffith mastered the full-length movie. Griffith's best-known movie is a controversial view of the Civil War, *The Birth of a Nation*.
- From 1910 to 1950, filmmakers like Noble and George Johnson and Oscar Micheaux produced movies specifically directed at African American audiences, called race films.

Movies Become Big Business

- The movie studios move from New York to Hollywood, where the climate is more favorable.
- The practice of block booking, led by Adolph Zukor, obligated movie houses to accept several movies at once, usually without previewing them first.
- The formation of United Artists by Mary Pickford, Charlie Chaplin, Douglas Fairbanks and D. W. Griffith was a rebellion against the big studios.
- UA distributed films for independent filmmakers.
- In the 1920s, the movie industry faced two crises: scandals involving movie stars and criticism that movie content was growing too explicit.
- The movie industry responded to the scandals and criticism about content by forming the Motion Picture Producers and Distributors Association under the direction of Will Hays.

- In 1930, the MPPDA adopted a production code, which created rules that governed movie content.
- Although standards have relaxed, the practice of self-regulation of content continues today.
- *The Jazz Singer*, the first feature-length motion picture with sound, premiered in New York City on October 6, 1927.

Big Five Studios Dominate

- As the studio system developed, the five largest Hollywood studios were able to control production, distribution and exhibition.
- In the 1930s, Walt Disney premiered the first feature-length animated film, *Snow White and the Seven Dwarfs*.
- Box office receipts sagged during the Depression, so theaters introduced the double feature—two movies for the price of one.

Labor Unions Organize Movie Workers

- In the 1930s, labor unions challenged studio control and won some concessions.
- Union agreements limited the studios' power over their employees.

Movies Glitter During the Golden Age

- The movies' golden age was the 1930s and 1940s, supported by the studio system and an eager audience.
- The most successful Hollywood studio was MGM, which concentrated on blockbuster movies such as *The Wizard of Oz* and *Gone with the Wind*.

Congress and the Courts Change Hollywood

- Three factors caused Hollywood's crash in the 1950s: the House Un-American Activities Committee hearings, the U.S. Justice Department's antitrust action against the studios, and television.
- At least 214 movie employees eventually were blacklisted as a result of the hearings of the House Un-American Activities Committee (HUAC).
- In 1948, the U.S. Supreme Court decision in *United States v. Paramount Pictures Inc., et al.* ended the studio system.

Movies Lose Their Audience to Television

- People abandoned the movies for television, and the trend of declining movie attendance continues today.
- Hollywood tried to lure audiences back to the movies in the 1950s with technological gimmicks, sultry starlets and spectaculars, but the rewards were temporary.
- Movie ratings were originally a response to criticism about immoral movie content, but the standards for these ratings have become blurred.

Movies and Money Today

- DreamWorks SKG, launched in 1994 by Steven Spielberg, Jeffrey Katzenberg and David Geffen, was the first major independent movie studio created in the United States since United Artists was formed in 1919. In 2006, DreamWorks was sold to Viacom, leaving the United States without a major independent movie studio.
- Today the number of moviegoers continues to decline, although DVD sales and rentals, as well as video game development, add to movie industry income.
- Most movies are funded in part by ancillary rights sales.
- The median cost to make a movie today is more than $100 million, and only two out of ten theatrical movies make money.
- Most movies are sold as packages, with all their potential media outlets underwriting the movie before it goes into production. This makes independent filmmaking difficult.

Movies at Work

- Movie production is the heart of the movie industry today.
- Screenwriters begin the moviemaking process; other jobs include producer, director, actor, technical production, marketing and administration.

Digital Technology Drives the Business

- New digital technologies affect production, distribution and exhibition of movies.
- Independent moviemakers can use computers to create movies inexpensively and distribute them on the Internet.
- Distribution companies send movies by satellite to satellite dishes on top of theaters and directly to consumers' homes.
- In 2008, Apple made first-run movie downloads available on its iTunes Web site for $2.99 each.
- In 2010, Netflix announced agreements with major studios to offer streaming service for new feature films. Subscription TV services also offer video-on-demand, available at home by subscription or pay-per-view.
- New Line Cinema and DreamWorks developed a new digital version of 3-D technology called RealD, which added more than $1 billion to industry income in 2010.

International Markets Bring Concentrated Power

- In 1993, the Federal Communications Commission voted to allow the TV networks to produce and syndicate their own programs. This opened the door for TV networks to enter the movie business.

- Overseas companies own two of the major studios.
- Foreign ownership gives these companies easier access to overseas markets.
- Overseas sales of American movies account for more than one-third of movie industry income.

- The movie and television industries have aligned themselves more closely to control all aspects of moviemaking.

Key Terms

These terms are defined in the margins throughout this chapter and appear in alphabetical order with definitions in the Glossary, which begins on page 373.

Ancillary Rights *143*	Blind Booking *139*	Star System *134*
Blacklisting *139*	Block Booking *134*	Studio System *133*

Critical Questions

1. Which audience age category is most attractive to today's moviemakers? Why?

2. What were race movies? Discuss the ways in which these films changed the perspective of African Americans in the films and for their audiences.

3. What was the effect of the practice of block booking on the movie industry? How and why did the practice end?

4. Why do you believe the Hollywood Ten became a target of the House Un-American Activities Committee? Could the same thing happen today? Why? Why not? Explain.

5. Describe how today's digital technologies are changing moviemaking, distribution and exhibition.

Working the Web

This list includes both sites mentioned in the chapter and others to give you greater insight into the movie industry.

Academy of Motion Picture Arts and Sciences
oscars.org

This honorary association of over 6,500 motion picture professionals is the home of the Oscars. The organization's goals include advancing the arts and sciences of motion pictures, recognizing outstanding achievement and promoting technical research of methods and equipment. The Web site includes Academy publications, information on the Academy Film Archive and an Academy Awards database.

DEG Digital Entertainment Group
dvdinformation.com

DEG is a nonprofit trade consortium composed of electronics manufacturers, movie studios and music companies whose goal is to explore opportunities in other digital technolo-

gies and represent all aspects of the home entertainment industry. Members include Philips Consumer Electronics, Paramount Home Entertainment and Sony BMG Music Entertainment.

The Internet Movie Database (IMDB)
imdb.com

Owned by Amazon.com, IMDB claims to be "the world's most popular and authoritative source for movie, TV and celebrity content with more than 103 million unique visitors each month." What started as a hobby project by movie fans has grown into a database of more than 15 million film and TV credits.

Lucasfilm
lucasfilm.com

This film and entertainment company founded by George Lucas in 1971 has produced such hits as *American Graffiti* and the *Star Wars* and *Indiana Jones* series. In addition to motion picture and television production, the company's businesses include Industrial Light & Magic (visual effects), Skywalker Sound and LucasArts (video games).

Motion Picture Association of America (MPAA) and Motion Picture Association (MPA)

mpaa.org

Advocates for the motion picture, home video and television industries, the MPAA and its international counterpart the MPA are responsible for the movie ratings and also work to protect copyrights and stem piracy of filmed works.

Netflix

netflix.com

The world's largest online movie rental source, Netflix provides subscribers access to more than 100,000 DVD titles and more than 10,000 instant downloads. DVDs are delivered free to subscriber households with a postage-paid return envelope, and there are no due dates or late fees.

Screenwriters Federation of America (SFA)

screenwritersfederation.org

Formerly the Screenwriters Guild of America, the SFA is an organization to promote the common interests of industry

professionals. Its goals are to educate screenwriters about their craft and about the entertainment business, to create a network for screenwriters and to administer standards for marketing scripts. The Web site includes news excerpts and links to Indiwire.com, the independent film community's news, information and social networking site. Users can also search imdb.com with one mouse click. Requires a log-in.

Sundance Institute

sundance.org

This nonprofit organization dedicates itself to discovering and developing independent moviemakers. Founder Robert Redford began hosting labs in 1981 where emerging filmmakers could work with leading writers and directors to develop their original projects. The Institute is now an internationally recognized independent artist resource and the host of the annual Sundance Film Festival.

Warner Bros.

warnerbros.com

This company founded by the four Warner brothers began as a silent-film distributor in 1903 and became a successful producer of "talkies" and animated cartoons. The company, now a division of Time Warner Inc., also produces television shows, animation, DVDs and interactive entertainment.

Impact/Action Videos are concise news features on various topics created exclusively for *Media/Impact*. Go online to access MindTap at cengagebrain.com. MindTap for Media/Impact sequences all of your learning tools—Chapter Readings with highlighting and note taking, Impact/Action Videos, activities and assessments—into chapter driven learning units that guide you through the curriculum.

TELEVISION:
CHANGING CHANNELS

8

Robyn Beck/AFP/Getty Images

In 2012 for the first time, many of television's Emmy awards went to non-network TV programming. The Internet is changing the way TV programs are delivered and consumed.

What's Ahead?

- Television Transforms Daily Life
- TV Delivers an Audience to Advertisers
- *Visual Radio* Becomes *Television*
- Television Outpaces Radio
- Quiz Shows Bring Ethics Scandals
- Ratings Target the Audience
- Newton Minow Criticizes TV as a "Vast Wasteland"
- Public Television Finds an Audience
- Satellites Make Transatlantic TV and Live Broadcasts Possible
- Television Changes National Politics
- TV News Images Bring Global Events into View
- Television at Work
- Audiences Drive TV Programming
- Digital Technology Expands TV's Focus
- Television Offers a New Vision

"I'm pretty tech savvy, but the TV industry with the cable and the television and the boxes, you don't know how to use their equipment. I try to go over to my grandma's place and teach her how to do it. I can't even figure it out myself."

—TRUCK DRIVER JAMES WEITZE, 31, WHO WATCHES TV PROGRAMS ONLY ON HIS IPHONE

"Television is the pervasive American pastime," writes media observer Jeff Greenfield. "Cutting through geographic, ethnic, class and cultural diversity, it is the single binding thread of this country, the one experience that touches young and old, rich and poor, learned and illiterate. A country too big for homogeneity, filled by people from all over the globe, without any set of core values, America never had a central unifying bond. Now we do. Now it is possible to answer the question, 'What does America do?' We watch television."

Television is turned on in today's American household, on average, more than eight hours a day, according to The Nielsen Company, which monitors television usage for advertisers. (See **Illustration 8.1**, "How Much Time Do People Spend Each Week Watching Traditional TV and Internet Video?," p. 154.) Even though people in your household may not watch TV this much, the percentage of households in the United States that use television a lot counterbalances the smaller amount of time people at your house spend with their television sets.

TELEVISION TRANSFORMS DAILY LIFE

It's not surprising that the effects of such a pervasive medium have attracted so much attention from parents, educators, social scientists, religious leaders, public officials and anyone else who wants to understand society's habits and values. TV has been blamed for everything from declines in literacy to rises in violent crime to the trivialization of national politics. Every once in a while it is praised, too, for giving viewers instant access to world events and uniting audiences in times of national crisis.

An industry with this much presence in American life is bound to affect the way we live. Someone who is watching television is not doing other things: playing basketball, visiting a museum, or looking through a telescope at the planets, for instance. Television can, however, bring you to a museum you might never visit or to a basketball game you cannot attend or to the surface of a planet you can only see through a telescope.

Television technology, by adding pictures to the sounds of radio, truly transformed Americans' living and learning patterns. The word *television*, which once meant programs delivered by antennas through over-the-air signals, now means a *television screen*, where several different types of delivery systems bring viewers a diversity of programs.

The programs Americans watch today are delivered by antennas, cables and satellites, but they all appear on the same television screen, and as a viewer, you can't tell how the program arrived at your television set and probably don't care. What you do know is that television gives you access to all types of programs—drama, comedy, sports, news, game shows and talk shows. You can see all types of people—murderers, public officials, foreign leaders, reporters, soldiers, entertainers, athletes, detectives and doctors. The television screen is truly, as scholar Erik Barnouw observed, a "tube of plenty."

TimeFrame

1884–TODAY

Television Remains the Nation's Primary Medium for News and Entertainment

Bernard Hoffman/Time & Life Pictures/ Getty Images

John Lamparski/WireImage/Getty Images

Timothy A. Clary/AFP/Getty Images

1884 In Germany, Paul Nipkow patents the Nipkow disk, which forms the basis for TV's development through the 1920s.

1907 The word *television* first appears in the June 1907 issue of *Scientific American*.

1939 NBC's David Sarnoff debuts television at the World's Fair in New York City. President Franklin D. Roosevelt, broadcasting from the fair, is the first U.S. president to appear on TV.

1947 NBC and CBS begin broadcasting television news.

1951 CBS launches *I Love Lucy*, a situation comedy, which becomes TV's most durable type of entertainment program.

1962 *Telstar I* sends the first transatlantic satellite broadcast.

1963 Public television begins broadcasting as National Educational Television. Network television provides nonstop coverage of the assassination and funeral of President John F. Kennedy.

1973 The television networks present live broadcasts of the Watergate hearings.

1979 Ted Turner starts Cable News Network. CNN's global reach gives the U.S. audience instant access to news about international events.

1983 More than 120 million people tune in for the final episode of *M*A*S*H*, the highest rated program ever.

1987 TV broadcasts the Iran-Contra hearings.

1993 More than 80 million people tune in for the final episode of *Cheers*.

2001 TV news offers nonstop, ad-free coverage of the terrorist attacks at the World Trade Center, the Pentagon and in rural Pennsylvania.

2003 TV broadcasts live news coverage of the Iraq War.

2006 Congress mandates that TV broadcasters switch totally to digital high-definition signals by February 17, 2009.

2008 More than 70 million people watch President-elect Barack Obama's election night victory on TV on November 4, a record audience for a presidential election night.

2009 The U.S. changes to a national high-definition television transmission standard (HDTV).

2010 Television manufacturers introduce 3-D television.

2012 Netflix offers original programming via video streaming.

TODAY HD is the standard for broadcast TV. Television programming is delivered on more than 125 channels by over-the-air broadcast, cable, satellite and the Internet.

IMPACT/Audience

Illustration 8.1

How Much Time Do People Spend Each Week Watching Traditional TV and Internet Video?

Americans spend an average of 33 hours a week watching traditional TV and video on the Internet. However, people who are 50 and older spend about twice as much time watching traditional TV as younger viewers (18–49). And younger viewers (18–49) spend more time than older viewers (50+) watching video on the Internet.

Source: *Free to Move Between Screens: The Cross-Platform Report*, March 2013, Nielsen.com.

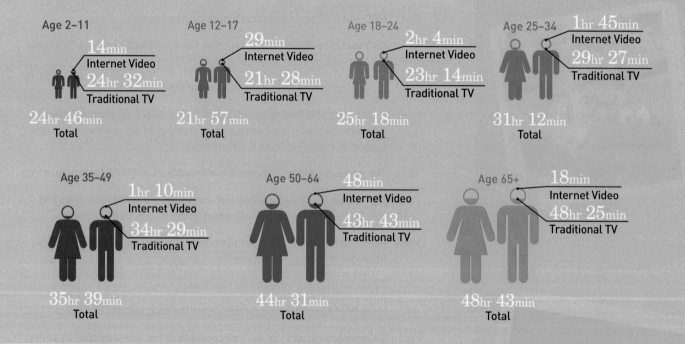

Age 2–11
14min Internet Video
24hr 32min Traditional TV
24hr 46min Total

Age 12–17
29min Internet Video
21hr 28min Traditional TV
21hr 57min Total

Age 18–24
2hr 4min Internet Video
23hr 14min Traditional TV
25hr 18min Total

Age 25–34
1hr 45min Internet Video
29hr 27min Traditional TV
31hr 12min Total

Age 35–49
1hr 10min Internet Video
34hr 29min Traditional TV
35hr 39min Total

Age 50–64
48min Internet Video
43hr 43min Traditional TV
44hr 31min Total

Age 65+
18min Internet Video
48hr 25min Traditional TV
48hr 43min Total

About 1,600 television stations operate in the United States. Three out of four of these are commercial stations, and the others are noncommercial stations. About half the commercial stations are affiliated with a network.

According to TV commentator Jeff Greenfield, "The most common misconception most people have about television concerns its product. To the viewer, the product is the programming. To the television executive, the product is the audience. Strictly speaking, television networks and stations do not make any money by producing a program that audiences want to watch. The money comes from selling advertisers the right to broadcast a message to that audience. The programs exist to capture the biggest possible audiences."

Robert Mankoff/The New Yorker Collection/Cartoonbank.com

"Maybe you set it up wrong."

TV Delivers an Audience to Advertisers

To understand why we get the programming we do, it is important to remember that *commercial television exists primarily as an advertising medium*. Programming surrounds the advertising, but it is the advertising that is being delivered to the audience. Commercial television, from its inception, was created to deliver audiences to advertisers.

Because television can deliver a larger audience faster than other mass media, television can charge higher rates than any other medium for its advertising—which makes TV stations rich investments. During a widely watched TV program like the 2013 Super Bowl (with an estimated audience of half the U.S. population and an even larger audience worldwide), a 30-second ad can cost as much as $3.8 million. Today, even the smallest independent television station is a multimillion-dollar operation. However, the television era began much more humbly, and with very little excitement, around the turn of the 20th century.

Visual Radio Becomes *Television*

The word *television* first appeared in the June 1907 issue of *Scientific American*. Before then, experiments in image transmission had been called "visual wireless," "visual radio" and "electric vision." Alexander Graham Bell's telephone and Samuel F. B. Morse's telegraph contributed to the idea of sending electrical impulses over long distances.

The first major technological discovery to suggest that pictures also could travel was the *Nipkow disk*. Twenty-four-year-old *Paul Nipkow* patented the Nipkow disk, which he called the "electrical telescope," in Germany in 1884. This disk, which formed the basis for television's development through the 1920s, was about the size of a phonograph record, perforated with a spiral of tiny holes.

Also crucial in television's (and radio's) development were *Guglielmo Marconi* and *Lee de Forest*. Marconi eliminated sound's dependence on wires and put sound on airwaves. De Forest contributed the Audion tube, which amplified radio waves so that people could hear the sound clearly.

In 1927, Secretary of Commerce Herbert Hoover appeared on a 2-inch screen by wire in an experimental AT&T broadcast. On September 11, 1928, General Electric broadcast the first dramatic production,

Epics/Hulton Archive/Getty Images

In 1939, RCA's David Sarnoff introduced TV at the 1939 New York World's Fair. Other manufacturers, including Emerson, followed, and television soon became an essential part of daily life.

"The Queen's Messenger"—the sound came over station WGY, in Schenectady, N.Y., and the picture came from experimental television station W2XAD. All the pictures were close-ups, and their quality could best be described as primitive.

Two researchers, one working for a company and one working alone, brought television into the electronic age. Then the same man who was responsible for radio's popularity, RCA's David Sarnoff, became television's biggest promoter.

Vladimir Zworykin was working for Westinghouse when he developed an all-electronic system to transform a visual image into an electronic signal that traveled through the air. When the signal reached the television receiver, the signal was transformed again into a visual image for the viewer.

Philo T. Farnsworth, working alone in California, developed the cathode ray tube (which he called a dissector tube). Farnsworth's cathode ray tube used an electronic scanner to reproduce the electronic image much more clearly than Nipkow's earlier mechanical scanning device. In 1930, 24-year-old Farnsworth patented his electronic scanner.

NBC television's commercial debut was at the 1939 World's Fair in New York City at the Hall of Television. On April 30, 1939, President Franklin D. Roosevelt formally opened the fair and became the first president to appear on television. Sarnoff also spoke, and RCA displayed its 5-inch and 9-inch sets, priced from $199.50 to $600 (equivalent to $2,950 to $8,870 in today's dollars).

NBC and CBS were the original TV networks. A *network* is a collection of radio or television stations that offers programs, usually simultaneously, throughout the country, during designated program times.

In 1943, ABC, the third major network, grew out of NBC's old Blue network. ABC labored from its earliest days to equal the other two networks but didn't have as many affiliates as NBC and CBS. The two leading networks already had secured the more powerful, well-established broadcast outlets for themselves. David Sarnoff and William Paley controlled the network game.

TELEVISION OUTPACES RADIO

By 1945, ten television stations were on the air in the United States. According to media historian Eric Barnouw, "By the late 1940s, television began its conquest of America. In 1949, the year began with radio drawing 81 percent of all broadcast audiences. By the year's end, television was grabbing 41 percent of the broadcast market. When audiences began experiencing the heady thrill of actually seeing as well as hearing events as they occurred, the superiority of television was established beyond doubt."

Black-and-white television replaced radio so quickly as the nation's major advertising medium that it would be easy to believe television erupted suddenly in a surprise move to kill radio. But remember that the two major corporate executives who developed television—Sarnoff and Paley—also held the country's largest interest in radio.

Network A collection of radio or TV stations that offers programs, usually simultaneously, throughout the country, during designated program times.

They used their profits from radio to develop television, foreseeing that television eventually would expand their audience and their income.

News with Pictures

Broadcast news, pioneered by radio, adapted awkwardly at first to the new broadcast medium—television. According to David Brinkley, a broadcast news pioneer who began at NBC, "When television came along in about 1947–1948, the big time newsmen of that day— H. V. Kaltenborn, Lowell Thomas—did not want to do television. It was a lot of work, they weren't used to it, they were doing very well in radio, making lots of money. They didn't want to fool with it. So I was told to do it by the news manager. I was a young kid and, as I say, the older, more established people didn't want to do it. Somebody had to."

In 1947, CBS launched *Television News with Douglas Edwards* and NBC broadcast *Camel News Caravan* (sponsored by Camel cigarettes) with John Cameron Swayze (see **Chapter 12**). Eventually, David Brinkley joined Swayze for NBC's 15-minute national newscast. He recalled, "The first broadcasts were extremely primitive by today's standards. It was mainly just sitting at a desk and talking. We didn't have any pictures at first. Later we began to get a little simple news film, but it wasn't much.

"In the beginning, people would call after a program and say in tones of amazement that they had seen you. 'I'm out here in Bethesda, and the picture's wonderful,'" Brinkley said. "They weren't interested in anything you said. They were just interested in the fact that you had been on their screen in their house."

At first, network TV news reached only the East Coast because there was no national hookup to deliver television across the country. By 1948, AT&T's coaxial cable linked Philadelphia with New York City and Washington, D.C. The 1948 political conventions were held in Philadelphia and broadcast to 13 eastern states. When the 1952 conventions were broadcast, AT&T's national coaxial hookups joined 108 stations across the country.

CBS had developed a strong group of radio reporters during World War II, and by 1950 many of them had moved to the new medium. CBS News also made a practice, more than the other networks, of using the same reporters for radio and television news. The major early news figure at CBS was Edward R. Murrow, who, along with David Brinkley at NBC, created the early standards for broadcast news. (See **Impact/Profile**, "Edward R. Murrow (1908–1965) Sets the Standard for Broadcast News," p. 157.)

IMPACT/Profile

Edward R. Murrow (1908–1965) Sets the Standard for Broadcast News

By Theodore H. White

Note: Edward R. Murrow had established a reputation for excellence as a CBS radio news broadcaster when he migrated to television news in 1951. In this profile, veteran journalist Theodore H. White outlines Murrow's broadcast career and its impact on television audiences.

It is so difficult to recapture the real Ed Murrow from the haze that now shrouds the mythical Ed Murrow of history.

Where other men may baffle friends with the infinite complexity of their natures, Ed was baffling otherwise. He was so straightforward, he would completely baffle the writers who now unravel the neuroses of today's demigods of television. When Ed was angry, he bristled; when he gave friendship, it came without withholding.

He could walk with prime ministers and movie stars, GIs and generals, as natural in rumpled GI suntans as in his diplomatic homburg. But jaunty or somber, to those of us who knew him he was just plain old Ed. In his shabby office at CBS cluttered with awards, you could loosen your necktie, put your feet up and yarn away. The dark, overhanging eyebrows would arch as he punctured pretension with a jab, the mouth would twist quizzically as he questioned. And then there were his poker games, as Ed sat master of the table, a cigarette dangling always from his lips—he smoked 60 or 70 a day—and called the bets.

Then—I can hear him now—there was the voice. Ed's deep and rhythmic voice was compelling, not only for its range, halfway between bass and baritone, but for the words that rolled from it. He wrote for the ear—with a

In the 1950s, Edward R. Murrow (right) established a very high standard for TV news. Murrow is shown here in 1950 with his long-time radio and television program producer Fred Friendly (left).

cadence of pauses and clipped, full sentences. His was an aural art but, in Ed, the art was natural—his inner ear composed a picture and, long before TV, the imagination of his listeners caught the sound and made with it their own picture.

We remember the voice. But there was so much more to Ed. He had not only a sense of the news but a sense of how the news fit into history. And this sense of the relation of news to history is what, in retrospect, made him the great pioneer of television journalism. . . .

He is very large now, for it was he who set the news system of television on its tracks, holding it, and his descendants, to the sense of history that give it still, in the schlock-storm of today, its sense of honor. Of Ed Murrow it may be said that he made all of us who clung to him, and cling to his memory still, feel larger than we really were.

Source: Excerpted from "When He Used the Power of TV, He Could Rouse Thunder," *TV Guide* 34, no. 3 (Jan. 18, 1986), pages 13–14. Reprinted by permission of Heyden White Rostow and David F. White.

The Honeymooners, which ran from 1955 to 1956 on CBS, is an early example of one of the most durable types of prime-time TV programming—the situation comedy (left to right: Jackie Gleason, Art Carney, Joyce Randolph and Audrey Meadows). *Big Bang Theory* is today's version of early topical TV sitcoms.

Public affairs programs like Murrow's *See It Now* continued to grow along with network news, and in 1956 NBC teamed David Brinkley with Chet Huntley to cover the political conventions. The chemistry worked, and after the convention, NBC put Huntley and Brinkley together to do the evening news, *The Huntley-Brinkley Report*. Brinkley often called himself "the other side of the hyphen."

Entertainment Programming

Early television entertainment also was the same as radio with pictures: It offered variety shows, situation comedies, drama, Westerns, detective stories, Hollywood movies, soap operas and quiz shows. The only type of show television offered that radio did not (besides movies, of course) was the talk show. (However, radio eventually created call-in programs, radio's version of the TV talk show.)

VARIETY SHOWS. The best radio stars jumped to the new medium. Three big variety show successes were Milton Berle's *Texaco Star Theater, The Admiral*

Prime Time The TV time period from 7 to 11 p.m. when more people watch TV than at any other time.

Situation Comedy A TV program that establishes a regular cast of characters typically in a home or work situation. Also called a sitcom.

Broadway Revue (later *Your Show of Shows*) with Imogene Coca and Sid Caesar, and Ed Sullivan's *Toast of the Town* (later *The Ed Sullivan Show*). These weekly shows featured comedy sketches and appearances by popular entertainers. *The Ed Sullivan Show*, for example, is where most Americans got their first glimpse of Elvis Presley and the Beatles. All of the shows were done live.

The time slot in which these programs were broadcast, 7 to 11 p.m., is known as ***prime time***. Prime time simply means that more people watch television during this period than any other, so advertising during this period costs more. Berle's 8 p.m. program on Tuesday nights often gathered 85 percent of the audience. *Texaco Star Theater* became so popular that one Laundromat installed a TV set and advertised, "Watch Berle while your clothes twirl."

SITUATION COMEDIES. Along with drama, the ***situation comedy*** (sitcom) proved to be one of TV's most durable types of programs. The situation comedy established a regular set of characters in either a home or work situation. *I Love Lucy*, starring Lucille Ball and Desi Arnaz, originated from Los Angeles because the actors wanted to live on the West Coast. In 1951, Ball began a career as a weekly performer on CBS that lasted for 23 years.

In 1955, Jackie Gleason launched *The Honeymooners*, a show based on his childhood experiences growing up in New York. *The Honeymooners* was only on for two years, but Gleason maintained the characters and featured them in skits on his variety program, *The Jackie Gleason Show*, beginning in 1961.

In 1960, CBS launched *The Andy Griffith Show*, which followed the adventures of widower and Mayberry sheriff Andy Taylor, who was raising his young son. It ran for eight seasons and is still shown today on the TV Land cable television network. *Modern Family* and *Portlandia* are examples of current situation comedy successes.

DRAMA. *The Loretta Young Show* offered noontime drama—broadcast live—every day in the 1950s. *The Hallmark Hall of Fame* established a tradition for high-quality, live dramatic presentations. For many years, TV dramas were limited to one- or two-hour programs. But in the 1970s, encouraged by the success of Alex Haley's *Roots*, which dramatized Haley's search for the story of his African ancestry, television began to broadcast as many as 14 hours of a single drama over several nights. Today, the series *The Good Wife* is an example of a popular prime-time drama.

WESTERNS. TV went Western in 1954, when Jack Warner of Warner Bros. signed an agreement with ABC to provide the network with a program called *Cheyenne*. The outspoken Warner had openly criticized TV's effect on the movie business, but when ABC asked Warner to produce programs for them, Warner Bros. became the first movie company to realize that the studios could profit from television.

DETECTIVE STORIES. *Dragnet*, with Sergeant Friday, was an early TV experiment with detectives, starting in 1951 and running for eight seasons. The genre became a TV staple: *Dragnet*'s successors today are programs like *CSI*.

MOVIES. The movie industry initially resisted the competition from TV, but then it realized there was money to be made in selling old movies to TV. In 1957, RKO sold 740 pre-1948 movies to television for $25 million. The other studios followed. Through various distribution agreements, movie reruns and movies produced specifically for television were added to television's program lineup.

SOAP OPERAS. Borrowed from radio serials, soap operas filled morning television programming. Today, game shows and reruns are more popular choices, but some soaps still survive. Soap operas have their own magazines, and some newspapers carry weekly summaries of plot development. Soap operas (*telenovelas*) also are an important feature of today's Spanish-language television.

TALK SHOWS. Sylvester "Pat" Weaver (actress Sigourney Weaver's father) created and produced television's single original contribution to programming: the talk show. Weaver's *Tonight Show* (originally *Jerry Lester's Broadway Open House*) first appeared in 1954. Through a succession of hosts from Lester to Steve Allen to Jack Paar to Johnny Carson to Jay Leno and (announced for 2014) Jimmy Fallon, *The Tonight Show* has lasted longer than any other talk show on television. Another modern-day successor of the late-night talk show format is, of course, David Letterman.

Trae Patton/NBC/Getty Images

The talk show is a very profitable TV program format. NBC announced in 2013 that Jimmy Fallon (right) will succeed current *Tonight Show* host Jay Leno in 2014. *The Tonight Show*, which has been on the air since 1954, is TV's longest-running late night talk show.

QUIZ SHOWS. In the mid-1950s, all three TV networks introduced quiz shows, on which contestants competed with each other for big-money prizes. Soon, the quiz shows were mired in controversy because of charges that the contestants had been given answers.

Quiz Shows Bring Ethics Scandals

Sponsored by Revlon, CBS's *$64,000 Question* premiered June 7, 1955. Contestants answered questions from a glass "isolation booth." Successful contestants returned in succeeding weeks to increase their winnings, and Revlon advertised its Living Lipstick. By September, the program was drawing 85 percent of the audience, and Revlon had to substitute an ad for another product because its factory supply of Living Lipstick had completely sold out.

As the most popular quiz show on early television, *$64,000 Question* engendered imitation: *Treasure Hunt, Giant Step* and *Twenty-One*. Winnings grew beyond the $64,000 limit; Charles Van Doren won $129,000 on *Twenty-One*. In the fall of 1955, CBS replaced Murrow's *See It Now* with a quiz program.

Sponsors produced many network quiz shows like *$64,000 Question* for the networks, and these programs usually carried the sponsor's name. In the 1958–1959 quiz show scandals, Revlon was implicated when a congressional subcommittee investigated charges that the quiz shows were rigged to enhance the ratings. Charles Van Doren admitted before the subcommittee that *Twenty-One*'s producer had fed him the answers. Staff members from other quiz shows confirmed Van Doren's testimony.

The quiz show scandals caused the networks to reexamine the relationship between advertisers and

Charles Van Doren (far left) won $129,000 on the quiz show *Twenty-One*, facing contestant Herb Stempel (far right). Contestants appeared in isolation booths, allegedly to keep them from hearing quiz answers from the audience. Van Doren and Stempel, who were fed answers beforehand by the show's producers, were central figures in the 1950s quiz show ethics scandals.

Rating The percentage of the total number of households *with TV sets* tuned to a particular program.

Share The percentage of the audience *with TV sets turned on* that is watching a particular program.

Sweeps The months when TV ratings services gather their most important ratings—February, May and November.

programs. Before the scandals, advertisers and their agencies produced one-quarter to one-third of network programming. As a result of the quiz show scandals, the networks turned to other sources, such as independent producers, for their programming.

By the late 1960s, advertisers provided less than 3 percent of network programming, and soon advertisers provided no network shows. The networks programmed themselves. They also used reruns of newly acquired studio movies to replace the quiz shows, but quiz shows resurfaced in 1983 with *Wheel of Fortune* and, in the 1990s, *Who Wants to Be a Millionaire?*

RATINGS TARGET THE AUDIENCE

After the quiz show scandals, the networks were criticized for being motivated only by ratings. Ratings give sponsors information about the audience they're reaching with their advertising—what advertisers are getting for their money.

By the late 1950s, The Nielsen Company dominated the television ratings business. The national Nielsen ratings describe the audience to advertisers; based on the Nielsens, advertisers pay for the commercial time to reach the audiences they want.

Today, Nielsen provides two types of numbers, known as rating and share. The *rating* is a percentage of the total number of households with television sets. If there are 95 million homes with TV sets, for example, the rating shows the percentage of those sets that were tuned in to a specific program. The share (an abbreviation for share-of-audience) compares the audience for one show with the audience for another. *Share* means the percentage of the audience with TV sets turned on that is watching each program.

For example, if TV sets in 50 million homes were turned on at 8 p.m. on Friday night, and 25 million homes were tuned to Program A, that program would have a rating of 26 (25 million divided by 95 million, expressed as a percentage) and a share of 50. (See **Illustration 8.2**, "What Do TV Ratings Mean for Advertisers?," p. 161.)

The most concentrated ratings periods for local stations are "sweeps" months—February, May and November. (Ratings are taken in July, too, but the numbers are not considered accurate because so many people are on vacation.) The sweeps provide an estimate of the local TV audience, and advertisers use that information when they decide where to place their commercials.

Sweeps are the months when the ratings services gather their most important ratings, so the networks and local stations often use these important months to

IMPACT/Money

Illustration 8.2

What Do TV Ratings Mean for Advertisers?

A TV program's rating determines how much a TV network or station can charge for an ad. Suppose that at 8 p.m. on Friday TVs are on in 50 million out of 95 million households and that 25 million TVs are tuned to Program A. Program A's rating is 26, meaning 26 percent of all TV households are tuned to Program A. Program A's share is 50, meaning that 50 percent of the total number of TV households watching TV are watching Program A.

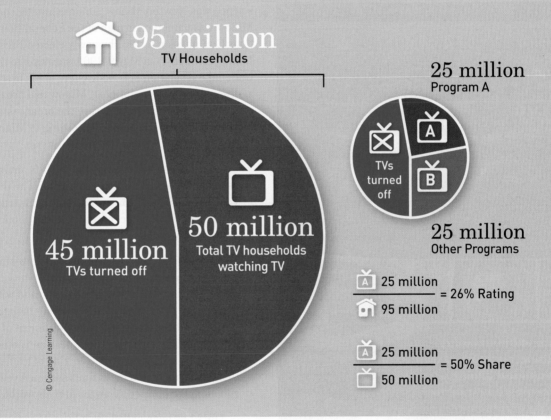

95 million
TV Households

45 million
TVs turned off

50 million
Total TV households
watching TV

© Cengage Learning

25 million
Program A

TVs
turned
off

A

B

25 million
Other Programs

$$\frac{A \quad 25 \text{ million}}{\text{🏠} \quad 95 \text{ million}} = 26\% \text{ Rating}$$

$$\frac{A \quad 25 \text{ million}}{\text{📺} \quad 50 \text{ million}} = 50\% \text{ Share}$$

showcase their best programs. This is when you are most likely to see a new one-hour episode of a popular series, for example, or a lavishly produced made-for-TV movie.

Today's Nielsen ratings work essentially the same as they did in the 1950s, except that the Nielsens now deliver very specific information on *demographics*— age, occupation and income, for instance—and Nielsen can deliver daily ratings information to any client willing to pay for it.

In 2007, The Nielsen Company expanded its tracking service to count people who watch TV outside the home, in places like bars, restaurants, airports, offices and retail stores. Nielsen also then announced in 2013 that it will track mobile viewing. "Nielsen has a mandate to follow the video wherever it goes," said Sara Erichson, executive vice president for client services at Nielsen Media Research North American.

Demographics Data about consumers' characteristics, such as age, occupation and income level.

Advertisers use this ratings information to target their most likely consumers. Nike shoes might create a new advertising campaign for the Super Bowl, for instance, and Nielsen could tell Nike, judging from previous Super Bowls, the projected demographics of the people who watch the game.

Criticism about the ratings persists. The main flaw today, critics contend, is the way the broadcast community religiously follows and uses ratings to determine programming.

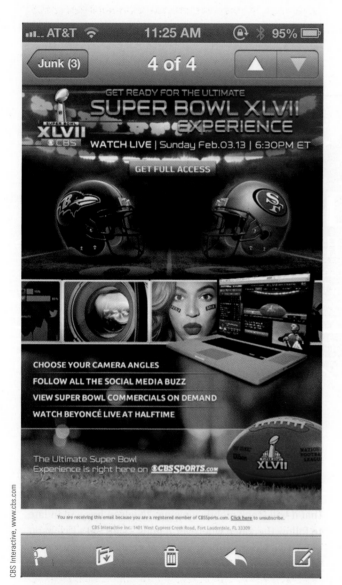

Live sports events are among the most profitable types of TV programming today because of their high audience ratings. In 2013, CBS Sports used an interactive Web site to promote Super Bowl XLVII.

Newton Minow Criticizes TV as a "Vast Wasteland"

The 1950s were a trial period for television, as the networks and advertisers tested audience interest in various types of programming. Captured by the miracle that television offered, at first audiences seemed insatiable; they watched almost anything that TV delivered. But in the 1960s, audiences became more discriminating and began to question how well the medium of television was serving the public.

Once it established itself throughout the country, television needed a public conscience. That public conscience was Newton Minow. An unassuming soothsayer, Minow was named chairman of the Federal Communications Commission in 1961 by newly elected President John F. Kennedy. On May 9, 1961, speaking to the National Association of Broadcasters in his first public address since his appointment, Minow told broadcast executives what he believed were the broadcasters' responsibilities to the public. According to Minow, in his book *Equal Time*, he told the broadcasters:

Your license lets you use the public's airwaves as trustees for 180 million Americans. The public is your beneficiary. If you want to stay on as trustees, you must deliver a decent return to the public— not only to your stockholders. . . .

Your industry possesses the most powerful voice in America. It has an inescapable duty to make that voice ring with intelligence and with leadership. In a few years this exciting industry has grown from a novelty to an instrument of overwhelming impact on the American people. It should be making ready for the kind of leadership that newspapers and magazines assumed years ago, to make our people aware of their world.

Ours has been called the jet age, the atomic age, the space age. It is also, I submit, the television age. And just as history will decide whether the leaders of today's world employed the atom to destroy the world or rebuild it for mankind's benefit, so will history decide whether today's broadcasters employed their powerful voice to enrich the people or debase them.

Minow then asked his audience of broadcast station owners and managers to watch their own programs. He said that they would find a "vast wasteland," a phrase that resurfaces today during any critical discussion of television.

PUBLIC TELEVISION FINDS AN AUDIENCE

The concept of educational television has been alive since the 1950s, when a few noncommercial stations succeeded in regularly presenting public service programs without advertisements, but the shows were low budget.

The educational network NET (National Educational Television) emerged in 1963 to provide some national programming (about ten hours a week), sponsored mainly by foundations, with some federal support. Then in 1967, the Ford Foundation agreed to help pay for several hours of live evening programming.

Also in 1967, the Carnegie Commission on Educational Television released its report *Public Television: A Program for Action*, which included a proposal to create the Corporation for Public Broadcasting (CPB). CPB would collect money from many sources—including the enhanced federal funds the Carnegie report suggested—and disburse the money to the stations.

President Lyndon Johnson's administration and several foundations added money to CPB's budget. The Public Broadcasting Service (PBS) was created to distribute programs. The extra money underwrote the creation of programs like *Sesame Street* and *The French Chef. PBS Newshour* became a weeknight staple. PBS also began to buy successful British television programs, which were

broadcast on *Masterpiece Theatre*. PBS programs actually started to show up in the ratings.

In 1995, members of Congress called for the "privatization" of public television, with the idea that eventually PBS would become completely self-sustaining. Today, the CPB, which oversees public television, still receives funding from the federal government. Local funding supplements this government underwriting, but within the past ten years, public donations to public television have been declining. This decline in funding has led public broadcasters to seek underwriting from more corporate donors, but companies accustomed to advertising on commercial networks are reluctant to advertise on a network that commonly attracts less than 3 percent of the national audience.

For the first time, public television began to pay attention to ratings. This attention to an audience of consumers means the pressure is building on public television executives to make each program profitable.

The FCC began liberalizing its rules for commercial announcements on public television in 1981. Now, corporate sponsors often make announcements, including graphics and video, at the beginning and the end of PBS-produced programs. The announcements often look the same as advertisements on commercial television. Critics of this commercialization of public television are calling for more government funding, but Congress seems unwilling to expand its underwriting. Today, public television is continuing to reinvent itself to compete for an audience.

SATELLITES MAKE TRANSATLANTIC TV AND LIVE BROADCASTS POSSIBLE

On July 10, 1962, *Telstar I* sent the first transatlantic satellite broadcast. Before *Telstar*, copper cable linked the continents, film footage from overseas traveled only by plane, and in most homes a long-distance telephone call was a special event. Today, *Telstar*'s descendants orbit at a distance of more than 22,000 miles. A single modern communication satellite can carry more than 30,000 telephone calls and three television channels. (Modern satellites make program services like CNN and satellite systems like DirecTV possible.)

By 1965, all three networks were broadcasting in color. Television demonstrated its technological sophistication in December 1968 with its live broadcast from the *Apollo* spacecraft while the spacecraft circled the moon, and seven months later television showed Neil Armstrong stepping onto the moon.

Slaven Vlasic/Getty Images

PBS began broadcasting as National Educational Television in 1963. Today *The PBS Newshour* provides an hour-long evening news broadcast, featuring Judy Woodruff, as an alternative to the traditional TV network evening news. PBS receives some government funding but relies mainly on private donations and corporate sponsors.

In 1962, technicians readied the *Telstar I* communications satellite for launch. *Telstar I* enabled the first transatlantic satellite broadcast. Today's modern satellites, the successors to *Telstar I*, make television delivery systems like DirecTV possible.

TELEVISION CHANGES NATIONAL POLITICS

Just as radio was first an entertainment medium and then expanded to cover important news events, television first established itself with entertainment and then developed a serious news presence. Franklin D. Roosevelt had been the first president to understand and use radio, and John F. Kennedy became the country's first television president. Some of Kennedy's predecessors had appeared on television, but he instinctively knew how to *use* television to promote his agenda.

Observers attributed Kennedy's 1960 presidential victory partly to his success in the televised presidential debates with Richard Nixon. Kennedy also was the first president to hold live televised news conferences. In July 1962, he oversaw the launch of the first communications satellite, *Telstar I*. One year later news organizations used that same satellite technology to broadcast live coverage of the news events following President Kennedy's assassination on November 22, 1963.

Television received credit for uniting the nation with its news coverage of the Kennedy assassination, but it also was blamed for dividing it. President Lyndon Johnson, beleaguered by an unpopular war in Vietnam, used television to make an announcement to the nation in 1968 that he would not run for a second term.

Johnson's successor, President Richard Nixon, had always been uncomfortable with the press. The Nixon administration often attacked the press for presenting perspectives on world affairs that the administration did not like. Upset with the messages being presented, the Nixon administration battled the messenger, sparking a bitter public debate about the role of a free press (especially television) in a democratic society.

Ironically, television's next live marathon broadcast chronicled the ongoing investigation of the Nixon presidency—Watergate. The Watergate scandal began when burglars broke into the offices of the Democratic Party's national headquarters in the Watergate complex in Washington, D.C., on June 17, 1972. Some of the burglars had ties to President Nixon's reelection committee as well as to other questionable activities originating in the White House.

In the months following the break-in, the president and his assistants sought to squelch the resulting investigation. Although Nixon denied knowledge of the break-in and the cover-up, the U.S. Senate hearings about the scandal, televised live across the country, created a national sensation. (See also **Chapter 12**.) Eventually, faced with the prospect of impeachment, Nixon announced his resignation on television on August 8, 1974.

In 1987, television repeated its marathon coverage of an important national investigation with the Iran-Contra hearings, a congressional investigation of the Reagan administration's role in illegally selling weapons to Iran and using the money to secretly finance Nicaraguan rebels, called contras.

Originally a very small part of television programming, television news today gives audiences access to 24-hour coverage of global events, such as the devastation caused by Hurricane Sandy in October 2012 on the nation's East Coast.

TV News Images Bring Global Events into View

Television news has matured from its early beginnings as a 15-minute newscast to today's 24-hour international coverage of events around the world.

On September 11, 2001, U.S. TV network news offered nonstop coverage of the terrorist events at New York's World Trade Center, the Pentagon and in rural Pennsylvania. Two years later, TV networks brought viewers even closer to events when TV reporters and photographers sent live battlefield images and stories during the Iraq War.

And in October 2012, news coverage of Hurricane Sandy on the nation's East Coast shared the storm's devastating damage with a worldwide audience. National events instantly become global events because of TV's international reach.

Television at Work

A typical television station has eight departments:

1. Sales
2. Programming (which includes news as well as entertainment)
3. Production
4. Engineering
5. Traffic
6. Promotion
7. Public affairs
8. Administration.

People in the *sales* department sell the commercial slots for the programs. Advertising is divided into national and local sales. Advertising agencies, usually based on the East Coast, buy national ads for the products they handle. An ad agency may buy time on a network for the Ford Motor Company, for instance, for a TV ad that will run simultaneously all over the country.

But local Ford dealers, who want you to shop at their showroom, buy their ads directly from the local station. These ads are called local (or spot) ads. For these sales, salespeople (called account executives) at each station negotiate packages of ads based on their station's advertising rates. These rates are a direct reflection of the station's position in the ratings.

The *programming* department selects the shows that you will see and develops the station's schedule. Network-owned stations, usually located in big cities (KNBC in Los Angeles, for example), are called *O & Os*, which stands for "owned and operated." O & Os automatically carry network programming. *Affiliates* are stations that carry network programming but are not owned by the networks. The networks pay affiliates to carry their programming, for which the networks sell most of the ads and keep the money. An affiliate is allowed to insert into the network programming a specific number of local ads, for which the affiliate keeps the income.

Because affiliates can make money on network programming and don't have to pay for it, many stations choose to affiliate themselves with a network. When they aren't running what the network provides, affiliates run their own programs and keep all the advertising money they collect from them.

Some of the nation's commercial TV stations operate as independents. Independent stations must buy and program all their own shows, but independents also keep all the money they make on advertising. Independents run some individually produced programs and old movies, but most of their programming consists of reruns such as *I Love Lucy* and *Cheers* that once ran on the networks. Independents buy these reruns from program services called *syndicators*.

Syndicators also sell independently produced programs such as *The Oprah Winfrey Show*. Independent programs are created and sold either by non-network stations or by independent producers. Stations pay for these first-run syndication programs individually; the price is based on the size of the station's market.

Local news usually makes up the largest percentage of a station's locally produced programming. In some large markets, such as Los Angeles, local news programming runs as long as two hours.

The *production* department manages the programs the station creates in-house. This department also produces local commercials for the station. The *engineering* department makes sure all the technical aspects of a broadcast operation are working: antennas, transmitters, cameras and any other broadcast equipment. The *traffic* department integrates the advertising with the programming, making sure that all the ads that are sold are aired when they're supposed to be. Traffic also handles billing for the ads.

O & Os   TV stations that are owned and operated by the networks.

Affiliates   Stations that use network programming but are owned by companies other than the networks.

Syndicators   Services that sell programming to broadcast stations and cable.

The *promotion* department advertises the station—on the station itself, on billboards, on radio and in the local newspaper. These people also create contests to keep the station visible in the community. The *public affairs* department helps organize public events, such as a fun run to raise money for the local hospital. *Administration* handles the paperwork for the station—paychecks and expense accounts, for example.

AUDIENCES DRIVE TV PROGRAMMING

Today's most-watched television programs are situation comedies, sports and feature movies. More than 120 million people tuned in for the final episode of the situation comedy *M*A*S*H* in 1983, making it the highest-rated television program ever. In 1993, the final episode of the sitcom *Cheers* garnered an audience of 80 million. Super Bowls generally grab about half the homes in the United States. In 2008, the surprise ratings leader was President-elect Barack Obama. More than 70 million people watched his election victory the night of November 4, 2008, a record number of viewers for a presidential election night.

Six developments promise to affect the television industry over the next decade: station ownership changes, the shrinking role of the networks, the accuracy of ratings, the growth of cable and satellite delivery, the profitability of sports programming and the growing audience for Spanish-language TV.

Station Ownership Changes and Mergers

The Telecommunications Act of 1996 (see **Chapter 14**) used a station's potential audience to measure ownership limits. The Act allowed one company to own TV stations that reach up to 35 percent of the nation's homes. Broadcasters also are no longer required, as they once were, to hold onto a station for three years before selling it. Today, stations may be sold as soon as they are purchased.

In 1999, the Federal Communications Commission (FCC) adopted new regulations that allow media companies to own two TV stations in one market, as long as eight separately owned TV stations continue to operate in that market after the merger. The rules said the four top-rated stations in one market cannot be combined under the same ownership, but a station that is among the four top-rated stations can combine with one that is not in the top four.

In 2003, the FCC relaxed ownership rules even further, leaving few restrictions on network ownership. As with radio, fewer companies are putting together larger and larger groups of TV stations. Today, most local TV stations are not owned by local companies, as they once were. Television is *concentrating* ownership, but it is also *shifting* ownership, as stations are bought and sold at an unprecedented rate. This has introduced instability and change to an industry that until 1980 witnessed very few ownership turnovers.

The Networks' Shrinking Role

Advertisers always have provided the economic support for television, so in 1986 the networks were disturbed to see the first decline in advertising revenues in 15 years. New and continuing developments—such as cable, satellite broadcast, DVDs, streaming—have turned the television set into a smorgasbord of choices. Audiences—and advertisers—began to desert the networks, and network ratings declined as a result.

Today, because there are so many sources of TV programming available, even the most popular shows attract a relatively small percentage of the overall audience. (See **Impact/Convergence**, "Broadcasters Worry About 'Zero TV' Homes Migrating to the Internet," p. 167.)

The networks' share of the audience for the evening news also is shrinking. The story is familiar, paralleling the decline in radio listening in the late 1940s when television first replaced radio and then television began competing with itself. Today more stations and more sources of programming mean the TV networks must expand their audience beyond the traditional prime-time evening time slot to stay profitable.

How Accurate Are TV Ratings?

People meters, first used in 1987 by The Nielsen Company to record television viewing, gather data through a 4-inch-by-10-inch box that sits on the television set in metered homes. People meters monitor the nation's Nielsen families (about 4,000 of them, which Nielsen says are a cross section of American viewers), and the results of these recorded viewing patterns are the ratings that establish the basis for television advertising rates.

Nielsen family members each push an assigned button in the set-top box when they begin to watch television. The system's central computer, linked to the home by telephone lines, correlates each viewer's number with information about that person stored in its memory.

Network ratings have plunged since people meters were introduced as a ratings system, and the networks complain that the people meters underestimate specific audiences, especially African Americans and Latinos. Still, Nielsen is the only company in the United States offering TV audience measurement.

IMPACT/Convergence

Broadcasters Worry About "Zero TV" Homes Migrating to the Internet

By Ryan Nakashima, Associated Press

Some people have had it with TV. They've had enough of the 100-plus-channel universe. They don't like timing their lives around network show schedules. They're tired of $100-plus monthly bills.

A growing number of them have stopped paying for cable and satellite TV service, and don't even use an antenna to get free signals over the air. These people are watching shows and movies on the Internet, sometimes via cell phone connections. Last month, the Nielsen Co. started labeling people in this group "Zero TV" households, because they fall outside the traditional definition of a TV home. There are 5 million of these residences in the U.S., up from 2 million in 2007.

While show creators and networks make money from this group's viewing habits through deals with online video providers and from advertising on their own Web sites and apps, broadcasters only get paid when they relay such programming in traditional ways. Unless broadcasters can adapt to modern platforms, their revenue from Zero TV viewers will be zero.

The Zero TV segment is increasingly important, because the number of people signing up for traditional TV service has slowed to a standstill in the U.S. Last year, the cable, satellite and telecoms providers added just 46,000 video customers collectively, according to research firm SNL Kagan.

Nielsen's study suggests that this new group may have left traditional TV for good. While three-quarters actually have a physical TV set, only 18 percent are interested in hooking it up through a traditional pay TV subscription.

Zero TVers tend to be younger, single and without children. Then there are the "cord-nevers," young people who move out on their own

Simon Bruty/Sports Illustrated/Getty Images

Michigan college basketball players Tim Hardaway, Jr. (foreground), and Jon Horford, use iPads to watch a rerun of the 2013 NCAA playoff game in which he played the night before. Hardaway is an example of what the Nielsen Ratings Company calls the Zero TV audience. Currently about 5 percent of the U.S. population, these people have no need for a traditional TV and instead watch programming on computers, tablets and mobile phones.

and never set up a landline phone connection or a TV subscription. They usually make do with a broadband Internet connection, a computer, a cell phone and possibly a TV set that is not hooked up the traditional way.

That brings us to truck driver James Weitze. The 31-year-old satisfies his video fix with an iPhone. He often sleeps in his truck, and has no apartment. To be sure, he's an extreme case who doesn't fit into Nielsen's definition of a household in the first place. But he's so divorced from the traditional TV ecosystem it could be hard to go back. It's become easier for him to navigate his smartphone than to figure out how to use a TV set-top box and the button-laden remote control.

"I'm pretty tech savvy, but the TV industry with the cable and the television and the boxes, you don't know how to use their equipment," he says. "I try to go over to my grandma's place and teach her how to do it. I can't even figure it out myself."

Source: Excerpted from Ryan Nakashima, "Broadcasters Worry about 'Zero TV' Homes," Associated Press, April 7, 2013. Retrieved from sacbee.com.

Cable and Satellite Delivery

Today's cable giants, ESPN (Entertainment and Sports Programming Network) and CNN, are descendants of America's first cable TV system, which was established in Pennsylvania and Oregon to bring TV signals to rural areas that couldn't receive an over-the-air signal. Soon, this community antenna television (*CATV*) system spread to remote areas all over the country where TV reception was poor.

By 1970, there were 2,500 CATV systems in the United States, and commercial broadcasters were getting nervous about what they called "wired TV." Cable operators were required by the FCC to carry all local broadcast programming, and programs often were duplicated on several channels. The FCC also limited the programs that cable could carry. One FCC ruling, for example, said that movies on cable had to be at least ten years old.

Believing that cable should be able to offer its own programming, Home Box Office (owned by Time Warner) started operating in Manhattan in 1972, offering a modest set of programs. Ted Turner's Turner Network Television (TNT) first relayed programs by satellite in 1976, and in 1979 Turner started Cable News Network (CNN). Today, more than 125 different program services, ranging from ESPN to 1930s and 1940s movies on American Movie Classics (AMC), are available by satellite.

Cable television as an alternative to the traditional networks moved to the center of the national news agenda in 1991 when CNN offered 24-hour coverage of the Gulf War in Iraq. CNN's fast response to world events underlined the new global role that CNN and many other cable companies will play in future television developments.

In 1982, the FCC authorized direct broadcast satellite (*DBS*), making direct satellite-to-home satellite broadcasts possible. In 1994, a company called DirecTV began offering services directly to the home by satellite for a monthly fee that is about the same as cable. Cable and satellite program delivery systems now are collectively called *subscription television* services.

Cable and satellite programming, which divides viewers into smaller segments than the networks, makes it easier for advertisers to target a specific audience.

CATV Community antenna television or cable television.

DBS Direct broadcast satellite.

Subscription Television A new term used to describe consumer services delivered by cable and satellite program delivery.

Programs like National Geographic's *The Dog Whisperer* starring Cesar Millan, for instance, bring dog lovers to any advertiser that wants to sell dog-related products. And the award-winning *Mad Men* series, which has run for seven seasons on AMC, has made the once-obscure channel very successful because of the upscale audience the program attracts.

Today, the number of satellite and cable subscribers has stopped growing because of the cost to subscribe and because many popular cable and satellite programs are available on the Internet.

Alberto E. Rodriguez/Getty Images

Cable channels began offering their own programming, separate from the traditional TV networks, in 1972. Today, more than 125 program services, including AMC, offer original programming via cable and satellite. The award-winning *Mad Men* on AMC is an example of successful original programming produced outside the traditional TV networks.

TV Changes Professional Sports

One of the most profitable types of television programming is sports because most sports programs are live events, and viewers tend to watch the entire program, including commercials. In 1964, CBS paid $28 million for television rights to the 1964–1965 National Football League (NFL) games. In 1990, the networks paid $3.6 billion to broadcast NFL football. In 2012, ESPN (owned by the Walt Disney Company) spent $5.6 billion for an eight-year contract to carry Major League Baseball on ESPN as well as radio, international and digital rights to the games.

Television fees fund most of the cost of organized sports today. Televised sports have become spectacularly complex entertainment packages, turning professional and college athletes as well as sports commentators into media stars. The expansion of sports programming beyond the networks to cable channels such as ESPN means even more sports programming choices for viewers and big pay-offs for American sports teams.

Spanish-Language Television Brings a New Audience

During the summer of 2005, Univision, the nation's largest Spanish-language network, drew more prime-time viewers in the 18–34 age group than all the traditional broadcast networks—NBC, CBS, ABC and Fox. This was the first time Spanish-language TV had surpassed the networks, and the main draw was *telenovelas*, or soap operas in Spanish.

This Spanish-language lead in prime time had been building for several years, as the nation's Latino population increased. According to *The New York Times*: "Market researchers say that Latinos—no matter their age or dominant language—tend to tune in to Spanish-language television for two main staples: newscasts, because networks like Univision and Telemundo cover Latino issues and Latin America with more breadth and resources than English-language networks, and telenovelas, which function like a kind of cultural touchstone.

"Whether you're U.S.-born and you're introduced to it by a parent or grandparent or whether you're foreign-born and you grew up with it, it's the kind of thing that's inherent in the culture," multicultural marketing consultant Derene Allen told the *Times*. "It's as Mexican as eating tortillas and as Venezuelan or Colombian as eating arepas."

As traditional audiences shrink, and advertisers try to find new ways to sell their products, Spanish-language TV is emerging as one of the few promising markets for new programming. In 2013, Univision and the Walt Disney Company announced the creation of a new 24-hour news and entertainment channel called Fusion, aimed specifically at English-speaking Latinos.

DIGITAL TECHNOLOGY EXPANDS TV'S FOCUS

When technological developments move like a rocket, as they have in the past decade, program delivery becomes easier and less expensive. New technologies have brought more competition. Several new delivery systems have been developed to bring more choices to consumers

Ralph Hagen/CartoonStock.com

IT'S A PROGRAM ON CONSERVING ENERGY.

than ever before—from the size of the screen to the clarity of the picture—and to change further the way people use television.

Digital Video Recorders

Digital video recorders (*DVRs*) download programming, using a set-top box that looks like a cable box and sits on or near the TV. DVRs use electronic storage to receive information from any program service (including the broadcast networks and satellite and cable programmers) to send viewers up-to-date information about what's on TV. DVRs transfer the information to an on-screen program guide, where viewers can decide what to watch and when, a practice called *time-shifting*.

One of the biggest features of a DVR is that it allows viewers to press the pause button during a show they're watching, leave the TV set on and then resume the program when they return or fast-forward through the recorded portion. DVRs change viewers' control over which programming they watch (and, most importantly, which commercials, if any).

"Although the DVR is a blessing for couch potatoes, it is more of a mixed blessing for the television industry," reports the *Los Angeles Times*. "The downside is that although DVRs enable viewers to catch shows they might otherwise miss, if someone is watching a recorded program it means they are not watching live TV.

DVR   Digital video recorders.

Time-Shifting   Recording a television program on a DVR to watch at a more convenient time.

"Networks still put great effort into designing lineups that will keep viewers tuned in to live TV. DVRs and other platforms have the potential to blow traditional viewing habits out of the water.

"And if viewers are using their DVRs more to watch TV, it also means they can easily skip through commercials, which has many advertisers worried."

High-Definition Television

A traditional television picture scans 525 lines across the screen. *High-definition television (HDTV)* scans at least 1,125 lines. CBS first demonstrated HDTV in the United States in 1982. HDTV, which offers a wider, sharper digital picture and better sound, requires more spectrum space than conventional television signals.

Digital TV also makes it easier for manufacturers to combine the functions of TV and the functions of a computer in the same piece of equipment. HDTV became the national industry standard in 2009.

Video Streaming and 3-D TV

In September 2010, Apple announced a push into the television market with Apple TV, a new device that uses video streaming and allows people to rent TV shows over the Internet for 99 cents each. Fox and Walt Disney make their shows available the day after they are broadcast over the air. The service requires users to buy a $99 Apple TV box, and Apple TV was called an "elementary effort" by Apple to enter the television business. Still, this is one more outlet for broadcast programming that wasn't available before and TV program downloads already are available on Apple's other devices, such as the iPad and the iPhone, and through iTunes.

In 2010 major television manufacturers started selling 3-D TVs, and several programmers announced plans to create 3-D shows to feed the new market. "Now that almost two-thirds of American homes have ditched their old tube televisions for flat-screens and high-definition sets, TV makers are trying to lure consumers back into the stores for the next big thing—3-D TV," reports *The New York Times*.

To see most 3-D television, consumers must have a 3-D set ($2,300), 3-D glasses ($150 each) and a special 3-D receiver box, although Toshiba announced plans to sell a

3-D TV that didn't require special glasses. Still, the cost for consumers is a barrier to the new technology, especially since many households have just absorbed the cost of their new HD sets. So far, 3-D TV accounts for less than 2 percent of new television sales in the United States.

TELEVISION OFFERS A NEW VISION

Forecasts for the future of television parallel the forecasts for radio—a menu board of hundreds of programs and services available to viewers at the touch of a remote-control button. In the 1990s, regional telephone companies (abbreviated as *telcos*) rushed to merge with cable TV companies to form giant telecommunications delivery systems.

To try to maintain their audience dominance, the TV networks have invested heavily in satellite TV and Internet program services to develop the capability to deliver programs to screens as small as a cell phone, and these new financial powerhouses can spend large sums of money for research to reach the audiences they want.

David Becker/Getty Images News/Getty Images

In 2013, Samsung previewed its new 84-inch Smart TV at the Consumer Electronics Show in Las Vegas. The touch-screen technology is interactive and offers access to broadcast and Internet programming services all on one screen.

High-Definition Television (HDTV)   The industry standard for digital television transmission as of 2009; it provides a picture with a clearer resolution than earlier TV sets.

Telcos   An abbreviation for "telephone company."

In 2006, when Congress passed a law that required TV broadcasters to switch totally to digital signals by 2009, only about 60 percent of U.S. households were capable of receiving a digital TV signal, according to the Consumer Electronics Association. Broadcasters resisted the 2009 deadline because they were afraid they would lose part of their audience—people without a digital TV—but the conversion happened without any major problems. Today, digital television is the new national standard. Television audiences seem to welcome new technology, even seek it out.

Digital technology makes high-quality television images available on screens as large as a wall and as small as a cell phone. HDTV televisions offer movie-quality pictures and CD-quality sound. Internet delivery offers programming that's mobile and can follow you wherever and whenever you want it.

And new players are entering the game. In 2012, Netflix offered a new original series, *House of Cards*, through its video streaming service, and Amazon Studios (created by online retailer Amazon) announced it has signed several pilot TV programs for Internet distribution.

In 2013, Samsung previewed an interactive Smart TV that allows consumers to use touch-screen technology to access Internet and over-the-air content all in one place—Samsung's new 84-inch TV screen (current price tag $40,000).

The definition of what we call "television" and "television program" is exploding. Lanny Smoot, an executive at Bell Communications Research, calls the future of television a *telepresence*. "This," he says, "is a wave that is not possible to stop."

Review, Analyze, Investigate

Reviewing Chapter 8

Television Transforms Daily Life

- The word *television*, which once meant programs delivered by antennas through over-the-air signals, today means a *television screen*, where a variety of delivery systems brings viewers a diversity of programs.

- Many groups are concerned that, because of its pervasiveness, television influences the nation's values, habits and behavior.

- About 1,600 television stations operate in the United States. Three out of four of these are commercial stations and about half of U.S. stations are affiliated with a network.

TV Delivers an Audience to Advertisers

- More than any other media industry today, commercial television exists primarily as an advertising medium.

- A 30-second ad during Super Bowl 2013 cost an advertiser as much as $3.8 million.

Visual Radio Becomes *Television*

- Guglielmo Marconi put sound on airwaves. Lee de Forest invented the Audion tube. Vladimir Zworykin turned an electronic signal into a visual image. Philo T. Farnsworth added the electronic scanner.

- The rivalry between David Sarnoff (RCA) and William S. Paley (CBS) is central to the early history of television.

- The ABC network was formed when the Federal Communications Commission (FCC) ordered David Sarnoff to sell one of his two networks (Red and Blue). The Blue network became ABC.

Television Outpaces Radio

- The first television news broadcasts were primitive compared to today's broadcasts. Television news, like radio news, developed its own standard of excellence, led by news pioneers Edward R. Murrow and David Brinkley.

- Most television entertainment programming was derived from radio.

- The only type of program that didn't come from radio was the talk show, which appeared on television first and then moved to radio. The situation comedy proved to be one of television's most durable types of programming.

Quiz Shows Bring Ethics Scandals

- A congressional investigation revealed that several 1950s TV quiz shows were rigged to enhance their ratings.

- The 1950s quiz show scandals caused the networks to eliminate advertiser-produced programming.

- Charles Van Doren, who admitted that he cheated, was a central figure in the quiz show scandals.

Ratings Target the Audience

- The Nielsen ratings determine the price that TV advertisers pay to air their commercials.

- TV audiences are measured as ratings and shares.

Newton Minow Criticizes TV as a "Vast Wasteland"

- In the 1960s, audiences grew more discriminating and began to question how well the medium of television was serving the public.

- An influential person who outlined TV's responsibility to its audience was then-FCC Chairman Newton Minow, who coined the phrase "vast wasteland" to describe television.

Public Television Finds an Audience

- National Educational Television (NET) is the predecessor of today's Corporation for Public Broadcasting (CPB).
- In 1981, the FCC loosened the rules for commercials on public television.

Satellites Make Transatlantic TV and Live Broadcast Possible

- In 1962, *Telstar I* sent the first transatlantic satellite broadcast.
- Modern satellites make CNN and DirecTV possible.

Television Changes National Politics

- In the 1960s, television drew criticism for the way it was perceived to influence politics and the dialogue about national issues.
- Television broadcast nonstop coverage of the Watergate hearings, President Nixon's resignation and investigations of the Iran-Contra scandal.

TV News Images Bring Global Events into View

- In 2001, U.S. TV network news offered nonstop coverage of the terrorist attacks at New York's World Trade Center, at the Pentagon and in rural Pennsylvania.
- In 2003, the TV networks brought viewers even closer to events when TV reporters and photographers sent live battlefield images and stories to viewers during the Iraq War.
- In 2012, TV showed people around the world the ominous devastation caused by Hurricane Sandy on the nation's East Coast.
- National events become global events because of TV's instant international reach.

Television at Work

- A typical TV station has eight departments: sales, programming, production, engineering, traffic, promotion, public affairs and administration.
- Many TV stations are affiliated with a network.

Audiences Drive TV Programming

- The most-watched TV programs are situation comedies, sports and feature movies.
- Deregulation, with relaxed ownership rules, means that instability, mergers and change have become major characteristics of the television industry.
- Network ratings have plunged since people meters were introduced as a ratings system, and the TV networks also must compete with the huge variety of program options vying for consumers' attention.
- More than 125 program services now offer alternatives to network programming.
- Television licensing fees fund most of the cost of the nation's college and professional sports.
- Spanish-language networks draw increasing numbers of prime-time viewers.

Digital Technology Expands TV's Focus

- Several technological developments are changing the way programs are delivered to consumers, including digital video recorders, high definition television and the Internet.
- HDTV offers better pictures, clearer sound and a flatter screen than traditional TV and became the national industry standard in 2009.
- Digital TV makes it easier for manufacturers to combine the functions of TV and the functions of a computer in the same TV set.
- In 2010, major television manufacturers started selling 3-D TVs, and several programmers announced plans to create 3-D shows to feed the new market.

Television Offers a New Vision

- Cable, satellite and Internet program services have developed the capability to deliver programs to screens as small as a cell phone.
- In 2012, Netflix offered a new original series, *House of Cards*, through its video streaming service, and Amazon Studios (created by online retailer Amazon) announced it has signed several pilot TV programs for Internet distribution.
- In 2013, Samsung previewed an interactive TV that allows consumers to use touch-screen technology to access Internet and over-the-air content all in one place.

Key Terms

These terms are defined in the margins throughout this chapter and appear in alphabetical order with definitions in the Glossary, which begins on page 373.

Critical Questions

1. Explain what media observer Jeff Greenfield means when he says, "To the television executive, the product [of television] is the audience."

2. How did the quiz show scandals of the 1950s affect the relationship between advertisers and the networks? Is the relationship between advertisers and the networks different or the same today? Explain.

3. Discuss the economic challenges facing public broadcasting and the various sources of funding on which individual public broadcast stations, as well as CPB and PBS rely. Summarize how public broadcasting has responded to the problems.

4. Explain the role of the Nielsen ratings in television, including such factors as ratings accuracy, advertiser dependence on ratings, and the effect of ratings on programming.

5. Describe how new technologies (such as video streaming and 3-D TV) will affect the television industry.

Working the Web

This list includes both sites mentioned in the chapter and others to give you greater insight into the television industry.

Disney/ABC Television Group

disneyabctv.com

Home to Disney's international entertainment and news properties, the Disney/ABC Television Group includes the ABC Television Network (Daytime, Entertainment and News divisions), Disney Channels Worldwide, ABC Studios and Hyperion Books. The Group also manages the Radio Disney Network and the company's equity interest in Lifetime Entertainment Services and A&E Television Networks.

Interactive Advertising Bureau (IAB)

iab.net

Established in 1996, the IAB is composed of more than 500 media and technology companies that are "responsible for selling 86 percent of online advertising in the United States." The IAB lobbies on behalf of these companies in Washington, D.C., and around the country, making recommendations on standards and practices as well as conducting its own research on the interactive advertising industry.

National Association of Broadcasters (NAB)

nab.org

The trade association for over-the-air radio and television broadcasters, the NAB provides networking opportunities, a career center and information about communication law. It also represents industry interests to government officials and provides research grants.

National Cable & Telecommunications Association (NCTA)

ncta.com

The principal trade association of the U.S. cable television industry, NTCA provides a unified voice for its members on all issues affecting cable and telecommunications. Its Web site includes information on other industry-related organizations, resources and services, as well legislative issues, filings and publications. Key issues for consumers include Internet regulation, TV parental controls and the digital television transition.

Nielsen Media Research

nielsen.com

This research company provides the Nielsen ratings, which measure the popularity of various television programs. Its founder, Arthur C. Nielsen, was one of the fathers of modern marketing research. Its data play a large part in determining how much can be charged for ads. Useful features on the Web site include a TV History Timeline and a searchable glossary of media industry acronyms and terms.

Parental Media Guide

parentalguide.org/movies.html

Sponsored by major entertainment industry associations such as the Motion Picture Association, NAB and Entertain-

ment Software Rating Board, this Web site provides a central resource for parents and caregivers seeking information on the voluntary parental guideline systems in place for television, movies, video games and recorded music.

Public Broadcasting Service (PBS)

pbs.org

This network of more than 350 noncommercial television stations reaches nearly 73 million viewers per week with content on air and online. PBS.org includes a program search, TV schedules and links to online-featured topics such as History, Culture & Society and News & Public Affairs. PBS Kids Online (pbskids.org) provides educational entertainment for children as well as comprehensive sections for parents and teachers.

Television Bureau of Advertising (TVB)

tvb.org

This trade association for broadcast groups, advertising sales reps, syndicators, international broadcasters and individual television stations provides audience analyses and a business databank. The Web site also offers advice for selling TV advertising, a job center and information on electronic business processes.

TV.com

tv.com

Powered by CNET, this fan-run site includes information about programs, episodes, actors, lines and trivia for TV shows from the 1940s to today. It has a wide variety of online forums sorted by show genre as well as news, celebrity photos, downloads and podcasts.

Impact/Action Videos are concise news features on various topics created exclusively for *Media/Impact*. Go online to access MindTap at cengagebrain.com. MindTap for *Media/Impact* sequences all of your learning tools—Chapter Readings with highlighting and note taking, *Impact/Action Videos*, activities and assessments—into chapter driven learning units that guide you through the curriculum.

DIGITAL MEDIA: WIDENING THE WEB

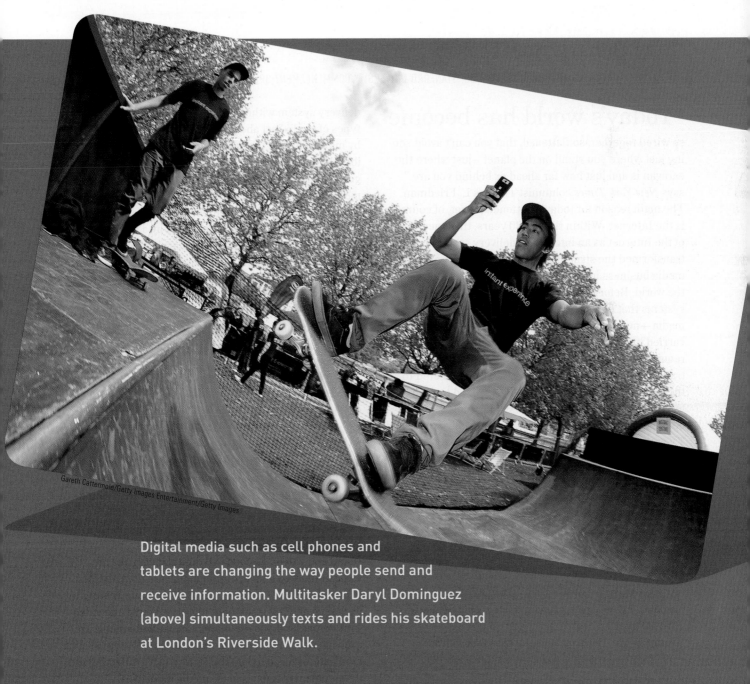

Gareth Cattermole/Getty Images Entertainment/Getty Images

Digital media such as cell phones and tablets are changing the way people send and receive information. Multitasker Daryl Dominguez (above) simultaneously texts and rides his skateboard at London's Riverside Walk.

"Stay Hungry. Stay Foolish"

—APPLE CEO STEVE JOBS, STANFORD UNIVERSITY COMMENCEMENT SPEECH, JUNE 12, 2005

"Today's world has become so wired together, so flattened, that you can't avoid seeing just where you stand on the planet—just where the caravan is and just how far ahead or behind you are," says *New York Times* columnist Thomas L. Friedman. The main reason for today's flattened planet, of course, is the Internet. Within the last 30 years, the emergence of the Internet as an interactive delivery system has transformed the structure and the economics of the media business in the United States and throughout the world. Before the 1970s, media were defined by the systems that delivered them. Paper delivered the print media—newspapers, magazines and books. Antennas carried broadcast signals—radio and television. Movies required film, and music traveled on round discs. These traditional media each were specifically connected to their own method of delivery and organized into different types of companies—newspaper, magazine and book publishers; recording and movie studios; radio and TV stations.

DIGITAL COMMUNICATION TRANSFORMS MEDIA

Today, the Internet delivers all types of media—print, broadcast, movies and recordings—using a single delivery system without barriers. You can receive all types of media just about anywhere you want, delivered by many different types of companies, carried on invisible electronic signals. The Internet has caused the emergence of new media products and new competition in the media business that were impossible to foresee when the Internet as a place for consumers first emerged in 1978. Originally the Internet was designed by a group of scientists who were simply hoping to share information.

The Internet combines millions of computer networks sending and receiving data from all over the world—competing interests joined together by a common purpose but no common owner. "No government or commercial entity owns the Net or directly profits from its operation," notes information designer Roger Fidler. "It has no president, chief executive officer or central headquarters."

In its global size and absence of central control, the Internet is completely different from traditional media. Originally developed to help researchers, scientists and educators communicate, the Internet has "evolved in a way no one planned or expected," says Fidler. "It is the relationships among people that have shaped the medium."

The term *digital media* describes all forms of communications media that combine text, pictures, sound and video using computer technology. Digital media read, write and store data electronically in numerical form—using numbers to code the data (text, pictures, sound and video). Because all digital media use the same numbered codes, digital media are *compatible*, which means they can function well with one another to exchange and integrate text, pictures, sound and video. This compatibility is the main reason digital media are growing so fast. Because of its rapid growth, digital communications has become the central factor affecting the development of today's mass media industries.

Digital Media All emerging communications media that combine text, graphics, sound and video using computer technology.

Compatible Media that can function well with one another to exchange and integrate text, pictures, sound and video.

TIMEFRAME

1978–TODAY

Digital Media Covers the Globe

SSPL/Science & Society Picture Library/Getty Images

1978 Nicholas Negroponte at MIT first uses the term *convergence* to describe the intersection of the media industries.

1988 Less than one-half of 1 percent of U.S. households is online.

1989 Tim Berners-Lee develops the first browser and programming languages that allow people to share all types of information online.

1992 Neil Papworth, a software programmer in England, sends the first text message.

1994 Marc Andreessen and his colleagues at the University of Illinois introduce the Mosaic browser.

1995 David Filo and Jerry Yang launch Yahoo! as a search engine company.

1996 Internet advertising reaches $200 million. Congress passes the Communications Decency Act.

1998 One in four U.S. households is online. Congress passes the Digital Millennium Copyright Act. Larry Page and Sergey Brin launch Google.

1999 The Recording Industry Association of America (RIAA) sues Internet file-sharing company Napster for copyright infringement.

David Paul Morris/Bloomberg/Getty Images

2000 The number of Internet businesses explodes.

2001 File-sharing company Napster shuts down. The number of Internet startups begins to shrink, and many existing companies close.

2003 The RIAA and the Motion Picture Association of America announce campaigns to aggressively fight online piracy.

2004 Mark Zuckerberg launches Facebook as a social networking site.

2005 File-sharing company Grokster shuts down, settling a landmark intellectual property case.

2006 Internet advertising reaches $17 billion.

2007 Apple introduces the iPhone.

2008 Google celebrates its 10th anniversary.

2010 Apple introduces the iPad and the iPhone 4.

David Paul Morris/Bloomberg/Getty Images

2011 Apple launches iCloud. Apple's App store reaches 25 billion downloads. Twitter hits 100 million users. Apple CEO Steve Jobs dies.

2012 Facebook has 150 million users.

2013 President Obama signs an executive order promoting cybersecurity.

TODAY Four out of five American adults use the Internet. Two-thirds of online adults use social media. Businesses spend more than $37 billion a year for Internet advertising.

The Internet offers people wireless access just about wherever and whenever they want it. New York City Mayor Michael Bloomberg announces on January 8, 2013 that Google has teamed with the city to provide free Wi-Fi throughout the Manhattan neighborhood of Chelsea.

Rather than the one-way communication of traditional media, communication on today's compatible digital networks means someone can receive and send information simultaneously, without barriers. Digital networks "free individuals from the shackles of corporate bureaucracy and geography and allow them to collaborate and exchange ideas with the best colleague anywhere in the world," said futurist George Gilder. "Computer networks give every hacker the creative potential of a factory tycoon of the industrial [turn-of-the-century] era and the communications power of a TV magnate of the broadcasting era."

In an interconnected digital world, the speed and convenience of the network redefines the mass media industries and erases all previous notions of how mass communications should work. Today's media are constantly evolving. Digital media forms "do not arise spontaneously and independently from old media," says media scholar Roger Fidler. Digital media are related and connected to old media. Fidler says today's media are members of an interdependent system, with "similarities

Convergence The melding of the communications, computer and electronics industries.

and relationships that exist among past, present and emerging forms."

Digital media are similar to traditional media yet different in ways that make them distinct from their predecessors. Because of the interdependence of today's mass media, all the media industries are transforming simultaneously.

DIGITAL MEDIA SUPPORT CONVERGENCE

In 1978, Nicholas Negroponte at the Massachusetts Institute of Technology was the first to identify a theory called **convergence**. This theory gave a name to the process by which the various media industries in the late 1970s were beginning to intersect, and MIT was among the first places to foresee and identify this trend. (See **Illustration 9.1**, "The Evolution of Today's Convergence: 1978 to 2014," p. 179.)

The media industries not only were combining economically, as media companies began to buy and sell each other, but the technology of the industries also was merging, according to MIT. This convergence meant that eventually the products the media companies produced began to resemble each other.

Negroponte also said that the combination of the traditional media industries with the computer industry would create a new type of communication.

To identify what was happening to the media industries, Negroponte created two models to show the position of the media industries in 1978 and his projected vision for those industries in the year 2000. He listed three segments of the media business: (1) print and publishing, (2) broadcast and motion pictures and (3) the computer industry.

The first diagram in Negroponte's model displays the alignment of the media industries in 1978, which shows them with a small amount of integrated territory. In the second diagram, which shows Negroponte's predictions for the year 2000, the three segments of the media industries completely overlap. Negroponte's forecast was a very accurate prediction, and it helped establish the framework for today's thinking about the Internet.

This early economic and technological convergence in the media industries is the most important reason for the development of today's digital media. By the year 2000, every media industry was equally well positioned to take advantage of new developments, and today every media industry benefits from convergence.

IMPACT/Convergence

Illustration 9.1

The Evolution of Today's Convergence: 1978 to 2014

The diagram on the left displays the alignment of the media in 1978, showing each media industry with very little overlapping territory. The middle diagram shows what MIT's Nicolas Negroponte predicted would happen by 2000, with the three types of industries—broadcast/motion pictures, printing/publishing and computers—merging further. The 2014 diagram shows what convergence looks like today—all three media segments are almost completely intersecting, with print, broadcast and movie industry products available through the Internet on a laptop, a tablet and a smartphone.

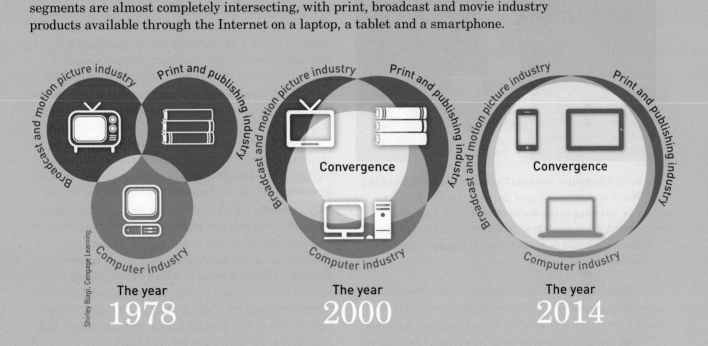

Shirley Biagi, Cengage Learning

The year 1978

The year 2000

The year 2014

20TH-CENTURY DISCOVERIES MADE INTERNET POSSIBLE

Several technological developments were necessary for people to be able to share text, graphics, audio and video online. These developments made the creation of the World Wide Web possible. The person most responsible for the World Wide Web is Tim Berners-Lee, a British native with an Oxford degree in physics. Working in 1989 in Geneva, Switzerland, at the CERN physics laboratory, Berners-Lee created several new programming languages.

One of these new computer-programming languages was *HTML* (hypertext markup language). Hypertext

transfer protocol (*HTTP*) allowed people to create and send text, graphics and video information electronically and also to set up electronic connections (called *links*) from one source of information to another. These developments were very important in the Web's early days, and today people who use the Internet don't even need to know the programming language that made the Web possible.

HTML	Hypertext markup language.
HTTP	Hypertext transfer protocol.
Links	Electronic connections from one source of information to another.

After he invented the language and mechanisms that would allow people to share all kinds of information electronically, Berners-Lee gave this invention its name—the World Wide Web. "The original goal was working together with others," says Berners-Lee. "The Web was supposed to be a creative tool, an expressive tool." Berners-Lee also created the first *browser*, which allows people to search electronically among many documents to find what they want.

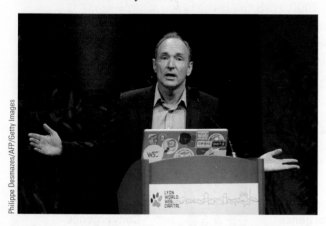

British computer scientist Tim Berners-Lee invented the World Wide Web and gave the Web its name. Berners-Lee, speaking at the World Wide Web 2012 international conference in Lyon, France, launched the World Wide Web Foundation to expand Internet access in developing countries.

Today, Berners-Lee still is involved in the Web's development, as founder of the World Wide Web Foundation, which promotes access to the Web throughout the world. "When you think about how the Web is today and dream about how it might be, you must, as always, consider both technology and people," says Berners-Lee. "Future technology should be smarter and more powerful, of course.

Browser   Software that allows people to display and interact with information on Web pages.

Search Engine   The tool used to locate information in a computer database.

Public Domain   Publications, products and processes that are not protected by copyright and thus are available free to the public.

Publishing   Placing items on the Web.

Home Page   The first page of a Web site, which welcomes the user.

But you cannot ethically turn your attention to developing it without also listening to those people who don't use the Web at all, or who could use it if only it were different in some way. The Web has been largely designed by the developed world for the developed world. But it must be much more inclusive in order to be of great value to us all."

Marc Andreessen and his colleagues at the University of Illinois further defined the browser, and in 1994 they introduced software called Mosaic, which allowed people to put text and pictures in the same online document. Three of the successors to Mosaic are Safari, Mozilla Firefox and Internet Explorer, which are among the most widely used commercial browsers.

Another level of help for Web access is the *search engine*. This tool locates information in computer databases. Two familiar search engines are Google and Yahoo! These systems turn your typed request for information into digital bits that then search for what you want and return the information to you. Yahoo!, founded in 1995 as a search engine company, today makes money through subscriptions, advertising and classified ads and employs more than 8,000 people around the world. Google, which has 20,000 employees, celebrated its 15th anniversary in 2013. Launched by entrepreneurs Larry Page and Sergey Brin in 1998 with four computers and $100,000, Google is now worth more than $150 billion.

To encourage people to use their systems, both Berners-Lee and Andreessen placed their discoveries in the *public domain*, which means that anyone with a computer and a modem can download them from the Internet and use them for free. *This culture of free information access, coupled with a creative, chaotic lack of direction, still permeates the Web today.*

The process of putting documents on the Web drew its terminology from print, the original mass medium. That's why placing something on the Web is called *publishing*, and the publication begins with a *home page*, the front door to the site—the place that welcomes the user and explains how the site works. However, even though Web sites are similar to published documents in the way they work, what is created on the Web has few of the legal limitations or protections that apply to other published documents. (See **Chapter 14**.)

WEB OPENS TO UNLIMITED ACCESS

Once Tim Berners-Lee had created the tools for access so that all types of text and video images could become available on the Web, it was left to anyone who could use the tools to create whatever they wanted and make it available to anyone who wanted it.

"Nobody ever designed the Web," says Canadian sociologist Craig McKie, who maintains his own Web site. "There are no rules, no laws. The Web also exists without national boundaries." Any type of information—video, audio, graphics and text—can travel virtually instantly to and from anyone who has a computer and access to the Internet anywhere in the world.

Universal access, limited only by the available technology, is what gives the Web the feeling and look of what has been called "anarchy"—a place without rules. The Web is a new medium, but its growth as a true *mass medium* for people seeking information and entertainment is limited only by digital technology and economics. Large media companies have huge amounts of money available to bankroll new technologies. These companies also have a shared interest in seeing their investments succeed. So convergence is continuing at a very rapid pace, which is the main reason new digital media products are being introduced so quickly.

Some of the digital media products that flood the marketplace succeed, and many do not. However, the potential reward if consumers adopt a digital media product is so large that all types of media companies are willing to take the risks associated with developing new products. For consumers, this means an array of products bombarding the marketplace simultaneously, such as the iPad and Internet TV.

Media and computer entrepreneurs try to capitalize on fast-moving developments to be the first to deliver new creative products that large numbers of people will want to use, and society struggles to adjust to the access to communication that new products create.

There are many parallels between the development of the Internet and the early history of traditional media, such as movies. Like traditional media, today's emerging technologies are being used to try to create new popular products that the public will crave.

In the early 1900s, when movies first were introduced as flickering images on a small screen, the moving images were something consumers hadn't seen before, but many people thought the silent movies were just a passing fad (see **Chapter 7**). The inventions Thomas Edison and his colleagues introduced at the time made the movies technologically possible, but the movies also needed creative minds like director D. W. Griffith

Aaron Bacall/CartoonStock.com

"Take out your phones. Open the American History app and turn to the page about George Washington."

and stars like Mary Pickford to create epic stories that people wanted to see. When new inventions brought sound to the movies, the success of the new medium was unstoppable.

This combination of technological development, creative expression and consumer demand was crucial for the movies' enduring prosperity. The same collision of economics, technology and creativity that drove the early days of the movie industry is behind today's race to develop digital media. (See **Impact/Global**, "Text Messaging Turns 20," p. 182.)

WHAT HAPPENS TO OLD MEDIA?

How does the development of digital media affect older, traditional media? Some scholars have predicted, for example, that print media are dead, yet book sales continue to be steady, and publishers have developed e-books to take advantage of the digital form. The history of the evolution of media shows that the introduction of a new medium or a new delivery system does not mean the end of the old. The continuous expansion of the media industries during the 20th century demonstrates this evolution.

When television was introduced, for example, radio did not disappear. Instead, radio adapted to its new place in the media mix, delivering music, news and talk. Today, radio exists alongside television. Movies, which also were threatened by the introduction of television, responded by delivering more spectacular and more explicit entertainment than people could see on

IMPACT/Global

Text Messaging Turns 20

By Tracy McVeigh, The Guardian (*United Kingdom*)

The text message is 20 years old. Long ago, back before Twitter, way before Facebook, in a time when people still lifted a receiver to make a call and telephone boxes graced streets where people didn't lock their doors, Neil Papworth, a software programmer from Reading, [United Kingdom,] sent an early festive greeting to a mate.

"Since mobile phones didn't yet have keyboards, I typed the message out on a PC. It read 'Merry Christmas' and I sent it to Richard Jarvis of Vodafone, who was enjoying his office Christmas party at the time," said Papworth.

On 3 December 1992, he had sent the world's first text message.

Text messaging turned 20 [on December 3, 2012]. More than 8 trillion were sent [in 2011]. Around 15 million leave our mobile screens every minute. There is now text poetry, text adverts and text prayers and an entire generation that's *SMS* [short messaging service] savvy.

SMS took off. According to a survey by mobile communication firm Acision, it is still the most popular way to message despite competition from email and social networking messaging services with 92 percent of smartphone users still preferring to text.

The act of typing and sending a brief, electronic message between two or more mobile phones or fixed or portable devices over a phone network is now one of the major means of communication in the world. Texting is the second most common use for a phone—the first being checking the time.

More than half (58 percent) of UK adults use text messages at least once a day.

James Thickett, Ofcom's director of research, said, "Our research reveals that in just a few short years, new technology has fundamentally changed the way that we communicate.

Tony Avelar/The Christian Science Monitor/Getty Images

About 15 million text messages are sent every minute, some of them while people are driving. First introduced in 1992, texting has changed the way people communicate throughout the world.

But texting has also brought some new social ills—cyber bullying, its use in stalking or "sexting" (sending sexually explicit messages), and car accidents caused by texting of both drivers and pedestrians.

Chance Bothe, 21, of Texas texted a friend while driving home from college: "I need to quit texting because I could die in a car accident and then how would you feel . . ."

Seconds later, Bothe's pickup veered off a bridge and dropped 35 feet down a ravine.

"I'm very lucky that I'm not gone for ever," said Bothe, who now campaigns on the dangers of texting and driving.

The 2008 LA commuter train crash which killed 25 people has been partly blamed on text messaging distracting crew members and an engineer who failed to stop at a signal.

Last month an Alaskan woman fell down a cliff while texting as she walked too close to the edge. Maria Pestrikoff, of Anchorage, survived and was rescued.

SMS Short messaging service.

Source: Tracy McVeigh, "Text Messaging Turns 20," *The Observer*, December 1, 2012. Retrieved from http://m.guardiannews.com.

Mark Makela/The New York Times/Redux Pictures

When newer forms of media emerge, older media systems evolve and adapt. However, discarded electronic gear like this pile of old computers and TV sets in Philadelphia, poses a challenge for recyclers.

television, and today movies still play an important role in the business of media.

"When newer forms of communication media emerge, the older forms usually do not die—they continue to evolve and adapt," says Roger Fidler. The different media compete for the public's attention and jockey for positions of dominance, but no medium disappears. Instead, each medium contributes to the development of its successors. Together, all media that now exist will contribute to media forms that are yet to be invented.

TRANSFORMATION TAKES 30 YEARS

Just how quickly consumers adopt new technologies is predictable, according to Paul Saffo, former director of the Institute for the Future in Menlo Park, Calif. Saffo theorizes that for the past five centuries the pace of change has always been 30 years, or about three decades, from the introduction of a new technology to its complete adoption by the culture.

Saffo calls his theory the ***30-year rule***, which he divides into three stages, with each stage lasting about 10 years. In the first stage, he says, there is "lots of excitement, lots of puzzlement, not a lot of penetration." In the second stage, there is "lots of flux, penetration of the product into society is beginning." In the third stage, the reaction to the technology is, "Oh, so what? Just a standard technology and everybody has it." By Saffo's standard, American society is in the third stage of acceptance of online technology because widespread

use of the Internet by consumers began in 1988, when less than one-half of 1 percent of the U.S. population was on the Internet. Today, 79 percent of the U.S. population is online.

Saffo's description of the third decade of acceptance coincides with the adaptability of today's media marketplace. New media is more familiar, and people seem better able to incorporate combinations of new and existing media technology into their lives. The technological transformation has stabilized.

WEB ACCESS LEAVES SOME PEOPLE BEHIND

The initial sign of the expansion of the Internet to consumer and educational users in the first decade of change—the early 1990s—was the adoption by businesses and private users of electronic mail, or *e-mail*, technology. With a computer, a modem and a telephone line, just about anyone could learn how to communicate electronically online.

"The driving force for achieving large subscriber gains is the incorporation of the Internet by consumers as part of their routine," according to Veronis Suhler Stevenson, a media research company. "The Internet has become a tool that allows users to economize on what has become their scarcest resource—time. Virtually all of the leading Internet applications allow users to accomplish tasks more quickly than they can through alternative means."

E-mail and text messaging at school, work or home still are how most people first experience communicating in an electronic environment. Just as telephone answering machines in the 1970s changed voice communication by allowing people to send and receive messages on their own time schedule, e-mail and text messaging allow people to communicate and receive information at their convenience.

E-mail and text messaging are easy to use, text-based systems, which means that people type in messages on a keyboard, which is a familiar tool. Familiarity and convenience are very important in the adoption of new technologies because people's fear of something they don't understand and misunderstandings about how new

30-Year Rule   Developed by Paul Saffo, the theory that it takes about 30 years for a new technology to be completely adopted within a culture.

E-mail   Mail that is delivered electronically over the Internet.

Ann Hermes/The Christian Science Monitor/Getty Images

Even though Internet access is everywhere, 21 percent of the U.S. population still has never gone online. The gap between people who use the Internet and people who don't is called the *digital divide*. In Worcester, Mass., Bancroft School student Jess Chang transfers work from her iPad to the school computer.

technologies work can keep them from changing their established habits.

According to the Pew Internet and American Life Project, one out of five American adults say they have never used the Internet or e-mail and do not live in an Internet-connected household. Some people avoid the Internet because they can't afford it or they're afraid to try it or they don't have access. People living with a disability also are less likely to go online. This gap between people who have Internet access and those who don't is called the ***digital divide***.

Pew calls these people "truly disconnected adults"—typically people who have less than a high school education, are over 65, or live in a rural area. "If they needed to get information from a Web site or other online source, they probably could not easily do so," says Susannah Fox, associate director of the Pew Internet Project.

Pew says that the main reason adults give for not going online is that "they don't think the Internet is relevant to them. Most have never used the Internet before, and don't have anyone in their household who does."

For children, the great equalizer is public education. Access to computers in the classroom guarantees they will be comfortable with the technology as they grow up. Mature adults and rural populations without access to

the technology can be disadvantaged unless government institutions, such as public libraries, close the gap.

INTERNET COMBINES COMMERCE, INFORMATION AND ENTERTAINMENT

What makes the Web as a mass medium different from traditional media is its capacity to combine commerce with access to information and entertainment. Not only can people buy products on the Web, but they can also learn new things and enjoy themselves.

Most people use an Internet service provider (*ISP*, also called an Internet access provider), such as a telephone, satellite or cable company, to organize and deliver Internet information and entertainment. Today, a major source of Web income is the money people pay their ISP to connect to the Web. There are three other potential sources of income on the Web: commerce (connecting sellers with potential buyers), advertising, and content.

Commerce

"Millions of Internet users are forsaking yard sales and the local dump for the prospect of selling their hand-me-downs and unwanted gear online," according to a report by the Pew Internet and American Life Project. "About one in six Internet-using adults have sold something online." This recent success of the Internet as a way for people to buy and sell things is only one example of the Internet's potential as a marketplace.

The most resilient commercial Internet operation is Amazon. It began as a place where people could buy media products such as books, CDs and DVDs, but today consumers also can shop on Amazon for just about anything—clothes, cosmetics and sports equipment, for example—often at discount prices from individuals as well as large retailers, such as Target. Amazon has grown into a vast international Internet department store.

Small retailers and even individual consumers also can use the Web to sell products directly, without setting up a store or spending a lot of money on expensive advertising on *eBay*, a Web site that began about 25 years ago as a place where individual sellers offered products—mostly collectibles—in an online auction atmosphere.

Today, eBay is another vast marketplace where individuals sell collectibles, but eBay also promotes direct consumer-to-consumer sales for products as varied as cars, houses, even used jeans. Most individual sellers on the site do not have retail stores. Their only outlet is eBay, yet the Internet gives eBay sellers access to buyers all over the world.

Convenience, reliability and affordability sustain both these Web sites as successful commercial ventures—

Digital Divide The lack of access to digital technology among low-income, rural and minority groups.

ISP Internet service provider, also called an Internet access provider.

Scott Olson/Getty Images

The Internet gives consumers access to a worldwide array of products and has changed the way many people shop and the way retailers advertise products. In the United States, Cyber Monday, the day after the Thanksgiving holiday, has become an online shopping tradition.

two examples of new types of businesses that thrive because of the Internet.

Advertising

When television was introduced to the public in the late 1940s, people assumed from the beginning that it would be a commercial medium—that is, advertisers who bought the commercials surrounding the programs would pay for the programming. This concept of using advertising to underwrite TV programs was a natural evolution from radio, where commercials also paid for the programming.

Advertisers follow the audience, so as consumers migrated to the Web, advertisers have tried to figure out how to follow them. Advertising is the second potential source of income on the Web.

Most commercial Web sites now carry some form of advertising. These appear as banners across the top of the Web site or run as borders alongside the site's pages. But just like traditional media, advertising can crowd out the original message and turn away consumers, and entrepreneurs continue to test the market to develop new Web advertising structures and designs that will pay the bills. (See **Illustration 9.2**, "How Much Do Businesses Spend Annually to Advertise on the Internet?," p. 186.)

Because the Web is such a targeted medium—the seller can gather a lot of information about the buyer—the Web holds better potential for monitoring consumers' buying habits than traditional methods of advertising. Ultimately, Web advertisers hope to "achieve the merchandiser's dream—targeting an audience far more precisely than it can with either newspapers or television by advertising a product only on sites that draw people

likely to be interested in that product," says media critic David Shaw, with "nearly instantaneous electronic feedback on whether their ads are effective: How many people saw the ad? How many 'clicked' on it and went on to a more detailed presentation? How many bought the product right then, online?"

Internet "tracking" offers advertisers information about their audiences. Commercial sites offer advertisers information about how many "hits" the sites receive—how many times people look at the site and how much time they spend. This information-gathering is so sophisticated that the data can even show an advertiser which specific user bought which specific products that were advertised on a specific site.

Companies also have developed "ad robots" that allow a business to, in effect, eavesdrop on chat room conversations while the user is online. If someone mentions a car problem online, for example, the robot recognizes the pattern of words in the discussion and sends the person an ad for car repair.

Always looking for new ways to target specific audiences, advertising agencies also offer services such as *search marketing*, which means placing client ads next to consumers' Internet search results so that when someone starts a search for SUVs, for example, the SUV car manufacturer's ad immediately appears on the screen next to the user's search results. Appearing within the SUV ad, of course, is a link to a Web site where the user can customize and order a car. By connecting consumers directly to advertisers, search marketers say, they can better trace and document the connection between Internet ads and their audiences, something many advertisers are demanding before they invest in the Internet audience.

Ad robots and search marketing are just two examples of the refined tools advertisers have developed to more accurately track and target the Internet consumer.

Content

The culture of the Web began with the idea that content would be available free, so it has taken a long time for consumers to embrace the idea that they should pay for media content on the Web.

Slate, the online literary magazine, tried to start charging subscribers in 1997, but then decided against it. Editor Michael Kinsley said, "It would be better to

Search Marketing Positioning Internet advertising prominently next to consumers' related online search results.

IMPACT/Money

Illustration 9.2

How Much Do Businesses Spend Annually to Advertise on the Internet?

Since 2000, advertisers have been racing to reach consumers by advertising products and services on the Internet. The amount that companies spend to advertise on the Internet today is more than four times what they spent in the year 2000.

Source: Interactive Advertising Bureau, iab.net.

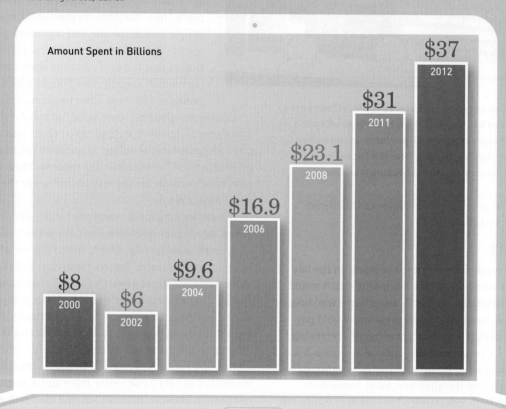

establish a brand name with wide readership first." *Slate* celebrated its 15th anniversary in 2010 and still does not charge subscribers.

Some explicit Web sites charge for access, and some news and information sites, such as *The Wall Street Journal*, charge subscribers an annual fee for access to archived online content older than seven days—beyond what's available free on the main *Journal* news site. *The New York Times* began charging for access to its site in 2011. Other sites, such as the sports network ESPN, give away some information and then charge for "premium" services. Internet game-makers, who offer video games on the Web, charge by the hour or use a tiered pricing structure—free, basic and premium.

In 2003, consumers showed they were willing to pay for music downloads when Apple founder Steve Jobs introduced iTunes, a music service for subscribers that allows people to download popular songs for a fee. Less than a year after its launch, iTunes celebrated its one-billionth music download. (See **Impact/Profile**, "'You've Got to Find What You Love,' Steve Jobs Says," p. 187.)

In 2010, when Apple introduced the iPad, an electronic tablet offering many more functions than its predecessor from Amazon (the Kindle), Apple sold 500,000 iPads in the first week. Tablet devices offer another mobile outlet for purchased media, such as books, newspapers and magazines. Book downloads sell for about $10, bringing a new source of revenue for book publishers.

IMPACT/Profile

"You've Got to Find What You Love," Steve Jobs Says

NOTE: This is a prepared text of the Commencement address delivered by Steve Jobs, CEO of Apple Computer and Pixar Animation Studios, on June 12, 2005. Jobs died on October 6, 2011. A video of Jobs' speech is available on the Stanford University Web site (see p. 189).

I am honored to be with you today at your commencement from one of the finest universities in the world. I never graduated from college. Truth be told, this is the closest I've ever gotten to a college graduation. Today I want to tell you three stories from my life. That's it. No big deal. Just three stories.

The first story is about connecting the dots.

I dropped out of Reed College after the first 6 months, but then stayed around as a drop-in for another 18 months or so before I really quit. So why did I drop out?

It started before I was born. My biological mother was a young, unwed college graduate student, and she decided to put me up for adoption. She felt very strongly that I should be adopted by college graduates, so everything was all set for me to be adopted at birth by a lawyer and his wife. Except that when I popped out they decided at the last minute that they really wanted a girl. So my parents, who were on a waiting list, got a call in the middle of the night asking: "We have an unexpected baby boy; do you want him?" They said: "Of course." My biological mother later found out that my mother had never graduated from college and that my father had never graduated from high school. She refused to sign the final adoption papers. She only relented a few months later when my parents promised that I would someday go to college.

And 17 years later I did go to college. But I naively chose a college that was almost as expensive as Stanford, and all of my working-class parents' savings were being spent on my college tuition. After six months, I couldn't see

Apple co-founder Steve Jobs poses in 1984 with Apple's first big success, the Macintosh computer.

Bernard Gotfryd/Premium Archive/Getty Images

the value in it. I had no idea what I wanted to do with my life and no idea how college was going to help me figure it out. And here I was spending all of the money my parents had saved their entire life. So I decided to drop out and trust that it would all work out OK. It was pretty scary at the time, but looking back it was one of the best decisions I ever made. The minute I dropped out I could stop taking the required classes that didn't interest me, and begin dropping in on the ones that looked interesting.

It wasn't all romantic. I didn't have a dorm room, so I slept on the floor in friends' rooms, I returned coke bottles for the 5¢ deposits to buy food with, and I would walk the 7 miles across town every Sunday night to get one good meal a week at the Hare Krishna temple. I loved it. And much of what I stumbled into by following my curiosity and intuition turned out to be priceless later on. Let me give you one example:

(continued)

Reed College at that time offered perhaps the best calligraphy instruction in the country. Throughout the campus every poster, every label on every drawer, was beautifully hand calligraphed. Because I had dropped out and didn't have to take the normal classes, I decided to take a calligraphy class to learn how to do this. I learned about serif and san serif typefaces, about varying the amount of space between different letter combinations, about what makes great typography great. It was beautiful, historical, artistically subtle in a way that science can't capture, and I found it fascinating.

None of this had even a hope of any practical application in my life. But ten years later, when we were designing the first Macintosh computer, it all came back to me. And we designed it all into the Mac. It was the first computer with beautiful typography. If I had never dropped in on that single course in college, the Mac would have never had multiple typefaces or proportionally spaced fonts. And since Windows just copied the Mac, it's likely that no personal computer would have them. If I had never dropped out, I would have never dropped in on this calligraphy class, and personal computers might not have the wonderful typography that they do. Of course it was impossible to connect the dots looking forward when I was in college. But it was very, very clear looking backwards ten years later.

Again, you can't connect the dots looking forward; you can only connect them looking backwards. So you have to trust that the dots will somehow connect in your future. You have to trust in something—your gut, destiny, life, karma, whatever. This approach has never let me down, and it has made all the difference in my life. My second story is about love and loss.

I was lucky—I found what I loved to do early in life. Woz and I started Apple in my parents garage when I was 20. We worked hard, and in 10 years Apple had grown from just the two of us in a garage into a $2 billion company with over 4000 employees. We had just released our finest creation—the Macintosh—a year earlier, and I had just turned 30. And then I got fired. How can you get fired from a company you started? Well, as Apple grew we hired someone who I thought was very talented to run the company with me, and for the first year or so things went well. But

then our visions of the future began to diverge and eventually we had a falling out. When we did, our Board of Directors sided with him. So at 30 I was out. And very publicly out. What had been the focus of my entire adult life was gone, and it was devastating.

I really didn't know what to do for a few months. I felt that I had let the previous generation of entrepreneurs down—that I had dropped the baton as it was being passed to me. I met with David Packard and Bob Noyce and tried to apologize for screwing up so badly. I was a very public failure, and I even thought about running away from the valley. But something slowly began to dawn on me—I still loved what I did. The turn of events at Apple had not changed that one bit. I had been rejected, but I was still in love. And so I decided to start over.

I didn't see it then, but it turned out that getting fired from Apple was the best thing that could have ever happened to me. The heaviness of being successful was replaced by the lightness of being a beginner again, less sure about everything. It freed me to enter one of the most creative periods of my life.

During the next five years, I started a company named NeXT, another company named Pixar, and fell in love with an amazing woman who would become my wife. Pixar went on to create the worlds first computer animated feature film, *Toy Story*, and is now the most successful animation studio in the world. In a remarkable turn of events, Apple bought NeXT, I returned to Apple, and the technology we developed at NeXT is at the heart of Apple's current renaissance. And Laurene and I have a wonderful family together.

I'm pretty sure none of this would have happened if I hadn't been fired from Apple. It was awful tasting medicine, but I guess the patient needed it. Sometimes life hits you in the head with a brick. Don't lose faith. I'm convinced that the only thing that kept me going was that I loved what I did. You've got to find what you love. And that is as true for your work as it is for your lovers. Your work is going to fill a large part of your life, and the only way to be truly satisfied is to do what you believe is great work. And the only way to do great work is to love what you do. If you haven't found it yet, keep looking. Don't settle. As with all matters of the heart, you'll know when

(*continued*)

you find it. And, like any great relationship, it just gets better and better as the years roll on. So keep looking until you find it. Don't settle.

My third story is about death.

When I was 17, I read a quote that went something like: "If you live each day as if it was your last, someday you'll most certainly be right." It made an impression on me, and since then, for the past 33 years, I have looked in the mirror every morning and asked myself: "If today were the last day of my life, would I want to do what I am about to do today?" And whenever the answer has been "No" for too many days in a row, I know I need to change something.

Remembering that I'll be dead soon is the most important tool I've ever encountered to help me make the big choices in life. Because almost everything— all external expectations, all pride, all fear of embarrassment or failure—these things just fall away in the face of death, leaving only what is truly important. Remembering that you are going to die is the best way I know to avoid the trap of thinking you have something to lose. You are already naked. There is no reason not to follow your heart.

About a year ago I was diagnosed with cancer. I had a scan at 7:30 in the morning, and it clearly showed a tumor on my pancreas. I didn't even know what a pancreas was. The doctors told me this was almost certainly a type of cancer that is incurable, and that I should expect to live no longer than three to six months. My doctor advised me to go home and get my affairs in order, which is doctor's code for prepare to die. It means to try to tell your kids everything you thought you'd have the next 10 years to tell them in just a few months. It means to make sure everything is buttoned up so that it will be as easy as possible for your family. It means to say your goodbyes.

I lived with that diagnosis all day. Later that evening I had a biopsy, where they stuck an endoscope down my throat, through my stomach and into my intestines, put a needle into my pancreas and got a few cells from the tumor. I was sedated, but my wife, who was there, told me that when they viewed the cells under a microscope the doctors started crying because it turned out to be a very rare form of pancreatic cancer that is curable with surgery. I had the surgery and I'm fine now.

This was the closest I've been to facing death, and I hope it's the closest I get for a few more decades. Having lived through it, I can now say this to you with a bit more certainty than when death was a useful but purely intellectual concept:

No one wants to die. Even people who want to go to heaven don't want to die to get there. And yet death is the destination we all share. No one has ever escaped it. And that is as it should be, because Death is very likely the single best invention of Life. It is Life's change agent. It clears out the old to make way for the new. Right now the new is you, but someday not too long from now, you will gradually become the old and be cleared away. Sorry to be so dramatic, but it is quite true.

Your time is limited, so don't waste it living someone else's life. Don't be trapped by dogma— which is living with the results of other people's thinking. Don't let the noise of others' opinions drown out your own inner voice. And most important, have the courage to follow your heart and intuition. They somehow already know what you truly want to become. Everything else is secondary.

When I was young, there was an amazing publication called *The Whole Earth Catalog*, which was one of the bibles of my generation. It was created by a fellow named Stewart Brand not far from here in Menlo Park, and he brought it to life with his poetic touch. This was in the late 1960's, before personal computers and desktop publishing, so it was all made with typewriters, scissors, and polaroid cameras. It was sort of like Google in paperback form, 35 years before Google came along: it was idealistic, and overflowing with neat tools and great notions.

Stewart and his team put out several issues of *The Whole Earth Catalog*, and then when it had run its course, they put out a final issue. It was the mid-1970s, and I was your age. On the back cover of their final issue was a photograph of an early morning country road, the kind you might find yourself hitchhiking on if you were so adventurous. Beneath it were the words: "Stay Hungry. Stay Foolish." It was their farewell message as they signed off. Stay Hungry. Stay Foolish. And I have always wished that for myself. And now, as you graduate to begin anew, I wish that for you.

Stay Hungry. Stay Foolish.

Thank you all very much.

Source: From "'You've Got to Find What You Love,' Jobs Says," Stanford University. All Rights Reserved. news.stanford.edu/news/2005/june15/jobs-061505.html.

Another major source of revenue generated by the Internet comes from the development and sale of video games. The video game industry is a hybrid that combines equipment (such as Xbox and PlayStation), software and Internet downloads. According to the Entertainment Software Association, computer and video game sales in the United States generated $24.75 billion in 2011, and the average game player is 30 years old and has been playing video games for 12 years.

Originally appealing to younger consumers, with war games for young adults and animated products for children, today's video game companies recently broadened their audience significantly by producing nonviolent kinetic games, such as Nintendo's Wii and Microsoft's Kinect. "The industry is saying we care about hard-core fans, but we have to go after the wide audience," says Brian Crescente, editor in chief of gaming Web site Kotaku. The shift is also economic—a way to escape the industry's reputation for exploiting violence by producing only "shooter" games and to blunt legislative attempts to control video game content and distribution.

MOBILE MEDIA CHASE THE AUDIENCE

Internet receivers have grown smaller and smaller, and retailers have expanded their ads to cell phones and tablets. Much like radio broadcasters who followed radio listeners from their homes into their cars when car radios were invented, Web site businesses are chasing today's mobile consumers.

The nation's millions of cell phone and tablet users make mobile media consumers an inviting target. Consumers use mobile media to send text messages,

Andreas Rentz/Getty Images Entertainment/Getty Images

Web developers cater to mobile media users because they are such a big audience. At a fashion show in Istanbul, Turkey, attendees use tablets and smartphones to go online.

take pictures, access the Internet and record video. This makes smartphones and other mobile media devices attractive media markets. (See **Illustration 9.3**, "How and Where Do People Use Mobile Media?," p. 191.)

Mobile media content has restrictions—content must be audible and/or clearly visible in the smaller viewing space of a cell phone or tablet screen. News and sports bulletins, short video clips and social media are perfectly suited for this media environment.

All four of the major TV networks and most subscription channels now offer most of their entertainment programs and news video online, on demand, for computer, cell phone and tablet viewing.

SOCIAL NETWORKS GROW GLOBALLY

A *social network* is an Internet community where people share information, ideas, personal messages, photographs, audio and video. Mobile applications (*apps*) make social network connections, such as Facebook, available to anyone anywhere in the world with a cell phone.

Social networks enable anyone who wants to create a podcast or a blog or a personal Web space to share information and ideas and, most often, to stay in touch with friends and family.

PODCASTS. Podcasting is the distribution of an audio or video file online. Individuals can easily use the Internet to create and share *podcasts*, and many news organizations, such as *PBS* and *The New York Times*,

---

Social Network   An Internet community where users share information, ideas, personal messages, photographs, audio and video.

App   Mobile application.

Podcast   An audio or video file made available on the Internet for anyone to download, often available by subscription.

IMPACT/Audience

Illustration 9.3

How and Where Do People Use Mobile Media?

Mobile media is the fastest-growing area of consumer media use. Americans spend more time watching their phones (144 minutes) than watching TV (141 minutes), and 70 percent of American consumers use their mobile phones *while* watching TV, according to InMobi, a mobile ad company.

Source: "Five Ways Mobile Devices Have Changed the Way Americans Consume Media." August 16, 2012, inmobi.com.

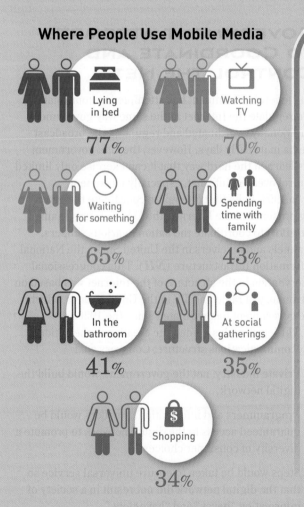

Where People Use Mobile Media

Lying in bed **77%**

Watching TV **70%**

Waiting for something **65%**

Spending time with family **43%**

In the bathroom **41%**

At social gatherings **35%**

Shopping **34%**

How People Use Mobile Media

General information and search **84%**

Social media **84%**

Games **83%**

Entertainment **77%**

E-mail **76%**

Local search **69%**

Shopping **55%**

Bill payment/mobile banking **37%**

frequently add podcasts to their Web sites as a way to expand coverage.

There also are podcast networks that feature several shows on the same feed, similar to a radio station. Consumers can download podcasts and listen to them whenever and wherever they want, which also makes podcasts an easy way to reach a mobile audience.

BLOGS. By one estimate, 80,000 new blog sites are launched daily, and the blog search engine Technorati tracks 29 million blog sites. A *blog* (short for Web log) is an online discussion group where people can post comments about a topic in a running conversation with each other.

Many news sites post live blogs to cover breaking news events. When Hurricane Sandy hit the East Coast in October 2012, several newspapers began blogs that invited people involved in the storm to contribute photos and news from their affected areas, as events were happening.

The text of the blog runs in reverse chronological order, with the most recent comments posted at the top of the blog so people can read through the previous postings for background on the topic, or they can start reading what follows after they join the group. Typically blogs do not carry advertising and are created as a way to enhance other content on the Web.

Blogs also have become frequent sources of information for news organizations seeking public reaction to ongoing events. The 2004 presidential election was the first time bloggers actually were accredited as part of the presidential press corps, indicating the importance of the bloggers' role as commentators on topical issues.

SOCIAL MEDIA SITES. In their report *Why Americans Use Social Media*, the Pew Internet and American Life Project said that two-thirds of adults who go online use social media sites such as Facebook, Twitter or LinkedIn. In 2012, Facebook and Twitter were among the most popular social media networks, but several competitors have emerged, such as Pinterest and LinkedIn. In 2012, Facebook reported the Web site had 150 million users. (See **Illustration 9.4**, "Why Do People Use Social Media?" and **Illustration 9.5**, "The Top 10 Social Networks Via Mobile Web," p. 193).

Blog   Short for Web log. A running Internet discussion group, where items are posted in reverse chronological order. Blogs usually focus on a specific topic.

NII   National Information Infrastructure.

CDA   Communications Decency Act.

Users create a personal page, a short blog for personal messages, plus they can add photos and video. Some sites, such as Facebook, are ad-supported; subscription fees support others, such as LinkedIn.

Podcasts, blogs and social media sites are the latest ways the media business has expanded its audience. It's important to remember that, in the history of the media business, advertisers always have followed consumers. To be successful, Internet providers know they must attract customers to be able to capitalize on the advertising potential the audience brings with it.

GOVERNMENT ATTEMPTS TO COORDINATE AND CONTROL THE NET

The federal government has attempted to coordinate and regulate the Internet in the same way government traditionally coordinated and regulated the broadcast media in its early days. However, the U.S. government has learned the hard way that it can exercise only limited control over the Internet, especially its content.

In 1994, in its first attempt to coordinate the growing presence of the Internet, the U.S. Congress named the effort to coordinate the nation's various senders, channels and receivers in the United States the National Information Infrastructure (*NII*). This congressional intervention in the structure of the Internet was based on the history of radio and TV in the United States, which the government had regulated since the 1920s.

Three principles guided the creation of the nation's telecommunications structure, Congress said:

1. Private industry, not the government, would build the digital network.

2. Programmers and information providers would be guaranteed access to the digital network to promote a diversity of consumer choices.

3. Steps would be taken to ensure universal service so that the digital network did not result in a society of information "haves" and "have-nots."

Then two years later, in its first attempt to control Internet content, Congress passed the Telecommunications Act of 1996. Included in that legislation was the Communications Decency Act (*CDA*), which outlined content that would be forbidden on the Internet. As soon as the act passed, civil liberties organizations challenged the law, and in 1997 the U.S. Supreme Court upheld the concept that the U.S. government could not control Internet content.

IMPACT/Audience

Illustration 9.4

Why Do People Use Social Media?

Most adults use social media to stay in touch with friends and family, but there are several other reasons people visit sites such as Facebook, Twitter and LinkedIn.

Source: Pew Internet & American Life Project, pewinternet.org.

91%
Stay in touch with current friends

87%
Stay in touch with family members

86%
Connect with old friends with whom they've lost touch

49%
Connect with others with shared hobbies or interests

43%
Make new friends

25%
Read comments by celebrities, athletes or politicians

16%
Find potential romantic or dating partners

Illustration 9.5

The Top 10 Social Networks Via Mobile Web

Source: The Social Media Report 2012, Nielsen, nielsen.com.

① Facebook
② Twitter
③ Blogger
④ Pinterest
⑤ Wordpress
⑥ LinkedIn
⑦ Tumblr
⑧ Wikia
⑨ Reddit
⑩ MySpace

A recent challenge to the distribution of Internet content came in 2005, when California passed a law prohibiting video game sales to minors. Federal courts declared the law unconstitutional, saying that the law interfered with freedom of expression, but the state appealed the precedent-setting challenge to the U.S. Supreme Court. Video game makers portrayed the law as a threat to First Amendment freedoms, and in 2011 the Supreme Court agreed, saying that the California law interfered with the First Amendment. (For more information about Congress and the U.S. Supreme Court's view of the Internet, see **Chapter 14**.)

PROTECTION SOUGHT FOR INTELLECTUAL PROPERTY RIGHTS

Money is the main reason the government wants to oversee the development of the Internet. Digitized bits, once they are widely available, can be easily stolen and reproduced for profit, which can means billions of dollars in lost revenue for companies and individuals who produce media content. Writers, moviemakers, singers and other creative people who provide the content for the media industries are especially concerned about their ideas being reproduced in several different formats, with no payment for their property.

This issue, the protection of what are called *intellectual property rights*, is a crucial part of the U.S. government's interest in the design of the Internet as a communications network. To protect online content, various copyright holders have used court challenges to establish their legal ownership, but some groups still are trying to avoid detection by keeping their online activities hidden from government scrutiny.

With access to copyrighted digital content, someone could capture video from a Disney movie sent over the Internet and join sections of that video with comedy bits from an episode of *Saturday Night Live*, putting the two casts together in a newly digitized program, for example. Once this content is captured and stored, it would be available to anyone who wants to use it.

The protection of content is one of the dilemmas created by digitized files that can be transmitted to anyone's storage system over an international network.

Intellectual Property Rights   The legal right of ownership of ideas and content published in any medium.

DMCA   Digital Millennium Copyright Act.

RIAA   Recording Industry Association of America.

MPAA   Motion Picture Association of America.

The creative people who contribute this content, and the people who produce and own these programs, are demanding laws and regulations structured to protect intellectual property rights.

The issue of who owns existing copyrighted material, such as recordings and movies, is particularly tricky on a medium like the Internet with global access and few controls. In 1998, Congress passed the Digital Millennium Copyright Act (*DMCA*) to make it illegal to share copyrighted material on the Internet. (For more information about the DMCA, see **Chapter 14**.) Using this law and provisions of existing copyright law, industries with a big stake in content ownership have sued to stop people from sharing copyrighted content on the Internet.

The Recording Industry Association of America (*RIAA*) and the Motion Picture Association of America (*MPAA*) have been especially aggressive in seeking to prosecute people who make copyrighted content available on the Web. In 1999, RIAA sued Napster, a company that provided a music-swapping service on the Internet. In 2001, after several appeals, the courts found that Napster was liable for "vicarious copyright infringement." Napster eventually shut down and then reopened as a subscription music service that pays royalties to companies that own rights to music available on the site.

© John McPherson/Distributed by Universal Uclick via CartoonStock.com 3-31

John McPherson/CartoonStock.com

Starbucks doubles its sales by devising a way to sell coffee over the Internet.

In 2001, the MPAA sued to stop publication of the digital code that allows a person to copy DVDs and place copies of movies on the Internet. The court agreed with the MPAA, saying that even if people possess the code but don't use it, they are committing piracy. This was an important legal precedent for content sharing on the Web and has led to more corporate attempts to seek wider protections over copyrighted content.

In 2003, Apple launched iTunes, a service that charges a fee to download songs legally. iTunes was created to respond to the various court actions since 1999, designed to end illegal *file sharing*, which means downloading files placed on the Internet by another person, not necessarily the original copyright holder.

In 2005, the music-file-sharing network Grokster shut down after reaching a settlement with the movie and music industries about online piracy. And in 2010, a federal judge ordered the major remaining music-file-sharing service, LimeWire, to shut its Web site. The court order required that LimeWire disable "searching, downloading, uploading, file trading and/or file distribution functionality."

In February 2013, the *Copyright Alert System (CAS)* in the United States was activated to warn consumers who try to download copyrighted material. Internet companies AT&T, Cablevision, Comcast, Verizon and Time Warner Cable created the system, which notifies offenders when they try to download a copyrighted file. Administered by the Center for Copyright Administration, the system tracks illegal downloaders and, after six warnings, the Internet service provider, such as Comcast, can block the offender's account. (For more information about file sharing and copyrights, see **Chapter 14**.)

FCC PROMOTES INTERNET NEUTRALITY

In 2010, the Federal Communications Commission (FCC) outlined rules for Internet service providers that require them to keep their networks open and available to carry all legal content from all carriers. These provisions, called Internet neutrality (often referred to as *Net neutrality*), mean that telecommunications companies, such as AT&T and Verizon, must maintain an open network. They cannot restrict access by other providers to their network nor can they limit the type or delivery of content they carry. There are three basic Open Internet rules, as defined by the FCC:

1. Transparency. Broadband providers must disclose information regarding their network management practices, performance, and the commercial terms of their broadband services.

2. No Blocking. Fixed broadband providers (such as DSL, cable modem or fixed wireless providers) may not block lawful content, applications, services or non-harmful devices. Mobile broadband providers may not block lawful Web sites or applications that compete with their voice or video telephone services.

3. No Unreasonable Discrimination. Fixed broadband providers may not unreasonably discriminate in transmitting lawful network traffic over a consumer's broadband Internet access service. The no blocking and no unreasonable discrimination rules are subject to limited exceptions for "reasonable network management."

For consumers, these rules mean, for example, that manufacturers such as Apple cannot require iPhone users to sign up exclusively with AT&T and that people with iPhones and tablets may use any carrier they chose.

In announcing the neutrality rules, FCC Chairman Julius Genachowski said, "Government should not be in the business of running or regulating the Internet." This signals that, under the Obama administration, the federal government plans minimal interference with Internet content, a shift from earlier government attempts to restrict it. (See **Chapter 14**.)

STORAGE, COMPATIBILITY AND SECURITY BRING CHALLENGES

Global government's support for net neutrality is an important issue for the future health of the Internet. The system faces at least three other major challenges: storage, compatibility and security.

Storage Capacity

The main technological advance that makes today's communications network possible is that electronic systems transform text, audio and video communication into the same type of digital file.

File Sharing The peer-to-peer distribution of copyrighted material on the Internet without the copyright owner's permission.

Copyright Alert System (CAS) A government-mandated warning to alert consumers who try to download copyrighted material.

Net Neutrality Rules for Internet service providers that require them to keep their networks open and available to carry all legal content. Under these rules, providers cannot restrict access to their network by other providers nor can they limit the type or delivery of content they carry.

Digital systems theoretically should be compatible, but many places in the world and many media systems have not yet totally converted to the technology that efficient digital delivery requires.

For example, digital delivery requires a huge amount of electronic storage space. To eliminate the need for so much storage, researchers developed a process called *data compression*. A copy of a major movie contains about 100 billion bytes of data. Compression squeezes the content down to about 4 billion bytes.

Data compression makes it much easier for a movie program service to keep movies available for use on demand. This helps make the movie affordable to deliver and usable for the customer.

Once the data are compressed, the company that delivers the service also must store the data. The next step in the process is equipment that grabs a movie the consumer has selected from a storage area and delivers it to the customer on request. This transfer equipment is called a *server* because it serves thousands of programs to millions of subscribers, on demand, all at the same time.

A recent innovation in data storage is called *cloud computing*, which allows one business to rent remote use of another company's computer space, operating "in the cloud." In 2011, Apple launched iCloud. Other large companies that can handle massive amounts of data over an online network, like Microsoft and Google, now provide cloud computing to businesses all over the world. Online video game and gambling sites, media producers and software designers, as well as video program providers (TV and cable networks) also are big consumers of cloud computing services.

Data streaming is the most familiar use of cloud computing. With video and audio data streaming, you can begin to play back a file without first completely downloading it. For example, you can start a movie on your laptop and immediately start to watch it. While

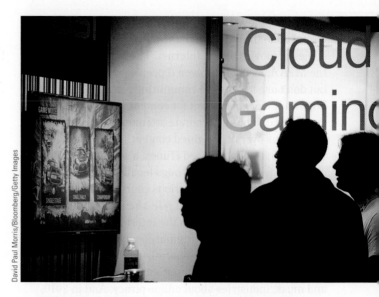

David Paul Morris/Bloomberg/Getty Images

The latest innovation in data storage is cloud computing. This allows one company to use another company's computer system, transferring information through the Internet to a "cloud"—the second company's secure online network. Attendees at the Game Developers Conference in San Francisco on March 27, 2013, look at an exhibit featuring video gaming on the cloud.

you are watching the movie, the file is downloading and stored on your computer. With a fast Internet connection, you can even stream live audio and video. Common streaming software brands are Real Audio and QuickTime.

Warehouses called *data farms* house the equipment that feeds the world's digital appetite. Often placed in remote, rural areas, tens of thousands of data centers throughout the world house millions of massive servers that process the data flowing over the Internet. According to *The New York Times*, these digital warehouses "use about 30 billion watts of electricity, roughly equivalent to the output of 30 nuclear power plants."

The United States contains about a third of these data centers, and many of them are running on local power grids, backed up by generators and lead-acid batteries in the case of a power failure. A basic necessity for the Internet's future will be the ability to maintain an efficient energy grid to feed the system's growing data storage needs.

Compatible Delivery

Today's global communications system is a mixture of old and new technologies. The current delivery system is a combination of coaxial cable, copper wire, fiber optics and cellular technology. Before the new communications

Data Compression The process of squeezing digital content into a smaller electronic space.

Server The equipment that delivers programs from their source to the programs' subscribers.

Cloud Computing The remote use by one business of another company's computer space, operating "in the cloud."

Data Streaming A common type of cloud computing that allows the user to play back an audio or video file without first completely downloading it.

Data Farms A location that houses data centers for the servers that process data flowing over the Internet.

network will be complete, new technology must completely replace old technology throughout the system. Some broadcasters, for example, still send signals over the airwaves with the same technology they have used since the 1930s, when broadcasting was first introduced. This technology is called *analog*.

Analog technology encodes video and audio information as continuous signals. Then these signals are broadcast through the air on specific airwave frequencies to a TV set, which translates them into pictures and sounds. Analog technology is very cumbersome because an analog signal needs a lot of space to travel on the airwaves. However, because analog signals travel through the air by transmitters, consumers can receive them free with just an antenna.

At least 10 million homes in the United States still receive only over-the-air broadcasts. They do not subscribe to cable or satellite. And although the federal government mandated that TV stations in large cities digitize their signals by 2009, by 2013 some smaller stations still had not made the costly transition to digital.

Cable companies eliminated the need for antennas by using coaxial cable, buried underground or strung from telephone poles. Some coaxial cable systems still use analog technology. Cable operators capture programming, such as HBO, from satellite systems, then gather analog broadcast signals from their local TV stations, and deliver this programming to the consumer using a combination of coaxial cable, copper wire and optical fiber.

Optical fiber is composed of microscopic strands of glass that transmit messages in digitized "bits"—zeroes and ones. Each fiber-optic strand carries 250,000 times as much information as one copper wire. A fiber-optics communication system is very efficient because fiber can carry digitized information easily and quickly from one place to another.

Satellite services use digital signals to carry their programming. Programs that are delivered to a home satellite dish follow a wireless electronic journey from the program source through one of the many telecommunications satellites hovering around the globe. Satellite delivery, however, still requires a telephone connection to deliver the programs and the menus for the programs to a home receiver.

Telephone companies have converted almost all their major communications delivery systems from coaxial cable and copper wire to fiber optics and cellular technology. However, the incompatibility between analog and digital technology means that any remaining analog signals must be converted first to digital signals so they can travel smoothly everywhere. Conversion is very expensive.

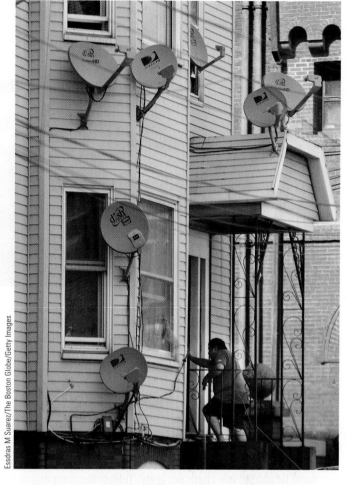

Essdras M Suarez/The Boston Globe/Getty Images

The transition to global digital delivery must overcome the incompatibility of existing media systems and new technology. Until all equipment is compatible and digital, the delivery system remains a mix of old and new. In East Boston, Mass., satellite dishes connected by antiquated wiring decorate the outside of an apartment building.

Digital technology is the most efficient method of delivery, but making the same system available throughout the world with a standardized delivery system is very complicated. Each competing system wants to control the entire delivery system because control of the delivery system means billions of dollars in revenue for whichever system consumers eventually adopt.

Analog   In mass communications, a type of technology used in broadcasting, whereby video or audio information is sent as continuous signals through the air on specific airwave frequencies.

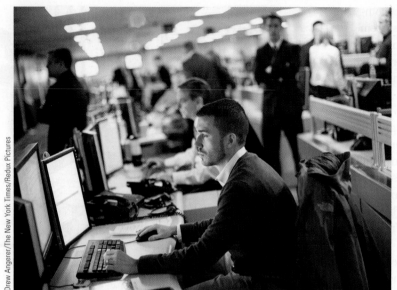

Drew Angerer/The New York Times/Redux Pictures

On February 12, 2013, President Obama signed an executive order to promote cybersecurity. At the nation's National Cybersecurity and Communications Integration Center in Arlington, Va., an agent monitors digital communications.

System Security

With all these different media delivery systems and services available, consumers, industry and governments must be able to use them securely. Telephone companies already have a complex system that matches people with the calls they make and carries conversations and texts on secure lines all over the world. To be effective, security for digital communications on the Internet must be at least as safe as current telephone communications.

Commercial operations, such as banks and retailers, have developed secure systems for transferring transaction records on the Internet. To protect consumers' banking records, banks use digital codes and dedicated transmission lines to secure the transactions from Internet hackers. Software companies have developed reasonably reliable systems to ensure that the personal records and content contained in interactive transactions are safe. An entirely new industry has evolved dedicated to the issue of Internet data security.

However, on January 30, 2013, *The New York Times* announced that Chinese hackers had infiltrated its computer systems and obtained passwords for its reporters and other employees. "The attacks appear to be part of

a broader computer espionage campaign against American news media companies that have reported on Chinese leaders and corporations," said *The Times*. Officials of the Chinese government denied the charges.

Less than a week later, Twitter said hackers had victimized about 250,000 of its accounts, including accounts for President Barack Obama, Vice President Joe Biden and House Speaker John Boehner. On February 12, 2013, President Obama signed an executive order to promote cybersecurity, which encourages the government and private companies to share information about data breaches that threaten national security.

The rules that individual nations develop to govern the security of this complex global communications network will have a profound impact on individuals, businesses, government and the media industries.

DISRUPTIVE TECHNOLOGIES REVOLUTIONIZE OLD CONCEPTS

The Internet affects consumers daily—how people shop, get their news, study, manage their money, and especially socialize with friends and family. For businesses, global information is instantly available to most companies simultaneously, making communication much easier, but inviting more intense competition.

For the media industries, the Internet places every element of the media business in transition. Today, owners and managers of the companies that make up the media industries are deciding daily how to invest in equipment, employees, research and development to protect current income while trying to ensure their companies adapt to the Internet's evolving demands.

Some digital entrepreneurs succeed, some create transitional products that will, in turn, spark new products, and many new ideas fail. Until the digital media landscape is clearer, however, it is important to follow ongoing developments because no one can predict exactly where digital media are headed. Four ongoing developments to watch are touch technology, Massive Open Online Courses (MOOCs), 3-D virtual reality systems, and wikis.

Touch Technology

Touch technology uses computing power to digitally enhance the five senses—touch, sight, hearing, taste and smell. Researchers at IBM and other companies are developing a system of cognitive computing, which uses artificial intelligence and advanced speech recognition to make a computer capable of learning.

Scientists say eventually you will be able to simulate the sensation of touch through your cell phone, for example. So when you look at a display of silk sheets on Amazon, you would be able to feel the fabric by touching your cell phone screen. And when an ad for pizza appears on your laptop, it will awaken your taste buds with digital sensors, sending the aroma of tomatoes and cheese and garlic.

Massive Open Online Courses

Massive open online courses (*MOOCs*) create huge online virtual classrooms, available to anyone with an Internet connection. Initially the courses have been offered free through established universities such as Princeton, Columbia and Duke. Typically the courses do not carry academic credit, but the idea is that eventually Internet classes would create a massive virtual university where students could sign up and receive credit for university-approved classes offered anywhere in the world via the Internet.

Three emerging companies, Coursera, edX and Udacity, are promoting MOOCs as an answer to the shortage of classes and increased tuition facing today's students. But there are critics and several unsolved problems. So far MOOCs have a very high dropout rate—nine out of ten students who enroll leave before the class is over. And how can one teacher effectively grade thousands of students or verify that the students who are enrolled are the students taking the tests or that they are, in fact, learning the material?

Still, some educators and entrepreneurs are investing in the idea that, for some college courses, a virtual classroom may offer a more efficient, cost-effective alternative to the traditional teacher-student classroom experience.

3-D Virtual Reality Systems

In the 1960s, computer flight simulators that trained military pilots were predecessors of today's *3-D virtual reality* (VR) systems. Virtual reality systems give the user the experience of being somewhere by creating a digital representation of reality and then placing a digital representative in that digital reality. In the Internet world, someone's digital representative is called an *avatar*. (The name comes from Hindu mythology, describing a deity who takes on human form.)

An Internet avatar is simply an icon or a representation of a user—a digital stand-in—that people create to represent their online identity. This new technology is especially promising in the field of science, where doctors can simulate an operation using a 3-D virtual reality avatar, for example, before using the procedure on a patient.

At the University of Illinois at Chicago, for example, scientists are developing a system that uses sophisticated 3-D glasses to allow a brain surgeon to take a virtual walk through an image of the human brain and a meteorologist to explore hurricanes from inside a digital image of the storm.

Wikis

The term *wiki* derives from a Hawaiian word that means "fast." This technology allows many users to collaborate to create and update an Internet page. A wiki Web site allows registered users to add and edit content on a specific topic. The best-known wiki is Wikipedia, an online encyclopedia where registered contributors may post additions and changes to any entry.

Wiki technology records the original material plus the material that contributors add over time. Wikis have great potential to gather together contributions worldwide from all the specialists on one subject, for example, but there are no safeguards that the material placed on the site is guaranteed accurate or reliable.

Touch Technology   Uses computing power to digitally enhance the five senses—touch, sight, hearing, taste and smell.

MOOCs   Massive open online courses.

3-D Virtual Reality   Creates a digital representative of reality and then places a digital representative (called an avatar) in that reality.

Avatar   An icon or representation of a user—a digital stand-in—that represents an online identity.

Wiki   Technology that allows many users to collaborate to create and update Internet pages.

AP Photo/PRNewsFoto/Netflix, Inc

Consumers Intersect with Technology

The future of digital media is bound only by the needs of consumers and the imaginations of media developers, as diverse as the people who are online today and going online tomorrow. The new media universe could become a purer reflection of the real universe than any medium yet created, with unprecedented potential, like all mass media, to both reflect and direct the culture.

"The Internet is still in its infancy, and its potential is enormous," writes media critic David Shaw. The

In 2013, Netflix announced plans to produce an original cartoon series for children based on the Dreamworks Animation movie *Turbo.* **The series, offered only through streaming on Netflix, will be available for children to watch all at once. Streaming video programs are an example of disruptive technology that can change the way consumers use media.**

Internet, says Shaw, could "revolutionize human communication even more dramatically than Johann Gutenberg's first printing press did more than 500 years ago."

Review, Analyze, Investigate

Reviewing Chapter 9

Digital Communication Transforms Media

• The emergence of the Internet within the last 30 years has transformed the structure and economics of the U.S. media business.

• The Internet today offers people wireless access to information just about wherever and whenever they want it.

• The Internet delivers all types of media using a single delivery system.

• The Internet is a combination of millions of computer networks sending and receiving data from all over the world.

• In its global size and absence of central control, the Internet is completely different from traditional media.

Digital Media Support Convergence

• Nicholas Negroponte at the Massachusetts Institute of Technology was the first person to identify the theory of convergence.

• The theory of convergence helped shape today's thinking about the Internet.

• Every media industry benefits from convergence.

20th-Century Discoveries Made Internet Possible

• The person most responsible for creating the World Wide Web is Tim Berners-Lee, who created the first browser and also gave the World Wide Web its name.

- Marc Andreessen at the University of Illinois created Mosaic, which allowed people to put text and pictures in the same online document.
- Both Andreessen and Berners-Lee placed their creations in the public domain, which meant that anyone with a computer and a modem could download them free.
- A culture of free information access, coupled with a creative, chaotic lack of direction, still permeates the Web today.

Web Opens to Unlimited Access

- Universal access, limited only by the available technology, is what gives the Web the feeling and look of what has been called "anarchy"—a place without rules.
- Today's media companies have a shared interest in seeing their investments in new technologies succeed.

What Happens to Old Media?

- The introduction of a new medium such as the Internet does not mean the end of the old.
- Older media forms continue to evolve and adapt to the new media environment.

Transformation Takes 30 Years

- Paul Saffo says the pace of change has consistently been about 30 years from the introduction of a new technology to its complete adoption by the culture.
- By Saffo's standard—the 30-year rule—American society is beginning to enter the third stage of acceptance, where the majority of the population has adapted to the new technology.

Web Access Leaves Some People Behind

- About 21 percent of Americans still do not go online— because either they can't afford it or they're afraid of it or they don't have access.
- The gap between people with online access and those who do not is called the *digital divide*.

Internet Combines Commerce, Information and Entertainment

- A major source of Web income is the money people pay their Internet service provider.
- Three other potential sources of income on the Web are commerce, advertising and content.
- Most commercial Web sites now carry some form of advertising.
- Tablet devices, such as the iPad, offer another outlet for purchased media.
- Another source of revenue generated by the Internet comes from the development and sale of video games.
- The video game industry is a hybrid that combines equipment (such as Xbox and PlayStation), software and Internet downloads.

- Computer and video game sales in the United States generated $24.75 billion in 2011.
- The average video game player is 30 years old and has been playing games for 12 years.
- Internet tracking tells advertisers about the audience's behavior.

Mobile Media Chase the Audience

- The latest targets for expanding Internet media use are mobile media—smartphones and tablets.
- Mobile media content must be audible and/or viewable in the small viewing space of a cell phone or tablet screen. News, sports bulletins and audio and video clips are perfectly suited for a mobile media environment.
- All four of the major TV networks and most subscription channels offer their entertainment and news programs online.

Social Networks Grow Globally

- A social network is an Internet community where people can share information, ideas, personal messages, photographs, audio and video.
- Two-thirds of adults who go online use social media sites.
- In 2012, Facebook and Twitter were among the most popular social media networks, but several competitors have emerged, such as Pinterest and LinkedIn.
- In 2012, Facebook reported the Web site had 150 million users.

Government Attempts to Coordinate and Control the Net

- The federal government has attempted to coordinate and regulate the Internet, but the U.S. government has limited control over the Internet, especially its content.
- In 1994, the U.S. Congress named the effort to coordinate the nation's various senders, channels and receivers the National Information Infrastructure (NII).
- In 1997, the U.S. Supreme Court upheld the concept that the U.S. government could not control Internet content.
- A recent challenge to Internet content started with the 2005 passage of a law in California that prohibited video game sales to minors. Federal courts declared the law unconstitutional. The state appealed the case to the U.S. Supreme Court, which ruled in 2011 that the ban was a violation of freedom of speech.

Protection Sought for Intellectual Property Rights

- Legal protections for digital content are called *intellectual property rights*.
- In 1998, Congress passed the Digital Millennium Copyright Act to make it illegal to share copyrighted material on the Internet.

- The Recording Industry Association of America and the Motion Picture Association of America have aggressively pursued copyright infringement.

- In 2003, Apple introduced iTunes, which allows people to download music legally.

- In 2005, the free music-file-sharing network Grokster shut down after reaching a settlement with the movie and music industries about online piracy.

- In 2010, a federal judge ordered the major remaining music-file-sharing service, LimeWire, to shut down its Web site.

- In February 2013, the Copyright Alert System (CAS) in the United States was activated to warn consumers who are trying to download copyrighted material.

FCC Promotes Internet Neutrality

- In 2010, the FCC adopted Internet neutrality rules to ensure that telecommunications companies maintain open Internet access.

- There are three basic Open Internet rules, as defined by the FCC: transparency, no blocking, and no unreasonable discrimination.

- The FCC's actions signal that the federal government plans minimal interference with Internet content.

Storage, Compatibility and Security Bring Challenges

- In 2006, Google agreed to let the Chinese government censor its online search results for Chinese customers. Yahoo! and MSN previously had agreed to similar restrictions in China.

- Researchers are developing a process called *data compression*, which collapses the size of data files so they are easier to download.

- A recent innovation in data storage is called *cloud computing*, which allows one business to rent remote use of another company's computer space, operating "in the cloud."

- Data streaming is the most familiar use of cloud computing.

- Today's communications system is a mixture of analog and digital technologies.

- At least 10 million homes in the United States still receive only over-the-air broadcasts. They do not subscribe to cable or satellite.

- On January 30, 2013, *The New York Times* announced that Chinese hackers had infiltrated its computer systems and obtained passwords for its reporters and other employees. Officials of the Chinese government denied the charges.

- Less than a week later, Twitter said hackers had victimized about 250,000 of its accounts, including accounts for President Barack Obama, Vice President Joe Biden and House Speaker John Boehner.

- On February 12, 2013, President Obama signed an executive order to promote cybersecurity.

- The rules that individual nations develop to govern the Internet will have a profound impact on individuals, businesses, government and the media industries.

Disruptive Technologies Revolutionize Old Concepts

- The Internet means that every element of the mass media industries is in transition.

- Four developments that are advancing consumers' use of the Internet are touch technology, 3-D virtual reality systems, massive open online courses (MOOCs) and wikis.

Consumers Intersect with Technology

- The future of digital media is bound only by the needs of consumers and the imagination of media developers.

- The new media universe has unprecedented potential to both reflect and direct the culture.

Key Terms

These terms are defined in the margins throughout this chapter and appear in alphabetical order with definitions in the Glossary, which begins on page 373.

Critical Questions

1. Explain the concept of the digital divide as outlined in this chapter. Why does the digital divide exist? How can the digital divide be eliminated?

2. Why does the Web show remarkable potential for revenue growth? Be specific.

3. Discuss Steve Jobs' contributions to the development of the Internet. List three contributions that he and/or his company, Apple Inc., contributed to the expansion of the Internet? What was his basic philosophy? Do you agree? Why or why not?

4. Discuss the role of the U.S. government in regulating activity on the Internet, including issues relating to copyright and intellectual property. Discuss areas where the government has been both successful and unsuccessful in regulating the Internet.

5. What communications role do social networks play in today's society?

Working the Web

This list includes both sites mentioned in the chapter and others to give you greater insight into the Internet industries.

Apple Inc.

apple.com

The main home page of Apple, this site's sections include Apple Store, iPod and iTunes, iPhone, Mac computers and software, and Support. Apple.com Worldwide allows users to shop internationally from Belgium to Portugal to Taiwan.

BuzzFeed

buzzfeed.com

Promoting itself as the "leading social news organization" that "reaches more than 25 million monthly unique visitors," BuzzFeed offers its own reports and information on topics trending on the Web, including politics, technology, entertainment and sports. The founder and CEO of the company was a co-founder of what is now one of its direct competitors, the *Huffington Post*.

CNET

cnet.com

A CBS Interactive site, CNET provides electronic technology news and reviews and does comparison-shopping for products. Its Tips & Tricks section includes more than 1,000 searchable tips with streaming video, online articles, forums and buying guides. Tips are designated by user level: all, beginner, intermediate and advanced.

Electronic Frontier Foundation (EFF)

eff.org

This nonprofit organization was created in 1990 to protect digital rights. EFF tackles issues including Free Speech (online anonymity), Innovation (patents) and Transparency (e-voting rights). The site lists legal cases with descriptions, outcomes, related documents, press releases and other resources.

Facebook

facebook.com

Founded in February 2004, Facebook is a social Web site with about 500 million users and 1,400 employees. The Palo Alto-based company uses Web-based technologies to help people create an online presence so they can share information with people who sign up to be "friends." Anyone can sign up for a free Facebook account.

iVillage

ivillage.com

iVillage Inc., a division of NBC Universal, is the first and largest media company dedicated exclusively to connecting women at every stage of their lives. Content ranges from health, parenting, beauty and style to fitness, relationships, food and entertainment. Interactive features include social networking and message boards that allow women to connect with others and to seek advice and support.

Journal of Electronic Publishing (JEP)

journalofelectronicpublishing.org

The Scholarly Publishing Office (SPO), a unit of the University of Michigan Library, produces this forum for research and discussion of contemporary publishing. When JEP began in 1995, it recognized the significant changes in print communication and the growing role of digital communication in transmitting published information. Journal articles present innovative ideas, best practices and progressive thinking about all aspects of publishing, authorship and readership.

MIT Media Lab Project

media.mit.edu

This innovative multidisciplinary research laboratory at the Massachusetts Institute of Technology explores human/computer interaction. Now in its third decade of operation, the Lab is focusing on "human adaptability" projects including initiatives to treat Alzheimer's disease and depression, sociable robots that can monitor the health of children or the elderly, and the development of prostheses that can mimic the capabilities of biological limbs.

Online Publishers Association (OPA)

online-publishers.org

A not-for-profit industry trade organization founded in 2001, the OPA represents online content providers to the advertising community, the press, the government and the public. Members, from ABCNews.com to *The Washington Post*, agree to abide by standards of quality and credibility. It also publishes the biweekly OPA Intelligence Report, which summarizes important news and research for the online publishing industry.

Pew Internet & American Life Project

pewinternet.org

Solely supported by the privately held Pew Charitable Trust, the Pew Internet Project explores the effect of the Internet on various aspects of life: children, families, communities, the work place, education, health care, and civic and political life. Information available on the site includes reports, presentations, data sets and current trends.

Quarter to Three

quartertothree.com

This site consists of a series of online forums on a variety of topics that "we stay up far too late to do," including video games, watching movies and television, reading and Internet browsing, but it is top-heavy in video game content. The site also has message boards and two weekly podcasts.

Technorati

technorati.com

Technorati acts as an online conduit, of sorts, with its own network of "member editors and writers." The site connects bloggers, social media Web sites and advertisers to one another and, in turn, offers access to its own online video and written content on a variety of topics, including politics, technology, sports and business.

The Verge

theverge.com

The Verge is one of the many online sites that have been established in the last few years to keep up with the craving for the immediacy of real-time breaking news, deliver information about the latest technology trends and products as well as share "community content" and information from a variety of locations around the world, including North and South America, Europe and Asia.

Whatis.com

whatis.techtarget.com

This self-education tool contains more than 4,500 individual information technology (IT) definitions, especially about the Internet and computers. Although the majority of its audience is IT professionals, even the layperson can search the site's encyclopedia for the most basic acronyms and terms. Users can find everything from a list of text messaging abbreviations to the definition of a zip drive.

 Impact/Action Videos are concise news features on various topics created exclusively for *Media/Impact*. Go online to access MindTap at cengagebrain.com. MindTap for Media/Impact sequences all of your learning tools—Chapter Readings with highlighting and note taking, Impact/Action Videos, activities and assessments—into chapter driven learning units that guide you through the curriculum.

ADVERTISING: 10
CATCHING CONSUMERS

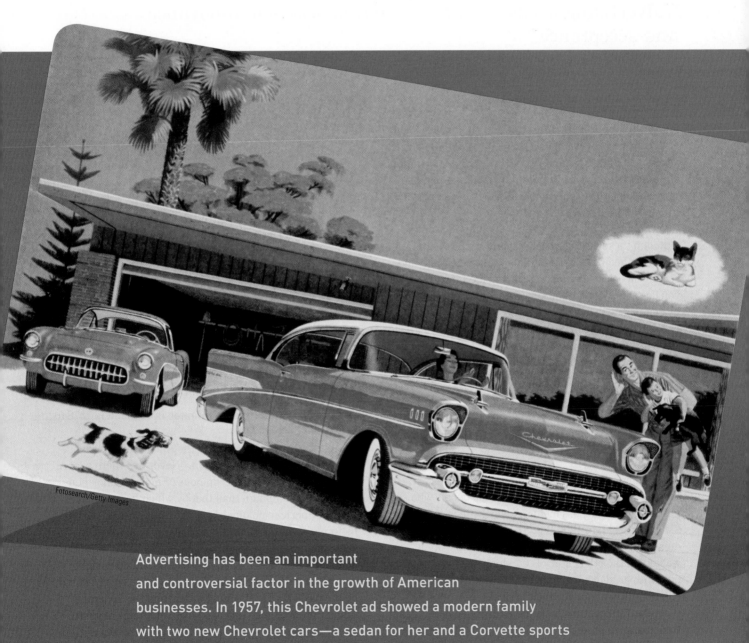

Fotosearch/Getty Images

Advertising has been an important
and controversial factor in the growth of American
businesses. In 1957, this Chevrolet ad showed a modern family
with two new Chevrolet cars—a sedan for her and a Corvette sports
car for him—which fit perfectly in their new modern house with its
two-car garage, a luxury for 1950s homeowners.

"Advertising needs to walk a fine line between annoyance and acceptance."

—ANTONY YOUNG, CEO, MINDSHARE NORTH AMERICA

American consumers pay

for most of their media (newspapers, magazines, radio and television) by watching, listening to and reading advertisements. The American Marketing Association defines advertising as "any paid form of non-personal presentation and promotion of ideas, goods or services by an identified sponsor."

You pay directly for books, movies and recordings, although these media use advertising to sell their products. But the broadcast programs you want to hear and see, the articles you want to read and the Internet sites you use every day are filled with advertisements placed by companies that want to sell you products. In 2012, U.S. businesses spent $161 billion—$512 per person—to advertise their products to American consumers, more than any other country in the world. (See **Illustration 10.1**, "What Are the World's Largest Markets for Advertising?," p. 207.)

ADVERTISING SUPPORTS MASS MEDIA

Advertising is not a mass medium. Advertising carries the messages that come to you from the people who pay for the American mass media. Advertising is at least 3,000 years old. In 1200 B.C., the Phoenicians painted messages on stones near paths where people often walked. In the 6th century B.C., ships that came into port with products on board sent criers around town with signboards to announce their arrival.

In the 13th century A.D., the British began requiring trademarks to protect buyers and to identify the makers of quality products. The first printed advertisement was

Marty Bucella/CartoonStock.com

"I don't know what it means, but sales have skyrocketed since I put the 'i' in front of it."

prepared by printer William Caxton in England in 1478 to sell one of his books.

Advertising became part of the American experience even before the settlers arrived. "Never was there a more outrageous or more unscrupulous or more ill-informed advertising campaign than that by which the promoters for the American colonies brought settlers here," writes historian Daniel J. Boorstin. "Brochures published in England in the 17th century, some even earlier, were full of hopeful overstatements, half-truths, and downright lies, along with some facts which nowadays surely would be the basis for a restraining order from the Federal Trade Commission. Gold and silver, fountains of youth, plenty of fish, venison without limit, all these were promised, and of course some of them were found."

IMPACT/Global

Illustration 10.1

What Are the World's Largest Markets for Advertising?

In 2012, marketers spent more money on advertising in the United States than any other country. The U.S. ranks second to Australia in the amount spent per person because Australia's population is so much smaller. And although China ranks third in the total amount spent on advertising, the country has such a large population that the amount spent per person is much lower than in the United States.

Source: "Ad Spending Per Person 1992–2013," *Advertising Age*, DataCenter, adage.com.

Canada
34M people
$11B spent
$324 per

United Kingdom
63M people
$20B spent
$309 per

France
66M people
$14B spent
$206 per

Germany
81M people
$26B spent
$315 per

China
1,343M people
$27B spent
$3 per

South Korea
49M people
$11B spent
$220 per

United States
*314M people
**$161B spent
$512 per

Japan
127M people
$52B spent
$404 per

Brazil
199M people
$19B spent
$93 per

Australia
22M people
$13B spent
$580 per

*Population in millions.
**$ spent rounded to the nearest billion

Advertising in Newspapers

The nation's first newspaper ad appeared in *The Boston News-Letter*'s first issue in 1704 when the newspaper's editor included an ad for his own newspaper. The penny press of the 1800s counted on advertising to underwrite its costs.

In 1833, the *New York Sun* candidly said in its first issue: "The object of this paper is to lay before the public, at a price within the means of everyone, all the news

of the day and at the same time afford an advantageous medium for advertising." Three years later, the *Phila-delphia Public Ledger* reported that "advertising is our revenue, and in a paper involving so many expenses as a penny paper, and especially our own, the only source of revenue."

Because they were so dependent on advertisers, newspapers in the 1800s accepted any ads they could get. Eventually, customers complained, especially about the patent medicines that advertised cures for every imaginable disease and often delivered unwelcome hangovers. (Many of these medicines contained mostly alcohol.)

Products like Anti-Corpulence pills claimed they would help someone lose 15 pounds a month: "They cause no sickness, contain no poison and never fail." Dr. T. Felix Couraud's Oriental Cream guaranteed it would "remove tan, pimples, freckles, moth patches, rash and skin diseases and every blemish on beauty."

The newspaper publishers' response to complaints was to develop an open advertising policy, which meant newspapers would accept advertising from anyone who paid for it. This allowed the publishers to continue accepting the ads and then criticize the ads on their editorial pages. The *Public Ledger* described its policy this way: "Our advertising columns are open to the 'public, the whole public, and nothing but the public.' We admit any advertisement of any thing or any opinion, from any persons who will pay the price, excepting what is forbidden by the laws of the land, or what, in the opinion of all, is offensive to decency and morals."

But some editors did move their ads, which had been mingled with the copy, to a separate section. Advertising historian Stephen Fox says: "Advertising was considered an embarrassment . . . the wastrel relative, the unruly servant kept backstairs and never allowed into the front parlor. . . . A firm risked its credit rating by advertising; banks might take it as a confession of financial weakness.

"Everyone deplored advertising. Nobody—advertiser, agent or medium— took responsibility for it. The advertiser only served as an errand boy, passing the advertiser's message along to the publisher: the medium printed it, but surely would not question the right of free speech by making a judgment on the veracity of the advertiser."

Advertising in Magazines

Until the 1880s, magazines remained wary of advertising, but Cyrus H. K. Curtis, who founded *The Ladies' Home Journal* in 1887, promoted advertising as the way for magazines to succeed.

Once when he was asked what made him successful, he answered, "Advertising. That's what made me whatever I am. . . . I use up my days trying to find men who can write an effective advertisement." When Curtis hired Edward Bok as editor, Bok began

a campaign against patent medicine ads and joined with *Collier's* and the American Medical Association to seek government restraints. Congress created the Federal Trade Commission (FTC) in 1914, and part of its job was to monitor deceptive advertising. The FTC continues today to be the major government watchdog over advertising (see "Federal Government Regulates Advertisers," p. 220).

Advertising on Radio

WEAF in New York broadcast its first advertisement in 1922, selling apartments in New Jersey. B. F. Goodrich, Palmolive and Eveready commercials followed. In September 1928, the Lucky Strike Dance Orchestra premiered on NBC, and Lucky Strike sales went up 47 percent. More cigarette companies moved to radio, and Camel cigarettes sponsored weekly, then daily, programs.

Sir Walter Raleigh cigarettes sponsored the Sir Walter Raleigh Revue. In one hour, the sponsor squeezed in 70 references to the product, according to Stephen Fox in *The Mirror Makers: A History of American Advertising and Its Creators.* "The theme song ('rally round Sir Walter Raleigh') introduced the Raleigh Revue in the Raleigh Theater with the Raleigh Orchestra and the Raleigh Rovers; then would follow the adventures of Sir Walter in Virginia and at Queen Elizabeth's court, with ample mention

David J. Griffin/Icon SMI/Corbis

The U.S. advertising industry collected $161 billion in 2012. Procter & Gamble, maker of Tide detergent, spends more money on advertising in the United States than any other company. The Tide logo covers this NASCAR race car.

of his cigarettes and smoking tobacco," according to Fox. In 1938, for the first time, radio collected more money from advertising than magazines did.

Advertising on Television

Television began as an advertising medium. Never questioning how television would be financed, the TV networks assumed they would attract commercial support. They were right. In 1949, television advertising totaled $12.3 million. In 1950, the total was $40.8 million. In 1951, advertisers spent $128 million on television. In 2012, television advertising revenue in the United States totaled $74 billion.

In a practice adopted from radio, television programs usually carried *direct sponsorship*. Many shows, such as *Camel News Caravan*, carried the sponsor's name in the title and advertised just one product (Camel cigarettes). Advertising agencies became television's programmers. "Given one advertiser and a show title often bearing its name, viewers associated a favorite show with its sponsor and—because of a 'gratitude factor'—would buy the products," writes Fox.

Alfred Hitchcock became legendary for leading into his show's commercials with wry remarks about the sponsor: "Oh dear, I see the actors won't be ready for another 60 seconds. However, thanks to our sponsor's remarkable foresight, we have a message that will fill in here nicely." But Hitchcock's sarcasm was the exception, and the television industry today relies heavily on advertising support.

Advertising on the Internet

Advertisers flocked to major Internet sites when they were first launched. They expected quick returns, as consumer use of the Internet skyrocketed. At first, advertisers primarily used banner advertising, which meant their advertising messages scrolled across a Web site or appeared in a box on the site.

Internet sites also tried *pop-up* advertisements, which meant an ad popped up either behind a Web site screen when someone left the site or on top of the Web site home page when someone first visited. Advertisers quickly learned, however, that no matter how they packaged the message, advertising on an Internet site didn't necessarily bring increased sales for their products.

What advertisers call the *click-through rate* (the rate at which someone who sees an advertising message on an Internet site actually clicks through to learn more) is less than 1 percent. This is a very disappointing return, especially because Web site advertising can be expensive. By 2012, Internet ad spending reached $37 billion. Advertisers today are still trying to figure out the magic formula to reach consumers on the Internet, and they're willing to spend a lot of money to try to find out what works.

Ford, BMW, Coca-Cola and Absolut Vodka created "advertainments" on their Web sites—short movies (2 to 11 minutes) featuring lots of action and familiar movie stars. Many marketers are using *viral marketing* to try to reach younger audiences. Viral marketing means creating an online message that is so entertaining or interesting that consumers pass it along through social networking sites, such as Facebook and MySpace, and by e-mail links. The message becomes an online "virus" that promotes a product without the expense of a paid commercial.

These new approaches are meant to make Internet advertisements seem less like advertisements—further blurring the line between information, entertainment and advertising. (See **Impact/Audience**, "Advertising Content Leads Consumers to the Internet," p. 210.)

ADS SHARE THREE CHARACTERISTICS

The word *advertise* originally meant to take note or to consider. By the 1700s, the word's meaning had changed. *To advertise* meant "to persuade." "If we consider democracy not just a political system," says Daniel J. Boorstin, "but as a set of institutions which do aim to make everything available to everybody, it would not be an overstatement to describe advertising as the characteristic rhetoric of democracy."

Boorstin says that advertising in America shares three characteristics: repetition, style and ubiquity.

Direct Sponsorship A program that carries an advertiser's name in the program title.

Pop-Up An advertisement on a Web site that appears on the screen either behind a Web page when someone leaves the site or on top of the Web site home page when someone first visits.

Click-Through Rate The rate at which people who see an ad on an Internet site click through to learn more.

Viral Marketing Creating an online message that is entertaining enough to get consumers to pass it on over the Internet like a virus.

IMPACT/Audience

Advertising Content Leads Consumers to the Internet

Antony Young, CEO, Mindshare North America

What's the next big thing? The 30-second ad has served us well as the staple for building awareness and driving brand familiarity. But the proliferation of devices to consume media, the increasing scale and influence of social platforms, and consumers' increasing control over their media are forcing us to re-think how brands must proceed.

If our role is to figure out how best to influence consumers, then we have to take a more strategic perspective of not just where to deliver ads, but what type of content and content formats will work best.

Home Depot and the Weather Channel. We are seeing examples of how marketers are adapting their messaging by combining data and creativity. Take what Home Depot is doing with The Weather Channel. Tapping the Home Depot banner on the Weather Channel's mobile app sends you to its mobile ecommerce site, which dynamically showcases products extracting weather conditions and location data of the user. Very cool.

Twitter Video. With one in three digital minutes now spent on a mobile device, advertising needs to walk a fine line between annoyance and acceptance. During college basketball's March Madness, the NCAA pushed out via Twitter video highlights of plays as they took place. Followers could click the tweeted link that ran five-second AT&T spots before the content.

Short Films. When Royal Caribbean—full disclosure: a Mindshare client—looked to get first-time cruisers to book, this presented some challenges. There are so many pre-conceptions about cruise liners that a 30-second spot alone couldn't easily overcome. Long-form storytelling was necessary to draw the consumer into the onboard experience. So Royal Caribbean agreed to develop two short films shot on their flagship

Victor J. Blue/Bloomberg via Getty Images

Mindshare agency CEO Antony Young suggests that advertisers have to find new ways to reach today's mobile media consumer. When someone taps Home Depot's banner on the Weather Channel's mobile app, the consumer is re-directed to Home Depot's site, featuring location-specific products.

"Allure of the Seas" ship, featuring Jenny McCarthy and James Brolin. The storyline incorporated the amenities onboard and gave viewers a more entertaining and organic view of the onboard experience.

TV Program Content. One of the important payouts in a content-first strategy is driving earned media. Consumers are more likely to share content than ads. Unilever—another Mindshare client—teamed up with AOL to support the "Makers" series of videos about empowering and inspirational women from Hillary Clinton to Ellen DeGeneres. The content program, a TV special on PBS and surrounding events drove advocacy among opinion formers, generating over 200 million earned impressions via editorial and social mentions.

Consumers are in control and brands need to up their game to engage them. As we navigate through more devices and platforms that consumers are using to access media, we need to be as dynamic and fluid in the way we communicate with them.

Source: Excerpted from Antony Young, "Content Has to Be Adapted to Fit the Consumer's Media Experience," April 12, 2013, adage.com.

Repetition

In 1851, when Robert Bonner bought the *New York Ledger*, he wanted to advertise his newspaper in the competing *New York Herald*, owned by James Gordon Bennett. Bennett limited all his advertisers to the same type size, so Bonner paid for an entire page of the *Herald*, across which he repeated the message "Bring home the *New York Ledger* tonight." This is an early example of advertising's widespread practice of repeating a simple message for effect.

An Advertising Style

At first, advertising adopted a plain, direct style. Advertising pioneer Claude Hopkins, says Boorstin, claimed: "Brilliant writing has no place in advertising. A unique style takes attention from the subject. . . . One should be natural and simple . . . [I]n fishing for buyers, as in fishing for bass, one should not reveal the hook." The plain-talk tradition is a foundation of what advertisers call modern advertising. But advertising today often adopts a style of hyperbole, making large claims for products. Boorstin calls this "tall-talk."

The tall-talk ad is in the P. T. Barnum tradition of advertising. Barnum was a carnival barker and later impresario who lured customers to his circus acts with fantastic claims. You may recognize this approach in some of the furniture and car ads on television, as an announcer screams at you that you have only a few days left until all the chairs or all the cars will be gone.

Both plain talk and tall-talk combine, Boorstin says, to create advertising's new myth. "This is the world of the neither true nor false—of the statement that 60 percent of the physicians who expressed a choice said that our brand of aspirin would be more effective in curing a simple headache than any other brand. . . . It is not untrue, and yet, in its connotation it is not exactly true."

Ubiquity

In America, advertising is everywhere. Advertisers are always looking for new places to catch consumers' attention. Ads appear on shopping carts, on video screens at sports stadiums, atop parking meters. Says Daniel Boorstin, "The ubiquity of advertising is, of course, just another effect of our uninhibited efforts to use all the media to get all sorts of information to everybody everywhere. Since the places to be filled are everywhere, the amount of advertising is not determined by the needs of advertising, but by the opportunities for advertising, which become unlimited."

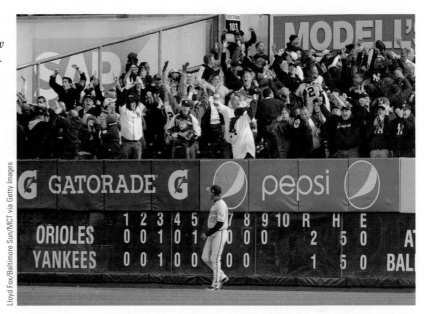

Lloyd Fox/Baltimore Sun/MCT via Getty Images

In the United States, advertising is everywhere—it is *ubiquitous*. Surrounded by advertising messages, fans at Yankee Stadium in New York cheer Raul Ibanez's game-tying home run in Game 3 of the American League Division Series on October 10, 2012.

In some cases, this ubiquity works to advertising's disadvantage. Many advertisers shy away from radio and TV because the ads are grouped so closely together. In 1986, in an attempt to attract more advertisers, TV began selling the "split-30" ad, which fits two 15-second ads into a 30-second spot. Even 10-second ads are available. Wherever these shorter commercials are sold, the station runs twice or three times as many ads for different products, crowding the commercial time even more. Too many ads that run together make it hard for one ad to grab consumers' attention.

ADS COMPETE FOR YOUR ATTENTION

To sell the products, advertisers must catch your eye or your ear or your heart (preferably all three). A study by the Harvard Graduate School of Business Administration reported that the average American is exposed to 500 ads a day.

With so many ads competing for your attention, the advertiser must first get you to read, to listen or to watch one ad instead of another. "The immediate goal of advertising [is to] tug at our psychological shirt sleeves and slow us down long enough for a word or two about whatever is being sold," says humanities and human sciences professor Jib Fowles in *Mass Advertising as Social Forecast*. Research shows there are at least 15 common ways ads appeal to consumers.

15 Ways Ads Appeal to Consumers

You make your buying decisions based on several sources of information besides advertising: friends, family and your own experience, for example. To influence your choices, the advertising message must appeal to you for some reason as you sift through the ads to make judgments and choose products. Fowles enumerated 15 appeals, which he calls an "inventory of human motives," that advertisers commonly use in their commercials:

1. **Need for sex.** Surprisingly, Fowles found that only 2 percent of the television ads he surveyed used this appeal. It may be too blatant, he concluded, and often detracts from the product.

2. **Need for affiliation.** The largest number of ads uses this approach: You are looking for friendship.

Advertisers use at least 15 different types of appeals to attract consumers. In 2012, Sleep Sheets launched an ad featuring tennis star Serena Williams with a billboard on Times Square. Which of the 15 ad appeals listed by Jib Fowles does the billboard use?

Ben Gabbe/Sleep Sheets/Getty Images

Advertisers can also use this negatively, to make you worry that you'll lose friends if you don't use a certain product.

3. **Need to nurture.** Every time you see a puppy or a kitten or a child, the appeal is to your maternal or paternal instincts.

4. **Need for guidance.** A father or mother figure can appeal to your desire for someone to care for you, so you won't have to worry. Betty Crocker is a good example.

5. **Need to aggress.** We all have had a desire to get even, and some ads give you this satisfaction.

6. **Need to achieve.** The ability to accomplish something difficult and succeed identifies the product with winning. Sports figures as spokespersons project this image.

7. **Need to dominate.** The power we lack is what we can look for in a commercial: "Master the possibilities."

8. **Need for prominence.** We want to be admired and respected, to have high social status. Luxury car ads and ads for diamond rings offer this potential.

9. **Need for attention.** We want people to notice us; we want to be looked at. Cosmetics are a natural for this approach.

10. **Need for autonomy.** Within a crowded environment, we want to be singled out, to be "a breed apart." This can also be used negatively: You may be too ordinary without a particular product.

11. **Need to escape.** Flight is very appealing; you can imagine adventures you cannot have. The idea of escape is pleasurable.

12. **Need to feel safe.** To be free from threats, to be secure is the appeal of many insurance and bank ads.

13. **Need for aesthetic sensations.** Beauty attracts us, and classic art or dance makes us feel creative, enhanced.

14. **Need to satisfy curiosity.** Facts support our belief that information is quantifiable, and numbers and diagrams make our choices seem scientific.

15. **Physiological needs.** Fowles defines sex (item no. 1) as a biological need, and so he classifies our need to sleep, eat and drink as physiological. Advertisements for juicy pizza are especially appealing late at night.

Marketers Use Demographics

Advertisers target their messages to an audience according to the audience's needs. But an advertiser also seeks to determine the audience's characteristics. This analysis of observable audience characteristics is called *demographics*.

Demographics are composed of data about a target audience's gender, age, income level, marital status, geographic location and occupation. These data are observable because they are available to advertising agencies through census data and other sources. Advertising agencies use demographic audience analysis to help advertisers target their messages.

A motorcycle dealer certainly wouldn't want to advertise in a baby magazine, for example; a candy manufacturer probably wouldn't profit from advertising in a diet and exercise magazine. Advertising agencies try to match a client's product to a thoroughly defined audience so each advertising dollar is well spent, such as matching an upscale bank with well-educated, high earners.

Defining the audience is very important because the goal of advertising is to market a product to people who have the desire for the product and the ability to buy it. Audience analysis tells an advertiser whether there are enough people who can be targeted for a product to make the advertising worthwhile.

Advertising Feeds Consumerism

According to Louis C. Kaufman, author of *Essentials of Advertising*, critics of advertising make three main arguments:

1. **Advertising adds to the cost of products**. Critics of advertising maintain that advertising, like everything that is part of manufacturing a product, is a cost. Ultimately, the consumer pays for the cost of advertising. But the industry argues that advertising helps make more goods and services available to the consumer and that the resulting competition keeps prices lower.

2. **Advertising causes people to buy products they do not need**. Says media scholar Michael Schudson, "Most blame advertising for the sale of specific consumer goods, notably luxury goods (designer jeans), frivolous goods (pet rocks), dangerous goods (cigarettes), shoddy goods (some toys for children), expensive goods that do not differ at all from cheap goods (non-generic over-the-counter drugs), marginally differentiated products that do not differ significantly from one another (laundry soaps), and wasteful goods (various un-ecological throw-away convenience goods)." The advertising industry contends the ultimate test of any product is the marketplace and that advertising may stimulate consumers to try a new product or a new brand, but consumers will not continue to buy an unsatisfying product.

3. **Advertising reduces competition and thereby fosters monopolies**. Critics point to the rising cost of advertising, especially on television, which limits which companies can afford to launch a new product or a new campaign. The industry argues that advertising is still a very inexpensive way to let people know about new products.

"The cost of launching a nationwide advertising campaign may be formidable," writes Louis C. Kaufman, "but the cost of supporting larger, nationwide sales forces for mass-marketed goods would be greater still."

Does advertising work? According to Schudson, "Apologists are wrong that advertising is simply information that makes the market work more efficiently—but so too are the critics of advertising who believe in its overwhelming power to deceive and to deflect human minds to its ends."

"Evaluating its impact," Kaufman says, "is more difficult than these simplicities of apology and critique will acknowledge."

Jean-Pierre Lescourret/Getty Images

Critics of advertising claim that it causes consumers to buy products they don't need. The advertising industry contends the ultimate test of any product is the marketplace because consumers won't continue to buy an unsatisfying product, such as this luxurious coat displayed on a Manhattan billboard.

Demographics Data about consumers' characteristics, such as age, gender, income level, marital status, geographic location and occupation.

ADVERTISING AT WORK

Several worldwide advertising agencies are based in the United States, but many advertising agencies are small local and regional operations. Advertising agencies buy time and space for the companies they represent. For this, they usually earn a commission (commonly 15 percent). Many agencies also produce television and radio commercials and print and Internet advertising for their clients.

Depending on the size of the agency, the company may be divided into as many as six departments:

1. Marketing research

2. Media selection

3. Creative activity

4. Account management

5. Administration

6. Public relations

Marketing research examines the product's potential, where it will be sold and who will buy the product. Agency researchers may survey the market themselves or contract with an outside market research company to evaluate potential buyers.

Media selection suggests the best combination of buys for a client—television, newspapers, magazines, billboards and/or Internet.

Creative activity thinks up the ads. The "creatives" write the copy for TV, radio, print and Internet. They design the graphic art, and often they produce the commercials. They also verify that the ad has run as many times as it was scheduled to run.

Account management is the liaison between the agency and the client. Account executives handle client complaints and suggestions and also manage the company team assigned to the account.

Administration pays the bills, including all the tabs for the account executives' lunches with clients. *Public relations* is an extra service that some agencies offer for companies that don't have a separate public relations office.

All these departments work together on an ad campaign. An ***advertising campaign*** is a planned advertising effort, coordinated for a specific time period. A campaign can last anywhere from a month to a year, and the objective is a coordinated strategy to sell a product or a service.

Advertising Campaign   A planned advertising effort, coordinated for a specific time period.

Typically, the company assigns the account executive a team of people from the different departments to handle the account. The account executive answers to the people who control the agency, usually a board of directors. The members of the campaign team coordinate all types of advertising—print and broadcast, for example—to make sure they share consistent content. After establishing a budget based on the client's needs, the campaign team creates a slogan, recommends a strategy for the best exposure for the client, approves the design of print and broadcast commercials and then places the ads with the media outlets.

Advertising agencies tend to be clustered in big cities such as New York, Los Angeles, San Francisco and Chicago. In part, this is by tradition. The agencies may want to be near their large clients in the cities. They also have access to a larger pool of talent and facilities such as recording studios, but today Internet technology enables greater flexibility for agency locations.

MASS MEDIA INDUSTRIES DEPEND ON ADVERTISING

The advertising business and the media industries are interdependent—that is, what happens in the advertising business directly affects the media industries. The advertising business also is very dependent on the nation's economic health. (See **Illustration 10.2**, "Top 10 Advertisers in the United States," p. 215.)

If the national economy expands, the advertising business and the media industries prosper. If the nation's economy falls into a recession, advertisers typically reduce their ad budgets, which eventually may lead to a decline in advertising revenue for the agencies and also for the media industries where the agencies place their ads. During a downturn, advertisers also may change their advertising strategies—choosing the Internet over television, for example, because the Internet is much less expensive.

The advertising industry today, therefore, must be very sensitive to economic and media trends. The success of an ad agency is best measured by the results an ad campaign brings. The agency must analyze the benefits of different types of advertising—broadcast, print, Internet—and recommend the most efficient combinations for their clients.

Commercials on Television

Even though the cost seems exorbitant, sponsors continue to line up to appear on network television. "Advertisers must use television on whatever terms they can get it, for television is the most potent merchandising vehicle ever devised," writes TV producer Bob Shanks in his

IMPACT/Money

Illustration 10.2

Top 10 Advertisers in the United States

Auto manufacturers, such as General Motors and Ford, always have spent a lot of money to advertise their products, but telecommunications companies such as Verizon (3), Comcast (4) and AT&T (5) spend nearly as much on advertising in the United States as General Motors (which ranked No. 2).

Source: "100 Leading National Advertisers 1992–2013," *Advertising Age*, DataCenter, adage.com.

book *The Cool Fire: How to Make It in Television*. Shanks is talking about national advertisers who buy network time—companies whose products can be advertised to the entire country at once.

Advertising minutes within every network prime-time hour are divided into 10-, 15- and 30-second ads. If an advertiser wants to reach the broad national market, television is an expensive choice because the average price for the TV time for a 30-second commercial in 2011 was $110,000. The price tag for a 30-second commercial reaches nearly $4 million for a widely watched program such as the 2013 Super Bowl.

National advertising on programs like CBS's *NCIS* is bought by national advertising agencies, which handle the country's biggest advertisers—Procter & Gamble

and McDonald's, for example. These companies usually have in-house advertising and public relations departments, but most of the advertising strategy and production of commercials for these companies is handled by the agencies. National agencies buy advertising space based on a careful formula, calculated on a cost-per-thousand (*CPM*) basis—the cost of an ad per 1,000 people reached (M is the Roman numeral for 1,000).

Making a TV commercial for national broadcast is more expensive per minute than making a television program because each company wants its ads to be different

CPM   Cost per thousand, the cost of an ad per 1,000 people reached. (M is the Roman numeral for 1,000.)

from the rest. The price to create a TV commercial can run more than $1 million a minute. That may be why, as one producer said, "the commercials are the best things on TV." Network television commercials certainly are the most visible type of advertising, but not everyone needs the reach of network television. The goal of well-placed advertising is to deliver the best results to the client for the lowest cost, and this may mean looking to other media.

Using Print and Radio

Different types of media deliver different types of audiences. Advertising agencies may buy time and space on local radio and in newspapers and magazines to target a specific audience by demographics: age, education, gender and income. A radio station with a rock format delivers a different audience than an easy-listening station does. *The New York Times* delivers a different reader than the *Honolulu Advertiser*. *Sports Illustrated* targets a different group than *Vogue*.

Language also can be a targeting factor. Some agencies use Spanish-language media to target Latino consumers, for example, on a Spanish-language radio station or in a Spanish-language newspaper.

With newspaper and magazine circulation declining, and over-the-air radio audiences migrating to satellite radio or listening to their iPods, Internet advertising is quickly becoming the fastest growing avenue for advertisers to reach consumers.

INTERNET DELIVERS DISPLAY, SEARCH AND SOCIAL NETWORKS

The Internet offers the largest potential audience, but consumers also can quickly click past ads on the Web so advertisers have become clever at placing Internet ads within and around the sites themselves. Internet ads run as banners that appear at the top of the page or alongside the copy. (See **Illustration 10.3**, "U.S. Consumers' Most Popular Online Destinations," p. 217.)

Another successful method of access to consumers through the Internet is *search advertising*, often called simply *search*. Advertisers pay Internet

---

Search Advertising Advertising in the form of a list and/or link to a company's site domain name through a specific online search word or phrase.

Branded Content, Content Marketing, Branded Entertainment A program or story that mimics regular commercial programming or standard journalism but is custom-produced by an advertiser to promote a specific product and may or may not be labeled as an advertisement.

Hagen/CartoonStock.com

Laugh all you want, but the advertising agency loved my idea: I'm making good money...

companies fees to list and/or link their company's site domain name to a specific search word or phrase. If a consumer searches for "Car Insurance," for example, the next screen will show information about car insurance, and the sides and top of the screen also might show ads for cars at the local dealership. Search advertising accounted for nearly half of all Internet advertising revenue, according to the Internet Advertising Bureau, which divides search advertising into four types:

1. Paid listings: Places links at the top or side of the screen next to search results.

2. Contextual search: Places text links in the article based on the context of the content.

3. Paid inclusion: Guarantees that a search engine indexes a marketer's URL, so that when someone searches for something, the marketer's URL shows up.

4. Site optimization: Fixes a site so search engines can more easily index the site.

Social networks such as Facebook, Twitter and YouTube offer even more marketing outlets. An ad campaign today can include a presence on Facebook, a YouTube video promoting the product or a carefully orchestrated Twitter campaign to take advantage of timely marketing moments (See **Impact/Audience**, "Social Media Places Marketing In-the-Moment," p. 218.)

Branded content has become another way that advertisers can promote products—by using either the Internet or traditional media. Also called *content marketing* and *branded entertainment*, branded content is a program or story that mimics regular commercial programming or standard journalism, but is

IMPACT/Audience

Illustration 10.3

U.S. Consumers' Most Popular Online Destinations

Despite the endless number of Web sites available, consumers tend to select a few favorites and return to them regularly, which makes them attractive to advertisers.

Source: Nielsen, "January 2013: Top U.W. Entertainment Sites and Web Brands," March 22, 2013, nielsen.com.

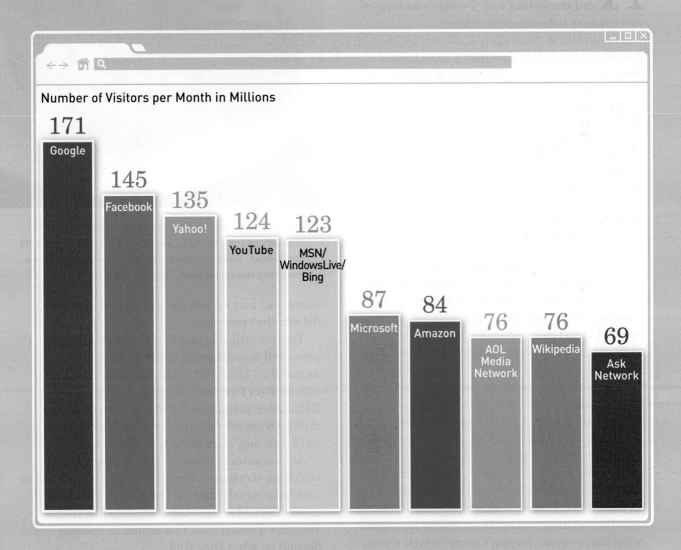

Number of Visitors per Month in Millions

Site	Visitors
Google	171
Facebook	145
Yahoo!	135
YouTube	124
MSN/WindowsLive/Bing	123
Microsoft	87
Amazon	84
AOL Media Network	76
Wikipedia	76
Ask Network	69

IMPACT/Audience

Social Media Places Marketing In-the-Moment

By Michael Learmonth

As a cultural force, Twitter has logged many defining moments. But as an ad platform and marketing tool, Twitter's coming-of-age appears to be happening now.

Slowly, but in plain sight, Twitter has opened a marketing window that didn't exist before, a window that allows marketers—or anyone—to exploit, in real time, moments both expected and completely unplanned.

Like search, this new frontier didn't exist before. Also like search, one company owns it, and that's Twitter. While brands have been dabbling in it for years, they're quickly moving from hobby to pro status. Marketers have even defined it with an acronym—*RTM*, or *real-time marketing*—which can lead to questions like, "So, what's your RTM budget?"

The shift to real-time marketing was on full display during the Super Bowl and during the Oscars, when brands like Pepsi, Samsung and Oreo had newsroom-like war rooms set up to interact with their audiences but also to react to the unexpected. During the Super Bowl, that moment came in the form of a blackout at the Mercedes-Benz Superdome, which created the opportunity for Oreo's "dunk in the dark" and PBS's reminder that *Downton Abbey* was just a flip of the dial away.

Marketers have long sought to attach themselves to context. In the pre-Twitter era, "you bought adjacencies next to news stories or, say, the style section during Fashion Week," said Ian Schafer, CEO of Deep Focus. Real-time advertising meant buying Google search terms, prodding bloggers or maybe some well-targeted online display ads.

But, as Twitter Revenue Chief Adam Bain put it, "Marketing has evolved to a series of 'now

Mandel Ngan/AFP/Getty Images

Advertising agencies have learned to use social media to their advantage. During an unexpected blackout at the 2013 Super Bowl, Twitter followers received the Oreo *real-time marketing* tweet that read, "You can still dunk in the dark."

moments,' and we are the platform that can deliver that moment."

Twitter still has just four revenue streams: promoted accounts and trends, which now run as much as $200,000 a day; promoted tweets; and its data fire hose, licensed by third parties. EMarketer estimates Twitter will earn $545 million from advertising (half from mobile) in 2013, but may soon raise that estimate.

As marketers get more serious about their real-time strategies, they'll get more serious about determining whether all the tweets, follows and retweets yield some kind of measurable result. Whether Twitter gets to a billion in revenue could depend on what they find.

"We are in the land-grab stage right now—we are still going to move to the results phase," Deep Focus's Mr. Schafer said. "It's not just enough to publish something and pat yourself on the back about it."

Source: Excerpted from Michael Learmonth, "When Did Twitter Grow Up? Answer: Now. Marketing Has Become an In-the-Moment Game, Thanks to One Company," February 25, 2013, adage.com.

RTM   Real-time marketing.

custom-produced by an advertiser to promote a specific product. The content may or may not be labeled as advertising, and, in most cases, the consumer may be unaware a product is being advertised. In one campaign for Jaguar Land Rover, for example, in a series called *Travel Channel's Road to the Unexpected*, a Travel Channel host drives a Land Rover on adventures in Bolivia, Britain, Jamaica and Quebec.

"Interactive advertising revenue is on a strong upward trajectory," according to Sherrill Mane of the Internet Advertising Bureau. "Nearly all types of ad formats are showing positive movement and marketers across all advertising categories, most notably consumer packaged goods and pharmaceuticals, are increasing their investment in digital media."

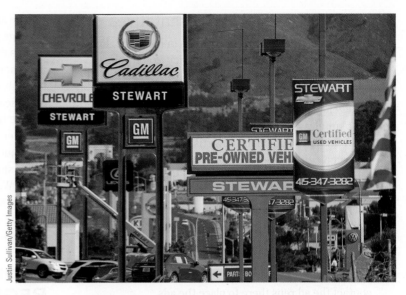

Justin Sullivan/Getty Images

Auto dealers are among the biggest spenders on local radio and TV advertising as well as the Internet. With Internet advertising, car dealers can reach consumers outside their local market.

Media Compete Fiercely for Clients

The competition among the media industries for advertisers is fierce:

- A study commissioned by the American Newspaper Publishers Association reveals that only one in five prime-time adult viewers could remember the last ad they had seen on television.

- Print advertisers claim that because viewers can so easily change channels and skip the ads, TV commercials are an unreliable way to deliver an audience.

- "Radio is the medium working women don't have to make time for," boasts the Radio Advertising Bureau (RAB). Whereas working women spend 15 percent of their daily media time reading a newspaper, they spend half of their media time with radio, says the RAB.

- The Internet Advertising Bureau says that mobile advertising is growing faster than any other type of marketing.

Advertising agencies gather demographic information provided by Nielsen for broadcast and the Internet and by the Alliance for Audited Media for print; the audience is converted into numbers. Based on these numbers, agencies advise advertisers about how to best reach buyers for their products, for example, by advertising locally or through an advertising sales representative. They may also suggest advertising online.

Advertising Locally

Danielle's health and fitness salon, a small downtown business, does not need to advertise on the *Late Show with David Letterman* or in *The New York Times*. Danielle and other local business owners only need to reach their local community. Businesses larger than the fitness salon, such as a car dealer or a furniture store, also may buy local television or radio time and set up an Internet site.

A local advertising agency can design a campaign, produce the ad and place the ad just as the national agencies do, but on a much smaller scale. Many small companies design and place their own ads directly with the local media. To attract customers, local media also help companies design their ads. Newspapers, for example, will help a small advertiser prepare an ad using ready-made art.

A radio or television station may include the services of an announcer or access to a studio in the price for a series of spot ads. Broadcast stations sometimes trade ads for services offered by the advertiser—dinner for two at the local restaurant in return for two spot ads, for example. Then the station gives the dinners away on one of its programs.

Advertising Sales Representatives

What if you manufacture sunglasses in Dubuque, Iowa, and you hire a local advertising agency to sell your product nationally? The agency tells you they've found a good market for your product on the West Coast. How is the agency going to find out the most efficient way to sell your sunglasses in Los Angeles?

In this situation, many advertising agencies would contact a *rep firm*—a company of advertising sales representatives who sell advertising time and space in their market to companies outside the area. The agency in Dubuque would first decide who were the most likely customers for your sunglasses. If the agency decided that L.A.-area males age 18 to 24 are the best potential customers, the agency would budget a certain amount of money for advertising in the Los Angeles area and then contact the ad reps there to place the ads.

The rep firm, in return, takes a percentage (usually 15 percent) of the advertising dollars for the ads they place. Ad reps are, in effect, brokers for the media in their markets. Each rep firm handles several clients. Some ad reps sell only broadcast advertising, and some specialize in print ads, but many rep firms sell all types of media.

In this case, each L.A. ad rep would enter the demographics ("demos") for your product into a computer. Based on ratings, readership and the price for the ads, each rep would come up with a CPM (cost per thousand people reached) for your product. The rep then would recommend the most efficient buy—how best to reach the people most likely to buy your sunglasses.

Each rep then presents an L.A. advertising plan for your product to the agency in Dubuque. Usually the buy is based on price: The medium with the lowest CPM gets the customer. But a rep who cannot match the lowest CPM might offer incentives for you to choose his or her plan. If you agree to provide 50 pairs of sunglasses, for example, the rep's radio station will give away the glasses as prizes during a local program, each time mentioning the name of your product. So even though the ad time you buy will cost a little more, you also will get promotional announcements every time the station gives away a pair of sunglasses. Other ad reps might offer different packages.

Rep Firm   A company of advertising sales representatives who sell advertising time and space in their market to companies outside their geographic area.

The agency in Dubuque then would decide which package is the most attractive and would present that proposal to you. This entire process can take as little as 24 hours for a simple buy such as the one for your sunglasses account, or as long as several weeks for a complicated campaign for a big advertiser.

The Internet has added another dimension. With Internet access, you can sell your local product from Dubuque anywhere in the world, without using a rep. Many small companies design their own Web sites, or hire a Web site designer. They also can list their products on a consumer Web site such as eBay or Amazon or place a product demonstration on a social networking site such as YouTube.

FEDERAL GOVERNMENT REGULATES ADVERTISERS

Government protection for consumers dates back to the beginning of the 20th century when Congress passed the Pure Food and Drug Act in 1906, mainly as a protection against patent medicine ads that magazines were running (see **Chapter 4**). The advertising industry itself has adopted advertising standards, and in some cases the media have established their own codes.

Government oversight is the main deterrent against deceptive advertising. This responsibility is shared by several government agencies: The Federal Trade Commission, the Food and Drug Administration and the Federal Communications Commission.

Federal Trade Commission

The mission of the Federal Trade Commission, established in 1914, is "to prevent business practices that are anticompetitive or deceptive or unfair to consumers; to enhance informed consumer choice and public understanding of the competitive process; and to accomplish this without unduly burdening legitimate business activity." If the FTC determines an ad is deceptive, the commission can order the advertiser to stop or revise the campaign.

The commission also can require corrective advertising to counteract the deception. In 2012, an administrative law judge issued a cease-and-desist order against the company that produced POM Wonderful juice, which the company advertised as offering health benefits that could treat, prevent or reduce the risks of heart disease and prostate cancer.

Karen Bleier/AFP/Getty Images

Advertisers in the United States are subject to FTC regulation. Based on an FTC complaint, in 2012 an administrative law judge issued a cease-and-desist order against the company that produced POM Wonderful beverage. The judge said the company had not proved that the product offered any of the health benefits the company advertised.

The order was based on a complaint filed by the FTC in 2010. The judge's order said the company "shall not make any representation, in any manner, expressly or by implication, including through the use of a product name, endorsement, depiction, illustration, trademark or trade name, about the health benefits, performance or efficacy of any covered product."

The Federal Trade Commission and the Bureau of Alcohol, Tobacco and Firearms (BATF) regulate the spirits industry, but neither agency has the authority to ban hard liquor ads on television. Although beer and wine advertisements have appeared on TV for decades, the TV networks traditionally did not advertise hard liquor. For three decades, the Distilled Spirits Council of the United States, operating under a voluntary Code of Good Practice, did not run television ads. In 1996, some

liquor companies challenged the voluntary ban by placing ads on local television.

Seagram's, the first company to question the ban, advertised Crown Royal whiskey on a local TV station in Texas. "We believe distilled spirits should have the same access to electronic media, just the same way beer and wine do," said Arthur Shapiro, executive vice president in charge of marketing and strategy for Seagram's in the United States.

Because hard liquor advertising means a great deal of revenue, the TV networks did not resist, and hard liquor ads are now quite common.

Food and Drug Administration

The Food and Drug Administration (FDA) oversees claims that appear on food labels or packaging. If the FDA finds a label is deceptive, the agency can require the advertiser to stop distributing products with that label. In the 2012 case against POM Wonderful, for example, the commission said the company had made health benefit claims on its labels that had not been reviewed by the Food and Drug Administration, and on that basis the government filed a claim against the company.

Chris Jackson/Getty Images

Ads for hard liquor, such as Jack Daniel's, did not start running on TV until 1996, when Seagram's challenged a 30-year voluntary Distilled Spirits Council policy of not advertising on television. Hard liquor ads are a lucrative source of TV revenue and now are commonplace on TV.

Sean Gallup/Getty Images

International advertising campaigns are becoming more common for global products. In Bucharest, Romania, on March 7, 2013, cars drive past a huge digital billboard on the side of a building.

Federal Communications Commission and Other Agencies

The Federal Communications Commission (FCC) enforces rules that govern the broadcast media. The FCC's jurisdiction over the broadcast industry gives the commission indirect control over broadcast advertising. In the past, the FCC has ruled against demonstrations of products that were misleading and against commercials the FCC decided were tasteless, but the FTC and the FDA are the primary enforcement agencies for advertising regulation. Other government agencies, such as the Environmental Protection Agency and the Consumer Product Safety Agency, also can question the content of advertisements.

Advertising agencies have formed the National Advertising Review Board (NARB) to hear complaints against advertisers. This effort at self-regulation among advertising agencies parallels those of some media industries, such as the movie industry's ratings code and the recording industry's record labeling for lyrics.

Global Marketing Delivers New Audiences

When U.S. products seek international markets, and international products want to reach American consumers, the marketers' job is to design appealing campaigns to reach those consumers. Global industries often also use American advertising agencies to help them sell products in the United States. American agencies today collect nearly half of the *world's* revenue from advertising.

International advertising campaigns are becoming more common for global products, such as Coca-Cola and McDonald's, and this has meant the creation of international advertising markets. Cable News Network (CNN) sells advertising on CNN worldwide, so that any company in any nation with CNN's service can advertise its product to a worldwide audience. Overall, billings outside the United States are commanding an increasing share of U.S. advertising agencies' business. (See **Illustration 10.1**, p. 207.)

The most important factor for the global advertising market is emerging technology. The widespread use of the Internet creates new outlets, and the advertising community is adapting.

Another factor in the future of advertising is shifting demographic patterns. As the ethnicity, education and wealth of global consumers shifts, marketing programs have to adapt quickly to reach target-specific audiences. Advertisers must find new ways to encourage product loyalty.

The challenges for the advertising business are as great as the challenges for the media industries. The advertising industry will do what it has always done to adapt—follow the audience. The challenge for advertising will be to learn how to efficiently and effectively match the audience to the advertising messages the media industries deliver.

Review, Analyze, Investigate

Reviewing Chapter 10

Advertising Supports Mass Media

- Advertising carries the messages that come to you from the sponsors who pay for the American media.
- In 2012, U.S. businesses spent a total of $161 billion to advertise their products to consumers—$512 per person, more than any country in the world.
- As early as 1200 B.C., the Phoenicians painted messages on stones to advertise.
- In the 6th century B.C., ship captains sent criers around to announce that their ships were in port.
- In the 13th century A.D., the British began requiring trademarks to protect buyers.
- In 1704, newspapers were the first medium to use advertising. Magazines, radio, television and the Internet followed in the 19th and 20th centuries.
- Advertisers flocked to major Internet sites when they first were established. They expected quick returns as consumer use of the Internet skyrocketed. Advertisers quickly learned, however, that no matter how they packaged the message, advertising on an Internet site didn't necessarily bring increased sales.
- What advertisers call the *click-through rate* (the rate at which someone who sees an advertising message actually clicks through to learn more) is less than 1 percent.
- In 2012, Internet ad spending reached $37 billion.
- Viral marketing is a form of advertising that involves creating an online message that consumers pass on—an online "word of mouth."
- Advertisers today are still trying to figure out the magic formula to reach consumers on the Internet. New approaches are meant to make advertisements seem less like advertisements—further blurring the line between information, entertainment and advertising.

Ads Share Three Characteristics

- Daniel Boorstin says that advertising in America shares three characteristics: repetition, an advertising style and ubiquity.
- The sheer number of ads sometimes works to advertisers' disadvantage because they can crowd each other so much that no individual ad stands out in consumers' minds.

Ads Compete for Your Attention

- To influence consumers, an advertising message must appeal to you for some reason.

- Advertising can catch your attention, according to Jib Fowles, in 15 ways, including playing on your need to nurture, your need for attention and your need for escape.

Marketers Use Demographics

- Advertisers target their messages according to an audience's characteristics.
- Demographics are composed of data about a target audience's gender, age, income level, marital status, geographic location and occupation.

Advertising Feeds Consumerism

- Advertising provokes three main criticisms: It adds to the cost of products; it causes people to buy products they do not need; and it reduces competition and thereby fosters monopolies.
- Because the audience is increasingly fragmented, advertisers have used other tactics—from the Internet to viral marketing.

Advertising at Work

- Many advertising agencies are small, local operations.
- Depending on the size of the company, an advertising agency may be divided into as many as six departments: marketing research, media selection, creative activity, account management, administration and public relations.

Mass Media Industries Depend on Advertising

- The advertising business and the media industries are interdependent—what happens in the advertising business directly affects the media industries.
- The advertising business is very dependent on the nation's economic health.
- The average price for the TV time for a 30-second commercial is $110,000. The price tag for a 30-second commercial can reach almost $4 million for a widely watched program such as the 2013 Super Bowl.
- The price to create a TV commercial can run as much as $1 million a minute.
- Different types of media deliver different types of audiences.

Internet Delivers Display, Search and Social Networks

- The most successful Internet access to consumers today is called *search advertising*, often called simply *search*.

- There are four types of search advertising: paid listings, contextual search, paid inclusion and site optimization.
- Advertising agencies have learned to use social media to their advantage with a technique called *real-time marketing*.
- Advertisers also use *branded content*, a program or story that mimics regular commercial programming or standard journalism but that is custom-produced by an advertiser to promote a specific product.

Media Compete Fiercely for Clients

- Advertising is divided into national and local categories.
- Advertising sales representatives broker local accounts to out-of-town advertisers.
- The media compete with each other for the advertising dollar, and some media are better than others for particular products.

Federal Government Regulates Advertisers

- Government protection for consumers dates back to the beginning of the 20th century.
- Protection for consumers from misleading advertising comes from government regulation (the Federal Trade Commission, Food and Drug Administration and Federal Communications Commission, for example), and from advertising industry self-regulatory groups (National Advertising Review Board, for example).

- In 1996, the distilled spirits industry challenged the 30-year-old industry-wide voluntary ban on hard liquor advertising on TV. The liquor industry placed the ads on local TV stations, and hard liquor ads are now commonplace on television.
- Neither the Federal Trade Commission nor the Bureau of Alcohol, Tobacco and Firearms, which regulate the spirits industry, has the power to stop liquor ads from appearing on TV.
- Based on an FTC complaint, in 2012 an administrative law judge issued a cease-and-desist order against the company that produced POM Wonderful beverage.

Global Marketing Delivers New Audiences

- The future of advertising will parallel the development of international markets, the refinement and expansion of new media technologies (especially the Internet) and changing demographics.
- Today's advertising agencies use sophisticated technology to track demographics to help deliver the audience the advertiser wants.
- International marketing is becoming more common for global products, such as Coca-Cola and McDonald's, and this means the creation of international advertising campaigns.

Key Terms

These terms are defined in the margins throughout this chapter and appear in alphabetical order with definitions in the Glossary, which begins on page 373.

Critical Questions

1. Why is advertising not a medium? What role does advertising play in the mass media?

2. What are the three main arguments given by advertising's critics and by its supporters?

3. What are the benefits to an advertiser of TV instead of print? Of radio instead of TV? Of the Internet instead of broadcast and print?

4. Discuss three of Jib Fowles' 15 psychological appeals for advertising in some detail, and present an example of an ad that demonstrates each of the three appeals you discuss.

5. Discuss government regulation and industry self-regulation of advertising. Which government agencies are involved in advertising regulation? Do you think government regulation or industry self-regulation is more effective at protecting consumer interests? Explain.

Working the Web

This list includes both sites mentioned in the chapter and others to give you greater insight into the advertising business.

Adrants

adrants.com

Adrants provides marketing and advertising news "with an attitude" through its Web site and daily e-mail newsletter. No-holds-barred commentary on the state of the advertising and media industries includes emerging advertising trends, effects of demographic shifts on advertising strategies and examination of paradigm shifts in the industry.

Advertising Age

adage.com

Adage.com is the Internet arm of *Advertising Age*, the weekly paper of advertising news. Other Ad Age platforms include events, webcasts, branded content and Datacenter, a primary research source for advertising industry statistics. The news on the Web site is updated throughout the day.

Advertising Council

adcouncil.org

As the leading producer of public service announcements, the nonprofit Ad Council has sponsored such familiar campaigns as "Friends Don't Let Friends Drive Drunk" and Smokey Bear's "Only You Can Prevent Forest Fires." Its clients are both nonprofit and governmental organizations.

American Advertising Federation (AAF)

aaf.org

With 100 corporate members, as well as clubs around the United States and about 225 college chapters, AAF is the oldest national advertising trade association in the country. "The Unifying Voice for Advertising," AAF educates members about the latest trends, honors advertising excellence, promotes diversity in advertising and "applies the communication skills of its members to help solve community concerns."

American Association of Advertising Agencies

aaaa.org

This management-oriented trade association provides research, media advice and information, and benefit programs such as liability insurance and retirement savings plans for its members. The Web site provides members with industry news, events (including webinars and speech transcripts),

career development opportunities and advice, and links to publications and research.

American Marketing Association (AMA)

marketingpower.com

Originally created in 1937 through a merger of the National Teachers of Advertising and the American Marketing Association, the AMA is a marketing association for individuals and organizations involved in the practice, teaching and study of marketing worldwide. AMA members are connected to a network of nearly 40,000 experienced marketers in academics, research and practice. Its Web site offers marketing data, articles, case studies, best practices and a job bank.

Association of Hispanic Advertising Agencies (AHAA)

ahaa.org

With the goal to "grow, strengthen and protect the Hispanic marketing advertising industry," the AHAA aims to raise awareness in the value of the Hispanic market to advertisers. Member agencies range from Acento (Los Angeles) to Zubi Advertising Services (Coral Gables, Fla.).

Clio Awards

clioawards.com

The most recognized global competition for advertising, the Clio Awards has celebrated excellence in a broad range of mediums for more than 50 years. Founded in 1959 by Wallace Ross, the program's name originates in Greek mythology: Clio was "the muse of history and the recorder of great deeds." Award categories include Interactive, Content & Contact, Billboard, Print, Radio and Television/Cinema/Digital. Students are awarded in limited categories, and Network, Agency, Production Company and Advertiser of the Year are also honored.

Federal Trade Commission (FTC)

ftc.gov

Created in 1914 to "bust the trusts," the FTC is the only U.S. government agency that protects consumers against fraud and misleading advertising and handles antitrust matters, through its Bureaus of Consumer Protection, Competition and Economics. It does not resolve individual disputes but rather looks for patterns of law violations. Mail order, telemarketing and used cars are among the businesses it regulates. Much of the information on the Web site is also available in Spanish.

MediaPost Communications
mediapost.com

An integrated publishing and content company, MediaPost is the leading advertising and media Internet portal provid-ing news, events, directories and a social network to help members better plan and buy both traditional and online advertising. The site's media directory includes information on more than 35,000 publications, stations, networks, Web sites and more.

Impact/Action Videos are concise news features on various topics created exclusively for *Media/Impact*. Go online to access MindTap at cengagebrain.com. MindTap for Media/Impact sequences all of your learning tools—Chapter Readings with highlighting and note taking, Impact/Action Videos, activities and assessments—into chapter driven learning units that guide you through the curriculum.

PUBLIC RELATIONS:
PROMOTING IDEAS

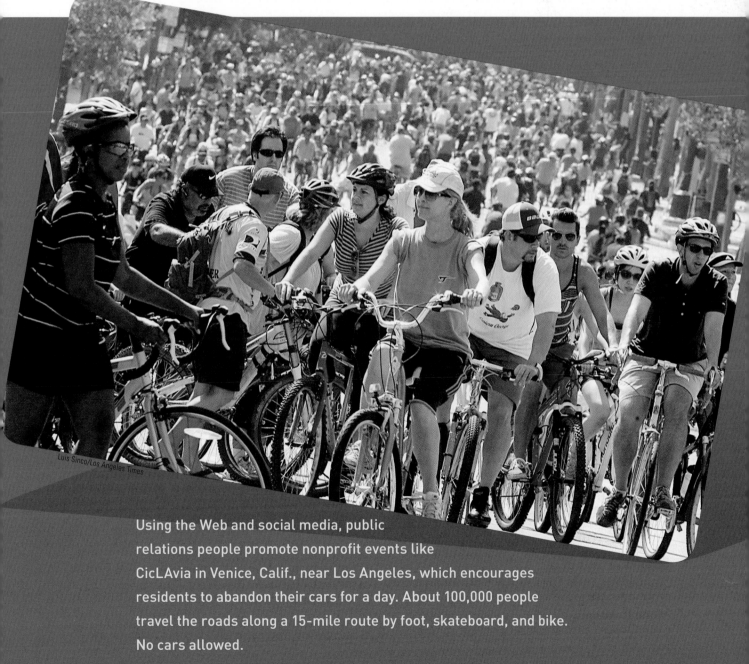

Luis Sinco/Los Angeles Times

Using the Web and social media, public relations people promote nonprofit events like CicLAvia in Venice, Calif., near Los Angeles, which encourages residents to abandon their cars for a day. About 100,000 people travel the roads along a 15-mile route by foot, skateboard, and bike. No cars allowed.

What's Ahead?

"Our job is to help [our clients] get more active in social media and stay on top of the trends."

—SAM FORD, DIRECTOR OF DIGITAL STRATEGY, PEPPERCOMM PUBLIC RELATIONS

You may think today's

cash rebates from car manufacturers are relatively new, but in 1914, Henry Ford announced that if he sold 300,000 Model Ts that year, each customer would receive a rebate. When the company reached its goal, Ford returned $50 to each buyer. This was good business. It also was good public relations. Like Henry Ford, public relations people today work to create favorable images—for corporations, public officials, products, schools, hospitals and associations.

There are three ways to encourage people to do what you want them to do: power, patronage and persuasion. Power involves ruling by law, but it also can mean ruling by peer pressure—someone does something because his or her friends do. Patronage is a polite term for bribery—paying someone with favors or money to do what you want. The third method—persuasion—is the approach of public relations. *Persuasion* is the act of using argument or reasoning to induce someone to do something.

Like advertising, the public relations business is not a mass medium. Public relations is a media support industry. In the classic definition, *public relations* involves creating an understanding for, or goodwill toward, a company, a person or a product.

Persuasion   The act of using argument or reasoning to induce someone to do something.

Public Relations   Creating understanding for, or goodwill toward, a company, a person or a product.

PR HELPS SHAPE PUBLIC OPINION

One of the first political leaders to realize the importance of public relations was Augustus Caesar, who in the 1st century commissioned statues of himself to be erected throughout the Roman Empire to enhance his image. Since then, many political leaders have ordered heroic images of themselves printed on coins and stamps.

Larry Lambert/CartoonStock.com

"Doctor, before you meet the press to explain your theory about space aliens communicating with us, maybe you should take the tin foil off of your head."

Today's public relations approach can be traced to the beginning of the 20th century. Journalists were an important reason for the eventual emergence of the public relations profession.

Before 1900, businesses believed they could work alongside the press, or even ignore it. Many stories that appeared in the press promoted companies that bought advertising. Then the Industrial Revolution arrived, and some industrialists exploited workers and collected enormous profits. Just before the turn of the 20th century, Ida Tarbell and Lincoln Steffens began to make businesspeople uncomfortable, writing stories for magazines like *McClure's* about the not so admirable characteristics of some companies, such as Standard Oil (see **Chapter 4**, p. 74).

According to *This Is PR: The Realities of Public Relations*, "No longer could the railroads butter up the press by giving free passes to reporters. No longer would the public buy whitewashed statements like that of coal industrialist George F. Baer, who in 1902 told labor to put their trust in 'the Christian men whom God in His infinite wisdom has given control of the property interests of the country.'"

President Theodore Roosevelt fed public sentiment—public opinion—against the abuses of industry when he started his antitrust campaigns. According to *Effective Public Relations*, "With the growth of mass-circulation newspapers, Roosevelt's canny ability to dominate the front pages demonstrated a new-found power for those with causes to promote.

"He had a keen sense of news and knew how to stage a story so that it would get maximum attention. His skill forced those he fought to develop similar means. He fully exploited the news media as a new and powerful tool of presidential leadership, and he remade the laws and the presidency in the process." Roosevelt used his skills at swaying public opinion to gain support for his antitrust policies.

PR PIONEER ISSUES DECLARATION OF PRINCIPLES

The first publicity firm was called The Publicity Bureau and opened in Boston in 1900 to head off growing public criticism of the railroad companies. The best-known early practitioner of public relations was Ivy Lee, who began his PR career by opening an office in New York with George F. Parker.

Lee and Parker represented coal magnate George F. Baer when coal workers went on strike. A former newspaper reporter, Lee issued a *Declaration of Principles* that he mailed to newspaper city editors. This declaration became a manifesto for early public relations companies to follow.

Reacting to criticism that The Publicity Bureau worked secretly to promote the railroads, Lee wrote in 1906 in *American Magazine*, "This [the firm of Lee & Parker] is not a secret press bureau. All our work is done in the open. We aim to supply news. . . . In brief, our plan is, frankly and openly, on behalf of business concerns and public institutions, to supply to the press and public of the United States prompt and accurate information concerning subjects which it is of value and interest to the public to know about."

Lee and Parker dissolved their firm in 1908, when Lee went to work as a publicity agent for the Pennsylvania Railroad. Eventually, John D. Rockefeller hired Lee to counteract the negative publicity that began with Tarbell's investigation of Standard Oil. (Lee worked for the Rockefellers until he died in 1934.)

The idea of in-house corporate public relations grew as Chicago Edison Company and American Telephone & Telegraph began promotional programs. The University of Pennsylvania and the University of Wisconsin opened publicity bureaus in 1904, and the YMCA of Washington, D.C., hired a full-time publicist to oversee fundraising in 1905—the first time someone hired a publicist to do fundraising.

GOVERNMENT RECRUITS PR PROFESSIONALS

During World War I (1914–1918), the U.S. government set up the Committee on Public Information, organized by former newspaper reporter George Creel, blurring the line between propaganda and publicity. Creel recruited journalists, editors, artists and teachers to raise money for Liberty Bonds and to promote the nation's participation in the war. One of the people who worked for Creel was Edward L. Bernays. Both Bernays and Ivy Lee have been called the father of public relations.

In 1923, Bernays wrote the first book on public relations, *Crystallizing Public Opinion*, and taught the first course on the subject. Bernays was interested in mass psychology—how to influence the opinions of large groups of people. Procter & Gamble, General Motors and the American Tobacco Company were among his clients. "Public relations," Bernays wrote in 1955, "is the

Bettmann/CORBIS

Edward L. Bernays wrote the first book on public relations, *Crystallizing Public Opinion*, and taught the first public relations course.

attempt, by information, persuasion and adjustment, to engineer public support for an activity, cause, movement or institution."

In 1985, Bernays further defined public relations as "giving a client ethical advice, based on research of the public, that will win the social goals upon which the client depends for his livelihood."

To sell the New Deal in the 1930s, Franklin D. Roosevelt used every tactic he knew. Comfortable with the press and the public alike and advised by PR expert Louis McHenry Howe, FDR "projected an image of self-confidence and happiness—just what the American public wanted to believe in. He talked to them on the radio. He smiled for the cameras. He was mentioned in popular songs. He even allowed himself to be one of the main characters in a Rodgers and Hart musical comedy (played by George M. Cohan, America's favorite Yankee Doodle Dandy)," according to *This Is PR*.

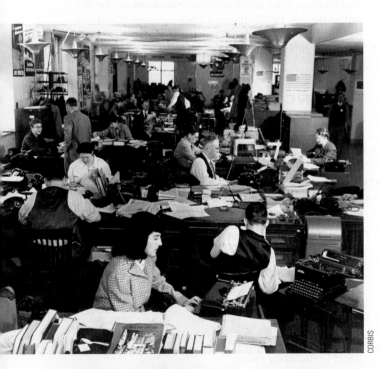

In what was the largest public relations drive of its time, the Office of War Information promoted the role of the United States in World War II. Today, the federal government is the largest employer of public relations people.

To gain support for the nation's entry into World War II (1939–1945), the federal government mounted the largest public relations drive in its history, centered at the Office of War Information, led by former newscaster Elmer Davis. After the war, the public relations business boomed along with the postwar economy.

WOMEN JOIN PR FIRMS

Doris E. Fleischman became one of the first women in public relations when she joined her husband, Edward L. Bernays, in his PR firm. Fleischman was an equal partner with Bernays in their public relations business. An early advocate of public relations as a profession for women, in 1931 Fleischman wrote, "One finds women working side by side with men in forming the traditions and rules that will govern the profession of the future."

Doris Fleischman, a public relations pioneer, began her career in the 1920s. Fleischman was an early advocate of public relations as a profession for women. Fleischman and her husband, Edward L. Bernays, were equal partners in their public relations business.

Two other women who were public relations pioneers were Leone Baxter and Anne Williams Wheaton. Baxter formed Baxter and Whitaker in San Francisco with her husband, Clem Whitaker—the first public relations agency to specialize in political campaigns. In 1957, President Dwight Eisenhower appointed Anne Williams Wheaton as his associate press secretary.

PROFESSIONALS PROMOTE ETHICS CODES

In the 1930s, the requirements to work in public relations were loose, and many people who said they worked in public relations were press agents who often used tricks to get attention for their clients. Henry Rogers, co-founder of what was then the world's largest entertainment PR firm, Rogers & Cowan (based in Beverly Hills), admitted that in 1939 he created a "best-dressed" contest to promote little-known actress Rita Hayworth.

There had been no contest, but Rogers dubbed Hayworth the winner of this fictional event. *Look* magazine gave Hayworth a ten-page spread. "Press agents, and that's what we were, would dream up all sorts of phony stories," he said. "Journalists knew they were phony but printed them because they looked good in print."

During the 1950s, the question of ethics in public relations arose publicly when Byoir and Associates, hired by a railroad company to counteract the expansion of trucking, was charged with creating "front" organizations to speak out against the trucking industry. In court, Byoir's agency argued they were exercising free speech. In 1961, the U.S. Supreme Court upheld Byoir's right to represent a client even if the presentation was dishonest, but this left the ethical issue of honesty unresolved.

The Public Relations Society of America (PRSA) established its first code of ethics in 1954 and expanded that code in 1959 with a *Declaration of Principles*. That ethics code still exists today to guide the business of public relations. (Excerpts from the PRSA code are in **Chapter 15**.) PR professionals continue to argue among themselves about the differences between the profession's beginnings as press agentry (which often meant fabricating stories) and the concept of ethically representing a client's business, as Edward L. Bernays described.

Public relations grew throughout the 1960s and 1970s with the encouragement of television, the federal government and corporate America. In 1961, for example, the federal government had about 1,000 people working as writer-editors and public affairs specialists. Today, *the federal government is the nation's largest single employer of public information people.* ("Public information" is the name given to the job of government public relations.)

PUBLIC RELATIONS AT WORK

Public relations is an industry of specialties. The most familiar public relations areas are financial public relations, product public relations and crisis public relations, but there are many other specialty areas.

Financial Public Relations

People in financial public relations provide information primarily to business reporters. "Business editors like a PR staff that can provide access to top management," wrote James K. Gentry in the *Washington Journalism Review*, "that knows its company well or can find needed information quickly, that demonstrates ethics and honesty and that knows and accepts the difference between news and fluff." Gentry then listed comments gathered from editors about what makes a bad PR operation:

- "Companies that think they can hide the truth from the public or believe it's none of the public's business."

- "I despise it when a PR person intercepts our calls to a news source but then isn't capable of answering our questions."

- "When they hire an outside PR firm to handle the job."

- "The 'no-comment' attitude. When they have little or no interest in going beyond the press release."

- "People who either get in the way of you doing your job, complain too much or are no help at all."

Product Public Relations

Product PR uses public relations techniques to sell products and services. Many companies have learned that seeking publicity for a product often is less expensive than advertising the product. Public relations "is booming partly because of price," reports *The Wall Street Journal*. A PR budget of $1 million for a substantial client is considered huge, whereas an ad budget that size is considered tiny.

Public relations often works better than advertising. For example, the Wieden & Kennedy agency in Seattle contracted Bigger Than Life, Inc., which makes large inflatables, to manufacture a 21-story pair of Nike tennis shoes. The company attached the shoes to the Westin Copley Place Hotel during the Boston Marathon and to the Westin Hotel in downtown Cincinnati during the March of Dimes walk-a-thon. Pictures of the shoes appeared in *The New York Times*, in *The Cincinnati Enquirer* and in newspapers as far away as Japan. Wieden & Kennedy estimated that buying the same advertising would have cost $7 million.

Crisis Public Relations

This aspect of public relations goes back as far as Edward Bernays responding to the charges against Standard Oil. The term *crisis public relations* (sometimes called *crisis communication*) describes the response to a public relations emergency facing a company because of an unexpected event that could seriously hurt the company's reputation.

In October 1996, beverage maker Odwalla Inc. faced a public relations crisis when *E. coli* bacteria was traced to unpasteurized apple juice that had been sold by the natural juice company. The death of a 16-month-old girl in Colorado and more than 50 cases of severe illness were eventually traced to the bacteria. Odwalla, the leading manufacturer of unpasteurized juices, had made its reputation on natural, unfiltered products. But as soon as Odwalla detected the bacteria, the company announced an immediate recall of 13 products in the seven western states and British Columbia.

Crisis Communication   A timely public relations response to a critical situation that could cause damage to a company's reputation.

Then the company worked with the Food and Drug Administration to scour the Odwalla processing facilities, which were found to be free of the bacteria. The company continued the investigation, including the processors who supplied fruit for the juice. One month after the outbreak, Odwalla took out full-page ads in several newspapers, an "open letter" to its customers, thanking them for their support and offering sympathy for people diagnosed with *E. coli*-related illnesses after drinking Odwalla juices. The Odwalla case is often used as an example of effective crisis public relations.

The year 2010 offered two classic corporate crisis public relations challenges—Toyota Motor Corp. and BP PLC (formerly called British Petroleum). Toyota and BP "exacerbated their woes by either declining to fess up promptly, casting blame elsewhere or striking adversarial postures with the public, the government and the news media," wrote Peter S. Goodman in *The New York Times*.

According to public relations experts, executives for BP (formerly British Petroleum) made many mistakes in the way they responded to the explosion on April 20, 2010, of their leased offshore rig near New Orleans Beach. Eleven people died and four people were critically injured. In 2013, BP agreed to pay a $4 billion criminal settlement for the damages.

In January 2010, Toyota recalled more than 2 million vehicles for accelerator flaws, a potentially huge public relations blow to its reputation for vehicle quality. The accelerator problems were linked to at least 51 deaths. There were reports that Toyota had known about the gas pedal problems much earlier but did not admit the problem publicly until the National Highway Traffic Safety Administration (NHTSA) issued a public alert.

Then, after the NHTSA disclosure, Toyota employed public relations techniques to try to contain the damage to its reputation. The company used a public relations firm to monitor comments posted on social networking sites. Still, critics charged the public relations effort came too late.

"Toyota blew it," communications expert Brad Burns told *The New York Times*. "It's been the proverbial death by a thousand cuts. They knew they had problems long ago, whether it was a mechanical issue or operator error, but they knew they had an issue they had to deal with. And rather than put public safety over profits, they appear to have listened to the product liability lawyers and they totally lost it. It's brand damage."

[Note: In July 2013 Toyota agreed to pay $1.6 billion to settle a class-action lawsuit for allegations about sudden-acceleration in its vehicles. (See **Impact/Audience**, "After Recalls, Toyota Monitors Social Media to Protect Its Reputation," p. 233.)]

On April 20, 2010, the British Petroleum Deepwater Horizon drilling platform exploded in the Gulf of Mexico, the biggest oil spill in the gulf's history. Eleven people died, four were critically injured, and millions of gallons of oil spilled into the gulf.

"It [BP] was one of the worst PR approaches that I've seen in my 56 years of business," said public relations expert Howard Rubinstein. "They tried to be opaque. They had every excuse in the book. Right away they should have accepted responsibility and recognized what a disaster they faced. They basically thought they could spin their way out of catastrophe. It doesn't work that way." In 2013, BP agreed to a $4 billion criminal settlement over the Gulf Oil Spill.

These three examples—Odwalla, Toyota and British Petroleum—indicate how important the specialty of crisis public relations is within the public relations business.

PUBLIC RELATIONS ADAPTS TO THE INTERNET

Because of its ability to deliver information quickly and directly, the Internet offers many benefits for public relations companies. Public relations people, in fact, often are very much involved in creating and modifying Web sites for their clients—creating a public face. News releases, product announcements and company profiles can be made available online, to be captured on demand by the press, stockholders, supporters and anyone else who is interested. Managing an Internet presence can also be risky because it is interactive, and public responses to posts on the sites are immediate.

IMPACT/Audience

After Recalls, Toyota Monitors Social Media to Protect Its Reputation

By Michael Bush

According to Doug Frisbie, Toyota Motor Sales USA's national social media and marketing integration manager, the automaker has actually grown its Facebook fan base more than 10 percent since late January [2010], around the time of the marketer's Jan. 21 recall announcement and its Jan. 26 stop-sale date.

That's a testament to the resilience of the brand, but also to Toyota's ability to quickly pick up one of the most important tools in a crisis-communications handbook: social media.

Toyota has been faulted for communicating too little and too late in traditional media, but it's gone all out when it comes to Twitter, Facebook, blogs and other social-media channels. Prior to the recall, Toyota didn't have a reputation as an aggressive social-media adopter, yet it's managed to increase the number of fans on its main Facebook presence (from 71,600 to 79,500) over the past five weeks and, starting Jan. 21, it became a far more active user on Twitter. On Feb. 22 alone, it tweeted 34 messages (by contrast, Honda has more than 300,000 Facebook fans).

Toyota's been able to be so aggressive in social media largely because around Feb. 1 [2010] it created a social-media response room, always staffed with six to eight people monitoring the online conversation and responding at all times. It's answering consumers on its four Facebook pages; it created a Twitter chat with Jim Lentz, Toyota Motor Sales USA president–chief operating officer; and it created two new platforms, one with Digg and the other on Tweetmeme called "Toyota Conversations" to aggregate online chatter and allow Toyota to respond directly.

Akio Toyoda, president of Toyota Motor Corp., speaks at a press conference in Toyota City, Japan, on March 30, 2010. Toyota used crisis communications, including social media, to try to overcome the public relations problems created by the massive recall of some of its vehicles for accelerator flaws linked to at least 51 deaths. In July 2013, Toyota agreed to a $1.6 billion settlement.

Mr. Frisbie recalls seeing the first tweets about the automaker's unintended acceleration issue toward the end of 2009, when Toyota recalled more than 4 million cars to fix and replace accelerator pedals. "The minute news hits the wires, it becomes a conversation," Mr. Frisbie said. "It's just a question of how high [the] volume [of] that conversation will become."

It didn't take long for Toyota to figure that out. According to Radian6, on Jan. 22, the day after the recall, buzz within the social web skyrocketed, with the number of posts about the automaker going from less than 100 to over 3,200.

"Just by virtue of the volume of conversation you see out there online, [social media] is probably the most important [crisis-communication] element in many cases," said Mr. Frisbie. "How you respond and react to those [social-media] conversations really has become perhaps the most important platform for dealing with a crisis like this."

Michael Bush, "The Cult of Toyota," *Advertising Age*, March 1, 2010, p. 1, Crain Communications.

In 2012, YouTube played a significant role in a public relations crisis for the cancer research charity, Susan G. Komen for the Cure. On January 31, 2012, Associated Press broke the story that Komen was eliminating most of its funding for Planned Parenthood. Within 48 hours, supporters flooded the Internet with negative comments and started a "Defund Komen" campaign. (See **Impact/ Money**, "Can Komen Recover from PR Crisis?," p. 235.)

Public Relations Monitors Brands

The Internet also brings hazards for companies' brand reputation. Disgruntled customers, pranksters and competitors can create their own sites to immediately challenge and even undermine a client's site. "In the pre-Internet days we used to say that a satisfied customer will tell one or two prospects but a dissatisfied customer will tell 10 or more," wrote G. A. Andy Marken, a public relations adviser, in *Public Relations Quarterly*. "With the Internet and the Web those same dissatisfied customers can tell millions of people . . . and they're doing it every day around the globe."

Marken says these attacks, which he calls *cyber- smears*, include anti-Disney, anti-McDonald's and anti- gun regulation sites, as well as chat rooms, discussion groups and online forums. In 2013, for example, hackers broke into the Burger King site and posted a message that said McDonald's had bought Burger King. (See **Impact/Convergence**, "Twitter Hacking Puts Focus on Security for Brands," p. 237).

To counter these negative messages, many businesses and organizations hire public relations firms to continu- ously monitor the Internet and alert their clients when negative information appears so the client can decide the best way to counter the information.

"It's a tedious task but any organization that isn't monitoring Internet traffic and Web activity could find itself in serious trouble," says Marken. "Companies and agencies spend hundreds and thousands of dollars on audio, video and print clipping services to analyze how their messages are being picked up, interpreted and used by the conventional media. They spend little or no time finding out what people are saying in real-time in cyberspace about them. . . . What you don't hear can hurt you . . . and it could be fatal."

By using public relations techniques, such as monitor- ing Internet social media like Facebook and Twitter for

Cybersmears Negative information organized and presented on the Internet as continuing attacks against a corporation.

negative comments about the company, public relations people often play a central role in trying to protect their clients from unfavorable publicity.

Ad Agencies and Public Relations Firms Merge

More than 150,000 people in the United States work in public relations, and about 4,000 firms throughout the nation offer PR-related services. The largest public relations firms employ more than 1,000 people. Several major corporations have 100 to 400 public relations spe- cialists, but most public relations firms have fewer than four employees.

Public relations people often deal with advertising agen- cies as part of their job, and because PR and advertising are so interrelated, several large public relations firms have joined several large advertising agencies. For example, J. Walter Thompson (advertising) joined Hill & Knowlton (public relations), and the London firm WPP Group PLC bought Young & Rubicam and now owns more than 250 public relations, advertising and marketing companies.

Combined agencies can offer both public relations and advertising services to their clients, and the trend toward advertising/public relations combinations continues today. The difference between public relations and adver- tising at the nation's largest agencies can be difficult to discern. Advertising is an aspect of marketing that aims to sell products. People in advertising usually *aren't* involved in a company's policy making. They implement the company's policies after company executives decide how to sell a product, a corporate image or an idea.

Public relations people, in comparison, usually are involved in policy. A PR person often contributes to deci- sions about how a company will deal with the public, the press and its own employees.

Variety of Clients Use Public Relations

Public relations people work for several types of clients, including governments, educational institutions, non- profit organizations, industry and business.

Government

The federal government is the nation's largest single employer of public information people. State and local governments also hire people to handle PR. Related to government are PR people who work for political candi- dates and for lobbying organizations. Media consultants also are involved in political PR. These people counsel candidates and officeholders about how they should pre- sent themselves to the public through the media.

IMPACT/Money

Can Komen Recover from PR Crisis?

Controversial Move, Confused Communication Damaged Reputation; Now Stability of Ties with Corporate Sponsors Hangs in the Balance

By Alexandra Bruell

Susan G. Komen for the Cure showed how a brand can boomerang from one of the most loved into one of the most reviled in a head-snapping two days.

The story of how Komen got consumers seeing red, rather than pink, says a lot about how social-media wildfire can singe even the most fireproof of brands. But it also demonstrates how inconsistent communications can fan the flames, and illustrates how quickly sponsors can become engulfed in controversy.

AP broke the story Jan. 31 [2012] that the charity was withdrawing funding from Planned Parenthood. Komen within 48 hours confirmed that it was pulling funding, contradicted itself in explaining its motive, and then backtracked on the decision following a groundswell of protest.

The first public response, a video of founder and CEO Nancy Brinker via YouTube, didn't help. PR executives said the background—a stuffy library—and Ms. Brinker's seemingly calculated statement was counterproductive.

A day later, Ms. Brinker told *The Washington Post* that the real reason for the funding cut "... has to do with the fact that [Planned Parenthood does] not provide mammograms to women, but only provides mammogram referrals." That same day, a Komen board member flip-flopped the message again. Lobbyist John D. Raffaelli told *The New York Times* that Komen "had become increasingly worried that an investigation of Planned Parenthood by Rep. Cliff Stearns, R.-Fla., would damage Komen's credibility with donors."

But Komen was doing a fine job of damaging that credibility on its own. What started as a communications crisis quickly flamed into a brand crisis as the organization went more than 24 hours without a tweet, during which time consumers besieged the Facebook pages of

A group of women protested outside the Susan G. Komen for the Cure headquarters in Dallas on February 7, 2012, after the Komen group announced it was eliminating most of its funding for Planned Parenthood, creating a public relations challenge for the organization.

Komen's corporate partners and voiced concerns on Twitter. As of Feb. 3, [2012,] there were 18,645 likes on the "Defund the Komen Foundation" Facebook page. New York Mayor Michael Bloomberg gave Planned Parenthood $250,000 out of his own pocket, indirectly admonishing the organization's decision.

"If they had quickly come out and communicated and said, 'Oops, we blew it,' that's one thing. But 48 hours is an eternity today with social media," said Kivi Leroux Miller, author and blogger at the website Nonprofit Marketing Guide.

Now its reputation—in a Harris poll last year Komen ranked second among nonprofits in terms of trust and tops in brand equity—and the stability of its relationships with corporate sponsors hangs in the balance.

Komen declined to comment.

"It's surprising that such an established organization didn't take a pulse check on different stakeholders," said Tara Greco, senior VP-corporate responsibility at APCO, a public-affairs firm.

Source: Excerpted from Alexandra Bruell, "Can Komen Recover from PR Crisis?," February 5, 2012, adage.com.

Education

Universities, colleges and school districts often hire public relations people to promote these educational institutions and to handle press attention from the consequences of decisions that educators make.

Nonprofit Organizations

Nonprofit organizations include hospitals, churches, museums and charities. Public relations organizations help raise money for charities such as Habitat for Humanity, which builds and remodels homes for low-income communities. Public relations for nonprofit organizations is growing especially fast as different charities compete with each other for donations.

Industry

Chicago Edison's early use of promotion was one type of industry PR. Many industries are government-regulated, so this often means that the industry PR person works with government agencies on government-related issues that affect the industry, such as utility rate increases or energy conservation programs.

Business

This is the best-known area of public relations. Large companies keep an in-house staff of public relations people, and these companies also often hire outside PR firms to help on special projects. Product publicity is one of the fastest-growing aspects of business-related public relations.

Within many large businesses are people who handle corporate PR, sometimes called financial PR. They prepare annual reports and gather financial data on the company for use by the press. They also may be assigned directly to the executives of a corporation to help establish policy about the corporation's public image. Many companies also sponsor charity events to increase their visibility in the community.

Athletic Teams and Entertainment Organizations

A professional sports team needs someone to travel with them and handle the press requests that inevitably come at each stop. Sports information people also are responsible for the coaches', the owner's and the team's relationship with the fans. College and university sports departments often hire public relations people to handle inquiries from the public and from the press. Athletic

Garrett W. Ellwood/NBAE via Getty Images

Public relations for athletic teams often involves organizing events to promote the team in the community. In 2013, Corey Brewer of the Denver Nuggets hosted second graders at the Denver Botanical Gardens as part of NBA Cares Green Week to teach children about gardening and protecting the environment.

teams also sponsor public relations events such as the National Basketball Association's Green Week.

As described earlier, in 1939 Henry Rogers learned how to use press agentry to gather publicity for actress Rita Hayworth. Today, entertainment public relations agencies promote movies and also handle TV personalities and well-known athletes who appear on the lecture circuit.

International

As the nation's consumer market broadens, more attention is being given to developing business in other countries. This means more opportunities in international PR. Hill & Knowlton and Burson-Marsteller, for example, are two big U.S. public relations firms that now also operate in Japan.

PUBLIC RELATIONS ORGANIZATIONS OFFER MANY SERVICES

Responsibilities of PR people include writing, editing, media relations and placement, special events, public speaking, production tasks, research, programming and counseling, training and management.

- Writing: Writing news releases, newsletters, correspondence, reports, speeches, booklet texts, radio and TV copy, film scripts, trade paper and magazine articles, institutional advertisements, product

IMPACT/Convergence

Twitter Hacking Puts Focus on Security for Brands

By Tanzina Vega and Nicole Perlroth

While most Americans were winding up their holiday weekends [in 2013], the phones at the Vancouver headquarters of HootSuite, a social media management company, began to ring.

Burger King's Twitter account had just been hacked. The company's logo had been replaced by a McDonald's logo, and rogue announcements began to appear. One was that Burger King had been sold to a competitor; other posts were unprintable.

What happened to Burger King is every brand manager's nightmare. While many social media platforms began as a way for ordinary users to share vacation photos and status updates, they have now evolved into major advertising vehicles for brands, which can set up accounts free but have to pay for more sophisticated advertising products.

Other prominent accounts have fallen victim to hacking, including those for NBC News, USA Today, Donald J. Trump, the Westboro Baptist Church and even the "hacktivist" group Anonymous.

Those episodes raised questions about the security of social media passwords and the ease of gaining access to brand-name accounts.

AP Photos/Ned Wiggins/Rex Features

Profile summary

McDonalds ✔
@BurgerKing
BURGER KING® USA official Twitter account. Just got sold to McDonalds because the whopper flopped =[FREDOM IS FAILURE*
mcdonalds.com
In a hood near you · info.bk.com/press/sold-to-…

| 1,301 | 613 | 85,066 |
| TWEETS | FOLLOWING | FOLLOWERS |

FISH McBites
HURRY, THEY WON'T LAST!

On March 18, 2013, hackers attacked the Burger King site and posted messages, including one that said Burger King had been sold to a competitor. Public relations plays an important role in protecting brand names.

"Twitter and other social media accounts are like catnip for script kiddies, hacktivists and serious cybercriminals alike," said Mark Risher, chief executive at Impermium, a Silicon Valley start-up that aims to clean up social networks. "Because of their deliberately easy access and liberal content policies, accounts on these networks prove irresistibly tempting."

Source: Excerpted from Tanzina Vega and Nicole Perlroth, "Twitter Hacking Puts Focus on Security for Brands," February 24, 2013, nytimes.com.

information and technical materials and developing content for Web sites.

- Editing: Editing special publications, employee newsletters, shareholder reports and other communications for employees and for the public.

- Media Relations, Placement and Internet Services: Contacting news media, magazines, Sunday supplements, freelance writers and trade publications with the intent of getting them to publish or broadcast news and features about or originated by clients; responding to media requests for information or spokespersons; charting Web site activity and monitoring social media for comments about clients.

- Special Events: Arranging and managing press conferences, convention exhibits, open houses, anniversary celebrations, fundraising events, special observances, contests and award programs.

- Public Speaking: Appearing before groups and arranging platforms for others before appropriate audiences by managing a speaker's bureau.

- Production Tasks: Creating art, photography and layout for brochures, booklets, reports, institutional advertisements and periodicals; recording and editing audio and Internet materials.

- Research: Gathering data to help an organization plan programs; monitoring the effectiveness of public relations programs. This fast-growing area of public relations includes focus groups to test message concepts; research to target specific audiences; surveys of a company's reputation for use in improving the company's image; surveys to determine employee and public attitudes; and shareholder surveys to improve relations with investors.

- Programming and Counseling: Establishing a program for effective public relations within the company.

- Training: Working with executives and other people within the organization to prepare them to deal with the media.

- Management: Overseeing the costs of running the public relations program; paying the bills.

PUBLICITY MEANS FREE MEDIA

Public relations work often means finding ways to attract the attention of the press. Seymour Topping, former managing editor of *The New York Times*, said, "PR people do influence the news, but really more in a functional manner rather than in terms of giving new editorial direction. We get hundreds of press releases every day in each of our departments. We screen them very carefully for legitimate news, and very often there are legitimate news stories. Quite a lot of our business stories originate from press releases. It's impossible for us to cover all of these organizations ourselves."

People in public relations provide *publicity*, which creates events and presents information so the press and the public will pay attention. Publicity and advertising differ: An advertising message is *paid for*; publicity is *free*. Advertising is a *controlled* use of media because the person or company that places the ad governs the message and where it will appear. Publicity is considered an *uncontrolled* use of the media because the public relations person provides information to the press but has no control over how the information will appear—the press presents the story.

"We know how the media work," says David Resnicow of the PR firm Ruder Finn & Rotman, "and we make judgments on that, providing access to events as it becomes necessary." It is precisely because people in the media and people in PR know how each other work that they debate about the role of public relations and the news.

"Of course, you realize that respectability for a sleazebag like yourself doesn't come cheap."

Bernard Schoenbaum/The New Yorker Collection/www.cartoonbank.com

Publicity Uncontrolled free use of media by a public relations firm to create events and present information to capture press and public attention.

PUBLIC RELATIONS GROWS GLOBALLY

Clever ways to attract attention are trademarks of today's successful public relations professional. Like advertising, the future of public relations is tied closely to the future of the media industries. The basic structure of the business will not change, but public relations practitioners find themselves facing the same challenges as people in the advertising business.

Growing international markets mean that many U.S. public relations firms have expanded overseas and that overseas companies seek help from American companies when faced with international marketing challenges. Global communications mean that public relations agencies often work internationally on some projects, and the agencies have to adjust to the cultural differences that global exposure brings.

"To be successful they need an education on how our market works, what is reputation and how do you build it and who are the people they need to know to have 'permission to operate' in both a formal and informal sense," according to Margery Kraus, global CEO of the independent agency APCO. "Many of these companies also have to overcome the fact that they are from countries that are misunderstood or feared by the U.S., such as Russia and China."

New technologies, especially the Internet, mean more ways to deliver public relations messages and to monitor public relations efforts globally.

In 2013, the Council of Public Relations Firms, an industry group, cited the top five issues facing the public relations industry today:

1. **The industry will need to deal with content overload.** "A piece of content doesn't carry the same weight that it did before and doesn't have the same impact," says Steve Rubel, Executive VP for global strategies and insights at Edelman.

2. **Brands will get increasingly visual.** "A really great visual can cross language and cultural barriers and be instantly relatable," says Janet Tyler, co-CEO of Airfoil.

3. **Real-time marketing will take off.** "We need not just make marketing plans for four months down the road, but to draft off what real people are talking about right now," says Jeff Beringer, executive director and global practice leader–digital at GolinHarris.

4. **Business-to-business marketing will move to embrace social media.** Sam Ford, director of digital strategy for Peppercomm, says his agency provides "content support" for their clients. "Our job is to help them get more active in social media and stay on top of the trends."

5. **As the social media space matures, consumer and marketer behavior will change.** "People are settling into the right behaviors for them and their connections, and to some degree user behaviors online have plateaued," says Mike Manual, senior VP of Voce Communications. Manual says not every social network is right for every company, and companies might see that Facebook or Twitter is a useful place for them, but not both.

Internet technology has streamlined delivery of print, audio and video, giving public relations agencies the same access to distributing information globally to news organizations that the news organizations themselves possess. As in the advertising industry, shifting demographic patterns also mean growing potential markets for public relations services around the world.

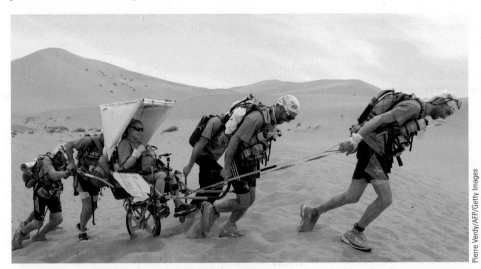

Pierre Verdy/AFP/Getty Images

Many public relations firms have expanded overseas. In April 2013, public relations promoted the United Nations International Children's Education Fund (UNICEF) 28th Marathon des Sables. Racers cross the dunes of Merzouga, Morocco, pulling a disabled young woman in her wheelchair, to raise donations for UNICEF.

Review, Analyze, Investigate

Reviewing Chapter 11

PR Helps Shape Public Opinion

- There are three ways to encourage someone to do what you want them to do: power, patronage and persuasion.

- Public relations people use persuasion to form public opinion about their clients.

- Modern public relations emerged at the beginning of the 20th century as a way for business to respond to the muckrakers and to Theodore Roosevelt's antitrust campaign.

PR Pioneer Issues *Declaration of Principles*

- President Roosevelt successfully used public relations to influence public opinion.

- The first U.S. publicity firm, called The Publicity Bureau, opened in Boston in 1900.

- The best-known practitioner of early public relations was Ivy Lee, who wrote a *Declaration of Principles* to respond to the secret publicity activities of The Publicity Bureau.

- The Chicago Edison Company and American Telephone & Telegraph were the first companies to begin in-house promotional programs.

Government Recruits PR Professionals

- Both Edward L. Bernays and Ivy Lee have been called the father of public relations.

- The Committee on Public Information, headed by George Creel, promoted the war effort during World War I.

- The Office of War Information, headed by newscaster Elmer Davis, promoted the country's efforts during World War II.

- Edward L. Bernays wrote the first book on public relations, *Crystallizing Public Opinion*.

- Franklin Roosevelt, assisted by public relations expert Louis McHenry Howe, successfully used public relations to promote the New Deal.

Women Join PR Firms

- Among the pioneering women in the public relations business were Doris E. Fleischman, Leone Baxter and Anne Williams Wheaton.

- Doris Fleischman and Edward L. Bernays were equal partners in their public relations firm.

- Doris Fleischman was an early advocate of public relations as a career for women.

Professionals Promote Ethics Codes

- The Public Relations Society established the profession's first code of ethics in 1954.

- Public relations expanded quickly in the 1960s and 1970s to accommodate television, the federal government and corporate America.

- The federal government is the largest single employer of public relations ("public information") people.

Public Relations at Work

- Three of the most common public relations specialties are financial public relations, product public relations and crisis public relations.

- Crisis public relations successfully repaired the public image of Odwalla Inc.

- Public relations experts criticized Toyota Motor Corp. and BP PLC for the way they handled their public relations crises in 2010.

Public Relations Adapts to the Internet

- Negative PR can spread very quickly on the Web, where anyone is free to post damaging comments about a company, organization or product.

- Toyota monitored social media to try to counteract negative comments about its auto recall in 2010.

- In 2012, YouTube was a significant factor in a public relations crisis for the cancer research charity, Susan G. Komen for the Cure.

Public Relations Monitors Brands

- Public relations plays an important role in protecting brand names.

- On March 18, 2013, hackers attacked the Burger King site and posted messages, including one that said Burger King had been sold to a competitor.

- Companies and agencies must be continually vigilant to monitor how their messages are being used and interpreted on the Internet.

Ad Agencies and Public Relations Firms Merge

- Today, more than 150,000 people work in public relations nationwide and about 4,000 firms in the U.S. offer PR-related services.

- Because PR and advertising are so interrelated, public relations people and advertising agencies often work together in the same company to offer advertising and marketing communications services.

Variety of Clients Use Public Relations

- Public relations people work in government, education, nonprofit agencies, industry, business, athletic teams, entertainment companies and international business.

Public Relations Organizations Offer Many Services

- Responsibilities of PR people include writing, Web site development, editing, media relations and placement, Internet monitoring, special events, public speaking, production tasks, research, programming and counseling, training and management.

Publicity Means Free Media

- The main difference between advertising and public relations is that advertising messages are controlled, and public relations messages are uncontrolled.

- Public relations people create publicity, which is considered an uncontrolled use of media.

Public Relations Grows Globally

- New technologies, especially the Internet, mean new ways to deliver public relations messages.

- Satellite technology has streamlined print, audio and video delivery, giving PR the same access to information distribution as news organizations.

- Global communications mean many public relations agencies work internationally on some projects and must adjust to cultural differences that global exposure brings.

- Growing international markets mean that many U.S. public relations firms have expanded overseas.

- In 2013, the Council of Public Relations Firms, an industry group, cited the top five challenges facing the industry: (1) The industry will need to deal with content overload. (2) Brands will get increasingly visual. (3) Real-time marketing will take off. (4) Business-to-business marketing will move to embrace social media. (5) As the social media space matures, consumer and marketer behavior will change.

- Shifting demographic patterns mean growing potential markets for public relations services.

Key Terms

These terms are defined in the margins throughout this chapter and appear in alphabetical order with definitions in the Glossary, which begins on page 373.

Critical Questions

1. How did each of the following people contribute to the development of public relations?
   a. Ivy Lee and George F. Parker
   b. Edward L. Bernays
   c. Doris E. Fleischman

2. Explain in some detail how the Office of War Information contributed to positive public relations for World War II.

3. When is it necessary for a company to apply crisis public relations techniques? Give an example from the public relations crises that developed at Toyota, BP or Susan G. Komen for the Cure.

4. Describe the ways that advertising and public relations are different. Describe the ways they are similar.

5. Describe one or more examples of how negative information on the Internet can create problems for public relations practitioners.

Working the Web

This list includes both sites mentioned in the chapter and others to give you greater insight into the public relations industry.

All About Public Relations

aboutpublicrelations.net

This site provides information and links to PR jobs, careers and internships as well as desk references, agencies and PR basics. Subject links range from a How-to PR Toolkit to online public relations campaigns and strategies.

Center for Media and Democracy: PRWatch.org

prwatch.org

This nonprofit, nonpartisan organization investigates and exposes "corporate and industrial public relations spin and government propaganda," and promotes media literacy and citizen journalism. The Center projects include *PR Watch*, a quarterly publication dedicated to investigative reporting on the PR industry; Latest News, Web-based daily reporting on PR propaganda and media spin; and SourceWatch, an online collaborative encyclopedia of people, groups and issues that shape the public agenda.

Chartered Institute of Public Relations

cipr.co.uk

The "eyes, ears and voice of the public relations industry," this professional organization for British public relations professionals provides training and events, a professional development program, PR policy and research, and a PR careers board. Its members sign an enforced code of conduct.

Institute for Public Relations

instituteforpr.com

This independent nonprofit organization sponsors and disseminates scientific research about public relations and sponsors the Commission on Public Relations Measurement and Evaluation, which establishes standards and methods for PR research and issues best-practices white papers. The Commission on Global Public Relations Research was formed in 2005 to study the practice of PR across regions, countries and cultures. The Institute also offers several awards for excellence in PR practice and research, including one for a master's thesis.

Online Public Relations

online-pr.com

This straightforward Web site provides free online resources for public relations professionals. It is developed and maintained by James L. Horton, a PR executive and educator who specializes in using technology and the Internet to enhance client service. This list of media, reference and PR resources contains thousands of links to reliable sources categorized by subject and alphabetically indexed.

PR Newswire

prnewswire.com

This association provides electronic distribution, targeting, measurement, translation and broadcast services for government, association, labor and nonprofit customers worldwide. PR Newswire provides search engine optimization, a professional community, user tracking, and multimedia and multicultural services to customers.

PRWeb

prweb.com

Founded in 1997 to help small businesses use the Internet to communicate their news to the public, PRWeb pioneered the direct-to-consumer news release. Clients can create a free account, access the site's search engine optimization tools and upload a press release for online distribution. PRWeb has helped more than 40,000 organizations of all sizes maximize the online visibility of their news. The service is owned by Vocus, a leader in on-demand PR software.

PRWeek

prweekus.com

A publication of Haymarket, producer of more than 100 international trade magazines, *PRWeek* is the company's first weekly in the United States. The magazine provides timely news, reviews, profiles, techniques and groundbreaking research for PR professionals. As the companion Web site for the magazine, PRWeek.com offers a searchable archive of editorials, news, features, industry research and special reports.

Public Relations Society of America (PRSA)

prsa.org

The world's largest organization for public relations professionals, PRSA was established in 1947 and has nearly 21,000 professional members organized into more than 110 chapters. Representing for-profit and not-for-profit organizations from areas including business and industry, government, health and education, its primary objectives are to advance the standards of the profession by providing members with professional development opportunities, to strengthen the society by increasing members and enriching member services and to establish global leadership in PR.

Public Relations Student Society of America (PRSSA)

prssa.org

An organization founded by the Public Relations Society of America for students, the PRSSA's goal is to help students become aware of current theories and procedures of the profession, appreciate ethical ideals and principles and understand what constitutes an appropriate professional attitude. It has more than 10,000 members at over 300 chapters on college campuses throughout the country and offers a number of scholarships and travel opportunities.

Impact/Action Videos are concise news features on various topics created exclusively for *Media/Impact*. Go online to access MindTap at cengagebrain.com. MindTap for Media/Impact sequences all of your learning tools—Chapter Readings with highlighting and note taking, **Impact/Action Videos**, activities and assessments—into chapter driven learning units that guide you through the curriculum.

NEWS AND INFORMATION: 12
CHOOSING SOURCES

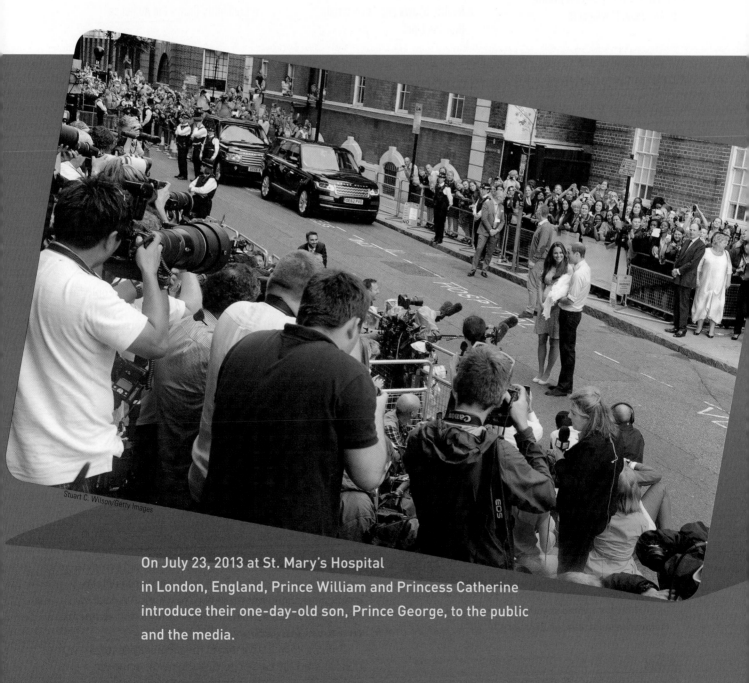

Stuart C. Wilson/Getty Images

On July 23, 2013 at St. Mary's Hospital
in London, England, Prince William and Princess Catherine
introduce their one-day-old son, Prince George, to the public
and the media.

What's Ahead?

"Hearing about things in the news from friends and family, whether via social media or actual word of mouth, leads to deeper news consumption."

—PEW RESEARCH CENTER'S PROJECT FOR EXCELLENCE IN JOURNALISM

Because the First

Amendment to the U.S. Constitution prescribes freedom of the press, it is important to understand the development of news reporting in this country. Today's news delivery is the result of a tug of war between audiences as they define the types of news they want and the news media that try to deliver it.

Vince Caligiuri/Getty Images Sport/Getty Images

Today the public's appetite for news means there are more news outlets gathering more types of news than ever before. Trainers parade racehorse Black Caviar before journalists for a photo shoot at Caulfield Racecourse in Melbourne, Australia, on February 14, 2013.

Cooperative News Gathering   Member news organizations that share the expense of getting the news.

Publick Occurrences, the nation's first newspaper, published only one issue in 1690 before the authorities shut it down. The nation's first *consecutively issued* newspaper (published more than once) was *The Boston News-Letter*, which appeared in 1704. In the first issue, editor John Campbell reprinted the queen's latest speech, some maritime news and one advertisement telling people how to put an ad in his paper.

From 1704 until the Civil War, newspapers spread throughout New England, the South and across the frontier. The invention of the telegraph, in 1844, meant news that once took weeks to reach publication could be transmitted in minutes.

EARLY NEWS ORGANIZATIONS COOPERATE TO GATHER NEWS

In 1848, six newspapers in New York City decided to share the cost of gathering foreign news by telegraph from Boston. Henry J. Raymond, who subsequently founded *The New York Times*, drew up the agreement among the papers to pay $100 for 3,000 words of telegraph news. Soon known as the New York Associated Press, this organization was the country's first *cooperative news gathering* association.

Being a cooperative meant the member organizations shared the cost of getting the news, domestic and foreign, returning any profits to the members. Today's Associated Press (AP) is the result of this early partnership. United Press, founded in 1884 to compete with AP, devised a different way of sharing information. United Press, which eventually became United Press International (UPI), was established not as a cooperative but as a privately owned, for-profit wire service. (Today wire services are called news services.)

Because news services now use digital delivery instead of the original telegraph machines, cooperative and for-profit news gathering is virtually instantaneous. Most American newspapers and broadcast news operations subscribe to at least one news service, such as AP. Many other news services send stories and broadcasts worldwide: Agence France-Presse (France), Reuters (Great Britain), ITAR-TASS (Russia), Agenzia-Nationale Stampa Associate (ANSA; Italy), Deutsche-Presse Agentur (Germany) and Xinhua (China).

The news services especially help small newspapers and broadcast stations that can't afford overseas correspondents. Large dailies with their own reporters around the world still rely on news services when they can't get to a story quickly. UPI had several owners and declined financially. AP today is still a cooperative, as it was when it began in New York and employs broadcast as well as print reporters. Associated Press is the nation's primary news service, constantly feeding stories to newspapers, broadcast outlets and Internet news services.

Some newspaper organizations in the United States—*The New York Times, The Washington Post* and the *Chicago Tribune*—also run their own news services. Subscribers publish each other's news service stories. For many newspapers, news service stories provide information at a relatively low cost because the subscribing newspaper doesn't need as many staff reporters to cover the news.

Civil War Brings Accreditation and Photojournalism

In the 1860s, interest in the emotional issues of the Civil War sent many reporters to the battlefront. Hundreds of correspondents roamed freely among the soldiers, reporting for the North and the South. Two important results of Civil War reporting were the accreditation of reporters and the introduction of photographs to enhance written reports.

Government Accredits Journalists

The issue of government interests versus press freedom surfaced early in the Civil War. In 1861, Union General Winfield Scott forbid telegraph companies from transmitting military information because he was afraid some stories would help the South. At the Battle of Bull Run in

1861, *New York Times* editor Henry J. Raymond, reporting the war from the front, mistakenly telegraphed a story that said the North had won. When he followed up with the correct story, military censors blocked the news, arguing the information should be kept secret. Then Union General William T. Sherman ordered *New York Herald* correspondent Thomas E. Knox arrested and held as a spy for sending sensitive military information.

President Lincoln intervened to reach a compromise that would balance the needs of the press with the needs of the nation through a process called *accreditation*. This meant that the federal government certified members of the press to cover the war. Accredited journalists were required to carry press passes issued by the military. The practice of accreditation continues today as the government's method of certifying war-reporting journalists. This concept of accreditation—that a journalist is someone who could be credentialed—served to add to a sense of professionalism among journalists.

Mathew B. Brady/CORBIS

Mathew Brady's photojournalism during the Civil War created a standard for future photojournalists to follow—using photo images to help capture a story's realism. In 1861, Brady photographed this group of men of the 71st New York Infantry outside their tent at Camp Douglas.

Photojournalism Is Born

Also at the Battle of Bull Run was photographer Mathew Brady, who convinced President Lincoln that a complete photographic record of the war should be made. Until the

Accreditation   The process by which the government certifies members of the press to cover government-related news events.

Civil War, photography had been confined primarily to studio portraits because of the cumbersome equipment and slow chemical processing. Brady photographed the battles of Antietam and Fredericksburg and sent photographic teams to other battles.

Newspapers did not yet have a method to reproduce the photographs, but Brady's pictures were published in magazines, making Brady the nation's first news photographer. His 3,500 photographs demonstrated the practicality and effectiveness of using images to help report a news story, although newspaper photographs did not become widely used until the early 1900s.

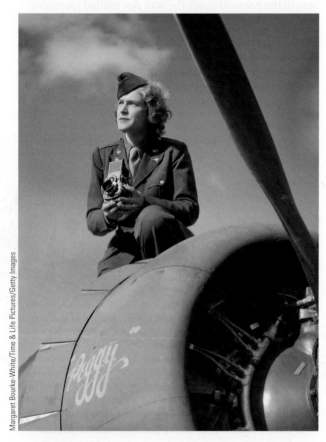

Photojournalist Margaret Bourke-White photographed stories for *Fortune* and *Time* magazines, establishing a 20th-century standard for photojournalism. Bourke-White, dressed in a military uniform, sits on top of a B-17 bomber in Northamptonshire, England, in 1942. Bourke-White covered World War II and the Korean War as a photojournalist.

Photojournalism   Using photographs to accompany text to capture a news story.

The marriage of images and text to tell a better story than either text or photographs could tell alone formed the beginnings of today's concept of *photojournalism*. It was photojournalism that made *Life* magazine, founded by *Time*'s Henry Luce, such a success and created stars out of gifted photographers like Margaret Bourke-White. The perfect image to accompany the words—the best photojournalism—has become an essential part of any good news story.

TABLOID NEWS TAKES OVER

The beginning of the 20th century brought the expansion of newspapers—New York City once had more than ten daily newspapers—and intensified competition. The introduction of the penny papers meant newspapers had to grab a bigger audience to survive. And, as described in **Chapter 3**, the race for readers ushered in yellow journalism—featuring stories about grisly crimes and illicit sex, often illustrated with large, startling photographs. Substantial newspapers, covering important stories, were being published all over the country, but today people still think first about tabloid journalism when they think about this period in newspaper history.

In the 1930s, people began to turn to radio for instant news headlines and information. Newspapers still flourished, but where they once had an exclusive corner on news, now they shared their audiences with radio. When World War II began, both radio and newspapers were in place to bring home expanded news of the war.

NEWSREELS BRING DISTANT EVENTS TO AMERICAN MOVIEGOERS

Beginning at the turn of the 20th century and lasting until television took over news coverage, movie newsreels showed audiences distant locations and newsworthy events. Produced by companies including British Pathé (from 1900 until 1970) and Fox Movietone News (between 1919 and 1960), newsreels were shown in movie theaters to audiences hungry for the pictures that radio couldn't provide. Newsreels and news features, such as *March of Time*, were usually no longer than 10 minutes, with running commentary by a narrator, updated every week.

Because it took time to assemble the stories and develop the film, newsreel footage usually reached audiences a week or more after the events took place. Movietone News, produced by Fox, offered the most popular newsreel in the United States, with more than 1,000 camera operators who roamed the globe to cover the news each day.

Before TV news, newsreels and news features were very popular with movie audiences. Shown in movie theaters before the main feature, newsreels, such as Movietone News, brought viewers closer to distant locations and newsworthy events. On November 2, 1932, Governor Franklin D. Roosevelt was interviewed for newsreel cameras at the executive mansion in Albany, N.Y.

Besides serious news stories, such as President Franklin Delano Roosevelt speaking to a national audience, newsreel photographers captured Hollywood celebrities, scoured exotic travel locations and produced sports and feature stories. Another newsreel company, All-American News, produced newsreels directed at African American audiences; often these were shown before feature movies in addition to, or instead of, Movietone newsreels.

Newsreels offered an important realistic glimpse at worldwide news and information events that audiences couldn't get anywhere else.

NEWSPAPERS AND RADIO PERSONALIZE WORLD WAR II

The most honored print journalist during World War II was Ernie Pyle, who worked for the Scripps Howard news organization. His reporting, which focused on the people who were fighting the war rather than battles and casualty counts, reached deep into the emotions of Americans who were stateside waiting for word from the

front. (See **Impact/Profile**, "Ernie Pyle: The War Correspondent Who Hated War," p. 250.)

Radio is the news medium that began to shine during World War II because radio news broadcasts meant that, for the first time, people could hear the action as it was happening. Imagine the date is September 8, 1940. World War II has begun its second year in Europe. You don't have a television set. You are sitting at home in the United States, listening to your radio.

CBS announces a special bulletin from journalist Edward R. Murrow, reporting the first bombing of London: 626 bombers have pounded the city, leaving more than 1,000 people dead and 2,000 people injured. You and your family listen intently in your living room as Murrow describes "men with white scarves around their necks instead of collars . . . dull-eyed, empty-faced women. . . . Most of them carried little cheap cardboard suitcases and sometimes bulging paper shopping bags. That was all they had left. . . .

During World War II, radio became the most immediate way for people to learn about current events. On July 5, 1942, radio commentators (left to right) Mark Hawley, William Shirer and John Charles Daly report on the day's war news from New York City.

"A row of automobiles with stretchers racked on the roofs like skis, standing outside of bombed buildings. A man pinned under wreckage where a broken gas main sears his arms and face. . . .

". . . the courage of the people, the flash and roar of the guns rolling down streets . . . the stench of air-raid shelters in the poor districts."

This was radio news reporting at its best. For 26 years, from 1921 until the advent of television news in

IMPACT/Profile

Ernie Pyle: The War Correspondent Who Hated War

By Dan Thomasson

Note: Ernie Pyle worked for Scripps Howard. Dan Thomasson, the editor of Scripps Howard News Service, wrote this reflection on Pyle's work to accompany a collection of Pyle's dispatches that was published in 1986.

The other day while going through some old files in our library, I came upon a yellowed and tattered dispatch.

It made me cry.

It was about the death of a Capt. Waskow during the Italian campaign of 1944. And it probably is the most powerful treatise on war and death and the human spirit I have ever read.

I took it out and had it treated and framed and I hung it in the office in a prominent position where now and then one of the younger reporters will come by and read it and try to hide the inevitable tear.

The man who wrote it, Ernest Taylor Pyle, is but a memory as distant as the war he covered so eloquently and ultimately died in.

But unlike so many who perished beside him, Pyle's contribution to what Studs Terkel calls "the last good war" remains with us in his work—thousands of words that will forever memorialize brave men and debunk the "glory" of war.

The column that says it best perhaps is the one drafted for the end of the fighting in Europe. It was found in his pocket by the foot soldiers who had risked their lives to retrieve his body on the Japanese island of Ie Shima in 1945:

"Dead men by mass production—in one country after another—month after month and year after year. Dead men in winter and dead men in summer.

War correspondent Ernie Pyle (1900–1945), the most honored journalist in the United States, died during the last days of World War II. Pyle (center, with goggles on his helmet) visits with a group of soldiers on the Anzio Beachhead in Italy.

"Dead men in such familiar promiscuity that they become monotonous.

"Dead men in such infinity that you come almost to hate them."

. . . When I was a kid starting out in this business, the trade magazines were full of job-seeking ads by those who claimed they could "write like Ernie Pyle." This was 10 years after his death and he was still everyone's model.

Source: From "Why They Still Write Ernie Pyle Books," *Honolulu Advertiser*, June 20, 1986, page A-1. Reprinted by permission of Scripps Howard News Service.

1947, radio reporters like Murrow painted pictures with words. (For more information about Murrow's career in television, see **Chapter 8**.)

During the first half of the 20th century, radio reporters described Prohibition and its repeal, the stock market crash, the Depression, the election of Franklin D. Roosevelt, the New Deal, the bombings of London and Pearl Harbor, the Normandy invasion, Roosevelt's funeral and the signing of the armistice that ended World War II.

Most radio stations maintained their own radio news departments, until the advent of format radio. Today, very few radio stations maintain full-time news departments, and radio stations with news formats tend to be concentrated in the nation's big cities. Still, the heritage of colorful, exciting radio news formed the foundation for TV news, which began to blossom in the 1950s.

TV NEWS ENTERS ITS GOLDEN AGE

The first network TV newscasts in the 1950s lasted only 15 minutes, but by the 1960s, TV network evening news had expanded to half an hour—the same amount of time the networks dedicate to national news today. Radio news stars like Edward R. Murrow moved from radio to television, and eventually the TV networks created large news departments with bureaus and correspondents spread throughout the United States and overseas.

What has been called the Golden Age of Television News was the decade that began in 1961, with President John F. Kennedy's inauguration. The Kennedy family was very photogenic, and they invited press coverage. Kennedy's victory as president, in fact, has been credited to his on-camera presence during the Kennedy-Nixon debates in 1960. So it was fitting that Kennedy would be the first president to play Cold War brinkmanship on television, when TV news grew to become a part of politics, not just a chronicler of political events.

TV and the Cold War

President Kennedy asked all three networks to clear him time on Monday, October 22, 1962, at 7 p.m. Eastern time. The president had learned that missile sites were being built in Cuba with Russian help. Kennedy used television to deliver his ultimatum to dismantle the missile bases.

"Using the word *nuclear* 11 times, Kennedy drew a panorama of devastation enveloping the whole hemisphere," according to media historian Eric Barnouw. "The moves that had made such things possible, said Kennedy, could not be accepted by the United States 'if our courage and our commitments are ever to be trusted again by either friend or foe.'"

Kennedy admonished Russian Premier Nikita Khrushchev and urged him to stop the ships the Soviet Union was sending to Cuba to help build the missile sites. Faced with such a visible challenge, the Soviet Union turned its ships around in the Atlantic and sent conciliatory messages in order to reach a settlement. The Cuban missile crisis was in fact a carefully constructed live television drama, in which Kennedy performed well.

TV News as a Window on the World

In 1963, television news was forced into an unexpected role as it conveyed a sense of collective national grief following President Kennedy's assassination. For four days beginning at 1:30 p.m. Eastern time on Friday, November 22, 1963, the country witnessed the aftermath of the assassination of the president. At 2:38 p.m., Vice President Lyndon Johnson was sworn in as president on television.

On Saturday, TV viewers watched the world's diplomats arrive for Kennedy's funeral. On Sunday, viewers watched the first murder ever broadcast live on television, as Jack Ruby killed assassination suspect Lee Harvey Oswald. Then, on Monday, November 25, 1963, came the president's funeral.

New York Daily News Archive/Getty Images

Television news provided a sense of collective national experience covering the events that followed the assassination of President Kennedy. On November 25, 1963, a crowd gathers in front of a giant television set in Grand Central Terminal to watch the funeral procession. The network news broadcasts during the events surrounding the Kennedy assassination have been called the finest four days of television news.

As many as nine out of ten television sets were turned on during the marathon events surrounding the president's funeral. The networks canceled all commercials. "Some television employees had slept as little as six hours in three nights," wrote media historian Eric Barnouw. "They went on, almost welcoming the absorption in the task at hand." The network news broadcasts during the events surrounding the Kennedy assassination were called the finest four days of television news. Television had become the nation's "window on the world," wrote Barnouw. "The view it offered seemed to be *the* world. They trusted its validity and completeness."

TV NEWS CHANGES THE NATION'S IDENTITY

In the late 1960s and early 1970s, television played a defining role in two very important stories—the war in Vietnam and the Watergate hearings.

Vietnam Coverage Exposes Reality

The longest-running protest program in the nation's history began appearing on television news as anti-Vietnam War marchers showed up on camera daily in the late 1960s. During live coverage of the Chicago Democratic Convention in 1968, demonstrators faced police in a march toward the convention hall. Television covered the resulting violence, which caused injuries to hundreds of protesters and to 21 reporters and photographers.

"When the war in Vietnam began to escalate in 1965," wrote TV critic Jeff Greenfield, "it was the television networks, covering the war with few official restrictions, that brought to American homes pictures of the face of war that had never been shown before: not friendly

troops welcomed by the populace, but troops setting fire to villages with cigarette lighters; troops cutting off the ears of dead combat foes; allies spending American tax money for personal gain."

Candid reporting from the war itself shook viewers as previous war reporting never had, but it also gave Americans an appetite for news and for live news coverage—instant information about events as they were happening.

Through live coverage of the Senate Judiciary Committee's Watergate hearings from May to August 1973, TV viewers got a close look inside the Nixon presidency as committee members examined evidence against the president. Nixon resigned in 1974.

Watergate Hearings Reveal Politics at Work

In 1973, live television news took another leap with the continuous broadcast of the U.S. Senate's Watergate hearings to investigate allegedly illegal activities of the Republican Committee to Re-elect the President (CREEP). A parade of government witnesses and political appointees fascinated viewers with descriptions of the inner workings of the Nixon presidency.

According to media scholars Christopher Sterling and John Kittross, "Running from May through August 1973, and chaired by North Carolina's crusty Sam Ervin, these hearings were a fascinating live exposition of the political process in America, and were 'must' television watching as a parade of witnesses told—or evaded telling—what they knew of the broad conspiracy to assure the reelection of Nixon and then to cover up the conspiracy itself." For more than a year the political drama continued to unfold on television's nightly news.

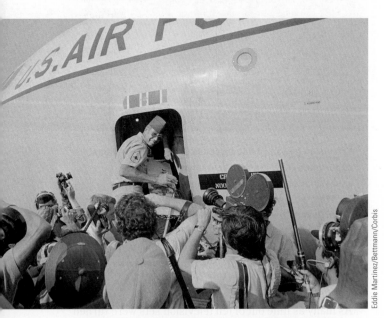

On March 29, 1973, news cameras recorded the last U.S. serviceman to leave Vietnam, Army Chief Master Sergeant Max Bielke. Graphic TV coverage of the Vietnam War shook American viewers as no previous war coverage had. It also gave them an appetite for live news coverage—instant information about events as they were happening.

Ultimately, the Judiciary Committee of the House of Representatives began a televised debate on whether to impeach the president. For the first time in its history, the nation faced the prospect of seeing a president brought to trial live on national television. On August 8, 1974, President Nixon brought the crisis to an end by announcing his resignation—on television.

TV News Expands and Contracts

Because viewers were hungry for news and wanted to watch it, local TV news operations expanded—some stations offering as much as two hours of local news plus the national news broadcasts. Throughout the 1970s and 1980s, networks and local news departments expanded. Then came broadcast deregulation in the 1980s. The networks were sold and consolidated, and local stations, many of which had been locally owned, became pieces of larger corporations.

In 1980, Ted Turner founded Cable News Network (CNN), which offered round-the-clock news on cable. CNN established overseas bureaus and the concept that all-news-all-the-time would grab an audience. Audiences responded, and CNN became an alternative to network news, often the first place audiences turned whenever there was a crucial international story that required constant updating.

In general, however, in the 1990s, the American public read fewer newspapers and watched less news on television. Network and local TV news audiences declined. News departments began to shrink. Soon, another medium replaced the public's seemingly insatiable need for instant news and information—the Internet.

Iraq War Produces "Embedded" Reporters

Since the Vietnam War, access to battlefield locations has been a battle between the press' aggressive need-to-know and the military's need-to-keep-secret. In 2003, military press relations took a new turn when the United States declared war on Iraq.

Before the battles began, the U.S. military announced a plan to *embed* more than 600 reporters with American troops. Embedding offered the reporters access to the frontlines but also kept them within the military's control. Still, it was a reversal of past Pentagon policy makers, who often had sought to keep the press far from military operations.

CNN and the major television networks offered nonstop coverage in the early days of the war, and people

watched. "A lot of people have been surprised at the access and cooperation we've had in the field," said Tony Maddox, Senior Vice President Europe, Middle East and Africa for CNN International. "It's produced some remarkable images."

Michael Macor/San Francisco Chronicle/Corbis

In 2003, during the Iraq War, the Pentagon embedded more than 600 reporters with American troops. Reporters prepared for Iraq duty by attending boot camp. On March 11, 2003, embedded journalists from throughout the world gathered at the Kuwait Hilton Hotel, waiting to join their assigned units.

Reality Shows and Advertorials Blur the Line

TV reality shows, such as *Undercover Boss*, blur the distinction between what is news and what is re-created drama. These shows use interviews and cover live action in a documentary style that imitates news stories. Reality shows, or docudramas, make it difficult for an audience to distinguish between packaged entertainment and spontaneous events.

Infomercials—programs that pretend to give viewers information but that are really advertisements for the sponsors' products—also are making it harder to discern what is reporting and what is advertising. The line between news and entertainment on television becomes even trickier when advertisers produce programs that

Embed During the Iraq War, a term used to describe journalists who were allowed to cover the war on the frontlines, supervised by the U.S. military.

look like news but are really advertisements. Paid advertising supplements in newspapers and magazines—called *advertorials*—also blur the line between news content and advertising. Although these supplements usually are labeled as advertising, they often look similar to the regular news pages.

"No, we don't have a TV, but we do have a news team."

This merging of news with entertainment and advertising, as well as the entertaining graphics and the lighthearted presentation style of most local TV newscasts, makes it more difficult for viewers and readers to separate fact from fiction, reality from reenactment, and news from advertising. The result may be a decline in the audience's trust in the news media to deliver accurate information. This makes it important that so-called pseudo-news be properly labeled so it doesn't mislead the public.

The Internet Transforms News Delivery

The immediacy of the Internet brought several changes to the news business. News became more personalized, and the Internet began to replace broadcast news because it is more immediate. The Internet also changed how journalists work because often they are required to

deliver several different types of stories simultaneously for print, broadcast and Internet formats. (See **Impact/Convergence**, "News Media and Social Media Become Part of a Real-Time Manhunt Drama," p. 255.)

According to the most recent study from the Pew Research Center, Internet news is attracting a large segment of the national audience. At the same time, many people are losing the news habit, according to the study. They pay attention to the news only when something important happens, and many watch broadcast news with the remote control nearby to skip uninteresting stories and move on to something they would rather watch.

Today, the Internet is a nonstop news and information machine. (See **Illustration 12.1**, p. 256.)

Anyone with access to the Internet can choose the sources and subjects to investigate. Yahoo! News, with a significant number of online subscribers, compiles headlines from television and print news outlets—photos and stories from major news organizations—as well as updated headline stories from news magazines like *Time* and *Bloomberg Businessweek*. For specialty information, and for more background, you can visit any corporation's, association's or nonprofit organization's Web site.

You can choose what to look for and also *when* you look. The Internet is available on your schedule—independent of any TV network or local broadcast time schedule. News rotates through CNN Headline News (HLN) on television in short segments, but you can check your computer or your cell phone and find just about anything you want to know—sports scores, the weather, international headlines—whenever you want it, and you control how much time you spend with each story.

The Internet, unlike any other form of news and information delivery, is completely self-directed—targeted to individual needs and not connected to a specific time of day or night. The Internet also is the place where people can get all the news in one location that they previously had to gather from several sources.

Today, one of four Americans lists the Internet as a main source of news (compared to just 15 percent in 2000), and 44 percent say they receive news reports from the Internet at least once a week, according to the Pew Project for Excellence in Journalism. At the same time, network evening television news viewership for the major TV networks is eroding. And in general, people who are interested in the news online tend to watch less network TV news.

Other important findings of the Pew news analysis were:

• As large numbers of Americans younger than age 30 turn to the Internet for news, people of all ages read the news online. Thirty-three percent of people younger than age 30 go online for news every day,

---

Advertorial   Paid advertising supplements in newspapers and magazines that often look similar to the regular news pages.

IMPACT/Convergence

News Media and Social Media Become Part of a Real-Time Manhunt Drama

By Brian Stelter

The all-consuming search in Massachusetts for the suspects in Monday's [April 15, 2013] Boston Marathon bombings gripped the nation with some of the most startling, and at times unnerving, news coverage in years. In the middle of it all were reporters, camera crews and ordinary citizens with cell phone cameras who were suddenly entwined with the story. When the second suspect was surrounded on Friday night [April 19, 2013], some reporters were so close to the scene that they could count the number of gunshots and flash bang sounds.

The close interaction of reporters with the unfolding events underscored the complex relationship the news media have had with law enforcement authorities this week. News organizations have been both scolded for irresponsible reporting and employed to relay information to the public, sometimes at the same news conference.

As thousands of police officers fanned out on Friday, the Massachusetts State Police asked local and national television networks to refrain from showing any live video of police movements, and for a time the Federal Aviation Administration restricted news helicopters from hovering above the area where one of the suspects was believed to be hiding.

The tension of the day also played out on Twitter, where seemingly every utterance from the local police scanners was repeated, often without any context.

There was at least one prominent case of mistaken identity late Thursday and early Friday.

That misstep came after several days of frenzied, sometimes inaccurate, reporting about the bombings. On Wednesday, the F.B.I. chastised news outlets that mistakenly reported an arrest in the case, saying it could have "unintended

Courtesy of the author

Public officials, members of the press and a local and global online audience became part of the hunt for two suspects in the 2013 bombings at the Boston Marathon. When police captured the second suspect, Boston Mayor Tom Menino tweeted the news.

consequences." But the next day, the authorities used the news media to help display photographs of the two men it was seeking as suspects.

On Friday, network programming was pre-empted most of the day for live coverage of the manhunt.

In places where reporters could not tread because of police restrictions, local residents filled in some of the audio and video gaps. From their front stoops and through their windows, they posted videos of an early-morning shootout and photographs of a vehicle said to be involved in a police chase. The material was quickly scooped up by local television stations and Twitter users.

At *The Boston Globe*, Brian McGrory, the editor, said that his staff had been working 16- to 18-hour days since the bombings on Monday.

"We are running on adrenaline, and every moment gets more urgent and more strange," he said. "For everyone in here, it's an unprecedented story."

Source: Excerpted from Brian Stelter, "News Media and Social Media Become Part of a Real-Time Manhunt Drama," April 19, 2013, nytimes.com.

IMPACT/Audience

Illustration 12.1

Top 10 Internet News Sites

The audience for news is swiftly migrating from newspapers and television to the Internet. Here is a list of the Internet news sites people visit most often.

Source: Nielsen.com

Unique Audience in Millions

62 Yahoo!-ABC News Websites

40 CNN Digital Network

34 HPMG* News Websites

30 MSNBC Digital Network

29.2 NYTimes.com

29 Huffington Post

22 Tribune Newspapers

21.5 Fox News Digital Network

16 Today

15 USA Today

* Huffington Post Media Group

but so do 27 percent of people in their 40s and 25 percent of people in their 50s.

- People who read online newspapers have a far less favorable view of network and local TV news programs than do people who read the print version of the daily newspaper.

More than half the TV audience say they turn to TV cable news, such as CNN, instead of the broadcast TV networks for breaking news, but the audience for cable news is still static.

INFORMATION ACCESS CREATES A NEWS EVOLUTION

This evolution in people's news habits has taken nearly a century and required several technological innovations. From print to radio to television to the Internet, as each new system of delivery emerged, the old systems still stayed in place. This means that today there's more news available from more news sources, delivered through more systems than ever before.

People can select the kinds of information they want, when they want it, creating personal news. The news business is becoming even more competitive. Consumers now have many sources—local, national and international plus the enormous variety of resources available on the Internet, such as social media sites—where they can look for what they want and need to know. (See **Impact/Audience**, "What the Explosion in Mobile Audiences Means for News," p. 258.)

JOURNALISTS AT WORK

The audience for news is shifting and in many cases declining (especially print news sources, such as newspapers and magazines). With so many sources of news available, news organizations must each be satisfied with a smaller piece of the audience. In a practical sense, this means lower revenues for media whose advertising rates are based on audience size—fewer readers, listeners or viewers means less money to hire people to write and report the news.

In today's media business, reporters often must work as *"all-platform" journalists*. They must be able to write the story and take photographs as well as produce video. In 2008, CNN assigned "digital journalists" to ten cities in the United States to report local stories. These journalists report live, using laptops and cell phone cameras. "We are harnessing technology that enables us to be anywhere and be live from anywhere," said Nancy Lane, senior vice president for newsgathering for CNN/U.S. "It completely changes how we can report."

News organizations like CNN and ABC News increasingly hire "all-platform journalists"—reporters who use laptops and shoot video to file articles for the Internet and broadcast simultaneously. Working on a dangerous assignment in Mogadishu, Somali journalist Abdukadir Hassan Abdirahman writes on a laptop with his video-camera and pistol nearby.

"Today, as they confront new competition on the Web, television networks are increasingly embracing portable—and inexpensive—methods of production," reports *The New York Times*. "A new breed of reporter, sometimes called a 'one-man band,' has become the new norm. Though the style of reporting has existed for years, it is being adopted more widely as these reporters act as their own producer, cameraman and editor, and sometimes even transmit live video."

The Pew Project for Excellence in Journalism has called today's transformation in the way journalists work "epochal, as momentous as the invention of television or the telegraph, perhaps on the order of the printing press itself."

In its 2013 *State of the News Media* report, the Project for Excellence in Journalism outlined six major trends that are affecting the news media today. (Excerpted from *The State of the News Media 2013: An Annual Report on American Journalism*, Project for Excellence in Journalism, journalism.org.)

1. **The effects of a decade of newsroom cutbacks are real—and the public is taking notice.** Nearly a third of U.S. adults, 31 percent, have stopped turning to a news outlet because it no longer provided them with the news they were accustomed to getting. With reporting resources cut to the bone and fewer specialized beats, journalists' level of expertise in any one area and the ability to go deep into a story are compromised.

2. **The news industry continues to lose out on the bulk of new digital advertising.** Two new areas of digital advertising that seemed to bring promise even a year ago now appear to be moving outside the reach of news: mobile devices and local digital advertising. Improved geo-targeting is allowing many national advertisers to turn to Google, Facebook and other large networks to buy ads that once might have gone to local media.

3. **The long-dormant sponsorship ad category is seeing sharp growth**. This is one area of growing digital ad revenue where news organizations have taken early steps to move in. Promoted tweets on Twitter account for some of the growth, along with the rise of native ads—the digital term for advertorials containing advertiser-produced stories—which often run alongside a site's own editorial content.

All-Platform Journalists Broadcast journalists who act as their own producer, cameraperson and editor, and sometimes even transmit live video.

IMPACT/Audience

What the Explosion in Mobile Audiences Means for News

By Amy Mitchell, Tom Rosenstiel and Laura Houston Santhanam of PEJ and Leah Christian of the Pew Research Center

The era of mobile digital technology has crossed a new threshold.

Half of all U.S. adults now have a mobile connection to the Web through either a smartphone or tablet, significantly more than a year ago, and this has major implications for how news will be consumed and paid for, according to a detailed new survey of news use on mobile devices by the Pew Research Center's Project for Excellence in Journalism (PEJ) in collaboration with The Economist Group.

At the center of the recent growth in mobile is the rapid embrace by Americans of the tablet computer. Nearly a quarter of U.S. adults, 22 percent, now own a tablet device—double the number from a year earlier. Another 3 percent of adults regularly use a tablet owned by someone else in their home. And nearly a quarter of those who don't have a tablet, 23 percent, plan to get one in the next six months. Even more U.S. adults (44 percent) have smartphones, according to the survey, up from 3 percent in May 2011.

News remains an important part of what people do on their mobile devices—64% of tablet owners and 62% of smartphone owners say they use the devices for news at least weekly, tying news statistically with other popular activities such email and playing games on tablets and behind only email on smartphones (not including talking on the phone). This means fully a third of all U.S. adults now get news on a mobile device at least once a week.

Mobile users, moreover, are not just checking headlines on their devices, although nearly all use the devices for the latest new updates. Many also are reading longer news stories—73 percent of adults who consume news on their tablet read in-depth articles at least sometimes, including 19 percent who do so daily. Fully 61 percent of smartphone news consumers at least sometimes read longer stories, 11 percent regularly.

And for many people, mobile devices are adding how much news they consume. More than four in ten mobile news consumers say they are getting more news now and nearly a third say they are adding new sources.

Perhaps most pressing for the industry, the survey shows continued resistance to paying for content on mobile devices. More mobile news users have print-only subscriptions than have digital ones. Just 24 percent of them are considering exchanging their print subscription for a digital one (though these tend to be younger subscribers, which suggests their numbers will grow).

Taken together, the data reveal that, even with a broadening population owning mobile devices that offer a range of activities, owners are still drawn heavily to news. What's more, there is a sizable cohort using mobile devices to broaden and strengthen their news experience, particularly male mobile news consumers who employ both apps and browsers, have a wireless data plan, get news multiple times throughout the day, and across a wide variety of platforms. (See **Illustration 12.2**, "The Growing Market for Mobile News in the United States," p. 259.)

Source: Amy Mitchell, Tom Rosenstiel, Laura Houston Santhanam and Leah Christian, "The Explosion in Mobile Audiences and a Close Look at What It Means for News," October 1, 2012, journalism.org.

IMPACT/Audience

Illustration 12.2

The Growing Market for Mobile News in the United States

Source: journalism.org/analysis_report/future-mobile-news

22% of adults own a tablet

64% of tablet owners get news on their device

66% of tablet or smartphone owners get news on their device

50% of adults own either a tablet or a smartphone

62% of smartphone owners get news on their device

44% of adults own a smartphone

4. **The growth of paid digital content experiments may have a significant impact on both news revenue and content.** After years of an almost theological debate about whether digital content should be free, the newspaper industry may have reached a tipping point in 2012. Indeed, 450 of the nation's 1,380 dailies have started or announced plans for some kind of paid content subscription or pay wall plan, in many cases opting for the metered model that allows a certain number of free visits before requiring users to pay.

5. **While the first and hardest-hit industry, newspapers, remains in the spotlight, local TV finds itself newly vulnerable.** Local TV audiences were down across every key time slot and across all networks in 2012. While local TV remains a top news source for Americans, the percentage is dropping— and dropping sharply among younger generations. Regular local TV viewership among adults under 30 fell from 42 percent in 2006 to just 28 percent in 2012. What's more, the topics people go there for most— weather and breaking news (and to a lesser extent

traffic)—are ripe for replacement by any number of web- and mobile-based outlets.

6. **Hearing about things in the news from friends and family, whether via social media or actual word of mouth, leads to deeper news consumption.** A majority of Americans seek out a full news story after hearing about an event or issue from friends and family.

JOURNALISTS CHANNEL THE PUBLIC'S ATTENTION

News organizations often are criticized for presenting a consistently shared view of the news. Often news values are shaped by the way news organizations are structured and the routines they follow. The press in America, it is generally agreed, doesn't tell people what to think but does tell people what and whom to think *about*. This is called *agenda-setting*. Agenda-setting works in two ways: the flow of information from one news organization to another and the flow of information from news organizations to their audiences.

In agenda-setting, the stories that appear in the nation's widely circulated print media provide ideas to the other media. For example, a widely circulated print media outlet, such as *The New York Times*, can identify specific stories as important by giving them in-depth attention, and this may set the news agenda on specific national issues.

Another type of agenda-setting occurs when a group of journalists, reporting the same story individually, presents a similar picture of the event they covered, rather than differing interpretations of events. This is called *consensus journalism*.

The emergence of the Internet as a news source, however, means that people now have more places to look for news—even overseas—which means more viewpoints on stories are available. This puts a bigger burden on the news consumer to seek out and verify the most reliable sources of information.

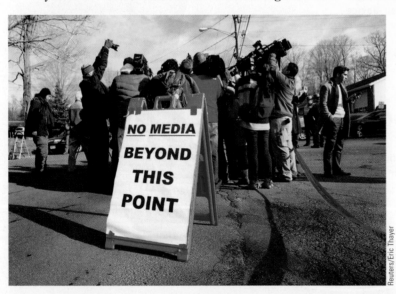

Ignoring the sign, journalists surround a woman who placed flowers outside the Sandy Hook school in Newtown, Conn., where 20 students died in a mass shooting in December 2012. Agenda-setting often occurs when a group of journalists, reporting the same story, present a similar view of events.

Agenda-Setting The belief that journalists don't tell you *what* to think but do tell you *what and whom to think about*.

Consensus Journalism The tendency among many journalists covering the same event to report similar conclusions about the event.

HOW THE PUBLIC PERCEIVES THE PRESS

It has not been shown in any comprehensive study of news gathering that journalists with liberal or conservative values insert their personal ideology directly into their reporting or that the audience unquestioningly accepts one point of view.

But the assumption that journalists' personal beliefs directly influence their professional performance is common. Although the reporting of some journalists, commentators and news organizations certainly can be cited to support this idea, the majority of journalists, says media scholar Herbert J. Gans, view themselves as detached observers of events:

Journalists, like everyone else, have values, [and] the two that matter most in the newsroom are getting the story and getting it better and faster than their prime competitors—both among their colleagues and at rival news media. Personal political beliefs are left at home, not only because journalists are trained to be objective and detached, but also because their credibility and their paychecks depend on their remaining detached.

Some press critics, in fact, argue that journalists most often present establishment viewpoints and are unlikely to challenge prevailing political and social values. The pressure to come up with instant analyses of news events also may lead to conformity in reporting—an unwillingness to think independently.

CREDIBILITY DRAWS THE AUDIENCE

Overall, the growing trust in Internet news sources and their expanding popularity as information sources may be connected. If Internet news can maintain this believability standard, even more of the audience—which was leaving the broadcast networks even before online news began—may gravitate to the Internet.

This is a familiar pattern: In the nation's news history, newspaper audiences added radio and newsreels, and then moved to television for news. Now news audiences have moved to the Internet. The Internet combines all the news outlets anyone could want in one place—news and information on the news consumer's own timetable, a trend the Pew Center calls a "digital tide."

Larry Lambert/CartoonStock.com

"Once again, there is no conclusive evidence of climate change. From Fairbanks, Alaska, this is Joe Matthews reporting."

Review, Analyze, Investigate

Reviewing Chapter 12

Early News Organizations Cooperate to Gather News

- The nation's first consecutively issued newspaper (published more than once) was the *Boston News-Letter*, which appeared in 1704.

- The invention of the telegraph in 1844 meant news that once took weeks to reach publication could be transmitted in minutes.

- In 1848, six newspapers in New York City formed the New York Associated Press, the first cooperative news-gathering association.

- Today, most American newspapers and broadcast news operations subscribe to at least one news service, such as Associated Press (AP).

- Some U.S. newspaper organizations also run their own news services, which allow subscribers to publish each other's stories for a fee.

Civil War Brings Accreditation and Photojournalism

- In 1861, during the Civil War, President Lincoln introduced the practice of accreditation for journalists.

- During the Civil War, Mathew Brady introduced the concept of photojournalism—using images to help capture a story.

Tabloid News Takes Over

- The competition for newspaper readers spawned yellow journalism—stories about grisly crimes and illicit sex, often accompanied by large, startling photographs.

- In the 1930s, newspapers began to share the audience for news with radio.

Newsreels Bring Distant Events to American Moviegoers

- Produced by companies including British Pathé (from 1900 until 1970) and by Fox Movietone News (between 1919 and 1960), newsreels were shown in movie theaters to audiences hungry for the pictures that radio couldn't provide. Audiences also watched news features such as *March of Time*.

- Newsreel footage usually took a week or more from the time it was shot to when audiences saw it.

Newspapers and Radio Personalize World War II

- In the 1930s, people began to turn to radio for instant news headlines and information.

- In the 1930s and 1940s, most radio stations maintained their own news departments until the advent of format radio.

- Journalist Ernie Pyle gave World War II the human touch because he wrote stories about the soldiers' lives, not troop movements.

- Very few radio stations today maintain full-time news departments, and radio stations with news formats tend to be concentrated in the nation's big cities.

TV News Enters Its Golden Age

- What has been called the Golden Age of Television News was the decade that began in 1961, with President John F. Kennedy's inauguration.

- In 1962, in what was called the Cuban missile crisis, President Kennedy used live television to deliver his ultimatum to Soviet leader Nikita Khrushchev, urging him to stop sending ships to Cuba to help build missile sites. Faced with this ultimatum, the Soviet Union turned its ships around.

- Television became a window on the world with its coverage of events in the days following the assassination of President Kennedy.

TV News Changes the Nation's Identity

- Coverage of the war in Vietnam gave Americans an appetite for live television news.

- The Watergate hearings showed viewers the inner workings of national politics.

TV News Expands and Contracts

- Ted Turner founded CNN in 1980, offering round-the-clock news on cable.

- The 1980s brought broadcast deregulation and consolidation of the TV networks.

- In the 1990s, in general, the American public read fewer newspapers and watched less news on television.

Iraq War Produces "Embedded" Reporters

- Before the war in Iraq began in 2003, the U.S. military announced a plan to embed more than 600 reporters with American troops.

- Embedding offered the reporters access to the front-lines but also kept them within the military's control.

Reality Shows and Advertorials Blur the Line

- Reality TV shows tend to blur the line between entertainment and news.

- TV infomercials and advertising supplements called "advertorials" in newspapers and magazines make it harder for readers to differentiate between news content and advertising.

- The merging of news with entertainment and advertising makes it more difficult for viewers to separate facts from fiction.

The Internet Transforms News Delivery

- The Internet, unlike any other form of news and information delivery, is completely self-directed news and information—targeted to individual needs.

- Pew Research Center studies reveal that network and local news viewership has dropped substantially. People, instead, are turning to the Internet for news.

- People who read online newspapers have a far less favorable view of network and local TV news programs than do people who read the print version of the daily newspaper.

Information Access Creates a News Evolution

- The immediacy of news on the Internet means people can personalize the news.

- Half of all U.S. adults now have a mobile connection to the Web through either a smartphone or tablet.

- The Internet is replacing broadcast news because of its immediacy and accessibility.

Journalists at Work

- The Pew Research Center's Project for Excellence in Journalism has described six major trends that are affecting the news media today.

1. The effects of a decade of newsroom cutbacks are real – and the public is taking notice.

2. The news industry continues to lose out on the bulk of new digital advertising.

3. The long-dormant sponsorship ad category is seeing sharp growth.

4. The growth of paid digital content experiments may have a significant impact on both news revenue and content.

5. While the first and hardest-hit industry, newspapers, remains in the spotlight, local TV finds itself newly vulnerable.

6. Hearing about things in the news from friends and family, whether via social media or actual word of mouth, leads to deeper news consumption.

- People today often use social media to share news.

- Half of Americans say they rely on the people around them to get at least some of their news.

Journalists Channel the Public's Attention

- The press in America doesn't tell you what to think. It does tell you what and whom to think about. This is called agenda-setting.

- Consensus journalism occurs when a group of journalists, reporting the same story individually, present a similar picture of the event rather than differing interpretations.

How the Public Perceives the Press

- It has not been shown in any comprehensive study of news gathering that journalists with liberal or conserva-

tive values insert their personal ideology directly into their reporting.

- Some press critics argue that journalists most often present establishment viewpoints and are unlikely to challenge prevailing political and social values.

Credibility Draws the Audience

- The growing trust in Internet news sources may be related to the Internet's increasing popularity as a source of news.

- If Internet news can maintain its believability, even more of the TV news audience may gravitate to the Internet.

Key Terms

These terms are defined in the margins throughout this chapter and appear in alphabetical order with definitions in the Glossary, which begins on page 373.

Accreditation 247

Advertorial 254

Agenda-Setting 260

All-Platform Journalists 257

Consensus Journalism 260

Cooperative News Gathering 246

Embed 253

Photojournalism 248

Critical Questions

1. List two specific ways in which news coverage changed during the Civil War.

2. List and explain three ways the Internet has changed consumers' news habits.

3. How is the decline in news budgets likely to affect the delivery of news?

4. Discuss three important trends for news identified in the 2013 report of the Pew Research Center's Project for Excellence in Journalism.

5. What is the relationship between mobile media and news delivery? Explain.

Working the Web

This list includes both sites mentioned in the chapter and others to give you greater insight into news and information media.

Committee to Protect Journalists

cpj.org

This nonpartisan organization is dedicated to protecting freedom of the press around the world. It publishes stories about imprisoned and threatened journalists, organizes public protests and works through diplomatic channels to effect change. It also publishes Attacks on the Press, an

annual survey of press freedom around the world. The Web site features links to news by country, special reports and a multimedia section with video, audio and slideshows.

CyberJournalist.net

cyberjournalist.net

This news and resource site focuses on how the Internet, convergence and new technologies are changing the media. Included on the Web site are tips, video and examples of good online journalism. Sections include Future of Media, Innovation and Social Media.

Fox Movietone News

foxnews.com/on-air/movietone-news/index.html.?cat=6

A portion of the Fox Movietone News film is housed in the University of South Carolina's Moving Image Research Collection. A sample of video clips—from Martin Luther King speaking on voting rights in May 1966 to a silent film of a suffrage rights group in New Orleans in September 1920—is available on the Web site.

Investigative Reporters and Editors (IRE)

ire.org

This organization, dedicated to improving the quality of investigative reporting, provides educational services to reporters and editors and works to maintain high professional standards. The Web site features news and publications, job and resource centers for members as well as a link to the National Institute for Computer-Assisted Reporting (NICAR).

The Online News Association (ONA)

journalist.org

ONA's members include news writers, producers, designers, editors, photographers and others who produce news for the Internet or other digital delivery systems. ONA partners with the Annenberg School of Communication at the University of Southern California to honor online journalistic excellence with their annual Online Journalism Awards.

Pew Research Center for People & the Press

people-press.org

This is an independent, nonpartisan public opinion research organization that studies attitudes toward the press, politics and public policy issues. The Web site includes Survey Reports by the Center on a variety of current issues. Findings of polls sponsored by media organizations also are available.

Pew Research Center's Project for Excellence in Journalism

journalism.org

This research organization uses empirical methods to evaluate and study the performance of the press. Its goal is to help journalists and consumers develop a better understanding of what the press is delivering. Features of the site include Journalism Resources—with links to organizations, schools and career information—and the project's annual report the *State of the News Media*.

Talking Points Memo (TPM)

talkingpointsmemo.com

The flagship blog of TPM Media, LLC, Talking Points Memo is a collection of comments on political events from a liberal perspective, gathered by writer Josh Marshall, who produces the Editors' Blog. Streaming video accompanied by written commentary is available on TPMtv, as well as current polling information.

Unity: Journalists for Diversity

unityjournalists.org

This alliance of four national associations—Asian American Journalists Association, National Association of Black Journalists, National Association of Hispanic Journalists and the Native American Journalists Association—advocates news coverage about people of color and challenges organizations at all levels to reflect the nation's diversity. Its goals include raising awareness and participation of the media industry in understanding diverse cultures, increasing and broadening news coverage focused on people of color, and dispelling racial and ethnic stereotypes and myths.

Vanderbilt University Television News Archive

tvnews.vanderbilt.edu

"The world's most extensive and complete archive of television news" holds network evening news broadcasts from ABC, CBS and NBC from 1968 to the present, as well as a daily news program from CNN (beginning in 1995) and Fox News Reports (beginning in 2004). DVD duplications of entire broadcasts as well as compilation videotapes of individual news stories may be borrowed for a fee.

Impact/Action Videos are concise news features on various topics created exclusively for *Media/Impact*. Go online to access MindTap at cengagebrain.com. MindTap for Media/Impact sequences all of your learning tools—Chapter Readings with highlighting and note taking, **Impact/Action Videos**, activities and assessments—into chapter driven learning units that guide you through the curriculum.

SOCIETY AND POLITICAL ISSUES:

SHAPING THE ARGUMENTS

13

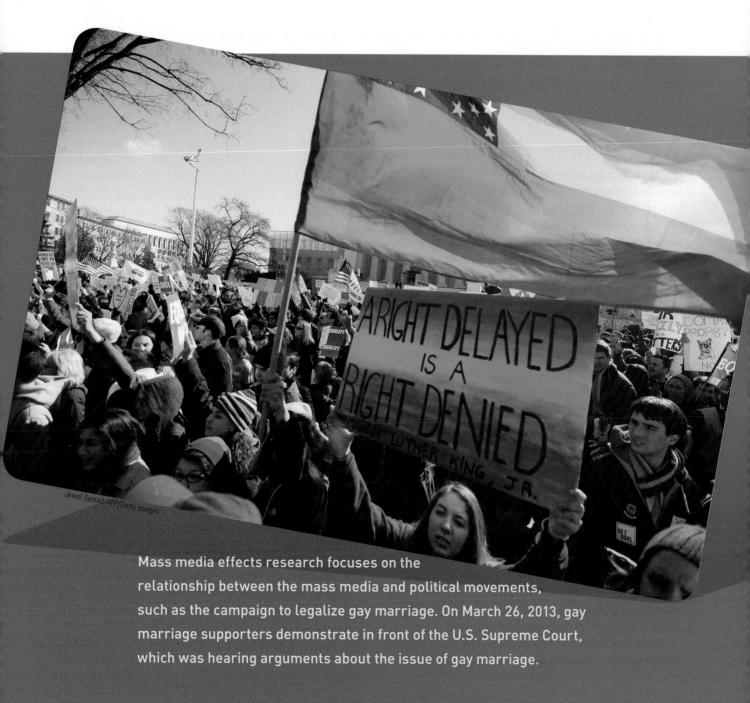

Jewel Samad/AFP/Getty Images

Mass media effects research focuses on the relationship between the mass media and political movements, such as the campaign to legalize gay marriage. On March 26, 2013, gay marriage supporters demonstrate in front of the U.S. Supreme Court, which was hearing arguments about the issue of gay marriage.

"Psychological studies purporting to show a connection between exposure to violent video games and harmful effects on children do not prove that such exposure causes minors to act aggressively."

—U.S. SUPREME COURT, 2011

Researchers at the

Southern Illinois University School of Medicine have identified a new psychiatric condition they have dubbed "celebrity worship syndrome." This affliction is an unhealthy interest in the rich and famous. People who admire celebrities often want to be just like them, even though some celebrities set examples that aren't very positive. Celebrity worship is just one example of the effect of media on our lives.

Today, scholars understand that the media have different effects on different types of people with differing results, and generalizations about the media's effects are easy to make but difficult to prove. "We do not fully understand at present what the media system is doing to individual behavior, much less to American culture," according to media scholars William L. Rivers and Wilbur Schramm. "The media cannot simply be seen as stenciling images on a blank mind. That is too superficial a view of the communication process."

EARLY MASS MEDIA STUDIES ASSESS IMPACT

The concept that the media have different effects on different types of people is relatively new. Early media observers were certain that a one-to-one relationship existed between what people read, heard and saw and what people did with that information. They also believed that the effects were the same for everyone.

The magic bullet theory, discussed later in the chapter (see "The Payne Fund Studies," p. 267) and sometimes called the hypodermic needle theory, alleged that ideas from the media were in direct causal relation to behavior. The theory held that the media could inject ideas into people the way liquids are injected through a needle. This early distrust of the media still pervades many people's thinking today, although the theory has been disproved.

Media research, like other social science research, is based on a continuum of thought, with each new study advancing slightly the knowledge from the studies that have come before. This is what has happened to the magic bullet theory. Eventually, the beliefs that audiences absorbed media messages uncritically and that all people reacted the same to each message were proven untrue. Research disclosed that analyzing media effects is a very complex task.

Some media research had been done before television use became widespread in the mid-1950s, but TV prompted scholars to take a closer look at media's effects. Two scholars made particularly provocative assertions about how the media influence people's lives: David M. Potter and Marshall McLuhan.

David Potter, a historian, arrived at just the right moment—when the public and the scholarly community were anxiously trying to analyze media's effects on society. In his book *People of Plenty*, published in 1954, Potter first articulated the idea that American society is a consumer society driven primarily by advertising.

Potter asserted that American advertising is rooted in American abundance: "Advertising is not badly needed in an economy of scarcity, because total demand is usually equal to or in excess of total supply, and every producer can normally sell as much as he produces. . . . It is when potential supply outstrips demand—that is, when abundance prevails—that advertising begins to fulfill a really essential economic function."

Potter also warned about the dangers of advertising: "Advertising has in its dynamics no motivation to seek the improvement of the individual or to impart qualities of social usefulness. . . . It has no social goals and no social responsibility for what it does with its influence." Potter's perspective was important in shaping the critical view of modern advertising. *People of Plenty* is still in print today.

Scholars Look for Patterns

Like Potter, Canadian author and educator Marshall McLuhan arrived at just the right moment. In the 1960s, McLuhan piqued the public's interest with his phrase "The medium is the message," which he later parodied in the title of his book *The Medium Is the Massage*. One of his conclusions was that the widespread use of television was a landmark in the history of the world, "retribalizing" society and creating a "global village" of people who use media to communicate.

McLuhan suggested that electronic media messages are inherently different from print messages—to watch information on TV is different from reading the same information in a newspaper. McLuhan never offered systematic proof for his ideas, and some people criticized him as a charlatan, but his concepts still are debated widely.

Scholars who analyze the media today look for patterns in media effects, predictable results and statistical evidence to document how the media affect us. Precisely because the media are ubiquitous, studies of their effects on American society are far from conclusive. In this chapter, you will learn about some of the major studies and some of the recent assertions about the role that the media play in our lives.

Mass media research today includes mass media effects research and mass media content analysis. *Mass media effects research* tries to analyze how people use the information they receive from the media—whether political advertising changes people's voting behavior, for example. *Mass media content analysis* examines what is presented by the media—how many children's programs portray violent behavior, for example. Sometimes these two types of analysis (effects research and content analysis) are combined in an attempt to evaluate the effect of a specific type of content on a specific audience.

The Payne Fund Studies

The prestigious Payne Fund sponsored the first major study of media in 1929. It contained 12 reports on media effects. One of these studies concentrated on the effects of movies on children. In his interviews, researcher Herbert Blumer simply asked teenagers what they remembered about the movies they had seen as children. Using this unsystematic approach, he reported that the teenagers had been greatly influenced by the movies because they *said* they had been greatly influenced.

Blumer's conclusion and other conclusions of the Payne Fund studies about the media's direct, one-to-one effect on people were accepted without question, mainly because these were the first major studies of media effects, and the results were widely reported. The Payne Fund studies were the source of the *magic bullet theory*, the belief that media messages directly and measurably affect people's behavior.

The Payne Fund studies also contributed ammunition for the Motion Picture Producers and Distributors Association production code, adopted in 1930, which regulated movie content.

The Cantril Study

The Martians who landed in New Jersey in the Mercury Theater "War of the Worlds" broadcast of October 30, 1939 (see **Chapter 6**, "*War of the Worlds* Challenges Radio's Credibility," p. 114), sparked the next major study of media effects, conducted by Hadley Cantril at Princeton University. The results of the Cantril study contradicted the findings of the Payne Fund studies and disputed the magic bullet theory.

Cantril wanted to find out why certain people believed the Mercury Theater broadcast and others did not. After interviewing 135 people, Cantril concluded that high critical-thinking ability was the key. Better-educated people were much more likely to decide the broadcast was a fake. This finding might seem to be self-evident today, but the importance of the Cantril study is that it differentiated among listeners: People with different personality characteristics interpreted the broadcast differently.

Mass Media Effects Research   An attempt to analyze how people use the information they receive from the media.

Mass Media Content Analysis   An attempt to analyze how mass media programming influences behavior.

Magic Bullet Theory   The assertion that media messages directly and measurably affect people's behavior.

IMPACT/Audience

Illustration 13.1

Lasswell's Model Asks Five Questions

The Lasswell model analyzes the communication process by asking five questions: Who? Says what? On which channel? To whom? With what effect?

Who?   Says what?   On which channel?   To whom?   With what effect?

Sender   Message   Listeners   Effect

Viewers   Effect

Readers   Effect

© Cengage Learning

The Lasswell Model

In 1948, political scientist Harold D. Lasswell designed a model to describe the process of communication that is still used today. Lasswell said the communication process could be analyzed by answering the five questions shown in **Illustration 13.1**.

Lasswell said you could analyze the process of communication by determining who the sender is and what the sender says. Next, you must identify which channel—or method—of communication the sender used. Then you must examine the audience and define the effect on that audience. Because Lasswell described the communication process so succinctly, most communications research still focuses on his five original questions.

HOW TV AFFECTS CHILDREN'S BEHAVIOR

The 1950s were a time of adjustment to the new medium of television, which at first was a novelty and then became a necessity. Since 1960, four of the major studies of the effects of television have focused on children.

Television in the Lives of Children

Published in 1961, by Wilbur Schramm, Jack Lyle and Edwin Parker, *Television in the Lives of Our Children* was the first major study of the effects of television on children. Researchers interviewed 6,000 children and 1,500 parents, as well as teachers and school officials.

Schramm and his associates reported that children were exposed to television more than to any other mass medium. On average, 5-year-old children watched television two hours every weekday. TV viewing time reached three hours by the time these children were 8 years old. In a finding that often was subsequently cited, Schramm said that from the ages of 3 to 16, children spent more time in front of the television set than they spent in school.

Children used television for fantasy, diversion and instruction, Schramm said. Children who had troubled relationships with their parents and children who were classified as aggressive were more likely to turn to television for fantasy, but Schramm could find no serious problems related to television viewing. Schramm also found, in support of Cantril, that different children showed different effects.

Television and Social Behavior

Television and Social Behavior, a study of the effects of television, was funded by $1 million appropriated by Congress in 1969, after the violent decade of the 1960s. The U.S. Department of Health, Education and Welfare, which sponsored the study, appointed a distinguished panel of social scientists to undertake the research.

The study's major findings, published in six volumes in 1971, concerned the effects of television violence on children. A content analysis of one week of prime-time programming, conducted by George Gerbner of the University of Pennsylvania, reported that eight out of ten prime-time shows contained violence.

Television and Social Behavior did not make a direct connection between TV programming and violent behavior, however. The report said there was a "tentative" indication that television viewing caused aggressive behavior. According to the study, TV violence affected only *some* children who were already classified as aggressive children and *only* in some environments.

Even though the report avoided a direct statement about violent behavior in children as a result of television viewing, the U.S. surgeon general called for immediate action against violence on television. The television industry dismissed the results as inconclusive.

The Early Window

Several studies since 1971 have suggested that television violence causes aggression among children. In their 1988 book *The Early Window: Effects of Television on Children and Youth*, psychologists Robert M. Liebert and Joyce Sprafkin urged caution in drawing broad conclusions about the subject:

> Studies using various methods have supported the proposition that TV violence can induce aggressive and/or antisocial behavior in children. Whether the effect will hold only for the most susceptible individuals (e.g., boys from disadvantaged homes) or whether it will hold for a wider range of youngsters obviously depends in part upon the measure being used. . . . The occurrence of serious violent or criminal acts results from several forces at once. Researchers have said that TV violence is *a* cause of aggressiveness, not that it is *the* cause of aggressiveness. There is no one, single cause of any social behavior.

Still, criticism of television's effects on children's behavior persists, especially the effects of advertising.

Television Advertising to Children

The effects of advertising on adults have been analyzed widely, but in 1979 the advertising of children's products became an object of serious government attention with Federal Trade Commission's release of the 340-page report *Television Advertising to Children*. The report, based on a two-year study, was designed to document the dangers of advertising sugar-based products to children, but embedded in the report was some provocative information about children's advertising.

Children are an especially vulnerable audience, said the FTC. The report concluded:

1. The average child sees 20,000 commercials a year, or about three hours of TV advertising a week.

2. Many children regard advertising as just another form of programming and do not distinguish between programs and ads.

3. Televised advertising for any product to children who do not understand the intent of the commercial is unfair and deceptive.

The report called for a ban on advertising to very young children, a ban on sugared products in advertising directed to children younger than age 12, and a requirement for counter-ads with dental and nutritional information to balance ads for sugared products.

Astrid Stawiarz/Getty Images Entertainment/Getty Images

Younger children are an especially vulnerable mass media audience because they tend to pay more attention to television advertising than older children. On January 24, 2013, *Sesame Street Live*'s Super Grover teaches children how to be super heroes.

The FTC report and subsequent research about children's advertising suggest that younger children pay more attention to television advertising than older children. But by sixth grade, children adopt what has been called a "global distrust" of advertising.

Linking TV to School Performance

There have been many studies about children and television, such as the National Institute of Mental Health (NIMH) report. In 1981, a California study suggested a link between television viewing and poor school performance.

The California Assessment Program (CAP), which tests academic achievement, included a new question: "On a typical weekday, about how many hours do you watch TV?" The students were given a choice ranging from zero to six or more hours. An analysis of the answers to that question from more than 10,000 sixth graders was matched with the children's scores on the achievement test.

The results suggested a consistent relationship between viewing time and achievement. Students who said they watched a lot of television scored lower in reading, writing and mathematics than students who didn't watch any television. The average scores for students who said they viewed six or more hours of television a day were six to eight points lower than for those children who said they watched less than a half-hour of television a day.

In 2010, new research further attempted to define whether children are poor students because they watch a lot of television or whether children who watch a lot of television are poor students for other reasons. Canadian researchers released a study in the May 2010 issue of the journal *Pediatrics and Adolescent Medicine* that linked a decline in classroom engagement with early television viewing. The study, "Prospective Associations Between Early Childhood Television Exposure and Academic, Psychosocial, and Physical Well-being by Middle Childhood," followed the TV viewing habits of 1,314 toddlers until they entered fourth grade.

From their analysis of the data, the researchers concluded that children who watched a lot of TV in their early years were less likely to perform well when they reached the fourth grade. The researchers noted that there were "long term risks associated with higher levels of [TV] exposure."

In 2011 a study conducted by Common Sense Media, a San Francisco nonprofit group, reported that children younger than 8 years old spend more time using media than ever, and more than half of these children have access to a mobile device like a smartphone, a video iPod or an iPad or other type of tablet. Still, according to the study, TV accounts for the largest amount of screen time.

According to *The New York Times*, "The report also documents for the first time an emerging 'app gap' in which affluent children are likely to use mobile educational games while those in low-income families are the most likely to have televisions in their rooms."

This is a new aspect of the digital divide (see **Chapter 9**)—the difference in media access between disadvantaged families and the rest of the nation—merits further study.

DO THE MASS MEDIA CAUSE VIOLENCE?

The search for a possible direct link between violent behavior and violence in the mass media has existed for more than 30 years. The first major modern study, *Television and Behavior: Ten Years of Scientific Progress and Implications for the Eighties*, published in 1982 by the NIMH, compiled information from 2,500 individual studies of television. According to NIMH, three findings of these 2,500 studies, taken together, were that:

1. A direct correlation exists between televised violence and aggressive behavior, yet there is no way to predict who will be affected and why.

2. Heavy television viewers are more fearful, less trusting and more apprehensive than light viewers.

3. Children who watch what the report called "pro social" programs (programs that are socially constructive, such as *Sesame Street* and *SpongeBob*) are more likely to act responsibly.

Most of the latest studies of the mass media's role have continued to reinforce the concept that different people in different environments react to mass media differently. (See **Impact/Audience**, "POW! CRACK! What We Know About Video Games and Violence," p. 271.)

RATINGS SYSTEMS AND PARENTAL CONTROLS ESTABLISHED

In 1994, cable operators and network broadcasters agreed to use an independent monitor to review programming for violent content. The agreement came after Congress held hearings on the subject in 1993, and threatened to introduce regulations to curb violence if the industry didn't police itself. The agreement also called for the development of violence ratings for TV programming and endorsed a v-chip—*v* for "violence"—technology that would be built into a television set to allow parents to block programs rated as violent.

The monitoring is qualitative rather than quantitative, according to the agreement. This means that the

IMPACT/Audience

POW! CRACK!
What We Know About Video Games and Violence

By Suzy Khimm

Do video games cause gun violence? There's little to no conclusive evidence that playing video games results in real-life violence, much less criminal acts. In 2011, the Supreme Court struck down a California law restricting the sale and rental of violent video games to minors in a 7-2 ruling.

Researchers like Chris Ferguson, a professor at Texas A&M International, believe that the research conducted over the past 20 years has been "quite inconsistent," leading the Supreme Court to dismiss such findings in its ruling.

In one 2012 article for the *Journal of Psychiatric Research*, Ferguson and his co-authors examined 165 participants over three years and found that playing violent video games was not linked to youth aggression or dating violence. Instead, they found that "depression, antisocial personality traits, exposure to family violence and peer influences were the best predictors of aggression-related outcomes."

That said, there is evidence that violent video games may have a tendency to make children who are already aggressive more hostile and more aggressive—at least in the context of playing a video game, Ferguson explains.

There are other researchers who believe there is a distinct and potentially dangerous link

Spencer Platt/Getty Images News/Getty Images

The debate about the relationship between violence portrayed in video games and violence in society gained national focus in 2013 when President Obama announced a plan to reduce gun violence that included more research into "links between video games, media images, and violence."

between video games and violent behavior. Brad Bushman, a professor at Ohio State University, was among the researchers who filed an amicus brief to the Supreme Court. While Bushman believes it's too simplistic to blame gun violence on video games, he says "it shouldn't be dismissed as a trivial cause either."

Source: Excerpted from Suzy Khimm, "POW! CRACK! What We Know About Video Games and Violence," January 17, 2013, washingtonpost.com.

programs are examined for content, not just for incidents of violence. The Telecommunications Act of 1996 established a television ratings code for content. The Entertainment Software Association, which represents video and computer game-makers, also has voluntarily created a ratings system. These ratings systems continue a tradition of media self-regulation. That is, the video game, broadcast, recording and movie media industries have responded—often reluctantly—to congressional pressure by offering to monitor themselves rather than invite the government to intrude on the content of their programs.

NATIONAL POLITICAL CAMPAIGNS DEPEND ON MASS MEDIA

The mass media have transformed politics in ways that could never have been imagined when President Franklin D. Roosevelt introduced what were called Fireside Chats in 1933. Roosevelt was the first president to use the media effectively to stimulate public support.

The newest technology introduced during FDR's era—radio—gave him immediate access to a national audience. Roosevelt's media skill became an essential element in promoting his economic programs. Today, politics and the media seem irreversibly dependent on each other, one of the legacies of Roosevelt's presidency.

The Fireside Chats

In March 1933, just after he was inaugurated, FDR looked for a way to avoid a financial panic after he announced that he was closing the nation's banks. For a week, the country cooled off while Congress scrambled for a solution. On the Sunday night eight days after his inauguration, Roosevelt used radio to calm the nation's anxiety before the banks began to reopen on Monday. FDR went down to the basement of the White House to give his first Fireside Chat. There was a fireplace in the basement, but no fire was burning. The president could not find his script, so he borrowed a mimeographed copy from a reporter.

In his first address to the nation as president, FDR gave a banking lesson to his audience of 60 million people: "I want to talk for a few minutes with the people of the United States about banking. . . . First of all, let me state the simple fact that when you deposit money in a bank, the bank does not put the money into a safe deposit vault. It invests your money in many different forms." When he finished, he turned to people in the room and asked, "Was I all right?" America had its first media president, an elected leader talking directly to the people through the media.

Roosevelt's chats are cited as a legendary example of media politics, yet he gave only eight Fireside Chats in his first term of office. His other meetings with the press also enhanced his reputation for press access: In 13 years in office, he held more than 900 press conferences.

The People's Choice

The first major study of the influence of media on politics was *The People's Choice*, undertaken precisely because FDR seemed to be such a good media politician. This comprehensive examination of voter behavior in the 1940 presidential election was quite systematic.

Researchers Paul Lazarsfeld, Bernard Berelson and Hazel Gaudet followed 3,000 people in rural Erie County, Ohio, from May to November 1940 to determine what influenced the way these people voted for president. The researchers tracked how people's minds changed over the six-month period and then attempted to determine why. (It is important to remember this study was undertaken before television.) Radio had become the prevailing medium for political advertising beginning in 1932, when the two parties spent more money for radio time than for any other campaign item. What effect, the researchers wanted to know, did the media have on people's choosing one candidate over another? The results were provocative.

In 1932, Paul Lazarsfeld and his colleagues studied people's voting habits to attempt to document the media's effect on their decisions. In 1942, Lazarsfeld (right) worked with Dr. Frank Stanton (left, future president of the CBS network) on an audience analysis project. Viewers pressed a button on the Lazarsfeld-Stanton Program Analyzer when they saw a program they liked, and the machine printed out the results. The machine never gained widespread use.

Lazarsfeld and his colleagues found that only 8 percent of the voters in the study were actually *converted* by the media. The majority of voters (53 percent) were *reinforced* in their beliefs by the media, and 14 percent were *activated* to vote. Mixed effects or no effects were shown by the remaining 25 percent of the people.

Lazarsfeld said opinion leaders, who got their information from the media, shared this information with their friends. The study concluded that instead of changing people's beliefs, the media primarily activate people to vote and reinforce already held opinions. *The People's Choice* also made the following findings:

- Family and friends have more effect on people's decisions than the media.

- The media have different effects on different people, reinforcing Cantril's findings.

- A major source of information about candidates is other people.

The finding that opinion leaders often provide and shape information for the general population was a bonus—the researchers hadn't set out specifically to learn this. This transmission of information and ideas from mass media to opinion leaders and then to friends and acquaintances is called the *two-step flow* of communication.

The Unseeing Eye

In 1976, a second study of the media and presidential elections, called *The Unseeing Eye: The Myth of Television Power in National Elections*, revealed findings that paralleled those of *The People's Choice*.

With a grant from the National Science Foundation, Thomas E. Patterson and Robert D. McClure supervised interviews with 2,707 people from early September to just before Election Day in the November 1972 race between George McGovern and Richard Nixon. The study did not discuss political media events, but it did analyze television campaign news and political advertising.

The researchers concluded that although political advertising influenced 16 percent of the people they interviewed, only 7 percent were manipulated by political ads. The researchers defined people who were *influenced* as those who decided to vote for a candidate based mostly on what they knew and only slightly on what the ads told them. The 7 percent of the people in the survey who were *manipulated*, according to Patterson and McClure, were people who cited political advertising as a major factor in their choices. Patterson and McClure concluded that political advertising on TV has little effect on most people:

By projecting their political biases . . . people see in candidates' commercials pretty much what they want to see. Ads sponsored by the candidate who shares their politics get a good response. They like what he has to say. And they like him. Ads sponsored by the opposing candidate are viewed negatively. They object to what he says. And they object to him.

Even though a minority of people are affected by political ads on TV, it is important to remember that in some elections the difference of a few percentage points can decide the outcome. Political advertising is designed to sway these swing voters. This is why political advertising continues to play such an important campaign role.

Election Campaigns on Television

So far, no convincing systematic evidence has shown that the mass media change the voting behavior of *large* groups of people. Yet, since John F. Kennedy debated Richard Nixon during the 1960 presidential campaign, many people deeply feel that the media—television in particular—have changed elections and electoral politics.

The series of debates in 1960 between Senator John F. Kennedy (right) and Vice President Richard Nixon (left) were the first widely televised debates of presidential candidates. Kennedy's performance on the telecast often is credited for his narrow victory in the election. Shown is the fourth and last Kennedy-Nixon debate on October 21, 1960.

Two-Step Flow The transmission of information and ideas from mass media to opinion leaders and then to friends.

The series of debates between Kennedy and Nixon in 1960 were the first televised debates of presidential candidates in American history. Kennedy's performance in the debates often is credited for his narrow victory in the election. In his book *Presidents and the Press*, media scholar Joseph C. Spear wrote:

> As the panel began asking questions, Nixon tended to go on the defensive, answering Kennedy point by point and ignoring his huge audience beyond the camera.

> Kennedy, by contrast, appeared rested, calm, informed, cocksure. Whatever the question, he aimed his answer at the millions of Americans viewing the program in their living rooms.

> It was an unmitigated disaster for Nixon. In the second, third and fourth debates, he managed to recover somewhat from his initial poor performance, but it was too late. Surveys showed that an overwhelming percentage of the television audience had judged Kennedy the victor.

One legacy of Kennedy's television victory was that national political campaigns came to depend almost entirely on TV to promote presidential candidates, and televised presidential debates became a staple of every presidential election.

Television is a very efficient way to reach large numbers of people quickly, but campaigning on television also distances the candidates from direct public contact. Instead of meeting the public in person to promote and debate issues, candidates can isolate themselves from public scrutiny by using television ads to portray their views.

Cost of Political Advertising Skyrockets

Television advertising also is very expensive. The cost of national and statewide campaigns—especially since the year 2000—has skyrocketed. Presidential, gubernatorial, congressional and senatorial candidates typically devote 40 to 60 percent of their campaign budgets to advertising.

Many candidates run in metropolitan areas like Los Angeles, where the media markets are much larger than their districts. Television advertising in large markets reaches a bigger audience than candidates need, so they also use direct mail. But a candidate running for Congress in Des Moines, Iowa,

might use mainly television because the entire district is included in the local TV station's coverage area. Historian James David Barber describes the public's role in politics:

> Particularly since television has brought national politics within arm's length of nearly every American, the great majority probably has at least some experience of the quadrennial passing parade. But millions vote their old memories and habits and interests, interpreting new perceptions that strike their senses to coincide with their prejudices and impulses.

> At the other end of the participation spectrum are those compulsive readers of *The New York Times* who delve into every twitch and turn of the contest. Floating in between are large numbers of Americans who pick up on the election's major events and personalities, following with mild but open interest the dominant developments.

> Insofar as the campaign makes a difference, it is this great central chunk of The People who swing the choice. They respond to what they see and hear. They are interested but not obsessed. They edit out the minor blips of change and wait for the campaign to gather force around a critical concern. They reach their conclusions on the basis of a widely shared common experience. It is through that middling throng of the population that the pulse of politics beats most powerfully, synchronizing to its insistent rhythm the varied vibrations of discrete events.

The rising cost of running for public office can exclude people without the means to raise huge sums of money. Since 1972, when political campaigns first began widespread

"That's an excellent prescreened question, but before I give you my stock answer I'd like to try to disarm everyone with a carefully rehearsed joke."

IMPACT/Money

Illustration 13.2

TV Political Campaign Spending in Presidential Elections, 1972–2012

The amount of money presidential candidates spend on advertising has soared since 1972. Of the $6 billion collected by all the candidates in the 2012 presidential campaign, a majority of the money went to pay for TV and Internet advertising.

Source: Center for Responsive Politics and opensecrets.org.

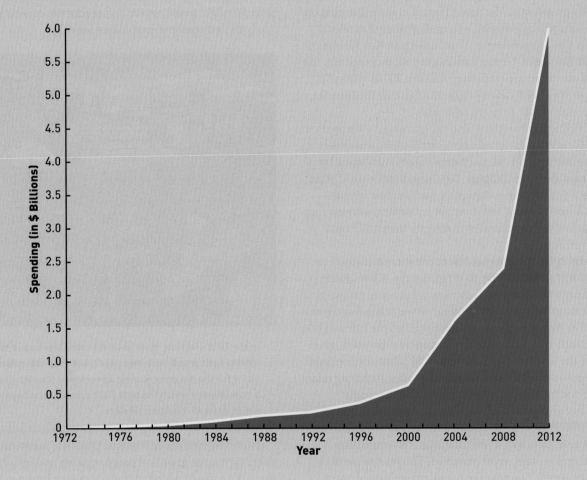

use of television advertising, presidential campaign expenditures have skyrocketed from less than $2 million in 1972 to $6 billion in 2012. (See **Illustration 13.2**.) Most of this money went to pay for TV and Internet advertising.

Today the mass media are an essential part of American politics, changing the behavior of politicians as well as the electorate, which raises important questions about the role of the nation's mass media in governance and the conduct of elections.

VOTERS AND CAMPAIGNS USE THE INTERNET AND SOCIAL MEDIA

The year 2004 was the first presidential election year when the Internet began to play a role in national politics, as citizen blogs became an outlet for political debate, and bloggers covered the presidential campaigns along with members of the established press corps.

The New York Times noted in 2004, "Democrats and Republicans are sharply increasing their use of e-mail, interactive Web sites, candidate and party blogs and text messaging to raise money, organize get-out-the-vote efforts and assemble crowds for rallies. The Internet, they say, appears to be far more efficient, and less costly, than the traditional tools of politics, notably door knocking and telephone banks."

The Pew Research Center reported that 75 million Americans used the Internet for political news during the 2004 presidential election. "The effect of the Internet on politics will be every bit as transformational as television was," Republican national chairman Ken Mehlman told *The Times*. "If you want to get your message out, the old way of paying someone to make a TV ad is insufficient: You need your message out through the Internet, through e-mail, through talk radio."

Political consultants also experimented with political podcasts that featured daily downloaded messages from candidates and viral marketing videos supporting the candidates (see **Chapter 10**). Supporters passed along the video messages through e-mail to their friends—an online chain of free Internet political messaging that reached young voters more directly than traditional advertising.

By 2008, the Internet had become a central force in national politics. "The 2008 race for the White House fundamentally upended the way presidential campaigns are fought in the United States," wrote Adam Nagourney of *The New York Times*. "It has rewritten the rules on how to reach voters, raise money, organize supporters, manage the news media, track and mold public opinion, and wage—and withstand—political attacks, including many carried by blogs that did not exist four years ago."

According to Mark McKinnon, a senior adviser to President George W. Bush's 2000 and 2004 campaigns, the year 2008 was when "campaigns leveraged the Internet in ways never imagined. The year we went to warp speed. The year the paradigm got turned upside down and truly became bottom up instead of top down." The Obama campaign especially used the Internet and social media, such as YouTube, as well as cell-phone text messaging. The Internet connection also helped the campaign raise record amounts of money.

Also in 2008, many younger voters sought alternative sources of information about the campaigns such as *The Daily Show* with Jon Stewart, and they shared blogs, video clips and online discussions through Facebook and YouTube, social media sites that were not a large factor in the 2004 election.

"According to interviews and recent surveys, younger voters tend to be not just consumers of news and current

events but conduits as well—sending out e-mailed links and videos to friends and their social networks. And in turn, they rely on friends and online connections for news to come to them," reported political writer Brian Stelter. "In essence, they are replacing the professional filter—reading *The Washington Post*, clicking on CNN.com—with a social one." "Young people also identify online discussions with friends and videos as important sources of election information," wrote Stelter. "The habits suggest that younger readers find themselves going straight to the source, bypassing the context and analysis that seasoned journalists provide."

In the 2012 election, most political campaigns used the Internet to spread their messages, but they still relied on TV for the majority of their advertising. Customers at a coin laundry watch the first 2012 presidential debate, which drew 67.2 million viewers.

However, even though Internet political marketing may reach large groups of people quickly and efficiently, there is no clear understanding yet of how Internet political messages can be used to change people's minds. In the 2012 election, most political campaigns used the Internet to spread their messages, but they still relied on television for the majority of their advertising, and expenditures on Internet advertising remained very small.

The total amount spent by presidential candidates for the 2012 elections reached $6 billion, more than twice what the candidates spent in 2008.

"Advertising veterans say the stakes are too high to experiment with a medium that, despite its ability to monitor the browsing habits of consumers, might not be effective," reported the *Los Angeles Times*. So, political campaigns are still spending more money on the controlled messages that television advertising provides rather than the uncontrolled environment of the Internet. However, in the 2012 election, 47 percent of voters said they turned to the Internet for campaign news. (See **Impact/Audience**, "Internet Grows, Newspapers Decline As Campaign News Source in 2012 Election," and **Illustration 13.3**, "Internet Grows as Campaign News Source," p. 278.)

MASS MEDIA REFLECT SOCIAL VALUES

Because media research is a continuing process, new ideas will emerge in the next decade from today's ideas and studies. Several provocative recent analyses have extended the boundaries of media research.

Silencing Opposing Viewpoints

Political scientist Elisabeth Noelle-Neumann has asserted that because journalists in all media tend to concentrate on the same major news stories, the audience is assailed on many sides by similar information. Together, the media present the consensus; journalists reflect the prevailing climate of opinion.

As this consensus spreads, people with divergent views, says Noelle-Neumann, may be less likely to voice disagreement with the prevailing point of view. Thus, because of a *"spiral of silence,"* the media gain more influence because opponents of the consensus tend to remain silent. The implication for future research will be to ask whether the media neutralize dissent and create a pattern of social and cultural conformity.

Losing a Sense of Place

In his book *No Sense of Place*, published in 1985, Joshua Meyrowitz provided new insight into television's possible effects on society. In the past, says Meyrowitz:

> Parents did not know what their children knew, and children did not know what their parents knew they knew. Similarly, a person of one sex could never be certain of what a member of the other sex knew. . . . Television undermines such behavioral distinctions because it encompasses children and adults, men and women and all other social groups in a single informational sphere or environment. Not only does it provide similar information to everyone, but, even more significant, it provides it publicly and often simultaneously.

This sharing of information, says Meyrowitz, means that subjects that rarely were discussed between men and

women, for instance, or between children and adults, have become part of the public dialogue.

A second result of television viewing is the blurred distinction between childhood and adulthood, says Meyrowitz. When print dominated the society as a medium, children's access to adult information was limited. The only way to learn about "adult" concepts was to read about them, so typically children were not exposed to adult ideas or problems, and taboo topics remained hidden from children.

Harley Schwardron/Cartoon Stock

"WE'RE DECREASING THE AMOUNT OF T.V. VIOLENCE BY ADDING MORE COMMERCIALS"

In a video world, however, any topic that can be portrayed in pictures on television challenges the boundaries that print places around information. This, says Meyrowitz, causes an early loss of the naïveté of childhood:

> Television removes barriers that once divided people of different ages and reading abilities into different social situations. The widespread use of television is equivalent to a broad social decision to allow young children to be present at wars and funerals, courtships and seductions, criminal plots and cocktail parties. . . . Television thrusts children into a complex adult world, and it provides the impetus for children to ask the meanings of actions and words they would not yet have heard or read about without television.

Meyrowitz concedes that movies offered similar information to children before television, but he says that

Spiral of Silence The belief that people with divergent views may be reluctant to challenge the consensus of opinion offered by the media.

IMPACT/Audience

Internet Grows, Newspapers Decline As Campaign News Source in 2012 Election

Television remains the leading source for news and information about the presidential campaign, but voters are increasingly turning to the Internet for election coverage. Television plays an even more dominant role in election-night coverage: Virtually all voters who followed election returns watched on television. Even among the roughly third of voters who tracked election returns on the Internet, most followed on TV as well.

The percentage naming television as a main source of campaign news has changed little from 2008 (68 percent then, 67 percent now [2012]).

Since 2008, the percentage using the Internet as a main campaign news source has increased 11 points, to 47 percent, making it the second

most frequently used news source by voters. Nearly three-in-ten voters (27 percent) name newspapers, while 20 percent cite radio and 3 percent magazines.

There continue to be large age differences in campaign news sources. More than six-in-ten (64 percent) voters under 30 name the Internet as a main source, while 56 percent cite television. Even among those 30 to 49, as many cite the Internet (65 percent) as television (60 percent). However, 74 percent of voters 50 and older name television as their main campaign news source, while just 31 percent cite the Internet.

Source: Excerpted from "News Sources, Election Night and Views of Press Coverage," The Pew Research Center for The People and The Press, November 15, 2012, people -press.org.

Illustration 13.3

Internet Grows as Campaign News Source

Source: Pew Research Center November 8–11, 2012, voter callback.

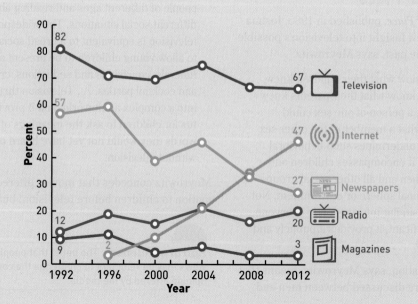

the pervasiveness of television today makes its effects more widespread.

Television is blurring social distinctions—between children and adults, and between men and women. Complicating the current study of media effects is the increase in the variety and number of available media sources.

Stereotyping

Journalists often use shorthand labels to characterize ethnic and other groups. In his 1922 book *Public Opinion*, political journalist Walter Lippmann first identified the tendency of journalists to generalize about other people based on fixed ideas.

> When we speak of the mind of a group of people, of the French mind, the militarist mind, the bolshevik mind, we are liable to serious confusion unless we agree to separate the instinctive equipment from the stereotypes, the patterns, the formulae which play so decisive a part in building up the mental world to which the native character is adapted and responds. . . . Failure to make this distinction accounts for oceans of loose talk about collective minds, national souls and race psychology.

The image of women portrayed by the media has been the subject of significant contemporary studies by many media researchers. Observers of the stereotyping of women point to past and current media portrayals showing very few women in professional roles or as strong, major characters.

The media's overall portrayal of women in mass culture is slowly improving, but in her book *Loving with a Vengeance: Mass-Produced Fantasies for Women*, Tania Modleski says that the portrayal in popular fiction of women in submissive roles goes back to 1740, with the British novel *Pamela*, which was published in America by Benjamin Franklin in 1744. Modleski analyzed the historical content of gothic novels, Harlequin romances and soap operas:

> In Harlequin Romances, the need of women to find meaning and pleasure in activities that are not wholly male-centered such as work or artistic creation is generally scoffed at.

> Soap operas also undercut, though in subtler fashion, the idea that a woman might obtain satisfaction from these activities [work or artistic creation]. . . . Indeed, patriarchal myths and institutions are . . . wholeheartedly embraced, although the anxieties and tensions they give rise to may be said to provoke the need for the texts in the first place.

The implication of Modleski's research is that women who read romance novels will believe they should act like the women in the novels they read. A stereotype that has existed since 1740 still shows up in today's mass media, often in advertising campaigns directed at women.

MEDIA SLOW TO REFLECT ETHNIC DIVERSITY

Beginning in the year 2000, the U.S. census allowed Americans to use more than one racial category to describe themselves, and the categories have been changed to reflect America's changing face. In the past, people were forced to choose one category from among the following: Black, White, Asian or Pacific Islander, American Indian or Alaskan Native, or "Other—specify in writing."

In the 2010 census, 9 million people chose more than one race, a change of about 32 percent since 2000. People who identify with more than one group also were able to check more than one description—African American and Asian, for example. All government forms are required to use the new categories.

This new census method allows people to identify themselves to the government and shows the evolving social landscape of the U.S. population. Yet the American media have been very slow to acknowledge America's changing population patterns.

Specific media outlets, such as African American and Latino newspapers and magazines, have been able to cater to specific audiences. But the mainstream media, especially daily newspapers and the TV networks, traditionally have represented the interests of the mainstream culture. Historically, scores of media studies have documented stereotypical representation and a lack of representation of people of color in all areas of the culture, even though the potential audience for ethnic media is very large.

Media scholar Carolyn Martindale, for example, in a content analysis of *The New York Times* from 1934 to 1994, found that most nonwhite groups were visible "only in glimpses." According to Martindale, "The mainstream press in the U.S. has presented minorities as outside, rather than a part of, American society."

After examining 374 episodes of 96 prime-time series on ABC, CBS, NBC, Fox, WB and UPN, the Center for Media and Public Affairs for the National Council of La Raza concluded that only 2 percent of prime-time characters during the 1994–1995 season were Latinos, and most of the roles played by those characters were minor. The study, *Don't Blink: Hispanics in Television Entertainment*, also revealed that although Latino characters were portrayed more positively than they had been in the past, they were most likely to be shown as poor or working class.

Based on a comprehensive analysis of the nation's newspapers, a 56-page *News Watch* report issued at a convention of the nation's African American, Asian, Latino and Native American journalists concluded that "the mainstream media's coverage of people of color is riddled with old stereotypes, offensive terminology, biased reporting and a myopic interpretation of American society."

To counteract stereotyping, the Center for Integration and Improvement of Journalism at San Francisco State University (which sponsored the study) offered the following Tips for Journalists:

- Apply consistent guidelines when identifying people of race. Are the terms considered offensive? Ask individual sources how they wish to be identified.

- Only refer to people's ethnic or racial background when it is relevant.

- When deciding whether to mention someone's race, ask yourself: Is ethnic/racial identification needed? Is it important to the context of the story?

- Consult a supervisor if you are unsure of the offensiveness or relevance of a racial or ethnic term.

- Use sensitivity when describing rites and cultural events. Avoid inappropriate comparisons. For example, Kwanzaa is not "African American Christmas."

- Be specific when using ethnic or racial identification of individuals. Referring to someone as Filipino American is preferred to calling that person Asian. The latter term is better applied to a group.

The issue of accurate reflection by mass media of a complex society invites analysis as the face of America grows more diverse every day.

MASS MEDIA FACE GAY AND LESBIAN ISSUES

In 1993, newspapers confronted an editorial dilemma when cartoonist Lynn Johnston, who draws the very popular syndicated strip *For Better or For Worse*, decided to reveal that Lawrence, one of the teenagers in the comic strip, was gay. Most newspapers published the strip, but 19 newspapers canceled their contracts for the comic, which was carried by Universal Press Syndicate of Kansas City.

One newspaper editor who refused to carry the strip explained, "We are a conservative newspaper in a conservative town." Another editor said he "felt the sequence condoned homosexuality 'almost to the point of advocacy.'" Responding to criticism that, by revealing Lawrence's sexual preference, she was advocating homosexuality, Johnston said, "You know, that's like advocating left-handedness. Gayness is simply something that exists. My strip is a reality strip, real situations, real crises, real people." One newspaper executive at a paper that carried the strip wrote, "It seems to me that what we're talking about here isn't the rightness or wrongness of homosexuality. It is about tolerance."

An understanding of the media portrayals of Americans' diverse lifestyles on television grabbed attention in 1997, when the program *Ellen* portrayed two women exchanging a romantic kiss. (Although promoted as the nation's first female television kiss, the first televised romantic lesbian relationship actually had been portrayed on the TV program *L.A. Law* in 1991.)

Same-sex relationship issues remained primarily a subject for the nation's lesbian and gay newspapers and magazines, although in 1996, *The New Yorker* ran a controversial cover that portrayed two men kissing on a Manhattan sidewalk. Bringing the issue to a mainstream audience, as the *Ellen* television program did, presented a dilemma for the TV networks because, when notified beforehand about the content of the program, some local TV stations refused to show the episode. The reluctance of mainstream television to portray alternative relationships was as much a reflection of the networks trying to protect their economic interests as it was a reflection of the nation's social values.

By 2003, society's strong reactions to the portrayals of gay people on television seemed to have subsided when Bravo introduced its series *Queer Eye for the Straight Guy*. The title itself would have been shocking just a few years earlier, but audiences seemed ready for programming that featured gay men who advise a straight man about fashion, home decor, cuisine and culture. Television programming traditionally has been slow to adapt to

At the request of his editor, cartoonist Dan Piraro supplied two different captions in 2005 for the same cartoon. Newspapers could choose which caption they wanted to use. Some newspaper editors objected to a caption on this cartoon that portrayed a same-sex male married couple.

changing social standards, trailing the culture's ability to accommodate its evolving diversity.

More than 10 years after the comic strip *For Better or Worse* revealed that one of its characters was gay, veteran cartoonist Dan Piraro confronted the issue of gay marriage. A Piraro cartoon drawn in 2005 appeared in newspapers in two different versions. The first version showed a doctor outside a surgery room talking to a man, saying, "Your husband is in the recovery room. You could go back and see him if you like, but our government-sanctioned bigotry forbids it."

Piraro's editor at King Features Syndicate, saying he had received complaints about Piraro's liberal bias, asked Piraro to draw a second version with the doctor talking to a man and saying, "She's going to be just fine—she's quite a fighter. The anesthesiologist has a black eye and I think she may have cracked my ribs."

Different papers chose which version to run, but some subscribers noticed the difference. "Not wishing to lose my voice entirely, I thought it was wise to send in a replacement caption for the same picture," Piraro said.

In 2012, Marvel Comics announced a wedding for its first openly gay hero, Northstar and his long-time boyfriend Kyle. In 1992, Northstar had become one of the first comic characters to reveal that he is gay. "The Marvel Universe has always reflected the world outside your window, so we strike to make sure our characters, relationships and stories are grounded in that reality," said Axel Alonso, Marvel's editor-in-chief. (See **Impact/Audience**, "Marvel Comics Plans Wedding for Gay Hero Northstar," p. 282.)

HOW TO ANALYZE MEDIA EFFECTS

Scholars once thought the effects of media were easy to measure, as a direct relationship between mass media messages and the effects of those messages. Contemporary scholars now know that the relationship between mass media and their audiences is complex.

Communications scholar Neil Postman poses some questions to ask about mass media's relationship to cultural, political and social issues:

- What are the main psychic effects of each [media] form?

- What is the main relation between information and reason?

- What redefinitions of important cultural meanings do new sources, speeds, contexts and forms of information require?

- How do different forms of information persuade?

- Is a newspaper's "public" different from television's "public"?

- How do different information forms dictate the type of content that is expressed?

These questions should be discussed, says Postman, because "no medium is excessively dangerous if its users understand what its dangers are. . . . This is an instance in which the asking of the questions is sufficient. To ask is to break the spell."

IMPACT/Audience

Marvel Comics Plans Wedding for Gay Hero Northstar

By Matt Moore, Associated Press

Wedding bells will ring this summer [2012] for Marvel Comics' first openly gay hero, super speedster Northstar, and his longtime boyfriend.

The New York-based publisher said that Canadian character Jean-Paul Beaubier will marry his beau, Kyle Jinadu, in the pages of "Astonishing X-Men" No. 51. That's due out June 20 [2012].

Northstar revealed he was gay in the pages of *Alpha Flight* No. 106 in 1992, one of Marvel Entertainment's first characters to do so.

Ten years later, in 2002, gay characters Apollo and the Midnighter were married in the pages of *The Authority* published by DC's Wildstorm imprint.

Since then, numerous comic book heroes and villains have been written as gay, lesbian or transgender—from DC Comics' Kate Kane, aka Batwoman, to Hulkling and Wiccan in the pages of "Young Avengers."

Comics, as a medium, have embraced gay, lesbian and transgender characters, including the introduction of Kevin Keller by Archie Comics. Comic strips have done likewise.

For Marvel, the upcoming wedding is a way to further embed same-sex issues in its contemporary universe. "The Marvel Universe has always reflected the world outside your window, so we strive to make sure our characters, relationships and stories are grounded in that reality," said Axel Alonso, Marvel's editor-in-chief.

Author Marjorie Liu, who is writing *Astonishing X-Men*, said the decision to have the pair marry was appropriate. "As a writer—and a romance novelist, no less—I've always found it a bit odd when characters in comic books remain in relationship limbo for years at a time," she said.

"Certainly, that happens in real life—some relationships just never grow—but the wonderful thing about stories is that they tend to move readers and characters forward," Liu said, adding

Marc Stamas/Getty Images

In 2012, Marvel Comics announced that their first openly gay hero, Northstar, would marry his longtime boyfriend Kyle. Northstar had revealed that he is gay in 1992, one of the first comic characters to do so. A poster showing Kyle and Northstar decorates a commemorative gay marriage ceremony on June 20, 2012, in New York City.

that Northstar pops the question in issue No. 50. "And, in this case, it was time to do the same to Northstar and Kyle, who have one of those rare comic book romances that actually works."

As for the event itself, Liu said the wedding will take place in New York City, where gay marriage is legal, but given that Northstar is one of the X-Men, it remains to be seen if the event will be trouble-free.

"As for the ceremony . . . well, what wedding ever goes off without a hitch?"

Source: Excerpted from Matt Moore, "Marvel Comics Plans Wedding for Gay Hero Northstar," May 23, 2012, Associated Press. Retrieved from Sacbee.com.

Review, Analyze, Investigate

Reviewing Chapter 13

Early Mass Media Studies Assess Impact

- Media scholars look for patterns in the effects of media rather than for anecdotal evidence.

- David Potter, in *People of Plenty*, described the United States as a consumer society driven by advertising.

Scholars Look for Patterns

- Canadian scholar Marshall McLuhan introduced the term *global village* to describe the way media bring people together through shared experience.

- The magic bullet theory, developed in the 1929 Payne Fund studies, asserted that media content has a direct causal relationship to behavior and that mass media affects everyone in the same way.

- Challenging the magic bullet theory, Hadley Cantril found that better-educated people listening to *War of the Worlds* were much more likely to detect that the radio broadcast was fiction. Today, scholars believe the media have different effects on different people.

- In 1948, political scientist Harold D. Lasswell described the process of analyzing communication as answering five questions: Who? Says what? On which channel? To whom? With what effect?

How TV Affects Children's Behavior

- In 1961, Wilbur Schramm and his associates revealed that children used TV for fantasy, diversion and instruction. Aggressive children were more likely to turn to TV for fantasy, said Schramm, but he could find no serious problems related to TV viewing.

- The 1971 report to Congress, *Television and Social Behavior*, made a faint causal connection between TV violence and children's violent behavior, but the report said that only some children were affected, and these children already had been classified as aggressive.

- Several recent studies have suggested that TV violence causes aggression among children. Researchers caution, however, that TV violence is not *the* cause of aggressiveness, but only *a* cause of aggressiveness.

- The Federal Trade Commission report *Television Advertising to Children* said that children see 20,000 commercials a year and that younger children are much more likely to pay attention to TV advertising than older ones.

- A study by the California Assessment Program of children's TV viewing habits seems to support the idea that children who watch a lot of TV do not perform as well in school as children who watch less television.

- A 2011 study by Common Sense Media reports that children younger than 8 years of age spend more time than ever using media, and more than half of these children have access to a mobile device.

Do the Mass Media Cause Violence?

- The summary study by the National Institute of Mental Health in 1982 asserted that a direct connection exists between televised violence and aggressive behavior, but there is no way to predict who will be affected and why.

- Most of the latest studies of the media's role have continued to reinforce the concept that different people in different environments react to the media differently.

Ratings Systems and Parental Controls Established

- In 1994, cable operators and network broadcasters agreed to use an independent monitor to review programming for violent content.

- The agreement called for the development of violence ratings for TV programming and endorsed a v-chip—*v* for "violence"—technology that eventually was required for all television sets to allow parents to block programs rated as violent.

- The Telecommunications Act of 1996 established a television ratings code for content.

- The Entertainment Software Association, which represents video and computer game-makers, also has voluntarily created a ratings system.

- These ratings systems continue a tradition of media self-regulation.

National Political Campaigns Depend on Mass Media

- Media politics began in 1933 with President Franklin Roosevelt's Fireside Chats. John F. Kennedy broadened the tradition when he and Richard Nixon appeared in the nation's first televised debate of presidential candidates, in 1960.

- The first major study of politics and the media, *The People's Choice*, concluded that only 8 percent of the voters in the study were actually converted by media coverage of the 1940 campaign.

- The 1976 study, *The Unseeing Eye*, revealed that only 7 percent of the people in the study were manipulated by TV ads. The researchers concluded that political advertising has little effect on most people.

- Television is a very efficient way to reach large numbers of people quickly, but campaigning through television also distances the candidates from direct public contact.

Cost of Political Advertising Skyrockets

- The rising cost of national political campaigns is directly connected to the expense of television advertising.
- Opinion leaders shape political views, a transmission of ideas that is called the *two-step flow* of communication.
- TV political advertising affects only a small percentage of people, but just a few percentage points decide many elections.
- Political spending by presidential candidates in 2012 totaled $6 billion.
- In most political contests, television advertising accounts for more than half of campaign spending, which means healthy earnings for local TV stations.

Voters and Campaigns Use the Internet and Social Media

- The 2004 presidential election was the first election where the Internet began to play a role in national politics. In that election, 75 million people used the Internet to obtain political news.
- Candidates use Web sites, e-mail, blogs, podcasts and social-networking sites such as MySpace, Facebook and YouTube to reach the public.

Mass Media Reflect Social Values

- Elisabeth Noelle-Neumann has asserted that due to what she calls a "spiral of silence" supporting the consensus point of view, the media have more influence because opponents of the consensus tend to remain silent.
- Joshua Meyrowitz says that television viewing blurs the distinction between childhood and adulthood.
- Walter Lippmann first identified the tendency of journalists to generalize about groups of people and create stereotypes.
- Scholar Tania Modleski says the media's inaccurate portrayals of women are not new but began in 1740 with the publication of *Pamela*, the first novel.

Media Slow to Reflect Ethnic Diversity

- In the 2010 census, 9 million people identified themselves as a member of more than one race.

- The mainstream media, especially daily newspapers and the TV networks, have traditionally represented the interests of the mainstream culture.
- A study of *The New York Times* from 1934 to 1994 found that most nonwhite groups were visible "only in glimpses."
- A study by the National Council of La Raza concluded that only 2 percent of prime-time characters during the 1994–1995 TV season were Latinos, and most of the roles played by those characters were minor.
- To avoid ethnic stereotyping, journalists should refer to people's ethnic or racial background only when it is relevant, use sensitivity when describing rites and cultural events and be specific when identifying someone's race or ethnicity, asking the person how he or she would like to be identified.

Mass Media Face Gay and Lesbian Issues

- The lesbian character on the TV program *Ellen* and the gay character Lawrence in the cartoon strip *For Better or For Worse* focused attention on media portrayals of gender issues in the 1990s.
- By 2003, the strong reactions to the portrayals of gay people on television seemed to have subsided when Fox Television introduced its series *Queer Eye for the Straight Guy*.
- The experience of the cartoonist Dan Piraro in 2005 is a reminder that same-sex issues still are sensitive topics for media. At the insistence of his editor, Piraro provided two captions for the same cartoon, one that reflected a male-female couple and one that showed a male-male married couple.
- In 2012, Marvel Comics announced a wedding for its first openly gay hero, Northstar and his longtime boyfriend Kyle.

How to Analyze Media Effects

- The relationship between media and their audiences is complex.
- Communications scholar Neil Postman says that scholars should continue to analyze the media's effects so people will not just accept what they see without question.

Key Terms

These terms are defined in the margins throughout this chapter and appear in alphabetical order with definitions in the Glossary, which begins on page 373.

Critical Questions

1. How did each of the following people contribute to media effects research?

   a. David M. Potter
   b. Marshall McLuhan
   c. Harold D. Lasswell
   d. George Gerbner

2. Describe three studies involving children and TV and discuss the results. Why are children often the subject of television effects research?

3. Discuss your understanding of the role of American media, especially television, in political campaigns.

Include reference to research about how political campaigns use media to try to influence voters.

4. Describe the nature and effects of the Internet on American politics.

5. How well and how fairly do you believe women, African Americans, Latinos and other ethnic groups are represented in American mass media today? How well and fairly do you believe gay and lesbian issues are portrayed in American mass media today? Give three specific examples.

Working the Web

This list includes both sites mentioned in the chapter and others to give you greater insight into social, cultural and political issues research.

Benton Foundation

benton.org

The foundation says that its mission is "to ensure that media and telecommunications serve the public interest and enhance our democracy." The foundation pursues this mission by "seeking policy solutions that support the values of access, diversity and equity, and by demonstrating the value of media and telecommunications for improving the quality of life for all." Its virtual library includes downloadable documents on issues ranging from the "digital divide" to telecommunications regulation and legislation to television/community media. The foundation was established by William Benton, whom pollster George Gallup called a father of advertising consumer research. Benton was also publisher of the *Encyclopedia Britannica* and a U.S. senator.

Center on Media and Child Health (CMCH)

cmch.tv

Dedicated to "understanding and responding to the effects of media on the physical, mental and social health of children through research, production and education," this center is located at Children's Hospital Boston along with Harvard Medical School and Harvard School of Public Health. Hot Topics in the site's section for parents and teachers include violence in video games, educational television and literacy, and obesity. The CMCH Database of Research catalogs current research on the relationship of media exposure to health-risk behaviors.

Joan Shorenstein Center on the Press, Politics and Public Policy (Harvard University)

shorensteincenter.org

Dedicated to "exploring and illuminating the intersection of press, politics and public policy in theory and in practice," this research center is based at the John F. Kennedy School of Government at Harvard University. Downloadable Research & Publications documents include books written by Center faculty, staff and associates, newsletters from the Center and a variety of reports, papers and case studies. The center offers some internships and scholarships for students.

Mediasmarts—formerly known as the Media Awareness Network (MNet)

mediasmarts.ca

This Canadian nonprofit organization promotes Internet and media education by producing online programs and resources, partnering with Canadian and international organizations, and speaking to audiences in Canada and around the world. MNet's focus is on providing educational information and materials empowering young people to develop the critical thinking skills needed to be "functionally literate" in media messages. The Web site deals with issues including media violence, online hate and media stereotyping (of ethnic minorities, girls and women, boys and men, and gays and lesbians).

Media Effects Research Lab at Penn State University

psu.edu/dept/medialab/

This research facility has conducted several experiments on hundreds of subjects testing the psychological effects of media content, form and technology. Research abstracts are available for viewing on a wide variety of subjects including Internet use and content credibility; cell phone usage and interaction with others; examinations of gender, racial and sexual minority stereotypes in the media; and fashion magazines' role in self-worth.

Media Research Hub (Social Science Research Council; SSRC)

mediaresearchhub.ssrc.org

Part of the SSRC's Necessary Knowledge for a Democratic Public Sphere program, the Media Research Hub works to ensure that debates about media and communication technologies are shaped by "high-quality research and a rich understanding of the public interest." Its Resource Database is a community-maintained field-mapping tool for work on the social dimensions of media, communications and technology. Research news, commentary and data are also available on the site. The program is run in partnership with the Center for International Media Action (CIMA) and the Donald McGannon Communication Research Center at Fordham University.

Moorland-Spingarn Research Center (MSRC) at Howard University

howard.edu/msrc

One of the largest repositories for "documentation of the history and culture of people of African descent in Africa, the Americas and other parts of the world," this site includes a link to the archives of the center's electronic journal (HUArchivesNet). Links to the Library Division and the Manuscript Division go to brief descriptions and samples of the center's holdings.

National Journal

nationaljournal.com

National Journal Group publishes nonpartisan magazines, newsletters, books and directories "for people who have a professional interest in politics, policy and government." Web site users can access online content from *National Journal Magazine*, *The Hotline* (daily news service for political insiders) and *CongressDaily*.

University of Iowa Department of Communication Studies: Political Communication and Campaigns

clas.uiowa.edu/commstudies/political-communication -campaigns

This resource site provides links to articles and a long list of Web sites relating to politics and to several political media consulting firms.

Impact/Action Videos are concise news features on various topics created exclusively for *Media/Impact*. Go online to access MindTap at cengagebrain.com. MindTap for *Media/Impact* sequences all of your learning tools—Chapter Readings with highlighting and note taking, **Impact/Action Videos**, activities and assessments—into chapter driven learning units that guide you through the curriculum.

LAW AND REGULATION:
REWRITING THE RULES

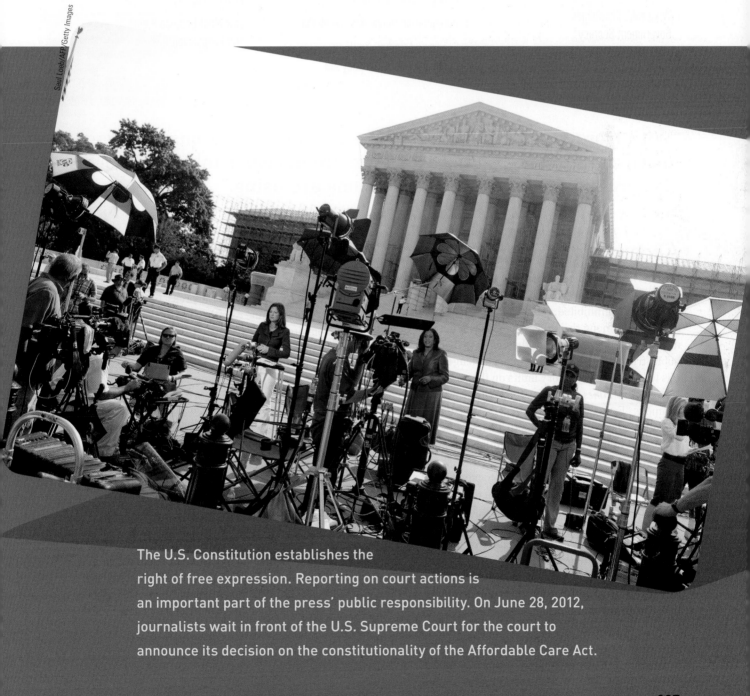

Saul Loeb/AFP/Getty Images

The U.S. Constitution establishes the right of free expression. Reporting on court actions is an important part of the press' public responsibility. On June 28, 2012, journalists wait in front of the U.S. Supreme Court for the court to announce its decision on the constitutionality of the Affordable Care Act.

What's Ahead?

"With more forms of expression, there are more reasons to engage in censorship if the people in charge are uncomfortable with forms of expression that younger generations are using."

—JOAN BERTIN, DIRECTOR, NATIONAL COALITION AGAINST CENSORSHIP

According to the precedent-

setting *New York Times v. Sullivan* case, which helped define press freedom in 1964, the U.S. media's role is to encourage "uninhibited, robust and wide-open" debate. Arguments among the public, the government and the media about the best way for the media to maintain this public trusteeship form the core of challenges and rebuttals to legal and regulatory limits on the media.

New York Times columnist Tom Wicker wrote, for example, "Even though absolute press freedom may sometimes have to accommodate itself to other high constitutional values, the repeal or modification of the First Amendment seems unlikely. . . . If the true freedom of the press is to decide for itself what to publish and when to publish it, the true responsibility of the press must be to assert and defend that freedom."

The media are businesses operating to make a profit, but these businesses enjoy a special trust under the U.S. Constitution. The legal and regulatory issues the media face are attempts by the government to balance this special trust with the interests of individuals and the interests of government.

U.S. CONSTITUTION SETS FREE PRESS PRECEDENT

All legal interpretations of the press' responsibilities attempt to determine exactly what the framers of the U.S. Constitution meant when they included the First Amendment in the Bill of Rights in 1791. The First Amendment established the concept that the press should operate freely:

> Congress shall make no law respecting an establishment of religion, or prohibiting the free exercise thereof; or abridging the freedom of speech, or of the press; or the right of the people peaceably to assemble, and to petition the Government for a redress of grievances.

In his book *Emergence of a Free Press*, Leonard W. Levy explains his interpretation of the First Amendment:

> By freedom of the press the Framers meant a right to engage in rasping, corrosive and offensive discussions on all topics of public interest. . . . The press had become the tribune of the people by sit-

ting in judgment on the conduct of public officials. A free press meant the press as the Fourth Estate, [as] . . . an informal or extra-constitutional fourth branch that functioned as part of the intricate system of checks and balances that exposed public mismanagement and kept power fragmented, manageable and accountable.

While efforts to interpret the Framers' meaning continue, as do challenges and rebuttals to subsequent laws and regulations, discussion of the restrictions and laws covering the press today can be divided into six categories: (1) federal government restrictions, (2) prior restraint, (3) censorship, (4) libel, (5) privacy and (6) the right of access.

GOVERNMENT TRIES TO RESTRICT FREE EXPRESSION

At least four times in U.S. history before 1964, the federal government felt threatened enough by press freedom to attempt to restrict the press' access to information. These four notable attempts to restrict the way the media operate were the Alien and Sedition Laws of 1798, the Espionage Act of 1918, the Smith Act of 1940 and the Cold War congressional investigations of suspected Communists in the late 1940s and early 1950s. All four challenges were attempts by the government to control free speech.

The Alien and Sedition Laws of 1798

Under the provisions of the Alien and Sedition Laws of 1798, 15 people were indicted, 11 people were tried, and 10 were found guilty. The Alien and Sedition Laws set a fine of up to $2,000 and a sentence of up to two years in jail for anyone who was found guilty of speaking, writing or publishing "false, scandalous and malicious writing or writings" against the government, Congress or the president. The laws expired in 1801, and when Thomas Jefferson became president that year, he pardoned everyone who had been found guilty under the laws.

The Espionage Act of 1918

Although Henry Raymond had challenged censorship of Civil War reporting (see **Chapter 12**), journalists and the general population during the Civil War had accepted government control of information. But during World

War I, Congress passed the Espionage Act of 1918. Not all Americans supported U.S. entry into the war, and to stop criticism, the Espionage Act made it a crime to say or write anything that could be viewed as helping the enemy. Under the act, 877 people were convicted. Many, but not all, of them were pardoned when the war ended.

The most notable person cited under the Espionage Act of 1918 was labor organizer and Socialist Party presidential candidate Eugene V. Debs, who was sentenced to two concurrent 10-year terms for giving a public speech against the war. At his trial, Debs said, "I have been accused of obstructing the war. I admit it. Gentlemen, I abhor war. I would oppose the war if I stood alone." Debs was released from prison by a presidential order in 1921.

The Smith Act of 1940

During World War II, Congress passed the Smith Act of 1940, which placed some restrictions on free speech. Only a few people were cited under it, but the members of the press were required to submit their stories for government censorship. President Franklin D. Roosevelt created the Office of Censorship, which worked out the voluntary Code of Wartime Practices with the press. The Code spelled out the kinds of information the press would not report about the war, such as troop and ship movements. The military retained power to censor all overseas war reporting.

The Office of Censorship also issued the Code of Wartime Practices for American Broadcasters, which were guidelines for news broadcasts and commentaries. (See **Impact/Audience**, "Excerpts from the 1943 Code of Wartime Practices for American Broadcasters," p. 290.) The government exercised influence over broadcasters because it licensed broadcast outlets.

HUAC and the Permanent Subcommittee on Investigations

The fourth major challenge to the First Amendment protection of free speech came in the late 1940s and early 1950s, culminating with the actions of the House Un-American Activities Committee (*HUAC*) against the Hollywood Ten (see **Chapter 7**) and the Senate's Permanent Subcommittee on Investigations presided over by Senator Joseph R. McCarthy.

HUAC   House Un-American Activities Committee.

IMPACT/Audience

Excerpts from the 1943 Code of Wartime Practices for American Broadcasters

Note: During World War II, the Office of War Information tried to control what was broadcast from the United States. Following are some of the rules radio broadcasters were expected to follow.

News Broadcasts and Commentaries

It is requested that news in any of the following classifications be kept off the air unless made available for broadcast by appropriate authority or specifically cleared by the Office of Censorship.

(a) Weather—Weather forecasts other than those officially released by the Weather Bureau.

(b) Armed forces—Types and movements of United States Army, Navy, and Marine Corps units, within or without continental United States.

Programs

(a) Request programs—No telephoned or telegraphed requests for musical selections should be accepted. No requests for musical selections made by word-of-mouth at the origin of broadcast, whether studio or remote, should be honored.

(b) Quiz programs—Any program which permits the public accessibility to an open microphone is dangerous and should be carefully supervised. Because of the nature of quiz programs, in which the public is not only permitted access to the microphone but encouraged to speak into it, the danger of usurpation by the enemy is enhanced.

Frederic Lewis/Getty Images

Under provisions of the 1943 Code of Wartime Practices for American Broadcasters, all live radio programs—including shows featuring performers such as Frank Sinatra (left) and comedian Fred Allen (right)—were subject to on-air censorship.

Foreign Language Broadcasts

(a) Personnel—The Office of Censorship, by direction of the president, is charged with the responsibility of removing from the air all those engaged in foreign language broadcasting who, in the judgment of appointed authorities in the Office of Censorship, endanger the war effort of the United Nations by their connections, direct or indirect, with the medium.

(b) Scripts—Station managements are requested to require all persons who broadcast in a foreign language to submit to the management in advance of broadcast complete scripts or transcriptions of such material.

Source: Excerpted from U.S. Government Office of Censorship, *Code of Wartime Practices for American Broadcasters*. Washington, D.C.: Government Printing Office, 1943, pages 1–8.

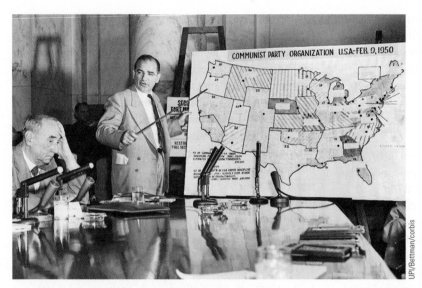

Senator Joseph McCarthy (at the easel) explained his theory of Communism during the Army-McCarthy hearings in 1954. Army counsel Joseph N. Welch, who was defending people who had been declared subversive by McCarthy, is seated at the table. News reports and Edward R. Murrow's exposure of McCarthy's investigative excesses eventually triggered public criticism of McCarthy's tactics, and his Senate colleagues censured him.

These congressional committees set a tone of aggressive Communist hunting. After television broadcasts of McCarthy's investigation of Communist influence in the Army and other reports eventually exposed his excesses, McCarthy's Senate colleagues censured him by a vote of 67 to 22. But while the hearings were underway, they established a restrictive atmosphere that challenged free expression.

PRIOR RESTRAINT RARELY USED

Prior restraint means government censoring of information before the information is published or broadcast. The Framers of the Constitution clearly opposed prior restraint by law. However, in 1931, the U.S. Supreme Court established the circumstances under which prior restraint could be justified.

Near v. Minnesota

J. M. Near published the weekly *Saturday Press*, which printed the names of people who were violating the

Prior Restraint   Government censorship of information before the information is published or broadcast.

nation's Prohibition laws. Minnesota authorities obtained a court order forbidding publication of *Saturday Press*, but the U.S. Supreme Court overturned the state's action. In *Near v. Minnesota* in 1931, the Court condemned prior restraint, although it acknowledged that the government could limit information about troop movements during war and could control obscenity. The Court also said that "the security of community life may be protected against incitements to acts of violence and the overthrow of orderly government."

Saturday Press had not violated any of these prohibitions, so the Minnesota court's order was lifted. But future attempts to stop other publications were based on the *Near v. Minnesota* decision, making it a landmark case.

In two important instances since *Near* (the Pentagon Papers and *United States v. The Progressive*), courts were asked to bar publication of information to protect national security. In the military offensives in Grenada and the Persian Gulf, the federal government took action to prevent journalists from reporting on the government's activities.

The Pentagon Papers

On June 13, 1971, *The New York Times* published the first installment of what has become known as the Pentagon Papers, excerpts from what was properly titled *History of U.S. Decision-Making Process on Vietnam Policy*. The Pentagon Papers detailed decisions that were made about U.S. involvement in Vietnam starting in the 1940s.

The documents were labeled top secret, but they were given to *The Times* by one of the report's authors, Daniel Ellsberg, a consultant to the Defense Department and the White House. Ellsberg said he believed the papers had been improperly classified and that the public should have the information. After the first three installments were published in *The Times*, Justice Department attorneys obtained a restraining order against *The Times*, which stopped publication of the installments for two weeks while *The Times* appealed the case. While the case was being decided, *The Washington Post* began publishing the papers, and *The Post* was stopped, but only until the U.S. Supreme Court decided the *Times* case.

In *New York Times Co. v. United States*, the Court said the government did not prove that prior restraint was necessary. *The Times* and *The Post* then printed the papers, but the Court action had delayed publication of the information for two weeks. This was the first time

UPI/Bettman/corbis

in the nation's history that the federal government had stopped a newspaper from publishing specific information. Legal fees cost *The Post* and *The Times* more than $270,000. Forty years later, on June 13, 2011, the U.S. government publicly released the complete set of documents once known as the Pentagon Papers.

The *Progressive* Case

The next instance of prior restraint happened in 1979, when editors of *The Progressive* magazine announced that they planned to publish an article by Howard Morland about how to make a hydrogen bomb. The author said the article was based on information from public documents and interviews with government employees. The Department of Justice brought suit in Wisconsin, where the magazine was published, and received a restraining order to stop the information from being printed (*United States v. The Progressive*). *The Progressive* did not publish the article as planned.

Before the case could reach the U.S. Supreme Court, a Wisconsin newspaper published a letter from a man named Charles Hansen that contained much of the same information as the Morland article. Hansen sent eight copies of the letter to other newspapers, and the *Chicago Tribune* also published the letter, saying that none of the information was proprietary. Six months after the original restraining order, *The Progressive* published the article.

GOVERNMENT MANAGES WAR COVERAGE

The U.S. government historically has tried to control its image during wartime. Four recent examples of government press management are Grenada, the Gulf War, Afghanistan and Iraq. In 2009, the U.S. government eased previous restrictions on press access when, with the family's consent, it allowed reporters to photograph caskets of fallen soldiers that were being returned home.

Restricting Press Access in Grenada

In an incident in 1983 that never reached the courts but that was a type of prior restraint, the Reagan administration kept reporters away from the Caribbean island of Grenada, where the administration had launched a military offensive. A press blackout began at 11 p.m. on October 24, 1983. The administration didn't officially bar the

press from covering the invasion on October 25, but the Pentagon refused to transport the press and turned back press yachts and airplanes that attempted to enter the war zone. About a dozen print journalists and photographers were able to get in, but no television crews were allowed.

More than 400 journalists from 170 news organizations around the world who couldn't get to Grenada were left on Barbados, waiting for the news to get to them. Charles Lachman of the *New York Post* flew to Barbados and then to St. Vincent. Then he and some other reporters paid $6,000 to charter a boat to Grenada. They arrived five days after the invasion and discovered that a hospital was one of the casualties of the military's action.

News Blackouts and Press Pools During the Gulf War

In the 1990s, the Gulf War posed another tough battleground for the rights of reporters versus the rights of the military to restrict access. On Saturday, February 23, 1991, about three weeks into the Gulf War, when the ground assault began, the Defense Department announced the first total news blackout in U.S. military history.

For 24 hours, defense leaders were told to issue no statements about the actions of U.S. troops. Military officials said that instantaneous transmission of information from the battlefield meant that Iraq would be able to pick up live TV pictures. Press organizations protested the ban, but the military argued that modern communications technology necessitated the blackout.

Pentagon rules for war coverage, reached in cooperation with journalists, imposed stricter limits on reporting in the Persian Gulf than in any previous U.S. war. Reporters had to travel in small "pools," escorted by public affairs officers. Every story produced by the pool was subject to military censorship. This system, called ***pool reporting***, had been created in response to reporters' complaints about news blackouts during the Grenada incident.

An unprecedented number of journalists—1,300 in Saudi Arabia alone—posed a challenge for military press officers. In a commentary protesting the restrictions, *The New Yorker* magazine said, "The rules, it is clear, enable the Pentagon to promote coverage of subjects and events that it wishes publicized and to prevent reporting that might cast it, or the war, in a bad light." Yet, in a *Los Angeles Times* poll of nearly 2,000 people two weeks after the fighting started, 79 percent approved of the Pentagon's restrictions, and 57 percent favored even further limits.

When the Persian Gulf War ended, many members of the U.S. press in the Middle East complained bitterly about their lack of access, but the military and the public seemed satisfied with the new rules for wartime coverage.

Pool Reporting   An arrangement that places reporters in small, government-supervised groups to cover an event.

War in Afghanistan

During the early days of the war in Afghanistan, especially in the months immediately following the September 11, 2001, terrorist attacks in the United States, the military carefully controlled press access to information, citing security reasons. The military used press pools and also provided its own video footage of troop landings, produced by the military's combat film teams.

"In World War II, accredited journalists from leading news organizations were on the front lines to give the public an independent description of what was happening," said *The New York Times*. "In the new war on terrorism, journalists have had limited access to many of the United States forces that are carrying out the war. . . . The media's access to American military operations is far more limited than in recent conflicts."

"Embed" Reporters During Iraq War

Beginning in 2003, during the Iraq War, the U.S. government adopted a system called *embedding*, which meant that members of the press traveled with the military, but the press' movements were restricted and managed by their military units.

Embedding was a reaction to the press' limited access in Afghanistan, but many journalists said they still had

U.S. Army Honor Guardsmen carry the flag-draped casket of Staff Sgt. Edward C. Kramer, who died in combat in Iraq. Because the ban on coverage of U.S. war casualties had been lifted and Kramer's family gave permission, the press was able to photograph this official transfer of his casket at Dover Air Force Base on July 1, 2009.

limited access to the real action in Iraq. However, the coverage left the impression with the public that the press was giving the whole story, when in fact the press had access to only a very limited view. (For more about embedded reporters, see **Chapter 12**.)

Photographs of War Fatalities

Twenty years ago during the Gulf War, the first Bush administration banned the media from covering the arrival of war fatalities as they were returned to the United States, saying the administration wanted to protect the families' privacy. Critics of the ban said that the government was trying to hide the consequences of war from public view. In 2009, the Obama administration lifted the ban and allowed the press access to photograph the returning soldiers, with family permission.

WikiLeaks Challenges Government Secrecy

Founded in 2006 by Australian Julian Assange, WikiLeaks is a whistle-blowing organization devoted to uncovering government secrets and publishing them on its Web site. Beginning in 2010, WikiLeaks began releasing classified U.S. diplomatic documents, including military information and State Department communications.

In late July 2010, WikiLeaks posted tens of thousands of confidential military documents about the wars in Iraq and Afghanistan. "The battlefield consequences of the release of these documents are potentially severe and dangerous for our troops, our allies and Afghan partners, and may well damage our relationships and reputation in that key part of world," Defense Secretary Robert M. Gates told Pentagon reporters.

On November 28, 2010, *The New York Times* began publishing a series of articles based on a new release of State Department documents. "Some 250,000 individual cables, the daily traffic between the State Department and more than 270 American diplomatic outposts around the world were made available to *The Times* by a source who insisted on anonymity," wrote *The Times* in an explanatory front page Note to Readers that accompanied the first article.

The Times acknowledged that WikiLeaks originally obtained the documents, but did not directly cite

Win McNamee/Getty Images

Rosie Hallam/Getty Images News/Getty Images

WikiLeaks founder Julian Assange makes a statement from the balcony of the Ecuadorian Embassy in London, England on August 19, 2012, where he was granted political asylum. Despite U.S. government objections, WikiLeaks published about 2,000 confidential State Department documents on its Web site in November 2010.

On August 21, 2013, Manning was sentenced to 35 years in prison.

On February 23, 2011, a British court ordered that Assange be extradited to Sweden. Assange appealed and the case is pending. He currently is living inside the Ecuadorian Embassy in London, where he has been granted political asylum. The U.S. government has not filed any charges against Assange for his role in publishing secret U.S. documents on the Internet.

When should the government be able to prevent military information from reaching the public? When should the press have access? The Supreme Court has never specifically addressed these questions, and the U.S. press and news organizations remain vulnerable to military restrictions.

LIBRARIANS RESIST THE PATRIOT ACT

In 2001, a few weeks after the terrorist attacks on the World Trade Center in New York City, Congress passed the USA PATRIOT Act (which stands for Uniting and Strengthening America by Providing Appropriate Tools Required to Intercept and Obstruct Terrorism Act), designed to give the U.S. government broad powers to track, detain and interrogate people who are deemed a threat to the country. Among the provisions of the act is Section 215, which allows the Federal Bureau of Investigation (FBI) to obtain "business records." These could include public library records, including computer log-ins and lists of books people check out, although the act does not specifically mention libraries.

Librarians said they were ready to cooperate with an investigation if they received a search warrant. However, they claimed the PATRIOT Act would allow officials to seize anything they wished without a search warrant, which librarians said would inhibit the use of public libraries—a limit on free expression.

WikiLeaks as *The Times'* source. "As daunting as it is to publish such material over official objections, it would be presumptuous to conclude that Americans have no right to know what is being done in their name," *The Times* explained.

Outraged at the leaks, several countries called for Assange's arrest. For months, he eluded authorities by traveling to various European countries. He eventually turned himself in to British authorities on December 7, 2010. According to *The New York Times*, as of December 28, 2010, WikiLeaks had posted 391,832 secret documents on the Iraq war, 77,000 classified Pentagon documents on the Afghan conflict and 250,000 State Department cables.

In July 2010, the U.S. military charged Pfc. Bradley Manning, an intelligence analyst, with downloading large amounts of classified information from a computer at a military base in Iraq and sharing the information with WikiLeaks. In February 2013, Manning pleaded guilty to 10 of the charges against him. On July 30, 2013, a military judge found Manning not guilty of "aiding the enemy," but found him guilty of 20 other charges, including six violations of the Espionage Act.

Some libraries posted signs to warn patrons that federal authorities might review their records; others systematically shredded patrons' sign-in sheets for using library computers. The American Library Association went on record opposing unwarranted government access to library records. The American Civil Liberties Union sued in several cities nationwide to keep library records private, and in 2004 a Los Angeles federal judge ruled that parts of the PATRIOT Act were unconstitutional violations of the First and Fifth amendments to the U.S. Constitution.

In 2005, the FBI demanded library records from Library Connection, a nonprofit library group in Bridgeport, Conn., saying the agency needed the information as part of a terrorism investigation under the PATRIOT Act. The American Civil Liberties Union challenged the request in court, saying the request was unconstitutional. Eventually the FBI withdrew its request.

The PATRIOT Act expired in late 2005, but in March 2006, Congress reauthorized the act for another four years, including Section 215. Opponents, including the American Library Association, vowed to renew their challenges to the most aggressive provisions of the act, especially Section 215, to stop what they said is an intrusion into important American civil liberties.

In 2007, a federal judge in New York struck down provisions of the PATRIOT Act that had authorized the government to issue so-called National Security Letters (*NSLs*), compelling businesses (such as Internet service providers, telephone companies and public libraries) to release customer information without a judge's order or grand jury subpoena. U.S. District Judge Victor Marrero said using the PATRIOT Act, even as rewritten and reauthorized in 2006, to obtain customer information without court authorization "offends the fundamental constitutional principles of checks and balances and separation of powers." President Obama signed a four-year extension of the PATRIOT Act on May 30, 2011.

What Is the Standard for Obscenity?

Different media industries historically have reacted differently to threats of *censorship*, the practice of suppressing material that is considered morally, politically or otherwise objectionable. Most threats of censorship concern matters of morality.

According to the American Library Association, the top three reasons critics try to challenge content are:

1. The material is considered "sexually explicit."

2. The material contains "offensive language."

3. The material is "unsuited to an age group."

In the United States, censorship almost always occurs after the fact. Once the material is printed or displayed,

the courts can be asked to review the content for obscenity. (See **Impact/Convergence**, "'Harlem Shake' Videos Lead to School Suspensions," p. 296.)

To try to avoid constant scrutiny, the motion picture and recording industries have accepted some form of self-regulation to avoid government intervention. The electronic media are governed by laws in the federal criminal code against broadcast obscenity, and the federal Cable Act of 1984 bars obscenity on cable TV.

Print media, including book publishers, have been the most vigorous defenders of the right to publish. The print media, of course, were the earliest media to be threatened with censorship, beginning with the philosopher Plato, who suggested in 387 B.C. that Homer's *Odyssey* be censored for immature readers.

Government efforts to block free expression happen on the local and federal levels.

Local Efforts

More than 2,000 years after Homer's *Odyssey* was threatened with censorship, Boston officials banned the sale of the April 1926 issue of H. L. Mencken's magazine *The American Mercury*. The local Watch and Ward Society had denounced a fictional story in the magazine as "salacious." The story featured "Hatrack," a prostitute whose clientele included members of various religious congregations who visited her after church.

In Boston, surrounded by his supporters, Mencken sold a copy of the magazine at a prearranged time to a member of the Watch and Ward. The chief of the Boston Vice Squad arrested Mencken and marched him to jail, where he spent the night before going to court the next morning. "Mencken passed an uneasy night," says Mencken's biographer Carl Bode, "knowing that he could be found guilty and perhaps even be imprisoned. . . . Returning to court he listened to Judge Parmenter's decision: 'I find that no offense has been committed and therefore dismiss the complaint.'"

Mencken spent $20,000 defending *The Mercury*, but according to Bode, "the net gain for both *The Mercury* and Mencken was great. *The Mercury* became the salient American magazine and Mencken the international symbol of freedom of speech."

NSL   National Security Letter.

Censorship   The practice of suppressing material that is considered morally, politically or otherwise objectionable.

IMPACT/Convergence

"Harlem Shake" Videos Lead to School Suspensions

By Hayley Tsukayama

I t's almost impossible to avoid a video of groups doing the "Harlem Shake" (at least the newest version of it) across the Web, but some students are finding that their 30-or-so seconds of online fame is coming at a fairly high cost.

According to the National Coalition against Censorship, about 100 students across the country have been suspended for making and posting their own version of the viral video on the Web. School districts have offered a variety of reasons for the suspensions, said NCAC Director Joan Bertin, with most saying that the videos, which feature suggestive dancing, are inappropriate. However, Bertin said, she believes that regardless of how the videos could be interpreted, decisions to suspend students and keep them out of class cross the line.

"It seems a rather disproportionate response by educators to something that, at most, I would characterize as teenage hijinks," Bertin said.

All technology shifts that give individuals a larger audience—from the printing press on, Bertin said—tend to make authority figures uncomfortable. More student censorship issues

Frederic Enneman/Demotix/Corbis

The National Coalition against Censorship reports that about 100 students in the United States were suspended for making and posting "Harlem Shake" videos on the Web, claiming the videos are inappropriate. Groups all over the world posted the videos. On February 23, 2013, people gathered at The Hague Central Station in the Netherlands to perform their version of the dance.

have emerged as young people gain more access to outlets for expression, such as the ability to post videos to YouTube, publish their thoughts on personal blogs and spread ideas through social media such as Facebook.

The best option, she thinks, would have been for schools to ignore the videos altogether.

Source: Excerpted from Hayley Tsukayama, "'Harlem Shake' Videos Lead to School Suspensions," March 4, 2013, washingtonpost.com.

Mencken was defending his magazine against local censorship. Until 1957, censorship in America remained a local issue because the U.S. Supreme Court had not considered a national censorship case.

U.S. Supreme Court Writes Obscenity Criteria

Today, censorship still is primarily a local issue, but two landmark Supreme Court cases—*Roth v. United States* and *Miller v. California*—established the major criteria for local censorship.

ROTH V. UNITED STATES. This decision in 1957 involved two separate cases. Samuel Roth was found guilty in New York of sending obscenity through the mail, and David S. Alberts was found guilty of selling obscene books in Beverly Hills. The case carries Roth's name because his name appeared first when the cases were combined for review. The U.S. Supreme Court upheld the guilty verdict and, according to legal scholar Ralph Holsinger, established several precedents:

- The First Amendment does not protect obscenity.

- Obscenity is defined as material "utterly without redeeming social importance."

- Sex and obscenity are not synonymous. Obscene material is material that appeals to "prurient [obsessively sexual] interest."

- A test of obscenity is "whether to the average person, applying contemporary community standards, the dominant theme of the material taken as a whole appeals to prurient interest." (This last description of obscenity has become known as the ***Roth test***.)

MILLER V. CALIFORNIA. In the late 1960s, a California court found Marvin Miller guilty of sending obscene, unsolicited advertising material through the mail. The case reached the U.S. Supreme Court in 1973. The decision described just which materials a state could censor and also set a three-part test for obscenity.

According to the Supreme Court, states may censor material that meets this three-part local test for obscenity. The local court, according to legal scholar Ralph Holsinger, must determine:

1. Whether "the average person, applying contemporary community standards," would find that the work, taken as a whole, appeals to the prurient interest.

2. Whether the work depicts or describes, in a patently offensive way, sexual conduct specifically defined by the applicable state law.

3. Whether the work, taken as a whole, lacks serious *L*iterary, *A*rtistic, *P*olitical or *S*cientific value—often called the ***LAPS test***.

The *Roth* and *Miller* cases together established a standard for obscenity, leaving the decision in specific obscenity challenges to local courts. The result is widely differing standards in different parts of the country because local juries and government regulators are free to decide what they consider offensive in their communities. Books and magazines that are available to young readers in some states may be unavailable in other states.

School Boards as Censors

Many censorship cases begin at schools and local-government boards, where parents' groups protest books, magazines and films that are available to students, such as these examples:

- Norwood High School in Colorado banned Rudolfo Anaya's award-winning book *Bless Me, Ultima* because of what the school considered "offensive language."

- A school board in New York removed 11 books from school libraries, including the novels *Slaughterhouse-Five* by Kurt Vonnegut and *Black Boy* by Richard Wright, plus a work of popular anthropology, *The Naked Ape* by Desmond Morris.

- A school district in Little Rock, Ark., removed Harry Potter books from its library because the school board claimed the tales of wizards and spells could harm schoolchildren.

- A school board in Minnesota banned four books, including *Are You There, God? It's Me, Margaret* by Judy Blume, a writer well known for her young adult books.

- The state of Alabama ordered 45 textbooks pulled from the shelves after a federal judge said the books promoted "secular humanism."

The American Library Association (ALA) fiercely opposes any attempt to censor or restrict access to information. Since 1990, the ALA and several other organizations have sponsored Banned Books Week to bring public attention to the issue of censorship.

Roth Test   A standard court test for obscenity, named for one of the defendants in an obscenity case.

LAPS Test   A yardstick for local obscenity judgments, which evaluates an artistic work's literary, artistic, political or scientific value.

"Censorship has no place in a free society," said ALA President Camila Alire. "Part of living in a democracy means respecting each other's differences and the right of all people to choose for themselves what they and their families read."

Most reported book challenges take place in schools and in public libraries, according to the ALA. These challenges usually are reversed when appealed, but while the specific issues are being decided, the books, magazines and videos are unavailable, and censorship efforts are growing nationwide. (See **Impact/Audience**, "Banned Books 2013: *Captain Underpants, Fifty Shades* Make List of Most-Challenged" and **Illustration 14.1**, "American Library Association's Top 10 Most Frequently Challenged Books," pp. 300–301.) For example, in August 2013 in an unprecedented move, the U.S. Army and Air Force announced that sex-themed magazines such as *Playboy* and *Penthouse* no longer will be sold at their military exchanges.

The *Hazelwood* Case

In 1988, the U.S. Supreme Court for the first time gave public school officials considerable freedom to limit what appears in student publications. The case, *Hazelwood v. Kuhlmeier*, became known as the *Hazelwood* case because the issues originated at Hazelwood High School in Hazelwood, Mo.

The high school paper, funded mostly from the school budget, was published as part of a journalism class. The principal at Hazelwood regularly reviewed the school paper before it was published, and in this case he deleted two articles the staff had written. One of the deleted articles was about student pregnancy and included interviews with three students who had become pregnant while attending school.

Although the article used pseudonyms instead of the students' names, the principal said he believed that the anonymity of the students was not sufficiently protected. He also believed that the girls' discussion of their use or nonuse of birth control was inappropriate for a school publication. By a vote of 5 to 3, the U.S. Supreme Court agreed.

The *Washington Post*, however, editorialized against the decision. "Even teenagers," the *Post* editorial said, "should be allowed to publish criticism, raise uncomfortable questions and spur debate on subjects such as pregnancy, AIDS and drug abuse that are too often a very real aspect of high school culture today."

Libel A false statement that damages a person's character or reputation by exposing that person to public ridicule or contempt.

The Hazelwood principal's action drew the attention of the *St. Louis Post-Dispatch*, which published the censored articles, bringing them a much wider audience than the students at Hazelwood High. Many states subsequently have adopted legislation to protect student newspapers from similar censorship. The Supreme Court decision is significant, however, because it may change the way local officials in some states monitor school publications.

LIBEL LAW OUTLINES THE MEDIA'S PUBLIC RESPONSIBILITY

"Americans have increasingly begun to seek the refuge and vindication of litigation," writes legal scholar Rodney A. Smolla in his book *Suing the Press*. "Words published by the media no longer roll over us without penetrating; instead, they sink in through the skin and work inner damage, and a consensus appears to be emerging that this psychic damage is serious and must be paid for." Four cases show why the media become targets of litigation:

1. In 1983, actress Carol Burnett sued the *National Enquirer* for $10 million for implying in an article that she was drinking too much and acting rude in a Washington, D.C., restaurant.

2. In late 1984, General William C. Westmoreland filed a $120 million suit against CBS, charging that he was defamed in a 1982 CBS documentary, *The Uncounted Enemy: A Vietnam Deception*.

3. In 1989, entertainer Wayne Newton was awarded $19.2 million in damages after he sued NBC-TV for a story that linked him to organized crime figures.

4. In September 2010, Republican U.S. Senate candidate Jeff Greene, a Florida real estate developer who lost the Democratic primary sued the *St. Petersburg Times* and *The Miami Herald* for $500 million, saying the newspapers' stories were part of "a coordinated and agreed upon plan to assassinate Greene's character."

These four cases involve the law of *libel*, which is one legal restraint on press freedom in the United States. (A libelous statement is one that unjustifiably exposes someone to ridicule or contempt.) The cases clearly indicate the media's legal vulnerability to charges of participating in and/or provoking irresponsible, damaging behavior. How can the country accommodate both the First Amendment concept of a free press and the right of the nation's citizens to keep their reputations from being unnecessarily damaged?

Sullivan Case Establishes a Libel Landmark

Modern interpretation of the free speech protections of the First Amendment began in 1964 with the landmark *New York Times v. Sullivan* case. With this case, the U.S. Supreme Court began a process that continues today to define how the press should operate in a free society. Many of today's arguments about the free press' role in a libel case derive from this decision.

The *Sullivan* case began in early 1960 in Alabama, where civil rights leader Dr. Martin Luther King, Jr., was arrested for perjury on his income tax form (a charge of which he was eventually acquitted). The Committee to Defend Martin Luther King bought a full-page ad in the March 29, 1960, *New York Times* that included statements about harassment of King by public officials and the police. The ad included a plea for money to support civil rights causes. Several notable people were listed in the ad as supporters, including singer Harry Belafonte, actor Sidney Poitier and former First Lady Eleanor Roosevelt.

L. B. Sullivan, who supervised the police and fire departments as commissioner of public affairs in Montgomery, Ala., demanded a retraction from *The Times* regarding the statements about King's harassment, even though he had not been named in the ad. *The Times* refused, and Sullivan sued *The Times* for libel in Montgomery County, where 35 copies of the March 29, 1960, *Times* had been distributed for sale. The trial in Montgomery County lasted three days, beginning on November 1, 1960. The jury found *The Times* guilty and awarded Sullivan $500,000.

Eventually, the case reached the U.S. Supreme Court. In deciding the suit, the Court said that although *The Times* might have been negligent because it did not spot some misstatements of fact that appeared in the ad, *The Times* did not deliberately lie—it did not act with what the Court called *actual malice*.

To prove libel of a public official, the official must show that the defendant published information with *knowledge of its falsity* or out of *reckless disregard* for whether it was true or false, the Court concluded. The *Sullivan* decision thus became the standard for subsequent libel suits: Public officials in a libel case must prove actual malice.

Redefining the *Sullivan* Decision

Three important cases further defined the *Sullivan* decision.

GERTZ V. ROBERT WELCH INC. The 1974 decision in Gertz v. Robert Welch Inc. established the concept that the expression of opinions is a necessary part of public

In the U.S., legal interpretation of free-speech protections of the First Amendment began with the landmark *New York Times v. Sullivan* case. L. B. Sullivan (second from right) appears in November 1960 with his attorneys. Although Sullivan's libel suit was successful in Alabama, the Supreme Court decided in 1964 that he had failed to prove malice on the part of *The New York Times.*

Bettmann/Corbis

debate, and so an opinion—an editorial or a restaurant review, for example—cannot be considered libelous. The Gertz case also expanded the definition of public official to public figure. Today, the difference between public figures and private figures is very important in libel suits.

People who are defined as private citizens by a court must show only that the libelous information is false and that the journalist or news organization acted negligently in presenting the information. Public figures must show not only that the libelous information is false but also that the information was published with actual malice—that the journalist or the news organization knew that the information was untrue or deliberately overlooked facts that would have proved the published information was untrue.

HERBERT V. LANDO. The 1979 decision in Herbert v. Lando established the concept that because a public figure suing for libel must prove actual malice, the public figure can use the discovery process (the process by which potential witnesses are questioned under oath before the trial to help define the issues to be resolved at the trial) to determine a reporter's state of mind in preparing the story. Because of this decision, today reporters are sometimes asked in a libel suit to identify their sources and to give up their notes and the tapes of the interviews they conducted to write their stories.

MASSON V. NEW YORKER MAGAZINE. In 1991, the U.S. Supreme Court reinstated a $10 million libel suit brought against *The New Yorker* magazine by

IMPACT/Audience

Banned Books 2013: *Captain Underpants, Fifty Shades* Make List of Most-Challenged

By Hillel Italie, Associated Press

NEW YORK—Here's a list *Fifty Shades of Grey* was destined to make: The books most likely to be removed from school and library shelves.

On Monday, E L James' multimillion-selling erotic trilogy placed No. 4 on the American Library Association's annual study of "challenged books," works subject to complaints from parents, educators and other members of the public. The objections: Offensive language, and, of course, graphic sexual content.

No. 1 was a not a story of the bedroom, but the bathroom, Dav Pilkey's *Captain Underpants* books (Offensive language, unsuited for age group). "It's pretty exciting to be on a list that frequently features Mark Twain, Harper Lee, and Maya Angelou," Pilkey said in a statement. "But I worry that some parents might see this list and discourage their kids from reading *Captain Underpants*, even though they have not had a chance to read the books themselves."

The library association's Office for Intellectual Freedom defines a challenge as a "formal, written complaint filed with a library or school requesting that a book or other material be restricted or removed because of its content or appropriateness." The office received 464 challenges last year, a jump of more 25 percent from 2011, but still low compared to the 1980s and '90s.

"One reason we think the number went up in 2012 is that we made challenges easier to report by including a portal on our Web page," said Barbara M. Jones, director of the OIF.

The *Fifty Shades* books were released last spring and public libraries in Georgia, Florida and elsewhere soon pulled the racy romance

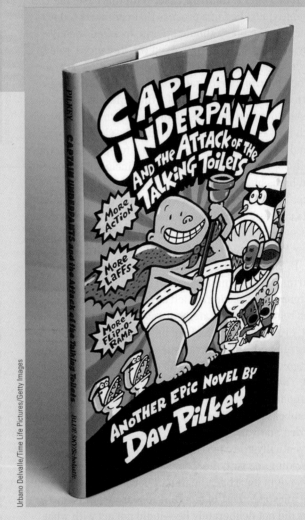

Urbano Delvalle/Time Life Pictures/Getty Images

Each year the American Library Association, along with several other organizations, sponsors Banned Books Week to bring public attention to the issue of censorship. Listed first on the 2013 Top 10 Most Frequently Challenged Books was the *Captain Underpants* series.

trilogy or decided not to order the books, saying they were too steamy or too poorly written. Local library representatives at the time denounced the novels as "semi-pornographic" and unfit for "community standards."

Young adult star John Green was on, for *Looking for Alaska* (Offensive language, sexually

(continued)

Illustration 14.1

American Library Association's Top 10 Most Frequently Challenged Books

Source: Excerpted from Hillel Italie, "Banned Books 2013: *Captain Underpants, Fifty Shades* Make List of Most Challenged," Associated Press, April 15, 2013, and American Library Association: ala.org.

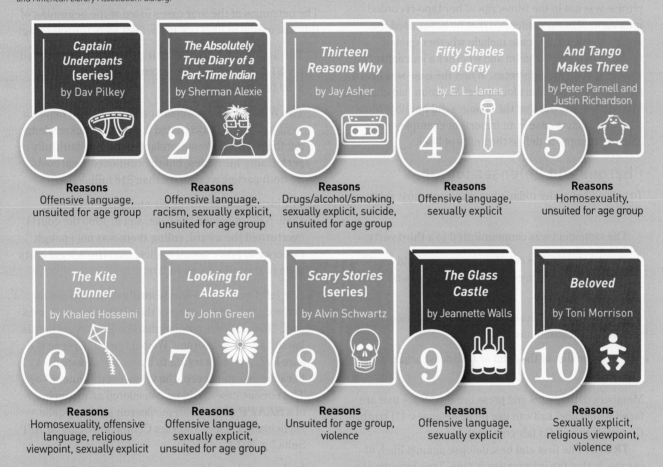

1 *Captain Underpants (series)* by Dav Pilkey
Reasons
Offensive language, unsuited for age group

2 *The Absolutely True Diary of a Part-Time Indian* by Sherman Alexie
Reasons
Offensive language, racism, sexually explicit, unsuited for age group

3 *Thirteen Reasons Why* by Jay Asher
Reasons
Drugs/alcohol/smoking, sexually explicit, suicide, unsuited for age group

4 *Fifty Shades of Gray* by E. L. James
Reasons
Offensive language, sexually explicit

5 *And Tango Makes Three* by Peter Parnell and Justin Richardson
Reasons
Homosexuality, unsuited for age group

6 *The Kite Runner* by Khaled Hosseini
Reasons
Homosexuality, offensive language, religious viewpoint, sexually explicit

7 *Looking for Alaska* by John Green
Reasons
Offensive language, sexually explicit, unsuited for age group

8 *Scary Stories (series)* by Alvin Schwartz
Reasons
Unsuited for age group, violence

9 *The Glass Castle* by Jeannette Walls
Reasons
Offensive language, sexually explicit

10 *Beloved* by Toni Morrison
Reasons
Sexually explicit, religious viewpoint, violence

explicit). The *Captain Underpants* books, which Green said he's currently reading to his 3-year-old son, have long been debated among parents and educators. Some praise the books because they encourage boys to read, others criticize them for their toilet humor and irreverent attitude; the title character is a superhero devised by two 4th graders about their grouchy principal, Mr. Krupp.

"I don't see these books as encouraging disrespect for authority. Perhaps they demonstrate the value of questioning authority," Pilkey said. "Some of the authority figures in the *Captain Underpants* books are villains. They are bullies and they do vicious things."

The president of Scholastic's trade division, Ellie Berger, said in a statement that the "appearance of Captain Underpants on the 2012 ALA list coincides with the publication of Dav Pilkey's first new *Captain Underpants* book in six years and the series' return to national bestseller lists—both of which are evidence that this longtime bestselling series continues to inspire a love of reading (and underpants) for a new generation of kids."

psychoanalyst Jeffrey M. Masson. Masson charged that author Janet Malcolm libeled him in two articles in *The New Yorker* and in a book when she deliberately misquoted him. Malcolm contended that the quotations she used were tape-recorded or were written in her notes.

Malcolm wrote, for example, that Mr. Masson said, "I was like an intellectual gigolo." However, this exact phrase was not in the transcript of her tape-recorded interview. Masson contended that he never used the phrase. Issues in the case include whether quoted material must be verbatim and whether a journalist can change grammar and syntax. When the case was heard again in 1994, the court found that Malcolm had changed Masson's words but that the changes did not libel Masson. The *Masson* case is an important example of the court's attempts to define the limits of libel.

Charges and Defenses for Libel

To prove libel under today's law, someone must show that:

- The statement was communicated to a third party.

- People who read or saw the statement would be able to identify the person, even if that person was not actually named.

- The statement injured the person's reputation or income or caused mental anguish.

- The journalist or the print or broadcast organization is at fault.

Members of the press and press organizations that are faced with a libel suit can use three defenses: (1) truth, (2) privilege and (3) fair comment.

TRUTH. The first and best defense against libel, of course, is that the information is true. True information, although sometimes damaging, cannot be considered libelous. Publishing true information, however, can still be an invasion of privacy, as explained later in this chapter. Furthermore, truth is a successful defense only if truth is proved to the satisfaction of a judge or jury.

PRIVILEGE. The press is free to report what is discussed during legislative and court proceedings, even though the information presented in the proceedings by witnesses and others may be untrue or damaging. This is called *qualified privilege*.

Qualified Privilege The freedom of the press to report what is discussed during legislative and court proceedings.

SLAPP Strategic lawsuit against public participation.

FAIR COMMENT. The courts also have carefully protected the press' freedom to present opinions. Because opinions cannot be proved true or false, the press is free to comment on public issues and to laud a play or pan a movie, for example.

Legal Outcomes Reflect Mixed Results

The outcomes of the four cases listed at the beginning of this discussion of libel law (on p. 298) were the following:

1. The jury in the Carol Burnett case originally awarded her $1.6 million, but the amount was reduced to $150,000 on appeal.

2. The William Westmoreland case was settled before it went to the jury. CBS issued a statement acknowledging that General Westmoreland had acted faithfully in performing his duties, but the combined legal costs for both parties were more than $18 million.

3. The jury awarded Wayne Newton $19.2 million in 1989. NBC appealed the case, and in 1990 the courts overturned the award, ruling there was not enough evidence to prove actual malice, but NBC's legal costs were in the millions of dollars.

4. The Jeff Greene case was dismissed. In responding to the charges, the editor of the St. Petersburg Times said, "It is our firm opinion that the allegations in this lawsuit are preposterous. We believe Jeff Greene is a sore loser and he's trying to blame the newspapers because he can't accept the verdict of the voters." The Greene case could be considered an example of a *SLAPP* suit—*strategic lawsuit against public participation*. (See "Internet Comments Bring SLAPP Suits," p. 303.)

In three of these four cases, the courts faulted members of the media for their reporting methods, even when members of the media and the media companies were not found legally responsible. All four cases show that journalists and media organizations must always be diligent about their responsibilities, and there are serious financial and professional consequences for news organizations that forget to act responsibly and heed the law.

Most successful libel judgments eventually are reversed or reduced when they are appealed. Often the major cost of a libel suit for the media is not the actual award but the defense lawyers' fees. Large media organizations carry libel insurance, but a small newspaper, magazine, book publisher, broadcast station or Internet site may not be able to afford the insurance or the legal costs.

"While most excessive trial awards are reduced in post-trial rulings or on appeal, the expense of litigating can be daunting. The danger is that excessive damage awards, and the cost of litigating and appealing them, may give editors and publishers pause when covering controversial people and topics," says Sandra S. Baron, executive director of the Libel Defense Resource Center.

Internet Comments Bring SLAPP Suits

Bloggers and other Internet users who post critical comments on a Web site like Facebook, Twitter and Yelp today may find themselves the target of what lawyers call a SLAPP. This is a common tactic of businesses and government officials because suing someone for defamation can intimidate the person with the prospect of an expensive court battle against a well-financed opponent.

Today, the Internet makes a person's critical comments available instantly, and some companies and public officials are threatening libel suits against their critics. There are 27 states with anti-SLAPP laws, which may require that the person who brings the suit pay the combined legal costs if the suit is dismissed.

Federal anti-SLAPP legislation, which would make protections uniform across the country, is being debated in Congress. "Just as petition and free speech rights are so important that they require specific constitutional protections, they are also important enough to justify uniform national protections against SLAPPs," said Mark Goldowitz, director of the California Anti-SLAPP Project.

INVASION OF PRIVACY DEFINED FOUR WAYS

The public seems to think invasion of privacy is one of the media's worst faults. However, libel suits are much more common in the United States than suits about invasion of privacy. Because there is no U.S. Supreme Court decision covering privacy like *The New York Times v. Sullivan* covers libel, each of the states has its own privacy protections for citizens and its own restrictions on how reporters can get the news and what can be published.

Privacy is an ethical issue as well as a legal one. (See **Chapter 15** for a discussion of the ethics of privacy.) Generally, the law says the media can be guilty of invasion of privacy in four ways:

1. By intruding on a person's physical or mental solitude.

2. By publishing or disclosing embarrassing personal facts.

3. By giving someone publicity that places the person in a false light.

4. By using someone's name or likeness for commercial benefit.

If they are successful, people who initiate privacy cases can be awarded monetary damages to compensate them for the wrongdoing. However, very few invasion of privacy cases succeed.

Physical or Mental Solitude

The courts in most states have recognized that a person has a right not to be pursued by the news media unnecessarily. A reporter can photograph or question someone on a public street or at a public event, but a person's home and office are private. For this reason, many photographers request that someone who is photographed in a private situation sign a release form, designating how the photograph can be used.

THE RESIDENTS OF SOHAN ARE BEGGING FOR PRIVACY ...GET IT ON PAGES THREE FOUR SIX AND EIGHT AND I WANT **PICTURES!**

Fran, Cartoon Stock

One notable case establishing this right of privacy is *Galella v. Onassis*. Jacqueline Onassis, widow of President John F. Kennedy, charged that Ron Galella, a freelance photographer, was pursuing her unnecessarily. He had used a telephoto lens to photograph her on private property, and he had pursued her children at private schools. In 1973, Galella was ordered to stay 25 feet away from Onassis and 30 feet away from her children.

Embarrassing Personal Facts

The personal facts the media use to report a story should be newsworthy, according to the courts. If a public official is caught traveling with her boyfriend on taxpayers' money while her husband stays at home, information about the boyfriend is essential to the story. If the public official is reported to have contracted AIDS from her boyfriend, the information probably is not relevant to the story and could be protected under this provision of privacy law.

In reality, however, public officials enjoy few legal protections from reporting about their private lives. Information available from public records, such as court proceedings, is not considered private. If the public official's husband testifies in court about his wife's disease, this information could be reported.

Bartnicki v. Vopper

In an important case for the press, *Bartnicki v. Vopper*, the U.S. Supreme Court in 2001 reaffirmed the media's right to broadcast information and to comment on that information, no matter how the information was obtained.

The case resulted from a cell phone conversation between Pennsylvania teachers' union negotiator Gloria Bartnicki and Anthony Kane, the union's president. The union was in the middle of negotiating a teachers' contract. During the conversation (which was intercepted and taped without Bartnicki's or Kane's knowledge), Kane is heard to say that if the school board didn't increase its offer, "We're going to have to go to their homes . . . to blow off their front porches."

A local activist gave the tape to radio station WILK-AM, and talk-show host Fred Vopper (who uses the on-air name Fred Williams) aired the tape. Bartnicki and Kane sued Vopper under the federal wiretap law, which provides civil damages and criminal prosecution for someone who disseminates information that is illegally intercepted. The case pitted the public's right to know versus the erosion of personal privacy by new technologies.

U.S. Supreme Court Justice John Paul Stevens wrote the opinion for the 6-3 majority that "a stranger's illegal conduct does not suffice to remove the First Amendment shield from speech about a matter of public concern." In this decision, the Court again reaffirmed the press' right to report information in the public interest.

False Light

A writer who portrays someone in a fictional version of actual events should be especially conscious of *false*

False Light   The charge that what was implied in a story about someone is incorrect.

---

light litigation. People who believe that what a writer or photographer *implies* about them is incorrect (even if the portrayal is flattering) can bring a false-light suit.

The best-known false-light suit is the first, *Time Inc. v. Hill*. In 1955, *Life* magazine published a story about a Broadway play, *The Desperate Hours*, which portrayed someone taking a hostage. The author of the play said he based it on several real-life incidents. One of these involved the Hill family, a husband and wife and their five children who had been taken hostage in their Philadelphia home by three escaped convicts. The Hills told police the convicts had treated them courteously, but the Hills were frightened by the events and eventually moved to Connecticut.

When *Life* decided to do the story about the play, the cast went to the Hills' old home, where *Life* photographed the actors in scenes from the play—one son being roughed up by the convicts and a daughter biting a convict's hand. None of these incidents had happened to the Hills, but *Life* published the photographs along with a review of the play.

The Hills sued Time Inc., which owned *Life* magazine, for false-light invasion of privacy and won $75,000, which eventually was reduced to $30,000. When the case went to the U.S. Supreme Court, the Court refused to uphold the decision, saying the Hills must prove *actual malice*. The Hills dropped the case, but the establishment of actual malice as a requirement in false-light cases was important.

In 1974, in *Cantrell v. Forest City Publishing Co.*, the U.S. Supreme Court held that a reporter for the Cleveland *Plain Dealer* had wrongly portrayed the widow of an Ohio man who was killed when a bridge collapsed. The story talked about the woman as if the reporter had interviewed her, although he had only interviewed her children. She was awarded $60,000 in her false-light suit, and the Supreme Court upheld the verdict.

"Eight justices held that a properly instructed jury had come to the correct conclusion in finding actual malice," writes legal scholar Ralph L. Holsinger. "There was enough evidence within the story to prove that the reporter's word portrait of Mrs. Cantrell was false. The story indicated that he had seen her and perhaps had talked with her. He had done neither." Only a few false-light cases have been successful, but the lesson for the press is that portraying events and people truthfully avoids the problem altogether.

Right of Publicity

This facet of privacy law is especially important in the advertising and public relations industries. A portable toilet seems a strange fixture to use to establish a point of law, but a case brought by former *Tonight Show* host

Johnny Carson demonstrates how the right of publicity protects someone's name from being used to make money without that person's permission.

In *Carson v. Here's Johnny Portable Toilets*, Carson charged, in 1983, that a Michigan manufacturer of portable toilets misappropriated Carson's name to sell the toilets. The manufacturer named his new line Here's Johnny Portable Toilets and advertised them with the phrase "The World's Foremost Commodian." Carson said he did not want to be associated with the product although he would be. Since he began hosting *The Tonight Show* in 1957, he said, he had been introduced by the phrase "Here's Johnny." The court agreed that "Here's Johnny" violated Carson's right of publicity.

The right of publicity can apply to a person's picture on a poster or name in an advertisement. In some cases, this right is covered even after the person dies, so that the members of the immediate family of a well-known entertainer, for example, are the only people who can authorize the use of the entertainer's name or likeness.

DEBATE CONTINUES OVER FAIR TRIAL, COURTROOM ACCESS AND SHIELD LAWS

The answers to three other questions that bear on press freedoms and individual rights remain discretionary for the courts:

1. When does media coverage influence a jury so much that a defendant's right to a fair trial is jeopardized?

2. How much access should the media be granted during a trial?

3. Should journalists be required to reveal information they obtained in confidence while reporting a story if a court decides that information is necessary to the judicial process?

Fair Trial

The best-known decision affecting prejudicial press coverage of criminal cases is *Sheppard v. Maxwell*. In 1954, Dr. Samuel Sheppard of Cleveland was sentenced to life imprisonment for murdering his wife. His conviction followed reams of newspaper stories, many of which proclaimed his guilt before the jury had decided the case. The jurors, who went home each evening, were told by the judge not to read newspapers or pay attention to broadcast reports, but no one monitored what the jurors did.

Twelve years later, lawyer F. Lee Bailey took Sheppard's trial to the U.S. Supreme Court, where the conviction was overturned on the premise that Sheppard had

been a victim of a biased jury. In writing the decision, Justice Tom C. Clark prescribed several remedies. He said that the reporters should have been limited to certain areas in the courtroom, that the news media should not have been allowed to interview the witnesses and that the court should have forbidden statements outside of the courtroom.

Courtroom Access

The outcome of the *Sheppard* case led to many courtroom experiments with restrictions on the press. The most widespread practices were restraining (gag) orders and closed proceedings. With a gag order, the judge limited what the press could report. Closed proceedings excluded the press from the courtroom. But since 1980, several court cases have overturned most of these limitations. Today the press is rarely excluded completely from courtroom proceedings, and the exclusion lasts only as long as it takes the news organization to appeal to a higher court for access.

Joshua Lott/Getty Images

Whether to allow cameras in the courtroom is a state-by-state decision. On July 23, 2012, Arapahoe County District Attorney Carol Chambers talks to reporters before going into a hearing for suspect James Holmes, charged with killing 12 people and injuring 58 in a movie theatre in Aurora, Colo. Cameras were not allowed in the proceedings.

While reporters usually gain access, the presence of cameras in the courtroom is a sticky issue between judges, who want to avoid the disruption of cameras, and broadcast news people, who want to photograph what is going on. The U.S. Supreme Court, for example, never

IMPACT/Audience

Illustration 14.2

**Cameras in the Courtroom:
A State-by-State Guide**

Most states allow at least some camera access to courtroom proceedings.
The U.S. Supreme Court does not allow cameras.

Source: Radio-Television Digital News Association, rtnda.org/pages/media_items/cameras-in-the-court-a-state-by
-state-guide55.php.

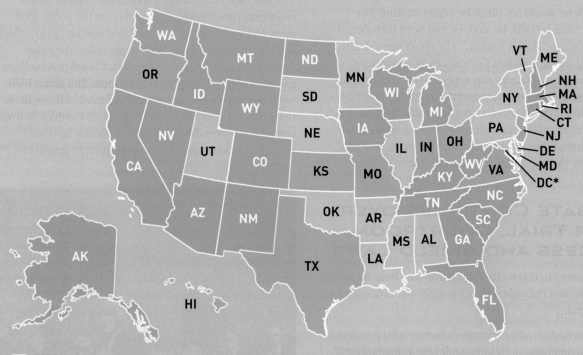

■ **TIER I:** States that allow the most coverage.

■ **TIER II:** States with restrictions prohibiting coverage of important types of cases, or prohibiting
coverage of all or large categories of witnesses who object to coverage of their testimony.

□ **TIER III:** States that allow appellate coverage only, or that have such restricting trial coverage
rules that essentially prevent coverage.

*The District of Columbia is the only jurisdiction that prohibits trial and appellate coverage entirely.

allows cameras. In some high-profile cases, cameras
have been allowed to record complete trials. In 1994, for
example, Court TV broadcast the entire murder trial of
O. J. Simpson. But in 2012, cameras were not allowed in
the proceedings against James Holmes, a suspect in the
Aurora, Colo., theater shootings, where 12 people died
and 58 were injured.

Whether to allow cameras in the courtroom is a state-
by-state decision. (See **Illustration 14.2**, "Cameras in
the Courtroom: A State-by-State Guide.") Some states

allow cameras during civil but not criminal trials. Other
states try to completely limit access. The U.S. courts and
the press are not yet completely comfortable partners.

Shield Laws

Traditionally, U.S. courts have been reluctant to ask journalists to reveal information they gather from confidential sources as part of their reporting on stories. In 1972,
in *Branzburg v. Hayes*, the U.S. Supreme Court ruled for
the first time that journalists do not have a constitutional

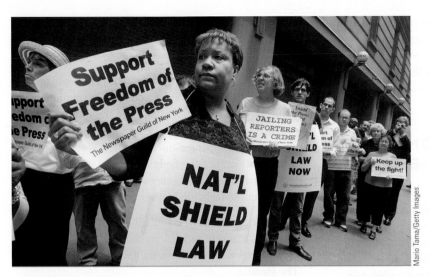

After several court challenges to reporters' ability to keep their sources confidential, journalists lobbied for a national shield law in front of *The New York Times* building in 2005. Although many states have shield laws to protect journalists' sources, there is no federal shield law.

privilege to refuse to testify but that there was "merit in leaving state legislatures free, within First Amendment limits, to fashion their own standards."

According to the Congressional Research Service, "31 states and the District of Columbia have recognized a journalist's privilege through enactment of press *'shield laws,'* which protect the relationship between reporters, their source, and sometimes, the information that may be communicated in that relationship." This means, for example, that reporters in California, Alaska and Colorado have state shield law protection, but reporters in Texas, South Dakota and Connecticut do not. There is no federal shield law that protects all U.S. journalists equally.

The role of shield laws in protecting journalists became particularly important in 2004–2005, when *New York Times* reporter Judith Miller refused to testify before a federal grand jury that was investigating whether Bush administration officials leaked the identity of a Central Intelligence Agency operative, Valerie Plame. In the summer of 2004, Miller was called before a Washington, D.C., grand jury that was investigating the leak of Plame's name; in the fall of 2004, Miller was held in contempt and served 85 days in jail the summer of 2005. In October 2005, Miller revealed to the grand jury that her source was I. Lewis Libby, Vice President Dick Cheney's chief of staff.

Even though Miller said she had received Libby's permission to reveal his name, which released her from her confidentiality agreement, some lawyers and

journalists expressed concern that Miller's actions had weakened journalists' lengthy legal history of protecting their sources.

Eventually Libby, who had testified to a grand jury about the case, was found guilty of perjury and obstruction of justice, but President Bush commuted his sentence in 2007.

After the Miller case, some members of Congress introduced legislation to create a federal shield law to protect journalists on a national level, but Congress never seriously considered the issue. This leaves journalists still at the mercy of individual state shield laws. (Valerie Plame's experiences formed the basis for the 2010 movie *Fair Game*, starring Naomi Watts and Sean Penn.)

FCC REGULATES BROADCAST AND CABLE

All the American media are expected to abide by the country's laws. Regulation of the media comes from government agencies that oversee aspects of the media business. The print industry is not regulated specifically by any government agency. The largest single area of regulation comes from the Federal Communications Commission (FCC), which oversees broadcasting. Other regulating agencies, such as the Federal Trade Commission, scrutinize specific areas that relate to the media, such as advertising.

Since 1927, the rationale for broadcast regulation has been that the airwaves belong to the public and that broadcasters are trustees operating in the public interest. The history of U.S. broadcast regulation can be traced to government's early attempt to organize the airwaves. The FCC, based in Washington, D.C., now has five commissioners who are appointed by the president and are approved by the Senate. Each commissioner serves a five-year term, and the president appoints the chairperson.

Today FCC regulation touches almost every aspect of station operations. Most important, U.S. broadcast stations

Shield Laws Laws that protect journalists from revealing their sources and the information that is communicated between journalists and their sources in a journalistic relationship.

must be licensed by the FCC to operate. Because the print media are unregulated by any government agency, the government exercises more direct control over the broadcast media than over the print media. Like the print media, broadcasters must also follow court rulings on issues such as libel, obscenity and the right of privacy.

Telecommunications Act of 1996 Changes the Marketplace

On February 8, 1996, President Clinton signed the Telecommunications Act of 1996, the most far-reaching reform in U.S. government regulation of mass media since the creation of the FCC. The act affects all aspects of the media industries, especially broadcast, cable, telephone and computer networks. The act is transforming the nation's media industries.

The last time the government intervened in a similar way to affect the development of the media business was in 1934, when Congress created the FCC to regulate broadcasting in the "public interest, convenience and necessity." The Telecommunications Act, however, is an extension of the philosophy of deregulation—that free competition, with less government regulation, eventually will improve consumers' choices, lower costs and encourage investment in new technologies. Critics, however, say the act helps large media companies get bigger because only the large companies can afford to upgrade their equipment and delivery systems to take advantage of new markets.

This philosophy of open competition, as established in the Telecommunications Act of 1996, governs the media industries in the 21st century. The strategies of providing multiple services and targeting select users are two examples of the effects of the act today.

Goal: To Sell Consumers "The Bundle"

"It's War!" declared *The Wall Street Journal* on September 16, 1996. The battlefield was telecommunications, and the goal was the *bundle*. In telecommunications, this term describes the combination of services the media industries can now offer. Following passage of the 1996 Telecommunications Act, large companies began

Bundle   The combination of telecommunications services that the media industries can offer consumers.

RBOC   Regional Bell Operating Companies.

positioning themselves to deliver the combination of telecommunications services that they think consumers want. The *Journal* reported:

> Thanks to a combination of deregulation and new technologies, war has broken out in the communications market. Everybody has joined the fray—long-distance telephone giants, the regional [local telephone] Bell companies and the cable-TV operators, the satellite outfits, the fledgling digital wireless phone firms and the Internet service providers. Even your old-fashioned power company.
>
> And they all want the same thing: to invade one another's markets and sell you one another's products and services. In short, they want to sell you The Bundle.

Your long-distance telephone company, such as AT&T or Sprint, would like to become your local telephone company, as well as your Internet service provider. This same long-distance company also wants to provide your TV programs, replacing the local cable system, adding these charges to your monthly telephone bill. Local telephone companies, the Regional Bell Operating Companies (*RBOC*), want their slice of revenue, too.

Lawrence K. Ho, *Los Angeles Times*/October 2, 2011

The Telecommunications Act of 1996 removed many regulations governing the services telecommunications companies provide. A telecommunications company can now offer Internet, telephone and TV together, called a "bundle," for power users, such as the Hartman family of Seal Beach, CA.

"The act so completely dismantles the existing regulatory structure that the telecommunications industry begins to look like a free-for-all," says Howard Anderson, founder and manager of Yankee Group, a Boston-based consulting firm. "Everyone is already trying to build multimedia networks to deliver everything from telephone and mobile services to Internet access and video-on-demand."

Targeting the Power User

This bundling of services means that you can pay one monthly bill for several types of media services to a single company, which, of course, dramatically increases that company's portion of media revenue. "The goal for these companies is twofold," says Richard Siber, a wireless analyst for Andersen Consulting in Boston. "One is locking in a customer for life and providing one-stop shopping. And the other is revenue maximization, getting you to use their products more and more."

BusinessWeek magazine called this intense competition for customers a "telescramble." The primary target is the so-called power user, someone who uses a lot of media at home or in business. While the average consumer spends about $100 a month on media services, an upscale customer averages $300 a month, or $3,000 to $3,500 a year.

The Telecommunications Act of 1996 created this battlefield for consumers' attention with huge financial incentives for the winners. The economic future of every media company in the country is, in some way, being affected by this battle. That is why it is so important to understand this single piece of legislation.

DEREGULATION UNLEASHES THE MEDIA

The major provisions of the Telecommunications Act affect telecommunications, broadcast and cable. The Communications Decency Act, which is part of the Telecommunications Act, attempts to regulate access to cable and television programming and monitor the content of computer networks, including the Internet.

Creates a Goal of Universal Service

The Telecommunications Act of 1996 established, for the first time in federal legislation, a goal of universal service—meaning that, as a matter of public policy, everyone in the United States should have access to affordable telecommunications services. The intent of the act is to make telecommunications available to everyone.

The FCC, of course, defines which type of access is offered in the "universal service" package. Does universal service mean only a telephone, or should universal service include access to the Internet? The FCC decides what exactly constitutes universal service and whether

access to the Internet will be part of that service guarantee, in an effort to use telecommunications to improve the economies of rural areas and central cities, as well as the rest of the nation.

Deregulates Free Media

The Telecommunications Act of 1996 continued a policy of deregulation of commercial radio and television ownership that began in the 1980s. Radio and over-the-air broadcast television are viewed as "free media." Unlike cable stations and satellite companies, which require extra equipment and charge consumers for their services, over-the-air broadcasting is available to anyone with a radio or television—and 99 percent of U.S. households have a TV set. Over-the-air broadcasting offers the largest potential audience for free media.

Relaxes Ownership and Licensing Rules

Previously, broadcast companies were allowed to own only 12 television stations. The act eliminated limits on the number of television stations one company could own and instead used a station's potential audience to measure ownership limits. The act said existing television networks (such as NBC and ABC) can begin new networks, but they cannot buy an existing network. NBC cannot buy ABC, for example, but NBC could begin a second network of its own, such as NBC2.

Before the act passed, radio broadcasters were allowed to own 20 AM or 20 FM radio stations nationwide. The act removed the limit on the number of radio stations a company can own, and in each market, the number of stations that one owner can hold depends on the size of the market. In a large market with 45 or more commercial radio stations, for example, a broadcaster may own 8 stations; in a market with 14 stations, a broadcaster may own up to 5 stations.

The act also allows *cross-ownership*. This means that companies can own television and radio stations in the same broadcast market. Companies also can own broadcast and cable outlets in the same market.

In 1999, the FCC further relaxed TV station ownership rules by allowing one broadcast company to own two TV stations in the same market, as long as eight

Cross-Ownership The practice of one company owning TV and radio stations in the same broadcast market.

"These new regulations will fundamentally change the way we get around them."

Peter C. Vey/Cartoonbank.com

other stations with different owners are still operating in the market after the deal. In 2002, the FCC began considering further relaxation of the ownership rules that, for example, would allow broadcasters to own newspapers. In 2010, a federal court lifted the ban on media cross-ownership altogether. The FCC is expected to announce a decision on cross-ownership rules in 2013.

In 2003, the FCC removed even more restrictions on broadcast ownership, making it easier for media companies to expand the number of stations they own, and included the provision that allows one company to own TV stations that reach 35 percent of the U.S. population. Today, the 35 percent limit still applies, although the industry continues to lobby to reduce the limitation or remove it completely.

The FCC licenses every broadcast station in the country—television and radio. In the past, renewal was a very complicated, rigorous process. Television stations were required to renew their licenses every five years and radio stations every seven. The Telecommunications Act extended the renewal period for both radio and television to every eight years.

Creates Local Phone Competition

Due to deregulation, cable, satellite and telephone companies today are competing to deliver telecommunications services to home customers.

Telco An abbreviation for "telephone company."

To encourage competition for delivery of video services, the Telecommunications Act of 1996 allowed local telephone companies to get into the video delivery business. The act repealed the FCC's "telco-cable cross-ownership" restrictions (***telco*** is an abbreviation for "telephone company"). Local telephone companies can deliver video services either by an agreement with a cable operator or by creating their own delivery system. In turn, the cable companies were allowed to enter the local telephone business. Large cable companies also may deliver new types of telephone services, such as carrying messages to and from wireless cell phones.

To add to competition in the local telephone business, the act also allowed long-distance carriers to offer local telephone service. Within two months of the act's passage, the long-distance carrier AT&T filed to be allowed to offer local telephone service in all 50 states. "If we get this right," said former FCC Chairman Reed Hundt, "you'll be buying communications services like shoes. Different styles, different vendors."

Until the market for telecommunications stabilizes, however, the choices are confusing for consumers and frustrating for people in the media industries who are trying to position themselves for a new future that isn't yet completely defined.

Ends Cable Rate Regulation

In an attempt to control spiraling cable charges to consumers, Congress passed the 1992 Cable Act to regulate rates. The cable companies, facing competition from the local telephone companies, argued that Congress should remove rate regulation to allow them to compete and to help raise cable income.

The Telecommunications Act of 1996 removed most rate regulation for all cable companies. All that remains is regulation to monitor the "basic tier" of cable service, often called "basic cable."

CONGRESS ATTEMPTS TO USE COMMUNICATIONS DECENCY ACT

Along with the major provisions of the Telecommunications Act to increase competition, Congress added several provisions to control content. These provisions, together called the Communications Decency Act (CDA), attempted to define and control users' access to specific types of programs and content. However, most provisions of the act subsequently were overruled by the Supreme Court as violations of the First Amendment.

Addresses Indecent Material on the Internet

The Communications Decency Act made it a felony to send indecent material over computer networks. The CDA also prohibited using a telecommunications device to:

- Make or initiate any communication that is obscene, lewd, lascivious, filthy or indecent with intent to annoy, abuse, threaten or harass another person.

- Make or make available obscene communication.

- Make or make available an indecent communication to minors.

- Transmit obscene material—including material concerning abortion—for any indecent or immoral use.

The act relied on a very broad definition of the word *indecent*, and courts have generally ruled that such speech is protected under the First Amendment. Under the act's provisions, violators could be charged with a felony and fined up to $250,000. More than 50 opponents of the act's indecency provision, including the American Library Association and the American Civil Liberties Union, went to court in Philadelphia to challenge the law.

On June 12, 1996, the three-judge panel unanimously declared that the Internet indecency provision was unconstitutional, and the judges blocked enforcement of the law. They issued a restraining order, which meant that the Internet indecency provision could not be enforced and that violations could not even be investigated.

The federal government had argued the Internet should be regulated like radio and television, but the judges said material on the Internet deserves the same protection as printed material. In presenting the court's opinion, Judge Stewart R. Dalzell made very strong arguments defending access to the Internet. "Just as the strength of the Internet is chaos," Judge Dalzell wrote, "so the strength of our liberty depends upon the chaos and cacophony of the unfettered speech the First Amendment protects."

In 1997, the U.S. Supreme Court struck down the indecency provision of the Communications Decency Act, making it much harder for Congress to limit Internet access in the future. What is interesting is that the courts are defining and protecting an electronic delivery system—the Internet—as if it were a print medium.

This effort is important because Congress and the president, through the FCC, historically have regulated the broadcast industries, but none of the regulations that apply to the broadcast media also apply to print. The content of the print media, by law and by practice, has historically remained unregulated because of the First Amendment's protection of free expression.

Child Online Protection Act Fails

In 1998, after the U.S. Supreme Court found the indecency provision of the Communications Decency Act unconstitutional, Congress passed the Child Online Protection Act (*COPA*), aimed at preventing minors from getting access to sexually explicit online material, even though the material is legal for adults. Congress based the legislation on the idea that the government has a responsibility to protect children from content that is legal for adults but could be considered harmful to minors.

Congress wanted to fine offenders $150,000 for each day they violated the law and face up to six months in prison. Among the law's provisions was the requirement that libraries and schools that receive federal funding must install filtering software on public computers. Several organizations, including the American Library Association and the American Civil Liberties Union, immediately challenged the law in court on First Amendment grounds, saying the law was too restrictive. In 2002, the U.S. Supreme Court agreed that Congress had no authority to limit Internet access.

Supreme Court Upholds Internet Filters for Public Libraries

One year later, however, the Supreme Court upheld another law that said that libraries that take federal funds must equip their computers with antipornography filters. The case was defended in court on behalf of 13-year-old Emalyn Rood, who logged onto the Internet in an Oregon library to research information on lesbianism, and Mark Brown, who found information about his mother's breast cancer on a Philadelphia library computer—information that might have been blocked by a commonly used Internet filter.

In a close 5-4 decision in *United States v. American Library Association*, the U.S. Supreme Court said the requirement for Internet filters is "a valid exercise of Congress' spending power." This decision allows the U.S. government to require Internet filters at libraries

---

COPA   Child Online Protection Act. A law aimed at preventing minors from getting access to sexually explicit online material.

that receive federal funding. Librarians argued that Internet filters are a form of censorship that blocks valuable information from people who need it.

TV Industry Agrees to Ratings and the V-Chip

Under pressure from Congress, television executives agreed to implement a voluntary ratings system for television programs by January 1997. The new ratings system *applies to all programming except sports, news magazines and news shows.*

The ratings divide programming into six categories, ranging from TVY (appropriate for all children but specifically designed for a very young audience, including children between the ages of 2 and 6) to TVMA (specifically designed to be viewed by adults and therefore possibly unsuitable for children younger than 17).

Unlike movies (which are rated by an independent board), TV shows are rated by producers, networks, cable channels, syndicators and other people who originate the programs. These ratings evaluate violence and sexual content, and the results are displayed on the screen at the beginning of each program and coded into each TV program. The codes are read by a v-chip, a microchip device required to be included with all new television sets. The v-chip allows parents to program the TV set to eliminate shows the parents find objectionable, although follow-up studies have shown that few parents use this option.

Six months after this rating system was adopted, the TV networks added a more specific rating for violent or sexual content. Today, the broadcast networks and program services post content ratings on most of their programs.

Government Monitors Broadcast Indecency

In early 2004, responding to congressional pressure for more government control over the airwaves, the Federal Communications Commission proposed a $775,000 fine against Clear Channel Communications for a Florida radio broadcast of various episodes of *Bubba the Love Sponge Show.* The FCC fined Clear Channel the maximum amount then allowed—$27,500 for each time the episode

ran (a total of $715,000) plus $40,000 for record-keeping violations at the station. Clear Channel said the programs were meant to entertain, not to offend its listeners.

FCC Chairman Michael Powell also urged Congress to increase the maximum fine for indecency to $275,000 per incident, saying the maximum fine of $27,500 per episode wasn't large enough to discourage objectionable programming.

Just a few days later, singers Janet Jackson and Justin Timberlake, performing on CBS-TV during halftime at the Super Bowl, caused another controversy when Timberlake reached over to Jackson and ripped off part of her costume, exposing her breast to an estimated 90 million Americans and a much bigger worldwide audience.

Jackson and Timberlake apologized for the incident, but FCC Chairman Powell launched an investigation. FCC rules say that radio and over-the-air TV stations may not air obscene material at any time. The rules also bar stations from broadcasting indecent material—references to sex or excretions—between 6 a.m. and 10 p.m., when the FCC says children are more likely to be listening or watching. Cable and satellite programming is not covered by the restrictions. The FCC fined CBS $550,000 for the Janet Jackson incident.

CBS appealed the Jackson fine in 2007 before the 3rd U.S. Circuit Court of Appeals in Philadelphia, saying the network had taken precautions beforehand to avoid any incidents, including a five-second audio delay. In 2008 a federal appeals court overturned the decision, saying, "The FCC cannot impose liability on CBS for the acts of Janet Jackson and Justin Timberlake, independent contractors hired for the limited purposes of the Halftime Show."

Then in a July 2010 ruling on a group of indecency cases, a federal appeals court in New York found that the FCC's indecency policy violated the First Amendment. The cases involved *fleeting expletives*, profanity uttered without warning on live television. In the instances cited, celebrities including Cher and Bono made impromptu remarks during awards shows on live television, and the FCC fined the networks that aired the shows.

The court said that the FCC's policy against indecency had a chilling effect on free speech "because broadcasters have no way of knowing what the FCC will find offensive."

These controversies highlight the difficulties that arise when a federal government agency attempts to monitor free expression and no clear national standards of broadcast obscenity have been established. The definition of broadcast indecency often is based on politics and public pressure at the FCC, which shifts emphasis from one presidential administration to another.

Fleeting Expletives   Profanity uttered without warning on live television.

In 2002, singer Cher appeared on the Billboard Music Awards and made some impromptu comments that included a profanity. The FCC fined the Fox television network, which broadcast the awards, for indecency. In July 2010, a three-judge panel in New York, hearing the Billboard Music Awards case and several others dealing with the issue of fleeting expletives, struck down the indecency rule, saying it had a "chilling effect" that interfered with freedom of expression.

The main issues are these: How much power should a government entity have to decide what's obscene or indecent and then to enforce those restrictions? And what effect, if any, will these decisions have on broadcast programming in a media environment with so many alternative, unregulated outlets available to consumers?

Intellectual Property Rights Affirmed

The right of ownership for creative ideas in the United States is legally governed by what are called *intellectual property rights*. Four recent developments—the Digital Millennium Copyright Act, the U.S. Supreme Court decision in *New York Times Co. v. Tasini* and decisions in *MGM v. Grokster* and *Arista Records v. Lime Group*—are beginning to define the issues of electronic copyright in the digital era. Additionally, independent progressive organizations have been working to give

copyright holders greater flexibility in handling their intellectual property.

Digital Millennium Copyright Act

Passed in 1998, the Digital Millennium Copyright Act (*DMCA*) is comprehensive legislation that begins to address the copyright issues provoked by the Internet. The law makes several changes in U.S. copyright law to bring it into compliance with two World Intellectual Property Organization (*WIPO*) treaties about digitally transmitted copyrighted and stored material. The WIPO is responsible for promoting the protection of intellectual property throughout the world.

The DMCA is designed to prevent illegal copying of material that is published and distributed on the Internet. The DMCA makes it illegal to circumvent technology that protects or controls access to copyrighted materials, such as the recordings shared on the Internet. The DMCA also makes it illegal to manufacture materials that will help people gain access to copyrighted materials. The DMCA became effective on October 28, 2000.

Supporters of the DMCA—which includes most of the media industries that hold copyrights on creative works, such as movies, books and recordings—say the DMCA is an important law that must be enforced to protect intellectual property. Opponents say the law goes too far and limits technological development.

In March 2007, media conglomerate Viacom, whose media properties include MTV, Comedy Central and Nickelodeon, sued Google and YouTube, saying the companies deliberately gathered a library of copyrighted video clips without permission. Earlier in 2007, Viacom asked YouTube to remove 100,000 clips that it said infringed on Viacom copyrights.

Google said the "safe harbor" provisions of the DMCA covered the company. Generally these provisions say that Web site owners are not liable for copyrighted material that others upload to their site if the Web site owners promptly remove the material when the copyright owner asks them to do so.

However, Google announced four months later that it was developing video recognition technology that could detect and remove copyrighted material from its site before it was posted.

Intellectual Property Rights The legal right of ownership of ideas and content published in any medium.

DMCA Digital Millennium Copyright Act.

WIPO World Intellectual Property Organization.

Still, illegal video sharing is very difficult to monitor and prevent. In December 2012, Torrentfreak.com, which tracks online piracy, listed the most-pirated TV shows of the year. First on the list was *Game of Thrones*, with 4.2 million downloads for a single episode. "The majority of TV-show piracy," reported TorrentFreak, "occurs outside the U.S.," by people who cannot receive the programs legally until after the shows air in America. *Game of Thrones*, aired on HBO, is available only to subscribers.

In December 2012, Torrentfreak.com, which tracks online piracy, said that *Game of Thrones* was the most-pirated TV show that year. To combat video piracy, the music and movie industries launched the Copyright Alert System in 2013. *Game of Thrones* actor Peter Dinklage promoted the series on March 19, 2013 in Hollywood, CA.

The most recent attempt to curtail illegal video file sharing was announced in February 2013, when the music and movie industries launched the Copyright Alert System, administered by the Center for Copyright Information. Music and movie companies monitor online traffic and then alert an Internet provider when a file is downloaded illegally.

There is an escalating series of six warnings after which the Internet provider is authorized to slow down or block the offender's Internet access. "We think there is a positive impact of (alert) programs like this, and that they can put money in the pocket of artists and labels," Jonathan Lamy, a spokesman for the Recording Industry Association, told *The New York Times*.

New York Times Co. v. Tasini

In 2001, a U.S. Supreme Court decision in *New York Times Co. v. Tasini* affirmed that freelance writers separately own the electronic rights to material they have written, even though a publisher has first published their writing in printed form. In 1993, freelance writer Jonathan Tasini, president of the National Writers Union, discovered that an article he had written for *The New York Times* was available on a database for Mead Data Center Corporation, which was paying royalties for the material to *The Times*. Tasini hadn't been paid for this use, so Tasini sued *The New York Times* and several other publishing companies (including Newsday Inc., the Atlantic Monthly Co. and Time Inc.).

The suit claimed the publishers had violated copyright law by using writers' work on electronic databases without their permission and that this limited the rights of freelance authors to have their articles published and receive payment for their work. Several writers' organizations, including the Authors Guild, joined Tasini in the suit. *The Times* claimed the digital versions of written works were simply "revisions" of paper copies, which meant the rights belonged to the publisher so the writers deserved no further compensation.

On June 25, 2001, by a vote of 7-2, the U.S. Supreme Court agreed with Tasini. Writing the majority opinion, Justices Breyer and Stevens said that upholding the freelance authors' copyright would encourage the development of new technologies and the creation of new artistic work. The Court said *The Times* must delete thousands of articles from its database for which it had not obtained the rights. "Once again, the legal system has come down in favor of the individual creator's rights in the digital age," Tasini told *Publishers Weekly*. "Everywhere you look, the law supports creators."

This case is very important—not only for freelancers but also for anyone who creates intellectual property. The Court established the legal concept that the right to reproduce creative material electronically is very distinct from the right to reproduce creative material in print and that writers and other creative artists should be compensated separately for electronic and print rights to their work.

Metro-Goldwyn-Mayer Studios Inc. v. Grokster Ltd. and Arista Records LLC v. Lime Group LLC

In 2005, the U.S. Supreme Court ruled in a unanimous decision in the *Grokster* case that a software company can be held liable for copyright infringement if someone uses the company's software to illegally download songs and movies, known as illegal file sharing. The decision effectively shut down the Internet sites Grokster and

StreamCast, also named in the suit. The companies provided free software that allowed users to download Internet content for free.

In 2010, a New York district court ordered that the major remaining file-sharing Web site, LimeWire, shut down in response to a suit by 14 recording companies, including Arista Records, Capitol Records and Virgin Records, who alleged that LimeWire was guilty of copyright infringement. (Lime Group LLC is the parent company of the Web site LimeWire.) The court required LimeWire to disable "searching, downloading, uploading, file trading and/or file distribution functionality." The same day, LimeWire removed its file-sharing function and closed the site.

The Grokster and LimeWire cases are two more examples of the strong legal tradition in the United States of guaranteeing intellectual copyright protection for creative content and the aggressiveness with which mass media companies pursue people who try to use intellectual property without permission or payment.

FCC Advocates Internet Neutrality

In December 2010, FCC Chairman Julius Genachowski proposed a regulatory plan that guarantees open access to the Internet and forbid Internet service providers from blocking any content that is considered lawful. This policy, called *Net neutrality* (also discussed in **Chapter 9**), requires Internet service providers to explain any restrictions they place on the content they carry. Under the plan, companies may charge more for premium services, such as streaming movies, but the FCC requires those companies to justify their rates.

The discussion about Net neutrality, and whether the FCC should even play a role in regulating the Internet, is based on whether Internet access services are classified as "information services" or "telecommunications services." The FCC has little power to regulate an information service company. But if Internet access is classified as a telecommunications service, the FCC may play a much larger role in its regulation, as it now does for traditional telephone companies. The FCC, for example, monitors rates and investigates service interruptions and restrictions on content. The new FCC open access rules took effect in November 2011.

Courts and Regulators Govern Advertising and PR

Advertising and public relations are governed by legal constraints and by regulation. *New York Times v.*

Sullivan (see p. 299) was a crucial case for advertisers as well as for journalists. Since that decision, two other important court cases have defined the advertising and public relations businesses—the *Central Hudson* case for advertising (which is defined as "commercial speech" under the law) and the *Texas Gulf Sulphur* case for public relations.

Central Hudson Case

In 1980, in *Central Hudson Gas & Electric Corp. v. Public Service Commission*, the U.S. Supreme Court issued the most definitive opinion yet on commercial speech. During the energy crisis atmosphere of the 1970s, the New York Public Utilities Commission had banned all advertising by public utilities that promoted the use of electricity. Central Hudson Gas & Electric wanted the ban lifted, so the company sued the commission.

The commission said the ban promoted energy conservation; the Supreme Court disagreed, and the decision in the case forms the basis for commercial speech protection today. "If the commercial speech does not mislead, and it concerns lawful activity," explains legal scholar Ralph Holsinger, "the government's power to regulate it is limited. . . . The state cannot impose regulations that only indirectly advance its interests. Nor can it regulate commercial speech that poses no danger to a state interest." The decision prescribed standards that commercial speech must meet to be protected by the First Amendment.

The main provisions of the standards are that (1) the advertisement must be for a lawful product and (2) the advertisement must not be misleading. This has become known as the *Hudson test*. To be protected, then, an advertisement must promote a legal product and must not lie. This would seem to have settled the issue, but controversy continues.

Should alcohol advertising be banned? What about advertisements for condoms or birth control pills? Courts in different states have disagreed on these questions, and no Supreme Court decision on these specific issues exists, leaving many complex questions undecided. The Hudson test remains the primary criteria for determining what is protected commercial speech.

Texas Gulf Sulphur Case

The most important civil suit involving public relations occurred in the 1960s in *Securities and Exchange*

Hudson Test   A legal test that establishes a standard for commercial speech protection.

Commission v. Texas Gulf Sulphur Company. Texas Gulf Sulphur (TGS) discovered ore deposits in Canada in late 1963 but did not announce the discovery publicly. TGS quietly purchased hundreds of acres surrounding the ore deposits, and TGS officers began to accumulate more shares of the company's stock.

Meanwhile, the company issued a press release that said that the rumors about a discovery were "unreliable." When TGS announced that it had made a "major strike," which boosted the price of the company's stock, the Securities and Exchange Commission took the company to court.

The U.S. Court of Appeals, Tenth Circuit, ruled that TGS officers had violated the disclosure laws of the Securities and Exchange Commission. The court also ruled that TGS had issued "a false and misleading press release." Company officers and their friends were punished for withholding the information. According to *The Practice of Public Relations,* "the case proved conclusively that a company's failure to make known material information (information likely to be considered important by reasonable investors in determining whether to buy, sell or hold securities) may be in violation of the antifraud provision of the Securities and Exchange Acts."

The *Texas Gulf Sulphur* case remains a landmark in the history of public relations law. The decision in the case means public relations people can be held legally responsible for information they do not disclose about their companies. Public relations people at publicly held corporations (businesses with stockholders) are responsible not only to their companies but also to the public.

Government Regulates Advertisers

The main regulatory agency for advertising and public relations issues is the Federal Trade Commission (FTC), although other agencies such as the Securities and Exchange Commission and the Food and Drug Administration sometimes intervene to question advertising practices.

In 1914, the Federal Trade Commission assumed the power to oversee deceptive interstate advertising practices under the Federal Trade Commission Act. Today, the FTC's policy covering deceptive advertising says, "The Commission will find an act or practice deceptive if there is a misrepresentation, omission or other practice that misleads the consumer acting reasonably in the circumstances, to the consumer's detriment."

The commission acts when it receives a complaint the staff feels is worth investigating. The staff can request a *letter of compliance* from the advertiser, with

the advertiser promising to change the alleged deception without admitting guilt. Next, the advertiser can argue the case before an administrative law judge, who can write a consent agreement to outline what the advertiser must do to comply with the law. A cease-and-desist order can be issued against the advertiser, although this is rare. The FTC can fine an advertiser who doesn't comply with an FTC order.

The Federal Trade Commission's five members serve seven-year terms. They are appointed by the president and confirmed by the U.S. Senate, and no more than three of the members can be from one political party. Because the FTC's members are presidential appointees, the commission's actions often reflect the political climate under which they operate. In the 1970s, the FTC became a very active consumer advocacy agency. This was challenged in the 1980s, when presidential policy favored easing regulations on business practices.

Under President Clinton in the 1990s, the FTC moved aggressively to cite companies for wrongdoing. For example, in 1997, the FTC conducted hearings to determine whether the government should impose safeguards on information access on the Internet to protect consumers' privacy.

In 2013, the FTC announced expanded federal safeguards to extend to children's apps and Web sites.

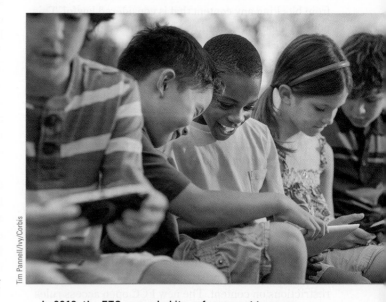

In 2013, the FTC expanded its enforcement to cover online access to personal information about children. New regulations require that online operators obtain parental consent before they gather photo, videos or audio recordings that could be used to identify, contact or locate a child.

The new rules mean that online operators must obtain parental consent before they gather information (such as photos, videos and audio recordings) that could be used to identify, contact or locate a child.

LAW MUST BALANCE RIGHTS AND RESPONSIBILITIES

Legal and regulatory issues governing advertising and public relations, then, are stitched with the same conflicting values that govern all aspects of mass media. The courts, the FCC, the FTC and other government agencies that monitor the media industries are the major arbiters of ongoing constitutional clashes.

Important legal decisions make lasting and influential statements about the role of law in protecting the constitutional guarantee of free expression in a country with constantly shifting public values. Through the courts and regulation, the government also must balance the business needs of the media industries with the government's role as a public interest representative.

Review, Analyze, Investigate

Reviewing Chapter 14

U.S. Constitution Sets Free Press Precedent

- The U.S. media's role is to encourage "uninhibited, robust and wide-open" debate.
- The legal and regulatory issues that media face are attempts to balance the media's rights and responsibilities.

Government Tries to Restrict Free Expression

- Before 1964, the First Amendment faced only four notable government challenges: the Alien and Sedition Laws of 1798, the Espionage Act of 1918, the Smith Act of 1940 and the Cold War congressional investigations of suspected communists in the late 1940s and early 1950s.
- All of these challenges were attempts to limit free expression.

Prior Restraint Rarely Used

- American courts rarely have invoked prior restraint. The two most recent cases involved the publication of the Pentagon Papers by *The New York Times* and the publication of directions to build a hydrogen bomb in *The Progressive* magazine.
- In both cases, the information eventually was printed, but the intervention of the government delayed publication.

Government Manages War Coverage

- Attempts by the Reagan administration to limit reporters' access to Grenada during the U.S. invasion in October 1983 were a subtle form of prior restraint.
- Pentagon rules for Gulf War coverage in 1991, reached in cooperation with journalists, imposed stricter restrictions on reporting than in any previous U.S. war.
- In 2001, the U.S. government controlled release of information to the American public about the war in Afghanistan even more than in the Gulf War.

- During the early months of the war in Afghanistan, the military used press pools and provided its own video footage of troop landings, produced by the military's combat film teams.
- During the Iraq War in 2003, the U.S. government used a system called embedding, which meant that members of the press traveled with the military, but the press' movements were restricted and managed by their military units.
- Twenty years ago during the Gulf War, the Bush administration banned the media from covering the return of war fatalities to the United States, saying they wanted to protect the families' privacy. Critics of the ban said the government was trying to hide the consequences of war from public view. In 2009, the Obama administration lifted the ban and now allows press coverage of the arrival of fallen soldiers, with family permission.

WikiLeaks Challenges Government Secrecy

- In 2010, WikiLeaks began releasing classified U.S. diplomatic documents about the Iraq and Afghanistan wars on its Web site.
- The U.S. government warned that the WikiLeaks postings could endanger military personnel and civilians.
- On November 28, 2010, *The New York Times* began publishing a series of articles based on a new release of U.S. State Department documents posted on WikiLeaks.
- On February 23, 2011, WikiLeaks founder Julian Assange was ordered extradited to Sweden, but eventually found asylum at the Ecuadorian Embassy in London. The U.S. government did not file any charges against Assange for publishing secret U.S. documents on the Internet.
- The U.S. military charged Pfc. Bradley Manning with downloading large amounts of classified information from a military database.

- In February 2013, Pfc. Manning pleaded guilty to 10 of the 22 charges against him.

Librarians Resist the PATRIOT Act

- Among the provisions of the PATRIOT Act is Section 215, which allows the Federal Bureau of Investigation to monitor business records, including computer log-ins and the lists of books people check out of public libraries.
- The American Library Association and the American Civil Liberties Union challenged Section 215 in court.
- In 2007, a federal district court agreed that some provisions of the PATRIOT Act go against constitutional principles of checks and balances and separation of powers.
- President Obama signed a four-year extension of the PATRIOT Act on May 30, 2011.

What Is the Standard for Obscenity?

- *Roth v. United States* defined obscenity as material that is "utterly without redeeming social importance."
- *Miller v. California* established a three-part local test for obscenity: whether "the average person, applying contemporary community standards," would find that the work, taken as a whole, appeals to the prurient interest; whether the work depicts or describes, in a patently offensive way, sexual conduct specifically defined by the applicable state law; and whether the work, taken as a whole, lacks serious literary, artistic, political or scientific value (often called the LAPS test).
- In the 1988 *Hazelwood* case, the U.S. Supreme Court gave public school officials considerable freedom to limit what appears in student publications.
- In 2013, the National Coalition against Censorship reported that about 100 students in the United States were suspended for making and posting "Harlem Shake" videos on the Web, claiming the videos are inappropriate.

Libel Law Outlines the Media's Public Responsibility

- In 1964, the *New York Times v. Sullivan* case set a precedent, establishing that to be successful in a libel suit, a public official must prove actual malice.
- The press can use three defenses against a libel suit: truth, privilege and fair comment.
- Most successful libel judgments eventually are reversed or reduced when they are appealed. Often the major cost of a libel suit is not the actual award but the defense lawyers' fees.
- *Gertz v. Robert Welch Inc.* established the concept that the expression of opinions is a necessary part of public debate.
- Because of the *Herbert v. Lando* decision, today reporters can be asked in a libel suit to identify their sources and to surrender their notes.
- The *Masson v. New Yorker Magazine* case addressed the journalist's responsibility for direct quotations.

- Businesses and public officials have used SLAPP suits to try to intimidate individuals and news organizations that write unfavorable stories or post critical comments on the Internet.

Invasion of Privacy Defined Four Ways

- Invasion-of-privacy lawsuits are much less common than libel suits.
- There is no U.S. Supreme Court decision that governs invasion of privacy, so each state has its own interpretation of the issue.
- Generally, the media can be guilty of invading someone's privacy by intruding on a person's physical or mental solitude, publishing or disclosing embarrassing personal facts, giving someone publicity that places the person in a false light or using someone's name or likeness for commercial benefit.
- In an important case for the press, *Bartnicki v. Vopper*, in 2001, the U.S. Supreme Court reaffirmed the media's right to broadcast information and to comment on that information, no matter how the information was obtained.

Debate Continues over Fair Trial, Courtroom Access and Shield Laws

- *Sheppard v. Maxwell* established the legal precedent for limiting press access to courtrooms and juries.
- In 2005, *New York Times* reporter Judith Miller spent 85 days in jail because she refused to reveal a confidential source to a Washington, D.C., grand jury. Eventually she revealed her source's name (I. Lewis Libby, Vice President Dick Cheney's chief of staff) after he released her from their confidentiality agreement. Libby was convicted of perjury and obstruction of justice, but President Bush commuted his sentence in 2007.
- In 1994, Court TV broadcast the entire murder trial of O. J. Simpson.
- In 2012, cameras were not allowed in the proceedings against James Holmes, a suspect in the Aurora, Colo., theater shootings.
- Individual state shield laws protect journalists from being compelled to reveal their sources, but no federal shield law guarantees these rights to every journalist nationwide.

FCC Regulates Broadcast and Cable

- Unlike print, the broadcast media are regulated by a federal agency, the Federal Communications Commission.
- Since 1972, the concept behind broadcast regulation has been based on the belief that broadcasters are trustees operating in the public interest.

Telecommunications Act of 1996 Changes the Marketplace

- The Telecommunications Act of 1996 was the most far-reaching reform in the way the U.S. government regulates mass media in more than 60 years.

- Following passage of the Telecommunications Act, large companies began positioning themselves to deliver the combination of telecommunications services they think consumers want.

- The major provisions of the Telecommunications Act of 1996 affect telecommunications, broadcast, satellite and cable.

Deregulation Unleashes the Media

- The FCC under President Clinton moved to a policy of deregulation of station ownership and regulation of broadcast programming.

- In 2003, the FCC adopted regulations that allow one company to control 35 percent of the broadcast audience. Those regulations are still in place today.

- In 2010, a federal court lifted the ban on media cross-ownership. The FCC is expected to announced a decision on cross-ownership in 2013.

Congress Attempts to Use Communications Decency Act

- The Communications Decency Act (CDA), which was part of the Telecommunications Act, attempted to regulate access to cable and TV programming and monitoring of computer networks, including the Internet.

- In 1997, the U.S. Supreme Court blocked enforcement of the Internet indecency provisions of the CDA.

- In 1998, Congress passed the Child Online Protection Act (COPA), aimed at preventing minors from getting access to sexually explicit material, even though the material is legal for adults. Several organizations, including the American Library Association and the American Civil Liberties Union, immediately challenged the law in court on First Amendment grounds. In 2002, the U.S. Supreme Court agreed that Congress has no authority to restrict Internet access.

- In 2003, the U.S. Supreme Court ruled that the federal government may withhold funding from schools and libraries that refuse to install Internet filters for pornography on their computers.

TV Industry Agrees to Ratings and the V-Chip

- Under pressure from Congress, television executives devised a voluntary system of ratings for TV programming.

- The new programming codes can be read by a v-chip, which allows parents to program a TV set to eliminate objectionable programs.

Government Monitors Broadcast Indecency

- In 2004, the FCC increased fines for broadcast programs the FCC determines are indecent.

- The FCC fined CBS-TV for Janet Jackson's "wardrobe malfunction" during the 2004 Super Bowl.

- In a July 2010 ruling on a group of indecency cases concerning fleeting expletives, a federal appeals court

in New York found that the FCC's indecency policy violated the First Amendment.

Intellectual Property Rights Affirmed

- The right of ownership of creative ideas in the United States is legally governed by what are called intellectual property rights. The Digital Millennium Copyright Act (DMCA), the U.S. Supreme Court decision in *New York Times Co. v. Tasini*, and the U.S. Supreme Court decision in *Metro-Goldwyn Mayer Studios Inc. et al. v. Grokster Ltd. et al.* have begun to define the issues of electronic copyright in the digital era.

- In 2010, a New York district court required LimeWire to shut down because of copyright infringement in response to a suit by 14 recording companies.

- All four cases affirm the strong legal tradition in the United States of guaranteeing intellectual copyright for creative content.

- To combat video piracy, the music and movie industries launched the Copyright Alert System in 2013.

FCC Advocates Internet Neutrality

- In December 2010, FCC Chairman Julius Genachowski proposed a regulatory plan to guarantee open access to the Internet and forbid Internet service providers from blocking any content that is considered lawful.

- The issue of Net neutrality, and whether the FCC should play a role in regulating the Internet, is based on whether Internet access services are classified as "information services" or "telecommunications services."

- The FCC's power to regulate an information service is limited, but the FCC has wider authority to regulate telecommunications services.

- Net neutrality rules took effect in November 2011.

Courts and Regulators Govern Advertising and PR

- The Hudson test for advertising means that to be protected by the First Amendment, an advertisement must promote a legal product and must not lie.

- The *Texas Gulf Sulphur* case established the concept that a publicly held company is responsible for any information it withholds from the public.

- The main government agency regulating advertising is the Federal Trade Commission. The agency today is becoming more aggressive about policing advertisers than it was during the previous 20 years.

- In 2013, the FTC expanded its enforcement to cover online access to personal information about children.

Law Must Balance Rights and Responsibilities

- The courts, the FCC and the FTC arbitrate the media's rights and responsibilities.

- Government must balance the media's business needs with the government's role to protect the interests of the public.

Key Terms

These terms are defined in the margins throughout this chapter and appear in alphabetical order with definitions in the Glossary, which begins on page 373.

Critical Questions

1. Cite five major events/legal decisions in the evolution of the interpretation of the First Amendment in America from its beginnings to today.

2. Why is *New York Times v. Sullivan* a precedent-setting case for the American media?

3. List and describe the four elements necessary to prove libel.

4. Why are the courts generally so reluctant to use prior restraint to stop publication? List two cases in which the courts did invoke prior restraint.

5. List and explain three specific cases that demonstrate how the U.S. legal system is responding to challenges created by the relationship between mass media and the Internet.

Working the Web

This list includes both sites mentioned in the chapter and others to give you greater insight into media law and regulation.

American Booksellers Foundation for Free Expression (ABFFE)
abffe.org

The self-described "bookseller's voice in the fight against censorship," this foundation participates in legal cases about First Amendment rights and provides education about the importance of free expression. Archived articles from the *ABFFE Update* and the downloadable Banned Books Week Handbook are available on the Web site.

American Library Association (ALA)
ala.org

This association's mission is to provide leadership for the development, promotion and improvement of library and information services and the profession of librarianship to enhance learning and ensure access to information for all. However, the ALA is open to any interested person or organization. Among the professional tools available on the Web site of this 130-year-old organization are articles, guidelines and other resources about such issues as censor-ship, copyright, diversity and equal access. ALA also sponsors a number of electronic discussion lists for participation by members and others with shared interests.

Federal Communications Commission (FCC)
fcc.gov

This U.S. government agency, established by the Communications Act of 1934, regulates interstate and international communications by radio, television, wire, satellite and cable. Its jurisdiction covers the 50 states, the District of Columbia and U.S. possessions. The site holds FCC news headlines—daily and archived—as well as links to media rules and regulations, strategic goals of the commission, bureaus and offices, advisory committees and even a kids' zone. The Consumer and Governmental Affairs Bureau (listed on the site under Bureaus and Offices) allows consumers to file or research individual informal complaints relating to FCC regulations.

FindLaw
findlaw.com

FindLaw provides legal information for the public on a host of topics, including intellectual property, copyright and the

Internet as well as civil rights, education law, employees' rights and criminal law. Users can find and share legal information on FindLaw Q&A.

Index (formerly Index on Censorship)

indexoncensorship.org

This Web site of a periodical founded in 1972 by a group of writers, journalists and artists describes itself as "one of the world's leading repositories of original, challenging, controversial and intelligent writing on free expression issues." Users can explore censorship issues and campaigns around the world. The organization gives annual Index Freedom of Expression Awards.

Media Center at New York Law School

nyls.edu/centers/projects/media_center

The Media Center sponsors pedagogy, scholarship and projects relating to evolving communication and information technologies and the laws that regulate them. Its goals are to promote scholarship, to preserve democratic values through effective media policy and to train lawyers to understand the law of media and the role of media in the law. The Center's Library holds comprehensive indexes of U.S. laws and cases, as well as articles and papers on various media law issues.

Media Law Resource Center (MLRC)

medialaw.org

This nonprofit information clearinghouse is a membership organization for media companies (publishers, broadcasters and web content providers), insurers and professional and public interest groups. Also available is an annual report on libel, privacy and related legal actions against the media.

National Freedom of Information Coalition (formerly Freedom of Information Center)

nfoic.org/foi-center/

Founded in 1958, the Center provides information to the general public and the media through a collection of more than 1 million articles and documents about access to government information at local, state and federal levels. The Web site features links to state and international FOI laws,

a media law guide and an index to research files that have been compiled since the Center's inception.

Silha Center for the Study of Media Ethics and Law (University of Minnesota)

silha.umn.edu/

The Silha Center examines the theoretical and practical applications of freedom and fairness in journalism. Major projects include media accountability, points of convergence of media ethics and law, and libel and privacy. The Web site includes articles from the quarterly *Silha Center Bulletin* and links to law-related and media-ethics-related Web sites as well as legislative testimony and briefs on a number of issues.

Student Press Law Center (SPLC)

splc.org

This advocate for student free press rights provides information, advice and legal assistance to students and educators. News Flashes link to current and archived articles about high school and college journalism controversies. The Web site also offers articles from the SPLC Blog. The Resource Center includes information about obtaining legal help, browsing through the online law library and testing your knowledge of student press law (30-minute quiz) and the First Amendment (10-minute quiz).

WikiLeaks

wikileaks.org

Funded as part of a "project of the sunshine press" and based in Melbourne, Australia, WikiLeaks publishes and comments on leaked documents alleging government and corporate misconduct. Unlike Wikipedia, source documents published on WikiLeaks cannot be edited or changed by the public. WikiLeaks claims that "transparency in government activities leads to reduced corruption, better government and stronger democracies." The site provides separate discussion and source pages for all of the content published on the site. In addition, WikiLeaks says that, as far as they are aware, "none of the thousands of WikiLeaks sources have been exposed, via WikiLeaks or any other method."

 Impact/Action Videos are concise news features on various topics created exclusively for *Media/Impact*. Go online to access MindTap at cengagebrain.com. MindTap for Media/Impact sequences all of your learning tools—Chapter Readings with highlighting and note taking, Impact/Action Videos, activities and assessments—into chapter driven learning units that guide you through the curriculum.

ETHICS:
PLACING
RESPONSIBILITY

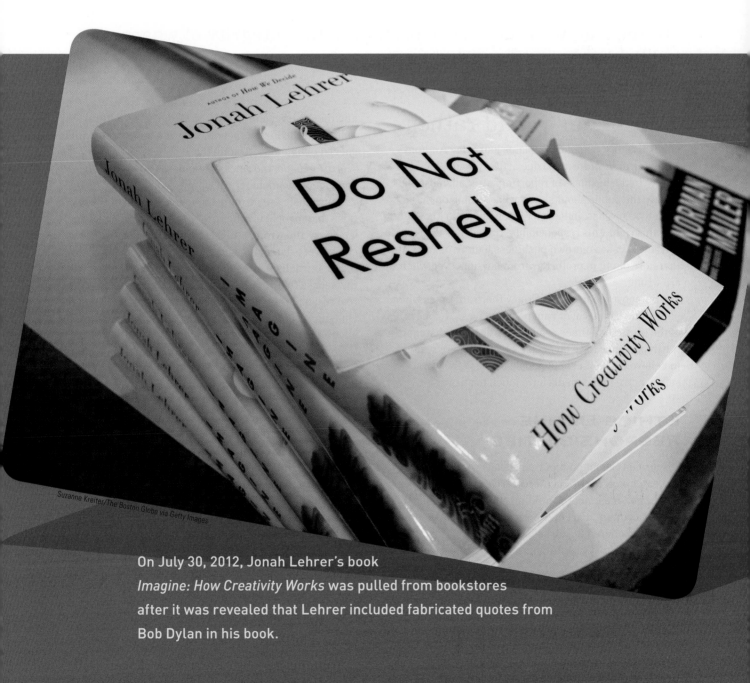

Suzanne Kreiter/The Boston Globe via Getty Images

On July 30, 2012, Jonah Lehrer's book
Imagine: How Creativity Works was pulled from bookstores
after it was revealed that Lehrer included fabricated quotes from
Bob Dylan in his book.

> "In the end, what is most important is the integrity of what we publish and what we stand for."
>
> —DAVID REMNICK, EDITOR, *THE NEW YORKER*

"Most of us would rather

publish a story than not," explains journalist Anthony Brandt in an *Esquire* magazine article about ethics. "We're in the business of reporting, after all; most of us believe the public should know what's going on, has a right to know, has, indeed, a responsibility to know, and that this right, this responsibility, transcends the right to privacy, excuses our own pushiness, our arrogance, and therefore ought to protect us from lawsuits even when we are wrong.

"But most reporters also know there are times when publishing can harm or ruin people's lives. Members of the press sometimes print gossip as truth, disregard the impact they have on people's lives, and are ready to believe the worst about people because the worst sells. . . . We in the media have much to answer for."

ETHICS DEFINE RESPONSIBILITIES

Discussions about how journalists answer for what they do center on *ethics*. The word derives from the Greek word *ethos*, meaning the guiding spirit or traditions that govern a culture. Part of America's culture is the unique protection offered to journalists by the First Amendment of the U.S. Constitution, so any discussion of ethics

and the American media acknowledges the cultural belief that the First Amendment privilege carries with it special obligations. Among these obligations are ***professional ethics***, the rules or standards governing the conduct of the members of a profession.

Journalists are no more likely to exploit their positions than people in other professions, but when journalists make the wrong ethical choices, the consequences can be very damaging and very public. "It may well be that if journalism loses touch with ethical values, it will then cease to be of use to society, and cease to have any real reason for being," writes media ethics scholar John Hulteng. "But that, for the sake of all of us, must never be allowed to happen."

Journalists sometimes make poor ethical judgments because they work quickly, and their actions can be haphazard because the lust to be first with a story can override the desire to be right; because they sometimes don't know enough to question the truthfulness of what they're told; because they may win attention and professional success quickly by ignoring ethical standards; and because journalists sometimes are insensitive to the consequences of their stories for the people they cover.

The media face four types of ethical issues:

1. Truthfulness

2. Fairness

3. Privacy

4. Responsibility

Consider these actual situations:

1. **Truthfulness.** A public relations agency hired by the U.S. government paid a commentator to promote

---

Ethics   The rules or standards that govern someone's conduct.

Professional Ethics   The rules or standards governing the conduct of the members of a profession.

a new federal education initiative. The contract also required the commentator to gain access for government officials to other journalists to convince the journalists about the new law's merits. By not disclosing the payment, did the commentator mislead his readers, or was he simply doing the job he was paid to do? Were the opinions he promoted truly his positions on the issues, or did he take the positions because he'd been paid to publicly promote a specific agenda?

2. **Fairness.** Two television commentators each admitted separately that they gave donations to political candidates. One commentator gave a donation to a Democratic candidate for national office and then questioned the candidate's opponent on the air. The second commentator gave money to friends who were running in local races and never covered these candidates. The TV network employers suspended each commentator for two days. The network said that company policy forbid the donations. Should commentators, who are expected to be partisan, be subject to the same ethical standards as news employees? Is their fairness on the job compromised if they make political donations?

3. **Privacy.** Reporters at a tabloid newspaper hacked into personal e-mail accounts and illegally obtained access to personal voice mails of celebrities and public officials. Did the reporters infringe on the person's privacy, or should public figures just expect this type of reporting?

4. **Responsibility.** A family that was hoping to be hired by a reality TV show concocted a story that their son had been swept away in a balloon-like object that resembled a flying saucer. This object had been built by the father, who told authorities that his son had crawled inside it without his knowledge. When the flying saucer was launched, the father said, he couldn't find his son, who was dubbed "Balloon Boy." The father told the journalists who arrived at the scene that he assumed the boy was inside the saucer.

Truth versus falsehood is the issue for the journalist who accepted payment to write stories in example 1. Fairness versus bias is the question for the commentators who gave the political donations in example 2. Personal privacy versus invasion of privacy is the debate facing the reporters who hacked e-mails and voice mails in example 3. Responsibility versus irresponsibility is the issue for the journalists who covered the Balloon Boy in example 4.

Some ethical debates are easier to resolve than others. These four incidents and several other examples described in this chapter demonstrate the amazing range of situations covered by media ethics and the different ways that media organizations get their jobs done.

Mike Twohy/The New Yorker Collection/Cartoon Bank.com

TRUTHFULNESS AFFECTS CREDIBILITY

Truthfulness in reporting means more than accuracy and telling the truth to get a story. Truthfulness also means not misrepresenting the people or the underlying motives of a story to readers and viewers, as well as not reporting disinformation. Another aspect of truthfulness is the belief that government officials should not use the media for their own ends by planting stories that aren't true.

Hidden Motives or Sponsors

The journalist described in example 1 (on p. 324) is syndicated columnist Armstrong Williams, who received $250,000 from a public relations firm to promote President George W. Bush's No Child Left Behind initiative to African Americans. In 2005, *USA Today* revealed that Williams' contract with the PR firm said he would "utilize his long-term working relationships with *America's Black Forum* [an African American news program] to encourage the producers to periodically address the No Child Left Behind Act."

When Williams' payment arrangement became public, Williams attributed the lapse to the fact that he was not trained as a journalist. He apologized for "blurring his roles as an independent conservative commentator and a paid promoter."

Misrepresentation

In July 2012, *Tablet* magazine revealed that Jonah Lehrer, 31, author of the best-selling book, *Imagine: How Creativity Works*, had fabricated quotes from musician Bob Dylan in his book. Only a month before, Lehrer, a writer for *The New Yorker*, had publicly apologized for taking some articles he had published in *The Wall Street Journal* and other publications and republishing them on his blog at *The New Yorker*.

After the *Imagine* fabrication was discovered, Lehrer admitted he had made up the quote and resigned from *The New Yorker*. "This is a terrifically sad situation," *New Yorker* Editor David Remnick said in a statement, "but, in the end, what is most important is the integrity of what we publish and what we stand for."

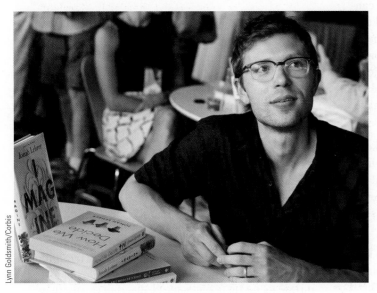

In July 2012, *New Yorker* writer Jonah Lehrer resigned after it was discovered that he had fabricated quotes for his book, *Imagine: How Creativity Works.*

Lehrer's publisher, Canongate Books, asked all its retailers to return the books; *Imagine* had sold 200,000 hardcover and e-book copies before it was pulled from the shelves.

In 2010, *The New York Times* suspended reporter Zachery Kouwe after editors said Kouwe had plagiarized portions of an article he had written for *The Times* from an article by another reporter that had appeared earlier online in *The Wall Street Journal*. When editors of *The Journal* contacted *The Times* about the similarity, *Times* editors investigated some of Kouwe's other stories and found more examples of plagiarism.

"In a number of business articles in *The Times* over the past year, and in posts on the DealBook blog on NYTimes.com, a *Times* reporter appears to have improperly appropriated wording and passages published by other news organizations," wrote *The Times* on its Corrections page. "A subsequent search by *The Times* found other cases of extensive overlap between passages in Mr. Kouwe's articles and other news organizations'. . . . Copying language directly from other news organizations without providing attribution—even if the facts are independently verified—is a serious violation of *Times* policy and basic journalistic standards. It should not have occurred." Kouwe resigned.

In another case of misrepresentation that involved a movie studio and several newspapers, Universal Pictures created a series of newspaper stories in 2009 purportedly taken from real Alaska news publications to promote its movie *The Fourth Kind*. The movie claimed to be a true story about alien abductions that allegedly occurred in Nome, Alaska, and the false news articles were used in movie ads to give the subject legitimacy. The *Fairbanks Daily News-Miner* explained what Universal did:

> To bolster that claim [that the story about the aliens was true], articles were posted that professed to be from real Alaska publications, but were actually created to bolster the movie's storyline. The articles included an obituary and a news story about the death of a character in the movie, Dr. William Tyler, which supposedly were from the *Daily News-Miner*. Neither the story nor the obituary ever appeared in the newspaper. Fake articles were listed from other newspapers in Alaska, including the *Nome Nugget*, alongside authentic new stories.

Universal paid $20,000 to the Alaska Press Club as part of a settlement with several Alaska newspapers once the deception was discovered. An attorney for the newspapers told the *Los Angeles Times*, "If people can't rely on the fact that when they look at a news article on the Web that it's from the newspaper it appears to be . . . it erodes confidence in the world of journalism."

Another celebrated case of misrepresentation happened in 2006 when author James Frey admitted that his personal memoir, *A Million Little Pieces*, contained many fabrications. In the book, selected by Oprah Winfrey in September 2005 for her book club, Frey detailed his battle with drug addiction and his ultimate recovery. The book quickly became a best-seller.

Lynn Goldsmith/Corbis

In 2006, author James Frey admitted to Oprah Winfrey that his memoir, *A Million Little Pieces*, contained fabrications. Frey's book had been chosen as an Oprah Book Club selection, and he previously had promoted the book on her TV show.

In January 2006, The Smoking Gun Web site posted information that disputed the truthfulness of many of the incidents Frey described. Frey's publisher, Doubleday, initially defended the book, but then Winfrey invited Frey to appear on her show, where Frey admitted he'd falsified many parts of *A Million Little Pieces*, including descriptions of time he spent in police custody and in jail.

He also admitted to Winfrey that the first pages of his just-published sequel, *My Friend Leonard*, were a fabrication, since *Leonard* started with Frey's 87th day in jail, which never occurred. Frey told Winfrey the invented stories "portrayed me in ways that made me tougher and more daring and more aggressive than in reality I was, or I am." He then publicly apologized to his readers.

Doubleday said it would include a detailed list of Frey's fabrications, compiled by the author, in all future copies of *A Million Little Pieces*. *The New York Times Book Review* continued to categorize the book in its nonfiction best-seller list, but the editors added a note saying, "Both author and publisher acknowledge that this memoir contains numerous fabrications."

A month after Frey admitted his mistakes on television, Riverhead Books, which published *Leonard* and had signed Frey to write two more books, cancelled the contract, and his agent dropped him. Sales of *A Million Little Pieces* dropped quickly after the *Oprah* confrontation; however, *The New York Times* reported in March

2006 that Frey's royalties for 2005 totaled more than $5 million.

The most well-known case of serious journalistic misrepresentation involved Jayson Blair, another *New York Times* reporter, six years before the Zachery Kouwe incident. On May 1, 2003, *The Times* published a front-page story, "*Times* Reporter Who Resigned Leaves Long Trail of Deception," which began: "A staff reporter for *The New York Times* committed frequent acts of journalistic fraud while covering significant news events in recent months, an investigation by *Times* journalists has found. The widespread fabrication and plagiarism represent a profound betrayal of trust and a low point in the 152-year history of the newspaper." *The Times* said that as a reporter for *The Times*, 27-year-old Blair had:

- Written stories purported to be filed in Maryland, Texas and other states, when often he was still in New York.

- Fabricated comments.

- Concocted scenes.

- Stolen material from other newspapers and wire services.

- Selected details from photographs to create the impression he had been somewhere or seen someone, when he hadn't.

The Times then published an exhaustive, unprecedented eight-page accounting of 73 significant falsehoods in Blair's stories *The Times* had published, detailing every traceable error, based on an internal investigation by its own reporters. In one story, for example, Blair had reported details from inside the National Naval Medical Center in Bethesda, Md., but the hospital said Blair had never been there. In another story about a stricter National Collegiate Athletic Association standard for class attendance, Blair quoted someone who said he had never talked to Blair and used quotes from another newspaper as his own.

When discussing Blair's case, Alex S. Jones, a former *Times* reporter and co-author of *The Trust: The Private and Powerful Family Behind The New York Times*, told the *Times*: "To the best of my knowledge, there has never been anything like this at *The New York Times*. . . . There has never been a systematic effort to lie and cheat as a reporter at *The New York Times* comparable to what Jayson Blair seems to have done."

Less than two months later, *The Times*' two top editors, who were responsible for hiring and supervising Blair, resigned.

Ulf Andersen/Getty Images

Misrepresenting the facts or creating false stories and attributing them to others can cause readers to question all information published by similar sources. Which are actual people and which are not? Is the story fiction or fact? Misrepresentation directly affects the credibility of the company that publishes the books, stories, even the ads and indirectly affects the credibility of all authors, all journalists and all publishers.

Disinformation

In October 1986, the press learned that two months earlier the Reagan administration had launched a *disinformation* campaign to scare Libyan leader Muammar Qaddafi. Selected U.S. government sources had planted stories with reporters that U.S. forces were preparing to strike Libya.

The first report about the bogus preparations appeared in the August 25, 1986, issue of *The Wall Street Journal*, which first used the word *disinformation* to describe the practice of government officials intentionally planting false information with reporters.

On the basis of a statement by White House spokesman Larry Speakes that the *Journal*'s article about an impending strike on Libya was "authoritative," other newspapers, including *The Washington Post*, carried the story. This example brings up the ethical question of the government's responsibility to tell the truth and not to use the news media for its own ends. State Department spokesman and former television reporter Bernard Kalb resigned when he learned about the disinformation campaign, saying, "Faith in the word of America is the pulse beat of our democracy."

Disinformation also was at the center of the 2007 trial of presidential adviser I. Lewis Libby, in which Libby was found guilty of perjury and obstruction of justice for leaking the name of CIA operative Valerie Plame to journalists and then denying before a Washington, D.C., grand jury that he had done so. (See **Chapter 14**.) President Bush commuted Libby's sentence. Former *New York Times* Executive Editor Max Frankel said the case showed "the shameless ease with which top-secret information is bartered in Washington for political advantage."

FAIRNESS MEANS EVENHANDEDNESS

Fairness implies impartiality—that the journalist has nothing personal to gain from a report, that there are no

---

Disinformation   The intentional planting of false information by government sources.

---

hidden benefits to the reporter or to the source from the story being presented or being withheld. Criticism of the press for unfairness results from:

- Close ties that develop between reporters and the stories they cover—called *insider friendships*.

- Reporters who accept personal or financial benefits from sources, sponsors or advertisers—called *conflicts of interest*.

- Reporters who pay their sources for stories—called *checkbook journalism*.

Insider Friendships

In June 2012, six months after her exclusive interview with President Bashar al-Assad of Syria, ABC News Correspondent Barbara Walters admitted that she had arranged an interview to help a former media advisor to al-Assad get a job as an intern at CNN and also gain admission to Columbia University. "I did offer to mention her to contacts at another media organization," Walters said in the statement, "though she didn't get a job or get into school. In retrospect, I realize that this created a conflict and I regret that." (See **Impact/Profile**, "Barbara Walters Apologizes for Helping Aide to Assad of Syria," p. 329.)

The TV commentators in example 2 (on p. 325) are Keith Olbermann and Joe Scarborough, who both worked for MSNBC. On November 5, 2010, MSNBC announced that it was suspending Olbermann without pay after MSNBC TV President Phil Griffin learned that Olbermann had violated newsroom policies by contributing to three Democratic congressional candidates.

Olbermann admitted he made three donations of $2,400 but issued a statement that said he did not use his influence in any other way. "I did not privately or publicly encourage anyone else to donate to these campaigns, nor to any others in this election or any previous ones, nor have I previously donated to any political campaign at any level," he said. MSNBC, which originally suspended him indefinitely, announced a two-day suspension. Olbermann resigned from NBC in January 2011.

Less than a month later, MSNBC announced another two-day suspension of the co-host of its morning program after the online site Politico reported that Joe Scarborough had donated $4,000 in recent years to three Republican candidates in Florida. The contributions, Scarborough said, "were not relevant to my work at MSNBC." He had not reported on any of the races to which he gave money, he said.

Scarborough's suspension "underscored the idiosyncrasy of a policy that seeks to protect NBC's journalistic

IMPACT/Profile

Barbara Walters Apologizes for Helping Aide to Assad of Syria

By Bill Carter

In the months after her exclusive interview [on December 7, 2011] with President Bashar al-Assad of Syria, Barbara Walters tried to intercede to get a television position for a former aide of his, who Ms. Walters acknowledged helped arrange the interview.

Ms. Walters, the longtime ABC News correspondent, issued a statement apologizing for reaching out to contacts to seek an internship with CNN and admission at Columbia University for Sheherazad Jaafari, who had been a media adviser for Mr. Assad. Ms. Jaafari, 22, is the daughter of the Syrian ambassador to the United Nations.

"I did offer to mention her to contacts at another media organization and in academia, though she didn't get a job or into school," Ms. Walters said in the statement. "In retrospect, I realize that this created a conflict and I regret that."

One longtime television news executive, who insisted on not being identified, said the circumstance was far from unusual in a business where favors are often requested on behalf of contacts.

"It's a little ugly to see how the sausage is made to land these big interviews," the executive said, adding that the favors appeared to be the result of an association established by the interview, not a quid pro quo for it.

Source: Excerpted from Bill Carter, "Barbara Walters Apologizes for Helping Aide to Assad of Syria," June 5, 2012, nytimes.com.

Michael N. Todaro/FilmMagic/Getty Images

In June 2012, ABC News Correspondent Barbara Walters admitted that, six months after airing an exclusive interview with Syrian President Bashar al-Assad, she had tried to help a former al-Assad media advisor get a job at CNN, an example of insider friendships.

integrity, but does not differentiate between news reporters and political commentators," wrote *The New York Times* (NBC owns MSNBC). MSNBC President Phil Griffin said, "As Joe recognizes, it is critical that we enforce our standards and politics." Scarborough said,

in a statement, "There is nothing more important than maintaining the integrity" of the news.

In the Olbermann and Scarborough examples, MSNBC was dealing with the potential public perception that insider contacts could affect its news coverage, even

In November 2010, MSNBC commentators Keith Olbermann (left) and Joe Scarborough (right) each were suspended for two days in separate incidents after it was discovered they had made campaign contributions to political candidates. Both said they had not used their influence to promote the candidates to whom they had given money. Olbermann resigned from MSNBC in January 2011.

though Olbermann and Scarborough are commentators, not news reporters. The network believed that political donations could interfere with the public's trust in the rest of its news organization. Even the appearance of insider friendships removes the very important element of a news organization's independence from the people and events it covers.

Conflicts of Interest

Reporters with conflicts of interest are divided between at least two loyalties, and the ethical question is, how will the stories the reporters write and the integrity of the organizations for which they work be affected?

One type of conflict of interest happens when reporters accept free meals and passes to entertainment events (freebies) and free trips (junkets). In one survey of newspapers, nearly half said they accepted free tickets to athletic events, and nearly two-thirds accepted free tickets to artistic events. In an editorial about junkets, *The New York Times* said, "Accepting junkets and boondoggles does not necessarily mean that a reporter is being bought—but it inescapably creates the appearance of being bought."

Accepting junkets and freebies creates an appearance of conflict of interest—even if the reporters don't write favorably about the places they visit. In 2010, however, a newspaper took the unusual step of taking

money from an advertiser to help pay for its coverage of the war in Afghanistan.

On September 27, 2010, the *New Hampshire Union Leader* (*UL*), the state's largest newspaper, announced that the paper had accepted underwriting from three major New Hampshire businesses so its publisher and a staff photographer could travel to Afghanistan to report on a New Hampshire National Guard unit serving there. One of the underwriters, BAE Systems, is the state's largest manufacturing firm and works mainly in the defense industry, according to a story about the incident published by The Newspaper Guild.

Citing declining revenue because of the recession, the newspaper's publisher wrote, "I had a hunch that I knew some companies that would feel the same way as the *Union Leader*, that the story of Charlie Company ought to be told and that, with their assistance, New Hampshire's newspaper and UnionLeader.com could and should tell it."

Many readers didn't agree. "The *UL* takes money from BAE and other companies? That is obvious conflict of interest," wrote one reader. "How can we trust the *UL* to report on these companies in an objective way when they are taking money from them? We can't. These stories will be nothing more than propaganda."

In a similar type of conflict of interest, *The Washington Post* in 2009 issued invitations to lobbyists, members of Congress and other influential people in Washington to attend a *Washington Post* "salon" at publisher Katharine Weymouth's home. Guests were invited to buy sponsorships ($25,000 for one or $250,000 for the entire series) to attend off-the-record dinners hosted by the newspaper's editor, Marcus Brauchli.

After a story on Politico (an online competitor) made the event public, *The Post* cancelled it, and Weymouth apologized to *The Post*'s readers, although she said Politico had characterized the invitation incorrectly. The planned event highlights the conflicts of interest that can develop when the business side of a media organization overlaps the news side.

Checkbook Journalism

In 2012, Alliance, the film company that represented actor Brad Pitt, requested £2,000 (approximately $3,000) from journalists who wanted to interview Pitt at the Cannes Film Festival, an example of checkbook journalism. Alliance claimed it was not a direct interview payment but helped cover some of the star's costs for the trip. This is an example of *checkbook journalism*—paying the interview source for access. (See **Impact/Money**, "Would I Pay £2,000 to Interview Brad Pitt? Not for More Boring Anecdotes," p. 332.)

In 2009, some journalists who were covering the kidnapping story of Jaycee Lee Dugard—a young girl who said she had been held in captivity for 18 years in Antioch, Calif.—offered payments to several neighbors near the place where she lived with her alleged kidnappers, Phillip and Nancy Garrido. Interview payments to witnesses are quite common in Europe, but they present serious ethical problems for reporters who cannot pay for information about the story they are covering.

According to the *Los Angeles Times*, one Garrido neighbor, Damon Robinson, was talking to reporters from CNN, the Associated Press and the *Times* when a British journalist offered Robinson $2,000 if he would stop talking with other reporters and give the British journalist an exclusive. According to the *Times*, "Robinson complied."

Two years later, when Jaycee Lee Dugard was ready to talk with the press, ABC News paid for exclusive rights to the interview.

Besides the ethical questions about whether actors, participants, witnesses and even criminals should profit financially from manufactured publicity, there are other hazards in any type of checkbook journalism. One danger is that a paid interviewee will sensationalize the information to bring a higher price, so the interviewee's truthfulness cannot always be trusted. A second hazard is that such interviews often become the exclusive property of the highest bidder, shutting out smaller news organizations and independent journalists from the information. A third possibility is that the person who is paid by the news organization to comment could possibly carry a hidden agenda.

PRIVACY INVOLVES RESPECT

Privacy for Electronic Communications

Privacy for e-mail and voice mail communications is a very important ethical and legal issue (see also **Chapter 14**). In July 2011, the British newspaper *The Guardian* reported that journalists at the competing British tabloid *News of the World* (owned by a subsidiary of Rupert Murdoch's News Corp.) repeatedly had hacked e-mails and voice mails belonging to British and U.S. celebrities and government officials. This is the case listed as example

Oli Scarff/Getty Images

In 2012, Rebekah Brooks, an executive at the now-defunct British tabloid *News of the World*, was charged with paying bribes of up to $160,000 to get access to public officials' e-mails and voice mails while she was at the paper. She faces a penalty of up to 10 years in prison.

3 on p. 325. There were at least 800 documented hacking victims, allegedly including Queen Elizabeth II, former Prime Minister Gordon Brown as well as actor Jude Law.

Murdoch printed a public apology and then shut down the 168-year-old newspaper. Parliament convened an investigatory commission, and the FBI opened an investigation into possible U.S. hacking victims. In January 2012, News Corp. agreed to pay substantial damages to 37 victims, including Jude Law, and in November 2012, prosecutors in London announced that two former top executives at the newspaper, Rebekah Brooks and Andy Coulson, would be charged with paying bribes of up to $160,000 to

Checkbook Journalism The practice of a news organization paying for an interview or a photograph.

IMPACT / Money

Would I Pay £2,000 to Interview Brad Pitt? Not for More Boring Anecdotes

By Simon Hattenstone

Brad Pitt's film company claims the payment covers costs such as private jets, hairdressers and makeup artists. Two grand for a 20-minute interview with Brad Pitt at Cannes. That's what film company Alliance is charging some journalists for the privilege. So if I took an hour and 20 minutes at £8,000, how many bangs would I expect for my buck? Quite a few, as it happens.

Alliance is quick to point out that we will not be paying Pitt Ltd per se. The payment is just a means of covering its star's costs – for example, flying from America to France in one's private jet with one's own army of hairdressers, makeup artists and agents, never mind the matching suits of armour for you and your son Maddox . . . well, it soon mounts up. And nobody would want Brad, estimated to be worth a paltry $150m last year, to suffer financially for his art.

Anyway, if you can't afford Pitt, you could always opt for an A-star bargain-basement interview—£1,200 for Nicole Kidman, and you still get the full 20 minutes.

In a way, there is nothing new about this. After all, interviews with celebrities have always been an exchange of sorts—you promote your movie, song, book, and we get pretty pictures, gossip and hopefully even an insight into said star. Some newspapers always preferred the cleaner deal of paying for interviews. Then you can whisk away your subject, hold them in captivity and interview the life out of them—because you've paid for it. The greatest ever television interview, David Frost's with Richard Nixon, was pure chequebook journalism—Nixon demanded $600,000 (£380,000) and 20 percent of any profits. No wonder Frost sweated for a confession out of him.

Sadly, the *Guardian* doesn't pay for interviews, which puts us at a distinct disadvantage in the Brad Pitt bidding wars. Not that we're totally

Vittorio Zunino Celotto/WireImage for Electrolux

The film company Alliance requested £2,000 for a 20-minute interview with actor Brad Pitt at Cannes in 2012, according to journalist Simon Hattenstone, whose newspaper doesn't pay for interviews. This is an example of checkbook journalism.

squeaky clean. I admit that in the past I have bribed potential subjects with monster bars of Toblerone. Strangely, it rarely did the trick, so I've had to rely on persistence, cheek, trust and fluke for any minor scoops.

Many interviewees, whether paid for or not, are not so obliging. Actors, in particular. (No offence, Brad.) They tend to spend the whole interview doing just that—acting; telling you yawningly boring anecdotes about the movie they've just made or talking in character, playing for time till the publicist informs you your time has run out and could you please leave the room NOW.

After 20 plus years in the job, I still love interviewing—talking to people who have achieved great things, trying to work out what makes them tick.

So back to the bangs per buck with Brad. If I were splashing out on a one-on-one hour with him, I certainly wouldn't be happy with the normal recycled claptrap . . . and I'd still expect change out of my 8 grand.

Source: Excerpted from Simon Hattenstone, "Would I Pay £2,000 to Interview Brad Pitt? Not for More Boring Anecdotes," May 29, 2012, guardian.co.uk/.

public officials, in addition to several earlier charges levied against them. More than two dozen suits still are pending.

"The charge of bribing a Defense Ministry official is potentially the most serious of all those drawn up by prosecutors so far in the scandal that has enveloped the Murdoch media empire in Britain," reported *The New York Times*. "Under a new bribery act passed by Parliament in 2010, described by British legal experts as one of the toughest statutes of its kind anywhere, the maximum penalty for bribing a public official or receiving a bribe is 10 years in prison and an unlimited fine, but the statute also provides for much lesser penalties."

Reporting on Rape

Reporting on rape is another examples of a complex ethical dilemma of privacy: How does the press balance the goal of truthfulness and fact-finding with the need for personal privacy? Is the private grief that such a report may cause worth the public good that can result from publishing the information?

Privacy is an important issue in reporting on rape cases. Common newsroom practice forbids the naming of rape victims in stories. In 1989, editor Geneva Overholser of *The Des Moines Register* startled the press community when she wrote an editorial arguing that newspapers contribute to the public's misunderstanding of the crime by withholding not only the woman's name but an explicit description of what happened.

In 1990, *The Register* published a five-part series about the rape of Nancy Ziegenmeyer, with Ziegenmeyer's full cooperation. Ziegenmeyer had contacted *The Register* after Overholser's column appeared, volunteering to tell her story. The Ziegenmeyer series provoked wide-ranging debate among editors about this aspect of privacy. Is there more benefit to society by printing the victim's name, with the victim's permission, than by withholding it? Should the press explicitly describe sexual crimes, or is that merely sensationalism, preying on the public's salacious curiosity?

The Brooks and Ziegenmeyer cases demonstrate how complex privacy issues in today's society have become. When do journalists' efforts to get a story go too far? Is it ever in the public interest to divulge personal information about private individuals? How important is the public's right to know?

RESPONSIBILITY BRINGS TRUST

The events journalists choose to report and the way they use the information they gather reflect on the profession's sense of public responsibility. Most reporters

realize that they often change the character of an event by covering that event. The mere presence of the media magnifies the importance of what happens.

A Staged Event

In October 2009, Richard and Mayumi Heene told authorities in Fort Collins, Colo., that they believed their young son Falcon was inside a runaway flying object that Richard Heene had designed. Reporters from all over the country rushed to cover the story. TV networks offered live coverage that showed video of the flying object (which resembled a small flying saucer). Soon, however, it was discovered that Falcon, who became known as "Balloon Boy," had never been in the flying object. Eventually the Heenes admitted the story was a hoax, designed to attract attention to the family in hopes of landing a reality TV show. This is example number 4 (on p. 325).

Chris Schneider/Getty Images

Richard Heene and Mayumi Heene walk out of a Colorado courtroom after being sentenced for their part in what became known as the "Balloon Boy" hoax. After the Heenes admitted the story was a hoax, Richard Heene was sentenced to some time in jail and community service work, plus probation.

Two months later, the Heenes were sentenced to some jail time and community service work and ordered to pay for the expense of police chasing the balloon and investigating the hoax, plus probation. The willingness of reporters to perpetuate the false story through their coverage pointed out how easily reporters can be fooled and how important it is for journalists to verify the information they report.

The media can be exploited by people in trouble or by people who covet the notoriety that media coverage brings. The media can exploit an event for its shock value to try to attract an audience, without adequately verifying the information in the story.

Staged events especially demonstrate the important responsibility that all members of the media share for what some of them do. The credibility of any news organization rests on the way the reporters get the story as much as on the story that's reported. Portraying inaccurate or staged information, even in just one story, ultimately causes readers and viewers to doubt the believability of all stories.

Sometimes reporters' rush to get a story or bad judgment causes serious mistakes to be aired or printed. During the 2004 presidential election campaign, two incidents proved that even large news organizations aren't immune to serious journalistic lapses.

Fabricated Documents

On September 8, 2004, CBS News correspondent Dan Rather presented documents on the CBS program *60 Minutes* that purported to show there were gaps in President Bush's Vietnam-era Texas Air National Guard service. Almost immediately after the broadcast, questions arose about whether the documents were authentic, but for several days CBS and Rather stood by the report.

The documents were supposed to have come from the files of Bush's squadron commander, but then the man who gave the files to CBS admitted that he lied about where the documents came from. A week later, Rather, who also anchored the *CBS Evening News* at the time, apologized during the evening newscast. "I want to say personally and directly I'm sorry," he said. "This was an error made in good faith." CBS appointed a fact-finding panel, which launched a three-month investigation into why Rather's *60 Minutes* producers did not substantiate the information before airing the story.

In January 2005, the panel issued its report, which found, among other things, that the program's primary producer, Mary Mapes, did not scrutinize the background of the person who had provided the documents and that the segment's producers did not report that four experts who looked at the documents could not guarantee their authenticity. CBS fired Mapes and asked three other producers who had been involved in the report to resign.

Rather, who said he previously had considered stepping down as *CBS Evening News* anchor, was replaced, but stayed on as a correspondent. CBS then instituted new procedures that required independent review for investigative stories and appointed a new vice president for Standards and Practices, Linda Mason. "Standards are not an end in themselves," Mason told *The New York Times*. "Standards are a way we can achieve fairness and accuracy."

Phony Web Story

In October 2004, less than a month after the CBS incident, Fox News was forced to apologize to visitors to the Fox News Web site after Fox's chief political correspondent Carl Cameron posted a story that quoted presidential candidate John Kerry saying, "Didn't my nails and cuticles look great? What a good debate!" after his October televised debate with President Bush. "Women should like me! I do manicures," the story also quoted Kerry as saying.

Fox quickly retracted the article, and Paul Schur, a network spokesman, said, "This was a stupid mistake and a lapse in judgment, and Carl regrets it." Schur said Cameron had been reprimanded, but Schur did not explain how such an irresponsible story managed to escape review before it appeared on the Fox site.

All news organizations must accept responsibility for a lack of editorial review and oversight of stories that should have been stopped before they reach the public. In the CBS case, producers hurried to get the story on the air before checking it thoroughly. At Fox News, an errant reporter called the credibility of the entire news organization into question, but the news organization itself ultimately is at fault for its lack of safeguards. Responsible news organizations encourage ethical behavior as well as constantly remind reporters about their special responsibility to the public and to their profession.

FIVE PHILOSOPHICAL PRINCIPLES GOVERN MEDIA ETHICS

Scholars can prescribe only general guidelines for moral decisions because each situation presents its own special dilemmas. First, it is important to understand the basic principles that underlie these philosophical discussions. In their book *Media Ethics*, Clifford G. Christians, Kim B. Rotzoll and Mark Fackler identify five major philosophical principles underlying today's ethical decisions: (1) Aristotle's golden mean, (2) Kant's categorical imperative, (3) Mill's principle of utility, (4) Rawls' veil of ignorance and (5) the Judeo-Christian view of persons as ends in themselves.

1. *Aristotle's golden mean:* According to Aristotle, virtue is "the mean between two extremes." This is a philosophy of moderation and compromise, often called the *golden mean*. The journalistic concept of fairness reflects this idea.

2. *Kant's categorical imperative*: "Act on that maxim which you will to become a universal law." Eighteenth-century philosopher Immanuel Kant developed this idea, an extension of Aristotle's golden mean. Kant's test—that you make decisions based on principles that you want to be universally applied—is called the *categorical imperative*. This means you choose an

action by asking yourself the question, what would happen if everyone acted this way?

3. *Mill's principle of utility*: "Seek the greatest happiness for the greatest number." In the 19th century, John Stuart Mill taught that the best decision is one with the biggest overall benefit for the most human beings.

4. *Rawls' veil of ignorance*: "Justice emerges when negotiating without social differentiations." John Rawls' 20th-century theory supports an egalitarian society that asks everyone to work from a sense of liberty and basic respect for everyone, regardless of social position.

5. *Judeo-Christian view of persons as ends in themselves*: "Love your neighbor as yourself." Under this long-standing ethic of religious heritage, people should care for one another—friends as well as enemies—equally and without favor. Trust in people and they will trust in you.

In American society, none of these five philosophies operates independently. Ethical choices in many journalistic situations are not exquisitely simple. What is predictable about journalistic ethics is their unpredictability. Therefore, journalists generally adopt a philosophy of situational ethics: Because each circumstance is different, a journalist must decide the best action to take in each situation.

Should the press adopt Rawls' idea of social equality and cover each person equally, or should public officials receive more scrutiny than others because they maintain a public trust? Is it a loving act in the Judeo-Christian tradition to allow bereaved parents privacy to grieve for their child's death by drowning, or is the journalist contributing to society's greater good by warning others about the dangers of leaving a child unattended? Questions like these leave the press in a continually bubbling cauldron of ethical quandaries.

MEDIA'S ETHICAL DECISIONS CARRY CONSEQUENCES

Ethical dilemmas might seem easier to solve with a rule book nearby, and several professional media organizations have tried to codify ethical judgments to ensure the outcomes in difficult situations. Codes of ethics can be very general ("Truth is our ultimate goal"—Society of Professional Journalists); some are very specific ("We will no longer accept any complimentary tickets, dinners, junkets, gifts or favors of any kind"—*The San Bernardino* [Calif.] *Sun*); and some are very personal

David Sipress/Cartoon Bank.com

("I will try to tell people what they ought to know and avoid telling them what they want to hear, except when the two coincide, which isn't often"—former CBS commentator Andy Rooney).

Some ethical decisions carry legal consequences—for example, when a journalist reports embarrassing facts and invades someone's privacy. First Amendment protections shield the media from government enforcement of specific codes of conduct, except when ethical mistakes also are judged by the courts to be legal mistakes. In most cases, however, a reporter or a news organization that makes an ethical mistake will not face a lawsuit.

The consequences of bad ethical judgments usually involve damage to the newsmakers and to the individual journalist, damage to the reputation of the news organization where the journalist works and damage to the profession in general.

PROFESSIONAL ASSOCIATIONS PROSCRIBE BEHAVIOR

Professional codes of ethics set a leadership tone for a profession, an organization or an individual. Several groups have attempted to write rules governing how the media should operate.

Television stations that belonged to the National Association of Broadcasters (*NAB*), for example, once subscribed to a code of conduct the NAB developed. This code covered news reporting and entertainment programming. One provision of the NAB code said, "Violence, physical or psychological, may only be projected

NAB National Association of Broadcasters, the lobbying organization that represents broadcasters' interests.

in responsibly handled contexts, not used exploitatively. Programs involving violence should present the consequences of it to its victims and perpetrators." Members displayed the NAB Seal of Approval before broadcasts to exhibit their compliance with the code.

In 1976, a decision by a federal-court judge in Los Angeles abolished the broadcast codes, claiming the provisions violated the First Amendment. Today, codes of ethics for both print and broadcast are voluntary, with no absolute penalties for people who violate the rules. These codes are meant as guidelines. Many media organizations, such as CBS News, the *Los Angeles Times*, and *The New York Times*, maintain their own detailed standards and hire people specifically to monitor ethical conduct. Other organizations use guidelines from professional groups as a basis to develop their own philosophies. Advertising and public relations organizations also have issued ethics codes.

Four widely used codes of ethics are the guidelines adopted by the Interactive Advertising Bureau, the Society of Professional Journalists, the Radio Television Digital News Association and the Public Relations Society of America.

Interactive Advertising Bureau Addresses Digital Ads

The Interactive Advertising Bureau (IAB)'s Code of Conduct is the most recent set of media guidelines, first established in 1996 to cover businesses that advertise on the Internet. The guidelines, last updated in 2003, are voluntary and self-regulatory and apply to all members of the IAB. The IAB says that more than 80 percent of interactive display ads follow IAB standards. The major principles of the IAB Code of Conduct are excerpted here.

> The IAB is committed to the continued growth of the interactive advertising ecosystem. The IAB believes that consumers and business are best-served when strong and flexible self-regulatory measures are in place when members and their business partners engage in digital behavioral advertising.

I. Education

Entities should participate in efforts to educate individuals and businesses about online behavioral advertising, including the actors in the ecosystem, how data may be collected, and how consumer choice and control may be exercised.

II. Transparency

A. Third Party and Service Provider Notice

Third parties and service providers should give clear, meaningful, and prominent notice on their own Web sites that describes their online behavioral advertising data collection and use practices.

III. Consumer Control

A. Third Party Choice for Behavioral Advertising

A Third party should provide consumers with the ability to exercise choice with respect to the collection and use of data for online behavioral advertising purposes or the transfer of such data to a non-Affiliate for such purpose.

IV. Data Security

A. Safeguards

Entities should maintain appropriate physical, electronic, and administrative safeguards to protect the data collected and used for online behavioral advertising purposes.

B. Data Retention

Entities should retain data that is collected and used for online behavioral advertising only as long as necessary to fulfill a legitimate business need, or as required by law.

V. Material Changes to Existing Online Behavior Advertising Policies and Practices

Entities should obtain consent before applying any material change to their online behavioral advertising data collection and use policies and practices prior to such material change.

VI. Sensitive Data

A. Children

Entities should not collect "personal information", as defined in the Children's Online Privacy Protection Act (COPPA), from children they have actual knowledge are under the age of 13 or from sites directed to children under the age of 13 for online behavioral advertising, or engage in online behavioral advertising directed to children they have actual knowledge are under the age of 13 except as compliant with the COPPA.

B. Health and Financial Data

Entities should not collect and use financial account numbers, Social Security numbers, pharmaceutical prescriptions, or medical records about a specific individual for online behavioral advertising without consent.

Society of Professional Journalists Outlines Conduct

This code lists specific canons for journalists. The code's major points follow.

Seek Truth and Report It. Journalists should be honest, fair and courageous in gathering, reporting and interpreting information. Journalists should:

- Test the accuracy of information from all sources and exercise care to avoid inadvertent error. Deliberate distortion is never permissible. . . .
- Identify sources whenever feasible. The public is entitled to as much information as possible on sources' reliability. . . .
- Make certain that headlines, news teases and promotional material, photos, video, audio, graphics, sound bites and quotations do not misrepresent. They should not oversimplify or highlight incidents out of context.
- Never distort the content of news photos or video. Image enhancement for technical clarity is always permissible. Label montages and photo illustrations.
- Avoid misleading reenactments or staged news events. . . .
- Never plagiarize. . . .
- Avoid stereotyping by race, gender, age, religion, ethnicity, geography, sexual orientation, disability, physical appearance or social status. . . .
- Distinguish between advocacy and news reporting. Analysis and commentary should be labeled and not misrepresent fact or context.
- Distinguish news from advertising and shun hybrids that blur the lines between the two.
- Recognize a special obligation to ensure that the public's business is conducted in the open and that government records are open to inspection.

Minimize Harm. Ethical journalists treat sources, subjects and colleagues as human beings deserving of respect. Journalists should:

- Show compassion for those who may be affected adversely by news coverage. Use special sensitivity when dealing with children and inexperienced sources or subjects.
- Be sensitive when seeking or using interviews or photographs of those affected by tragedy or grief.
- Recognize that gathering and reporting information may cause harm or discomfort. Pursuit of the news is not a license for arrogance. . . .
- Show good taste. Avoid pandering to lurid curiosity. . . .
- Balance a criminal suspect's fair trial rights with the public's right to be informed.

Act Independently. Journalists should be free of obligation to any interest other than the public's right to know. Journalists should:

- Avoid conflicts of interest, real or perceived.
- Remain free of associations and activities that may compromise integrity or damage credibility.
- Refuse gifts, favors, fees, free travel and special treatment, and shun secondary employment, political involvement, public office and service in community organizations if they compromise journalistic integrity. . . .

Be Accountable. Journalists are accountable to their readers, listeners, viewers and each other. Journalists should:

- Clarify and explain news coverage and invite dialogue with the public over journalistic conduct.
- Encourage the public to voice grievances against the news media.
- Admit mistakes and correct them promptly.
- Expose unethical practices of journalists and the news media.
- Abide by the same high standards to which they hold others.

Radio Television Digital News Association (RTDNA) Code Covers Electronic News

The RTDNA Code of Ethics and Professional Conduct, last updated in September 2000, offers general principles for electronic news reporters ("Professional electronic journalists should recognize that their first obligation is to the public"), as well as specific guidelines ("Professional electronic journalists should not

Frederic J. Brown/AFP/Getty Images

Professional codes of ethics provide guidelines for how journalists should do their jobs. On April 18, 2013, Texas Attorney General Greg Abbott (center) briefs reporters in West, Texas, about a massive explosion at a fertilizer factory that killed 12 people and destroyed dozens of homes.

manipulate images or sounds in any way that is misleading"). Following is the RTDNA ethics code, reprinted in its entirety.

PREAMBLE

Professional electronic journalists should operate as trustees of the public, seek the truth, report it fairly and with integrity and independence, and stand accountable for their actions.

PUBLIC TRUST: Professional electronic journalists should recognize that their first obligation is to the public.

Professional electronic journalists should:

- Understand that any commitment other than service to the public undermines trust and credibility.
- Recognize that service in the public interest creates an obligation to reflect the diversity of the community and guard against oversimplification of issues or events.
- Provide a full range of information to enable the public to make enlightened decisions.
- Fight to ensure that the public's business is conducted in public.

TRUTH: Professional electronic journalists should pursue truth aggressively and present the

news accurately, in context, and as completely as possible.

Professional electronic journalists should:

- Continuously seek the truth.
- Resist distortions that obscure the importance of events.
- Clearly disclose the origin of information and label all material provided by outsiders.

Professional electronic journalists should not:

- Report anything known to be false.
- Manipulate images or sounds in any way that is misleading.
- Plagiarize.
- Present images or sounds that are reenacted without informing the public.

FAIRNESS: Professional electronic journalists should present the news fairly and impartially, placing primary value on significance and relevance.

Professional electronic journalists should:

- Treat all subjects of news coverage with respect and dignity, showing particular compassion to victims of crime or tragedy.
- Exercise special care when children are involved in a story and give children greater privacy protection than adults.
- Seek to understand the diversity of their community and inform the public without bias or stereotype.
- Present a diversity of expressions, opinions, and ideas in context.
- Present analytical reporting based on professional perspective, not personal bias.
- Respect the right to a fair trial.

INTEGRITY: Professional electronic journalists should present the news with integrity and decency, avoiding real or perceived conflicts of interest, and respect the dignity and intelligence of the audience as well as the subjects of news.

Professional electronic journalists should:

- Identify sources whenever possible. Confidential sources should be used only when it is clearly in the public interest to gather or convey important information or when a person providing information might be harmed. Journalists should keep all commitments to protect a confidential source.
- Clearly label opinion and commentary.
- Guard against extended coverage of events or individuals that fails to significantly advance a story,

place the event in context, or add to the public knowledge.

- Refrain from contacting participants in violent situations while the situation is in progress.
- Use technological tools with skill and thoughtfulness, avoiding techniques that skew facts, distort reality, or sensationalize events.
- Use surreptitious newsgathering techniques, including hidden cameras or microphones, only if there is no other way to obtain stories of significant public importance and only if the technique is explained to the audience.
- Disseminate the private transmissions of other news organizations only with permission.

Professional electronic journalists should not:

- Pay news sources who have a vested interest in a story.
- Accept gifts, favors, or compensation from those who might seek to influence coverage.
- Engage in activities that may compromise their integrity or independence.

INDEPENDENCE: Professional electronic journalists should defend the independence of all journalists from those seeking influence or control over news content.

Professional electronic journalists should:

- Gather and report news without fear or favor, and vigorously resist undue influence from any outside forces, including advertisers, sources, story subjects, powerful individuals, and special interest groups.
- Resist those who would seek to buy or politically influence news content or who would seek to intimidate those who gather and disseminate the news.
- Determine news content solely through editorial judgment and not as the result of outside influence.
- Resist any self-interest or peer pressure that might erode journalistic duty and service to the public.
- Recognize that sponsorship of the news will not be used in any way to determine, restrict, or manipulate content.
- Refuse to allow the interests of ownership or management to influence news judgment and content inappropriately.
- Defend the rights of the free press for all journalists, recognizing that any professional or government licensing of journalists is a violation of that freedom.

ACCOUNTABILITY: Professional electronic journalists should recognize that they are accountable for their actions to the public, the profession, and themselves.

Professional electronic journalists should:

- Actively encourage adherence to these standards by all journalists and their employers.
- Respond to public concerns. Investigate complaints and correct errors promptly and with as much prominence as the original report.
- Explain journalistic processes to the public, especially when practices spark questions or controversy.
- Recognize that professional electronic journalists are duty-bound to conduct themselves ethically.
- Refrain from ordering or encouraging courses of action that would force employees to commit an unethical act.
- Carefully listen to employees who raise ethical objections and create environments in which such objections and discussions are encouraged.
- Seek support for and provide opportunities to train employees in ethical decision-making.

Public Relations Society of America Sets Standards

The Code of Professional Standards, first adopted in 1950 by the Public Relations Society of America, has been revised several times. Here are some excerpts:

- A member shall deal fairly with clients or employers, past, present, or potential, with fellow practitioners and with the general public.
- A member shall adhere to truth and accuracy and to generally accepted standards of good taste.
- A member shall not intentionally communicate false or misleading information, and is obligated to use care to avoid communication of false or misleading information.
- A member shall be prepared to identify publicly the name of the client or employer on whose behalf any public communication is made.
- A member shall not guarantee the achievement of specified results beyond the member's direct control.

MEDIA ORGANIZATIONS RESPOND TO CRITICISM

Prescriptive codes of ethics are helpful in describing what journalists should do, and informal guidelines can supplement professional codes. Many journalists use good judgment, but what happens when they don't? People with serious complaints against broadcasters sometimes appeal to the Federal Communications Commission, but what about complaints that must be handled more quickly? The press has offered three solutions: news councils, readers' representatives and correction boxes.

News Councils

News councils originated in Great Britain. They are composed of people who formerly worked or currently work in the news business, as well as some laypeople. The council reviews complaints from the public, and when the members determine that a mistake has been made, the council reports its findings to the offending news organization.

In 1973, the Twentieth-Century Fund established a National News Council in the United States, which eventually was funded through contributions from various news organizations. The council was composed of 18 members from the press and the public. The council was disbanded in 1984, largely because some major news organizations stopped giving money to support it but also because several news managers opposed the council, arguing that the profession should police itself.

Today, only two news councils exist in the United States, the Minnesota News Council and the Honolulu Community Media Council. The Minnesota council is older. Since 1970, the council's 24 members, half of them journalists and half of them public members such as lawyers and teachers, have reviewed complaints about the state's media. Half of the complaints have been ruled in favor of the journalists. The council has no enforcement power, only the power of public scrutiny.

Media ethics scholar John Hulteng offers this evaluation of news councils:

> It would seem that—as with the [ethics] codes—the great impact of the press councils is likely to be on the responsible editors, publishers and broadcasters who for the most part were already attempting to behave ethically. . . . An additional value of the councils may be the mutual understanding that grows out of the exchange across the council table between the members of the public and the managers of the media. These values should not be dismissed as insignificant, of course. But neither should too much be expected of them.

Readers' Representatives

The *readers' representative* (also called an ombudsperson or public reporter) is a go-between at a newspaper who responds to complaints from the public and regularly publishes answers to criticism in the newspaper.

About two dozen newspapers throughout the country, including *The Washington Post, The New York Times, The Kansas City Star* and the Louisville *Courier-Journal*, have tried the idea, but most newspapers still funnel complaints directly to the editor.

The *Los Angeles Times* publishes a regular blog called *Readers' Representative Journal*, which the newspaper

says is designed to "help readers understand the thinking behind what appears in the *Times*, and to provide insight for the newsroom into how readers respond to their reporting."

Correction Boxes

The *correction box* is a device that often is handled by a readers' representative but also has been adopted by many papers without a readers' representative. The box is published in the same place, usually a prominent one, in the newspaper every day and on the newspaper's Web site with the corrected story and a note about the correction.

As a permanent feature of the newspaper, the correction box leads readers to notice when the newspaper retracts or modifies a statement. It is used to counter criticism that corrections sometimes receive less attention from readers than the original stories.

The New York Times, for example, regularly publishes a small correction box to fix small errors in its stories. But when *The Times* discovered in 2010 that its reporter Zachery Kouwe had plagiarized stories from *The Wall Street Journal* (see p. 326), *The Times* published a specific explanation as a lengthy Editor's Note, which gave the incident more prominent attention.

PROFESSIONAL CODES PRESERVE MEDIA CREDIBILITY

News councils, readers' representatives and correction boxes help newspapers handle criticism and avert possible legal problems that some stories foster, but these solutions address only a small percentage of issues and only for print journalism. In newsrooms every day, reporters face the same ethical decisions all people face in their daily lives—whether to be honest, how to be fair, how to be sensitive and how to be responsible.

The difference is that, unlike personal ethical dilemmas that people can debate privately, reporters and editors publish and broadcast the results of their ethical judgments, and those judgments become public knowledge—in newspapers, magazines and books and on radio, television and the Internet. So the media's ethical decisions have the potential to affect society.

A profession that accepts ethical behavior as a standard helps guarantee its future. The major commodity the press in America has to offer is information, and when the presentation of that information is weakened by untruth, bias, intrusiveness or irresponsibility, the press gains few advocates and acquires more enemies.

Writes John Hulteng:

> The primary objective of the press and those who work with it is to bring readers, listeners and viewers as honest, accurate and complete an account of the day's events as possible. . . . The need to be informed is so great that the Constitution provides the press with a First Amendment standing that is unique among business enterprises. But as with most grants of power, there is an accompanying responsibility, not constitutionally mandated but nonetheless well understood: that the power of the press must be used responsibly and compassionately.

Review, Analyze, Investigate

Reviewing Chapter 15

Ethics Define Responsibilities

- The word *ethics* derives from the Greek word *ethos*, which means the guiding spirit or traditions that govern a culture.

- When journalists make the wrong ethical choices, the consequences are very public.

- Journalists' ethical dilemmas can be discussed using four categories: truthfulness, fairness, privacy and responsibility.

Truthfulness Affects Credibility

- Truthfulness means more than telling the truth to get a story. Truthfulness also means not misrepresenting the people or the situations in the story for readers or viewers.

- Syndicated columnist Armstrong Williams received $250,000 from a public relations firm to promote President Bush's No Child Left Behind initiative to African Americans. In 2005, after *USA Today* revealed the arrangement, Williams attributed his lapse to the fact that he was not trained as a journalist.

- Truthfulness means that government agencies should not knowingly provide disinformation to the press.

- In July 2012, *New Yorker* writer Jonah Lehrer resigned after it was discovered that he fabricated quotes for his book, *Imagine: How Creativity Works*.

- In 2010, *The New York Times* suspended reporter Zachery Kouwe after editors said Kouwe had plagiarized portions of an article he had written for *The Times* from an article by another reporter that had appeared online in *The Wall Street Journal*. Kouwe resigned.

- In 2009, Universal Pictures posted fake stories purported to be from Alaska news publications to promote its movie *The Fourth Kind*. When the fabrications were discovered, Universal paid the Alaska Press Club a $20,000 settlement.

- Disinformation was the issue at the 2007 trial of presidential advisor I. Lewis Libby.

- In 2006, author James Frey admitted he had fabricated many incidents in his memoir *A Million Little Pieces*. Frey apologized.

- A classic example of a journalistic misrepresentation is Jayson Blair, a reporter for *The New York Times*, who admitted in May 2003 that he had fabricated comments, concocted scenes, stolen material from other newspapers and news services and selected details from photos to create an impression he had been in certain places and interviewed people when he hadn't.

Fairness Means Evenhandedness

- Fairness implies impartiality—that the journalist has nothing personal to gain from a report and that there are no hidden benefits to the reporter or to the source from the story being presented.

- Criticism of the press for unfairness results from insider friendships, conflicts of interest and checkbook journalism.

- In June 2012, six months after her exclusive interview with President Bashar al-Assad of Syria, ABC News Correspondent Barbara Walters admitted she had arranged an interview to help a former media advisor to al-Assad get a job as an intern at CNN and also gain admission to Columbia University.

- As examples of insider friendships, in 2010, MSNBC commentators Keith Olbermann and Joe Scarborough each were suspended for two days after it was discovered that they had made campaign contributions to political candidates.

- In another example of insider friendship, in 2010, the *New Hampshire Union Leader* accepted underwriting from three major New Hampshire businesses including BAE Systems, a defense contractor, so the newspaper's publisher and a staff photographer could travel to Afghanistan to report on a New Hampshire National Guard unit serving there.

- In 2009, *The Washington Post* lost credibility when its publisher invited sponsorships in exchange for attendance at an exclusive "salon" at her home. *The Post* eventually cancelled the event and printed an apology.

- In 2012, Alliance, the film company that represented actor Brad Pitt, requested £2,000 (approximately $3,000) from journalists who wanted to interview Pitt at the Cannes Film Festival, an example of checkbook journalism.

- In 2011, ABC News paid kidnapping victim Jaycee Lee Dugard for exclusive rights to an interview, another example of checkbook journalism.

Privacy Involves Respect

- Privacy for personal communications such as e-mails and voice mails became a big issue in 2011 when reporters at Rupert Murdoch's *News of the World* hacked celebrity e-mails and voice mails.

- In November 2012, prosecutors in London announced that two former top executives at *News of the World*, Rebekah Brooks and Andy Coulson, would be charged with paying bribes of up to $160,000 to public officials, in addition to several earlier charges levied against them.

- An important invasion-of-privacy issue is the publication of names of rape victims.

- Reporters must decide whether the public interest is served by revealing victims' names.

Responsibility Brings Trust

- Responsibility means that reporters and editors must be careful about the way they use the information they gather.

- Live events, such as the "Balloon Boy" hoax, offer especially perilous ethical situations for reporters because they must verify information quickly and are vulnerable to mistakes.

- During the 2004 presidential campaign, CBS's *60 Minutes'* undocumented report of President Bush's Air National Guard service and Fox News' phony report about presidential candidate Senator John Kerry are two examples of news organizations forgetting their responsibilities to the public.

Five Philosophical Principles Govern Media Ethics

- Five philosophical principles underlying the practical application of ethical decisions are (1) Aristotle's golden mean, (2) Immanuel Kant's categorical imperative, (3) John Stuart Mill's principle of utility, (4) John Rawls' veil of ignorance and (5) the Judeo-Christian view of persons as ends in themselves.

- Journalists adopt a philosophy of situational ethics.

Media's Ethical Decisions Carry Consequences

- Some ethical decisions carry legal consequences, such as when a journalist reports embarrassing facts and invades someone's privacy.

- In most cases, a reporter or a news organization that makes an ethical mistake will not face a lawsuit.

Professional Associations Proscribe Behavior

- Several media professions have adopted ethics codes to guide their conduct.

- Four of these ethics codes are the guidelines adopted by the Interactive Advertising Bureau, the Society of Professional Journalists, the Radio Television Digital News Association and the Public Relations Society of America.

Media Organizations Respond to Criticism

- The three responses of the U.S. press to criticism have been to create news councils, to employ readers' representatives and to publish correction boxes in the printed newspaper and online.

- The National Press Council, created to hear consumer complaints about the press, was created in 1973 but disbanded in 1984. Today only two news councils still exist in the United States—the Minnesota News Council and the Honolulu Community Media Council.

Professional Codes Preserve Media Credibility

- The media's ethical decisions can broadly affect society.

- The major commodity the American press has to offer is credibility, and when the presentation of information is weakened by untruth, bias, intrusiveness or irresponsibility, the press gains few advocates and acquires more enemies.

Key Terms

These terms are defined in the margins throughout this chapter and appear in alphabetical order with definitions in the Glossary, which begins on page 373.

Critical Questions

1. When you read about high-profile media ethics cases like the ones in this chapter, do you ever think about the possibility that what you're reading, hearing or seeing in the mass media may not be true, or at least not what you understand it to be? How does this affect the way you obtain or use information?

2. How does checkbook journalism affect the quality of reporting?

3. Pick any of the ethical situations specified in this chapter and describe how each of the following philosophical principles would define your decision.

    a. Aristotle's golden mean
    b. Kant's categorical imperative
    c. Mill's principle of utility
    d. Rawls' veil of ignorance

4. What is your opinion about the question in the Ziegenmeyer case of releasing the name of a victim of rape with the victim's consent? How would you balance the protection of victims with the public's interest in the non-anonymous comments of the victim? Should rape victims be more deserving of anonymity than victims of other crimes? Explain.

5. What effect do you believe ethics codes, such as those described in this chapter, have on the professionals for whom they have been developed?

Working the Web

This list includes both sites mentioned in the chapter and others to give you greater insight into media ethics.

Columbia Journalism Review (CJR)
cjr.org

The mission of this publication from Columbia University Graduate School of Journalism is "to encourage and stimulate excellence in journalism in the service of a free society." The Web site's search capabilities allow users to access all past posts from *CJRDaily.org* and Campaign Desk (political journalism coverage), as well as back issues. Its resources include Who Owns What, a guide to what the major media companies own; Language Corner, a guide to writing in English; and CJR study guides for journalism students. The site promises fresh media analysis and criticism every day as well as specials and interactive features about the performance and problems of the press.

EthicNet, European Ethics Codes
ethicnet.uta.fi/

This databank holds links to English translations of journalism codes of ethics from most European countries (maintained by the Department of Journalism and Mass Communication, University of Tampere, Finland). There are also links to press councils' Web sites, Ethics on the World Wide Web from California State University at Fullerton (eth-icnet.uta.fi/links).

Fairness & Accuracy In Reporting (FAIR)
fair.org

This national media watch group offers "well-documented criticism of media bias and censorship." An anticensorship organization, FAIR is a progressive group that believes structural reform is needed to promote strong nonprofit sources of information. FAIR's critique of the current state of the media is explained in its overview, What's FAIR? Viewers can browse archived articles on issues from Abortion to Youth.

Freedom Forum
freedomforum.org

This nonpartisan foundation is dedicated to "free press, free speech and free spirit for all people." The Freedom Forum is the main funder of the Newseum, an interactive museum of news in Washington, D.C. (newseum.org); the First Amendment Center, which features current news and commentary as well as a First Amendment glossary and lesson plans (first amendmentcenter.org); and the Diversity Institute, based at the John Seigenthaler Center at Vanderbilt University in Nashville, Tenn., dedicated to developing and retaining a diverse workforce in U.S. newsrooms (freedomforumdiversity.org).

Indiana University Index of Journalism Ethics Cases
journalism.indiana.edu/resources/ethics/

This set of cases was created to help teachers, researchers, professional journalists and consumers of news explore ethical issues of journalism. The issues include sensitive news topics, covering politics, invading privacy and being first.

Poynter Online

poynter.org

This Web site of the St. Petersburg, Fla., center for journalists, future journalists and journalism teachers features news and tips for students about reporting and writing, ethics and diversity, journalism education and more. The training section includes information on seminars and webinars, career coaching and Poynter publications. Users can connect with an online community of groups based on various journalism topics.

Project for Excellence in Journalism: Ethics Codes

journalism.org/resources/ethics_codes

This is a direct Web link to a list of professional ethics codes used throughout various media industries in the U.S. and Europe. Includes sites for specific U.S. news organizations (such as the *Los Angeles Times*, *The New York Times*, the *Detroit Free Press*, and the Corporation for Public Broadcasting) as well as international ethics codes, such as the BBC Editorial Guidelines and the International Federation of Journalists' Declaration of Principles on the Conduct of Journalists.

Radio Television Digital News Association (RTDNA; formerly Radio-Television News Directors Association)

rtdna.org

RTDNA is a professional organization that serves the electronic news profession. Its membership consists of more than 3,000 news directors, associates, educators and students. The association's educational foundation, RTDNF, was created to help members uphold ethical journalism standards in the newsroom. Ethics information—including the association's Code of Ethics and Professional Conduct, details on the Journalism Ethics Project, and coverage guidelines—is available in the Web site's Best Practices section.

Society of Professional Journalists (SPJ)

spj.org

The nation's most broad-based journalism organization, SPJ is dedicated to "encouraging the free practice of journalism and stimulating high standards of ethical behavior." Features include freedom of information; ethics (including the SPJ Code of Ethics); *Rainbow Diversity Sourcebook*, *Journalists Toolbox*, SPJ blogs and other publications including the current issue of the association's online magazine *Quill*.

Impact/Action Videos are concise news features on various topics created exclusively for *Media/Impact*. Go online to access MindTap at cengagebrain.com. MindTap for Media/Impact sequences all of your learning tools—Chapter Readings with highlighting and note taking, **Impact/Action Videos**, activities and assessments—into chapter driven learning units that guide you through the curriculum.

GLOBAL MEDIA:
DISCOVERING
NEW MARKETS

Trevor Snapp/Bloomberg/Getty Images

Pedestrians pass a giant advertise-
ment for Samsung Electronics Co. in Nairobi, Kenya,
on March 1, 2013. Mobile phones are a central factor in the expansion
of mass media around the world.

"The Internet will pass newspapers to become the second-largest global ad medium, behind television."

—ADVERTISING AGE

In the United States,

many students assume that mass media in most countries operate like the U.S. media, but media industries in different countries are as varied as the countries they serve. Can you identify the countries in the following media situations?

1. People in this country have access to more wireless Internet *hot spots* than anywhere else in the world. (A hot spot is a public area like a restaurant or hotel where a wireless Internet router allows people with laptops and hand-held Internet devices, such as smartphones, to use the Internet without a wired connection.)

2. This country produces more movies every year—1,100—than any other nation in the world.

3. This company is the world's biggest advertiser and spends more than $11 billion a year to market is products.

4. This country's TV license police can knock on people's doors, fine them approximately $250 and threaten them with jail if they don't pay the annual TV license fee.

Hot Spot A public area like a restaurant or hotel where people with laptops and hand-held Internet devices can connect to the Internet without a wire.

WORLD MEDIA SYSTEMS VARY

The country with the largest number of wireless locations (example 1) is South Korea, according to JiWire, a leading hot spot directory. In the United States, the place with the most wireless locations (hot spots) is New York City with 1,657—nearly three times the number of hot spots that are available in Los Angeles (637).

The country that produces the most movies (example 2) is India, which celebrated its 100th year of moviemaking in 2013.

The company that spends the most money to advertise globally (example 3) is Procter & Gamble, makers of Tide detergent, among other household products. Procter & Gamble is also the United States' biggest advertiser. (See **Illustration 16.2**, "Top 10 Global Marketers," p. 365.)

People who live in the United Kingdom are responsible for paying a yearly TV license fee (example 4). The fee is due at the post office each year, so the collectors who enforce the fee are actually members of the post office. The government collects more than $2 billion a year from the fees, which allows the British Broadcasting Corporation to operate several radio and TV stations without advertising.

These examples help demonstrate the complexity of defining today's international media marketplace, which clearly is a marketplace in rapid transition. This chapter examines various aspects of global media, including political theories and the media, world media systems, news and information flow and global media markets.

Five Political Theories Describe How World Media Operate

No institution as sizable and influential as the mass media can escape involvement with government and politics. The media are not only channels for the transmission of political information and debate but also significant players with a direct stake in government's regulatory and economic policies, as well as government's attitude toward free speech and dissent.

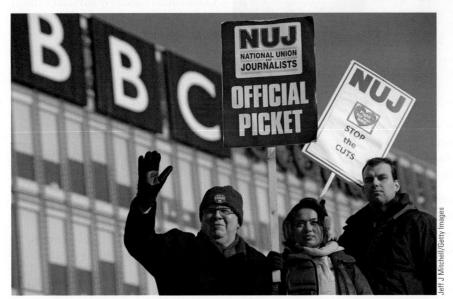

In Britain, radio and TV users pay an annual license fee to support the British Broadcasting Corporation (BBC). In 2011, the faltering economy forced the BBC to cut 2,000 jobs. Journalists in the UK are represented by the National Union of Journalists, which protested the job cuts outside the BBC offices in Glasgow, Scotland.

Remember that *the way a country's political system is organized affects the way the mass media within that country operate*. Media systems can be divided broadly into those systems that allow dissent and those that do not.

To categorize the political organization of media systems, scholars often begin with the 1956 book *Four Theories of the Press*, by Fred S. Siebert, Theodore Peterson and Wilbur Schramm. These four theories, which originally were used to describe the political systems under which media operated in different countries, were (1) the Soviet theory, (2) the authoritarian theory, (3) the libertarian theory and (4) the social responsibility theory. Scholars recently added a fifth description, the more modern (5) developmental theory, to update the original categories used to help describe the world's mass media systems.

The Soviet Theory

Historically in the Soviet Union (which dissolved in 1991 into several independent nations and states), the government owned and operated the mass media. All media employees were government employees, expected to serve the government's interests.

Top media executives also served as leaders in the Communist Party. Even when the press controls loosened in the 1980s, the mass media were part of the government's policy. Government control came *before* the media published or broadcast; people who controlled the media could exercise *prior restraint*. They could review copy and look at programs before they appeared.

This description of the Soviet press system was conceived before the events of the 1990s challenged the basic assumptions of Soviet government. Many Eastern bloc countries, such as Romania, Slovakia and the Czech Republic, which once operated under Soviet influence, based their media systems on the Communist model. Today, the media systems in these countries are in transition.

The Authoritarian Theory

Media that operate under the authoritarian theory can be either publicly or privately owned. This concept of the press developed in Europe after Gutenberg. Until the 1850s, presses in Europe were privately owned, and the aristocracy (which governed the countries) wanted some sort of control over what was printed about them. The aristocracy had the financial and political power necessary to make the rules about what would be printed.

The first idea was to license everyone who owned a printing press so the license could be revoked if someone published something unfavorable about the government. The British crown licensed the first colonial newspapers in America. Licensing wasn't very successful in the United States, however, because many people who owned presses didn't apply for licenses.

The next authoritarian attempt to control the press was to review material after it was published. A printer who was discovered publishing material that strongly challenged the government could be heavily fined or even put to death. Today, many governments still

China has 538 million Internet users, and the government has placed various controls on Web site access. A newspaper stand in Shanghai advertises Wi-Fi access through ChinaNet on January 8, 2013.

maintain this type of rigid control over the media. Most monarchies, for example, operate in an authoritarian tradition, which tolerates very little dissent. Media systems that serve at the government's pleasure and with the government's approval are common.

The Libertarian Theory

The concept of a libertarian press evolved from the idea that people who are given all the information on an issue will be able to discern what is true and what is false and will make good choices. This is an idea embraced by the writers of the U.S. Constitution and by other democratic governments.

"Watching people argue about the world situation night after night makes me feel I'm doing something about it."

This theory assumes, of course, that the media's main goal is to convey the truth and that the media will not cave in to outside pressures, such as from advertisers or corporate owners. This theory also assumes that people with opposing viewpoints will be heard—that the media will present all points of view, in what is commonly called the free marketplace of ideas.

The First Amendment to the U.S. Constitution concisely advocates the idea of freedom of the press. Theoretically, America today operates under the libertarian theory, although this ideal has been challenged often by changes in the media industries since the Constitution was adopted.

The Social Responsibility Theory

This theory accepts the concept of a libertarian press but prescribes what the media should do. Someone who believes in the social responsibility theory believes that members of the press will do their jobs well only if periodically reminded about their duties.

The theory grew out of the 1947 Hutchins Commission Report on the Free and Responsible Press. The commission listed five goals for the press, including the need for truthful and complete reporting of all sides of an issue. The commission concluded that the American press' privileged position in the Constitution means that the press must always work to be responsible to society.

If the media fail to meet their responsibilities to society, the social responsibility theory holds that the government should encourage the media to comply. In this way, the libertarian and the social responsibility theories differ. The libertarian theory assumes the media will work well without government interference; the social responsibility theory advocates government oversight for media that don't act in society's best interest.

The Developmental Theory

The most recent description for media systems is the developmental or Third World theory. Under this theory, named for the developing nations where it is most often found, the media *can* be privately owned but usually are owned by the government.

The mass media in the developmental category are used to promote the country's social and economic goals and to direct a sense of national purpose. For example, a developmental media system might be used to promote birth control or to encourage children to attend school.

The media are an outlet for some types of government propaganda, then, but in the name of economic and social progress, as defined by the government.

Although the theory that best describes the American media is the libertarian theory, throughout their history the American media have struggled with both authoritarian and social responsibility debates: Should the press be free to print secret government documents, for example? What responsibility do television networks have to provide worthwhile programming to their audiences? The media, the government and the public continually modify and adjust their interpretations of just how the media should operate.

It has been nearly seven decades since scholars began using the political theories of the press to define the world's media systems. With today's transitional period in global history, even the recent addition of the developmental theory still leaves many media systems beyond convenient categorization.

Media systems vary throughout the world. The print media form the basis for press systems that developed in North America, Australia, Western Europe and Eastern Europe—where two-thirds of the world's newspapers are published. Many developing countries matured after broadcast media were introduced in the 1920s, and newsprint in these countries often is scarce or government-controlled, making radio their dominant communications medium. Radio receivers are inexpensive, and many people can share one radio.

Television, which relies on expensive equipment, is widely used in prosperous nations and in developing countries' urban areas. Yet many countries still have only one television service, usually run by the government. In many developing countries, all broadcasting—television and radio—is owned and controlled by the government.

The Internet is blurring international media borders because it is very difficult to control the flow of digital information across geographical and ideological boundaries, although some countries try.

What follows is a description of today's media systems by geographic region: Western Europe and Canada; Eastern Europe; the Middle East and North Africa; Africa; Asia and the Pacific; and Latin America and the Caribbean.

WESTERN EUROPE AND CANADA ARE SIMILAR TO THE UNITED STATES

Western European and Canadian media prosper under guarantees of freedom of expression similar to the First Amendment, but each nation has modified the idea to

In Western Europe, newspapers tend to be partisan, and journalists often reflect strong points of view. On January 17, 2013, Fiat SpA chief executive Sergio Marchionne talks to the press in Milan, Italy, to announce a joint venture to manufacture and sell Jeep SUVs in China.

reflect its values. For example, in Great Britain the media are prohibited from commenting on a trial until the trial is finished, and in 2003, Britain banned all tobacco advertising in newspapers, on billboards and on the Internet.

France and Greece, unlike the United States, give more libel protection to public figures than to private citizens. Scandinavian journalists enjoy the widest press freedoms of all of Western Europe, including almost unlimited access to public documents.

Of the Western nations, Canada is the most recent country to issue an official decree supporting the philosophy of press freedom. In 1982, Canada adopted the Canadian Charter of Rights and Freedoms. Before 1982, Canada did not have its own constitution and instead operated under the 1867 British North America Act, sharing the British free press philosophy. In 2010, however, Canada's Supreme Court ruled that Canadian reporters do not have a constitutional right to offer their sources blanket confidentiality. Like the United States, Canada does not have a national shield law.

Print Media

Johannes Gutenberg's invention of movable type rooted the print media in Western Europe. Today, Western European and Canadian media companies produce many fine newspapers. *The Globe and Mail* of Toronto, *The Times* of London, *Frankfurter Allgemeine* of Germany, *Le Monde* of France and Milan's *Corriere della Sera* enjoy healthy circulations.

Whereas Canadian journalists have adopted the U.S. values of fairness and balance as a journalistic ethic, Western European newspapers tend to be much more partisan than the U.S. or Canadian press, and newspapers (and journalists) are expected to reflect strong points of view.

Broadcast Media

As in the United States, the print media in Western Europe are losing audiences to the broadcast media, cable and the Internet. Government originally controlled most of Western Europe's broadcast stations. A board of governors, appointed by the queen, supervises the British Broadcasting Corporation (*BBC*), for example.

To finance the government-run broadcast media, countries like the United Kingdom tax the sale of radios and TVs or charge users an annual license fee, which funds the broadcasts. The BBC collects 3.6 billion British pounds annually in license fees, but in 2010, because of government budget cuts, the BBC governing board reduced staff positions and proposed cuts to employee pensions. The BBC's 4,100 reporters, who are members of the National Union of Journalists, announced a series of 48-hour strikes in protest, and BBC management was forced to replace scheduled live shows with pre-recorded programs during the strikes.

ITV is the largest commercial network in the United Kingdom, with four separate channels. ITV is a "public service broadcaster," which means the network is required to offer public service programming and is regulated by the government, but the channels are very similar to commercial networks in the United States.

Western Europeans watch less television than people in the United States—an average of three hours a day per household in Europe, compared with seven hours a day per household in the United States. One reason for the difference in viewing time is that some Western European TV stations don't go on the air until late afternoon. In the many countries, commercials are shown back to back at the beginning or the end of a program.

Europe gets some of its programming from the United States. Of the 125,000 hours of TV broadcast in Western Europe each year, less than half are produced in Europe. Many of the programs come from America, with a few shows imported from Australia and Japan. U.S. imports

are attractive because buying U.S. programs is cheaper than producing new programming within the country.

The European Union (EU) constitutes a single, unified European market. The policy adopted by the EU is Television Without Frontiers, which promotes an open marketplace for television programs among countries in the EU and between EU countries and the United States.

Some members of the EU (especially France) have proposed quotas to limit imported TV programs, charging that U.S. imports are an example of "cultural imperialism." Countries that favor quotas fear that the importation of U.S. programs imposes a concentration of U.S. values on their viewers.

The United States opposes such quotas, of course, because Western European commercial broadcasting offers a seemingly insatiable market for recycled U.S. programs. Broadcasting in Western Europe is slowly evolving to private ownership and commercial sponsorship.

EASTERN EUROPE IS IN TRANSITION

The democratization of Eastern Europe is transforming the print and broadcast media in these countries at an unprecedented pace. Everette E. Dennis, executive director of the Gannett Center for Media Studies, and Jon Van-den Heuvel described the Eastern European challenges in a report issued after a Gannett-sponsored fact-finding trip: "Mass communication in the several countries

Chung Sung-Jun/Getty Images

American officials often invite press coverage overseas. On April 12, 2013, U.S. Secretary of State John Kerry appeared at a joint press conference with South Korean foreign minister Yun Byung-Se in Seoul, South Korea.

BBC British Broadcasting Corporation, the government-funded British broadcast network.

of the region was reinventing itself. While grassroots newspapers and magazines struggled for survival, new press laws were being debated and enacted; elements of a market economy were coming into view; the media system itself and its role in the state and society were being redefined, as was the very nature of journalism and the job description of the journalist, who was no longer a propagandist for the state."

Eastern Europe today is in transition, defining a new balance between a desire for free expression and the indigenous remnants of government-controlled systems. In many of these countries, mass media played a central role in upsetting the established power structure. Often one of the first targets of the revolutionary movements is a nation's broadcast facilities.

For example, in Romania in 1989, opposition leaders of the National Salvation Committee and sympathetic employees barricaded themselves in a Bucharest TV station, rallying the audience to action. "Romania was governed from a hectic studio littered with empty bottles, cracked coffee mugs and half-eaten sandwiches, and run by people who had not slept in days," the Associated Press reported.

Print Media

Print media were strictly controlled under Communism, with high-ranking party officials forming the core of media management. Because paper supplies were limited, newspapers rarely exceeded 12 pages. Revolutionary leader Vladimir Lenin, who said a newspaper should be a "collective propagandist," a "collective agitator" and a "collective organizer," founded *Pravda*, the Soviet Union's oldest newspaper, in 1912. The Eastern European nations developed their press policies following the Soviet model.

In the late 1980s, Soviet President Mikhail Gorbachev relaxed media controls as part of his policy of *glasnost*. In 1988, the first paid commercials (for Pepsi-Cola, Sony and Visa credit cards) appeared on Soviet TV, and in 1989, the Soviet daily newspaper *Izvestia* published its first Western ads (including ads for perfume and wines from the French firm Pechiney and for Dresdner, a German bank).

In 1990, the Supreme Soviet, the legislative body, outlawed media censorship and gave every citizen the right to publish a newspaper. Within five months, more than 100 newspapers began publication. Then, showing how quickly government positions can change, in early 1991, Gorbachev asked the Supreme Soviet to suspend these press freedoms, but they refused. Less than a year later, Gorbachev's successor, President Boris Yeltsin, again

began to relax government control of the press. In 1996, facing bankruptcy, *Pravda* ceased publication.

Today Russian officials, such as Prime Minister Vladimir Putin, maintain a tight rein on the press, and several reporters who have written critically about the government have been brutally injured or killed, although the government disavows any connection to the attacks. Putin "thinks that democracy stands in his way," former Soviet leader Mikhail S. Gorbachev told *The New York Times* in an interview published on October 26, 2010. "I am afraid that they [Prime Minister Putin and President Dmitri A. Medvedev] have been saddled with this idea that this unmanageable country needs authoritarianism. They think they cannot do without it."

Broadcast Media

Television in the Eastern bloc countries developed under Communist direction because the Communist governments were in power before TV use was widespread. Radio broadcasting also was tightly controlled, although foreign broadcasts directed across Eastern European borders, such as Voice of America and Radio Free Europe, usually evaded jamming attempts by Radio Moscow. Today Eastern Europe is creating a new media environment.

As Eastern European governments change and realign themselves, the adjustments facing Eastern European media are unprecedented. According to Everette E. Dennis and Jon Vanden Heuvel: "Once the revolution came, among the first acts of new government was to take (they would say liberate) electronic media and open up the print press. Permitting free and eventually independent media was a vital beginning for democracy in several countries and a clear break with the past. The freeing up of the media system, speedily in some countries and incrementally in others, was the lifting of an ideological veil without saying just what would replace it."

MIDDLE EASTERN AND NORTH AFRICAN MEDIA WORK UNDER GOVERNMENT CONTROLS

Press history in the Middle East and North Africa begins with the newspaper *Al-Iraq*, first published in 1817, although the first *daily* newspaper didn't begin publishing until 1873. With one exception, development of the press throughout this region follows the same pattern as in most developing countries: More newspapers and magazines are published in regions with high literacy rates than in regions with low literacy rates.

The exception is Egypt, where less than half the people are literate. Yet Cairo is the Arab world's publishing center. *Al Ahram* and *Al Akhbar* are Egypt's leading government-controlled daily newspapers.

Print Media

The Middle Eastern press is tightly controlled by government restrictions, through ownership and licensing, and it is not uncommon for opposition newspapers to disappear and for journalists to be jailed or to leave the country following political upheaval.

According to global media scholar Christine Ogan, "Following the revolution in Iran, all opposition and some moderate newspapers were closed, and according to the National Union of Iranian Journalists (now an illegal organization), more than 75 percent of all journalists left the country, were jailed, or no longer work in journalism." The Palestinian press was subject to censorship by the Israeli government, and all Palestinian newspapers and magazines at one time required permission from the Israeli government to be published.

In Syria, where rebels were fighting the government of President Bashar al-Assad, opposition journalists began publishing weeklies in 2012, hoping to counteract government-controlled media. The papers are supported by donations and distributed free in Syria and by paid subscription abroad. (See **Impact/Global**, "Syrian Newspapers Emerge to Fill Out War Reporting," p. 353.)

Broadcast Media

The foreign-language press is especially strong in the Middle East because of the large number of immigrants in the area, and foreign radio is very popular. Governments within each country control radio and television almost completely, and television stations in Sudan and Yemen, for example, broadcast for only a few hours a day beginning in mid-afternoon.

In the larger Arab states (Jordan, Lebanon, Saudi Arabia and Egypt), TV stations typically broadcast from early morning until midnight. Radio signals beamed from Europe have become one of the region's alternative, affordable sources of news. According to the *Los Angeles Times*, "Because of tight censorship, newspapers and television stations in the Arab world frequently reflect the biases or outright propaganda of their governments. But radio broadcasts from outside the region travel easily across borders and long distances, and many Arabs regard those stations as the most reliable sources of unbiased news." The BBC (based in London) and Radio

Monte Carlo Middle East (based in Paris) are the main Western European across-the-border program sources.

In the Middle East, as in other developing regions, government-owned media are often perceived as instruments of each country's social and political structure. When demonstrators calling for the ouster of President Hosni Mubarak filled Tahrir Square in Cairo, Egypt, in late January 2011, the government quickly shut down access to the Internet. Officials blamed social media, such as Twitter and Facebook, for mobilizing the demonstrators. This marked the first time that a government had deliberately denied Internet communications access to an entire country.

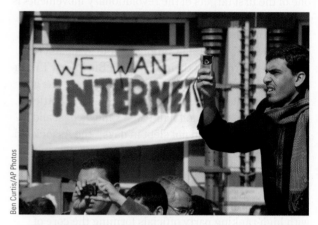

On January 27, 2011, thousands of demonstrators filled the streets of Cairo, Egypt, demanding that President Hosni Mubarak step down. The government quickly shut off Internet access, blaming social media outlets like Facebook and Twitter for the uprising. Mubarak eventually resigned.

Within 24 hours of the Internet shutdown, a new voice-based social media platform, Saynow, joined with Google and Twitter to create an alternative way to communicate. Saynow distributed three phone numbers Egyptians could call to record messages that were then distributed using cell phone access, a modern telephone tree.

In July 2013, i24news went on the air in Israel, the first international broadcast channel dedicated to an Israeli point of view. It is privately funded and its founders say they hope to provide a multi-dimensional view of the country. "What I want to do is to connect Israel to the world and connect the world to the Israeli reality," i24news' chief executive Frank Melloni told the Associated Press.

The Arabic-language channel Al Jazeera, founded in 1996 as an independent satellite TV channel based in Doha, Qatar, is the Middle East's most-watched

IMPACT/Global

Syrian Newspapers Emerge to Fill Out War Reporting

By Neil MacFarquhar

Absi Smesem became the editor in chief of a new weekly Syrian newspaper hoping to leave behind what he disparaged as the "Facebook phase" of the uprising. The tall tales and outright misinformation that tainted so much reporting from Syria convinced him that more objective coverage was essential to bolster the effort to overthrow President Bashar al-Assad.

"There are no objective sources of information on either side, neither with the regime nor the rebels," said Mr. Smesem, 46.

It was in the spirit of objectivity that Mr. Smesem's newspaper, *Sham*, another name for Syria in Arabic, began publishing in February [2013]. It was one of several publications introduced at roughly the same time.

Another weekly paper, *Free Syria*, published in nearby Gaziantep, Turkey, shares an ideological viewpoint with the *Sham* weekly by endorsing pluralism, moderate Islam and democracy.

Mr. Smesem said he relied on 15 reporters from throughout Syria.

"The distribution is a bit random," Mr. Smesem said, with delivery inside Syria often determined by which roads are safe. Of the 6,000 copies printed, up to 4,000 are distributed free throughout Syria, with the rest available by subscription abroad.

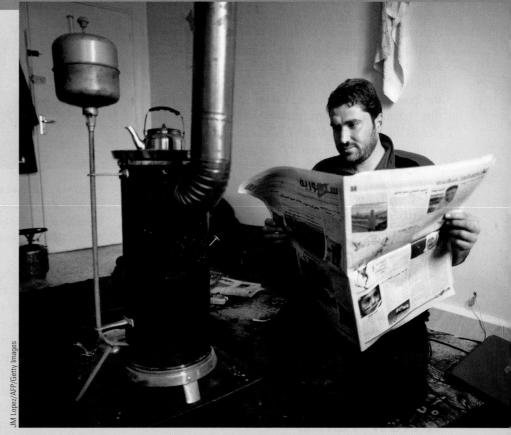

JM Lopez/AFP/Getty Images

In Syria, opposition newspapers like *Free Syria* and *Sham* (another name for Syria in Arabic) have emerged to counteract government-controlled media reporting during the Syrian conflict. *Free Syria* chief editor Khaled al-Khatib poses with a copy of his paper in rebel-held Aleppo, Syria, on January 6, 2013.

"The revolution has started to give what it was started for," said the paper's managing editor, speaking anonymously to avoid any repercussions. "What we don't know is what will happen after the regime falls."

Source: Excerpted from Neil MacFarquhar, "Syrian Newspapers Emerge to Fill Out War Reporting," April 1, 2013, nytimes.com.

TV network. Al Jazeera, available since 2006 in an English-language version at english.aljazeera.net, has made its reputation through comparatively independent news reporting and coverage of events in the region. Al Jazeera was widely credited with extensive video coverage of the January 2011 Cairo protests, although the network experienced continued disruptions in transmission of its signal during its live coverage of the demonstrations.

Al Jazeera blamed the interruptions on "powers that do not want our important images pushing for democracy and reform to be seen by the public," but did not specify who the "powers" were. Al Jazeera did tell *The New York Times* that "signals on the Nilesat platform were cut, and frequencies on the Arbsat and Hotbird platforms were disrupted continually forcing millions of viewers across the Arab world to change satellite frequencies throughout the day."

In an unprecedented show of solidarity with Al Jazeera, ten other channels in the region interrupted their own programming to simulcast Al Jazeera coverage of the demonstrations live to their viewers. The government efforts failed to stop the demonstrations and eventually President Mubarak resigned.

The rapid spread of technological developments, such as the growing availability of DVDs, wider access to the Internet, and the ongoing influence of new media outlets such as the satellite network Al Jazeera, demonstrate serious challenges to traditional government authority over mass media in the Middle East.

AFRICAN MEDIA FIND A NEW VOICE

Most of the new nations of Africa were born after 1960. African history is a record of colonialism, primarily by the British, French, Dutch and Portuguese, and the early print media were created to serve the colonists, not the native population.

Print Media

The first English-language newspaper in sub-Saharan Africa, the *Capetown Gazette and African Advertiser*, appeared in South Africa in 1800. A year later, the first black newspaper, the *Royal Gazette and Sierra Leone Advertiser*, appeared in Sierra Leone.

French settlement in Africa is reflected in the pages of more than 60 newspapers, including *Fraternité-Matin*, French Africa's major daily. A Portuguese settler founded *Noticias*, published in Mozambique. In Kenya, three tabloid newspapers enjoy wide circulations with relative independence: the English-language *Daily Nation* and *The Standard* and the Swahili daily *Taifa Leo*.

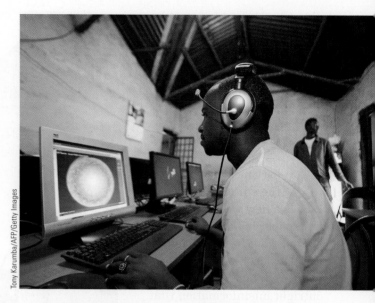

Less than 5 percent of Africa's population has access to the Web, and Internet access is concentrated in urban areas. In Nairobi, Kenya, customers use the Internet at a cyber café that provides computers as well as beverages.

According to media scholar L. John Martin, Africans have never had an information press. Theirs has always been an opinion press. Advocacy journalism comes naturally to them. To the extent that they feel a need for hard news, that need is satisfied by the minimal coverage of the mass media, especially radio.

African culture is very diverse, with an estimated 800 to 2,000 language dialects, making it impossible to create a mass circulation newspaper that can appeal to a wide readership. One publication with a wide circulation in the continent is a magazine called *Drum*, published in South Africa but also distributed throughout Africa.

From 1985 to 1990, the South African government demonstrated its distaste for dissident speech when it instituted strict limits on domestic and international news coverage in the region. Because of violent demonstrations supporting the opposition African National Congress, President P. W. Botha declared a state of emergency in the country in 1985. In 1988, the government suspended the *New Nation* and four other alternative publications. The suspensions and regulations that prevented journalists from covering unrest show the power of government to limit reporting on dissent.

Today, most newspapers in South Africa, for example, are published either in English or in Afrikaans, a language that evolved from South Africa's 17th-century Dutch settlers. South Africa's first Afrikaans newspaper, *Di Patriot*, began in 1875. South Africa's highest circulation newspaper is *The Star*. Avusa Limited publishes the *Sowetan*, a handsome newspaper based in Johannesburg, with color graphics, an appealing design and a healthy circulation. Many of the *Sowetan*'s original editors spent time in jail for speaking out against apartheid. Avusa also owns South Africa's biggest-selling weekly newspaper, the *Sunday Times*, and a daily print and Internet newspaper, *The Times*.

Broadcast Media

Radio is a very important medium in Africa. One reason for radio's dominance over print is that literacy rates are lower in Africa than in many other regions of the world. Radio is also very accessible and the cheapest way for people to follow the news. Some governments charge license fees for radio sets, which are supposed to be registered, but many sets go unregistered. Most stations accept advertising, but the majority of funding for radio comes from government subsidies.

A relatively small percentage of the African public own a TV set, and less than 5 percent of Africa's population has access to the Internet. "Attempts to bring affordable high-speed Internet service to the masses have made little headway on the [African] continent," according to journalist Ron Nixon. "A lack of infrastructure is the biggest problem. In many countries, communications networks were destroyed during years of civil conflict, and continuing political instability deters governments or companies from investing in new systems." Media in the region are concentrated in urban areas, although the growing availability of cell phone signals throughout Africa has the potential to expand communications rapidly, once the political unrest subsides.

MEDIA EXPLODE IN ASIA AND THE PACIFIC

The development of media in this region centers primarily in four countries: Japan, with its prosperous mix of public and private ownership; Australia, where media barons contributed their entrepreneurial fervor; India, which has seen phenomenal media growth; and the People's Republic of China, with its sustained government-controlled media monopoly.

Japan

Japan boasts more newspaper readers than any other nation in the world. Japan's three national daily newspapers—*Asahi Shimbun, Yomiuri Shimbun* and *Mainichi Shimbun*—are based in Tokyo. These three papers, each of them more than 100 years old, account for almost half the nation's newspaper circulation. Broadcast media in Japan developed as a public corporation called the Japanese Broadcasting Corporation (NHK). During World War II, NHK became a propaganda arm of the government, but after the Japanese surrender, the United States helped establish the direction for Japanese broadcasting.

Japan created a licensing board similar to the Federal Communications Commission, but an operating board similar to that of Great Britain's BBC. Japan also decided to allow private broadcast ownership. As a result, Japan today has a mixed system of privately owned and publicly held broadcast media. NHK continues to prosper and, according to broadcast scholar Sydney W. Head, "NHK enjoys more autonomy than any other major public broadcasting corporation. In a rather literal sense, the general public 'owns' it by virtue of paying receiver fees.

"The government cannot veto any program or demand that any program be aired. It leaves the NHK free to set the level of license fees and to do its own fee collecting (which may be why it rates as the richest of the world's fee-supported broadcasting organizations)."

Private ownership is an important element in the Japanese media, and newspaper publishers own many broadcasting operations. NHK owns many more radio properties than private broadcasters do; NHK shares television ownership about equally with private investors. Japan has very few cable systems, which has hindered access to global communications networks in the past, but its cellular and Internet networks are growing rapidly. Japan is ranked eighth in the world in the number of wireless hot spots available to the public (see p. 361). Tokyo also is the home of Sony Corp., which owns Sony Music and Sony Pictures and is one of the world's largest manufacturers of electronic products, including television sets and PlayStation 3. Sony has 167,000 employees worldwide.

Australia

In Australia, acquisitions by media moguls such as Rupert Murdoch skyrocketed in the 1980s. The Murdoch empire controls 60 percent of Australia's newspaper circulation, which includes the *Daily Telegraph* in Sydney and *The Herald-Sun* in Melbourne. Murdoch, although somewhat burdened with debt because of his media investments in the 1980s, emerged in the 1990s as Australia's uncontested print media baron.

Australian Broadcasting Corporation (*ABC*), modeled after the BBC, dominates broadcasting in Australia. Three nationwide commercial networks operate in the country. All three suffered financial difficulty in the 1990s, a legacy "of the heydays of the 1980s, when aspiring buyers, backed by eager bank lenders, paid heady

ABC   Australian Broadcasting Corporation.

prices for broadcast and print assets," reported *The Wall Street Journal*. But they have recovered and today are very prosperous.

India

Entrepreneurship is an important element in the print media of India, which gained independence from Britain in 1947. Forty years after independence, in 1987, Indian print media had multiplied 1,000 times—from 200 publications in 1947 to nearly 25,000.

Broadcasting in India follows its British colonial beginnings, with radio operating under the name All India Radio (AIR) and TV as Doordarshan ("distance view"). Doordarshan uses satellite service to reach remote locations, bringing network TV to four out of five people in the country. As in most developing countries, the network regularly broadcasts programs aimed at improving public life, covering subjects such as family planning, health and hygiene.

One of the most prosperous industries in India today is filmmaking. The film industry, which produces 1,100 films a year (more than twice as many as Hollywood), is centered around a place called Film City near Mumbai, where 16 film studios employ thousands of people working at dozens of sprawling sets. The industry popularly is known as Bollywood, a mix of Bombay, the former name of Mumbai, and Hollywood.

India has a rich history of filmmaking. In April 2013 in New Delhi, attendees pay tribute to the career of legendary filmmaker Satyajit Ray at the Centenary Film Festival, celebrating 100 years of filmmaking in India. Ray wrote all his films, in addition to designing the costumes and composing the music.

People's Republic of China

Social responsibility is a very important element of media development in the People's Republic of China, where a media monopoly gives government the power to influence change. At the center of Chinese media are the two Communist Party information sources, the newspaper *People's Daily* and Xinhua, the Chinese news agency. These two sources set the tone for the print media throughout China, where self-censorship maintains the government's direction.

Broadcasting in China, as in India, offers important potential for social change in a vast land of rural villages. China's three-tier system for radio includes a central national station; 100 regional, provincial and municipal networks; and grassroots stations that send local announcements and bulletins by wire to loudspeakers in outdoor markets and other public gathering places.

A television set is a prized possession in China. The Chinese have bought some U.S. TV programs and accepted some U.S. commercials, but they produce most of the programming themselves. Chinese media today sometimes use information and entertainment programming from the West to show the dangers of Western influence, proving the power and the reach of a government media monopoly. In the new market economy in China, there are ten times as many newspapers and magazines today as there were in 1978.

With the increased competition for readers, some of the print media are beginning to look like Western tabloids, running sensationalist stories. This sensationalism has angered Communist Party officials, who are trying to maintain control over what is published. In 1996, the president of the popular newspaper *Beijing Youth Daily* was disciplined after the paper ran a story about a poisoning case involving a state-run business. "The leadership of the news media must be tightly held in the hands of those who are loyal to Marxism, the party and the people," said President Jiang Zemin.

With the inevitable influx of Western media during the 2008 Beijing Olympics, the Chinese government originally pledged to open up media outlets completely but still restricted journalists' access to many Western news outlets. In 2012, when *The New York Times* reported that Chinese premier Wen Jiabao's family controlled assets worth at least $2.7 billion, the country blocked the *Times'* main and Chinese language Web sites and banned English and Chinese language searches for "New York Times" on blogs. (See **Impact/Convergence**, *"New York Times* Blocked by China After Report on Wealth of Wen Jiabao's Family," p. 358.)

China has 538 million Internet users, and the government has placed various controls on Web site access, especially for social networking sites, such as Facebook and Twitter, but technology-savvy people in the country often manage to find ways around the government's limits.

Government, Large Corporations and Family Dynasties Control Latin American and Caribbean Media

In Latin America, where hectic political change is the norm, media have been as volatile as the region. Media are part of the same power structure that controls politics, business and industry. In some Latin American countries, such as Brazil, a family dynasty dominates the media, and in many countries one corporation is allowed to control several different types of media outlets.

For example, Televisa, based in Mexico, owns more than 258 affiliated TV stations, 31 pay TV channels and 158 publications. Organization Editorial Mexicana owns 70 newspapers, 24 radio stations and 43 Internet sites.

Print Media

In Santiago, Chile, the newspaper *El Mercurio* was founded in 1827. Today the El Mercurio company owns nine newspapers and 32 radio stations. *O Estado de São Paulo* in Brazil, owned by the Mesquita family, has represented editorial independence in the region for more than 100 years and often is mentioned as one of the country's best newspapers. Argentina's *La Prensa* refuses government subsidies and has survived great conflicts with people like dictator Juan Perón, who shut down the newspaper from 1951 to 1955.

Home delivery for newspapers and magazines is uncommon in Latin America; the centers of print media merchandising are street-corner kiosks, where vendors offer a variety of publications. *Manchete*, published in Brazil, is one of the most widely circulated national magazines, similar in size and content to America's *Life* magazine.

Broadcast Media

Broadcasting operates in a mix of government and private control, with government often owning a few key stations and regulating stations that are privately owned, but the pattern varies.

Cuba's broadcast media are controlled totally by the government, for example. In Costa Rica and Ecuador, almost all the broadcast media are privately owned. In Brazil, private owners hold most of the radio stations and television networks, including TV Globo Network, which claims to be the world's fourth largest television network (after the United States' original three TV networks—ABC, CBS and NBC).

Leo Ramirez/AFP/Getty Images

In Latin America, broadcast media operate under a mix of public and private control. On April 25, 2013, newly elected Venezuelan President Nicolas Maduro speaks to the media in Caracas.

IMPACT/Convergence

New York Times Blocked by China After Report on Wealth of Wen Jiabao's Family

By Tania Branigan

China's foreign ministry has accused the *New York Times* of smearing the country by reporting that the premier Wen Jiabao's extended family has controlled assets worth at least $2.7 billion.

A spokesman, Hong Lei, said the report "blackens China's name and has ulterior motives." Authorities have also blocked the news organization's main and Chinese-language Web sites and banned searches for "New York Times" in English and Chinese on microblogs.

"China manages the Internet in accordance with laws and rules," Hong told reporters at a daily briefing when asked why the sites were inaccessible.

The New York Times reported that several of Wen's close relatives had become extremely wealthy since his ascent to leadership. But in many cases their holdings were obscured by layers of partnerships and investment vehicles involving friends, colleagues or business partners, it said, in a detailed and lengthy account based on an extensive review of company and regulatory filings.

A single investment held on paper by Wen's 90-year-old mother Yang Zhiyun—a retired schoolteacher—was worth $120 million five years ago, *The New York Times* said. It added it was unclear if Yang was aware of the holdings in her name.

AFP/AFP/Getty Images

After *The New York Times* reported that Chinese premier Wen Jiabao's family controlled assets of $2.7 billion, the Chinese government blocked access to *The Times'* Web sites within China. Savvy Chinese users often circumvent the government's attempt to control Internet content. Shown is an online café in Jiashan, Zhejiang province on November 2, 2012.

It is the latest in a string of unwelcome revelations about the vast wealth amassed by those around senior leaders.

Authorities blocked the Bloomberg Web site earlier this year [2012] after it exposed the multimillion-dollar assets held by the extended family of Xi Jinping, heir-apparent to the presidency. The news agency has also reported that relatives of the disgraced politician Bo Xilai accumulated at least $136 million in assets.

Source: Excerpted from Tania Branigan, "New York Times Blocked by China After Report on Wealth of Wen Jiabao's Family," guardian.co.uk, October 26, 2012.

INTERNATIONAL HERALD TRIBUNE SEEKS A GLOBAL AUDIENCE

One of the largest global media presences is the *International Herald Tribune* (**IHT**), based in Paris and published in English. Called "the world's daily newspaper," the *International Herald Tribune* was founded in 1887 by American entrepreneur J. Gordon Bennett, Jr., and today is the world's largest English-language newspaper. Known for its independence, the newspaper was co-owned by *The Washington Post* and *The New York Times* until 2003, when *The New York Times* became the paper's sole owner.

The *IHT* is the first truly global newspaper, published at 35 sites around the world and covering international news every day. With a global outlook and available by subscription in an electronic edition, the *IHT* counts most of the world's opinion leaders and decision makers among its subscribers.

The paper has a circulation of 241,000 and an international readership in 180 countries throughout Europe, Asia, the Middle East, Russia, Africa and the Americas. The biggest regular audience for the print edition is American tourists traveling abroad, and the Internet edition receives 7 million visitors a month. (See **Impact/Global**, "*International Herald Tribune* Timeline 1887–Today," p. 360.)

CRITICS CITE WESTERN COMMUNICATIONS BIAS

Countries in many developing nations, such as Cuba, historically have criticized what they believe is a Western bias to the flow of information throughout the world. These countries charge that this practice imposes cultural imperialism, centered in Western ideology. In fact, many of the major international news services are based in the West.

The Associated Press, Reuters (Great Britain), Agence France-Presse (France), Deutsche Presse-Agentur (Germany) and Agencia Efe (Spain) supply news to the print and broadcast media. Visnews, based in Great Britain, the U.S.-based Cable News Network and World International Network (WIN) offer international video services. Sky TV in Europe and Star TV in Asia deliver programs by satellite. The Internet, of course, ignores all national borders.

Despite Western dominance of global news organizations, many regions of the world support information services within their own countries and even within their regions. Middle East News Agency (MENA), based

in Egypt, serves all the countries of the Middle East, while News Agency of Nigeria (NAN) limits services to Nigeria, for example.

Within the past 50 years, news services outside the Western orbit have been created—Russian Information Agency (RIA); Asian-Pacific News Network in Japan; Caribbean News Agency (CANA); Pan-African News Agency (PANA); Non-Aligned News Agency (NANA), linking the nonaligned nations with the national news agencies, based in Yugoslavia; and Inter Press Service (IPS), based in Rome as an "information bridge" between Europe and Latin America.

Even with the creation of these added sources of information and the Internet, Western news services dominate. Critics of the system of news and information flow have called for a New World Information and Communications Order (**NWICO**), saying that the existing system is *ethnocentric*, or promotes the superiority of one ethnic group (in this case, the Western world) over another.

According to Robert G. Picard in *Global Journalism: Survey of International Communication*, "Developing world media and governments have argued that Western ethnocentrism creates an unequal flow of information by providing a large stream of information about events in the developed world but only a very small flow from the developing world." Internet access to news outlets like the *International Herald Tribune* and the availability of original Internet news reports from throughout the world could potentially change the balance. (See **Illustration 16.1**, p. 361.)

INTERNET EXPANDS MEDIA'S GLOBAL REACH

When communication stays within borders, it is easier for governments to control information, but the Internet makes it possible for information and entertainment to travel effortlessly across borders.

Until recently, most developing countries were limited to traditional mass media delivery systems—print and broadcast. These systems were regional by nature because they were confined by geography and economics. Print media could travel only through the mail and by carrier. Radio and television were limited by the

IHT *International Herald Tribune*, the world's largest English-language newspaper.

NWICO New World Information and Communications Order. The concept that mass media should include all areas of the world, not just the West.

Ethnocentric Promoting the superiority of one ethnic group over another.

IMPACT/Global

International Herald Tribune Timeline 1887–Today

- **1887** On October 4, American entrepreneur J. Gordon Bennett, Jr., publishes the first issue of the *New York Herald*'s European edition in Paris.
- **1928** The *Herald* becomes the first newspaper distributed by airplane, with copies flown to London from Paris in time for breakfast.
- **1940** The occupation of Paris interrupts publishing.
- **1944** Publishing resumes.
- **1959** The *New York Herald Tribune* and its European edition are sold to John Hay Whitney, the U.S. ambassador to Britain.
- **1966** The New York paper closes. The Whitney family keeps the Paris paper going through partnerships. In December *The Washington Post* becomes a joint owner.
- **1967** In May, *The New York Times* becomes a joint owner, and the newspaper becomes the *International Herald Tribune*, emphasizing its global perspective.
- **1974** The *IHT* pioneers the electronic transmission of facsimile pages across countries with the opening of a printing site near London. A second site is opened in Zurich in 1977.
- **1980** The *IHT* begins sending page images via satellite from Paris to Hong Kong, making it the first daily newspaper to be electronically sent across continents and simultaneously available to readers on opposite sides of the world.
- **1991** *The Washington Post* and *The New York Times* become sole and equal shareholders of the newspaper.
- **2003** *The New York Times* acquires full ownership of the *International Herald Tribune*.
- **2005** On the 25th anniversary of the *International Herald Tribune*'s publication in

Kostas Tsironis/Bloomberg/Getty Images

The *International Herald Tribune*, published in Paris and owned by *The New York Times*, is the largest general circulation, English-language daily in the world. *IHT* runs through the printing presses at the Kathimerini printing plant in Palania, Greece, on January 17, 2013.

Asia the *IHT* opens its Hong Kong newsroom, allowing *IHT* to be published in both Paris and Hong Kong.
- **2006** *IHT* becomes the first international daily newspaper to be printed in Russia, ensuring early morning distribution with the *Moscow Times*.
- **2008** *IHT* and Reuters join forces to launch Business with Reuters and Business Asia with Reuters. Seven million users visit iht.com each month.
- **2009** IHT launches the global edition online, in coordination with *The New York Times*. The paper is edited in New York, Paris and Hong Kong.
- **2012** *IHT* celebrates its 125th anniversary.
- **Today** The *IHT* is available in 180 countries and on the Web.

Source: *International Herald Tribune*, ihtinfo.com.

IMPACT/Convergence

Illustration 16.1

Top 10 Countries with Public Wireless Locations (Hot Spots)

South Korea has more public wireless locations (hot spots) than any other country, and the U.K. (ranked second) has more hot spots than the United States. South Korea has 20 times more hot spots than Sweden, which is ranked tenth.

Source: Hotstats as of April 22, 2013, Jiwire.com.

Sweden
9,546 locations

United Kingdom
182,603 locations

France
35,433 locations

Germany
15,095 locations

Russian Federation
16,829 locations

China
104,107 locations

South Korea
186,759 locations

Japan
15,735 locations

United States
136,984 locations

Taiwan
24,148 locations

reach of their towers and depended on people having enough money to purchase receivers. Information from outside the country was limited to reports filtered through each nation's print and broadcast outlets; similarly, news and information about other countries reached the United States only through traditional print and broadcast organizations.

A country with government controls on the mass media can use those controls to combat dissent and limit awareness. But digital signals carried on the Internet break down international barriers because the delivery system knows no limits. Information on the Internet is controlled by individuals rather than by institutions, which is precisely why many governments are afraid

of the influence that access to the Internet will have if allowed to operate unchecked within their countries.

Governments that are accustomed to controlling information, especially in developing countries, have tried to stop the information flow by pricing Internet access beyond what most people can afford. According to the World Bank, the average consumer pays about $22 a month for Internet access, but in Tanzania, for example, the price is $95 a month, and in South Africa the cost is $60 a month.

Also, many countries simply don't have reliable telecommunications technology in place—telephone, broadband, cellular or satellite connections—to handle Internet traffic. None of the countries in South America or Africa is listed among the countries with the highest number of wireless hot spots available to the public, for example.

This often means that in poorer countries, only the wealthy and powerful have access to the international flow of information that the Internet offers. As digital technology grows more affordable, however, it will be difficult even for developing countries to stop information from seeping across their borders. The most promising new and simplest technology today is the mobile phone.

MOBILE PHONES OPEN COMMUNICATIONS CHANNELS

In 2002, for the first time, the number of mobile phones in the world exceeded the number of landline phones, according to the World Bank. Wireless networks offer the easiest way for developing countries to modernize their communications systems because these countries have never had extensive wired networks. "The mobility, ease of use, flexible deployment, and relatively low and declining rollout costs of wireless technologies enable them to reach rural populations with low levels of income and literacy," reports the World Bank.

"From Kenya to Colombia to South Africa . . . cell phones are becoming the truly universal technology," according to Anand Giridharadas, reporting for *The New York Times*. "The number of mobile subscriptions in the world is expected to pass five billion this year [2010], according to the International Telecommunication Union, an intergovernmental organization. That would mean more human beings today have access to a cell phone than the United Nations says have access to a clean toilet."

According to Giridharadas, "The phone has also moved to the center of community life in many places. In Africa, churches record sermons with cell phones and then transmit them to villages to be replayed. In Iran and Moldova, phones helped to organize popular uprisings against authoritarian governments."

The World Bank points out the interrelationship between reliable communications systems and economic development. Farmers can price and sell goods to markets they could never reach otherwise; city dwellers can transfer money to rural relatives through an online banking network; and smartphones give users access to the Internet, music downloads, movies, radio, games and information services.

Josep Lago/AFP/Getty Images

Today mobile phones are the world's fastest growing communications technology. An Android character poses for a picture with visitors at the Mobile World Congress, a global trade show, in Barcelona, Spain, on February 27, 2013.

While access to information from outside the country is a major benefit of wireless networks, many governments consider outsiders—and the information they offer—a threat. Digital technology is much more difficult for governments to restrict. Governments often try to limit which messages pass the country's borders, usually with little success. Today, information can travel from anywhere in the world to almost anywhere in the world and back again via the Internet.

The Internet is as near as a smartphone, which is becoming an indispensable tool in the developing world for individuals, businesses and governments. For developing countries especially, today's digital technology offers a faster path to economic growth, increased literacy and freedom of expression.

REPORTERS RISK THEIR LIVES TO REPORT WORLD EVENTS

Journalists in many developing countries are often targets for political and terrorist threats, where a reporter's life is very hazardous.

According to *Global Journalism: Survey of International Communication*, "Threats to journalists come not only from governments but from terrorist groups, drug lords and quasi-government hit squads as well. Numerous news organizations have been bombed, ransacked and destroyed by opponents. Dozens of Latin American journalists have been murdered for their beliefs or for

IMPACT/Profile

Committee to Protect Journalists Monitors Reporters Killed in 2012

The Committee to Protect Journalists (CPJ) reports the number of journalists killed each year while on assignment. In 2012, magazine journalist Regina Martinez was among the journalists who died.

CPJ statistics are divided into "motive confirmed" and "motive unconfirmed." A *motive confirmed* death is one where CPJ finds that the reporter was killed "in direct reprisal for his/her work; was killed in crossfire during a combat situation; or was killed on a dangerous assignment." If the motive is unclear, but it is possible that the journalist was killed because of his/her work, the case is classified as *motive unconfirmed*. A *media worker* is someone who supports reporters, such as a translator or driver.

AP Images/Felix Marquez

A photograph of slain journalist Regina Martinez is displayed on a cross during a vigil in her honor outside government offices in Xalapa, Mexico, on April 29, 2012. Police found Martinez's body inside her home. She was a highly respected reporter who covered Mexican drug trafficking for *Proseco* magazine.

70	Journalists Killed, Motive Confirmed
31	Journalists Killed, Motive Unconfirmed
2	Media Workers Killed
103	Total Number of Journalists and Media Workers Killed in 2012

Source: Adapted from Committee to Protect Journalists, cpj.org/killed/2012/.

writing articles that contain those beliefs." (See **Impact/Profile**, "Committee to Protect Journalists Monitors Reporters Killed in 2012.")

According to the Committee to Protect Journalists, which tracks deaths and injuries suffered by journalists throughout the world, 103 journalists and media workers were killed in 2012.

Journalists face danger because the mass media often represent a challenge to the political power of a country's leadership or they uncover criminal activity that is being ignored by the government. In all parts of the world, the dangers that journalists face to report unraveling news events form a central part of each nation's political history.

GLOBAL MEDIA CHASE INTERNATIONAL CONSUMERS

International communication on the Internet is just the beginning of an easy, affordable and accessible transfer of information and entertainment back and forth between other countries and the United States. Media companies in the United States also are looking longingly at the large populations in other countries that are just beginning to acquire the tools of communication, creating millions of potential consumers for all types of products. (See **Impact/Money**, "Ten Things You Need to Know About the Global Advertising Market," p. 364.)

IMPACT/Money

10 Things You Need to Know About the Global Advertising Market

Advertising Age

Here are 10 things to keep in mind about the global ad market.

1. **Advertising is a $500 billion market.** Worldwide ad spending topped the half-trillion mark in 2012.

2. **Consensus ad growth is 3.9 percent in 2012 and 2013.** Forecasts suggest the worldwide advertising market will grow 3.9 percent in both years.

3. **Worldwide ad spending is at an all-time high**. Advertising is expected to set new records each year through at least 2017.

4. **Regional spending is a mixed picture**. Advertising in Asia/Pacific and Latin America has rocketed past pre-recession levels, reflecting growth in emerging markets.

5. **Emerging markets are set to pass the U.S**. The world's emerging markets in 2014 will account for one-third of ad spending, surpassing the U.S. share of advertising. Developing markets will account for 61 percent of global ad spending growth between 2012 and 2015.

6. **A giant BRIC**. **B**razil, **R**ussia, **I**ndia and **C**hina account for nearly half of emerging-market ad spending. By 2017, [forecasters] expect the BRIC bloc to comprise four of the world's 10 largest ad markets, with China No. 2 behind the U.S.

7. **Digital captures one in five ad dollars**. The Internet in 2013 will pass newspapers to become the second-largest global ad medium, behind television. Internet media will get 19.8 percent of the 2013 spending pie and Internet advertising [will] account for 59 percent of growth in worldwide ad spending between 2012 and 2015.

8. **TV's share of global advertising peaked in 2012**. [Forecasters] expect TV's share to hold steady at about 40 percent through 2015. Even with a flat share, TV is likely to score solid gains in revenue because the overall ad market is growing.

9. **Number of billion-dollar advertisers: 46.** That's how many companies had 2011 worldwide measured-media spending above $1 billion. The group includes 43 Global 100 multinational, multi-region advertisers; and three big marketers (AT&T, Berkshire Hathaway, Verizon Communications) that don't appear in the global ranking because their measured spending is virtually all in a single region (U.S.).

10. **Personal care cleans up**. It's the world's biggest advertising category, followed by automotive and food, and makes up one-fourth of 2011's Global 100 spending. The three biggest global advertisers have the world in a lather: Procter & Gamble Co., Unilever and L'Oréal (see **Illustration 16.2**, p. 365).

Source: Adapted from *Advertising Age*, "10 Things You Need to Know About the Global Market: Amid Uncertainty, There Are Bright Spots and Emerging Opportunities," December 9, 2012, adage.com.

(continued)

Illustration 16.2

Top 10 Global Marketers

Source: *Advertising Age*, DataCenter, 1992–2013, Adage.com.

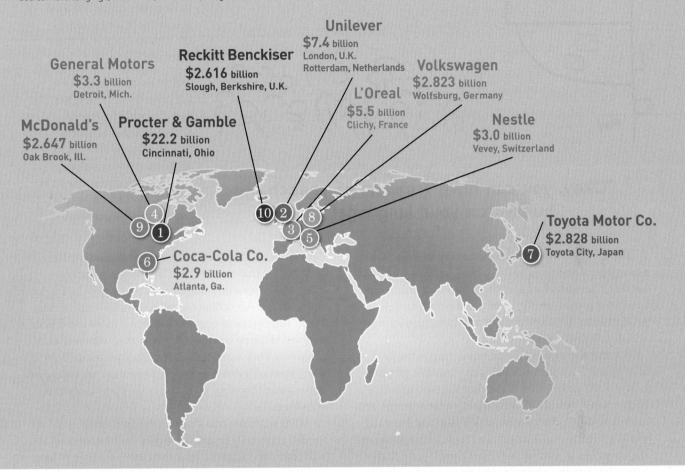

Unilever
$7.4 billion
London, U.K.
Rotterdam, Netherlands

General Motors
$3.3 billion
Detroit, Mich.

Reckitt Benckiser
$2.616 billion
Slough, Berkshire, U.K.

Volkswagen
$2.823 billion
Wolfsburg, Germany

L'Oreal
$5.5 billion
Clichy, France

McDonald's
$2.647 billion
Oak Brook, Ill.

Procter & Gamble
$22.2 billion
Cincinnati, Ohio

Nestle
$3.0 billion
Vevey, Switzerland

Toyota Motor Co.
$2.828 billion
Toyota City, Japan

Coca-Cola Co.
$2.9 billion
Atlanta, Ga.

Today's media markets are increasingly global. U.S. media companies are searching for new markets overseas at the same time that overseas media companies are purchasing pieces of media industries in the United States and other countries. Here are some recent examples:

- Walt Disney Co. joined with China's largest Internet company, Tencent Holdings Ltd., in an initiative to develop China's animation industry. "Our philosophy is to operate as the Chinese Walt Disney Company," according to Stanley Cheung, managing director of Disney China.

- IBM announced plans to supply computing technology and services to upgrade the cell phone network across 16 nations in sub-Saharan Africa.

- The Russian government launched a news cable channel called Russia Today, financed by the Russian government and available to viewers in the United States, reporting news in America from a Russian perspective. Its advertising slogan is "Question More."

- In 2007, a nonprofit group called One Laptop Per Child, based in Cambridge, Mass., launched an effort to provide children in the developing world with laptops. By 2013, the organization had distributed 2.4 million laptops in 42 countries.

- The British advertising and public relations firm Shandwick is the largest agency in the United Kingdom and more than half of Shandwick's business comes from the United States.

"Okay, you can have freedom of speech, but watch your language!"

All these companies have positioned themselves to take advantage of emerging global media markets. This marketplace includes news and information services, print, broadcast programming, movies and music, as well as products and the advertising to sell them, plus Internet access to deliver them.

Fueling the move to global marketing is the decision by the European countries to eliminate all trade barriers. A further sign of the times is the shrinking proportion of worldwide advertising expenditures generated by the United States, which has long been the world's advertising colossus. In recent years, advertising spending by companies *outside* the United States has overtaken the amount spent by companies *in* the United States.

IDEAS TRANSCEND BORDERS

Along with the transfer of information in the new global communications future, however, comes the transfer of ideas. Says the *Los Angeles Times*:

Historically, the empowered elite have always sought to suppress the wider distribution of ideas, wealth, rights and, most of all, knowledge. This is as true today as it was . . . when the German printer Gutenberg invented movable type to print the Bible. For two centuries afterward, government tightly controlled what people could read through the widespread use of "prior restraint." . . .

Just as censorship of the printed word could not continue with the emergence of democracy in 17th century Britain and 18th century America, so today suppression of the electronic media is thwarted by technology and rapidly growing economies around the world.

Governments that are accustomed to controlling the information that crosses their borders face unprecedented access within their countries to global information sources. According to media theorist Ithiel de Sola Pool, "International communications is often considered a mixed blessing by rulers. Usually they want technical progress. They want computers. They want satellites. They want efficient telephones. They want television. But at the same time they do not want the ideas that come with them."

Many governments that control their country's media, especially broadcast media and the Internet, will continue to govern access to the messages as long as they can regulate newsprint and satellites, but this is becoming increasingly difficult. As more national media boundaries disappear throughout the world, news, information and entertainment will be able to move instantly from each home country to become part of an interactive global dialogue. Today the mass media industries operate in a media marketplace without boundaries, using a global delivery system that is truly "transnational." According to *The Economist* magazine, "Nothing is inevitable about this technology except its advance. . . . As the universe behind the screen expands, it will be the people in front who shape the soul of the new machine."

Review, Analyze, Investigate

Reviewing Chapter 16

World Media Systems Vary

- Media industries in different countries are as varied as the countries they serve.

- The United States isn't necessarily always the leader in adopting innovative technologies.

- The Internet is blurring international media borders because it is very difficult to control the flow of digital information across geographical and ideological boundaries, although some countries try.

Five Political Theories Describe How World Media Operate

- The original four theories on the press (the Soviet theory, the authoritarian theory, the libertarian theory and the social responsibility theory) plus the developmental theory still leave many press systems beyond specific categorization.

- The global media theory that best describes the American media is the libertarian theory, although American media also have struggled with authoritarian and social responsibility debates.

Western Europe and Canada Are Similar to the United States

- Until the 1850s, presses in Europe were privately owned.

- The print media form the basis for press development in North America, Australia, Western Europe and Eastern Europe.

- Today Western European and Canadian media prosper under guarantees of freedom of expression similar to the First Amendment of the U.S. Constitution, although each nation has modified the idea to reflect differing values.

- In 1982, Canada adopted the Canadian Charter of Rights and Freedoms, becoming the most recent Western country to issue an official decree supporting the philosophy of press freedom.

- Scandinavian journalists enjoy the widest press freedoms of all of Western Europe, including almost unlimited access to public documents.

- Western European newspapers tend to be much more partisan than U.S. or Canadian newspapers.

- To finance the government-run broadcast media, countries like the United Kingdom tax the sale of radios and TVs or charge users an annual license fee, which funds the broadcasts.

- ITV, a "public service broadcaster," is the largest commercial network in the United Kingdom, with four separate channels.

- Western Europeans watch less television than people in the United States.

- Some TV stations in Europe don't go on the air until late afternoon.

- Some Western European programming comes from the United States.

- U.S. programs are attractive to European broadcasters because buying U.S. programs is cheaper than producing their own.

- Some members of the European community have proposed quotas on the importation of U.S. programs.

Eastern Europe Is in Transition

- Many Eastern European nations developed their press policies following the Soviet model.

- Eastern Europe is defining a new balance between the desire for free expression and the remnants of government control.

- In many Eastern European countries, the media play a central role in upsetting the established power structure.

- Television in the Eastern bloc countries developed under Communist direction because the Communist governments were in power before TV use was widespread; radio broadcasting also was tightly controlled.

- *Pravda*, the Soviet Union's oldest newspaper, was founded in 1912. In 1996, facing bankruptcy, *Pravda* ceased publication.

Middle Eastern and North African Media Work Under Government Controls

- Press history in the Middle East and North Africa begins with the newspaper *Al-Iraq*, first published in 1817, although the first daily newspaper didn't begin publishing until 1873.

- In the Middle East and North Africa, more newspapers and magazines are published in regions with high literacy rates than in regions with low literacy rates; the one exception is Cairo, Egypt, which is the Arab world's publishing center.

- Radio often is the dominant medium in developing countries; television is in widespread use in prosperous nations and in urban areas of developing countries. Yet many countries still have only one TV service, usually run by the government.

- Radio Monte Carlo and the BBC offer alternative radio programming across Middle Eastern borders.

- The Middle Eastern press is tightly controlled by government restrictions, through ownership and licensing.

- Al Jazeera is the Middle East's most-watched TV network and has made its controversial reputation by promising independent news reporting and coverage.

- In the Middle East, as in other developing regions, the mass media are perceived as instruments of each country's social and political agendas.

- In Syria, where rebels were fighting the government of President Bashar al-Assad, opposition journalists began publishing weeklies in 2012, hoping to counteract government-controlled media.

African Media Find a New Voice

- The first English-language newspaper in sub-Saharan Africa appeared in Capetown, South Africa, in 1800; a year later, the first black newspaper appeared in Sierra Leone.

- African culture is very diverse, making it impossible to create a mass circulation newspaper that can appeal to a wide readership.

- In Africa, radio is a much more important medium than print because it is an inexpensive way for people to follow the news.

- Suspension of five publications in South Africa throughout the state of emergency from 1985 to 1990 demonstrates the power of government to limit reporting on dissent.

- People in Africa have limited access to the Internet. Internet access is mostly available in urban areas.

Media Explode in Asia and the Pacific

- Japan's three major newspapers are each more than 100 years old.

- The three major Japanese national dailies account for almost half the nation's newspaper circulation.

- Japan today has a mixed system of privately owned and publicly held broadcast media.

- Entrepreneurs, including Rupert Murdoch, control large segments of Australia's media.

- The Australian Broadcasting Corporation (ABC) dominates broadcasting in Australia.

- Since India's independence in 1947, the number of publications has increased 1,000 times.

- Broadcasting in India follows its British colonial beginnings.

- The most successful media business in India is filmmaking, an industry nicknamed Bollywood. The industry is based in Film City, a settlement near Mumbai.

- Chinese media operate under a government monopoly, supported by a belief in the media's social responsibility.

- China has 538 million Internet users.

Government, Large Corporations and Family Dynasties Control Latin American and Caribbean Media

- Media in Latin America are part of the power structure, and family dynasties as well as large corporations control many media industries.

- Dictator Juan Perón shut down Argentina's independent newspaper *La Prensa* from 1951 to 1955.

- In Santiago, Chile, for example, the Edwards family has owned *El Mercurio* since 1880.

International Herald Tribune Seeks a Global Audience

- The *International Herald Tribune* was founded in 1887 by American entrepreneur J. Gordon Bennett, Jr., and today is the world's largest English-language newspaper.

- The *IHT* was co-owned by the *Washington Post* and *The New York Times* until 2003, when *The New York Times* became the paper's sole owner.

- The *IHT* is the first truly global newspaper, published at 35 sites around the world and covering world news every day.

Critics Cite Western Communications Bias

- Some developing nations criticize the news media for their Western slant.

- Despite Western dominance of global news organizations, many regions of the world have their own news services.

- The New World Information and Communications Order (NWICO) advocates parity for the media in all countries.

Internet Expands Media's Global Reach

- Governments that are used to controlling information, especially in developing countries, have tried to stop the information flow by making Internet access too expensive for the average consumer.

- South Korea has more public wireless locations (hot spots) than any other country, and the U.K. (ranked second) has more hot spots than the United States.

- Many countries simply don't have reliable telecommunications technology in place—telephone, broadband, cellular or satellite connections—to handle Internet traffic.

- More than any other factor, the economic potential of the Internet guarantees its future as a global communications medium.

Mobile Phones Open Communications Channels

- In 2002, for the first time, the number of mobile phones in the world exceeded the number of landline phones.
- Wireless networks offer the easiest way for developing countries to modernize their communications systems because these countries have never had extensive wired networks.

Reporters Risk Their Lives to Report World Events

- Journalists in Latin America and many other developing countries face danger because the media represent a challenge to political power.
- In 2012, 103 journalists and media workers were killed on the job.

Global Media Chase International Consumers

- U.S. media companies are looking for markets overseas at the same time that overseas media companies are purchasing pieces of media industries in the United States and other countries.
- Procter & Gamble spends more money on global advertising than any other company.
- Fueling the move to global marketing is the decision by the European countries to eliminate all trade barriers.

Ideas Transcend Borders

- Along with the transfer of information in the new global communications future comes the transfer of ideas.
- Governments that are accustomed to controlling the information that crosses their borders face unprecedented access within their borders to global information sources.
- Today the media industries operate in a marketplace that is "transnational."

Key Terms

These terms are defined in the margins throughout this chapter and appear in alphabetical order with definitions in the Glossary, which begins on page 373.

ABC *355*	Ethnocentric *359*	*IHT 359*
BBC *350*	Hot Spot *346*	NWICO *359*

Critical Questions

1. In what ways might a nation's media system be shaped by its government's political philosophy? Cite three specific examples.

2. Compare the evolution of mass media in the various regions of the world. Give three specific examples.

3. Discuss the role of radio in developed and less-developed countries. Cite three specific examples.

4. Explain how the *International Herald Tribune* became one of the largest global media presences. What will the *IHT* have to do to stay competitive in the growing global media market?

5. Discuss the global consequences of international access to the Internet, including the impact of the Internet on government control of information and ways that developing countries attempt to deal with the loss of control.

Working the Web

This list includes both sites mentioned in the chapter and others to give you greater insight into global media.

BBC News

bbc.co.uk

The British Broadcasting Company's Web site with a U.K. and an international version is customizable with content choices including news, sports, weather, radio, TV, entertainment, history and blogs. The international version, which offers news and audio in 32 languages, has links to BBC TV and radio channels around the world. Its Country Profiles (located in the News section) provide background on every nation in the world. A complete A–Z directory of BBC sites is also available.

Foreign Policy Magazine

foreignpolicy.com

A bimonthly magazine about global politics and economics, *Foreign Policy*'s mission is to explain "how the process of globalization is reshaping nations, institutions, cultures, and, more fundamentally, our daily lives." Articles from current issues are available for free as well as Special Reports, which combine *Foreign Policy* articles and links to other sources, and topical stories and columns from international and regional news sources.

Global Media Journal (GMJ)

globalmediajournal.com

A journal published since 2002 by Professor Yahya R. Kamalipour, currently head of the Department of Communication and Creative Arts at Purdue University Calumet, *GMJ* aims to publish works that assess global media concentration, global media and consumer culture, media regulations, alternative media and other timely issues. *GMJ* has established African, American, Arabic, Australian, Canadian, Chinese, Indian, Pakistan, Persian, Polish, Spanish, Mexican, Mediterranean and Turkish editions.

Global Media Monitor (GMM)

lass.purduecal.edu

Serving as a "clearinghouse for numerous issues related to global communication and mass media studies," the GMM Web site was founded by editor Yahya R. Kamalipour of Purdue University Calumet while working on his e-journal *Global Media Journal*. The Web site houses numerous reference links to a variety of mass media subjects including international news and programs, news agencies, organizations, scholars and experts.

International Center for Journalists

icfj.org

This nonprofit professional organization promotes quality journalism around the world and believes that "independent, vigorous media are crucial in improving the human condition." It offers programs, seminars and fellowships for journalists in the United States and abroad, as well as online resources and instructor-led and distance courses in English, Arabic and Persian.

International Herald Tribune (IHT)

iht.com

The "global edition of *The New York Times*," the *International Herald Tribune* is the world's daily newspaper for global readers with articles from its own correspondents and *New York Times* reporters. Its sections are those of any local paper (Business, Tech/Media, Travel, Style, Culture, Health, Sports and Opinion), but the content is international (including a currency converter in the Business Market Tools section). The Web site includes four regional versions: Europe, the Americas, Asia-Pacific and Africa and Middle East.

International Women's Media Foundation (IWMF)

iwmf.org

This organization raises awareness about, creates opportunities for and builds networks of female journalists around the world. "No press is truly free unless women share an equal voice" is its motto. Online resources include links to online training, tips and guides, statistics and studies, links to Web sites of interest to women in the media, and publications and newsletter articles.

Internews

internews.org

An international media development organization based in California, Internews has offices in 23 countries in Africa, Asia, Europe, the Middle East and North America. Its goal is to "empower local media worldwide to give people access to information they need." Current Internews activities include providing training for media professionals in journalism, production and management; supporting media infrastructure; and adopting and implementing fair media laws and policies.

Funders of projects have included the Bill and Melinda Gates Foundation, the National Science Foundation, UNICEF, the World Bank, and many others. A long list of related organizations is available on the Web site.

Reporters Without Borders

rsf.org

An international organization that works for freedom of the press around the world, Reporters Without Borders defends journalists who are threatened, imprisoned or persecuted; works to improve the safety of journalists in war zones; and opposes censorship. The Web site provides news and online petitions in five languages about attacks on press freedom and journalists in Africa, the Americas, Asia, Europe and the former USSR, the Middle East and Northern Africa, within the United Nations and on the Internet.

Worldpress.org

worldpress.org

Worldpress.org is a digest of world news from the world's newspapers. The site contains originally written material and articles reprinted from the press outside the United States. Besides the latest news stories, resources include world headlines (updated every 15 minutes), a directory of world newspapers, World Press and other RSS (Really Simple Syndication) news feeds, country maps and profiles (from the *CIA World Factbook*), the texts of documents in the news and links to think tanks and nongovernmental organizations. The homepage also has a link to world cartoons, a currency converter and Worldtimeserver.com. The site's most recent feature is World Blogs.

Impact/Action Videos are concise news features on various topics created exclusively for *Media/Impact*. Go online to access MindTap at cengagebrain.com. MindTap for Media/Impact sequences all of your learning tools—Chapter Readings with highlighting and note taking, Impact/Action Videos, activities and assessments—into chapter driven learning units that guide you through the curriculum.

3-D Virtual Reality   Creates a digital representative of reality and then places a digital representative (called an avatar) in that reality.

30-Year Rule   Developed by Paul Saffo, the theory that it takes about 30 years for a new technology to be completely adopted within a culture.

AAM   Alliance for Audited Media (formerly Audit Bureau of Circulations). An independent agency of media market research that verifies and publishes circulation figures for member magazines.

ABC   Australian Broadcasting Corporation.

Accreditation   The process by which the government certifies members of the press to cover government-related news events.

Advance   An amount the publisher pays the author before the book is published.

Advertising Campaign   A planned advertising effort, coordinated for a specific time period.

Advertorial   Paid advertising supplements in newspapers and magazines that often look similar to the regular news pages.

Affiliates   Stations that use network programming but are owned by companies other than the networks.

Agenda-Setting   The belief that journalists don't tell you *what* to think but do tell you *what and whom to think about*.

All-Platform Journalists   Broadcast journalists who act as their own producer, cameraperson and editor, and sometimes even transmit live video.

Alternative (Dissident) Press   Media that present alternative viewpoints that challenge the mainstream press.

Analog   In mass communications, a type of technology used in broadcasting, whereby video or audio information is sent as continuous signals through the air on specific airwave frequencies.

Ancillary Rights   Marketing opportunities related to a movie, in addition to direct income from the movie itself.

App   Mobile application.

ASCAP   American Society of Composers, Authors and Publishers.

Audiobooks   Abridged or complete versions of classic books and popular new titles available on CDs and as Internet downloads.

Avatar   An icon or representation of a user—a digital stand-in—that represents an online identity.

BBC   British Broadcasting Corporation, the government-funded British broadcast network.

Blacklisting   Studio owners' refusal to hire someone who was suspected of taking part in subversive activities.

Blanket Licensing Agreement   An arrangement whereby radio stations become authorized to use recorded music for broadcast by paying a fee.

Blind Booking   The practice of renting films to exhibitors without letting them see the films first.

Block Booking   The practice of requiring theaters to take a package of movies instead of showing the movies individually.

Blockbuster   A book that achieves enormous financial success.

Blog   Short for Web log. A running Internet discussion group, where items are posted in reverse chronological order. Blogs usually focus on a specific topic.

BMI   Broadcast Music, Inc., a cooperative music licensing organization.

Branded Content, Content Marketing, Branded Entertainment   A program or story that mimics regular commercial programming or standard journalism but is custom-produced by an advertiser to promote a specific product and may or may not be labeled as an advertisement.

Browser   Software that allows people to display and interact with information on Web pages.

Bundle   The combination of telecommunications services that the media industries can offer consumers.

CATV   Community antenna television or cable television.

CDA   Communications Decency Act.

CD-RW (Re-Writable) Drives   Computer drives that are used to read data and music encoded in digital form and can be used to record more than once.

Censorship   The practice of suppressing material that is considered morally, politically or otherwise objectionable.

Checkbook Journalism   The practice of a news organization paying for an interview or a photograph.

Click-Through Rate   The rate at which people who see an ad on an Internet site click through to learn more.

Cloud Computing   The remote use by one business of another company's computer space, operating "in the cloud."

Company Magazines   Magazines produced by businesses for their employees, customers and stockholders.

Compatible   Media that can function well with one another to exchange and integrate text, pictures, sound and video.

Concentration of Ownership   The current trend of large companies buying smaller companies so that fewer companies own more types of media businesses.

Conglomerates   Companies that own media companies as well as businesses that are unrelated to the media business.

Consensus Journalism   The tendency among many journalists covering the same event to report similar conclusions about the event.

Consumer Magazines   All magazines sold by subscription or at newsstands, supermarkets and bookstores.

Convergence   The melding of the communications, computer and electronics industries. Also used to describe the economic alignment of the various media companies with each other to take advantage of technological advancements.

Cooperative News Gathering   Member news organizations that share the expense of getting the news.

COPA   Child Online Protection Act. A law aimed at preventing minors from getting access to sexually explicit online material.

Copyright Alert System (CAS)   A government-mandated warning to alert consumers who try to download copyrighted material.

CPM   Cost per thousand, the cost of an ad per 1,000 people reached. (M is the Roman numeral for 1,000.)

Crisis Communication   A timely public relations response to a critical situation that could cause damage to a company's reputation.

Cross-Ownership   The practice of one company owning TV and radio stations in the same broadcast market.

Cybersmears   Negative information organized and presented on the Internet as continuing attacks against a corporation.

Data Compression   The process of squeezing digital content into a smaller electronic space.

Data Farms   A location that houses data centers for the servers that process data flowing over the Internet.

Data Streaming   A common type of cloud computing that allows the user to play back an audio or video file without first completely downloading it.

DBS   Direct broadcast satellite.

Demographics   Data about consumers' characteristics, such as age, gender, income level, marital status, geographic location and occupation.

Deregulation   Government action that reduces government restrictions on the business operations of an industry.

Digital Audio Broadcast   A new form of audio transmission that eliminates all static and makes more program choices possible.

Digital Communication   Data in a form that can be transmitted and received electronically.

Digital Divide   The lack of access to digital technology among low-income, rural and minority groups.

Digital Media   All emerging communications media that combine text, graphics, sound and video using computer technology.

Direct Sponsorship   A program that carries an advertiser's name in the program title.

Disinformation   The intentional planting of false information by government sources.

DMCA   Digital Millennium Copyright Act.

Drive-Time Audiences   People who listen to the radio in their cars during 6 to 9 a.m. and 4 to 7 p.m.

DVR   Digital video recorders.

E-books   Electronic books.

E-mail   Mail that is delivered electronically over the Internet.

Embed   During the Iraq War, a term used to describe journalists who were allowed to cover the war on the frontlines, supervised by the U.S. military.

Ethics   The rules or standards that govern someone's conduct.

Ethnocentric   Promoting the superiority of one ethnic group over another.

False Light   The charge that what was implied in a story about someone is incorrect.

FCC   Federal Communications Commission.

Feedback   A response sent back to the sender from the person who receives the communication.

File Sharing   The peer-to-peer distribution of copyrighted material on the Internet without the copyright owner's permission.

Fleeting Expletives   Profanity uttered without warning on live television.

Freelancers   Writers who are not on the staff of a magazine but who are paid for each individual article published.

HD Radio   Hybrid digital technology that improves sound quality and makes it possible for radio stations to transmit real-time text messaging along with their programming.

High-Definition Television (HDTV)   The industry standard for digital television transmission as of 2009; it provides a picture with a clearer resolution than earlier TV sets.

Home Page   The first page of a Web site, which welcomes the user.

Hot Spot   A public area like a restaurant or hotel where people with laptops and hand-held Internet devices can connect to the Internet without a wire.

HTML   Hypertext markup language.

HTTP   Hypertext transfer protocol.

HUAC   House Un-American Activities Committee.

Hudson Test   A legal test that establishes a standard for commercial speech protection.

IHT   *International Herald Tribune*, the world's largest English-language newspaper.

Illuminations   Hand-colored decorative drawings used to enhance printed text.

Intellectual Property Rights   The legal right of ownership of ideas and content published in any medium.

Interactive   A message system that allows senders and receivers to communicate simultaneously.

Internet   An international web of computer networks.

ISP   Internet service provider, also called an Internet access provider.

LAPS Test   A yardstick for local obscenity judgments, which evaluates an artistic work's literary, artistic, political or scientific value.

Libel   A false statement that damages a person's character or reputation by exposing that person to public ridicule or contempt.

Libelous   A statement is libelous if it damages a person's character or reputation by exposing that person to public ridicule or contempt.

Links   Electronic connections from one source of information to another.

LP   Long-playing record.

Magic Bullet Theory   The assertion that media messages directly and measurably affect people's behavior.

Mass Communication   Communication from one person or group of persons through a transmitting device (a medium) to large audiences or markets.

Mass Media Content Analysis   An attempt to analyze how mass media programming influences behavior.

Mass Media Effects Research   An attempt to analyze how people use the information they receive from the media.

Mass Media Industries   Eight types of media businesses: books, newspapers, magazines, recordings, radio, movies, television and the Internet.

Media   Plural of the word *medium*.

Medium   The means by which a message reaches the audience. Also, the singular form of the word *media*.

Message Pluralism   The availability to an audience of a variety of information and entertainment sources.

MOOCs   Massive open online courses.

MPAA   Motion Picture Association of America.

MPA   The Association of Magazine Media, originally the Magazine Publisher's Association.

Muckrakers   Investigative magazine journalists who targeted abuses by government and big business.

NAB   National Association of Broadcasters, the lobbying organization that represents broadcasters' interests.

Narrowcasting   Segmenting the radio audience.

Net Neutrality   Rules for Internet service providers that require them to keep their networks open and available to carry all legal content. Under these rules, providers cannot restrict access to their network by other providers nor can they limit the type or delivery of content they carry.

Network   A collection of radio or TV stations that offers programs, usually simultaneously, throughout the country during designated program times.

NII   National Information Infrastructure.

Noise   Distortion (such as static) that interferes with clear communication.

NSL   National Security Letter.

NWICO New World Information and Communications Order. The concept that mass media should include all areas of the world, not just the West.

O & Os TV stations that are *o*wned and *o*perated by the networks.

Pass-Along Readership People who share a magazine with the original recipient.

Payola The practice of accepting payment to play specific recordings on the air.

Paywall A fee-for-access system set up by a newspaper to charge readers for Internet content.

Penny Press or Penny Paper A newspaper produced by dropping the price of each copy to a penny and supporting the production cost through advertising.

Persuasion The act of using argument or reasoning to induce someone to do something.

Phonetic Writing The use of symbols to represent sounds.

Photojournalism Using photographs to accompany text to capture a news story.

Pictograph A symbol of an object that is used to convey an idea.

Podcast An audio or video file made available on the Internet for anyone to download, often available by subscription.

Point-of-Purchase Magazines Magazines that consumers buy directly, not by subscription. They are sold mainly at checkout stands in supermarkets.

Pool Reporting An arrangement that places reporters in small, government-supervised groups to cover an event.

Pop-Up An advertisement on a Web site that appears on the screen either behind a Web page when someone leaves the site or on top of the Web site home page when someone first visits.

Prime Time The TV time period from 7 to 11 p.m. when more people watch TV than at any other time.

Prior Restraint Government censorship of information before the information is published or broadcast.

Professional Ethics The rules or standards governing the conduct of the members of a profession.

Public Domain Publications, products and processes that are not protected by copyright and thus are available free to the public.

Publicity Uncontrolled free use of media by a public relations firm to create events and present information to capture press and public attention.

Public Relations Creating understanding for, or goodwill toward, a company, a person or a product.

Publishing Placing items on the Web.

Qualified Privilege The freedom of the press to report what is discussed during legislative and court proceedings.

Rating The percentage of the total number of households *with TV sets* tuned to a particular program.

RBOC Regional Bell Operating Companies.

Recording Industry Association of America (RIAA) Industry association that lobbies for the interests of the nation's major recording companies. Member companies account for 95 percent of all U.S. recording company sales.

Rep Firm A company of advertising sales representatives who sell advertising time and space in their market to companies outside their geographic area.

Roth Test A standard court test for obscenity, named for one of the defendants in an obscenity case.

Royalty An amount the publisher pays an author, based on an established percentage of the book's price; royalties run anywhere from 6 to 15 percent.

RPM Revolutions per minute.

RTM Real-time marketing.

Satellite Radio Radio transmission by satellite, with limited or no advertising, available by subscription.

Search Advertising Advertising in the form of a list and/or link to a company's site domain name through a specific online search word or phrase.

Search Engine The tool used to locate information in a computer database.

Search Marketing Positioning Internet advertising prominently next to consumers' related online search results.

Seditious Language Language that authorities believe could incite rebellion against the government.

Selective Perception The concept that each person processes messages differently.

Server The equipment that delivers programs from their source to the programs' subscribers.

Share The percentage of the audience *with TV sets turned on* that is watching a particular program.

Shield Laws Laws that protect journalists from revealing their sources and the information that is communicated between journalists and their sources in a journalistic relationship.

Situation Comedy   A TV program that establishes a regular cast of characters typically in a home or work situation. Also called a sitcom.

SLAPP   Strategic lawsuit against public participation.

SMS   Short messaging service.

Social Network   An Internet community where users share information, ideas, personal messages, photographs, audio and video.

Spiral of Silence   The belief that people with divergent views may be reluctant to challenge the consensus of opinion offered by the media.

Star System   Promoting popular movie personalities to lure audiences.

Studio System   An early method of hiring a stable of salaried stars and production people under exclusive contracts to a specific studio.

Subscription Television   A new term used to describe consumer services delivered by cable and satellite program delivery.

Subsidiary Rights   The rights to market a book for other uses—to make a movie or to print a character from the book on T-shirts, for example.

Sweeps   The months when TV ratings services gather their most important ratings—February, May and November.

Syndicates   News agencies that sell articles for publication to a number of newspapers simultaneously.

Syndicators   Services that sell programming to broadcast stations and cable.

Tabloid   A small-format newspaper that features large photographs and illustrations along with sensational stories.

Telco   An abbreviation for "telephone company."

Time-Shifting   Recording a television program on a DVR to watch at a more convenient time.

Touch Technology   Uses computing power to digitally enhance the five senses—touch, sight, hearing, taste and smell.

Trade, Technical and Professional Magazines   Magazines dedicated to a particular business or profession.

Two-Step Flow   The transmission of information and ideas from mass media to opinion leaders and then to friends.

Vertical Integration   An attempt by one company to simultaneously control several related aspects of the media business.

Viral Marketing   Creating an online message that is entertaining enough to get consumers to pass it on over the Internet like a virus.

Webzines   (also called **zines**) Online magazines available only on the Internet.

Wi-Fi   An abbreviation for *Wi*reless *Fi*delity. The new mass media are as convenient as your cell phone, complete with graphics and sound, offering massive choices of information, entertainment and services whenever and wherever you want them.

Wiki   Technology that allows many users to collaborate to create and update Internet pages.

WIPO   World Intellectual Property Organization.

Yellow Journalism   News that emphasizes crime, sex and violence; also called jazz journalism and tabloid journalism.

This guide offers a selection of current information sources to help research mass media topics. Many of these are print resources that also are available as e-books and online. Also included is a list of associations that provide information, including job listings, for specific media industries.

The study of mass media covers a wide range of scholarship besides journalism and mass communication. Historians, psychologists, economists, political scientists and sociologists, for example, often contribute ideas to media studies. This guide therefore includes a variety of research sources from academic and industry publications as well as from popular periodicals.

These Research Sources Give a Good Overview

The New York Times is the best daily source of information about the media industries, especially the paper's Business section, where you will find regular reports on earnings, acquisitions and leaders in the media industries. *The New York Times* archive online helps locate the articles you need. *The International Herald Tribune*, published by *The New York Times*, offers the best global English-language coverage of mass media worldwide.

The *Los Angeles Times'* daily Calendar section follows the media business very closely, especially television and movies, because many video production companies are based in Los Angeles.

The Wall Street Journal and *The Washington Post* also carry media information, and both archives are indexed online. *The Wall Street Journal* charges users for access to most of its articles.

Advertising Age publishes special issues throughout the year focusing on newspapers, magazines, broadcasting and the Internet, as well as periodic estimates of total advertising revenue in each industry throughout the year. *Advertising Age* has an online index at *adage.com* but charges a fee and requires user registration for some articles and most statistical tables.

Columbia Journalism Review and *American Journalism Review* regularly critique developments in the print, broadcast and Internet industries. *Columbia Journalism Review* is published by New York's Columbia University Graduate School of Journalism. *American Journalism* is published by the University of Maryland Foundation with offices in the Philip Merrill College of Journalism.

Communication Abstracts, *Communication Research*, *Journal of Communication* and *Journalism Quarterly* offer scholarly articles and article summaries about media issues. Journals that cover specific media topics include *Journal of Advertising Research*, *Newspaper Research Journal* and *Public Relations Review*.

These Resources Offer Specific Media Industry Information

Editor & Publisher, updated regularly online at *editorand publisher.com*, follows the newspaper business, including information about industry revenue.

Broadcasting & Cable Yearbook was an annual compilation of material about the broadcast industry that also included syndicators, brokers, advertising agencies and associations. The yearbook stopped publishing in 2010 but an archive of issues is available free online at *american radiohistory.com*.

Encyclopedia of American Journalism, edited by Stephen L. Vaughn (Routledge, 2007) is the only single-volume reference work covering the history of journalism in the United States and is available in paperback and as a Kindle e-book. The *Encyclopedia* documents the historical distinctions between print media, radio, television and the Internet and their roles in the formation of a variety of social movements in the United States, including peace and protest, civil and consumer rights, environmentalism and globalization.

Ulrich's Periodicals Directory lists journals, magazines and newspapers alphabetically and by subject and is available in most libraries. Its online counterpart, *Ulrichs web.com*, is continually updated with new information and includes an archive.

ASCAP (The American Society of Composers, Authors and Publishers) publishes a magazine called *Playback* that chronicles the recording industry.

Hollywood Screenwriting Directory is a compilation of contact information for what the publisher calls "Hollywood buyers," including street and e-mail addresses.

For annual compilations of movie listings and reviews, check *Roger Ebert's Movie Yearbook* (Andrews McMeel, 2012) and *Leonard Maltin's 2014 Movie Guide* (Signet, 2013).

The National Association of Broadcasters (NAB) produces some publications that cover the radio and television industries, including advocacy papers on subjects the NAB lobbies in Congress.

Advertising Red Books is a database of advertisers and advertising agencies, available at *redbooks.com*.

Digital Media Wire publishes daily online newsletters and updated directories covering the business of digital media (including music, videos, gaming and mobile media).

THESE RESOURCES HELP UNCOVER U.S. MEDIA HISTORY AND CULTURE

John P. Dessauer's *Book Publishing: What It Is, What It Does* (R. R. Bowker, 1981) succinctly explains the history of the book publishing business. Another historical perspective and overview is available in *Books: The Culture & Commerce of Publishing* by Lewis A. Coser et al. (Basic Books, 1982). *Book Business: Publishing Past, Present and Future* by Jason Epstein (Norton, 2002) assesses the past and present book business. *The Book Publishing Industry* by Albert N. Greco, 2nd edition (Erlbaum, 2004) discusses marketing, production and changing technology.

The Journalist's Bookshelf by Roland E. Wolseley and Isabel Wolseley (Berg, 1986) is a comprehensive listing of resources about American print journalism.

The classic early history of American magazines is Frank Luther Mott's *History of American Magazines* (Appleton, 1930). *Pages from the Past: History and Memory in American Magazines* by Carolyn Kitch (University of North Carolina Press, 2008) examines the role of magazines in creating collective memory and identity for Americans.

The Music Business and Recording Industry by Geoffrey Hull, Thomas Hutchinson and Richard Strasser (Routledge, 2010) is a textbook that examines the economics of today's recording industry. *Appetite for Self-Destruction: The Spectacular Crash of the Record Industry in the Digital Age* by Steve Kopper (Soft Skull Press, 2009) offers a critical look at the last 30 years of the music business. *This Business of Music* by M. William Krasilovsky, Sidney Shemel, John M. Gross and Jonathan Feinstein (Billboard Publications, 2007) explains how the recording industry works.

Listening In: Radio and American Imagination by Susan J. Douglas (University of Minnesota Press, 2004) and *Radio Reader: Essays in the Cultural History of Radio* by Michele Hilmes (Routledge, 2001) specifically discuss the cultural impact of radio in the 20th century.

A History of Films by John L. Fell (Holt, Rinehart & Winston, 1979) and *Movie-Made America: A Cultural History of American Movies,* revised edition (Vintage, 1994) by Robert Sklar provide a good introduction to the history of movies. Works examining the cultural, social and economic impacts on American society include *Movies and American Society* edited by Steven J. Ross (Wiley-Blackwell, 2002) and *American Film: A History* by Jon Lewis (Norton, 2007). *Hollywood Stories: A Book about Celebrities, Gossip, Directors, Famous People and More!* by Stephen Schochet (Hollywood Stories Publishing, 2010) is a chatty compilation of stories and useful information, available in hardback and as an e-book.

International Film Guide (International Film Guide, 2012) is an encyclopedic source for global movie information. Another good movie information resource is *The Film Encyclopedia* (Collins, 2012), currently in its 7th edition, by Ephraim Katz.

The Columbia History of American Television by Gary Edgerton (Columbia University Press, 2009) follows the technological developments and cultural relevance of TV from its early days to today. *From Daytime to Primetime: The History of American Television Programs* by James W. Roman (Greenwood, 2008) offers comprehensive coverage of TV history before 2008. The classic television history is Eric Barnouw's *Tube of Plenty* (Oxford University Press, 1975). Christopher H. Sterling and John M. Kittross provide another overview of radio and television history in *Stay Tuned: A History of American Broadcasting*, 3rd edition (Routledge, 2001).

Confessions of an Advertising Man by David Ogilvy (Southbank, 2004) is the classic insider's view of the business. Three other histories of American advertising are *The Making of Modern Advertising* by Daniel Pope (Basic Books, 1983), *Advertising the American Dream* by Roland Marchand (University of California Press, 1986) and *The Mirror Makers: A History of American Advertising and Its Creators* by Stephen Fox (University of Illinois Press, 1997). In 2011, Yale University Press published a current critique of advertising by Joseph Turow, *The Daily You: How the New Advertising Industry Is Defining Your Identity and Your Worth*.

In 1923, Edward L. Bernays wrote the first book specifically about public relations, *The Engineering of Consent* (University of Oklahoma Press, reprinted in 1955). For an understanding of today's public relations business, you can read *This Is PR: The Realities of Public Relations* by Doug Newsom, Judy Turk and Dean Kruckeberg (Cengage, 2012).

A Social History of the Media: From Gutenberg to the Internet by Peter Burke and Asa Briggs, 2nd edition (Polity, 2005) and *Convergence Culture: Where Old and New Media Collide* by Henry Jenkins (NYU Press, 2008) discuss the emergence and evolution of communications media, their social impact and the relationship between media producers and consumers. For recent analysis of the Internet's effects on society, read *The Filter Bubble:*

How the New Personalized Web Is Changing What We Read and How We Think by Eli Pariser (Penguin, 2011) and *The Shallows: What the Internet Is Doing to Our Brains* by Nicholas Carr (W. W. Norton, 2011).

To learn more about newsreels and to view the actual films, visit the University of South Carolina Web site, *sc.edu/library/newsfilm*. Other major newsreel collections exist at the National Archives and Records Administration Web site at archives.gov and at the Library of Congress, *loc.gov/library/libarch-digital.html*. British Pathé newsreels are located at *britishpathe.com*.

The most comprehensive academic journals specifically devoted to media history are *American Journalism*, published by the American Journalism Historians Association, and *Journalism History*, published by the E. W. Scripps School of Journalism at Ohio University, with support from the History Division of the Association for Education in Journalism and Mass Communication.

For information about historical events and people in the media who often are omitted from traditional histories, you can refer to *Up from the Footnote: A History of Women Journalists* by Marion Marzolf (Hastings House, 1977); *Great Women of the Press* by Madelon Golden Schilpp and Sharon M. Murphy (Southern Illinois University Press, 1983); *Taking Their Place: A Documentary History of Women and Journalism* by Maurine Hoffman Beasley and Sheila Jean Gibbons, 2nd edition (Strata Publishing, 2002); *Journalistas: 100 Years of the Best Writing and Reporting by Women Journalists*, edited by Eleanor Mills (Seal Press, 2005); *Black Journalists: The NABJ Story* by Wayne Dawkins, updated edition (August Press, 1997); *Ladies' Pages: African American Women's Magazines and the Culture that Made Them* by Noliwe M. Rooks (Rutgers University Press, 2004); *Minorities and Media: Diversity and the End of Mass Communication* by Clint C. Wilson and Felix Gutiérrez (Sage, 1985); *Gender, Race and Class in Media* by Gail Dines and Jean M. Humez (Sage, 2002); and *Facing Difference: Race, Gender and Mass Media* by Shirley Biagi and Marilyn Kern-Foxworth (Pine Forge Press, 1997).

THESE WEB SITES FOLLOW CURRENT MEDIA INDUSTRY NEWS

Thousands of Web sites on the Internet offer useful material about the mass media. What follows is an alphabetical list of the specific sites that also appear at the end of each chapter. If you can't reach the Web site at the address listed, search using the site's name, listed in **bold type**. To find Web sites on a specific media topic, check **Working the Web** at the end of each chapter.

Academy of Motion Picture Arts and Sciences
oscars.org

Adrants
adrants.com

Advertising Age
adage.com

Advertising Council
adcouncil.org

All About Public Relations
aboutpublicrelations.net

AllYouCanRead.com
allyoucanread.com

Amazon
amazon.com

American Advertising Federation (AAF)
aaf.org

American Association of Advertising Agencies
aaaa.org

American Booksellers Association (ABA)
bookweb.org

American Booksellers Foundation for Free Expression (ABFFE)
abffe.org

American Library Association (ALA)
ala.org

American Marketing Association (AMA)
marketingpower.com

American Society of Journalists and Authors (ASJA)
asja.org

American Society of News Editors (ASNE)
asne.org

American Top 40 with Ryan Seacrest
at40.com

AOL Music
music.aol.com

Apple.com/iTunes
apple.com/itunes

Apple Inc.
apple.com

Association of American Publishers
publishers.org

Association of Hispanic Advertising Agencies (AHAA)
ahaa.org

Barnes & Noble
barnesandnoble.com

BBC News
bbc.co.uk

Benton Foundation
benton.org

Biblio
biblio.com

Billboard
billboard.biz and *billboard.com*

BookFinder
bookfinder.com

The Broadcast Archive
oldradio.com

BuzzFeed
buzzfeed.com

Canadian Broadcasting Corporation (CBC)
Radio-Canada
cbc.ca/radio

CBS Corporation
cbscorporation.com

CBS Radio
cbsradio.com

Center for Media and Democracy: PRWatch
prwatch.org

Center on Media and Child Health (CMCH)
cmch.tv

Chartered Institute of Public Relations
cipr.co.uk

Clio Awards
clioawards.com

CNET
cnet.com

Columbia Journalism Review (CJR)
cjr.org

Comcast Corporation (owner of NBC Universal)
comcast.com

Committee to Protect Journalists
cpj.org

CondéNet—Web Site for Condé Nast Publications
condenet.com

CyberJournalist.net
cyberjournalist.net

The Dallas Morning News
dallasnews.com

DEG Digital Entertainment Group
dvdinformation.com

Disney–ABC Television Group
disneyabctv.com

Electronic Frontier Foundation (EFF)
eff.org

EthicNet, European Ethics Codes
ethicnet.uta.fi/

Facebook
facebook.com

Fairness & Accuracy in Reporting (FAIR)
fair.org

Federal Communications Commission (FCC)
fcc.gov

Federal Trade Commission (FTC)
ftc.gov

FindLaw
findlaw.com

Folio: The Magazine for Magazine Management
foliomag.com

Foreign Policy Magazine
foreignpolicy.com

Fox Movietone News
foxnews.com/on-air/movietone-news/index.html
foxnews.com

Freedom Forum
freedomforum.org

Friday Morning Quarterback (FMQB)
fmqb.com

Gannett Company, Inc. (owner of USA Today)
gannett.com

Global Media Journal (GMJ)
globalmediajournal.com

Global Media Monitor (GMM)
lass.purduecal.edu

Google Book Search
books.google.com

Hearst Corporation
hearst.com

Honolulu Star-Advertiser
staradvertiser.com

Index (formerly Index on Censorship)
indexoncensorship.org

Indiana University Index of Journalism Ethics Cases
journalism.indiana.edu/resources/ethics

IndieBound
indiebound.org

Inside Radio
insideradio.com

Insound
insound.com

Institute for Public Relations
instituteforpr.com

Interactive Advertising Bureau
iab.net

International Center for Journalists
icfj.org

International Herald Tribune
iht.com

International Women's Media Foundation (IWMF)
iwmf.org

The Internet Movie Database (IMDB)
imdb.com

Internews
internews.org

Investigative Reporters and Editors (IRE)
ire.org

iVillage
ivillage.com

Joan Shorenstein Center on the Press, Politics and Public Policy (Harvard University)
shorensteincenter.org

Journal of Electronic Publishing (JEP)
journalofelectronicpublishing.org

Los Angeles Times
latimes.com

Lucasfilm
lucasfilm.com

Media Center at New York Law School
nyls.edu/centers/projects/media_center

Media Effects Research Lab at Penn State University
psu.edu/dept/medialab/

Media Law Resource Center (MLRC)
medialaw.org

MediaPost Communications
mediapost.com

Media Research Hub (Social Science Research Council; SSRC)
mediaresearchhub.ssrc.org

MediaSmarts [formerly known as the Media Awareness Network (MNet)]
mediasmarts.ca

The Miami Herald
miamiherald.com

MIT Media Lab Project
media.mit.edu

Moorland-Spingarn Research Center (MSRC) at Howard University
howard.edu/msrc

Motion Picture Association of America (MPAA) and Motion Picture Association (MPA)
mpaa.org

MPA—The Association of Magazine Media and the American Society of Magazine Editors (ASME)
magazine.org

National Association of Broadcasters (NAB)
nab.org

National Cable & Telecommunications Association (NCTA)
ncta.com

National Freedom of Information Coalition (formerly Freedom of Information Center)
nfoic.org/foi-center

National Journal
nationaljournal.com

National Public Radio
npr.org

Netflix
netflix.com

News Corporation
newscorp.com

Newspaper Association of America (NAA)
naa.org

Newsweek
thedailybeast.com/newsweek

The New York Times
nytimes.com

Nielsen Media Research
nielsen.com

The Online News Association (ONA)
journalist.org

Online Public Relations
online-pr.com

Online Publishers Association (OPA)
online-publishers.org

Pandora: Radio from the Music Genome Project
pandora.com

Parental Media Guide
parentalguide.org/movies.html

Pew Internet & American Life Project
pewinternet.org

Pew Research Center for People and the Press
people-press.org/reports

Pew Research Center's Project for Excellence in Journalism
journalism.org

Poynter Online
poynter.org

PR Newswire
prnewswire.com

Project for Excellence in Journalism: Ethics Codes
journalism.org/resources/ethics_codes

PRWeb
prweb.com

PRWeek
prweekus.com

Public Broadcasting (PBS)
pbs.org

Public Relations Society of America (PRSA)
prsa.org

Public Relations Student Society of America (PRSSA)
prssa.org

Quarter to Three
quartertothree.com

Radio Advertising Bureau (RAB)
rab.com

Radio Lovers
radiolovers.com

Radio Television Digital News Association (RTDNA; formerly Radio-Television News Directors Association)
rtdna.org

Radio Time
radiotime.com

Recording Industry Association of America (RIAA)
riaa.com

Reporters Without Borders
rsf.org

Rhapsody Inc.
rhapsody.com

Salon
salon.com

Scholastic Corporation
scholastic.com

Screenwriters Federation of America (SFA)
screenwritersfederation.org

Silha Center for the Study of Media Ethics and Law (University of Minnesota)
silha.umn.edu/

Sirius XM
siriusxm.com

Slate
slate.com

Society of Professional Journalists (SPJ)
spj.org

Sony Corporation of America
sony.com

Sports Illustrated
sportsillustrated.cnn.com

Student Press Law Center (SPLC)
splc.org

Sundance Institute
sundance.org

Talking Points Memo (TPM)
talkingpointsmemo.com

Technocrati
technocrati.com

Television Bureau of Advertising (TVB)
tvb.org

Time Warner Inc.
timewarner.com

Topix
topix.net

Tribune Company
tribune.com

TuneIn
tunein.com

TV.com
tv.com

Twitter
twitter.com

Unity: Journalists for Diversity
unityjournalists.org

Universal Music Group (UMG)
universalmusic.com

University of Iowa Department of Communication Studies: Political Communication and Campaigns
clas.uiowa.edu/commstudies/political-communication-campaigns

U.S. Census Bureau Statistical Abstract: Information and Communications
census.gov/compendia/statab/cats/information_communications.html

Vanderbilt University Television News Archive
tvnews.vanderbilt.edu

The Verge
theverge.com

Viacom Inc. (owner of Nickelodeon, Comedy Central and Nick at Nite)
viacom.com

Walt Disney Company (owner of ABC)
disney.go.com

Warner Bros.
warnerbros.com

The Washington Post
washingtonpost.com

Whatis.com
whatis.techtarget.com

WikiLeaks
wikileaks.org

Worldpress.org
worldpress.org

YouTube
youtube.com

MORE MEDIA RESEARCH SOURCES YOU CAN USE

Many magazines and journals publish information about the mass media industries. The following is a listing of the major magazine and journal titles in each subject area. All of these publications offer companion Web sites.

Advertising

Adweek
adweek.com

Journal of Advertising
tandfonline.com

Journal of Advertising Research
journalofadvertisingresearch.com

Broadcasting

Broadcasting and Cable
broadcastingcable.com

Emmy, published by the Academy of Television Arts and Sciences
emmys.tv/emmy-magazine

Journal of Broadcasting and Electronic Media
beaweb.org/jobem.htm

RTDNA Communicator
rtdna.org

TV Guide
tvguide.com

Magazine and Book Publishing

Folio Magazine
foliomag.com

Publishers Weekly
publishersweekly.com

Movies

Film Comment
filmcomment.com

Hollywood Reporter
hollywoodreporter.com

Variety
variety.com

Video Age
videoageinternational.com

Newspapers

Editor & Publisher
editorandpublisher.com

Journalism and Communication Monographs
jmo.sagepub.com

Newspaper Research Journal
newspaperresearchjournal.org

Presstime
naa.org/news-and-media/presstime-update.aspx

Quill
spj.org/quill.asp

Public Relations

PR Week
prweekus.com

Public Relations Journal
prsa.org/Intelligence/PRJournal

Recordings

Billboard
billboard.com

Down Beat
downbeat.com

Music Index
ebscohost.com/public/music-index

Rolling Stone
rollingstone.com

Digital Media and the Web

AI Magazine
aaai.org/Magazine/magazine.php

Communications Daily
warren-news.com

Information Today
infotoday.com

MacWorld
macworld.com

PC Magazine
pcmag.com

PC World
pcworld.com

Technical Communication
techcomm.stc.org

Wired
wired.com

Global Media

Advertising

International Journal of Advertising
internationaljournalofadvertising.com

Broadcasting

Cable and Satellite International
csimagazine.com/csi/index.php

Ofcom (Independent regulator and competition authority for the UK communications industries)
ofcom.org.uk

Movies

Cineaction, Canada
cineaction.ca

Empire Magazine
empireonline.com/magazine

Film Ink, Australia
filmink.com.au

Film, Ireland
filmireland.net

Recordings

Musical America Worldwide
musicalamerica.com

Other

OPMA Overseas Media Guide, England
opma.co.uk

Media-Related Topics

Censorship News (published by the National Coalition Against Censorship—available to download as a PDF or by e-mail subscription)
ncac.org

Communication Research (online editions available through Sage Publications)
sagepub.com/content/current

News Media and the Law (published by Reporters Committee for Freedom of the Press)
rcfp.org/magazine-archive

Nieman Reports (published by the Nieman Foundation for Journalism at Harvard University)
nieman.harvard.edu/reports.aspx

Chapter 1 Mass Media and Everyday Life

Bagdikian, B. (1980, Spring). Conglomeration, concentration, and the media. *Journal of Communication*, 60.

Bagdikian, B. (1983). *The media monopoly*. Boston: Beacon Press.

Carr, D. (2007, January 15). 24-hour newspaper people. *The New York Times*, C1.

Carr, D. (2011, January 2). The great mashup of 2011. NYTimes.com.

Elliott, S. (2013, January 14). Super Bowl commercial time is a sellout. NYTimes.com.

eMarketer (2011, January 4). Online ad spending set to break records. eMarketer.com.

Gilder, G. (1994, February 28). Life after television, updated. *Forbes*, 17.

Graham, J. (2005, May 20). Google gets personal. *USA Today*, 6B.

Greene, J. (2003, April 28). The year of living wirelessly. BusinessWeek.com.

Grobart, S. (2012, May 30). Daddy, what were compact discs? NYTimes.com.

Gustin, S. (2010, February 23). One-third of Americans lack high-speed Internet access. DailyFinance.com.

Hernandez, D. (2011, August 6). Too much Facebook time may be unhealthy for kids. LATimes.com.

Ives, N. (2010, June 28). Mounting web woes pummel newspapers. *Advertising Age*, 6.

Jenkins, H. (2000, March). Digital land grab. *Technology Review*, 103.

Johnson, B. (2012, October 1). Your guide to the leading media companies 2012. Adage.com.

Kharif, O. (2005, June 21). Nearly everything gets unplugged. BusinessWeek.com.

Kim, R. (2005, May 28). Sales of cell phones totally off the hook. *San Francisco Chronicle*, C1.

Kirkpatrick, D. D. (2003, April 14). Murdoch's first step: Make the sports fan pay. *The New York Times*, C1.

Lang, B. (2010, September 20). Ipsos OTX study: People spend more than half their day consuming media. TheWrap.com.

Liebling, A. J. (1961). *The press*. New York: Ballantine.

Lohr, S. (2010, March 16). How privacy vanishes online. NYTimes.com.

Lohr, S. (2011, October 23). More jobs predicted for machines, not people. NYTimes.com.

Los Angeles Times (2011, January 26). Mobile app revenue will triple to $15 billion this year, Gartner says. LATimes.com.

New York Times, The (2013, February 25). Social media, made mobile, B-8.

Nielsenwire (2009, December 21). Study: More cellular-only homes as Americans expand mobile media usage. Nielsenwire.com.

Plato (1961). *Collected works*. Princeton, N.J.: Phaedrus.

Raine, G. (2005, September 27). Net ad revenues grow steadily. *San Francisco Chronicle*, D1.

Rose, L. (2007, February 7). The best-paid talking heads. Forbes.com.

Rosenbloom, S. (2010, February 27). Cell phone applications let shoppers point, click and purchase. *The New York Times*, A1.

Scott, A. O. (2008, November 23). The screening of America. *The New York Times Magazine*, 21.

Siebert, T. (2007, February). World wide web: Hearing is believing. MediaPost.com.

Siklos, R. (2005, August 1). Behind Murdoch rift, a media dynasty unhappy in its own way. *The New York Times*, C1.

Siklos, R. (2007, May 13). Tilting at a digital future. *The New York Times*, 3-1.

Siklos, R., & Holson, L. (2005, August 8). NBC Universal aims to be prettiest feather in G.E.'s cap. *The New York Times*, C1.

Smith, A. (1980). *Goodbye Gutenberg*. New York: Oxford University Press.

Soto, M. (2000, May 4). Microsoft executive Nathan Myhrvold resigns. SeattleTimes.nwsource.com.

Story, L. (2007, January 15). Anywhere the eye can see, it's now likely to see an ad. *The New York Times*, A1.

Stout, H. (2010, May 2). Antisocial networking? *The New York Times*, ST2.

Sutel, S. (2005, September 20). *New York Times* to cut 4 percent of work force. Associated Press, AOL Business News. AOL.com.

Timberg, C. (2013, February 25). Mobile device connections growing quickly. WashingtonPost.com.

Tsukayama, H. (2013, January 2). Trends to watch at CES 2013. WashingtonPost.com.

Verrier, R. (2011, January 28). Movie ticket prices reach new milestone. LATimes.com.

Zinuda, N. (2013, March 11). Ad spending rises 3% in 2012: Kantar Media. Adage.com.

Chapter 2 Books: Rearranging the Page

Andriani, L. (2009, August 14). Cengage Learning to rent print textbooks. PublishersWeekly.com.

Anton, M. (2012, April 14). Even e-reader owners still like printed books, survey finds. LATimes.com.

Associated Press (2009, August 20). Microsoft, Yahoo, Amazon to fight Google book deal. SFGate.com.

Associated Press (2010, November 9). Publishers to get 70 percent of sales on Kindle. WSJ.com.

Associated Press (2011, August 30). Books-A-Million will assume 14 Borders leases. SFGate.com.

Auletta, K. (2010, April 26). Publish or perish. NewYorker .com.

Bosman, J. (2010, August 3). Biggest U.S. book chain up for sale. NYTimes.com.

Bosman, J. (2010, December 8). Lusty tales and hot sales: Romance e-books thrive. NYTimes.com.

Bosman, J. (2011, June 23). Rowling releases *Harry Potter* into the ether on Pottermore. NYTimes.com.

Bosman, J. (2012, June 4). Amazon buys Avalon Books, publisher in romance and mysteries. NYTimes.com.

Boss, S. (2007, May 13). The great mystery: Making a best-seller. *The New York Times*, 3-1.

Bradley, T. (2009, September 21). Opposition mounting against Google books settlement. SFGate.com.

Clifford, S., & Bosman, J. (2011, February 27). Publishers look beyond bookstores. NYTimes.com.

Coser, L. A., Kadushin, C., & Powell, W. F. (1982). *Books: The culture and commerce of publishing*. New York: Basic Books.

Davis, K. C. (1984). *Two-bit culture: The paperbacking of America*. Boston: Houghton Mifflin.

Dessauer, J. P. (1974). *Book publishing: What it is, what it does*. New York: R. R. Bowker.

Donadio, R. (2008, April 27). You're an author? Me too! *The New York Times Book Review*, 27.

Flood, A. (2011, August 18). James Patterson brand makes him world's best-paid writer. Guardian.co.uk.

Galassi, J. (2010, January 3). There's more to publishing than meets the screen. NYTimes.com.

Hart, J. D. (1950). *The popular book*. Berkeley: University of California Press.

Helft, M. (2009, April 29). U.S. opens inquiry into Google books deal. *The New York Times*, B5.

Helft, M. (2009, September 24). Google books settlement delayed indefinitely. NYTimes.com.

Helft, M. (2011, March 22). Judge reject's Google's deal to digitize books. NYTimes.com.

Hoffman, J. B. (2012, October 9). Long live paper. NYTimes .com.

Hyde, C. R. (2010, November 2). The (paltry) economics of being a novelist. DailyFinance.com.

Itzkoff, D. (2009, September 8). Not a typo: James Patterson signs 17-book deal. NYTimes.com.

Kaufman, L. (2013, February 20). Independent booksellers sue Amazon and publishers over e-books. NYTimes .com.

Mackay, R. (2010, December 27). Julian Assange's 1.3 million reasons to write. NYTimes.com.

Mahler, J. (2010, January 24). James Patterson Inc. NYTimes.com.

McMurtrie, H. (2009, March 15). The Kindle 2: A thin read. SFGate.com.

Miller, C. C. (2010, July 19). E-books top hardcovers at Amazon. NYTimes.com.

Miller, C. C., & Bosman, J. (2011, May 19). E-books outsell print books at Amazon. NYTimes.com.

Pfanner, E., & Chozick, A. (2012, October 29). Random House and Penguin merger creates global giant. NYTimes.com.

Publishers Weekly (2012, June 25). The global 50: The world's largest book publishers, 2012. Publishers weekly.com.

Randolph, E. (2008, June 18). Reading into the future. NYTimes.com.

Reuters (2010, August 24). Book chain reports loss as it fights with investor. NYTimes.com.

Rich, M. (2009, May 17). Steal this book (for $9.99). *The New York Times*, WK3.

Rich, M. (2010, February 19). Judge hears arguments on Google book settlement. *The New York Times*, B4.

Rich, M. (2010, February 22). Textbooks that professors can rewrite digitally. *The New York Times*, B4.

Rich, M. (2010, March 1). Math of publishing meets the e-book. *The New York Times*, B1.

Richtel, M., & Miller, C. C. (2010, September 1). Of two minds about books. NYTimes.com.

Stelter, B. (2010, December 27). WikiLeaks founder signs book deal. NYTimes.com.

Stone, B. (2009, October 7). New Kindle to download books beyond U.S. NYTimes.com.

Stone, B., & Wortham, J. (2010, January 27). Apple reveals the iPad tablet. NYTimes.com.

Streitfield, D. (2005, July 17). Publisher loses ruling on e-books. LATimes.com.

Sweeney, M. (2013, March 26). *Fifty Shades of Grey* publisher Random House posts record profits. Guardian news.com.

Tedeschi, B. (2010, May 13). E-reader applications for today, and beyond. *The New York Times*, B10.

Trachtenberg, J. A. (2010, May 21). E-books rewrite book-selling. WSJ.com.

Trachtenberg, J. A. (2010, September 28). Authors feel pinch in age of e-books. WSJ.com.

Trachtenberg, J. A. (2010, December 6). Google opens online bookstore. WSJ.com.

Turow, S. (2013, April 7). The slow death of the American author. NYTimes.com.

Weinberg, S. (2010, March 16). Enhanced e-books: A boon for readers, a headache for agents. DailyFinance.com.

Weinberg, S. (2010, August 2). Amazon's new Kindles sell out in just five days. DailyFinance.com.

White, E. B. (1976). *Letters of E. B. White*. New York: Harper & Row.

Chapter 3 Newspapers: Expanding Delivery

Ahrens, F. (2009, March 26). *Washington Post* to offer new buyouts to employees. WashingtonPost.com.

Associated Press (2010, January 16). MediaNews holding company filing Chapter 11. SFGate.com.

Associated Press (2010, February 12). *USA Today* mandates staff furloughs to save money. NYTimes.com.

Associated Press (2010, August 27). *USA Today* plans overhaul to emphasize mobile devices. NYTimes.com.

Associated Press (2012, December 30). Tribune to leave bankruptcy after four years. SacBee.com.

Associated Press (2013, August 3). Red Sox owner enters $70M deal for *Boston Globe*. SFGate.com.

Auletta, K. (2005, October 10). Fault line. *The New Yorker*, 51.

Avriel, E. (2007, July 2). *N.Y. Times* publisher: Our goal is to manage the transition from print to Internet. Haaretz.com.

Carr, D. (2010, October 5). At flagging Tribune, tales of a bankrupt culture. NYTimes.com.

Carr, D. (2011, April 11). At Gannett, furloughs but nice paydays for brass. NYTimes.com.

Carr, D. (2013, May 12). Newspaper monopoly that lost its grip. NYTimes.com.

De Falco, B. (2011, January 11). Gannett to cut staff at 3 N.J. papers by nearly half. SFGate.com.

De La Merced, M. (2009, December 8). Tribune files for bankruptcy. NYTimes.com.

Dertouzos, J., & Quinn, T. (1985, September). Bargaining responses to the technology revolution: The case of the newspaper industry. *Labor management cooperation brief*. Washington, D.C.: U.S. Department of Labor.

Elliott, S. (2012, November 14). Renaming the circulation overseer. NYTimes.com.

Haughney, C. (2013, April 4). Cleveland paper to trim delivery and cut staff. NYTimes.com.

Johnson, K. (2009, February 27). Part of Denver's past, the Rocky says goodbye. NYTimes.com.

Kessler, K. (1984). *The dissident press*. Beverly Hills, Calif.: Sage.

Kirchhoff, S. M. (2010, September 9). *The U.S. newspaper industry in transition*, Congressional Research Service, Washington, D.C.

Marzolf, M. (1977). *Up from the footnote*. New York: Hastings House.

Oneal, M., & Puzzanghera, J. (2012, July 14). Bankruptcy judge to confirm Tribune reorganization plan. LATimes.com.

Perez-Peña, R. (2007, May 1). Newspaper circulation in steep slide across nation. *The New York Times*, C10.

Perez-Peña, R. (2009, March 12). As cities go from two newspapers to one, some talk of zero. *The New York Times*. A1.

Perez-Peña, R. (2010, January 21). *The Times* to charge for frequent access to its web site. NYTimes.com.

Peters, J. W. (2010, September 5). Some newspapers, tracking readers online, shift coverage. NYTimes.com.

Peters, J. W. (2010, October 25). Newspaper circulation falls broadly but at slower pace. NYTimes.com.

Peters, J. W. (2012, February 11). A newspaper, and a legacy, reordered. WashingtonPost.com.

Pew Research Center's Project for Excellence in Journalism, *The State of the News Media* 2013. Stateofthemedia.org/2013.

Plambeck, J. (2010, April 27). Newspaper circulation falls nearly 9 percent. *The New York Times*, B3.

Rainey, J. (2011, February 5). Consolidation seen as inevitable for Southern California newspapers. LATimes.com.

Reuters (2010, May 21). Tribune facing legal battle with creditors. *The New York Times*, B4.

Reuters (2011, December 12). To reorganize debt, publisher of papers files for bankruptcy. NYTimes.com.

Richman, D., & James, A. (2009, March 16). *Seattle P-I* to publish last edition Tuesday. SeattlePI.com.

Rutherford, L. (1963). *John Peter Zenger*. Gloucester, Mass.: Peter Smith.

Saltmarsh, M. (2010, March 26). Murdoch finalizes paywall for two British papers. NYTimes.com.

Schilpp, M. G., & Murphy, S. M. (1983). *Great women of the press*. Carbondale: Southern Illinois University Press.

Seelye, K. Q. (2005, September 21). Times company announces 500 job cuts. *The New York Times*, C5.

Seelye, K. Q., & Sorkin, A. R. (2007, April 2). Tribune accepts real estate magnate's bid. NYTimes.com.

Smith, A. (1980). *Goodbye Gutenberg*. New York: Oxford University Press.

Stelter, B. (2011, October 13). *New York Times* plans staff reductions. NYTimes.com.

Swanberg, W. A. (1971). *Citizen Hearst*. New York: Bantam Books.

Sweeney, M. (2012, December 3). News Corp. to close iPad newspaper *The Daily*. Guardiannews.com.

Wells, I. B. (1970). *The crusade for justice: The autobiography of Ida B. Wells*. Chicago: University of Chicago Press.

Woodward, C. (2013, August 6). A family dynasty gives up *The Washington Post*. SFGate.com.

Yardley, W., & Perez-Peña, R. (2009, March 17). In Seattle, a newspaper loses its paper routes. *The New York Times*, A1.

Zezima, K. (2005, August 8). Abolitionist's family celebrates a legacy of nonconformity. *The New York Times*, A10.

Chapter 4 Magazines: Targeting the Audience

Bercovici, J. (2009, October 5). Condé Nast closes beloved *Gourmet* magazine and three others. DailyFinance.com.

Bercovici, J. (2010, August 2). *Newsweek* gets sold to Sidney Harman. So long, *Newsweek*. DailyFinance.com.

Biagi, S. (1987). *NewsTalk I*. Belmont, Calif.: Wadsworth.

Carr, D. (2011, May 9). *The New Yorker* begins to offer iPad subscriptions. NYTimes.com.

Chozick, A. (2013, March 6). Time Warner ends talks with Meredith and will spin off Time Inc. into separate company. NYTimes.com.

Clifford, S. (2010, February 9). Newsstand sales and circulation fall for magazines. *The New York Times*, B3.

Clifford, S. (2010, May 6). As *Newsweek* goes on block, an era fades. *The New York Times*, A1.

Clifford, S. (2010, May 16). Fans of *Gourmet Magazine* accept no stand-ins. NYTimes.com.

Dredge, S. (2013, March 27). Flipboard 2.0 looks to make everyone the editor of their own magazine. Guardian news.com.

Haber, M. (2012, December 7). *Ebony* looks to its past as it moves forward. NYTimes.com.

Haughney, C. (2012, August 7). Women's magazines lead overall decline in newsstand sales. NYTimes.com.

Holson, E. (2007, May 25). OMG! Cute boys, kissing lips and lots of pics as magazines find a niche. *The New York Times*, C1.

Ives, N. (2012, November 30). Digital subs rising, *The Economist* unbundles tablet editions from print. Adage.com.

Ives, N. (2013, January 3). Digital cracks 50% of ad revenue at *Wired* magazine. Adage.com.

Ives. N. (2013, February 7). Magazines' digital circ soars . . . to 2.4% of total. Adage.com.

Kobak, J. B. (1985, April). 1984: A billion-dollar year for acquisitions. *Folio*, 14, 82–95.

Lee, F. R. (2005, August 10). He created a mirror for black America. *The New York Times*, B1.

Mechanic, M. (2001, March 19). Doing the bare minimum media: Magazines are rethinking the Internet. *Newsweek*, 62F.

O'Brien, K. J. (2007, March 18). Magazine publishers see future, but no profit in shift to Internet. IHT.com.

Olivarez-Giles, N. (2010, November 30). *Project*, Richard Branson's iPad-only magazine, now available in Apple's app store. LATimes.com.

Paneth, D. (1983). *Encyclopedia of American journalism*. New York: Facts on File.

Perez-Peña, R. (2008, July 20). Undercover publisher. *The New York Times*, BU1.

Peters, J. W. (2010, November 29). Magazines take a shot at the net. *The New York Times*, B6.

Peters, J. W. (2011, January 16). For magazines, a bitter pill in iPad. NYTimes.com.

Peters, J. W. (2011, November 13). *Newsweek*, mired in red ink, cancels longtime political series. NYTimes.com.

Peters, J. W. (2011, November 20). At 154, a digital milestone. NYTimes.com.

Pogue, D. (2012, April 11). A buffet of magazines on a tablet. NYTimes.com.

Rose, M. (2000, November 6). Problems for magazines come into view. *The Wall Street Journal*, B18.

Sarno, D. (2012, April 5). Five magazine publishers jointly release tablet app. LATimes.com.

Schilpp, M. G., & Murphy, S. M. (1983). *Great women of the press*. Carbondale: Southern Illinois University Press.

Seelye, K. Q. (2007, January 19). Time Inc. cutting almost 300 magazine jobs to focus more on Web sites. NYTimes.com.

Seelye, K. Q. (2007, February 23). New Republic to cut back publication schedule. NYTimes.com.

Seelye, K. Q. (2007, March 27). *Life* magazine, its pages dwindling, will cease publication. NYTimes.com.

Smith, S. (2010, December 14). Has the age of uber-cocooning begun? Digital media October boxscores. MinOnline.com.

Swanberg, W. A. (1972). *Luce and his empire*. New York: Scribner's.

Tarbell, I. (1939). *All in the day's work*. New York: MacMillan.

Wyatt, E. (2005, June 2). 80 years of *The New Yorker* to be offered in disc form. *The New York Times*, B3.

Chapter 5 Recordings: Demanding Choices

Associated Press (2008, July 26). Merger of Sirius and XM approved by FCC. NYTimes.com.

Chmielewski, D. C. (2004, October 27). iPod's rock and rollout. MercuryNews.com.

Denisoff, R. S. (1975). *Solid gold*. New Brunswick, N.J.: Transaction Books.

Evangelista, B. (2003, April 25). Apple kicks off online music store. *San Francisco Chronicle*, B1.

Evangelista, B. (2003, September 3). RIAA decries drop in CD sales. *San Francisco Chronicle*, B1.

Frost, L. (2007, January 26). Music industry pauses over ad-funded downloads. Money.aol.com.

Gomes, L. (2001, February 13). Napster suffers a rout in appeals court. *The Wall Street Journal*, A3.

Gomes, L. (2001, March 5). Judge starts process of silencing Napster. *The Wall Street Journal*, B6.

Holloway, L. (2003, June 26). Recording industry to sue Internet music swappers. *The New York Times*, C4.

Karnowski, S. (2009, June 18). Jury rules against Minn. woman in download case. SFGate.com.

Kopytoff, V. (2003, September 4). Music lawsuits snare 18 in Bay Area. *San Francisco Chronicle*, A1.

Kravels, D. (2013, March 18). Supreme Court OKs $222K verdict for sharing 24 songs. Wired.com.

Lee, E. (2007, March 22). Music industry threatens student downloaders at UC. SFGate.com.

Leeds, J. (2005, November 8). Grokster calls it quits on sharing music files. *The New York Times*, C1.

Leeds, J. (2007, February 19). Music labels offer teasers to download. *The New York Times*, C1.

Leeds, J. (2007, May 28). Plunge in CD sales shakes up big labels. *The New York Times*, B1.

Leeds, J. (2007, October 5). Labels win suit against song sharer. NYTimes.com.

Lowensohn, J. (2013, January 17). *Rolling Stone* lands on iPad with iTunes integration in tow. Cnet.com.

McBride, S., & Smith, E. (2008, December 19). Music industry to abandon mass suits. WSJ.com.

Metz, R. (1975). *CBS: Reflections in a bloodshot eye*. Chicago: Playboy Press.

Mostrous, A. (2010, March 1). Music industry needs clear strategy and control over illegal downloads. Business .TimesOnline.co.uk.

Pareles, J. (2005, August 23). Swaggering past 60, unrepentant. *The New York Times*, B1.

Pfanner, E. (2009, April 18). File-sharing site violated copyright, court says. NYTimes.com.

Pfanner, E. (2009, July 20). Music industry lures "casual" pirates to legal sites. NYTimes.com.

Pfanner, E. (2013, February 26). Music industry records first revenue increase since 1999. NYTimes.com.

Pham, A. (2011, May 10). Warner Music Group debt is downgraded. LATimes.com.

Plambeck, J. (2010, February 26). 10 billionth download for iTunes. *The New York Times*, C5.

Plambeck, J. (2010, May 31). As CD sales wane, music retailers diversify. *The New York Times*, B5.

Pogue, D. (2005, August 7). Britney to rent, lease or buy. *The New York Times*, 2-1.

Recording Industry Association of America (2010, May 12). Federal court issues landmark ruling against LimeWire. RIAA.com.

Rendon, J. (2003, July 20). From a store with 300,000 titles, a big music lesson. *The New York Times*, BU5.

Sabbagh, D. (2008, June 18). Music sales fall to their lowest level in over 20 years. Timesonline.com.

Sachs, T., & Nunziato, S. (2007, April 5). Spinning into oblivion. NYTimes.com.

Satter, R. G. (2011, January 21). IFPI: Growth in digital music sales is slowing. SFGate.com.

Segal, D. (2010, April 25). They're calling almost everyone's tune. *The New York Times*, BU1.

Sisario, B. (2012, September 21). U.S. and European regulators approve Universal's purchase of EMI. NYTimes.com.

Sisario, B. (2013, January 28). As music streaming grows, royalties slow to a trickle. NYTimes.com.

Sisario, B. (2013, January 28). For many digital music services, free is not a choice. NYTimes.com.

Sloan, P. (2013, March 12). Spotify: Growing like mad, yet so far to go. Cnet.com.

Smart, J. R. (1977). *A wonderful invention: A brief history of the phonograph from tinfoil to the LP*. Washington, D.C.: Library of Congress.

Smith, E. (2004, October 11). Concert industry blames creeping prices for slow summer. *The Wall Street Journal*, B1.

Smith, E. (2011, December 15). Sony, Warner join suit against Grooveshark music service. WSJ.com.

Sweeney, M., & Sabbagh, D. (2011, November 11). Universal and Sony reach deal to buy EMI for 2.5 billion British pounds. Guardian.co.uk.

Trachtenberg, J. A. (1994, August 2). Music industry fears bandits on the information highway. *The Wall Street Journal*, B21.

Veiga, A. (2003, May 2). Students settle music suit. *San Francisco Chronicle*, B1.

Veiga, A. (2003, October 9). New version of Napster service debuts. AOL Business News. AOL.com.

Wood, M. (2009, October 25). Making the U2 set so big that it's invisible. LATimes.com.

Chapter 6 Radio: Riding the Wave

Associated Press (2007, April 14). $12.5 million "payola" fine. *San Francisco Chronicle*, C2.

Barnouw, E. (1978). *Tube of plenty*. New York: Oxford University Press.

Bittner, J. (1982). *Broadcast law and regulation*. Englewood Cliffs, N.J.: Prentice Hall.

De La Merced, M. J. (2012, December 18). Nielsen to buy Arbitron for $1.26 billion. NYTimes.com.

Dow Jones Newswire (2005, May 16). XM satellite radio surpasses 4 million subscribers; nears target. AOL Business News. AOL.com.

Engleman, E., & Fixmer, A. (2012, November 27). Pandora, musicians clash over fees. SFGate.com.

Fabrikant, G. (2009, April 30). Radio giant faces crisis in cash flow. NYTimes.com.

Farhi, P. (2011, November 16). CBS Radio to start all-news station in D.C. area. WashingtonPost.com.

Feder, B. J. (2002, October 11). FCC approves a digital radio technology. *The New York Times*, B1.

Fixmer, A. (2013, February 28). Pandora caps free listening as royalty costs soar. Bloomberg.com.

Fleishman, G. (2005, July 28). Revolution on the radio. *The New York Times*, C11.

Fornatale, P., & Mills, J. E. (1980). *Radio in the television age*. New York: Overlook Press.

Frere-Jones, S. (2010, June 14 & 21). You, the D. J. *The New Yorker*, 138.

Jensen, E. (2010, April 26). Classical music's comeback, on public radio. *The New York Times*, B7.

Leeds, J. (2005, July 28). Payola or no, edge still to the big. *The New York Times*, B1.

Leeds, J. (2007, March 6). Broadcasters agree to fine over payoffs. *The New York Times*, C1.

Leeds, J., & Story, L. (2005, July 26). Radio payoffs are described as Sony settles. *The New York Times*, A1.

Levine, R. (2007, March 19). A fee per song can ruin us, Internet radio companies say. *The New York Times*, C4.

MacFarland, D. R. (1979). *The development of the top 40 radio format*. New York: Arno Press.

Manly, L. (2005, July 31). Spin control: How payola went corporate. *The New York Times*, 4-1.

McMahan, T. (2009, July 14). Pandora sings new tune with royalty agreement, funding. Blogs.WSJ.com.

McMahan, T. (2009, October 2) A venture firm's gift to Pandora. Blogs.WSJ.com.

Miller, C. (2010, March 8). How Pandora slipped past the junkyard. *The New York Times*, B1.

Mindlin, A. (2007, May 7). Counting radio listeners stirs controversy. *The New York Times*, C4.

Norris, F. (2007, February 23). Satellite radio: Good music, bad investment. *The New York Times*, C1.

Pickler, N. (2001, September 26). First satellite radio service begins. *San Francisco Chronicle*, B3.

Plambeck, J. (2010, April 19). Saving the neglected history of FM radio's unsung pioneer. *The New York Times*, B7.

Rainey, J. (2010, October 20). Public radio is enjoying boom times. LATimes.com.

Settel, L. (1960). *A pictorial history of radio*. New York: Citadel Press.

Shenon, P. (2008, March 25). Justice Dept. approves XM merger with Sirius. *The New York Times*, C1.

Sisario, B. (2012, September 23). Proposed bill could change royalty rates for internet radio. NYTimes.com.

Spencer, K. (2011, November 4). College radio heads: Off the dial. NYTimes.com.

Sperber, A. M. (1986). *Murrow: His life and times*. New York: Freundlich.

Stelter, B. (2012, October 14). Unique morning show on NPR thrives as others slip. NYTimes.com.

Stimson, L. (2010, September 1). AM HD radio has stalled; now what? *Radio World*. RWOnline.com.

Chapter 7 Movies: Picturing the Future

Arango, T., & Carr, D. (2010, November 25). Netflix's move onto the web stirs rivalries. *The New York Times*, A1.

Associated Press (2012, September 6). Small theaters struggle as Hollywood goes digital. SFGate.com.

Balio, T. (1976). *The American film industry*. Madison: University of Wisconsin Press.

Barnes, B. (2010, July 24). In Hollywood, everybody's a digital revolutionary. NYTimes.com.

Burrows, P. (2010, December 5). Will Netflix kill the Internet? *Bloomberg Businessweek*. SFGate.com.

Child, B. (2013, February 5). Yoda not far, soon you will be with him—when his own *Star Wars* movie he has. Guardiannews.com.

Chinnock, C. (1999, August 9). Lights! Camera! Action! It's the dawn of digital cinema. *Electronic Design*, 32F.

Chmielewski, D. C. (2011, June 6). Disney film studio layoffs expected soon. LATimes.com.

Cieply, M. (2010, March 3). 3-D films fuel a rise in box office revenues. *The New York Times*, C2.

Cieply, M. (2011, July 31). Charging a premium for movies, at a cost. NYTimes.com.

Cieply, M. (2012, October 30). Disney buying Lucasfilm for $4 billion. NYTimes.com.

Dargis, M. (2007, March 18). The revolution will be downloaded (if you're patient). *The New York Times*, C1.

Denby, D. (2007, January 8). Big pictures. *The New Yorker*, 54.

Ellis, J. C. (1985). *A history of American film*, 2nd ed. Englewood Cliffs, N.J.: Prentice Hall.

Fabrikant, G., & Waxman, S. (2005, December 9). Viacom's Paramount to buy DreamWorks for $1.6 billion. NYTimes.com.

Fritz, B. (2010, May 31). Summer box office sees its worst Memorial Day weekend in 17 years. LATimes.com.

Fritz, B. (2011, July 9). Not much demand yet for premium video on demand. LATimes.com.

Goldstein, P. (2010, January 30). Is this a box-office record with an *? LATimes.com.

Guthman, E. (2003, January 20). Sundance grows up. *San Francisco Chronicle*, D1.

Halbfinger, D. M. (2008, March 13). With theaters barely digital, studios push 3-D. *The New York Times*, B1.

Helft, M. (2007, January 16). The shifting business of renting movies, by the disc or the click. *The New York Times*, C1.

Holson, L. M. (2005, July 22). Film studios said to agree on digital standards. *The New York Times*, C9.

Keegan, R. (2011, September 25). 3-D makeover coming to aging Hollywood blockbusters. LATimes.com.

Kehr, D. (2011, March 6). It's delivery, stupid: Goodbye, DVD. Hello, future. *The New York Times*, AR14.

Kopytoff, V. G. (2010, September 26). Shifting online, Netflix faces new competition. NYTimes.com.

LaSalle, M. (2005, July 13). Blame the economy, the product, the theaters—We're just not going to movies the way we used to. SFGate.com.

Leeds, J. (2007, March 1). A comeback in 3-D, but without those flimsy glasses. *The New York Times*, B9.

Leonhart, D. (2010, March 1). Why "Avatar" is not the top-grossing film. NYTimes.com.

McGrath, C. (2010, May 23). A gamer's world, but a dramatist's sensibility. *The New York Times*, AR18.

Motion Picture Association of America (1954). *Motion picture production code*.

Nakashima, R. (2009, March 10). Sony Pictures to cut nearly 350 jobs. SFGate.com.

Schuker, L. A. E., & Smith, E. (2010, May 22). Hollywood eyes shortcut to TV. WSJ.com.

Scott, A. O. (2007, March 18). The shape of cinema, transformed at the click of a mouse. *The New York Times*, 2-1.

Sklar, R. (1975). *Movie-made America*. New York: Random House.

Smith, D. (2010, April 23). Streaming putting video stores out of business. SacBee.com.

Solomon, C. (2011, August 16). A little lamp lights the way for Pixar's success. LATimes.com.

Sorkin, A. R., & Chozick, A. (2013, January 13). "South Park" creators to start company, Important Studios. NYTimes.com.

Squire, J. E. (ed.). (1983). *The movie business book*. New York: Simon & Schuster.

Stelter, B. (2010, August 10). Netflix to stream films from Paramount, Lions Gate, MGM. NYTimes.com.

Trumbo, D. (1962). *Additional dialogue: Letters of Dalton Trumbo, 1942–1962.* New York: M. Evans.

Verrier, R. (2010, May 7). FCC paves way for studios to push movies into the home, rattling theaters. LATimes.com.

Verrier, R. (2013, March 21). International box office revenues soared in 2012, MPAA reports. LATimes.com.

Waxman, S. (2007, April 26). Hollywood's shortage of female power. *The New York Times,* B1.

Chapter 8 Television: Changing Channels

Arango, T. (2009, February 28). Broadcast TV faces struggle to stay viable. *The New York Times,* A1.

Associated Press (2010, August 24). Toshiba developing no-glasses 3-D televisions. SFGate.com.

Associated Press (2011, April 6). Hit show "Mad Men" will be streamed on Netflix. SFGate.com.

Associated Press (2013, June 13). 3-D TV falls flat; ESPN to kill 3-D broadcasts. SacBee.com.

Barnes, B., & Jordan, M. (2005, May 2). Big four TV networks get a wake-up call—in Spanish. WSJ.com.

Barnouw, E. (1975). *Tube of plenty.* New York: Oxford University Press.

Bauder, D. (2007, May 9). 2.7 million TV viewers missing this spring. *San Francisco Chronicle,* A2.

Bauder, D. (2009, November 30). Jay Leno losing his audience to DVR machines. WashingtonPost.com.

Biagi, S. (1987). *NewsTalk II.* Belmont, Calif.: Wadsworth.

Brooks, T. (2011, April 18). Is TV still a "vast wasteland"? *Advertising Age.*

Brown, L. (1971). *Television: The business behind the box.* New York: Harcourt Brace Jovanovich.

Carr, D. (2011, December 24). New rules for the ways we watch. NYTimes.com.

Carter, B. (2011, February 21). Networks have lost key viewers at 10 p.m. *The New York Times,* B1.

Chen, K., & Peers, M. (1999, August 6). FCC relaxes its rules on TV station ownership. *The Wall Street Journal,* A3.

Chmielewski, D., & Guynn, J. (2010, August 18). Google TV plan is causing jitters in Hollywood. LATimes.com.

Chozick, A. (2013, February 11). Univision and Disney give details of Fusion, a channel for Latinos. NYTimes.com.

Chozick, A., & Stelter, B. (2013, February 12). Comcast buys rest of NBC in early sale. NYTimes.com.

FitzGerald, T. (2011, May 4). Pac-12 gets richest TV deal. SFGate.com.

Flint, J. (2012, August 28). ESPN shells out $5.6 billion to keep Major League Baseball. LATimes.com.

Fritz, B., & Verrier, R. (2011, March 2). DirecTV prepares to launch premium video on demand; theater executives alarmed. LATimes.com.

Greenfield, J. (1977). *Television: The first fifty years.* New York: Abrams.

Hart, K. (2009, June 7). Your antenna's big day. Washington Post.com.

Helft, M. (2010, September 5). Apple faces many rivals for streaming to TVs. NYTimes.com.

James, M., & Flint, J. (2009, December 3). Comcast strikes deal to buy NBC Universal from GE. LATimes.com.

Jensen, E. (2011, February 28). Public broadcasters start to sweat, as a budget threat looks serious. *The New York Times,* B4.

Jensen, E. (2011, May 30). PBS plans promotional breaks within programs. NYTimes.com.

Kantor, J. (2005, October 30). The extra-large, ultra-small medium: What happens when television becomes a matter of extremes. *The New York Times,* 2-1.

McGrath, C. (2008, February 17). Is PBS still necessary? *The New York Times,* AR1.

Minow, N. (1964). *Equal time: The private broadcaster and the public interest.* New York: Atheneum.

Newman, J. (2010, August 23). TV makers predicting a bright future for 3-D sets. NYTimes.com.

Nielsen (2013, March). Free to move between screens: The cross-platform report. Nielsen.com.

Richtel, M., & Stelter, B. (2010, August 23). In the living room, hooked on pay TV. NYTimes.com.

Sandomir, R. (2011, June 7). NBC wins TV rights to four more Olympics. NYTimes.com.

Severo, R. (2003, June 13). David Brinkley, 82, newsman model, dies. *The New York Times,* A26.

Sherr, I. (2010, September 1). Apple makes Internet-TV push. WSJ.com.

Sorkin, A. R. (2003, April 10). Murdoch adds to his empire by agreeing to buy DirecTV. *The New York Times,* C1.

Stelter, B. (2009, May 8). PBS to shorten time commitments for sponsorships. *The New York Times,* B3.

Stelter, B. (2010, January 5). Discovery, Imax and Sony form 3-D television channel. NYTimes.com.

Stelter, B. (2011, January 2). TV viewing continues to edge up. NYTimes.com.

Stelter, B. (2013, February 11). A CBS deal bolsters Amazon's challenge to Netflix. NYTimes.com.

Stelter, B. (2013, March 4). Don't touch that remote: TV pilots turn to net, not networks. NYTimes.com.

Stelter, B. (2013, April 9). Two networks hint at leaving the airwaves. NYTimes.com.

Stelter, B., & Stone, B. (2010, January 6). Television begins a push into the 3rd dimension. NYTimes.com.

Sterling, C., & Kittross, J. (1990). *Stay tuned: A concise history of American broadcasting,* 2nd ed. Belmont, Calif.: Wadsworth.

Story, L. (2007, January 29). At last, television ratings go to college. *The New York Times,* C1.

Story, L. (2007, June 1). Agencies and networks ponder Nielsen ad ratings. *The New York Times,* C6.

Taub, E. A. (2007, January 11). On display, the video frontier. *The New York Times,* C11.

Tsukayama, H. (2011, October 5). TV on your Xbox, coming soon. WashingtonPost.com.

Villarreal, Y. (2012, October 27). TV giant Don Francisco celebrates 50 years of "Sabado Gigante." LATimes.com.

Chapter 9 Digital Media: Widening the Web

Arango, T. (2009, March 23). Rights clash on YouTube, and videos disappear. *The New York Times*, B1.

Arango, T. (2010, October 28). Judge tells LimeWire, the file-trading service, to disable its software. NYTimes.com.

Arthur, C. (2012, September 5). Tim Berners-Lee: The internet has no off switch. Guardiannews.com.

Associated Press (2009, May 6). A fifth of U.S. homes have cell phones, no landlines. NYTimes.com.

Associated Press (2011, December 4). Study confirms many of us go online for no reason. SFGate.com.

Barnes, B. (2013, February 13). Netflix teams with Dream Works on cartoon series for children. *The New York Times*, B3.

Barnes, R. (2011, June 28). Court strikes down law on violent video games. WashingtonPost.com.

Batteiger, J. (2009, February 18). Landlines losing to cellular. SFGate.com.

Chmielewski, D. C. (2011, June 8). Online advertising to reach $31 billion in 2011. LATimes.com.

Cohen, N. (2007, March 12). After false claim, Wikipedia to check degrees. *The New York Times*, C6.

Cohen, N. (2009, August 25). Wikipedia to limit changes to articles on people. NYTimes.com.

Dewey, C. (2012, December 21). Holiday smartphone shoppers set records for mobile retail. WashingtonPost.com.

Edwards, J. (2012, August 15). People now spend more time watching their phones than watching TV. Business insider.com.

Fidler, R. (1997). *Mediamorphosis*. Thousand Oaks, Calif.: Pine Forge Press.

Fitzhugh, M. (2010, April 16). Seas of spam keep rising, despite efforts to hold back the flood. DailyFinance .com.

Gnatek, T. (2005, October 5). Darknets: Virtual parties with a select group of invitees. *The New York Times*, E2.

Guynn, J. (2012, April 1). Facebook's Sheryl Sandberg has a talent for making friends. LATimes.com.

Hansell, S. (2009, May 22). Counting down to the end of Moore's Law. NYTimes.com.

Hardy, Q. (2011, November 14). Will cloud computing make everything (and everyone) work harder? NYTimes .com.

Helft, M. (2010, May 27). Apple is no. 1 in tech, overtaking Microsoft. *The New York Times*, B1.

Isaacson, W. (2011, October 29). The genius of Jobs. NYTimes.com.

Itzkoff, D. (2012, December 24). "Game of Thrones" is named year's most pirated show. NYTimes.com.

Johnson, C. K. (2013, February 20). Future science: Using 3-D worlds to visualize data. SacBee.com.

Johnson, F. (2009, September 21). FCC Chairman proposes "net neutrality" rules. WSJ.com.

Johnson, F. (2009, October 22). FCC adopts open net rules. WSJ.com.

Kang, C. (2011, October 11). U.S. has more cell phones than people. WashingtonPost.com.

Kim, R. (2010, June 17). Keeping core gamers while expanding audience. SFGate.com.

Lewsin, T., & Markoff, J. (2013, January 15). California to give web courses a big trial. NYTimes.com.

Liptak, A. (2010, November 2). Justices debate video game ban. NYTimes.com.

Lohr, S. (2012, December 17). IBM looks ahead to a sensor revolution and cognitive computers. NYTimes.com.

Lopez, S. (2009, May 6). The rigors of life unplugged. LATimes.com.

Markoff, J. (2010, March 2). U.S. to reveal some rules on security for Internet. *The New York Times*, A14.

Markoff, J. (2011, October 5). Steve Jobs, Apple visionary, dies at 56. NYTimes.com.

Milian, M. (2010, June 17). E3: Nintendo booth tour, 3Ds wow crowds. LATimes.com.

Musli, S. (2013, February 4). Twitter hack may have targeted elected officials, journalists. Cnet.com.

Nielsen (2012, December 3). State of the media: The social media report. Nielsen.com.

Nielsen (2013, February). The mobile consumer: A global snapshot. Nielsen.com.

Sherr, I. (2012, November 17). Activision's "Call of Duty" sets sales record. Wsj.com.

Stone, B. (2009, March 29). Is Facebook growing up too fast? *The New York Times*, BU1.

Stone, B. (2010, May 23). Google: Sure it's big, but is that bad? *The New York Times*, B1.

Stone, B., & Vance, A. (2010, April 19). "Cloud" computing casts a spell. *The New York Times*, B1.

Urbina, I. (2013, March 18). Unwanted electronic gear rising in toxic piles. NYTimes.com.

Wachter, S. (2010, October 24). Beaming to the cloud all the mess that is our digital life. NYTimes.com.

Wollman, D. (2010, October 20). UN report: Internet users to surpass 2B in 2010. WashingtonPost.com.

Wright, R. (1997, May 19). The man who invented the Web. *Time*, 68.

Wyatt, E. (2013, March 22). Backer of an open internet steps down as FCC chief. NYTimes.com.

Chapter 10 Advertising: Catching Consumers

Associated Press (2010, November 15). Facebook enters e-mail, messaging arena. LATimes.com.

Atwan, R. (1979). Newspapers and the foundations of modern advertising. In *The commercial connection*, ed. J. W. Wright. New York: Doubleday.

Beatty, S. G. (1996, June 11). Seagram flouts ban on TV ads pitching liquor. *The Wall Street Journal*, B1.

Boorstin, D. J. (1986). The rhetoric of democracy. In *American mass media: Industries and issues*, 3rd ed., ed. R. Atwan, B. Orton, & W. Vesterman. New York: Random House.

Cardwell, A. (2001, February 1). The new ad game: Online games are more than just a good time; they're the hottest new ad space on the web. *Ziff Davis Smart Business for the New Economy*, 53.

Carter, B., & Vega, T. (2011, May 13). In shift, ads try to entice over-55 set. NYTimes.com.

Clifford, S. (2009, March 4). Your ad here, not there. *The New York Times*, B1.

Clifford, S. (2009, March 11). Advertisers get a trove of clues in smartphones. *The New York Times*, A1.

Clifford, S. (2010, March 12). Instant ads set the pace on the web. *The New York Times*, B1.

Elliott, S. (2002, March 31). Advertising's big four: It's their world now. *The New York Times*, 3-1.

Elliott, S. (2005, November 3). Liquor ads move to satellite radio. *The New York Times*, C6.

Elliott, S. (2013, March 19). Using "sponsored content" to keep viewers watching. NYTimes.com.

Feder, B. (2007, January 29). Billboards that know you by name. *The New York Times*, C4.

Flint, J., Branch, S., & O'Connell, V. (2001, December 14). Breaking longtime taboo, NBC network plans to accept liquor ads. *The Wall Street Journal*, B1.

Fowles, J. (1985). Advertising's fifteen basic appeals. In *American mass media: Industries and issues*, 3rd ed., ed. R. Atwan, B. Orton, & W. Vesterman. New York: Random House.

Fox, S. (1984). *The mirror makers: A history of American advertising and its creators*. New York: Morrow.

Georgiadis, A. (2010, November 1). Why marathons are hot spot to chase consumers. *Advertising Age*, 1.

Guynn, J., & Sarno, D. (2010, April 8). Apple launches ad system for mobile devices in race with Google. LATimes.com.

Hof, R. (2013, January 9). Online ad spending tops $100 billion in 2012. Forbes.com.

Internet Advertising Bureau (2010, October 12). Internet ad revenues break records, climb to more than $12 billion for first half of '10. IAB.com.

James, M. (2012, July 8). Digital advertising agencies are built for the internet age. LATimes.com.

Jones, E. R. (1979). *Those were the good old days*. New York: Simon & Schuster.

Kaufman, L. (1987). *Essentials of advertising*, 2nd ed. New York: Harcourt Brace Jovanovich.

Kiley, D. (2005, March 7). A green flag for booze. *BusinessWeek*, 95.

Li, S., & Sarno, D. (2011, August 21). Advertisers start using facial recognition to tailor pitches. LATimes.com.

Nielsen (2013, March 22). January 2013: Top US entertainment sites and web brands. Nielsen.com.

Nielsenwire (2010, January 20). Survey: Most Super Bowl viewers tune in for the commercials. Blog.Nielsen.com.

Pfanner, E. (2009, July 4). Internet companies and ad agencies go from old enemies to new friends. *The New York Times*, B7.

Pfanner, E. (2011, March 9). British television opens a door for product placement in shows. *The New York Times*, B3.

Schudson, M. (1984). *Advertising: The uneasy persuasion*. New York: Basic Books.

Silverstein, B. (2012, December). Branding in 2013: Convergence, content, gaming, big data and other big trends. Brandchannel.com.

Singer, N. (2011, September 10). On campus, it's one big commercial. NYTimes.com.

Steel, E. (2012, December 3). Ad groups cut 2013 growth outlook. FT.com.

Stelter, B. (2010, January 25). Court ruling invites a boom in political ads. *The New York Times*, B1.

Story, L. (2007, April 28). Overture to an untapped market. *The New York Times*, B1.

Story, L. (2008, March 10). To aim ads, web is keeping closer eye on what you click. *The New York Times*, A1.

Strom, S. (2012, May 21). Judge says Pom Wonderful's advertising is misleading. NYTimes.com.

Stross, R. (2009, February 8). Why television still shines in a world of screens. *The New York Times*, BU3.

Sweney, M. (2011, July 27). Advertising watchdog orders L'Oreal to drop airbrushed ads. *The Guardian*, National–13.

Sylvers, E. (2007, February 14). The ad-free cell phone may soon be extinct. *The New York Times*, C5.

Turow, Joseph. (2011). *The daily you: How the new advertising industry is defining your identity and your worth*. New Haven, Conn. & London: Yale University Press.

Vega, T. (2011, November 6). A site to help marketers appeal to African-Americans. NYTimes.com.

Vega, T. (2013, February 25). Twitter hackings put focus on security for brands. *The New York Times*, B1.

Vega, T. (2013, April 7). Sponsors now pay for online articles, not just ads. NYTimes.com.

Watercutter, A. (2013, February 4). How Oreo won the marketing Super Bowl with a timely blackout ad on Twitter. Wired.com.

Chapter 11 Public Relations: Promoting Ideas

Acohido, B., & Swartz, J. (2011, May 10). PR firm's Google attack fails. *USA Today*, B1.

Ambrosio, J. (1980, March/April). It's in the *Journal*, but this is reporting? *Columbia Journalism Review*, 18, 35.

Associated Press (2012, March 22). Komen executives resign in aftermath of decision to eliminate money for Planned Parenthood. WashingtonPost.com.

Bernays, E. L. (1955). *The engineering of consent.* Norman: University of Oklahoma Press.

Berr, J. (2010, January 28). Facing its "Tylenol Moment," Toyota needs to move fast. DailyFinance.com.

Blyskal, B., & Blyskal, M. (1985). *PR: How the public relations industry writes the news.* New York: Morrow.

Bumiller, E. (2003, February 9). War public relations machine is put on full throttle. *The New York Times,* A1.

Bumiller, E. (2003, April 20). Even critics of war say the White House spun it with skill. *The New York Times,* B14.

Bush, M. (2010, March 1). The cult of Toyota. *Advertising Age,* 1.

Bush, M. (2010, March 1). Internal communication is key to repairing Toyota reputation. *Advertising Age,* 1.

Clifford, S. (2010, January 25). Corporate antagonism goes public. *The New York Times,* B1.

Council of Public Relations Firms (2012, November 12). The PR factor 2012: The expanding power of public relations. Adage.com.

Fleischman, D. E. (1931, February). Public relations—A new field for women. *Independent woman.* As quoted in S. Henry, *In her own name: Public relations pioneer Doris Fleischman Bernays.* Paper presented to the Committee on the Status of Women Research Session, Association for Education in Journalism and Mass Communication, Portland, Ore., July 1988.

Foster, L. G. (1983, March). The role of public relations in the Tylenol crisis. *Public Relations Journal,* 13.

Glover, M. (1996, March 6). Juice maker in PR mode: Odwalla's ads explain status. *The Sacramento Bee,* B6.

Goldsborough, R. (2001, June). Dealing with Internet smears. *Campaigns & Elections,* 50B6.

Goodman, P. S. (2010, August 21). In case of emergency: what not to do. NYTimes.com.

Graham, J. (2007, March 9). Apple buffs marketing savvy to a high shine. *USA Today,* 1B.

Kaufman, J. (2008, June 30). Need press? Repeat: "green," "sex," "cancer," "secret," "fat." NYTimes.com.

Krauss, C. (2010, April 30). Oil spill's blow to BP's image may eclipse out-of-pocket costs. *The New York Times,* B1.

Krauss, C. (2010, May 7). For BP, a technological battle to contain leak and an image fight, too. *The New York Times,* A16.

Krauss, C. (2013, January 29). Judge accepts BP's $4 billion criminal settlement over Gulf oil spill. NYTimes.com.

Lee, C. (2005, March 15). Administration rejects ruling on PR videos. WashingtonPost.com.

Los Angeles Times Staff (2012, December). Toyota to pay at least $1.2 billion to settle sudden-acceleration lawsuit. LATimes.com.

Lozano, C. (2013, April 20). Motorists encouraged to park their cars for CicLAvia. LATimes.com.

Marken, A. (1998, Spring). The Internet and the web: The two-way public relations highway. *Public Relations Quarterly,* 31–34.

McDonough, S. (2005, May 26). Paid promotions sneaking into broadcasts. *San Francisco Chronicle,* C6.

Miller, C. (2009, July 5). Spinning the web: PR in Silicon Valley. NYTimes.com.

Morse, S. (1906, September). An awakening on Wall Street. *American Magazine,* 460.

Newsom, D., Turk, J., & Kruckeberg, D. (2009). *This is PR: The realities of public relations,* 11th ed. Boston: Cengage Learning.

O'Brien, T. (2005, February 13). Spinning frenzy: PR's bad press. *The New York Times,* 3-1.

Parekh, R., & Lee, E. (2010, May 10). How to succeed when it's time to make your social-media mea culpa. *Advertising Age,* 1.

Pear, R. (2005, October 1). Buying of news by Bush's aides is ruled illegal. *The New York Times,* A1.

Peters, J. W. (2010, June 9). Efforts to limit the flow of spill news. NYTimes.com.

Pilon, M., & Lehren, A. W. (2013, February 15). Livestrong not immune from turmoil surrounding its founder. NYTimes.com.

Pizzi, P. (2001, July 23). Grappling with "cybersmear." *New Jersey Law Journal,* S12.

Randall, C. (1985, November). The father of public relations: Edward Bernays, 93, is still saucy. *United,* 50.

Rutten, T. (2010, February 20). Tiger and Toyota: Rebuilding the brands. LATimes.com.

Seitel, F. P. (1984). *The practice of public relations,* 2nd ed. Columbus, Ohio: Merrill.

Tracy, T. (2010, September 1). BP tripled its ad budget after oil spill. WSJ.com.

Trop, J. (2013, July 19). Toyota will pay $1.6 billion over faulty accelerator suit. NYTimes.com.

Vellinga, M. L. (2012, May 7). Komen race numbers show sharp decline. SacBee.com.

Vittachi, I. (2011, June 13). Horse marches through John Wayne Airport to mark air service to Canada. LATimes.com.

Wallis, D. (2012, November 8). Komen Foundation struggles to regain wide support. NYTimes.com.

White, R. D. (2010, April 30). For BP, oil spill is a public relations catastrophe. LATimes.com.

Chapter 12 News and Information: Choosing Sources

Bennett, S. (2003, July 1). How the Iraq War was seen overseas. *World and I,* 62.

Carr, D. (2013, June 16). Big news forges its own path. NYTimes.com.

Carvajal, D. (2007, March 7). 1,000 journalists killed in ten years while reporting. *The New York Times,* A3.

Charles, D. (2005, September 7). Federal government seeks to block photos of dead. Reuters on AOL News. AOL.com.

Chmielewski, D. C. (2010, May 4). Murdoch to unveil paywall for news content soon. LATimes.com.

Cohen, N. (2010, May 24). Through soldiers' eyes, "The first YouTube war." *The New York Times*, B3.

Daragahi, B. (2011, March 8). Libya keeps foreign journalists on tight leash. LATimes.com.

Faiez, R. (2009, September 9). NYT reporter freed; Afghan aide killed in rescue. SFGate.com.

Fathi, N., & Landler, M. (2009, May 12). Iran releases journalist convicted of spying for U.S. NYTimes.com.

Gans, H. (1985, December). Are U.S. journalists dangerously liberal? *Columbia Journalism Review*, 32–33.

Gans, H. (1986). *The messages behind the news.* In *Readings in mass communication*, 6th ed., ed. M. Emery & T. Smythe. Dubuque, Iowa: Brown.

Garwood, P. (2005, January 21). Deadline passes with no word on reporter's fate. Associated Press on AOL News. AOL.com.

Gerth, J., & Shane, S. (2005, December 1). U.S. is said to pay to plant articles in Iraq papers. *The New York Times*, A1.

Goodman, T. (2011, March 18). Japan disaster shows U.S. journalists unprepared. SFGate.com.

Gordon, M. (2001, October 31). Military is putting heavier limits on reporters' access. *The New York Times*, B3.

Johnston, D. C. (2005, July 11). Most editors say they'd publish articles based on leaks. NYTimes.com.

Just, M., & Rosenstiel, T. (2005, March 26). All the news that's fed. *The New York Times*, A27.

Keller, B. (2011, May 5). The inner lives of wartime photographers. NYTimes.com.

Kuttab, D. (2003, April 6). The Arab TV wars. *The New York Times Magazine*, 45.

Lewis, N. A., & Shane, S. (2007, January 31). Ex-reporter for *Times* testifies for prosecutor who jailed her. *The New York Times*, A1.

Lippmann, W. (1965). *Public opinion.* New York: Free Press.

Liptak, A. (2005, February 16). Jailing of reporters in CIA leak case is upheld by judges. *The New York Times*, A1.

Liptak, A. (2005, June 30). Judge gives reporters one week to testify or face jail. *The New York Times*, A12.

Liptak, A. (2005, July 1). Time Inc. to yield files on sources, relenting to U.S. *The New York Times*, A1.

Liptak, A. (2005, July 11). For Time Inc. reporter, a frenzied decision to testify. NYTimes.com.

Lipton, E. (2007, March 7). Members of a sympathetic jury describe emotional but inevitable conclusion. *The New York Times*, A17.

McDermott, T. (2007, March 17). Blogs can top the presses. LATimes.com.

McFadden, R. D. (2005, July 9). Newspaper withholding two articles after jailing. NYTimes.com.

O'Connor, J. D. (2005, July). "I'm the guy they called Deep Throat." *Vanity Fair*, 86.

Perez-Peña, R. (2010, February 3). Some news sites to try charging readers. *The New York Times*, B2.

Perlez, J., & Schmitt, E. (2011, July 4). Pakistan's spies tied to slaying of a journalist. NYTimes.com.

Perlroth, N. (2013, January 30). Hackers in China attacked *The Times* for last four months. NYTimes.com.

Peters, J. W. (2011, August 22). Journalists keep in hotel as battle rages outside. NYTimes.com.

Pew Research Center for the People & the Press (2012, September 27). In changing news landscape, even television is vulnerable. People-press.org.

Pew Research Center's Project for Excellence in Journalism. *The state of the news media 2013.* Stateofthemedia.org.

Pincus, W., & VandeHei, J. (2005, July 21). Plame's identity marked as secret. *Washington Post*, A1.

Purdum, T. S. (2005, June 3). Three decades later, "Woodstein" takes a victory lap. *The New York Times*, A14.

Purdum, T. S., & Rutenberg, J. (2005, June 2). In the prelude to publication, intrigue worthy of Deep Throat. *The New York Times*, A1.

Quinn, P. (2006, January 7). American journalist kidnapped in Iraq. Associated Press on AOL News. AOL.com.

Raines, H. (2010, March 14). Why don't honest journalists take on Roger Ailes and Fox News? WashingtonPost.com.

Rich, F. (2005, July 24). Eight days in July. NYTimes.com.

Rutenberg, J. (2003, April 20). Spectacular success or incomplete picture? Views of TV's war coverage are split. *The New York Times*, B15.

Rutten, T. (2003, April 5). A 24/7 war pulls viewers to cable news. *Los Angeles Times*, C1.

Salamon, J. (2003, April 6). New tools for reporters make war images instant but coverage no simpler. *The New York Times*, B13.

Sang-Hun, C. (2009, June 9). N. Korea sentences 2 U.S. journalists to 12 years of hard labor. NYTimes.com.

Sanger, D. E. (2010, January 26). In digital combat, U.S. finds no easy deterrent. *The New York Times*, A1.

Schmitt, E. (2005, December 2). Senate summons Pentagon to explain effort to plant reports in Iraqi news media. *The New York Times*, A10.

Schmitt, E. (2005, December 13). Military admits planting news in Iraq. *The New York Times*, A11.

Seelye, K. Q. (2005, March 14). Fewer sources go nameless in the press, survey shows. *The New York Times*, C6.

Seelye, K. Q. (2005, August 1). Newsrooms seek ways to shield identities. *The New York Times*, C1.

Seelye, K. Q. (2005, August 15). Editors ponder how to present a broad picture of Iraq. *The New York Times*, C2.

Seelye, K. Q. (2005, October 4). Freed reporter says she upheld principles. *The New York Times*, A23.

Seelye, K. Q. (2005, November 10). *Times* reporter agrees to leave the paper. *The New York Times*, A21.

Shane, S. (2007, March 8). Debate over possible pardon erupts after verdict on Libby. *The New York Times*, A1.

Steinberg, J. (2005, June 30). Writer in sources case laments threat to jail 2. *The New York Times*, A12.

Steinberg, J. (2005, July 7). Response from journalists is not unanimous. *The New York Times*, A17.

Steinberg, J. (2008, June 8). For new journalists, all bets, but not mikes, are off. *The New York Times*, WK3.

Stelter, B. (2010, May 1). Job cuts at ABC leave workers stunned and downcast. *The New York Times*, B2.

Stelter, B. (2011, May 10). For journalists, a call to rethink their online models. NYTimes.com.

Stelter, B. (2011, October 3). ABC News and Yahoo News announce deal to share content. NYTimes.com.

Stelter, B. (2012, May 26). You can change the channel, but local news is the same. NYTimes.com.

Stelter, B. (2013, April 16). A Pulitzer Prize, but without a newsroom to put it in. NYTimes.com.

Stolberg, S. G. (2007, March 7). Libby, ex-Cheney aide, guilty of lying in CIA leak case. *The New York Times*, A1.

Woodward, B. (2005, June 2). How Mark Felt became "Deep Throat." *Washington Post*, A1.

Worth, R. F. (2005, September 20). Reporter working for *Times* abducted and slain in Iraq. NYTimes.com.

Yost, P. (2005, July 6). Judge orders *New York Times* reporter jailed. Associated Press on AOL News. AOL.com.

Chapter 13 Society and Political Issues: Shaping the Arguments

Alexander, H. E. (1983). *Financing the 1980 election*. Lexington, Mass.: Heath.

Alexander, H. E., & Haggerty, B. (1987). *Financing the 1984 election*. Lexington, Mass.: Heath.

Angelo, M. (2010, May 30). At TBS, diversity pays its own way. *The New York Times*, AR17.

Barber, J. D. (1986). *The pulse of politics: Electing presidents in the media age*. New York: Norton.

Barnes, R. (2013, March 19). In copyright case, Supreme Court rules that goods made overseas can be resold here. WashingtonPost.com.

Carey, B. (2011, October 18). Parents urged again to limit TV for youngest. NYTimes.com.

Carr, D. (2012, November 20). Election audience votes, and web clobbers print. NYTimes.com.

Cieply, M. (2007, April 13). Report says the young readily buy violent games and movies. *The New York Times*, C3.

Cox, A. M. (2012, November 29). How the Obama White House has won the hashtag wars. Guardiannews.com.

Fairfield, H., & Palmer, G. (2008, July 6). Cashing in on Obama and McCain. *The New York Times*, BU1.

Fetler, M. (1985). Television viewing and school achievement. *Mass communication review yearbook*, vol. 5. Beverly Hills, Calif.: Sage.

Flood, A. (2012, May 31). Gay superheroes under fire from US pressure group. Guardiannews.com.

Greenhouse, S. (2013, January 21). Even if it enrages your box, social net speech is protected. NYTimes.com.

Hamburger, T. (2012, December 6). Manic spending marked end of 2012 campaigns, FEC reports show. WashingtonPost.com.

Healy, M. (2010, May 4). Toddler TV time linked to poorer fourth-grade classroom attention, math and exercise. LATimes.com.

Hua, V. (2005, June 6). Audience for ethnic media huge. *San Francisco Chronicle*, A7.

James, M. (2010, October 29). TV still the favored medium for political ad spending. LATimes.com.

Khimm, S. (2013, January 17). POW! CRACK! What we know about video games and violence. Washington Post.com.

Krueger, A. B. (2005, August 18). Fair? Balanced? A study finds it does not matter. *The New York Times*, C2.

Liebert, R. M., & Sprafkin, J. (1988). *The early window*, 3rd ed. New York: Pergamon Press.

Linn, S. (2013, January 22). Invitation to a dialogue: Media violence. NYTimes.com.

Lippmann, W. (1965). *Public opinion*. New York: Free Press.

Martindale, C. (1995, August). *Only in glimpses: Portrayal of America's largest minority groups by The New York Times 1934–1994*. Paper presented at the Association for Education in Journalism and Mass Communication Annual Convention, Washington, D.C.

Meier, B., & Martin, A. (2012, December 24). Real and virtual firearms nurture a marketing link. NYTimes.com.

Meyrowitz, J. (1985). *No sense of place*. New York: Oxford University Press.

Mindlin, A. (2007, January 15). Boys and girls use social sites differently. *The New York Times*, C3.

Modleski, T. (1982). *Loving with a vengeance: Mass-produced fantasies for women*. New York: Methuen.

Moore, M. (2012, May 23). Marvel comics plans wedding for gay hero Northstar. SacBee.com.

Nauman, A. (1993, April 11). Comics page gets serious. *The Sacramento Bee*, B1.

Patterson, T., & McClure, R. (1976). *The unseeing eye: The myth of television power in national elections*. New York: Putnam.

Pham, A., Zeitchik, S., & Fritz, B. (2012, July 28). Hollywood trying to avoid villain role in film violence. LATimes.com.

Pham, S. (2010, November 8). Political TV ad spending sets record. ABCNews.go.com.

Postman, N. (1985). *Amusing ourselves to death*. New York: Viking Penguin.

Potter, D. M. (1954). *People of plenty*. Chicago: University of Chicago Press.

Reyes, L. I., & Rampell, E. (2007, February 23). Movies' multicultural milestone year. *San Francisco Chronicle*, B11.

Rivers, W. L., & Schramm, W. (1986). The impact of mass communications. In *American mass media: Industries and issues*, 3rd ed., ed. R. Atwan, B. Orton, & W. Vesterman. New York: Random House.

Sanger, D. E., Barboza, D., & Perlroth, N. (2013, February 18). Chinese Army unit is seen as tied to hacking against U.S. NYTimes.com.

Scott, A. O. (2010, April 18). Brutal truths about violence. *The New York Times*, AR1.

Sidoti, L. (2011, April 4). Obama announces 2012 re-election bid in web video. Aolnews.com.

Simon, S., & Stein, P. (2010, September 4). From grass roots to goofball: Politicians pitch on YouTube. WSJ.com.

Spear, J. (1984). *Presidents and the press*. Cambridge, Mass.: M.I.T. Press.

Stanley, A. (2008, June 8). No debate: It's great TV. *The New York Times*, MT1.

Stein, M. L. (1994, August 6). Racial stereotyping and the media. *Editor & Publisher*, 6.

Stelter, B. (2008, March 27). Finding political news online, young viewers pass it along. *The New York Times*, A1.

Stelter, B. (2010, August 1). CBS adds 3 gay roles. NYTimes.com.

Stone, B. (2009, February 8). Disclosure, magnified on the web. *The New York Times*, BU3.

Terdiman, D. (2012, October 4). Obama, Romney debate (and Big Bird) generate 10 million tweets. Cnet.com.

Vanacore, A. (2010, October 29). Sick of campaign ad avalanche? TV stations aren't. SFGate.com.

Vega, T. (2011, September 19). Newsroom diversity groups in partnership. NYTimes.com.

Wardhwa, T. (2012, November 7). Nate Silver and the rise of political data science. Forbes.com.

Wright, J. W. (1979). *The commercial connection*. New York: Dell. (Synopsis of FTC staff report on television advertising to children.)

Wyatt, E. (2009, March 18). No smooth ride on TV networks' road to diversity. NYTimes.com.

Chapter 14 Law and Regulation: Rewriting the Rules

Abrams, J. (2011, May 30). Obama, in Europe, signs Patriot Act extension. Associated Press, SFGate.com.

Aitkenhead, D. (2012, December). Julian Assange: The fugitive. Guardiannews.com.

American Library Association (2007, September 6). Federal judge declares NSL gag order unconstitutional. ALA.org.

American Library Association (2009, September 21). Attempts to ban books in U.S. continue. ALA.org.

Ardito, S. C. (2001, November). The case of Dmitry Sklyarov: This is the first criminal lawsuit under the Digital Millennium Copyright Act. *Information Today*, 24.

Associated Press (2005, December 30). Justice Department opens inquiry into leak of domestic spying. NYTimes.com.

Associated Press (2006, June 8). Fines to rise for indecency in broadcasts. *The New York Times*, C7.

Associated Press (2007, September 6). Judge strikes down part of Patriot Act. NYTimes.com.

Associated Press (2007, December 18). FCC relaxes media ownership rule. NYTimes.com.

Associated Press (2009, May 4). High court throws out ruling on Janet Jackson. WashingtonPost.com.

Associated Press (2010, April 6). Court rules against FCC in "net neutrality" case. NYTimes.com.

Associated Press (2010, April 26). FCC asks court to revisit a ruling against an indecency policy. NYTimes.com.

Associated Press (2010, October 31). Supreme Court to hear violent video game case. NYTimes.com.

Associated Press (2011, October 24). Financial woes may sink WikiLeaks, Assange says. NYTimes.com.

Associated Press (2012, July 24). Judge bars cameras from shooting suspect's hearing. SacBee.com.

Associated Press (2013, May 13). U.S. secretly obtains two months of A.P. phone records. NYTimes.com.

Barnes, R. (2011, October 4). Supreme Court copyright case will decide fate of millions of once-public works. WashingtonPost.com.

Benton Foundation (1996). *The Telecommunications Act of 1996 and the changing communications landscape*. Washington, D.C.: Author.

Birnbaum, M. (2010, March 17). Historians blast proposed Texas social studies curriculum. WashingtonPost.com.

Bode, C. (1969). *Mencken*. Carbondale: Southern Illinois University Press.

Braestrup, P. (1985). *Battle lines: Report of the Twentieth Century Fund Task Force on the Military and the Media*. New York: Priority Press.

Brick, M. (2010, May 21). Texas School Board set to vote textbook revisions. *The New York Times*, A17.

Burns, J. F., & Somaiya, R. (2010, December 7). British court denies bail to Assange. NYTimes.com.

Chu, H. (2011, November 2). Julian Assange ordered extradited in sex case. LATimes.com.

Climan, L. (2001, September). Writers battle media companies. *Dollars & Sense*, 6.

Cloud, D. S. (2011, March 2). Soldier in WikiLeaks case charged with aiding the enemy. LATimes.com.

Coile, Z. (2007, February 17). House Dems back federal shield law. *San Francisco Chronicle*, A5.

Congressional Research Service (2005, March 8). Journalists' privilege to withhold information in judicial and other proceedings: State shield statutes. Library of Congress, Washington, D.C.

Cowan, A. L. (2005, September 1). At stake in the court, the use of the Patriot Act to get library records. *The New York Times*, A18.

Cowan, A. L. (2005, September 10). Plaintiffs win round in Patriot Act lawsuit. NYTimes.com.

Crary, D. (2013, August 1). *Playboy, Penthouse* get the ax at military stores. SacBee.com.

Crawford, K. (2005, June 27). Hollywood wins Internet piracy battle. Money.CNN.com.

Davis, J. (2001, April 9). Decision: A defining moment in libel law. *Editor & Publisher*, 9.

Deutsch, L. (2004, January 26). Judge rules part of Patriot Act unconstitutional. Associated Press, SacBee.com.

Dishneau, D., & Jelinek, P. (2013, August 21). Manning sentenced to 35 years in WikiLeaks case. SacBee.com.

Dombey, D. (2010, December 3). U.S. counts cost in week of leaks. FT.com.

Dunn, N. (2010, September 23). Banned books week 2010: Which books drew the most fire last year? CSMonitor.com.

Evangelista, B. (2005, April 20). House passes piracy measure. *San Francisco Chronicle*, C1.

Fitzgerald, M. (2001, July 2). "Tasini" reality test. *Editor & Publisher*, 11.

Flaherty, A. (2013. February 26) Music, movie industry to warn copyright infringers. SFGate.com.

Gerhardt-Powals, J. (2000, November 27). The Digital Millennium Copyright Act: A compromise in progress. *New Jersey Law Journal*, 28.

Greenhouse, L. (2004, December 11). Justices agree to hear case on sharing of music files. *The New York Times*, B1.

Greenwald, G. (2013, June 6). NSA collecting phone records of millions of Verizon customers daily. Guardiannews.com.

Hellwege, J. (2001, June). Civil liberties, library groups challenge the latest law restricting web access. *Trial*, 93.

Holsinger, R. (1996). *Media law*, 4th ed. New York: McGraw-Hill.

Hulse, C. (2005, June 16). House blocks provision for Patriot Act inquiries. *The New York Times*, A17.

Italie, H. (2013, April 15). Banned books 2013: *Captain Underpants*, *Fifty Shades* make list of most challenged. HuffingtonPost.com.

Keller, B. (2011, January 26). Dealing with Assange and the WikiLeaks secrets. NYTimes.com.

Khatchadourian, R. (2010, June 7). No secrets: Julian Assange's mission for total transparency. NewYorker.com.

Kitigaki, P. (2003, September 22). Librarians step up. *The Sacramento Bee*, A1.

Labaton, S. (2007, June 5). Decency ruling thwarts FCC on vulgarities. *The New York Times*, A1.

Lessig, L. (2007, March 18). Make way for copyright chaos. *The New York Times*, WK12.

Levin, M. (2005, January 27). Lawsuits take aim at ads for alcohol. LATimes.com.

Levine, R. (2007, March 12). Old concerts on new media lead to lawsuits. IHT.com.

Levy, L. (2004). *Emergence of a free press*. Lanham, Md.: Ivan R. Dee.

Lewis, P. (1996, June 13). Judges turn back law intended to regulate Internet decency. *The New York Times*, A1.

Lichtblau, E. (2005, August 26). FBI demands library records. *San Francisco Chronicle*, A5.

Lichtblau, E. (2006, January 17). Groups file lawsuits over eavesdropping. NYTimes.com.

Lichtblau, E. (2007, September 9). FBI data mining reached beyond initial targets. *The New York Times*, A1.

Lichtblau, E. (2013, January 11). Makers of violent video games marshal support to fend off regulation. NYTimes.com.

Lichtblau, E., & Shenon, P. (2008, May 10). From places unexpected, support for the press. *The New York Times*, A11.

Liptak, A. (2007, December 31). In the fight over piracy, a rare stand for privacy. NYTimes.com.

Liptak, A. (2012, June 21). Supreme Court rejects F.C.C. fines for indecency. NYTimes.com.

McKinley, J. C. (2010, March 13). Conservatives on Texas panel carry the day on curriculum changes. *The New York Times*, A9.

McMasters, P. K. (2006, January 1). Prying by the press exposes spying on Americans. FirstAmendment Center.org.

Milliot, J. (2000, November 6). Decision supports web copyrights. *Publishers Weekly*, 56.

New York Times, The (2010, November 28). A note to readers: The decision to publish diplomatic documents. NYTimes.com.

Nohlgren, S. (2010, September 2). Jeff Greene files suit against *St. Petersburg Times*, *Miami Herald*. Tampa Bay.com.

Peek, T. (1999, January). Taming the Internet in three acts. *Information Today*, 28.

Penenberg, A. L. (2011, January 28). Wikileaks' Julian Assange: "Anarchist," "agitator," "arrogant," and a journalist. WashingtonPost.com.

Pike, G. H. (2001, October). Understanding and surviving *Tasini*. *Information Today*, 18.

Pilkington, E. (2013, February 28). Manning plea statement: Americans had a right to know "true cost of war." Guardiannews.com.

Puzzanghera, J., & James, M. (2010, July 14). FCC indecency rule struck down by appeals court. LATimes.com.

Reid, C. (2001, October 15). Writers 2, publishers 0. *Publishers Weekly*, 12.

Reuters (2007, September 11). "Wardrobe malfunction" goes to court. NYTimes.com.

Risen, J., & Lichtblau, E. (2005, December 16). Bush lets U.S. spy on callers without courts. NYTimes.com.

Risen, J., & Lichtblau, E. (2009, June 17). Extent of e-mail surveillance renews concerns in Congress. *The New York Times*, A1.

Rousseau, C. (2003, April 23). *Harry Potter* back in schools. *San Francisco Chronicle*, A2.

Rushe, D. (2012, June 22). Google reports "alarming" rise in censorship by governments. Guardiannews.com.

Savage, C. (2013, June 3). WikiLeaks source put soldiers at risk, prosecutor says. NYTimes.com.

Savage, C. (2013, July 30). Manning is acquitted of aiding the enemy. NYTimes.com.

Schmidt, M. S., & Perlroth, N. (2013, February 13). Obama order gives firms cyberthreat information. *The New York Times*, A-16.

Shane, S. (2007, July 3). Bush commutes Libby sentence, saying 30 months "is excessive." *The New York Times*, A1.

Shane, S. (2011, January 13). Accused soldier in brig as WikiLeaks link is sought. NYTimes.com.

Shane, S. (2011, December 16). Private in WikiLeaks spying case goes to court. NYTimes.com.

Singer, N. (2012, December 19). F.T.C. broadens rules for online privacy of children. NYTimes.com.

Sisario, B. (2010, December 4). LimeWire to shut subscription music service at year-end. *The New York Times*, B2.

Sisario, B. (2013, February 25). Online piracy alert system to begin this week. NYTimes.com.

Smith, R. J. (2007, March 7). Cheney's suspected role in security breach drove Fitzgerald. WashingtonPost.com.

Smolla, R. (1987). *Suing the press*. New York: Oxford University Press.

Stern, C. (1996, February 12). The V-chip First Amendment infringement vs. empowerment tool. *Broadcasting & Cable*, 8.

Stone, B., & Helft, M. (2007, February 19). New weapon in Web war over piracy. *The New York Times*, C1.

Stout, D. (2009, April 29). Supreme Court backs FCC on indecency rule. NYTimes.com.

Stutz, T. (2010, September 24). Texas Board of Education OKs resolution against pro-Islamic references in textbooks. DallasNews.com.

Swett, C. (2008, January 2). F.C.C. auction may reshape telecom field. SacBee.com.

Tsukayama, H. (2013, March 4). "Harlem Shake" videos lead to school suspensions. WashingtonPost.com.

Ungar, S. (1975). *The papers and the papers: An account of the legal and political battle over the Pentagon papers*. New York: Dutton.

Van Natta, D., Liptak, A., & Levy, C. J. (2005, October 16). The Miller case: A notebook, a cause, a jail cell and a deal. *The New York Times*, A1.

Varian, H. R. (2007, May 31). Copyrights that no one knows about don't help anyone. *The New York Times*, C3.

Woodward, C., & Lardner, R. (2011, June 13). 40 years after leak, the Pentagon Papers are out. Associated Press, SFGate.com.

Wyatt, E. (2010, August 5). FCC Chief opposes fees for Internet priority. NYTimes.com.

Wyatt, E. (2010, December 1). FCC Chairman sets a framework for regulating broadband providers. NYTimes.com.

Wyatt, E. (2011, June 27). Justices agree to consider F.C.C. rules on indecency. NYTimes.com.

Chapter 15 Ethics: Placing Responsibility

Alter, J., & McKillop, P. (1986, August). AIDS and the right to know. *Newsweek*, 46.

Associated Press (2007, March 12). *New York Times* says former reporter's link to source included a $2,000 payment. IHT.com.

Associated Press (2010, November 19). MSNBC suspends host Scarborough for GOP donations. SFGate.com.

Barry, D. (2003, May 1). *Times* reporter who resigned leaves long trail of deception. *The New York Times*, A1.

Barstow, D., & Stein, R. (2005, March 13). Government video reports blur media ethics. *The New York Times*, A5.

Brandt, A. (1984, October). Truth and consequences. *Esquire*, 27.

Buettner, R. (2011, February 24). Affidavits say Fox News chief told employee to lie. NYTimes.com.

Calame, B. (2007, March 25). Money, a source and new questions about a story. *The New York Times*, WK12.

Carr, D. (2010, November 8). Olbermann, impartiality and MSNBC. *The New York Times*, B1.

Carter, B. (2010, November 9). Olbermann, on air again, criticizes NBC for its policy. *The New York Times*, B2.

Carter, B. (2012, June 5). Barbara Walters apologizes for helping aide to Assad of Syria. NYTimes.com.

Christians, C., Rotzoll, K., & Fackler, M. (1987). *Media ethics*, 2nd ed. New York: Longman.

Chu, H. (2011, September 6). James Murdoch knew of wider phone hacking, ex-colleagues say. LATimes.com.

Cowell, A., & Burns, J. F. (2012, November 20). Two former top Murdoch aides will be charged with bribery of public officials. NYTimes.com.

Deans, J., Hill, A., & O'Carroll, L. (2012, January 19). Phone hacking: News International to pay out to 37 victims. Guardiannews.com.

Freeman, S. (2005, April 9). Newspaper panel to investigate Mitch Albom. Associated Press on AOL. AOL.com.

Friedman, J. (2007, March 10). Blogging for bucks stirs uproar over ethics. Reprinted from the *Los Angeles Times* in *The Sacramento Bee*.

Garside, J. (2011, October 10). Campaign grows to oust Murdoch. Guardiannews.com.

Goldstein, P. (2009, November 13). An embarrassment for Universal: Fabricated news stories. LATimes.com.

Halbfinger, D. M., & Weiner, A. H. (2005, June 9). As paparazzi push ever harder, stars seek a way to push back. *The New York Times*, A1.

Hulteng, J. (1985). *The messenger's motives: Ethical problems of the news media*. Englewood Cliffs, N.J.: Prentice Hall.

Ives, N. (2005, April 11). Meeting a deadline, repenting at leisure. NYTimes.com.

Kelly, K. J. (2006, January 13). *People*'s baby scoop: Mag wrote sizeable check for Angelina's pet charity. NYPost.com.

Kirkpatrick, D. D. (2007, January 29). Feeding frenzy for a big story, even if it's false. *The New York Times*, A1.

Kornblut, A. E., & Barstow, D. (2005, April 15). Debate rekindles over government-produced "news." NYTimes.com.

Kurtz, H. (2009, October 18). *Post*'s canceled series of "salon" dinners again called into question. WashingtonPost.com.

Lunzer, B. (2010, October 5). New Hampshire newspaper publishes Afghanistan series with corporate backers. NewsGuild.org.

Lyall, S. (2011, November 14). Pattern of illegality is cited at *News of the World*. NYTimes.com.

Macropoulos, A. (2007, April 2). A misfired memo shows close tabs on reporter. *The New York Times*, C4.

Maerz, M. (2011, January 24). Keith Olbermann's departure and the unanswered questions. LATimes.com.

New York Times, The (2010, February 17). *Times* business reporter accused of plagiarism is said to resign. NYTimes.com.

O'Carroll, L. (2011, December 10). Phone-hacking victims to number 800. Guardian.co.uk.

Prendergast, A. (1987, January/February). Mickey Mouse journalism. *Washington Journalism Review, 9*, 32.

Preston, J. (2011, March 27). Ethical quandry for social sites. NYTimes.com.

Public Relations Society of America Member Code of Ethics (2000).

Radio-Television Digital News Association Code of Ethics and Professional Conduct (September 14, 2000).

Reuters (2011, November 23). James Murdoch resigns from U.K. newspaper boards. NYTimes.com.

Rich, F. (2005, February 20). The White House stages its "Daily Show." NYTimes.com.

Rubenstein, S., Lee, H. K., & King, J. (2007, April 19). The video: Should it have been shown? *San Francisco Chronicle*, A14.

Sabbagh, D. (2011, October 27). James Murdoch a "dead man walking" following shareholder vote. Guardian.co.uk.

Seelye, K. Q. (2012, December 28). Newspaper on Cape Cod apologizes for a veteran reporter's fabrications. NYTimes.com.

Society of Professional Journalists Code of Ethics (September 1996).

Sonne, P., Whalen, J., & Orwall, B. (2011, August 17). New issues emerge for News Corp. in Britain. WSJ.com.

Steinberg, J. (2003, June 6). *Times*' top editors resign after furor on writer's fraud. *The New York Times*, A1.

Stelter, B. (2010, November 10). 2nd MSNBC host suspended over campaign donations. *The New York Times*, B1.

Stone, A. (2010, November 5). Keith Olbermann suspended for giving political donations. AOLNews.com.

Volz, M. (2012, April 18). Author faces civil suit over "Three Cups of Tea." SacBee.com.

Chapter 16 Global Media: Discovering New Markets

Abdulrahim, R., & Gorman, A. (2009, August 6). Journalists freed by North Korea back in U.S. SFGate.com.

Andrews, E. L. (2007, April 7). Piracy move on China seen as near. *The New York Times*, B1.

Arango, T. (2008, December 1). Friend, foe or just a fan: World falls for American media, even as it sours on America. *The New York Times*, B1.

Arthur, C. (2013, June 4). Turkish protesters using encryption software to evade censors. Guardiannews.com.

Associated Press (2010, January 25). Cable TV station critical of Chavez is shut down. *The New York Times*, A5.

Associated Press (2010, November 10). Rights groups blast Egypt detention of blogger. WashingtonPost.com.

Associated Press (2011, January 30). Egypt bans Arabic broadcaster Al Jazeera. AOLNews.com.

BBCNews (2010, May 6). "Historic" day as first non-Latin Web addresses go live. News.BBC.co.uk.

Bloomberg (2013, March 22). China passes Japan to become world's no. 2 movie market. Bloomberg.com.

Branigan, T. (2012, October 26). *New York Times* blocked in China after report on wealth of Wen Jiabao's family. Guardiannews.com.

Bulos, N. (2013, August 2). Syria opens new front in social media war: Instagram. LATimes.com.

Carr, D. (2012, November 25). Using war as cover to target journalists. NYTimes.com.

Chen, A. C., & Chaudhary, A. G. (1991). Asia and the Pacific. In *Global journalism: Survey of international communication*, 2nd ed. New York: Longman.

Chivers, C. J. (2007, August 29). Russia arrests ten in killing of Putin critic. NYTimes.com.

Committee to Protect Journalists (2013, April 28). 70 journalists killed in 2012/motive confirmed. Cpj.org.

Cowell, A. (2003, July 31). Independent for 81 years, the BBC is facing a challenge. *The New York Times*, A3.

DeGiorgio, E. (2000, April). The African Internet revolution. *African Business*, 30.

Dennis, E., & Vanden Heuvel, J. (1990, October). Emerging voices: East European media in transition. *Gannett Center for Media Studies*, 2.

Fanner, E. (2013, February 10). With a focus on its future, Financial Times turns 125. NYTimes.com.

Fathi, N. (2005, June 29). Women writing novels emerge as stars in Iran. *The New York Times*, B1.

Foster, P. (2010, February 26). BBC signals an end to era of expansion. Business.TimesOnline.co.uk.

French, H. W. (2007, December 7). As Chinese media grow, foreign news is left out. *The New York Times*, A4.

Fuller, T. (2007, April 5). Thailand blocks users' access to YouTube. *The New York Times*, C12.

Garside, J. (2011, July 27). Vodafone under fire for bowing to Egyptian pressure. *The Guardian*, 27.

Gerth, J. (2005, December 11). Military's information war is vast and often secretive. *The New York Times*, A1.

Glanz, J., & Markoff, J. (2011, June 12). U.S. underwrites Internet detour around censors. *The New York Times*, A1.

Hamilton, R. (2010, November 10). In Radio Dabanga raid, Sudan targets last uncensored media outlet on the ground. WashingtonPost.com.

Hassan, A. (2010, June 1). Arabic Web addresses expected to draw millions of new users to Internet. LATimes.com.

Hauser, C. (2011, February 1). New service allows Egyptian voices to be heard. NYTimes.com.

Hays, L., & Rutherford, A. (1991, January 1). Gorbachev bids to crack down on Soviet press. *The Wall Street Journal*, A8.

Head, S. W. (1985). *World broadcasting systems*. Belmont, Calif.: Wadsworth.

Heller, A. (2013, July 31). New TV channel tells Israel's side of the story. SFGate.com.

Hindley, A. (1999, April 23). Breaking the taboos. *Middle East Economic Digest*, 6.

Hindley, A. (2000, February 11). Internet usage, the boom in access. *Middle East Economic Digest*, 27.

Ivry, S. (2007, April 16). Now on YouTube: The latest news from Al Jazeera, in English. *The New York Times*, C5.

Khalil, M., Dongier, P., & Zhen-Wei Qiang, C. (2009). *Information and communications for development 2009: Extending reach and increasing impact.* World Bank Publications, Washington, D.C.

Kirkpatrick, D. D. (2011, May 31). Egypt's military censors critics as it faces more scrutiny. NYTimes.com.

Kirkpatrick, D. D., & Goodman, J. D. (2011, February 3). Reporters in Egypt under broad assault. NYTimes.com.

Kramer, A. E. (2007, March 22). Editor of Russian edition of Forbes guilty of defamation. *The New York Times,* C4.

Kramer, A. E. (2010, November 9). On video, Russian journalist is seen being brutally beaten. *The New York Times,* A8.

Kulish, N. (2012, October 18). Twitter blocks Germans' access to neo-Nazi group. NYTimes.com.

LaFraniere, S. (2010, January 20). China to scan text messages to spot "unhealthy content." *The New York Times,* A5.

Landler, M. (2010, January 22). Clinton urges global response to Internet attacks. NYTimes.com.

Levy, C. J. (2010, May 18). In culture of graft and impunity, Russian journalists pay in blood. *The New York Times,* A1.

Lowndes, F. S. (1991). The world's media systems: An overview. In *Global journalism: Survey of international communication,* 2nd ed. New York: Longman.

Lyall, S., & Pfanner, E. (2011, April 23). BBC, under criticism, struggles to tighten its belt. NYTimes.com.

MacFarquhar, N. (2006, January 15). In tiny Arab state, web takes on ruling elite. NYTimes.com.

Mackey, R. (2012, November 4). Crowdfunding citizen journalism in Cairo. NYTimes.com.

Malkin, E. (2009, September 29). Honduras shuts down 2 news outlets. NYTimes.com.

Markoff, J. (2007, January 29). At Davos, the squabble resumes on how to wire the Third World. *The New York Times,* C1.

Martin, L. J. (1991). Africa. In *Global journalism: Survey of international communication,* 2nd ed. New York: Longman.

McDowall, A. (2001, April 20). Uncorking the bottlenecks. *Middle East Economic Digest,* 45.

Mista, N. (2003, September 15). India's film city is gobbling tribal land. *San Francisco Chronicle,* D1.

Nordland, R. (2012, February 22). Two journalists are among the dead in Syrian shelling. NYTimes.com.

Ogan, C. (1991). Middle East and North Africa. In *Global journalism: Survey of international communication,* 2nd ed. New York: Longman.

Paraschos, M. (1991). Europe. In *Global journalism: Survey of international communication,* 2nd ed. New York: Longman.

Pfanner, E. (2011, December 13). O.E.C.D. calls on members to defend Internet freedoms. NYTimes.com.

Picard, R. G. (1991). Global communications controversies. In *Global journalism: Survey of international communication,* 2nd ed. New York: Longman.

Pierson, D. (2010, January 16). Despite censorship, cracks in China's great firewall. LATimes.com.

Pintak, L. (2007, April 27). Reporting a revolution: The changing Arab media landscape. ArabMediaSociety.com.

Richburg, K. B. (2011, April 12). Chinese editors detail censors' hidden hand. WashingtonPost.com.

Richtel, M. (2011, January 28). Egypt cuts off most Internet and cell service. NYTimes.com.

Romero, S. (2007, May 27). Chavez's move against critic highlights shift in media. NYTimes.com.

Sabbagh, D. (2009, March 20). BBC must cut spending by £400 million, says Mark Thompson. TimesOnline.co.uk.

Sabbagh, D. (2009, April 16). Digital economy bill to pave way for shake-up of rules governing media mergers. TimesOnline.co.uk.

Saltz, R. (2007, April 21). Using Bollywood ideas to portray today's India. *The New York Times,* A19.

Salwen, M. B., Garrison, B., & Buckman, R. (1991). Latin America and the Caribbean. In *Global journalism: Survey of international communication,* 2nd ed. New York: Longman.

Shadid, A., Addario, L., Farrell, S., & Hicks, T. (2011, March 22). 4 Times journalists held captive in Libya faced days of brutality. NYTimes.com.

Shane, S. (2011, January 29). Spotlight again falls on Web tools and change. NYTimes.com.

Siebert, F., Peterson, T., & Schramm, W. (1963). *Four theories of the press.* Urbana: University of Illinois Press.

Sobranes, R., & Palafox, G. G. (2013, April 28). Mexican journalists march against attacks on press. SacBee.com.

Stelter, B. (2011, February 1). Channels join fight to broadcast Al Jazeera in Egypt. NYTimes.com.

Stelter, B. (2013, January 2). Al Jazeera seeks a U.S. voice where Gore failed. NYTimes.com.

Strobel, W. P. (2005, April 18). Arab satellite channel Al Jazeera goes global. MercuryNews.com.

Stross, R. (2010, April 19). Two billion laptops? It may not be enough. *The New York Times,* BU5.

Sweis, R. F., & Rudoren, J. (2013, June 3). Jordan blocks local access to news sites. NYTimes.com.

Tavernise, S. (2010, May 21). Pakistan, citing "sacrilegious content," widens online ban to include YouTube. *The New York Times,* A12.

Timmons, H. (2008, May 20). Newspapers on upswing in developing markets. *The New York Times,* C6.

Tunstall, J. (2008). *The media were American.* New York: Oxford University Press.

Wallace, C. (1988, January 7). Radio: Town crier of the Arab world. *Los Angeles Times,* 1.

Wan, W. (2011, March 4). Egypt's Facebook revolution faces identity crisis. WashingtonPost.com.

Warren, M. (2010, August 28). Argentine president moves to control newsprint. SFGate.com.

Werdigier, J. (2010, November 5). BBC staff strikes over changes to pension plan. NYTimes.com.

Wilkinson, T. (2012, May 20). Six journalists killed in Mexico in under a month. LATimes.com.

ethics (*continued*)
    public relations, 230–231, 339
    radio, 118, 123
    responsibility, 325, 333–334
    truthfulness, 324–328
ethnic diversity, 279–280. *see also individual*
    ethnic genres of media
ethnic newspapers, 53
ethnocentric news, **359**
European Union (EU), 350
Eveready, 208
The Evolution of Today's Convergence:
    1978 to 2014, *179*
expletives, fleeting, **312**

F

Faber's Golden Female Pills, 72
fabricated documents, 334
Facebook, 177, 190, 203, 276
    advertising, 257
    Crabb, Stuart, 21
    globally, 352, 353, 357
    marketing, 209, 216
    popularity, 192, *217*
    and public relations, 233, 234, 235, 239
    and SLAPP, 303
    why people use, *193*
Fackler, Mark, 334–335
Fairbanks, Douglas, *136*
Fairbanks Daily News-Miner, 326
fair comment, 302
Fair Game, 307
fairness, 325, 328–331
Fairness & Accuracy in Reporting (FAIR),
    343
fair trial, 305
Fallon, Jimmy, 159
false light, **304**
Family Circle, *77*, 79
Farnsworth, Philo T., 156
FCC. *see* Federal Communications
    Commission (FCC)
Federal Bureau of Investigation (FBI),
    294–295
Federal Communications Commission
    (FCC)
    advertising, 222
    broadcast indecency fines, 312–313
    cable television, 168
    commercial announcements on public
        television, 163
    defined, **11, 113**
    deregulation, 13
    establishment of, 113, 208
    Internet (Net) neutrality, **195**,
        315
    music content labeling, 97
    radio, 91, 113, 120–121
    role of, 307–308
    TV and radio station ownership rules,
        166, 309–310
    TV network production and syndication,
        147
    Web site, 320
Federal Radio Commission, 113
Federal Trade Commission (FTC)
    role of, 220–221, 316–317
    Television Advertising to Children,
        269–270
    Web site, 225

feedback, **7**, 17
Ferguson, Chris, 271
Fessenden, Reginald Aubrey, 109, 110
Fey, Tina, 39
Fidler, Roger, 176, 178, 183
Fifty Shades of Grey (James), 300
file sharing, **97**–99, 194, **195**,
    314–315
Fillmore, Millard, 54
film. *see* movies
Filo, David, 177
financial public relations, 231
FindLaw, 320–321
Fireside Chats, 272
First Amendment, 140–141, 194, 246, 288,
    312, 336. *see also* freedom of press
First Amendment Center, 343
Fitch Ratings, 60
fleeting expletives, **312**
Fleischman, Doris E., 230
Fleischmann, Raoul, 75
FM radio, 116, 118, 124
Folio: The Magazine for Magazine
    Management, 86
Food and Drug Administration (FDA),
    221, 316
Food Network, 82
Food Network Magazine, 82
Forbes, 83
For Better or For Worse, 280
Ford, Henry, 228
Ford, Sam, 228, 239
Ford Foundation, 163
Fordham University, 119, 286
Ford Motor Company, 209, *215*
Foreign Policy magazine, 370
format radio, 117
Forrester Research, 41
Fortune, 70, 71, 76, 79, 91, *248*
45s (records), 91
42 (the movie), *146*
4XD (Charlotte), 111
Four Theories of the Press (Siebert,
    Peterson and Schramm), 347
The Fourth Kind, 326
Fowles, Jib, 212
Fox
    Fox Broadcasting Co., 11, 12, 13
    Fox Movietone News, 248–249, 264
    Fox News, 334
    Fox News Digital Network, *256*
Fox, Stephen, 208–209
Fox, Susannah, 184
France
    advertising market, *207*
    broadcast media, 350
    freedom of press, 349
Frankel, Max, 328
Frankfurter Allgemeine, 349
Franklin, Benjamin, 11, 30, 50, 72
Franklin, James, 50, 52
Fraternité-Matin, 354
Fredericksburg, Battle of, 248
Freed, Alan, 118
Freedom Forum, 343
Freedom of Information Act, 67
Freedom of Information Center, 321
freedom of press, 51, 288–307
    censorship, 295–298
    constitutional basis, 348

    courtroom access, 305–306
    federal government restrictions, 192,
        289–291
    libel law, 298–303
    PATRIOT Act and, 294–295
    prior restraint, 291–292
    privacy, 303–305
    shield laws, 306–307
    in Soviet Union, 351
    during war, 289, 292–293
    in Western Europe and Canada, 349
    WikiLeaks and, 293–294
Freedom's Journal, 54
freelancers, **79**, 314
free media, 309
Free Speech and Headlight, 54
Free Syria, 353
The French Chef, 163
Frey, James, 326–327
Friday Morning Quarterback (FMQB),
    127
Friedman, Thomas L., 176
Friendly, Fred, *157*
Frisbie, Doug, 233
frontier journalism, 52
Frost, David, 332
FTC. *see* Federal Trade Commission (FTC)
fulfillment, 35

G

Galella v. Onassis, 303
Gallup, George, 285
Game Developers Conference, *196*
Game Informer Magazine, *77*
Game of Thrones, *314*
Gannett Center for Media Studies, 350
Gannett Co., 11, 12, 24, 49, 59, 61, 68
Gans, Herbert J., 260
The Garden Island, *62*
Garrido, Nancy, 331
Garrido, Phillip, 331
Garrison, William Lloyd, 53, 54
Gates, Robert M., 293–294
Gaudet, Hazel, 272–273
gays and lesbians
    marriage, *265*
    media coverage, 280–281
    newspapers, 58
Geffen, David, *136*, 141
Genachowski, Julius, 195, 315
gender issues. *see* gays and lesbians;
    women
General Electric (GE), 111, 115, 155
General Magazine, 72
general managers, radio, 118
General Motors, 14, *215*, *356*
Gentry, James K., 231
Georg von Holtzbrinck, *34*
Gerbner, George, 268
German-language newspapers, 53
Germany, advertising market, *207*
Gertz v. Robert Welch Inc., 299
Gilder, George, 6, 178
Gillmor, Dan, 38
Giridharadas, Anand, 362
Glamour, 70, 76, 79, *83*
glasnost, 351
Gleason, Jackie, 116, 158
Global Journalism: Survey of International
    Communication, 362–363